SOCIAL STRATIFICATION

SOCIAL STRATIFICATION

The American Class System in Comparative Perspective

Daniel W. Rossides

Bowdoin College

Prentice Hall, *Englewood Cliffs, New Jersey 07632*

Library of Congress Cataloging-in-Publication Data

Rossides, Daniel W.
    [American class system]
    Social stratification : the American class system in comparative
perspective / Daniel W. Rossides.
        p.   cm.
    Previously published: The American class system. Boston : Houghton
Mifflin, c1976.
    ISBN 0-13-817578-0
    1. Social classes--United States. 2. Social classes--Cross
-cultural studies.   I. Title.
HN90.S6R68 1990
305.5'0973--dc20   89-38274
                                                    CIP

Editorial/production supervision: *Carolyn Serebreny*
Interior design: *Janet DiBlasi*
Cover design: *20/20 Services Inc.*
Manufacturing buyer: *Ed O'Dougherty*

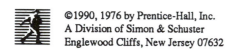 ©1990, 1976 by Prentice-Hall, Inc.
A Division of Simon & Schuster
Englewood Cliffs, New Jersey 07632

Printed in the United States of America
10 9 8 7 6 5 4 3 2 1

ISBN 0-13-817578-0

Prentice-Hall International (UK) Limited, *London*
Prentice-Hall of Australia Pty. Limited, *Sydney*
Prentice-Hall Canada Inc., *Toronto*
Prentice-Hall Hispanoamericana, S.A., *Mexico*
Prentice-Hall of India Private Limited, *New Delhi*
Prentice-Hall of Japan, Inc., *Tokyo*
Simon & Schuster Asia Pte. Ltd., *Singapore*
Editora Prentice-Hall do Brasil, Ltda., *Rio de Janeiro*

For Marilyn, as always

Contents

Preface

Social stratification has been studied scientifically and with considerable success on a relatively sustained basis since the 1920s, but it cannot be said that a consensus has emerged about the main issues in the field. However, it is no longer as necessary as it was during the early 1970s, when the first edition of this text was written, to argue the case that social classes are real. Today, almost all sociologists accept the reality of social classes and reject the classless ideology that still controls most popular and most elite opinion. This development is to the good since the achievements of stratification analysts are considerable and make up one of the best (if not the best) ways to understand the nature of individual societies as well as their relations to each other.

As a text, this study is designed for students with some background in social science and is especially directed at the introductory social stratification course. Although its focus is on the American class system and on the current state of the field of social stratification, it contains considerable amounts of historical-comparative material and could easily be used as the main text in a comparative stratification course. For one thing, the full-scale analysis of the American class system is put in a comparative setting wherever possible. In addition, there is a chapter on stratification through history, a chapter on stratification among societies (including a discussion of dependency theory and case studies of two variations on dependency in the Third World—underdevelopment in El Salvador and dependent development in the Republic of Korea), and an extended case study of a developed socialist society, the Soviet Union. Finally, one of the concluding chapters compares the adaptive capacity of the United States and the Soviet Union to raise the question: Must stratified societies always fail? And the last chapter uses the links between domestic and intersocietal stratification to show that solving world problems requires an understanding of world stratification.

No study can avoid organizing assumptions even when presented in the name of science (as this one is). Accordingly, I have tried to state where I stand as early and as clearly as possible. The book's basic theoretical framework is derived from two aspects of Max Weber's work (as well as the work of others): one, Weber's insistence on clear analytical models, which in the case of stratification analysis means an insistence that the dimension of class (the economic hierarchy), prestige or status (subjective forms, consumption, and interaction in social groups), and power (political-legal hierarchies) be kept analytically separate; two, Weber's unique comparative-historical perspective, which not only provided an empirical foundation to his work but also led him to stress the diversity, relativity, and instability of social phenomena. To focus all these aspects of social phenomena in contemporary stratification language, Weber had both a conflict and a functional approach to industrial (capitalist) society, seeing it, on the whole, as inherently unstable because of its rich, complex, and contradictory institutions, but at the same time as subject to deep stabilizing pressures from bureaucratization and state centralization.

In adopting the Weberian orientation, I have not interpreted his multidimensional approach to mean that modern society is a hodgepodge of hierarchies with no coherent or structured system of inequality, or that it can be understood in terms of functional differentiation. And in adopting his anti-Marxian perspective, I have tried to avoid the temptation (which is so strong in American society and sociology) to overemphasize subjective (prestige) factors or to give them priority over economic (class) variables. Weber himself was more than aware of the preeminent role of economic forces and would no doubt have disavowed some of the uses that have been made of his multicausal approach in stratification analysis.

In analyzing the American class system, I have tried to present a balanced and relatively full treatment of the nature and interrelations of all three major stratification dimensions. Not only do areas hitherto neglected, such as law, politics, government, and legislation, receive extensive treatment, but also there is a relatively full treatment of class variables, such as income, wealth, occupation, and education, as well as prestige variables, such as self-perception and attitudes, consumption, and differences in associational life. My analysis also contains a major emphasis on minorities. There is an extended discussion of black Americans and Mexican-Americans, and a summary of the social class position and prospects of racial and ethnic minorities in general. There is a major focus on sexual stratification as well as discussions of the problems of age groups, the handicapped, and homosexuals, which can be expanded to suit the interests of instructors.

I have also given considerable attention to the impact of foreign relations on the American class system and to what appear to be profound and historic changes in the American economy (economic slowdown, declining standard of living, loss of industrial competitiveness). Indeed, both the analysis and the interpretation of these changes and their causes (the shift to a service economy, growing social overhead, the internationalization of the American economy, the obvious shortfalls in American foreign policy) are major themes of the text.

In tackling the broad and complex materials of social stratification, every effort has been made to introduce ideas in an orderly sequence and to allow students to extend their grasp of these materials in a cumulative manner. I have also assumed that a pedogogically effective text must provide background on specialized topics; thus, I discuss marriage and the family as a context for understanding the relation of economic class to family life, the sociology of law and deviance as a context for understanding the relation between class and law, and so on. Above all, I have tried to suggest overall images of where modern society is headed and where the levers of power are located so that knowledge can be wedded to policy.

Given the lack of consensus about social stratification, I have tried to represent rival positions as accurately and as fairly as possible, hoping in this way to let readers form their own judgments about the complex issues of stratification analysis while at the same time making it as easy as possible for instructors to follow their own bent in designing their courses. As a further aid toward this latter end, and to stimulate and reinforce student interest, there are extensive bibliographic notes flowing directly out of the text as well as numerous references to research topics and areas.

With the growth and establishment of liberal democracy, most people (more certainly among the general public in the United States) have come to believe that equality either has been or can be achieved within the near future. As the reader will see, this view is questionable, as are many other beliefs about modern stratification structures and processes. Perhaps the major conclusion of our study is that the United States is a highly unequal society, in many ways running counter to its basic ideals, and that on balance there appears to be no evidence that it is making any progress toward more equality, putting aside for the moment the special issue of racial inequality. Our study also broaches the possibility (cautiously and reluctantly) that the United States is incapable of modifying its structure of inequality—that far from being a dynamic system progressively realizing its ideals, it may well be a nondirectional class society, a permanent halfway house mired in the mud of ascriptive property relations and liberal ideology.

Daniel W. Rossides

SOCIAL STRATIFICATION

CHAPTER 1

An Introduction
to Stratification Analysis

Inequality is a pervasive feature of human society and a subject that has fascinated both social theorists and laypeople from time immemorial. Social inequality is the stuff of which the drama of history is made: the power and pageantry of kingship, the struggle for supremacy among feudal barons, the executioner's block, the stench and brutality of a slave galley, the vast chasm between Brahman and untouchable, the mind-deadening routine of an assembly line, the factory owner, and the welfare mother all evoke vivid images of the ways in which stratification has been manifested at different times and places.

American history also evokes dramatic images of inequality, such as the bonded servant, the plantation owner and slave, the robber baron, the immigrant, the Depression, and the Dust Bowl. Americans have also witnessed some unique efforts to institute relations of equality, such as the Bill of Rights, the Homestead Act, the Fourteenth and Fifteenth Amendments, the sit-down strike, collective bargaining, the war on poverty, and the civil rights movement. In trying to understand these and other manifestations of the ceaseless drama of inequality and equality, sociologists must ask many questions: Who or what process determines who shall work in the fields and who in a factory, office, or laboratory? Who or what process decides who shall stand in an unemployment line or suffer the humiliation of welfare allotments? How is it possible in a democracy that millions have second homes while many live in rat-infested tenements or are homeless? Why do people tolerate hardship in the face of plenty when they have the franchise? Has rising prosperity made Americans more nearly equal? Have reforms made any headway against the forces of ascription, exploitation, and unequal opportunity? Is the United States a meritocracy, and if not, is it making progress in that direction?

As a distinct discipline within modern social science, sociology has long studied such questions. Despite decades of creative research and theorizing, however, there is still no integrated body of research and theory to account for the way in which social inequality is produced, maintained, and transmitted from one generation to the next. Given the complexity of this subject, it is understandable that there are many rival theories about the nature and destiny of social inequality, ranging from those that describe industrial society as spearheading a long-term drive toward equality, personal achievement, and consensus to those that interpret it as characterized by privilege, conflict, and repression.

All these questions and controversies will be discussed in some depth in the chapters that follow. The major purpose of this chapter is to provide an overview of the main issues and goals of stratification, and a working definition of social stratification. We shall begin by considering a theme basic to Western social thought—the attempt to understand the relationship between human nature and inequality. Because the literature that addresses this theme is exceedingly rich, we can do no more than discuss representative examples of the two major positions: the view that seeks to explain social inequality in terms of factors in human nature (the biopsychological position) and the view that seeks to explain it in terms of social variables (the sociocultural position). It will become apparent that each of these orientations is quite complex, and that particular theories often combine elements of these two general positions.

INEQUALITY FROM HUMAN NATURE

The Biopsychological Explanation of Inequality

The type of stratification theory that is most pervasive and influential in Western society attributes inequality to various alleged differences among individuals *qua* individuals. This explanation can be called *biopsychological* (or *naturalistic* or *ahistorical* or *nonsocial*) in that it argues that deep innate differences exist among human beings and that society derives (or should derive) its structure from the hierarchy of "talent" identifiable among human beings. This position assumes, in other words, that one can equate behavior and human nature: Behavior is a function of human nature, and differences in the behavior of individuals result from differences in their natures.

One of the most famous and influential expressions of the biopsychological view is Plato's *Republic*, in which he introduced many of the fundamental elements of social inquiry and supplied Western thought with many of its basic concepts. One of the most enduring of these concepts is his definition of society as a network of cooperation, a complex exchange of goods and services for mutual benefit. In the language of modern sociology, Plato thought of society as a system of interdependent functions.

Plato was not the first to articulate the ancient idea that there is a congruence between human nature and society, but he gave it a revolutionary cast by combining it with the novel assumption that the nature of that congruence could be identified by means of rational analysis. Society, argued Plato, has always been nonrational, or even irrational, based more on blind than on conscious cooperation. Instead of being founded on and governed by reason, society is governed by myth and custom. And because human beings have not understood themselves, they have not understood the nature of society. As a result, they have argued over the worth of their respective roles in the social division of labor, causing widespread inefficiency, instability, and civil war. To bring about the good society, Plato insisted, one must derive social and ethical conclusions from rational analysis. The division of labor that is the essence of society has an analogue in the division of labor in the human personality, or soul. According to Plato, the structure of the personality is hierarchical: Reason is at the top, followed by the "spirited" or executive capacity, and then the appetites. This specialization within the human being is matched by specialization *among* human beings. In the aggregate, human beings have different aptitudes: Some men and women have the capacity to reason, some are specially equipped to manage, and others are suited for work and work alone. In his famous metallic analogy, Plato described the hierarchy of human talent as composed of three groups of individuals who correspond respectively to gold, silver, and iron-brass.

The structure of society, therefore, corresponds to the division of labor in the human personality. In order to function, it must have a reasoning element (philosopher-king or -kings), administrators (guardians), and workers (presumably farmers, merchants, artisans, and slaves). To establish a rational society, one must see to it that the human beings suited by nature to each of these functions are identified and appropriately educated. To do so, however, would not have been as easy as it might seem, since Plato complicated his prescription by introducing a number of other revolutionary ideas. Gold parents, he argued, can have iron-brass children, and iron-brass parents can have gold or silver children; in other words, the distribution of talent is not determined by family birth, nor is it insured by property or a function of sex. For Plato, society could not be constituted on any of the traditional grounds. Only when the innate hierarchy of individual ability (enhanced by education) matches the intrinsic hierarchy of social functions can one speak of the good—and thus stable, just, and happy—individual and society.

Plato's interpretation of society as a functional system, staffed by those innately equipped to perform certain social functions, has had a long and varied career in Western social theory. But it is one thing to posit an ideal society free from the practices of history and another thing to talk about how people and societies actually behave. As we shall see when we examine some contemporary thinking about inequality, whenever a functional definition of society predominates (for example, those of John of Salisbury and other feudal social theorists, Adam Smith, James Madison, fascist corporate theorists, Joseph Stalin, and some contemporary stratification theorists), the concept of social class—especially its emphasis on illegitimate and exploitative ascriptive factors—is relegated to a secondary position.[1] And we will also find that the rulers of society invariably prefer to have their dominions depicted as characterized by a harmonious, equitable, and natural division of functions based on human nature and to avoid forms of thought that stress ascription, exploitation, and conflict. In brief, this social philosophy takes the form of what Ossowski has called *nonegalitarian classlessness,* or the belief that social inequality is based on natural factors and not on arbitrary definition or the use of force.[2] In the United states, nonegalitarian classlessness is expressed as the belief that inequality is determined by the innate differences in individuals as revealed by equal opportunity and competition.

Biopsychological Inequality: The Liberal World View

In the modern world, the biopsychological explanation has developed in a unique way. The emergence of capitalism gave rise to the novel proposition that society and social position should directly reflect the personal natures of individuals as individuals, a social philosophy known as liberalism[3] or bourgeois social theory. Expressed in its fullest earliest form in the social contract theories of Thomas Hobbes (1588–1679) and John Locke (1632–1704), this revolutionary redefinition of human nature (and thus of society) gradually broadened and deepened, and eventually triumphed over the feudal view of human nature and society. Expressed in terms of stratification theory, liberal thought attacked the hereditary principle and fixed hereditary estates of feudal society, and in their place sought to establish the achieve-

---

[1] For an historical survey of functional stratification thought that notes this similarity between apologists for very different social systems, see Stanislaw Ossowski, *Class Structure in the Social Consciousness,* trans. Sheila Patterson (New York: Free Press, 1963), pp. 172–180.

[2] Ossowski, *Class Structure in the Social Consciousness,* chap. 7. A similar idea is found in Pareto's biopsychic theory of "the circulation of elites."

[3] The meaning of the term *liberalism* will unfold gradually, especially over the next few pages. Essentially, it refers to the acceptance of private property, private economic motives and actions, and political and legal equality as central social institutions. Thus, both Democrats and Republicans in the United States are liberals; that is, both accept the validity and superiority of capitalist (liberal) society while disagreeing on how to run it. For a fuller discussion of historical and European developments in liberal social thought, see George H. Sabine's unsurpassed commentary, *A History of Political Theory,* 4th ed. (New York: Dryden, 1973).

ment ethic. Henceforth, it declared, inequality was to be a function of personal ability, especially in economic pursuits.

The new focus on achievement in the West acquired a deep biopsychological cast in the period between 1650 and 1850. During this unusually creative period in social thought, theorists in their efforts to explain behavior and inequality catalogued an enormous variety of biological and psychological forces: pugnacity, reason, hunger, sex, the will to power, self-interest, moral traits, genius, mental power, and so on. In French thought, the fathers of sociology, Saint-Simon (1760–1825) and Auguste Comte (1798–1857), found the explanation for behavior and inequality directly in human nature. Both theorists divided human beings into brain men, sensory men, and motor men, each category having special functions to perform for society.[4] According to Saint-Simon and Comte, these three biopsychic capacities, while shared by all individuals, are distributed unevenly. Education can develop the dominant capacity in individuals but it cannot change the category in which nature has placed them.

In English social thought, the biopsychological approach is a prominent feature of the work of Herbert Spencer (1820–1903) and Francis Galton (1822–1911). Spencer never developed a rigid classification of biopsychological types, but his thought—the first to be based on the scientific theory of evolution—was heavily influenced by biological analogies. (The basic capacity, according to Spencer, is the ability to adjust to conditions, a capacity that is not solely a function of thinking.) For Spencer, the individual is a real but unknown quantity in the operation of society. Because it is not possible to identify the capacities of individuals precisely, it is necessary for society to provide competitive situations; thus Spencer's emphasis on the law of contract, the free market, private property, limited government, and open competition. Francis Galton, who worked in the early period of quantitative social science, argued on the basis of statistical data that "genius" (by which he meant ability in general) is biological in nature and is distributed differently among individuals, races, and nations. By examining the families of eminent Englishmen, Galton concluded that ability is clustered in families and is transmitted by biological inheritance, especially from father to male offspring.

The idea that inequality stems from differences among individuals is the dominant theme of American political and social theory. James Madison, for example, argued in the *Federalist* paper number 10 that government is necessary because of conflicts over property, and that differences in amounts and types of property individuals own are due to "diversity in the faculties of men." Because social conflict has this natural basis, it cannot be eliminated without doing violence to nature. "The protection of these faculties is the first

---

[4]Comte used the terms *men of intellect, men of feeling,* and *men of action*.

object of government," argued Madison, and its proper role is to contain or control the effects of conflict, not to eliminate conflict as such. The main virtue of representative government, Madison concluded, is that it transfers natural economic conflicts and inequalities to a different arena and mitigates their impact on the body politic.

In American sociology, the thought of William Graham Sumner (1840–1910) best exemplifies the biopsychological approach. Like Madison, Sumner emphasized the importance of economic conflict in human behavior. History, he argued, is a struggle between economic interests, though only in the modern period has society evolved to a point at which this struggle can be made explicit and thus more "rational." All societies, according to Sumner, are divided into the masses and the classes; the former embody the society's *mores* and resist change, while the latter introduce variation and change. Society cannot change individuals, but it can select and develop those who best serve its interests. There is a natural distribution of human talent, ranging from the few individuals of genius and talent to the defective and delinquent. Modern society, which has evolved from a system based on customary status to one based on rational contract, provides individuals with an opportunity to prove themselves. Merit is inherent in the individual; society merely brings it out by means of education and competition. Thus, concluded Sumner, all schemes to help the weak and less talented are wrongheaded interferences with nature.

The biopsychological approach constituted the core of the liberal world view from the seventeenth through the nineteenth centuries, and was deeply related to the needs of emerging capitalism. At its inception, the liberal emphasis on equality of opportunity and inequality of native endowment was both a metaphysical attack on feudalism and a legitimation of the emerging liberal society. With the consolidation of liberal society, the same position was used to attack theories of reform and assorted forms of socialist thought.[5] Eventually, however, the biopsychological explanation of social inequality had to be drastically modified, not only on scientific grounds but also because it no longer suited the needs of a maturing industrial society. A complex industrial society requires a great deal of coordination, and many of its members require long years of preparation for adult roles. It is not surprising, therefore, that the idea that society should simply reflect the natures of individuals was gradually questioned and modified. The shift to a more sociocultural explanation of behavior has been the major trend in liberal intellectual-scientific circles during the past century.

---

[5]Antisocialist arguments are prominent in the thought of such leading sociologists as Georg Simmel, Max Weber, Emile Durkheim, William Graham Sumner, Vilfredo Pareto, Charles Horton Cooley, Franklin Henry Giddings, and Talcott Parsons.

INEQUALITY AS A SOCIAL PHENOMENON

Rousseau and the Sociocultural Explanation of Inequality

The other influential theme in Western social theory treats inequality as the outcome of social variables. Rousseau's remarkable essay, the *Discourse on the Origin of Inequality* (1754), is an early modern expression of a mode of thought that has become the cornerstone of creative social science. In brief, Rousseau argued that those who attribute inequality to human nature are mistaken; they are confusing the effects of society on human beings with their original constitution. Humans in their original state, Rousseau suggests, can only be hypothesized about. At best, they are merely compassionate bundles of emotions motivated by their own welfare and self-preservation, and repelled by others' pain and death. By and large, they are equal to their fellows in their weakness and nakedness. Only in the society of others do they develop language, property, law, and inequality; in this process their original nature is distorted and corrupted by reason and civilization. Above all, the division of labor and the attendant convention of property create mutual dependence and enslave not merely the subordinate groups in society but everyone.

Rousseau's thesis is an outstanding example of the sociocultural view of behavior and inequality. Of special importance is the fact that his analysis contains a conception of the division of labor totally different from Plato's (and from those of most "functional" theorists). While Rousseau defined society as a network of functional specialization, unlike Plato he saw the division of labor as resulting not in mutual profit or peace but only in corruption, injustice, and violence. He was an adherent of the "conflict school of inequality," which regards social factors, and often the basic structure of society, as detrimental to human beings and incompatible with social harmony and justice.

Sociocultural Inequality: Karl Marx and Max Weber

The sociocultural explanation of inequality has many sources, but its most influential contributors have been Karl Marx (1818–1883) and Max Weber (1864–1920). Indeed, the basic conceptual elements both of the contemporary sociocultural explanation of social stratification and of conflict theory are found in their original forms in the theories of these two men. Both Marx and Weber explicitly rejected the Anglo-American liberal view that capitalist society and the inequality that characterizes it stem from the individual. Despite serious disagreements, both theorists maintained that the biopsychological approach was a thorough mistake. The reasons for their rejection of it transcend the undoubted genius of these two men. Gradual economic growth and small-scale enterprise had misled English and American theorists into believing that individualism had caused capitalism. As Germans, Marx and Weber had not grown up in a social environment permeated by the logic of individualistic explanations. The growth of capitalism in Germany was an abrupt, disruptive process spawned largely by military and political considerations. Lacking the long phase of small-scale enterprise characteristic of capitalist growth in other countries, German capitalism took the form of a relatively large-scale factory system from the outset. This abrupt growth, due to corporate formation and state action, made it as impossible for Germans to develop a theory of individualism and laissez-faire as it was for them to explain capitalism and its resulting system of social stratification in biopsychological terms.[6]

Karl Marx: Social Classes as Property Relations

Though Marx and Weber agreed that behavior is the outcome of sociocultural forces, they disagreed markedly about the nature of these forces. Marx, who was greatly influenced by such classical liberal economists as Adam Smith and David Ricardo, by and large accepted their definition of society as a functional division of economic and social labor.[7] But Marx rejected the notions that an individual's place in the functioning of society rested on his or her innate talents and that the division of labor (as found in any known society) was compatible with social harmony and justice. For Marx the key determinant of human behavior and human consciousness is the relationship of humans to nature. Marx referred to this relationship as *the forces of production* or *the material conditions of life* (resources, technology, and technical skills). A given level of production, he argued, leads to a distinctive set of social relations or *mode of production*. The core of these social relations is the legal order, especially property forms; forms of the state; and the ideological order, including religion, philosophy, and art. In brief, as Marx put it, "the hand mill will give you a society with the feudal lord, the steam mill a society with the industrial capitalist."

History is essentially the story of the changing relation of humans to nature. As the forces of production change, they come into conflict with the mode of production (or superstructure), leading to a conflict between classes and eventually to revolution. As the forces of production crystallize into a new modal technology, they give rise to a new set of social relations that corresponds to the new needs it creates, including a new type of human being. For Marx, therefore, society derives its essential structure from the prevailing level of technology, and it is the individual's relation to the means

---

[6]In this connection, see Norman Birnbaum, "Conflicting Interpretations of the Rise of Capitalism: Marx and Weber," *British Journal of Sociology* 4 (June 1953): 125–141.

[7]The substance of Marx's theory of social stratification may be found in *The Communist Manifesto* and, on a more sophisticated level, in *The German Ideology*.

of production, rather than innate abilities or drives, that determines one's class level, personality, and consciousness. Rather than seeing economic and social structures as the result of human talents, drives, or needs, Marx always focused on social variables, particularly technology and the economic system in which it was embedded.

Strictly speaking, the crucial factor in the creation of classes is not technology as such but the ownership of technology, or the means of production. The simple dichotomy between owner and nonowner is the ultimate basis of Marx's conception of social stratification. All other factors, such as income, occupation, education, and political power, are derivative and secondary. Fundamental to Marx's conception of class is the fact that all material value is the result of labor. But because of the power inherent in property, the owners of the means of production receive more than they produce by their own labor. Therefore their interests and those of the nonpropertied producers of labor are inherently antagonistic.[8]

Economic classes (determined on the basis of the ownership and nonownership of land, tools, factories, and the like) are synonymous with social classes, according to Marx, because beliefs and values (consciousness) and overt behavior outside of work correspond to economic behavior, beliefs, and values. Also crucial to Marx's explanation of class formation, as well as his theory of the dynamics of class struggle and social change, is his assumption that one can distinguish between progressive and reactionary technological forces. The basic criterion that Marx used to make this distinction is the concept of *human fulfillment.* Some technological forces (and the social systems that embody them) retard and some promote the progress of human beings toward emancipation from historical necessity. A class is progressive when it represents the emergence of new forms and levels of liberating technology; an example is the middle class between the sixteenth and nineteenth centuries. Inevitably, however, such a class becomes conservative and reactionary—a "ruling class"—because it can make larger and larger profits without distributing the fruits of the machine to the general populace; an example is the "upper middle" class or *grande bourgeoisie* in the nineteenth century. In other words, individuals are subject to a distortion of their nature as long as material scarcity exists. Technology, Marx argued, is the key to the reduction and eventual elimination of both material and moral scarcity. Once material abundance is achieved, historical systems of inequality (caste, estate, and class), and the corresponding structures of moral scarcity (original sin, noble versus ignoble birth, master-slave, lord-serf, owner-worker, government-citizen, policeman-criminal) will also disappear and a "classless" society of human fulfillment will emerge.

---

[8]The importance of wealth, or the income and power derived from the ownership of the means of production, was neglected by American stratification theorists until quite recently. For its importance and for attempts to incorporate it into stratification theory, see Chapter 5.

Max Weber: Social Classes as Multicausal and Nondirectional

Marx's identification and analysis of economic causation was perhaps the most important contribution to social science in the nineteenth century. However, the monocausal or deterministic version of economic causation that he proposed had to be considerably modified before it was accepted into stratification theory and sociology. The theorist largely responsible for its modification was Max Weber. While acknowledging the importance of economic causes in the formation of social strata, Weber insisted that noneconomic sociocultural variables are not only influential but often more influential than economic factors in controlling the distribution of material and symbolic benefits. Religious beliefs and values, for example, significantly influence the relationship of humans to nature, the definition of work, and the worth of material values. And such factors as family beliefs and values, canons of taste or consumption, considerations of race or ethnicity, and philosophical, political, legal, or military beliefs and values can often exert powerful controls over economic forces.

Weber developed his multicausal theory of behavior in a lifelong analysis of the rise and nature of capitalism.[9] While acknowledging the importance of the economic factor, Weber came to the conclusion that the economic breakthrough to capitalism would have been impossible had medieval Europe not possessed a congenial religious and social tradition. With regard to social stratification, Weber concluded that a simple economic determinism was not consonant with the historical record.[10] He insisted, therefore, that the analysis of social inequality required the analytical separation of three major causal variables: class (market factors, property, technology, income, wealth), status (cultural evaluations expressed in group life, involving such matters as family, religion, race, morality, ethics, consumption, breeding, and general style of life), and party (access to the state, ability to create and enforce law). In developing this analytical model, Weber raised all the problems that confront contemporary stratification theory, especially those associated with his stress on multiple causation. The multiplicity of causes influencing the formation and composition of social classes and the reciprocal relations between causes, he argued, make it necessary to posit a scheme of causation characterized by mutual action and reaction. Economic wealth, for example, can be used to obtain prestige and political-legal power, and, conversely, one can use prestige (in the form, say, of noble birth or skin color) to secure

[9]For Weber's summary of the rise of capitalism, see his *General Economic History*, trans. Frank H. Knight (New York: Greenberg, 1927), Collier paperback, 1961, pt. 4.

[10]Weber's theory of stratification is outlined in his influential essay "Class, Status, Party," in H. H. Gerth and C. Wright Mills, trans. and ed., *From Max Weber: Essays in Sociology* (New York: Oxford University Press, 1946), chap. 7. The introduction to this volume by Gerth and Mills is invaluable.

economic wealth or political-legal benefits. So too, one can use political-legal power (such as military skill or the ability to organize voters) to secure economic benefits or prestige.

Weber's insights into social stratification illuminate further shortcomings of a simple economic explanation of social class. A wealthy individual, such as a junk dealer, may have low prestige, and a person of high prestige, such as a clergyman, may have an inferior class (economic) position. Poorly paid workers and even the unemployed, though their class and prestige position is inferior to other classes, can nonetheless enjoy equal political-legal benefits (the vote, due process of law) on a formal level and to some extent in practice. But there is no need either to pursue these difficulties now or to stress any further the differences between Marx and Weber. It is their similarities that are relevant to our present task of distinguishing the theories that focus on human nature from those that focus on society as the cause of inequality. Marx and Weber agreed that no such phenomenon as human nature can be identified as a cause of behavior; what we call human nature is the result of sociocultural forces, and the deep observable differences among human beings are the *result* of social stratification, not its cause.

A WORKING DEFINITION OF SOCIAL STRATIFICATION

It should be apparent from the foregoing that social theorists are deeply divided over the root causes of inequality. This is not surprising, given the complexity of the problem and the fact that a thorough discussion of inequality touches on every topic that human beings consider important. Despite decades of scientific research, social scientists are still far from unanimous about how and why human beings become unequal. Thus it seems wise to adopt an explicit working definition of social stratification in order to illuminate the maze of materials and issues we will encounter later. Toward this end, we must first distinguish between inequality in general and social stratification in particular.

Social Differentiation and Social Stratification

All human societies are differentiated by various forms of specialization, only one of which should be called *social stratification*. The advantages of specialization are obvious and every society is characterized by a division of labor, no matter how rudimentary. Simple societies invariably use sex, age, and kinship to ascribe rights and duties to their members. That these three biological attributes are universally used to assign people to social functions, however, does not mean that sex, age, and kinship actually cause behavior. We have become too aware of the wide variations in behavior within each of the sexes and age groups, and among parents and children, to accept a simple biopsychological explanation of behavior. The way in which power groups *define* these human attributes is the crucial determinant of how people are assigned to social functions. Despite historical variations, the differentiation of social tasks on the basis of age, sex, and kinship leads to certain forms of inequality. Specifically, the old are usually given authority over the young, parents over children, and males over females.

When differentiation results in a more complex division of economic and social labor, some people become subordinate to other people. The social pattern becomes even more complex when the young acquire power over the old, female employees gain authority over males, or a great industrialist becomes subject to the authority of a doctor or a meter maid. For various reasons, those who hold certain positions in the range of tasks (for example, those of priest, landlord, warrior, doctor, factory owner) tend to receive more material and moral benefits than those in lower positions. Given the existence of families and a structure of differential rewards based on *alleged* differences in functional importance, there emerges a distinct form of inequality that we call social stratification. *Essentially, social stratification is a hierarchical configuration of families (and in industrial societies in recent decades, unrelated individuals) who have differential access to whatever is of value in the society at a given point and over time, primarily because of social, not biopsychological, variables.*

It is simple to illustrate the difference between inequality resulting from social stratification and inequality resulting from differentiation. While a society may declare all women inferior to men, the processes of social stratification make some women superior not only to many other women but to many men as well: One need only compare the wives of lawyers, business executives, and generals, for example, to lower- and working class wives and their husbands to see social stratification in operation. To take another example, a servant in a millionaire's home will have two sources of authority over the children of his or her employer—adulthood and functional position—but the children under his or her authority occupy a much higher position in the total hierarchy of values. To use Max Weber's telling term, their *life chances*—measured in terms of material comfort and security, personal fulfillment, occupation, and so on—are superior to the servant's or his or her children's.

Still another way to understand the nature of social stratification is to imagine an unstratified hunting and gathering tribe in which all males are fairly equal in hunting ability, and therefore equal socially. Then imagine the appearance of an individual who is exceptionally fleet of foot and keen of vision. Social stratification begins when he becomes the leader of the hunting party and is given authority, prestige, and a larger share of the catch. It is crucial to note that both he and his family will rank above those who are average in ability and who in turn will rank above those who are lame or nearsighted. But such a stratification hierarchy is only a partial system because the superior hunter cannot ensure his son's future position as a leader. His wife and children will enjoy more food and prestige during his lifetime, but unless the son inherits his father's physical traits he will sink in the hierarchy upon reaching adulthood. Indeed, if no biologically superior or inferior individuals emerge in our hypothetical society, the stratification hierarchy itself will disappear. A full system of social stratification emerges only when parents can see to it that their children inherit or acquire a social level equal or superior to their own regardless of innate ability.

The key to intergenerational transfer of social level is the development of high occupational positions that can be filled only by those who possess or acquire a given range of *social* assets, such as property, leisure, motivation, education, personality traits, noble birth, military or other skills, and so on (or those who have socially defined, valued, and cultivated biopsychological abilities associated with such occupations as basketball player, opera singer, or mathematician). Thus, *stratification inequality* is the condition in which social positions are ranked in terms of importance, rewarded differentially, acquired by individuals (and thus their families), and transmitted over generations quite independently of biological or psychological attributes. Furthermore, the definition of what is functionally important and the ways specified to achieve given social functions are quite arbitrary and based as much on force as on rationality, moral insight, or social necessity. The fact that modern society allows some individuals to rise above their parents' station (or to drop below it) does not alter the fact of social stratification. There is far less mobility than is popularly believed, and it neither diminishes the distance between tops and bottoms nor interferes much (despite considerable rhetoric to the contrary) with the hereditary transmission of stratification level.

Caste, Estate, and Class Forms of Stratification

Once a society abandons direct dependence on nature, social stratification inequality emerges prominently.[11] Economic surplus is easily translated into prestige and power and readily transmitted from one generation to the next. On the other hand, those who elevate themselves above others by the exercise of personal qualities (such as hunting, military, or religious skills) cannot easily transmit their prestige or power to their offspring unless the transfer also has an economic base. In short, economic surplus provides the wherewithal for social stratification: If property is esteemed, parents can guarantee that their children will be esteemed by giving them property; if abstinence from economic work is valued, those who can live off property or the work of others will be elevated above those who must work; if education

[11]For an ethnographic study of fourteen aboriginal Polynesian cultures that finds a direct relationship between productivity and degree of social stratification, see Marshall D. Sahlins, *Social Stratification in Polynesia* (Seattle: University of Washington Press, 1958). This general point has been usefully elaborated by Gerhard Lenski; for a fuller discussion of his work, see Chapter 4.

is necessary to attain high occupations, those whose parents can motivate and support them through long years of schooling will have a decided edge over those who cannot.

Though economic variables are crucial to social stratification, they do not function in any mechanical or unitary fashion. As Weber pointed out, moral relationships (status or, in our terms, prestige) emerge to legitimate property relations and often become strong enough to disguise and even counteract economic forces. The diversity of causation and the variety of structures that social stratification assumes make it difficult to impose conceptual order on this form of inequality. However, for our immediate purpose of developing a brief working definition of social class, we need only note that it is generally accepted that social stratification, considered in the abstract, takes three general forms:

1. Caste stratification, in which an agrarian society defines social level and function in terms of a hierarchy of religous worth (or a hierarchy of racial worth in some approximations).
2. Estate stratification, in which an agrarian society defines social level and function in terms of a hierarchy of family worth.
3. Class stratification, in which an industrial society defines social level and function in terms of a hierarchy of differential achievement by individuals, especially in economic pursuits.

Analysis of Class Stratification

Class stratification appears in societies with expanding economies and is a phenomenon peculiar to industrial society. Both the development and the nature of class stratification have varied by country, and one can detect interesting variations in class structure among England, France, Germany, the United States, and Eastern Europe.[12] Essentially, however, an expanding economy requires functional expertise in many sectors of its specialized occupational system, and needs flexibility in its labor, commodity, and credit markets (to use Weber's breakdown of class variables). Because of these needs, expanding economies undermine feudal norms and practices based on static lineage, prestige, and legal criteria. Thus the emergence of class over estate stratification occurred in modern Western Europe.

Much of the widespread confusion over the meaning of class inequality results from a failure to note two things: (1) class stratification emerged primarily in societies with well-developed systems of estate stratification; and (2) class stratification in such countries has undergone two distinct stages: an initial period during which classes crystallized into relatively

---

[12]For a pioneering comparison of the historical development of class stratification in the United States and Europe, see Norman Birnbaum, *The Crisis of Industrial Society* (New York: Oxford University Press, 1969).

self-conscious antagonistic strata,[13] followed by a stage in which an expanding standard of living, political-legal equality, and state welfare programs have succeeded in muting class hostility.

Though the United States was spared the early stage of class crystallization experienced by most European nations, it would be a mistake to assume that social classes do not exist in the United States. The essence of class stratification is that economic status prevails openly, steadily, and strongly over all other statuses. What Americans are worth on the labor, commodity, and credit markets is the primary determinant not only of their standard of living but also of their worth in the realms of prestige and power. As we shall see, American social classes do not form a strict and clearly defined set of strata. There are multiple dimensions of inequality, which, while under the general sway of economic status, remain distinct and somewhat independent. Thus our overall analytical model is based on the general orientation provided by Max Weber. Our model assumes, first, that the causes of behavior are sociocultural rather than biopsychological, and it accepts the primacy of economic factors even as it stresses multiple causation. Because of the number of factors affecting social stratification, analysis is made easier if these factors are grouped under three broad headings—class, prestige, and power, each of which has subdimensions. (See Table 1–1.)

In the abstract, the values within the dimensions of class range from affluence and economic power and security at the top to destitution and economic powerlessness at the bottom. Some of the variables or subdimensions of class are listed in Table 1–1. A fuller list of class-related variables would include not only income, wealth, occupation, education, family stability and values, and the education of children, but also basic personality structure, physical and mental health, and life expectancy. In analyzing this domain, we are interested in the variables that determine life chances in all dimensions. None of these variables has any scientific meaning, however, until we specify a relationship to something else; a given income, for example, has little meaning unless we relate it to the total universe of incomes or to other variables. In general, class refers to those who have similar life chances (goods, living conditions, personal experiences) because of a similar ability or power to turn goods or skills into income in a given economic system.

The variables that compose the dimension of prestige are occupational prestige, certain aspects of personality, associational life, and consumption or style of life. Again, these variables are not intrinsic entities; they must be understood in relation to each other and to variables in other dimensions. At one end of this scale of values are those who tend to have integrated personalities and to enjoy personal fulfillment through valued associations and

---

[13]The terms *social class* and *social stratum* will be used interchangeably throughout this text, though this is not always the case in the literature of stratification.

TABLE 1-1   Basic Dimensions of Social Stratification (with examples of values in the top and bottom classes within each dimension and examples of subdimensions)[a]

	(ECONOMIC) CLASS VARIABLES						PRESTIGE VARIABLES							(POLITICAL-LEGAL) POWER VARIABLES				
	INCOME	WEALTH	OCCUPATION	EDUCATION	FAMILY STABILITY	EDUCATION OF CHILDREN	OCCUPATIONAL PRESTIGE	SUBJECTIVE DEVELOPMENT	CONSUMPTION	PARTICIPATION IN GROUP LIFE	EVALUATIONS OF RACE, RELIGION, ETHNICITY		POLITICAL PARTICIPATION	POLITICAL ATTITUDES	LEGISLATION AND GOVERNMENTAL BENEFITS	DISTRIBUTION OF JUSTICE	
HOUSEHOLDS IN THE UPPER SOCIAL CLASS	Affluence: economic security and power, control over material and human investment Income from work but mostly from property						More integrated personalities, more consistent attitudes, and greater psychic fulfillment due to deference, valued associations, and consumption						Power to determine public policy and its implementation by the state, thus giving control over the nature and distribution of social values				
HOUSEHOLDS IN THE LOWER SOCIAL CLASS	Destitution: worthlessness on economic markets						Unintegrated personalities, inconsistent attitudes, sense of isolation and despair; sleezy social interaction						Political powerlessness, lack of legal recourse or rights, socially induced apathy				

[a]For expository purposes, religious-ethnic and racial rankings are omitted.

consumption. At the other end are those who tend to have distorted, underdeveloped personalities and to live lives of isolation and despair.

The dimension of power is made up of rights to political participation and access to public office, political attitudes, legislative benefits, and governmental treatment, including the distribution of justice. In all areas, and perhaps especially in this one, it is necessary to see beyond the rhetoric of formal institutional analysis to the operational reality. As we will see in abundant detail later, the people at the upper end of this scale have far more power to influence the state, and thus the distribution of values in all dimensions, than do those at the bottom, protestations of democracy and equal rights notwithstanding.

Weber's cross-cultural comparisons and his acute eye for historical variations enabled him to see things that most stratification theorists overlooked. He not only insisted that prestige and political-legal factors were important in modifying and even counteracting economic forces, but also stressed the importance of distinguishing between three kinds of economic markets—credit, commodity, and labor. For Weber, class was no simple dichotomy between the propertied and nonpropertied (though he, like Marx, considered this phenomenon central to social stratification), but rather a series of hierarchies that interact to produce the inequality of social stratification. Even the central economic markets of credit, commodities, and labor could be powerfully influenced by prestige and political-legal forces. This suggests the importance of Weber's insistence that the various dimensions and sub-dimensions of social stratification be kept analytically separate so that their relationships could be disclosed on an empirical rather than verbal basis.

Weber quite rightly stressed the diversity among societies, as well as *within* society. But Weber also sensed the strengthening grip of rationality—the efficient coordination of means and ends—on Western life, and he feared that it would usher in an "age of icy darkness," by which he meant meaning-less efficiency and centralization. The main agency of this trend, according to Weber, was bureaucratization. We shall stress both aspects of Weber's work, the need to give due regard to the empirical complexity of society and the need to see the empirical interconnectedness that constitutes a social system. Since Weber's day it has become apparent that industrial society has found ways to stabilize itself. In short, while we will keep the dimensions of class, prestige, and power analytically separate, we will assume that coordinating mechanisms and processes at strategic points connect them empirically to form an identifiable system.

We will differ from Weber, however, in a number of respects. Weber tended to regard education as a prestige phenomenon even when it was used as the basis for occupation, the classic example being his analysis of the Chinese literati, the scholar-civil servants of Imperial China. For our part, we will regard education primarily as a class phenomenon. Since Weber's day diplomas and degrees, whether functionally necessary or not, have become the prime qualification for occupational status at many levels, thus making education an explicit class phenomenon. Education is also the main means by which families pass on their class positions to their children, and therefore an indispensable part of the process of class continuity and consolidation of advantage. And it is quite clear that both students and educators (more, perhaps, in the United states than elsewhere) look upon education as a way to enhance economic status. But education is not totally a class phenomenon, and we will note its implications for prestige and power as well.

Our use of the key but ambiguous term *power* will also vary somewhat from Weber's. In differentiating the major variables of social stratification, Weber used the terms *class, status,* and *party* (rather than *power*), and his discussion of party was quite fragmentary. Implicit in his analysis of stratifi-cation and in his work as a whole, however, was the recognition that political institutions have much to do with social stratification. The term *power,* there-fore, will refer to any and all political-legal forces that stratify a population in the political realm and that influence stratification elsewhere. However, Weber would also have insisted, and rightly, that all three realms—the economic, the social, and the political—are complexes of power. Furthermore, it must be understood that in a class system the most important form of power as such is economic power; as a matter of fact, it is crucial in all societies. Thus, while we will speak of power as a separate dimension for analytical purposes, the concept of *social* power refers to the combined effects of class, prestige, and power variables.

Whatever terminology is used, however, the basic objectives of stratification analysis are to locate a population along the axes of class, prestige, and power and to understand the causal processes that produce any given distribution of values. Location on any one dimension, while important, cannot be relied on to yield a social class—that is, a class of units characterized by common benefits and behavior across the dimensions of class, prestige, and power. In addition to avoiding a monocausal emphasis on economic status (class), or any other variable, we must also guard against a semantic difficulty that characterizes the use of the concept of class: For one thing, the word *class* is used to refer both to the economic dimension and to the general system of stratification in an industrial society. A closely related complication is the use of the term *class* to denote both economic class and social class. And to make matters worse, the word *class* can refer both to the type of society that provides freedom and opportunities for individuals to transcend their origins (the liberal achievement ethic as opposed to caste and estate systems based on family, sexual, religious, ethnic, or racial ascription) *and* to the ascriptive advantages or disadvantages that attend birth in an economic class. Every effort has been to keep these diverse meanings clear and distinct in the following pages, and the reader is urged to examine each such usage carefully.

SPECIAL PROBLEMS OF AGE AND SEX STRATIFICATION

In recent years a number of neglected areas of social inequality, notably age and sex, have come into prominence—thanks in good measure to the growing awareness and militancy of the affected parties. No model or depiction of the American structure of social stratification would be complete if it did not treat the relationship between social stratification and age-related and sexual stratification. Inequalities based on age and sex are not as totally distinct from social stratification as we might have implied earlier.

Age, for example, importantly influences the economic, and thus class, status of individuals. There is a tendency, too, for those who are born poor to be poor when they are old and for those who are born rich to remain so as they age. But unlike social stratification, which allows for individuals and families to move upward or downward or to remain stationary in the scheme of rewards, age is a one-way irreversible process. By and large, the inequalities of age do not have to correspond to the inequalities of social stratification—the old can be either poor or rich, and so on. Perhaps the most important point about age is that its meaning can vary enormously from one society to another: For example, in different societies a fourteen-year-old male can be either a married adult or a child with many years of school ahead of him; an elder can be revered as a fount of wisdom or put to death as an economic burden; and so on. Because age has an obvious bearing on an individual's worth on economic, prestige, and political markets, stratification analysts must keep an eye on norms and values that define stages in the life cycle (for example, school-leaving or retirement age) and on factors that affect longevity (for example, sanitation, nutrition, and medical care). There is another way in which age exerts a significant influence on social stratification: If large numbers of young or elderly people lack secure economic statuses, this fact will be reflected in all other stratification hierarchies. If large numbers of affluent or impoverished elderly cluster in retirement centers, this phenomenon will have repercussions at all political levels. And, to take a final example, a life expectancy of eighty, instead of thirty-five to forty, means that women's lives do not begin and end with bearing and raising children, and allows them to pursue other goals. In sum, it should be apparent that age and social stratification are distinct but related phenomena. However, the analysis of the relation between age and social inequality is in a preliminary stage and much remains to be done.[14]

After long neglect, the analysis of the relationship between sexual and social stratification is now well under way. Social stratification theorists have always identified the family as the ranking unit, and by and large this stance is correct. As we indicated earlier, the rationale for this position is that all family members are equals in terms of class (or estate or caste). Thus, to repeat our earlier argument, even when a prejudiced and discriminatory society makes women subordinate to men, the nature of social stratification makes some women (mostly the wives of successful men and women with careers of their own) superior in significant ways to other women and to many men as well. As long as women are subordinated to men in the family system, and as long as families can be ranked in terms of differences in economic, prestige, and power values, social and sexual stratification will remain two distinct forms of sociocultural inequality.[15]

However, women are no longer as fully subordinated in the family system as they once were. Thanks to forces that have been gestating for

---

[14]For a discussion of the process of aging in relation to social class membership, see James J. Dowd, *Stratification Among The Aged* (Belmont, Calif.: Wadsworth, 1980).

[15]In defining *social stratification*, we may seem to imply that age-related and sexual stratification are not social. Nevertheless, age and sex are culturally defined and thus overwhelmingly "social" in nature.

generations, many women now fill roles outside the home and marriage. The thrust of industrial society is to individualize behavior, and stratification theorists can no longer assume that the family is the only unit of social stratification. It is not just that one must account for the many individuals whose lives are lived outside of marriage and family life; of perhaps greater significance is the increase in individualism *within* the family, especially at middle-class levels. It is significant that the women's liberation movement is primarily a middle-class phenomenon. The reason for this is not difficult to discern: Middle (especially upper-middle) class parents tend to treat their male and female children alike, even to the extent of providing both with higher education and the motivation to pursue careers. As a consequence, middle-class females have experienced a deep contradiction between, on the one hand, an upbringing focused on personal worth and training for productive citizenship, and, on the other, subordination to a husband and children, what some feel is the relatively degrading role of housewife, and institutionalized inferiorities and inequalities in economic, political, legal, and moral statuses.

Seen from the standpoint of individuals, women are an exploited portion of the labor force even after education, type of work, and lifetime experience are taken into account. That women are concentrated in low-paying occupations is not the main issue here; so are many men, for that matter. Central to the relation between sex and social stratification is the fact that women are not treated as men's equals once they enter the labor force. They receive less pay for the same work, are not subject to the same standards of evaluation and promotion as men, and are prevented from entering certain occupations. Furthermore, when their husband dies or disappears they must assume the extraordinary burden of heading the household (which means that many widows and abandoned mothers and their children sink to and remain at the bottom of the social hierarchy). When we analyze the relation between sex and social stratification we must distinguish between inequalities, just and unjust, to which men and women are both subject and those that pertain only to women (or, for that matter, only to men).[16]

Seen from the standpoint of class structure, however, a different picture of the relation between the sexes emerges. Women from the upper classes have the resources to compete for the better jobs and thus enjoy a class advantage over males (and females) from the lower classes. In addition, individuals from similar class backgrounds tend to marry and thus there is a tendency for the better jobs to cluster in upper-level households. Here again we see the need to keep sex and class stratification separate.

---

[16]For example, men are uniquely subject to military service, and inequitably burdened by muscular and dangerous wage labor and the anxieties and hurts of economic insecurity and failure.

STRATIFICATION OF RELIGIOUS-ETHNIC AND RACIAL GROUPS

The inequality of ethnic and racial groups can be related to social stratification much more easily than can age or sex, for a simple reason. In a society with an ethnic-religious or racially diverse population, a hierarchy based on ethnic-religious or racial status is easily established using the traditional ranking unit, the family.

An upper class must contain all ages and sexes, but it need not include all ethnic, religious, and racial groups. Thus, a relatively sharp hierarchy based on ethnicity, religion, or race can easily be established and maintained over generations. Indeed, the clustering of economic and political power around distinctive ethnic, religious, or racial statuses is a commonplace of social stratification, not only in the United States but in all societies that are or have been heterogeneous in these regards. In industrial societies such stratification is an important aspect of the prestige dimension, sometimes coinciding with class and power stratification and sometimes not. In preindustrial societies, religious-ethnic and racial stratification more often coincide with class and power stratification and thus partake of the more explicit and thorough separation of strata characteristic of such societies.

THE SPECIAL PROBLEM OF INEQUALITY AND THE HANDICAPPED

The handicapped of the United States number over 35 million (approximately 15 percent of the total population). They are extremely diverse, ranging from those with learning disabilities, the severely and mildly retarded, the physically disabled, including the blind and deaf, the physically different, and the mentally ill. We will assume that the handicapped are largely, indeed mostly, the products of society (of poverty, especially inadequate prenatal care, of dangerous work, of dangerous leisure, of unsafe consumer products, of biased professional judgments,[17] of faulty socialization, and contradictory norms and values). To be handicapped is to stay at the bottom of the class system or, if well off, to sink to the bottom or to lose out on many of the benefits of social life. Class analysis helps us identify how society generates handicapped people and thus how the social production of disease and

---

[17]For a brilliant analysis of learning disability—which shows how most of it is based on arbitrary professional judgments connected to similar naturalistic, biased professional judgments about IQ, mental retardation, mental illness, physical disabilities, the gifted, crime, sexual deviation, educational potential and problems, which altogether allow the professions, the schools, and the state to create and reproduce a particular kind of unequal society—see James G. Carrier, *Learning Disability: Social Class and the Construction of Inequality in American Education* (Westport, Conn.: Greenwood Press, 1986).

disability can be prevented. It also helps us in understanding the many ways in which the handicapped can lead more productive lives.

THE SPECIAL PROBLEM OF INEQUALITY AND SEXUAL LIFE-STYLE

Societies have also treated unequally those individuals who prefer members of their own gender for companionship and sex. Here we cannot have class stratification since there are no offspring to transmit class position to. However, gays (as homosexuals prefer to be called) are denied important social benefits despite the fact that sexual preference appears to be irrelevant for the performance of occupation roles, and now that reproduction is not as vital for social survival as it was in the past, irrelevant for citizenship too. Our knowledge about gays is still limited, and because their relevance for social stratification is not central, we will have little to say about them (for a brief discussion, see Chapter 9).

STRATIFICATION ANAYSIS: A SUMMARY

The purpose of this chapter was to provide a broad overview of the general field of social stratification. To do so we have examined and discussed the relative merits of the biopsychological and sociocultural explanations of inequality, finding the latter more persuasive. In developing a working definition of social stratification, we relied heavily on Max Weber, and especially on his insistence that the various areas of inequality—the economic (class), the social (prestige), and the political (power)—be kept analytically separate. We explained that the purpose of stratification analysis is to locate social units on each of these three dimensions (and their subdimensions) over time, and to relate the various hierarchies to each other, also over time. Again following Max Weber, we assumed that though these dimensions vary in importance over the course of history, they tend with time to coalesce and form either castes, estates, or classes—that is, aggregates of households whose members share given social benefits across all three dimensions.

All this means that the popular explanation for American inequality is unacceptable: Americans are not made unequal by their biopsychological natures but by social variables, which are for the most part ascriptive in nature. In other words, social class at birth explains success or failure for Americans in the aggregate better than does the idea of talent or the philosophy of nonegalitarian classlessness. Social stratification, as the institutionalized ranking of family units containing both sexes and all ages, was carefully distinguished from sexual and age-related inequality. It was also pointed out that since religious-ethnic and racial aggregates are composed of family units, they can be stratified as aggregates by more powerful religious-ethnic or racial groups. We pointed out too that the handicapped are a numerous and varied group who also suffer from a socially induced and maintained inequality. Finally, we added a brief word about inequality on the basis of sexual preference.

CHAPTER 2

Stratification Through History

SOCIAL INEQUALITY AND TYPE OF SOCIETY

In the following analysis, each of the major types of stratification will be depicted in ideal-typical terms—that is, in terms of how each would work if it adhered to its basic principles—and also in terms of how it actually works. Following Max Weber's usage, it should be noted that the use of an ideal type is not a value judgment. An ideal type is simply a freely and logically constructed model in which the constitutive principles of the phenomena under examination are identified and formulated purely, even exaggeratedly, so that the empirical world can be brought into relief more easily.

As always, the best way to break the stranglehold of our familiar social world is to compare it with other worlds (whose members also take their societies for granted). In stratification analysis, this means analyzing how forms of inequality vary by type of society and by stage of social development.

HUNTING AND GATHERING SOCIETY

Imagine a hunting and gathering society based on age and sex differentiation. Men and women both perform important economic duties. All work hard and there is little economic surplus. By and large, families in hunting-gathering societies are equal—equally poor, equally rich, equal in a shared scarcity. Those who have outstanding abilities that can be directly seen as beneficial to society will stand out. An outstanding male hunter may well get a larger share of the catch and some prestige because of his hunting ability. People will listen to him when it comes time to organize hunts. A female hunter who is more dextrous (in hunting small animals) will also gain some extra benefits and be listened to with extra attention. The families of these individuals will share their fortune, and one can thus see the beginnings of economic, political, and social stratification. But a full system of social stratification cannot appear because these successful individuals have no way to guarantee the superiority of their spouses or offspring after they themselves die. It is possible of course that they can pass on their attributes to their children through biological inheritance. But there is no guarantee.

COMPLEX HORTICULTURAL SOCIETY

The domestication of plants gave human beings a revolutionary new source of power—an efficient and readily available mechanism for harnessing solar energy. The cultivation of plants provided more than a dependable supply of food—it was also the basis for other advances in utilizing and controlling nature. And it had large implications for how humans would organize themselves as societies.

The movement away from hunting-gathering to simple and then complex horticultural society and eventually (in some places) to agrarian society took centuries. Simple horticultural societies produce food in family plots using simple tools and methods (and sometimes by herding animals). The emergence of more advanced methods of plant cultivation between 9,000 and 6,000 years ago soon led to complex or advanced horticultural societies. A key technological element in crossing the threshold to complex society was the development of metallurgy.[1]

The advanced horticultural societies of Mesopotamia, Egypt, India, China, Mesoamerica, and Peru were marked by permanent settlements, population increase, a marked growth in specialized occupations, technological and normative creativity, and the emergence of separate political institutions. In all six societies there appeared a full-fledged, autonomous state generated from internal sources alone. Four of these, the societies of the Tigris-Euphrates, the Nile, the Indus, and the Yellow rivers, eventually went beyond advanced horticulture to become agrarian societies (which we will discuss shortly).

[1] I am indebted to Gerhard and Jean Lenski, *Human Societies: An Introduction to Macrosociology*, 5th ed. (McGraw-Hill, 1987), Chaps. 5, 6, and 7, for their concise and informative analysis of horticultural and agrarian societies.

One of the striking features of the more advanced horticultural societies is the large increase in nonproductive activities: warfare, religious ritual and ceremonies, prestige practices and consumption, and administration. Also striking is the growth of specialized occupations: political heads, priests, warriors, tax collectors, merchants, artisans, servants, tenant-workers, serfs, slaves, entertainers, prostitutes, and bandits.

Perhaps the most striking feature of advanced horticultural society is the growth and formalization of special economic and political statuses. These statuses, which revolve around property rights, the organization of the labor force, and political authority, represent a significant change in power relations. Of special significance is the fact that these statuses become the attributes and transferable possessions of private individuals. Society is not only reconstituted but also its operation and maintenance over time are achieved through hereditary rights and processes. Another striking feature of advanced horticultural (and advanced herding societies) is the development of *monotheism* (doctrine or belief that there is one God). In some advanced horticultural societies there is also the momentous development of writing and mathematics, both outcomes of the need to record and direct complex economic and social transactions.

Complex horticultural societies are marked by considerable internal rivalry among elites, by population pressures both internal and external, and by economic problems (water shortages, pests, plant disease). The basic flow of resources is toward the top although there are some downward redistribution processes, most of them token and symbolic. The essential power structure derives from ownership of or control over land, which in turn leads to occupations dependent on land ownership or control either directly or indirectly: king, nobility, priests, artisans, servants, serfs, slaves. The essential problem of power in this type of society (not necessarily seen clearly or fully) is how to maintain the overhead of nonproductive activities in the face of population growth, disease, crop failure, water shortages, and so on.

The power groups of advanced horticultural societies establish granaries to provide for lean years, institute welfare programs, undertake public works, some with direct economic significance such as irrigation and road-building projects, and expand their economic base by conquest and plunder. The association of advanced horticultural society (out of which grew some of the great agrarian civilizations) with irrigation and flood control is striking. Also striking is the independent emergence of an autonomous state in societies that geared their economies to water control.[2]

---

[2]Morton H. Fried, "On the Evolution of Social Stratification and the State," in Robert A. Manners and David Kaplan, eds., *Theory in Anthropology* (Chicago: Aldine, 1968), pp. 251–260. For more general discussions, see Morton H. Fried, *The Evolution of Political Society* (New York: Random House, 1967), and Elman R. Service, *Origins of the State and Civilization: The Process of Cultural Evolution* (New York: W.W. Norton, 1975).

COMPLEX AGRARIAN SOCIETY

Five Thousand Years of Hereditary Landlords and Servile Labor

The first agrarian societies emerged out of advanced horticultural societies in the Middle East approximately 5,000 years ago. An agrarian society is unique because it can produce food, tools, and other things, including belief and value systems, on a scale far exceeding even an advanced horticultural society. New technology, especially iron metallurgy and the plow, along with other productive techniques such as irrigation and the harnessing of animal energy—combined with such economically central sociocultural inventions as slave and serf labor, family-tenant labor, administrative structures, standing armies, forms of taxation (including forced labor), money, writing, mathematics, religion, and legal codes—result in a unique type and level of social existence.

The revolution implicit in the domestication of plants and animals soon expressed itself in the "domestication" of human beings. A sedentary farm or village life became the characteristic form of human behavior in a number of places. Within a few thousand years there emerged that momentous transformation in the quality and quantity of social interaction, namely the city. The unique advantages of an urban division of labor augmented technological advances.[3] Once established, the new agrarian economy became the basis for a continuous growth of the productive arts (despite setbacks) until a series of technological-economic plateaus were reached in the high civilizations of India, China, and medieval Europe.

The complex agrarian society develops a considerable economic surplus, thanks to an advanced technology and division of labor. Literacy, restricted to the elite in power, leads to the accumulation of technical knowledge and of a corpus of sacred writings, all easily transmissible under the custody of a privileged profession of priests or scholars. Agrarian society is characterized by mighty public works such as aqueducts, temples, roads, and fortresses, but little accumulation of productive capital; most production is for consumption. Any surplus over subsistence is expended on luxury, on "public" buildings glorifying the upper estates and the beliefs and values that benefit them, and on warfare. The surplus produced by the masses, in other

---

[3]Two essays, by Robert J. Braidwood, "The Agricultural Revolution," and Robert M. Adams, "The Origins of Cities," both in *Scientific American*, September 1960 (reprints 605 and 606), give quick introductions to this period. For fuller treatments, see the highly readable accounts by V. Gordon Childe, *Man Makes Himself*, rev. ed. (New York: Mentor, 1951), and *What Happened in History*, rev. ed. (Baltimore: Penguin, 1954); William Howells, *Back of History* (New York: Doubleday, 1954); and Leslie A. White, *The Evolution of Culture* (New York: McGraw-Hill, 1959).

words, is used to reinforce and perpetuate the system that dominates and exploits them.

Advanced agrarian societies (as found, for example, in the river-valley civilizations of the Middle East, India, and China) are typically large both in population and territory and exhibit a marked degree of institutional specialization. Above all, they everywhere exhibit a sharp cleavage between a small governing elite and a large unarmed peasant mass. Other features are a significant increase in food production and an increase in craft specialization. The most important development, however, is the increased specialization of the dominant landlord stratum, an important mechanism for effective control of the many by the few.

Advanced agrarian societies derive their productive economies from a number of sources. Irrigation is a pervasive feature of agrarian civilizations. Feudal-absolutism (or state feudalism) was given considerable impetus by the development of centralized irrigation and water-control systems. The so-called hydraulic societies[4] everywhere set up a leader and a state machine that legitimated itself in terms of an alleged derivation from both the supernatural and the people, and an alleged devotion to their service.

In addition to advances in technology, agrarian society develops a variety of labor forms: The tenant family is the most productive unit where crops require intensive labor; a militarized slave force is productive in some forms of agriculture and transportation (slave galley), in mining, road building, and other public works. Productivity is also enhanced by the emergence of specialized crafts. The outstanding characteristic of advanced agrarian society is a concentration of land worked in a variety of ways by human and animal muscle. The essential economic power relation is between the owners/controllers of land and the landless. As a result, the goods and services produced by the economy are not distributed equally nor are they distributed widely enough to raise per capita living standards. The essential flow of goods and services is upward into the coffers and service of the landlord (in the form of rent, interest, labor, or goods).

Advanced agrarian societies are marked by pronounced expansionist tendencies.[5] Once productive levels reach their limits, the only way to increase an elite's holdings—to make up for reverses caused by drought or disease, to replenish a labor force, or to gain psychic benefits—is physical expansion, invariably through conquest. A key perspective on complex

---

[4]Karl Wittfogel, *Oriental Despotism: A Comparative Study of Total Power* (New Haven, Conn.: Yale University Press, 1957).

[5]Complex societies in general tend to be expansionist—see Chapter 3 for a discussion of the imperialism of empire (found among advanced horticultural, agrarian, and early capitalist societies and the imperialism of the world-market economy (found among contemporary industrial systems).

agrarian societies is that they have the technological and organizational capacity to utilize their own as well as captured labor forces.[6]

The high agrarian civilizations are also marked by fully developed universalist, monotheistic religions. Montheism and monarchy support and reinforce each other, and religious and political institutions are formally intertwined; indeed, religious values and norms permeate all institutional areas. In addition, complex agrarian society develops practices and symbols in the realms of law, education, and art that reinforce and maintain elite domination. A marked feature of these developments is the explicit division of a population into two static categories, a tiny elite and a huge mass, and the explicit parallel between inequality in law, education, and art with the sharp inequality in economic and political power. Ultimately, the basic symbolic system portrays the interests of the monarch and elite as synonymous with the interests of the masses.[7]

The central problem in building an agrarian state is the decentralizing thrust of the local, self-sufficient economy. The central authority must subdue not the masses but the local landlords, who in turn are intent on subduing the masses on their self-sufficient estates. Because the power that accrues to those who control land is enormous, the agrarian state never succeeds in fully freeing itself from its social base—its essential characteristic is a tension-filled collaboration between hereditary landlords and a central power (the-monarch who is also an hereditary landlord).

Nonetheless, a developed agrarian society is characterized by a nobility that has been harnessed to serve a centralized state. In addition to civil servants and the military, there is further specialization and professionalization—for example, priesthood, astronomers and astrologers, theologians, physicians, mathematicians, scholars, philosophers, and artists. Though king and nobility are at odds in some ways, their interests are reconciled somewhat by the fact that the upper reaches of the various professions are recruited either by law or de facto from the hereditary stratum of landlords. *The essential definition of complex agrarian society is domination by a landed propertied group that has specialized to control all functional areas—or, expressed differently, the propertied elite monopolizes the means of production, administration, warfare, belief, and meaning.*[8]

---

[6]Industrial societies also know how to utilize foreign labor at home (immigrants, brain drain, guest labor, illegal aliens). In addition, industrial capitalists use foreign labor abroad by exporting capital to compliant countries with large pools of cheap labor; for example, American capital goes abroad to manufacture television sets in Taiwan, textiles in the Republic of Korea, and automobile engines in Mexico.

[7]The historic middle class of the modern West did much the same—it proclaimed a universal humanity and gave itself as the definition of the human.

[8]Important continuities and similarities between state feudalism and liberal democracy will be pointed out in due course.

Agrarian societies are stable and yet comparative standards of stability are difficult to establish either in contrast to simpler societies or to industrial systems (whose time span has so far been very small). Advanced agrarian systems, however, experience unique types of instability. In addition to the palace rivalries that occur in horticultural systems, advanced agrarian societies face a new problem—challenges from below. A marked feature of advanced agrarian feudalism is peasant and slave revolt (and crime). Stated more broadly, class polarization and struggle are widespread in advanced agrarian society.

Advanced agrarian society is also more politicized than earlier societies. Government takes an active role in managing the economy, providing public works, and storing food and other provisions for time of need. Despite notable achievements, however, agrarian society has instability built directly into its power relations—the masses work hard, do not receive much in return, and can identify their oppressors.[9] Many reforms are "revolutions from above"—segments of the dominant oligarchy seeking to oust other segments, to institute "reforms." A characteristic feature of Greece and Rome, for example, is *caesarism*—a reform movement initiated at the top in populist language but which leaves class relations substantively intact and distracts the masses by providing bread, circuses, and moral exhortation as substitutes for equality and justice.[10]

These societies never solved the economic problem that was the cause of their malfunctioning. The best-documented pictures of the instability caused by economic troubles and inequality are for ancient Greece and Rome. Strictly speaking, these are both hybrid societies (that is, they have complex economies consisting not only of subsistence horticulture and agriculture, but extraction, construction, moneylending, manufacturing, and export agriculture and manufacturing) and complex political-legal institutions (that stemmed largely from the need to manage their complex economies). Nonetheless, their essential system of inequality was based on land and unfree labor (slaves and a variety of semi-free serfs, tenants, and laborers). Without the consensus that marked this relation in the more straightforward agrarian systems, such as Egypt or China, this system was regarded as illegitimate (exploitative) by many and resulted in a chronic condition of class struggle.

The cleavage between rich and poor not only led to internal dissension but also spilled out to cause instability among the Greek city-states and

---

[9]These are also the conditions that lead to economic and technological stagnation and which propel elites toward war as a way to maintain revenues.

[10]The similarity with reform in contemporary liberal and socialist societies will be noted in due course. And revolution from above is a distinctive feature of contemporary modernizing societies.

between Rome and its neighbors.[11] Under pressure to pay higher taxes, the wealthier elements were always ready to lead and unite with the poor to seek booty in war. This relation between inner and outer power relations is a characteristic feature of all complex societies down to the present day.

Agrarian society has two similar yet different forms of social stratification—the caste and estate system—and each deserves a special word.

The Caste System: India

The most explicit, thoroughgoing, and inflexible structure of social stratification is the *caste system*. A caste system forms when an ascriptive condition, usually religious birth or condition of servitude, becomes an unalterable and inviolate basis for the unequal distribution of all social benefits. While a number of societies (for example, Ceylon, parts of Africa, Japan, and the United States) have developed approximations of caste stratification, probably the only true example is India.[12]

Disregarding origins and historical irregularities, what appears to have happened on the Indian subcontinent is that the Hindu religion crystallized in such a way as to transcend class and power, and came not only to express economic and political forces but also to dominate them. This is not to minimize the importance of economic and political factors. Reading the following description of the underlying religious rationale for caste, it should be kept in mind that India was an agrarian society, the vast bulk of whose population worked in a labor-intensive, low-technology agricultural economy. Given a static village economy, it is not surprising that a complex, sophisticated religion such as Hinduism could provide the simple productive system with a religious sanction and eventually envelop it altogether. And the same thing is true of family, governmental, and military relations: Together with economic functions, these realms too were eventually absorbed into a hierarchic mosaic of religiously defined castes and subcastes. With behavior in all areas of life subject to a religiously determined division of social labor, the individual castes were self-sufficient in terms of marriage and reproduction, the socialization of the young, eating patterns, kin obligations and mutual help, the settlement of disputes, and the practice of religion

---

[11] Alvin W. Gouldner, *Enter Plato: Classical Greece and the Origins of Social Theory* (New York: Basic Books, 1965), pt 1; Robert Antonio, "The Contradiction of Domination and Production in Bureaucracy: The Contribution of Organizational Efficiency to the Decline of the Roman Empire," *American Sociological Review* 44 (December 1979):895–912; Andrew Lintott, *Violence, Civil Strife and Revolution in the Classical City* (Baltimore: Johns Hopkins University Press, 1981); G.E.M. de Ste. Croix, *The Class Struggle in the Ancient Greek World: From the Archaic Age to the Arab Conquests* (Ithaca, N.Y.: Cornell University Press, 1981); and Alexander Fuks, *Social Conflict in Ancient Greece* (Jerusalem: Hebrew University Press, 1984).

[12] For a wide-ranging historical and comparative analysis of various stratification systems, which sees class forces behind caste divisions including racial slavery in the American South, see Oliver Cromwell Cox, *Caste, Class and Race* (Garden City, N.Y.: Doubleday, 1958).

per se, while at the same time they were committed to occupations and caste relations that incorporated them into villagewide, regional, and all-India divisions of social labor.

In all societies always, there is a basic thrust toward consistency of class, prestige, and power (especially at the upper levels), and India was no exception. Modern empirical research has revealed considerable inconsistency—even conflict and mobility—in twentieth-century India, but evidence suggests a high degree of consistency in the classic period among the statuses of each caste and subcaste in each dimension of stratification. The system of caste and subcaste cannot be described exactly. On a very abstract and relatively unrealistic level, Indian society was a hierarchy composed of four *varnas* (broad all-India castes) and the *untouchables* (the outcaste). This scheme was derived from a religious literary tradition about 3,000 years old; while it is not accurate empirically—the reality of Indian stratification is its thousands of subcastes—it provides a first approximation of the essential spirit of caste.[13]

Formally speaking, therefore, the classic caste system of India was based on the all-pervasive importance of religious status at birth (Hinduism). Both the Hindu religion and the social system it eventually brought under its sway were vastly different from the religions and societies that Westerners are accustomed to. They lacked the theology, explicit organizational structures, functional staff (clergy, civil servants), and degree of legalization and formal political authority that Westerners associate with religion and society. Despite the apparent formlessness of the Indian caste system, however, it effectively controlled Indian society for well over 2,000 years. This is all the more remarkable in light of the fact that the caste and subcastes could never be precisely identified, described, ranked, or even numbered. Each of the four main castes—the Brahmans (priests and scholars), the Kshatriyas or Rajputs (princes and warriors), the Vaishyas (merchants), and the Sudras (peasants, artisans, laborers)—contained many subcastes, and the total numbered in the thousands. Below these, the outcastes (untouchables) made up approximately 20 percent of the population.

It is impossible to understand the absolute inequality that prevails under the Indian caste system without understanding the main tenets of Hinduism:

1. *Samsara,* or reincarnation, is life after death—in this world not another.
2. *Dharma,* or correct ritual behavior, specifies the behavior appropriate to one's caste.

[13]For an excellent formal description of the Indian caste system, see Egon E. Bergel, *Social Stratification* (New York: McGraw-Hill 1962), pp. 35–67. For a theoretical discussion of caste, see Anthony de Reuck and Julie Knight, eds., *Caste and Race: Comparative Approaches* (London: J. and A. Churchill, 1967), especially chaps. 1, 5, and 7. Probably the best introduction for the beginning reader is Taya Zinkin, *Caste Today* (London: Oxford University Press, 1962).

3. *Karma,* or causality, is dependent on how well one adheres to correct ritual behavior (dharma) independently of social conditions.

In Hinduism, there is no supreme creator: Life, or the soul, has always existed and manifests itself in caste. One can improve one's caste in the next (social) life, and failure to adhere to the dharma of one's caste can cause one to be downgraded either in this social life or the next one, but no one can climb the social hierarchy during any given lifetime.

There is little that is obligatory for all Hindus. All must respect the Brahmans, believe in the sacredness of the cow, and accept the castes into which they are born. The main thrust of Hinduism (and thus of Indian culture) is toward prescribing different modes of behavior and different benefits for each caste. There is no universal standard of right and wrong, and no improvement is possible in this life, all deprivations and hardships are ordained and explained by religion, and the only recourse against worldly suffering and the only avenue to social mobility is the possibility of a better life in some future reincarnation. Unlike Christianity, which has universal moral rules (the Ten Commandments), universal ethical ideals (love and brotherhood), and declares all individual souls equal before God, Hinduism sets a radically different course for each caste and subcaste, saying in effect that different castes are worth different amounts in the divine scheme of things.

The enormous power and stability of the Indian caste system resulted from the extension of religion into every aspect of behavior, occupation, marriage, eating and drinking, friendship, and many other pursuits explicitly regulated by caste status. The radical particularism of religion thus resulted in a social and cultural particularism so deep that it precluded even a minimal degree of equality. The Indian subcaste was a prestige group without parallel in the history of stratification. It constituted the consciousness of its members and controlled their economic and political relationships down to the smallest particular. A Westerner's deeply implanted sense of the public, ingrained universalism, and easy use of abstractions in dealing with oneself, others, and nature make the cultural diversity (particularism) represented by India's thousands of subcastes almost incomprehensible. Nevertheless, the caste system was not random or unpatterned. Relations between the subcastes were strictly prescribed according to a logic provided by the Hindu concept of ritual purity—a concept blurred obviously by such phenomena as conquest, migration, British imperial control, urbanization, and industrialization.

Given this strict and narrow definition of identity, there is no formal consistency between the hierarchies of class, prestige, and power. Formally, each of the top three castes monopolized the top of one hierarchy and each was formally positioned hierarchically in relation to the others: Brahmans (prestige), Kshatriyas or Rajputs (power), and Vaishyas (class). But beneath the forms of the Indian caste system there is a general consistency of status in the major dimensions of stratification: All three of the top castes, for example, enjoyed high or substantial economic status and were roughly equivalent in their other statuses. Only a minority of Brahmans, for example, followed a priestly calling; while Brahmans could not pursue certain occupations, such as medicine and moneylending, without jeopardizing their caste positions, they were landlords and practiced all the learned professions. Of course, there was a considerable amount of both rivalry among castes and subcastes and upward and downward mobility (of subcastes, not individuals) due to military conquest, the settlement of new lands, the emergence of new occupations, and British rule. But all this notwithstanding, the classic Indian caste system was a uniquely rigid system of virtually total inequality.

Stratification by Estates: Feudal and Feudal-Authoritarian Societies

Inequality by estates is the most commonplace system of stratification among precommercial horticultural and agricultural societies. Two subtypes can be distinguished:

1. *Feudalism,* or the highly localized and personalized lord-vassal relation based on hereditary linkages to land, in which the lord has explicit governmental, religious, military, and economic power over his dependents.
2. The *feudal-authoritarian* form, in which a relatively strong central government emerges and is superimposed on the feudal system. Ordinarily, an hereditary absolute monarchy rules bureaucratically through officials recruited from the nobility.[14]

A feudal or *simple* agrarian society is not much different from a horticultural society—in some ways it is less differentiated and less developed culturally. A simple feudal system is centered on the economically self-sufficient *latifundia, manor,* or *hacienda.* It has a natural economy—little is produced for exchange. Simple feudal society is also marked by political self-sufficiency: The local lord (or patron, or gentry) enforces laws and settles disputes. Decentralized feudalism generates simple market relations, mostly of a local character. Its outstanding characteristic is that land and labor are not commercialized. Work and nature are given fixed definitions and the economy is embedded in political, religious, and family institutions.[15]

---

[14]For a broad sociological analysis of an example of the feudal-authoritarian form of estate stratification, see Hsiao-Tung Fei, "Peasantry and Gentry: An Interpretation of Chinese Social Structure and Its Changes," *The American Journal of Sociology* 52 (July 1946): 1–17.

[15]For a useful distinction between types of economies and their societies, see C.B. Macpherson, "Status, Simple Market, and Possessive Market Societies," in his book *The Political Theory of Possessive Individualism: Hobbes to Locke* (London: Oxford University Press, 1962), pp. 46–68. As we will see in Chapter 3, societies with a horticultural or simple feudal background (black Africa and Latin America) have had a more difficult time "modernizing" than have societies with a feudal-authoritarian background (Western Europe and Sino-based societies).

Like the caste system, the estate system is focused formally on prestige rather than economic status. However, institutionalized inequality in estate society relies much more explicitly and heavily than does caste society on power (monarch, magistrate, state religion, tax collector, the military). Although economic variables are important in the orgination of such societies, they eventually succumb to such power and prestige variables as military force, law and administration, a mighty religion, styles of consumption, traditions of family honor, intellectual-educational forces, and the like.

The estate system of stratification is similar to the caste system in other ways, too, though a full silhouette requires contrasts with class society. Both caste and estate societies lack a coherent and viable state or system of public authority relative to modern society. When estate stratification is compared only with the Indian caste system, however, one finds in the former a much higher degree of formal definition, especially in the area of law. While the estate system is also governed by ascription, it is family, not religious status at birth, that is the crucial determinant of social position in an established estate system.

Medieval society in the West contains both subtypes of estate stratification. Because of the prime social importance of force during the settlement of barbarian Europe after the Fall of Rome, skill at warfare became the most important form of social behavior. The retreat into the countryside and the primitive technology of the time made land the most important economic value. The warrior soon turned his skill at violence into an economic asset through plunder and control of land under a system in which protection was exchanged for food and labor, and eventually succeeded in legalizing and legitimizing his ascendant position through chivalry, *noblesse oblige*, and privilege or superior legal rights.

While the full-fledged estate system has a relatively higher degree of explicit social specialization than does the caste system, it is much less specialized and differently specialized than modern society. The modern social system specializes the behavior of individuals according to an intricate occupational system, but also demands considerable versatility from individuals. Thus, individuals (especially males) are Jacks-of-all-functions in that they must obtain education, work, attend to the formation and functioning of their families, be responsible for the legality and morality of their actions, seek out salvation, participate in public affairs, and fight in their nation's wars. The feudal system specializes a population by families. In the feudal system the upper stratum of noble families (its males) did the fighting, administered the manors, dispensed justice, engaged in "politics," and did the thinking and praying.[16] The serfs were a dependent group who followed the decrees of

---

[16]The upper clergy were eventually drawn only from noble families. Thus, the disputes between Church and State, however real, were disputes between two estates that shared fundamental stratum (class, prestige, and power) attributes and interests.

custom and lord. They raised families, of course, and went to church, and were even pressed into military service on occasion, but by and large the normative tradition and social practice confined them to manual work, a dishonorable activity regarded as punishment for sin.

The estate legal system in the West stipulated that legal status was a function of family birth and provided for different rights and duties (privilege) depending on social position. The noble was not subject to arrest or trial in the same manner as were commoners; his fiefs were not inherited in the same way as were other properties; his rank gave the nobleman exclusive access to high religious position; his person was specially protected against his inferiors; he had the right of private vengeance; he enjoyed special rights with regard to consumption and personal adornment; and he was able to substitute military service for the usual burdens of taxation.

The feudal idea of privilege must be seen in the context of a pronounced system of cultural particularism. Feudalism was characterized by few abstractly defined functional institutions, and there was little that was shared by all. Its emphasis, rather, was on the different rights and duties of the different strata. The relation between lord and serf was a highly personal, rigid, and pervasive structure of supersubordination that encompassed all spheres of existence. Of great significance to this system was the privatization of political power; what today is defined as public authority or public office was defined under feudalism as the attribute or possession of private persons.

Despite the static nature of feudal stratification, a certain measure of social mobility was both possible and legitimate. In the Western estate system, for example, marriage between social unequals (strictly forbidden in a caste system) was possible though not common, non-nobles could be knighted in exceptional circumstances (usually military), noble status and high office could be purchased, and the nature of the Christian Church blurred the strict distinction between noblemen and serfs by permitting the latter to become priests. Furthermore, Christianity tended to give all people a common religious and moral status, thus lending the moral force of religion to a minimal acknowledgment of equality.

Western feudalism was modified, of course, by the emergence of absolutism or feudal-authoritarian society. Attempts to impose absolute monarchy on feudalism account for a great deal of the histories of England, France, Prussia, Russia, and other countries. The essential new contribution by the authoritarian estate system was bureaucratic administration in government, a hierarchy of governmental occupations requiring training and other ways to attach individuals to a centralized means of administration. While this subtype emerged throughout the world, it developed most fully in the West, where it was eventually transformed into the class system when the "state" passed out of the hands of the monarch and nobility into the hands of the middle class. As Gideon Sjoberg[17] points out, however, the emergence of liberal democracy represented less of a break with the past than we imagine. Agrarian societies are exceedingly durable. Despite large-scale problem-solving failures, they successfully resist revolt from below and changes from above. In only one place—the West—did agrarian society succumb to a new form of society and even there it imparted many of its characteristics to its successor. With their monopolistic control of symbol formation, technical intelligence, and administrative-military-legal-political skills, along with their highly developed forms of etiquette and taste, it is not surprising that agrarian feudal elites were highly influential in shaping the modern West. In England the feudal aristocracy had a profound impact on liberal society and one must think in terms of the blending of interests and values between the feudal elite and the developing middle class rather than an abrupt break and reversal.[18] The feudal nobility was a powerful force in France well after the French Revolution, while feudal elites remained dominant in industrial Germany[19] and Japan. Thus, while the class system of stratification will be treated as a distinct type, important continuities and similarities with the estate system will be noted.

INEQUALITY IN THE MODERN WORLD: CAPITALIST AND SOCIALIST NATION-STATES

The concept *modern world* refers to the developed world of capitalist and socialist nation-states (it could also refer to all 165 countries in the contemporary world). The socialist nation-state is fairly recent, in many ways an offshoot of capitalism, and the developed socialist societies represent only a small portion of the industrial world. Clearly, the modern world is primarily the story of capitalist society. The struggle to explain capitalism is also the main story of social science ever since the seventeenth century.

Understanding capitalism presents special problems for Americans. Liberalism established itself so fully during the course of American history that the basic structure of capitalist society has merged with the American conception of human nature, history, religion, and human destiny. Both of the two major political parties in the United States regard capitalism as

[17]Gideon Sjoberg, "Folk and 'Feudal' Societies," *American Journal of Sociology* 58, no. 3 (November 1952): 231–239.

[18]Walter L. Arnstein, "The Survival of the Victorian Aristocracy" in F. C. Jaher, ed., *The Rich, the Well Born, and the Powerful* (Urbana, Illinois: University of Illinois Press, 1973), pp. 203–57.

[19]For an interesting analysis of how feudal and bourgeois values of inequality blended in Germany, which has implications for all modern societies, see Walter Struve, *Elites Against Democracy: Leadership Ideals in Bourgeois Political Thought in Germany, 1890–1933* (Princeton, N.J.: Princeton University Press, 1973).

natural, and neither party raises questions about its core values and beliefs (for example, private property, individualism, and economic growth). The same is true of most Americans, including the majority of American social scientists. To gain a perspective on capitalism, it is necessary to get outside it.

The Rise of Capitalism

The transformation of feudal to industrial society is the most momentous event ever directly experienced and reflected upon by human beings (if we are right in assuming that the advent of agriculture was too gradual and too absorbed in mythology to stimulate much reflection). Many social scientists in the eighteenth and nineteenth centuries interpreted the rise of modern (capitalist or liberal) society as the outcome of "individualism." They assumed that human nature, suppressed for millennia by the forces of ignorance and superstition, had at last freed itself. Human beings they felt were now manifesting their natural biopsychological structures (or drives, instincts, needs, rights). Today, a sociological perspective would insist that the order of causality be reversed, that capitalism emerged first and then developed individualism (including the full range of vices and virtues termed the *modern Protestant-bourgeois personality*) as its necessary personality type. If there's no human nature, then, where did capitalism come from?

Our best answer comes from Max Weber. According to Weber, capitalism was the outcome of the following conditions that came together by chance during the late Middle Ages:

1. Greek philosophy with its emphasis on abstraction, its assumptions about the lawfulness of human nature and nature, and its well-developed structures of logic (teleology and mathematics).
2. Greek and Roman political and legal theories with their distinctions between law and other types of norms, between the responsible and irresponsible exercise of power, and between public and private offices and norms.
3. The Judaic-Christian religious-moral orientation with its abstract theology (rational monotheism), its this-worldly counterbalance to excessive other-worldliness, and its sharp separation among the realms of God, human nature, and nature.
4. An advanced material culture (plows, carts, the harness, hearths, bellows, wind and watermills, ships).
5. A favorable natural environment (good soil, adequate rainfall, a temperate climate; good energy and other resources such as timber and ores; cheap water transportation).
6. Military factors.
7. Luxury trade.
8. But "in the last resort the factor which produced capitalism is the rational permanent enterprise, rational accounting, rational technology and rational law, but again not these alone. Necessary complementary factors were the

rational spirit, the rationalization of the conduct of life in general, and a rationalistic economic ethic."[20]

Indispensable to the capitalist spirit, argued Weber, was Protestantism.
Protestant Christians, especially Calvinists, were called on, one and all, to do
God's work in this world and to accept the world's problems as a challenge
to their character. As Protestants they could neither withdraw from the world
into mysticism nor accommodate themselves to it under the guidance of
others (the medieval Catholic Church). Given the need to avoid creatural
temptations, Calvinism soon came to see work as a calling in which one
administers what God has given. Eventually, argued Weber, there emerged a
methodical, impersonal, individualist type of conduct, especially in economic affairs, which, combined with a religious brake on personal consumption, stimulated both capital formation and the spirit of capitalism. Out of the
Reformation came a merger of religious and economic behavior in which
economic success signified religious worth and religious status provided
economic motives and credentials.

Weber did not think of religion either as the only or even as the major
cause of capitalism. If anything, his major emphasis was on economic factors,
followed by political and then religious factors. But while his approach was
multicausal, he put no emphasis on establishing priorities or on finding the
unifying thread of human history as Marx had done. If anything, argued
Weber, capitalism occurred because a large number of causes came together
by chance. Thus, he emphasized such economic factors as the emergence of
technology, especially in the textile industry; the preeminent importance of
coal and iron, which freed industry from inorganic and organic limitations;
and the rise of new forms of economic organization such as the joint-stock
company. But he also cited political factors such as law, administration,
warfare, and types of urban existence as important causes. All these, along
with Protestantism, said Weber, caused capitalism.

Weber (as did Marx) emphasized *internal* factors in his explanation of
the rise of capitalism. In recent years theorists have argued that capitalism
could not have risen without the help of factors *outside* society. Societies are
not only interdependent but it is difficult to think of any complex society as
autonomous. No understanding of the rise of capitalism is complete, therefore, until international trade and imperial expansion are included.[21] And the
rise of science was also dependent on an international network of stimulation
and support.[22]

[20]Weber's only summary of his position is in his *General Economic History*, trans. F.H.
Knight, 1927 (New York: Collier, 1961), pt. 4. The quotation is on p. 260.

[21]This perspective will be developed more fully in Chapter 3.

[22]Robert Wuthnow, "The Emergence of Modern Science and World System Theory,"
Theory and Society 8 (September 1979): 215–243.

The Nature of Capitalism

The essence of capitalism is the private ownership of aspects of nature (land, water, mineral or grazing rights, air space, and so on), technology, including knowledge, and labor power (including professional skills), and their employment for gain (profit, rent, salaries, wages) through exchange relationships. Understood differently, capitalism means the transformation of nature and human nature into productive forces. Under a capitalist (market or exchange) economy, the bulk of productive property (land, animals, factories, offices, and so on) is in private hands and its owners strive to profit from the use of their property. Under capitalism, work is performed by legally free individuals who sell their labor time. In the classic capitalist tradition, it is assumed that economic units are small and competitive, and that the free exchange of goods, services, and labor is the most rational way to allocate resources. The reality of capitalism is otherwise: The vast bulk of economic activity is conducted by giant, oligarchic corporations and there are numerous distortions and barriers to the free exchange of goods, services, and labor; distortions and barriers that are both legal and illegal and which often represent other respectable social values.

Another distinctive feature of capitalism is its many-sided process of capital formation. Unlike even the highly productive agrarian society, capitalism channels significant portions of economic surplus into productive uses. While part of its surplus goes toward a rising standard of living and part for social overhead, part also goes for capital investment. Paying labor less than it produces, thrift, safeguarding property rights, tax policies that favor investments, norms of efficiency, the substitution of technology for labor, the subsidization of necessary but unprofitable capital investments (such as canals, railroads, highways, airports, water supply, sanitation, fire and military protection) by public revenues are all part of the process of capital formation.

Historic capitalism based itself on a number of key beliefs: that its institutions expressed fundamental forces in human nature, that science and knowledge embedded in capitalist institutions are an unmixed good, and that the encouragement of self-interest is compatible, indeed, a requisite for social health. These beliefs were based on the master assumption that a hidden logic synthesizes the selfish, short-term initiatives of profit-oriented egos. The magical belief in the hidden logic of social institutions, especially economic markets (laissez-faire market economy), political markets (representative government), and intellectual markets (competitive education, professionalism, research, free press), has tended to protect capitalist society from scrutiny and evaluation.

If capitalism is not rooted in human nature and does not represent the unfolding of a rational process rooted in the cosmos, then capitalism becomes simply another type of society. Placed in a more contemporary light, the historical uniqueness of capitalism means that economic growth is not necessarily inherent in the destiny of humanity. Far from being in the nature of things for humans to exploit nature and ride the crest of endless economic growth, it is now recognized (at least by some) that the planet is finite and that it may not be able to sustain economic growth at current levels much longer. Perhaps more important is the fact that neither capitalist nor socialist societies can look for answers in alleged natural laws of economics, society, or history. All this has enormous implications for the modern system of social stratification.

The Nation-State: Its Nature and Varieties

The nation-state emerged slowly in the West during the Middle Ages and reached its mature development during the nineteenth century. After 1945 the nation-state spread rapidly outside the West. Today, all societies have assumed (or are struggling to assume) the shape of a nation-state. What is a nation-state? Despite variations (and the fact that many societies are only partially developed nation-states), today's societies are all marked by centralized states. A centralized state means political mechanisms for reconciling power conflicts and producing a legitimate government, a legal code that expresses the results of the reconciliation process and that is sovereign vis-à-vis to all other types of norms, and a bureaucratic form of administration (civil and military) to interpret, administer, and enforce the complex criminal, civil, and legislative elements in that code. Despite differences, all nation-states identify themselves with a given piece of geography, and all display nationalistic or patriotic emotions and beliefs—that is, deep, common, emotional-cognitive commitments to their constitutive values and norms and to the piece of geography on which they are located.

Despite these common elements, nation-states take distinctive forms. Two types can be distinguished: liberal and socialist nation-states.

The Liberal (Capitalist) Nation-State

It should be repeated that the term *liberalism* refers to the philosophic world view of the middle class and not to the political program or platform of political parties or organizations. In broad terms, the basic assumption behind the liberal world view is that human beings can achieve a mastery of themselves and of nature through the proper exercise of human reason (science) and the proper set of values (Protestant-bourgeois ethic). Translated into institutions, the liberal world view equates social health with private property, individualism, a market economy (with or without explicit public direction), and private scientific-intellectual life.

Ideally speaking, liberal society is secular, scientific, and dynamic. Geared to effect a mastery over nature and over human nature, liberal society institutionalizes individual achievement, futurism, and a highly specialized division of economic and social functions. Its general symbolic and status structure contains distinct public and private spheres of action and does not assume an identity of interest between individuals and groups. Its unity is based on universal (often excessively abstract and vague) values and beliefs as well as on specific mechanisms for ensuring social control and reconciliation (police, schools, courts, political parties, legislatures, government). Its social constitution is made up of hundreds of thousands (millions, counting families and economic units) of groups that cooperate, jostle, and disagree about this or that issue. Both competitive and managed economic markets settle many of the issues between groups and classes. The political system serves as a further arena of negotiation among groups and the results of the political process become law. There is an explicit generation and use of law (as distinct from agrarian societies, which discover law), and legal norms—as distinct from other norms—are publicly enforced by coercive, allegedly referee structures and constitute the ultimate control system of liberal society. Private groups also play an important part in the process of social control since they develop fairly explicit norms to control their members. As Emile Durkheim pointed out, much of the stability of a differentiated society comes from the social control exerted by occupational groupings over their members.

Inequality in capitalist society allegedly derives from the natural hierarchy of ability in human beings. The biopsychological explanation of inequality often takes the form of racism and sexism. Capitalist ideology and imperialism have even produced an unusual hybrid, the Republic of South Africa (see Box 2–1). Inequality in capitalist societies is deep and often at variance with their ideals. The evidence of the past decades also suggests that these societies have made little progress in living up to their ideals and, further, that they may be incapable of bringing themselves in line with their normative value system. While there is much talk of equality of opportunity in all spheres and a strong normative tradition stressing equality of competition, in reality most competition takes place *within* classes, and there is considerable concentration of economic, social, and political power. While a powerful ideology stresses individual achievement, in reality the majority of wealthy individuals inherited their property. In addition, occupational placement is also hereditary, either directly or through class-based socialization processes, including the private and public educational systems.

The Socialist Nation-State

Imperial Russia was undergoing a transformation toward industrialization and parliamentary democracy when it suffered a crushing military defeat in World War I. As a result, the tiny Communist party headed by Lenin came to power and began the task of establishing a Marxian society. Between 1917 and the 1960s, the USSR developed as a one-party totalitarian state in

BOX 2–1. *SOUTH AFRICA: A CLASS-CASTE HYBRID*

South Africa was colonized by the English and Boers during the late nineteenth century. After World War II the English lost control of the country to the Dutch Calvinist Boers, who instituted a rigid system of racial segregation called *apartheid*. Today the 83 percent of the population that is black is kept in a subordinate position by the white population. What makes this a peculiar case is that the dominant whites are committed to economic development.

South Africa has representative government but blacks cannot vote. Blacks are forced to live in impoverished areas, must use segregated facilities, and until recently even had to carry passports. Interracial marriage and sex are illegal. Tension in South Africa is high because the white elite needs black labor to run their advanced economy. Even though whites monopolize the good jobs, blacks must be brought into cities, factories, and mines to work. Advanced societies develop "free" labor, that is, a labor force composed of individuals who are free to sell their labor and move to where there is work. South Africa's attempt to combine "slave" labor and a specialized, interdependent economy in which the majority must work hard for few rewards (and which knows that this is going on) is fundamentally flawed.[23]

[23]For background, including a valuable comparison with the United States, see G.M. Frederickson, *White Supremacy: A Comparative Study in American and South African History* (New York: Oxford University Press, 1981).

relative isolation from the rest of the world (save for the brief New Economic Period when it invited outside help). Since the 1960s the Soviet Union has become authoritarian rather than totalitarian.[24] In general perspective, the Soviet Union is a case where industrialization succeeded with neither capitalism nor political democracy.

Between 1917 and 1939 the USSR was the world's only society committed to socialism. After 1945 a number of Eastern European nations occupied by the Soviet Army became similar one-party Marxist societies. In addition, a number of societies committed to socialism emerged in various parts of the world: China, Yugoslavia, Albania, Cuba, Tanzania, Vietnam, and assorted Arab countries. Socialist societies are quite diverse. Marxist Yugoslavia has a one-party state that emphasizes a market economy, decentralized decision making, and mass citizen participation. There are also variations inside Soviet-dominated Eastern Europe; Marxist Hungary has instituted many of the features of a market economy. In Poland the Communist party, government, and military face strong opposition from the Roman Catholic Church

[24]For an extended case study of the USSR, and the recent steps taken toward representative government, see Chapters 18 and 19.

and a politicized trade-union movement. More recently, China has adopted some "capitalist" practices to help it modernize.

Socialist societies are based on public property, public control of investment priorities, and comprehensive public planning and direction. Socialist society hopes to achieve many of the values of capitalism by removing what it believes is the chief obstacle of those values—private property. For socialists, private property fragments populations into selfish, warring, wasteful units (individuals, groups, classes) and makes it impossible for society to achieve unity and self-direction, to eliminate both poverty and unemployment, or fully realize the ideals of individual fulfillment. Some socialist movements (for example, in Great Britain, France, and Germany) hope to combine liberal democracy with substantial social ownership of the economy. Socialist government in Sweden has ignored public ownership of economic units and has focused instead on reducing inequality through taxation and social services. And socialism elsewhere is associated with centralized political and economic forms without civil and political freedoms or rights. Variations on this latter pattern exist in the USSR, East Germany, Poland, the People's Republic of China, Syria, Algeria, and Cuba. A more "liberal" socialist system exists in Tanzania, Yugoslavia, and Hungary.

Socialist societies also claim to be meritocracies, to be based on an inequality related to ability and social functions. But like capitalist societies, they too have inequalities at wide variance with their legitimating ideology.

STRATIFICATION THROUGH HISTORY: A SUMMARY

Inequality varies with type of society. Inequality increases with economic development and reaches its high point in agrarian and industrial societies. It is a mistake to think that modern society (whether capitalist or socialist) has more equality than in the past.

The economic system determines inequality though sometimes it is disguised as an estate system (stratification by an hereditary family system) or caste system (stratification by religious birth).

The modern class system resulted from the rise of capitalism and eventual industrialization.

Modern society and its class system took the form of the nation-state. Today, developed societies take the form of capitalist (or liberal) nation-states and socialist nation-states.

CHAPTER 3

Stratification Among Societies

Societies are characterized by "political" relations; they discuss, argue, and moralize among themselves, negotiate trade and military agreements, and agree or disagree on matters as varied as air rights, mail, customs, the rights of citizens, cultural and scientific exchange, and so on. Societies spy on each other and finance political movements in other countries that favor their interests. Political relations among societies can lead to mutual respect, a concern for the rights of the weak and of minorities, including political opponents, and a willingness to compromise. But intersocietal relations are also characterized by domination, conquest, exploitation, and dependence, in short, by stratification and imperialism.

INTERSOCIETAL STRATIFICATION: EMPIRE AND WORLD-MARKET SYSTEMS

The fact that societies interpenetrate as part of larger systems, culminating in imperialism, has received various explanations. Karl Deutsch has identified them as:

1. folk theories (biologic-instinctive, demographic-Malthusian, geographic-strategic, cultural organicism, or the people as a psychological entity), theories that today command little respect;

2. conservative theories (Julie Ferry, Disraeli, Rhodes, Kipling), which advocated imperial expansion to provide economic stability at home;
3. liberal theories (John Hobson and Norman Angell), which argued that imperialism was unnecessary and stood in the way of competition;
4. a sociological/psychological theory (associated with Joseph Schumpeter), which argued that imperialism was learned behavior and thus not inevitable;
5. Marxian theories of imperialism (especially those of Vladimir Lenin, Jon Galtung, and Samir Amin), which argue that capitalist economies necessarily reach outward to acquire colonies to support themselves (with Leninists arguing that imperialist nations weaken themselves by investing abroad and other Marxists arguing that they strengthen themselves by creating dependent, complementary colonial economies and societies).[1]

Perhaps the first systematic analysis of imperialism to influence mainsteam sociology is Immanuel Wallerstein's *The Modern World System: Capitalist Agriculture and the Origins of the European World Economy in the Sixteenth Century*.[2] Wallerstein argues that a society's internal development is greatly affected by its relations with other societies. The uniqueness of capitalism is its commitment to economic growth through economic activity. The empires acquired by the capitalist societies were not ordinary empires. They were part of a new international division of labor roughly divided into technically advanced countries and countries that specialized in food, staples, ores, fuel, and labor. Gradually modern imperialism shifted to a new kind of imperialism, one in which advanced societies could dominate others through new imperialist mechanisms such as free markets, trade agreements, loans, and investments (as well as in conquest and colonies). Historically, the imperialism of the new world-market economy emerged as a mercantile-financial operation (*portfolio investment*, or loans to the governments of colonies and dependent countries, characteristic of British imperialism) and then shifted to *direct investment* in productive, especially industrial enterprises (characteristic of American imperialism).

In analyzing international stratification, therefore, one must distinguish between the imperialism of an empire, in which a society expands by absorbing other societies (often becoming a larger society composed of different ethnic, religious, or linguistic groups), and the imperialism of the capitalist era in which a society expands by developing an economic superiority to other societies (as well as by territorial expansion) within an international division of labor.

[1] For a valuable analysis of these theories, including the fine shades of meaning that my summary has obscured, see Karl W. Deutsch, "Theories of Imperialism and Neocolonialism," in Steven J. Rosen and James R. Kurth, eds., *Testing Theories of Economic Imperialism* (Lexington, Mass.: D.C. Heath, 1974), chap. 2.

[2] New York: Academic Press, 1974; two more of the projected 4 volumes have appeared: Vol. II, *The Modern World System: Mercantilism and the Consolidation of the European World Economy, 1600–1750* (New York: Academic Press, 1980) and Vol III, *The Modern World System: The Second Era of Great Expansion of the Capitalist World Economy, 1730–1840s* (New York: Academic Press, 1988).

AGRARIAN EXPANSIONISM: THE IMPERIALISM OF EMPIRE

Empires in some form or another have existed for 5,000 years and were made possible by the advent of agriculture. Their beginnings are the great river-valley civilizations in the Middle East and their endings are in the dissolution of the Hapsburg Empire in 1918, the collapse of Imperial China between 1900 and 1945, the containment and contraction of the Ottoman Empire between 1450 and the 1920s, the dissolution of the British Empire and the overthrow of the French Empire after World War II, and the end of Portugal's empire in 1975. The essence of an empire is expansion through military or political conquest, and an attempt to control and profit from the economy of a conquered territory through military and political means. Empires are not able to integrate themselves through homogenization (because of feudal particularism and because they invariably contain a variety of racial and ethnic groups) though they are often accompanied by religious, missionary zeal (world religion).

Empires often last for considerable periods, but they exhibit chronic internal turmoil and all have decayed and disintegrated. Empires are marked by considerable economic surplus since they are based on a well-developed agriculture and a relatively advanced technology (irrigation, aqueducts, metallurgy, power from animals, water, wind, and sail, and from human muscle, especially serfdom and slavery). Characteristically, economic surplus is consumed in nonproductive activities: war, luxurious life-styles, inefficient administration, public spectacles, art, and the construction of monuments, arenas, palaces, temples, churches, and tombs. Indeed, the costs of these activities, especially the military and administrative costs of maintaining empires, invariably become so great that they stagnate the economy. A stagnant or declining economy creates political and social unrest that requires more coercion, more unproductive activities, and more conquest.

Empires may expand in terms of geographical size, population, and production but they are not dynamic systems. Unlike modern industrial systems they do not result in increased per capita living standards and do not provide incentives for productivity, technological advance, or capital investment. Actually, they institutionalize *disincentives* for production and efficiency. Their servile serf and slave labor, nonbureaucratic (nonrational) administration, punitive systems of tribute and taxation, other-worldly values, and institutionalized "waste" (prestige and military-political expenditures militate against productivity, efficiency, and capital formation). The elites of feudal systems see the acquisition of territory as the main way to enlarge the economic pie (which means that enemies are created because someone else's pie shrinks).

The mounting and conflicting claims that converge on the central state of empires lead to more inefficient centralization, political intrigue and conflict, ethnic and class rivalries, labor repression, and the suppression of political dissent through force. Ultimately, the military and political costs of running such a system outstrip the economy's ability to sustain them.

THE NEW IMPERIALISM: THE CAPITALIST WORLD-MARKET SYSTEM

New insight into the rise and nature of capitalism, modern class formation, the nation-state, imperialism, and international stratification is provided by Wallerstein's concept of a capitalist world economy, or as we will refer to it, the world-market system. Using neo-Marxian ideas concerning imperialism, Wallerstein argues that solitary societies (except for simple subsistence societies) are not ultimate entities. On the contrary, all contemporary societies must be conceived as part of a uniquely modern international division of labor. Unlike the inner structure of a single (precapitalist) society in which economic and political institutions are explicitly related, capitalist society separates its economy and politics both in its domestic life and in the relations among societies. The essence of the international system is that an expansive world economy comes into being in which all benefit, but because unequal units are transacting business, the more powerful benefit disproportionately. And because there is no government common to the unequal and often exploitive economic relations of the world-market economy, there is no way to focus conflicts, bring about compromises, assign blame and responsibility, and the dominant societies do not (at least at first) have to pay the full costs of maintaining order or institutionalizing exploitation.

Core, Semi-Periphery, and Periphery

According to Wallerstein, three different types of units interact in the capitalist world-market system that emerged in the sixteenth century: *core states, peripheral areas,* and *semi-peripheral areas.* The core state develops an expanding economy based on capitalist agriculture (gentry, yeoman farmers), trade (for example, the East India and Hudson's Bay companies), manufacture (textiles, china, and ironware), and services (banking and insurance). A large component of this expanding economy is made up of foreign trade. Essentially, a core state specializes its economy (and its internal system of social stratification) to complement the specialization of its international trading partners. Over time it acquires many trading partners, whereas peripheral and semi-peripheral areas acquire few. Gradually, its labor force is upgraded in skills and responsibilities, and a strong state emerges to supply the conditions of internal economic expansion (roads, law, currency) and external economic expansion (army, navy, foreign ministry).

Peripheral areas are marked by a distinctive form of development known as *underdevelopment.*[3] Development for them means the creation of unskilled, coerced, slave, or serf labor organized in extraction (for example, silver, gold, tin, oil, bauxite, copper) or in the production and export of labor and agricultural staples (slaves, cheap "immigrant," "migrant" or "guest" labor, sugar, cotton, coffee, rubber, tea, bananas, or cash crop specialty fruits and vegetables). Such areas are also politically underdeveloped: At first they are colonies but even after independence they are governed by a native upper and middle class that benefits from and thus has a stake in the new international division of labor.

The term *semi-peripheral* denotes societies that for one reason or another were able to avoid being subordinated by the capitalist core long enough to develop as core states themselves (Russia and Japan), or societies that are large enough, developed enough, or have enough special assets to have some of the features of core societies (India, the People's Republic of China, Brazil, Spain, Greece, Turkey, South Korea, and others). Here one is dealing with *dependent development* as opposed to underdevelopment. The society in question has a growing economy, perhaps with considerable industry, and an active national state. Nonetheless, it is still subject to both its own past and to the imperatives of the world market.

The concept of semi-periphery also serves as a caution against a mechanical one-way conception of the imperialist causal process. Every state no matter how weak has unique traditions and sources of strength and resilience. Thus, dependent societies all have some power vis-à-vis dominant countries even if it only means the ability to participate in setting the terms of their dependence.

Nationalism and Middle-Class Dominance

Caste and estate systems of social stratification explicitly promote strata consciousness and identification. A class system of stratification is markedly different. A society with an expanding economy cannot allow fixed values to develop. The historic middle class created a new political and social consciousness to help it rise against a feudal aristocracy, but it did not want the masses to rise on their own. It needed a strong state but had to prevent both feudal elites and the masses from using it for their own purposes. The basic solution adopted by the middle class was to define itself as the universal

---

[3]In this respect Wallerstein's work builds on the revisionist wing of Marxist imperialist theory; for two pioneering essays, see Paul A. Baran, "On the Political Economy of Backwardness," *Manchester School of Economics and Social Studies* (January 1952), reprinted in Robert I. Rhodes, ed., *Imperialism and Underdevelopment: A Reader* (New York: Monthly Review Press, 1970), pp. 285–301, and Andre Gunder Frank, "The Development of Underdevelopment," *Monthly Review* (September, 1966), reprinted in Andre Gunder Frank, ed., *Latin America: Underdevelopment or Revolution: Essays on the Development of Underdevelopment and the Immediate Enemy* (New York: Monthly Review Press, 1969), pp. 3–17.

class, as human nature, as rational, as normal, as the spearhead of an emerging humanity, and as the agent of progress. The net result of liberal social theory was to make aristocrats and workers look peculiar, warped, privileged, parasitic, dysfunctional, backward. Once in power, the middle class's orientation was to homogenize its population (one language, one law, one education, one government, one value-belief system, one mode of labor, standardized consumption, one nation). Nationalism is a fundamental bourgeois emotion because it helps to promote all of the above. And while ensuring middle-class dominance internally, nationalism also provided motives and justifications for dominance over foreign countries.[4]

The Disruption of Preindustrial Economies

The impact of the advanced nations of the West on preindustrial societies has been varied. British imperialism stressed elite control through British administration in cooperation either with a native elite or a white-settler elite. British colonial government tended to be relatively efficient and honest. In addition, roads and ports were built and hygienic measures were instituted. The French thought of their colonies as extensions of French civilization and tended to avoid the overt racism and ethnocentrism of Britain. Variations of the British and French models can be found in the imperial policies of Portugal, Spain, Germany, the Netherlands, Belgium, and Italy. Russian and then later Soviet imperialism is somewhat different in that Czarist and Soviet Russia simply incorporated conquered lands into Russian society. English imperialism also consisted of incorporating contiguous areas, succeeding with Scotland and Wales, failing with Ireland. The United States has also expanded by incorporating new territory unto itself, some through conquest, some through purchase.

Despite variations, Western imperialism has had one outstanding feature: Everywhere traditional subsistence economies were transformed into export-oriented economies. From relative self-sufficiency, traditional societies became dependent on world markets (and internally, rural and urban areas became dependent on each other). Colonial powers everywhere introduced and promoted cash-crop agriculture and (where resources permitted) the extraction and export of raw materials. The colonial powers developed an infrastructure of roads, water and power supply, sanitation and medicine, currency, ports, railroads, land-use patterns, law, tax and other money incentives, and education, all of which furthered economic development in keeping with their needs. Even the white-settler colonies of British North America (the American colonies, Canada), Australia, and New Zealand were shaped to suit the needs of England.

[4]Here we are referring to the original nationalisms of developing capitalist Europe. Nationalism has also arisen in former colonies and has served to rally a variety of subjugated peoples against foreign domination.

The dissolution of the European empires after World War II changed little in the economic relations between developed and developing nations. The former colonies were now independent nations, but their economies were still geared to the world economy. Most former colonial powers adopted foreign aid programs, especially for their former colonies, and development loans were now made through international (Western-dominated) bodies such as the World Bank. The developing countries were still subject to private groups: multinational corporations, churches, universities, and foundations, professional groups, and so on. The basic thrust of development aid—whether in the form of loans, grants, education, technical aid, or capital investment—has been the same—to develop the human and natural resources of the developing world in keeping with the needs of the developed world.

SOCIETIES IN THE CONTEMPORARY WORLD: FIRST, SECOND, AND THIRD WORLDS

Three terms, *First, Second,* and *Third* World, have gained currency as a shorthand for the world's countries. While usage varies, the term *First World* refers to the industrialized capitalist nations led by the United States (see Table 3–1). All are liberal (capitalist) democracies. With the exception of Japan, all are white and derive from the European Judaic-Christian, Greco-Roman tradition. The basic economic interests of the developed capitalist countries are threefold: economic growth through private capital and an exchange economy, trade and investment abroad, and the importation of raw materials. The small group of developed capitalist countries outproduce by far the rest of the world, conduct most of the world's trade among themselves, and consume far more of the earth's resources than the rest of the world combined. The United States alone, for example, with only 6 percent of the world's population, consumes 33 percent of its energy.

The *Second World* is made up of the more developed socialist countries and is led by the USSR (see Table 3–2). All are one-party authoritarian regimes. All are white and derive from the European Judaic-Christian tradition although their version of this tradition is distinctly less liberal and humanistic than its counterpart in Western Europe. The basic economic problem of these countries is to sustain economic growth in the face of popular restiveness over low living standards. Economically, the state-socialist societies have developed extensive trade with the First World because of their decision (derived from need) to import Western capital, technological expertise, and food. As a result, the Second World is an exporter of raw materials (to help pay for its imports) and many Second World countries have incurred sizable debts to First World banks.

The term *Third World* originated during the Cold War period soon after

TABLE 3-1.   The First World (Industrial Capitalist Countries) Ranked By GDP[a]
(With Per Capita Income and Population), 1985.

	GDP (1985) (IN BILLIONS, U.S.)	PER CAPITA INCOME (1985)	POPULATION (ROUNDED IN MILLIONS)
1. The United States	$3,947	$14,565	239
2. Japan	1,325	9,452	121
3. The Federal Republic of Germany	625	8,950	61
4. France	512	8,126	55
5. United Kingdom	456	7,156	57
6. Italy	359	5,592	57
7. Canada	349	11,788	25
8. Australia	156	9,196	16
9. The Netherlands	125	7,710	14
10. Sweden	100	10,315	8
11. Switzerland	93	13,720	6
12. Belgium	81	7,408	10
13. Austria	66	7,631	8
14. Norway	57.9	11,784	4
15. Denmark	57.8	9,709	5
16. New Zealand	22	6,100	3
17. Luxembourg	4	11,960	.36

Source: *The World In Figures*, editorial information compiled by *The Economist* (Boston: G. K. Hall, 1988), pp. 8, 9, 13.

[a]Gross Domestic Product (GDP) differs from Gross National Product (GNP) in that it excludes property income from other countries. All such figures are dependent on exchange rates (modified by purchasing power indices) and should be used to obtain gross ratios among nation state economies.

World War II and took on political reality in 1955 at the Bundung Conference led by Tito of Yugoslavia, Nehru of India, and Sukarno of Indonesia. Calling themselves nonaligned, a number of developing countries proclaimed their right to act independently of the two superpowers. Since 1955 the nonaligned nations (now numbering approximately 125) have met formally to coordinate their efforts. The term *Third World* is also a catchall term for all nonindustrialized countries (which number approximately 140).

The outstanding characteristics of most Third World countries are their low technological levels, low energy consumption, an unskilled and surplus labor force, specialized economies geared toward exporting food and raw materials, and their inability to create capital fast enough to yield self-sufficiency and self-direction. Many of these characteristics have their origin in foreign economic (and political-military-educational-religious) penetration, and all are reinforced by continued outside influences.

The countries of the Third World are highly diversified by size, natural

TABLE 3–2. The Second World (The More Developed Socialist Countries)[a] Ranked By GDP[b] (With Per Capita Income and Population), 1985.

	GDP (IN BILLIONS, U.S.)	PER CAPITA INCOME	POPULATION (ROUNDED IN MILLIONS)
1. The Union of Soviet Socialist Republics	$1,200	$4,200	279
2. The Democratic Republic of (East) Germany	100	5,400	17
2. Czechoslovakia	100	6,000	16
3. Poland	78	1,900	37
4. Romania	69	2,687	23
5. Bulgaria	31	3,200	9
6. Hungary	21	1,722	11

Source: *The World In Figures*, editorial information compiled by *The Economist* (Boston: G. K. Hall, 1988), pp. 8, 9, 13.

[a]Yugoslavia is a developed socialist society but does not follow the lead of the USSR.

[b]GDP figures are estimates and are even less reliable than usual because the Soviet bloc uses different accounting methods.

environment, previous forms of social development, including experience with imperialism, and by the nature of their economy. Some, like the People's Republic of China, India, Brazil, and Nigeria, are very large and exert considerable influence on world and regional affairs. Others are oil-rich, whereas some are extremely poor with bleak prospects. Some nations are semi-developed with good prospects, while still others are floundering and in revolutionary ferment. (For data on the diversity of the Third World, see Table 3–3).

The impact of imperialism on the non-West is extremely complex, and its interpretation has understandably become a source of considerable controversy. Probably the best strategy in assessing the impact of imperialism is to keep the issues in close contact with concrete cases. Two studies are presented in the following sections illustrating the two forms of dependency (underdevelopment and dependent development) and their respective systems of internal stratification.

UNDERDEVELOPMENT: EL SALVADOR

An inflow of technology, money, and know-how into a simple feudal society results in economic concentration, especially in land. A road, a new supply of water, tractors, or a dependable customer for a product—each in its own way makes land more valuable. Before the arrival of imperial powers, the landlord had to develop labor-intensive methods of utilizing the land. Landlords

TABLE 3-3.   The Diversity of the Third World (By Per Capita Income and Average Life Expectancy, 1986.

Low Income Countries (Total[a] 39; av. inc. $270; income range $120-420; av. life expectancy 52 excluding China and India)

Ethiopia, Burma, Tanzania, Niger, India, Kenya, China[b], Sri Lanka, Vietnam, Senegal

Lower Middle Income Countries (Total 35; av. inc. $750; income range $460-1570; av. life expectancy 59)

Indonesia, Philippines, Zimbabwe, Nigeria, Nicaragua, El Salvador, Peru, Turkey, Cuba, Chile, Syria

Upper Middle Income Countries (Total 20; av. inc. $1890; income range $1810-7410; av. life expectancy 67)

Brazil, Malaysia, South Africa[c], Yugoslavia, Republic of Korea, Greece, Israel, Iraq, Mexico, Algeria, Singapore

High Income Oil Exporters (Total 4; av. inc. $6740; income range $6950-14,680; av. life expectancy 64)

Saudia Arabia, Libya, Kuwait, United Arab Emirates

Source: World Bank, *The World Bank Development Report, 1988* (New York: Oxford University Press, 1988), Table 1.

[a]Totals include only countries with a population of 1 million or more.

[b]China is not a typical low-income country—it not only has a life expectancy of 69 years and can feed itself but it is presently making a transition to industrialization.

[c]South Africa is a developed country but its general per capita income puts it in the Third World. It is peculiar also because its income distribution is skewed in favor of its white minority by South Africa's explicit racial policies.

and serf-tenants needed each other. The introduction of Western technology and supporting institutions made the land more valuable and labor cheaper. Everywhere in such societies landlords began to abrogate traditional relations with tenants, serfs, and other forms of labor. Unneeded labor was dispossessed and a gradual concentration of land took place in keeping with economic power and the economies of scale. Today, most such societies are in a peculiar position: Food production, even where it has risen dramatically, can no longer keep up with population growth (which has also risen spectacularly because of Western sanitation and medicine). Neither the Green Revolution nor food from abroad (whether bought or given free) seems to help.

Like much of Central and South America, El Salvador has outgrown its social form, namely the simple feudal society. *Simple feudalism* is a customary society centered on subsistence farming. The society is decentralized and revolves around a series of haciendas or large self-sufficient estates. The *patron* is head of the hacienda, similar to the lord of the manor of yesteryear. He (invariably male) supervises an estate that is labor-intensive and provides for its own needs—furniture, clothing, leather goods, repairs, sickness, old age, and so on. A rudimentary polity, created and operated by large land-owners, provides a few services. There is no government in the sense of national educational, health, transportation, postal, or energy services (some of these are provided especially in the few urban centers).

From the nineteenth century on, but especially in the past fifty years or so, El Salvador gradually developed a more specialized division of labor, and its simple feudal system eventually broke at the seams. In clear view of the United States government (actually with its help), American and other foreign companies brought new technology to El Salvador and introduced new products and services. The El Salvador government grew to provide more services to handle the increased economic activity, but ominously there was no extension of political participation. Essentially, political power remained in the hands of a few landowners and the tiny urban business and professional elite. Economic development resulted in a changeover from subsistence, labor-intensive farming to cash-crop, export-oriented, technologically inten-sive farming. As in the rest of the Third World, the *patron* asserted absolute legal ownership of the estate and renounced all customary rights based on the previous feudal, patron-tenant relations. This was a preliminary, of course, to dispossessing the peasants and turning the estate into a business.

Gradually a new economy emerged under the euphemism of the *Green Revolution*. The Green Revolution refers to the many-sided effort by the United States (and other industrial countries) to increase the agricultural output of Third World countries through technology (new seeds, fertilizer, irrigation systems, tractors, harvesters). The same technology has made the United States incredibly productive in food and staples. When Third World countries needed more food, the United States simply assumed that what worked here would work there. But even in the United States the Green Revolution has not been an unmixed blessing. Millions of Americans, for example (of all skin colors and ethnic backgrounds), were dispossessed by the surge of agricultural technology and forced to enter cities that were only partially ready for them.

The Green Revolution in El Salvador (and in the Third World) did not have an industrial revolution to soak up the labor it dispossessed from the countryside. Although it raised agricultural production, the Green Revolu-tion seems to have had the ironic outcome of increasing food dependency, making people poorer than they were and hungrier as well. The Green Revolution has promoted cash-crop agriculture, which means production to stock the pantries and dining tables of America, Europe, and Japan: coffee, sugar, cotton, bananas, cocoa, nuts, artichokes, and so on. The Green Revolu-tion means economic concentration in land and the dispossession of former tenants. The Third World landlords import seed, fertilizer, and farm ma-chinery and pay for them by exporting food and staples. The World Bank, other international agencies, the United States government, and a landlord-dominated home government provide ports, energy, and roads. The police become a National Guard to protect the economy. The value of the exports can never match the value of what is being imported (farm technology, Coca-Cola, television sets, arms for the National Guard), and a classic example of a dependent right-wing society has been helped into being by the Green Revolution.

When food aid is sent either by the United States government or private charities to feed the dispossessed masses, the basic power structure is reinforced. The free or subsidized food is used to keep the National Guard, the civil service, and urban workers fed and quiet. Some of the food is used to put rural labor to work—building roads, for example. But roads benefit landlords who can now get their crops out to be sold abroad. Food aid simply postpones the day of reckoning—the day the masses question a society in which economic growth produces poverty for most of the people.

Despite some growth of industry and urban services, El Salvador's new economy could not absorb the dispossessed labor. People crowded into the cities, most of them as squatters without jobs. Government employees and other workers are insecure and dependent because their jobs are precarious—a slight change in the price of coffee or energy and many are out of work. The government is under the influence of landlords, banks, import companies, and manufacturing firms, many of them branches of multinational (mostly American) corporations. But all efforts by civil servants, workers, and peasants to obtain a voice in setting government policy are rebuffed. Gradually, a revolutionary situation develops in plain sight of all, including the United States Embassy, and American executives and professionals.

The major trend is clear: The fruits of economic growth were being hogged by a small set of oligarchic elites. The masses, who were always poor, are now poor in a new way: Their poverty lacks meaning—they are idle while things around them are humming. Workers and civil servants are insecure, surrounded by consumer goods they cannot afford. Both the poor and the insecure employed can see the flow of profits to both native and foreign elites. Eventually, after repeated demands for reform are rebuffed, increasingly by violent means, the situation becomes polarized. Armed insurrection breaks out (using weapons supplied from abroad, especially the Soviet Union and Cuba, but also purchased from private dealers in the United States or stolen from the inept El Salvador military). There is also support from social democratic governments and forces in Europe as well as from the one-party conservative government of Mexico. The El Salvador government quickly schedules elections, which nobody takes seriously. It also beefs up its antiquated National Guard (with emergency aid from the United States) in an effort to suppress the rebellion.

Official United States policy is that El Salvador is trying to develop representative government and that Soviet and Cuban forces are causing all the trouble. But the American government is not believed by even its own people let alone the rest of the world. Everyone knows that the main problem lies in the outmoded, unworkable institutions of El Salvador itself, an institutional disarray that the United States has helped to produce. Everyone knows that it is too late for meaningful elections. Tens of thousands have been murdered (by all accounts most of the blame is laid on the El Salvador military) and hatred consumes all parties. The United States, the world's oldest democracy, finds itself on the side of an incompetent, greedy, feudal elite. The feudal elite gasps for breath as the American government funnels in the supplies it needs to stay alive. On February 25, 1982, President Reagan makes a bold proposal to invigorate the economies of the Caribbean countries, especially El Salvador, so as to bring prosperity and stability to the region. As he throws gasoline on the fire, there is not even a hint of understanding that prosperity without democracy is the main cause of the problem, that the civilian government is in deep trouble because it has been unable to change the oligarchic economy and find a place in it for the large majority of the El Salvadorean people.[5]

DEPENDENT DEVELOPMENT: THE REPUBLIC OF (SOUTH) KOREA

Land and People

Korea[6] occupies a peninsula on the northeast coast of Asia. Korea has a distinctive language and culture although it has been massively influenced by its giant neighbors, China and Japan.

The population of South Korea in 1986 was estimated at 43.3 million.[7]

[5]For a brief but meaty background on El Salvador, see Roland H. Ebel, "Political Instability in Central America," *Current History* 81 (February 1982): 56ff. For more extensive data on the extreme and growing inequality in El Salvador, the brutality with which the tiny elite rules, and the complicity of the United States in perpetuating an unworkable system, see Enrique A. Baloyra, *El Salvador in Transition* (Chapel Hill: The University of North Carolina Press, 1982); Tommie Sue Montgomery, *Revolution in El Salvador: Origins and Evolution* (Boulder, Colo.: Westview Press, 1982); Robert Armstrong and Janet Shenk, *El Salvador: The Face of Revolution* (Boston: South End Press, 1982); and Raymond Bonner, *Weakness and Deceit: U.S. Policy and El Salvador* (New York: Times Books, 1984). For an eyewitness account by a priest of the role of local Christian communities in supporting insurrection in El Salvador, Guate mala, and Nicaragua (influential in the latter's success), see Philip Berryman, *The Religious Roots of Rebellion: Christians in Central American Revolutions* (Maryknoll, N.Y.: Orbis Books, 1984).

[6]*South Korea: A Country Study*, 3rd ed. (Washington, D.C.: U.S. Government Printing Office, 1982), compiled by Foreign Area Studies of The American University, provides invaluable background on all aspects of Korean history, culture, and society, including the division of North and South Korea after World War II. An indispensable companion to this volume is *North Korea: A Country Study*, 3rd ed. (Washington, D.C.: U.S. Government Printing Office, 1981). Other sources will be cited below, but towering over all accounts is the sophisticated and comprehensive analysis by Norman Jacobs, *The Korean Road to Modernization and Development* (Urbana: University of Illinois Press, 1985).

[7]The population of North Korea in 1988 was estimated at 21.9 million.

The religion of South Korea is primarily Buddhist but Confucianists and Christians represent sizable minorities. South Korea is not well endowed with natural resources. It lacks minerals and fuels, its topography is mountainous, its soil poor, and overcutting has denuded it of trees. Aside from its hardworking, disciplined people, perhaps its most valuable resource is its fishing waters.

Korea has a continuous history of settlement that stretches back into Paleolithic times. The various groups on the Korean peninsula were united in the seventh century, and Korea remained a unified kingdom until 1905 when it was occupied by Japan (Korea was formally annexed by Japan in 1910). Feudal Korea was similar to Imperial China and in general conformed to authoritarian or state feudalism rather than manorial, decentralized, stateless feudalism. Land is the basis of power under all forms of feudalism. In advanced agrarian systems[8] large landowners supplement their local power by participating in a central power structure. Under the Chinese system the landowning gentry prepared their sons to take rigorous examinations in the classics, the gateway to highly prized positions in the Emperor's civil service. Confucianism supplied the legitimating ideology for China's power structure. As is common in feudal symbolic systems, Confucianism gave central position to the family, or rather the patriarchical family. The authority of the father, and thus the superiority of males, is the linchpin of the entire system. Filial piety is the most important obligation, and the hierarchical family is the model for thinking about society. The ultimate image in Confucian as well as feudal thought in general is of a harmonious, finished hierarchy that extends from one end of human nature to nature at large. The essential value for all to seek, in keeping with their station in life, is the world's harmony.

Feudal Korea was a highly concentrated society dominated by a handful of large landowning families. The concentration of power continued under Japanese rule and has continued into the present despite Korea's independence and industrialization.

With the defeat of Japan in World War II, the Soviet Union occupied the northern half of the Korean peninsula and the United States occupied the southern half. Present-day Korea is divided into the Republic of (South) Korea and the People's Republic of (North) Korea.

Economy

For various reasons, including influence and pressure from the outside, Korea's economy[9] and polity tended to promote concentrated landholding. For much of its history feudal Korea was subsistence oriented. Perhaps the

---

[8]For a discussion of agrarian society, see Chapter 2.

[9]For indispensable background and analysis of all of Korea's institutions, see Norman Jacobs, *The Korean Road to Modernization and Development* (Urbana: University of Illinois Press, 1985).

chief activity in its simple market economy was money lending. There is evidence of increased market activity in the nineteenth century as Korea experienced other foreign influences besides China, most notably Japan and Western countries.

Under Japanese rule Korea developed as a typical colonial economy. Japan treated Korea as booty—it took over all land, businesses, and government, and colonized it with a thick strata of Japanese who occupied all important positions. The Korean agricultural sector became export-centered to supply Japan with food and staples while Japan supplied Korea with manufactured products.

World War II and the Korean War of 1950 to 1953 brought new forms of economic devastation to Korea. After the stalemate and negotiated peace of 1953, massive American aid and investment in the 1970s wrought a significant transformation in the Korean economy. During the 1960s Korea had one of the highest economic growth rates in the world. Essentially its economy was oriented toward exporting from a labor-intensive manufacturing sector. Using imported capital, Korea also imported most of its raw materials and exported them in the form of finished goods.

Korea's agricultural sector was bypassed by its industrial boom. Land reform after World War II had ended its long history of large feudal landholding. Korea took back its economy after the defeat of Japan and redistributed the large Japanese-held lands to its own people. The effect, however, was not to produce a balanced economy or a greater equality of political power. Korean autocracy and elitism switched from agriculture to industry and services. As always, Korea was dependent on outsiders. The impact of China during Korea's early history had helped to produce a hierarchical, concentrated bureaucratic agrarian economy and society. The Japanese reinforced this structure by deliberately using it to dominate and exploit Korea between 1910 and 1945 (the United States also relied on the feudal-authoritarian tradition during its occupation between 1945 and 1948, thereby giving it added legitimacy. Korea's modernization after 1948, based on its own efforts, massive American aid and military protection, and American and Japanese investment, took place within this feudal-authoritarian system.[10]

Korea's economic development deviates considerably from other Third World countries. Significant steps toward industrialization have been taken; its standard of living has shown a steady increase; and its inequality, while considerable, is more in line with developed rather than developing coun-

---

[10]For a brilliant analysis of how and why Korea modernized without developing (a useful distinction), see Norman Jacobs, *The Korean Road to Modernization and Development* (Urbana: University of Illinois Press, 1985). By *modernization* Jacobs means adopting new ways of achieving old values, and by *development* he means maximizing the potential of a society regardless of existing values or organizational structures (one has to conclude that what Jacobs means by this is development into a capitalist democracy).

tries. Its gross national product (GNP) of $91.7 billion (1986 estimate) yielded a per capita income of $2,032 (1985). Korea's economic success is due to a number of factors. Japan's occupation, which lasted to 1945, and land reform brought about by the American occupation following World War II, left Korea without a landed oligarchy to oppose modernization and industrialization. In addition, an uprooted population fell back on a cultural tradition that stressed discipline, hierarchy, state service, and respect for education. And Korea's government has provided a wide variety of support facilities and services, including reliable statistics and planning services. In an important sense, Korea, like Japan and Germany (and perhaps the Soviet Union), derived significant benefits from the devastation of war (and in Korea's case from colonial exploitation). The destruction of Japanese and German industry during World War II allowed both countries to build the world's most modern factories following war's end. Together with guilt and shame over their defeat, a traditional sociocultural system that stressed discipline, employee loyalty, and a hierarchical world, together with massive American aid, including military protection, both Japan and Germany channeled their efforts into industry. Much the same can be said of the Republic of Korea.

It should be noted that Korea's economic success since the 1960s is no miracle of free enterprise and should not be considered to result from Korean efforts alone. Korea's economic success should also not be attributed to abstract forces like Confucian values or education. Korea (like any society) is a product of history.

Chinese hierarchical feudal forms certainly played a part. But Korea is also a result of Japan's imperial expansion from the late nineteenth century through World War II. The Japanese conquest and colonization provided Korea with much of what it needed to become part of the capitalist world. Korea is also a result of American policy since World War II. The United States' major foreign-policy goal in Asia has been to contain and rollback communism. To that end it fought the Korean war and it supported Korea with massive economic aid of various sorts, including making its own giant market available to Korean exports.[11]

A World Bank analysis attributes Korea's competitive edge to private-public cooperation, or rather to the Korean government's skill in providing incentives to private producers oriented toward export markets. The analysis stresses the importance to these producers of being able to rely on long-term government support of the export-oriented manufacturing sector. It also cites the importance of Korea's work force, with its Confucian-derived beliefs in loyalty, punctuality, hard work, and respect for authority, and of foreign

---

[11]For a valuable analysis placing the economic success of Korea (as well as Taiwan and Japan) into its historical context, including the role played by Japanese and American imperialism, see Bruce Cumings, "The Origin and Development of the Northeast Asian Political Economy: Industrial Sectors, Product Cycles, and Political Consequences", *International Organization* 38, (Winter 1984): 1–40.

capital. The report fails to note that the Korean government is authoritarian, that Korean labor is managed in a military manner, works a 54- to 60-hour week, and is consistently repressed and unable to organize. The World Bank also fails to note that Korea's export-centered economy has made it vulnerable (dependent) to the world market, put it deeply in debt, and is not connected to, and thus not producing benefits for, Korean society in general. Needless to say, the report fails to place Korea in history or in the context of Japanese and American imperial expansion and policies.[12]

A number of other liberal analyses have also failed to explain Korea's economic "miracle". In addition to specific deficiencies, these studies also fail to place Korea in history or to cite the enormous impact that Japan and the United States have had in preparing Korea for economic expansion (and dependency).[13]

There can be little doubt about one thing, however: Korea's economic success is real and puts it in a select group of Third World countries that have managed to achieve significant growth, *including relative gains against the developed world.* As is true of the various capitalist countries, Korea's industrial sector is not organically linked to the Korean people. In Korea, as in other parts of the developing capitalist world, American and First World aid and investment have promoted a highly concentrated dual economy and an authoritarian political regime.

Polity

Korea's political institutions, like its economy, have been massively influenced by outsiders.[14] Korea did not develop as a decentralized, self-sufficient feudal society. The landed elite of a self-sufficient manorial economy fears the state and retards its growth as it develops enough state power to maintain the status quo. In the modern world, oligarchies whose power is

[12]Yung Rhee, Bruce Ross-Larson, and Garry Pursell, *Korea's Competitive Edge: Managing The Entry Into World Markets* (Baltimore: The Johns Hopkins University Press, 1984), a World Bank report.

[13]L.L. Wade and B.S. Kim, *Economic Development of South Korea: The Political Economy of Success* (New York: Praeger, 1978) provide a useful analysis of Korea's economic "miracle," including invaluable comparisons with other developing countries but it too fails to mention Korea's authoritarian-repressive political regime and the major handicap such a regime presents for coping with economic difficulties. The volume by Edward S. Mason *et al., The Economic and Social Modernization of the Republic of Korea* (Cambridge Mass: Council on East Asian Studies, Harvard University, 1980), which summarizes seven studies of Korea's modernization, is another example of the complacent liberal view of modernization. Relying on scanty, biased data and ignoring dependency theory, this book exaggerates Korean income equality, the spread of benefits to the population at large, and the role of education, and has few misgivings about the export economy (no mention is made of Korea's huge debt) or the repressive political system.

[14]For an analysis of Korean political institutions that provides valuable historical contrasts and continuities, see Gregory Henderson, *Korea: The Politics of the Vortex* (Cambridge, Mass: Harvard University Press, 1968); Edward Reynolds Wright, ed., *Korean Politics in Transition* (Seattle: University of Washington Press, 1976), and especially Norman Jacobs, *The Korean Road to Modernization and Development* (Urbana: University of Illinois Press, 1985).

based on self-sufficient estates or derived from horticulture have had great difficulty in developing successful nation-states. It is quite different with societies with a feudal-authoritarian background. Political institutions in China, Korea, Japan, Prussia, and Russia were based on the absolute authority of the ruler, an authority, it must be noted, that extended over the nobility and not just the masses. Korea, following China's practice, developed an employee mentality among its entire population—the elite prepared for examinations for state service while the remainder of the population worked for their superiors in a hierarchy headed by a supreme ruler.

The most successful modernizers among the above group of nations were Prussia and Japan. Both countries developed an efficient, centralized, bureaucratically organized system of state power in the service of feudal values, and both countries managed to escape dependence on outside powers. In both countries modernization led to movement away from feudal values and into liberal democracy only through defeat in war.

Korea has also modernized successfully, owing in large part to its feudal-authoritarian experience. Korea's social order and political system came largely from its giant neighbor China. That system was reinforced by Japan and the United States. Korea's status as a Japanese colony strengthened the authoritarian system and deprived Korea of valuable political experience. The Japanese monopoly of all important positions also meant a lack of Korean administrators, although Japan established Japanese-oriented schools and Korean military figures went to Japanese military schools.

The American occupation after World War II did not alter the feudal-authoritarian system. Independence led to a liberal political constitution and land reform (similar to the pattern that occurred in the American military occupation of Japan). But land reform had no real significance (except perhaps to facilitate the neglect of the agricultural sector), and the liberal political constitution became a dead letter thanks to the Korean War and to the fact that electoral politics threatened the power of Korea's tiny elite.

Korea has an extremely large military-police establishment. With considerable American aid and with huge expenditures of its own, the South Korean military defends the nation against both North Korea and its own people. Violent political protests in 1987 finally forced the government to agree to free elections. Whether and how soon Korea develops viable representative government remains to be seen. In 1988, the right-wing (authoritarian) party won the presidential election by a plurality but lost control of the legislature.

Family, Religion, and Education

As is common in countries with a well-established agrarian tradition, the family has first claim on the energies, time, and resources of Koreans.[15] The Korean family is male-oriented and is explicitly conceived as the perma-

---

[15]Both for this and the concluding section, the key source is still Norman Jacobs.

nent foundation of society over time. In the ideal agrarian Korea, the household is a three-generation extended family. In practice, the eldest son and his family (as the eventual inheritors of the family property and authority) continue to live with his parents while other sons establish separate households (primogeniture). Further reflecting Confucian values and beliefs, age and sex were carefully defined as a hierarchy: Grandparents received considerable respect while elder brothers had authority over younger brothers, brothers over sisters, and husbands over wives.

Given the large concentration in landholding in feudal Korea, the hierarchical, ascriptive family form was generalized into a model for all social relations. Confucian religion and philosophy stressed filial piety and argued that all social relations must be modeled on authority relations derived from a father-headed family. Social harmony would ensue if all obeyed the obligations of their ascriptive stations in life.

In today's Korea the family has changed in keeping with urbanization and industrialization. As in other countries experiencing economic growth, Korea's urban families have become neolocal (married couples establish their own residence), nuclear (the family consists of parents and children), smaller, and the status of Korea's urban women has been changing, though slowly.

Korea's religious institutions are relatively diverse, ranging from shamanism and nativist eclectic forms to Buddhism, Confucianism, and Christianity. While the largest group of religious adherents are Buddhist, the most influential has been Confucianism. Ever since the end of the nineteenth century a significant Christian sector has established itself largely because Christianity brought with it Western values that Koreans wanted.

Education is highly valued by both Korea's elite and its people. However, the Chinese practice of gearing education to the development of officials has been a burden. Confucian educational precepts emphasized the memorization of classics and the acquisition of basic ethical norms. The goal of education was wisdom, and it was assumed that wise officials could solve problems through the application of what they had learned from the classics.

Nonetheless, after 1945, Korea witnessed an extraordinary development of education leading to mass literacy. The educational system is no doubt part of the explanation for Korea's economic success. Education is highly graded and extremely competitive, with a pronounced emphasis on credentials, although it is still deficient in scientific and vocational programs. The emphasis on academic learning has two consequences. First, it cuts back on the supply of qualified (that is, credentialed) job applicants, for it is easier to inflate academic as opposed to technical requirements; and, second, it created a reservoir of politically active students who brought down one government and has challenged others from the 1970s on.

Despite Korea's traditional preference for the classics (which has been carried into the present), it has not lacked trained technical personnel. Whether derived from training programs in Korea, or through its own efforts, Korea's economic success is in no small measure due to its supply of trained economists, civil servants (including military, intelligence, and police), engineers, and technically oriented business leaders. It is also important to note that Korea appears far more successful than other countries in getting its citizens to extract meaning and benefits from utilitarian, lower-level schooling.[16]

Class and Dependency

Korea is an unequal country with a considerable disparity among the upper and lower reaches of its system of social stratification. Analyzing inequality even when quantitative income distribution data are used is very difficult unless reference points are clear and explicit. Thanks to its unusual history (Japanese occupation, the ouster of Japan, and land reform in the post–World War II period, and the Korean War), Korea began its development as a relatively more equal society than most other Third World countries. And although economic expansion has raised living standards, it has also led to a considerable amount of income inequality.

Perhaps the most remarkable thing about Korean inequality is the ease with which authoritarian-feudal forms have transferred themselves to urban-industrial conditions.[17] In any case, the fruits of economic growth have not been distributed evenly to the Korean people nor has economic growth equalized income and wealth. This pattern is not uncommon, especially in capitalist countries, both developed and underdeveloped—economic expansion raises general living standards without producing more equality.

Korea is one of the few developing countries whose class system has been studied in some depth. In making this study, Hagen Koo has argued that we cannot simply use Marx's central criterion of property owner vs. nonproperty owner and purchaser vs. seller of labor power to understand social stratification. One must also analyze the occupational system, especially nonmanual vs. manual status. Combining these criteria, Koo argues, yields these basic social classes: capitalist and state elite, new middle class, petty bourgeoisie, working class, marginal class, plus farmers who are relatively equal. Between 1965 and 1975 the new middle class (white collar), petty bourgeoisie, and the marginal class all grew while the working class expanded rapidly and farmers declined significantly.

Household income inequality declined during the 1960s (largely because manufacturing reduced the number of unemployed and underemployed) but

---

[16]R. P. Dore, "South Korean Development in Wider Perspective," *Pacific Affairs* 50 (Summer 1977):196–198.

[17]This has parallels in the West as we saw in Chapter 2.

increased during the 1970s. The top 20 percent of households increased their share of the total from 41 to 45 percent while the bottom 40 percent declined from 19 to 16 percent. Beyond income inequality, Korea's class structure went from one that was relatively fluid and amorphous to one with more clearly defined boundaries and overall hierarchy. First, there is an extremely wealthy and politically powerful capitalist class anchored in highly concentrated economic groupings called *Jaebols* (the largest twenty Jaebols, for example, controlled 33 percent of total manufacturing). By and large, the capitalist class refers to large industrialists as well as the political elite who are joined at the hip. Hagen Koo notes that there is considerable resentment of this class by the Korean people, more than any resentment of foreign capital. The people resent this class because they know it has received its wealth through political favoritism. Second, there is now a distinct working class. By and large, Korean workers receive higher wages than their counterparts in other developing countries, but there is still considerable resentment over the injustice of its relative share in Korea. The white-collar class has enjoyed a good share of economic growth along with the owners of small businesses. Farmers, marginals, and especially industrial workers have lost out.

Koo argues that while Korea is a case of dependent development, it is different from such dependency in other countries, most notably in Latin America.[18] Korea's development is a result primarily of state action with foreign capital and multinationals playing only a small role. The other difference with dependency elsewhere is that development has not led to a dual economy and the marginalization of significant portions of the population. The benefits of economic growth have been distributed widely though not fairly or equally.[19]

Korea's dependency takes a number of forms. One, it is dependent on world markets and has accumulated considerable debt (which its economy can service as long as its exports remain strong). And it is dependent in the sense that it is still subject to what outsiders do. Dependence on outside powers is such a marked feature of Korean history that it is remarkable that Korea could emerge as a distinct ethnic-linguistic group. American policy since 1945 has openly supported South Korea's survival and development as part of larger American interests in the Far East.[20] Although President Carter

[18]For an original contribution to the theory of dependent development, see Peter Evans, *Dependent Development: The Alliance of Multinational, State, and Local Capital in Brazil* (Princeton, N.J.: Princeton University Press, 1979).

[19]Hagen Koo, "Transformation of the Korean Class Structure: The Impact of Dependent Development," in Robert V. Robinson, ed., *Research in Stratification and Mobility*, vol. 4 (Greenwich, Conn.: JAI Press, 1985), pp. 129–148. Koo focuses on 1960 to 1980 and cannot be completely faulted for failing to put Korea's development in deeper historical context, including the role of Japanese and American imperialist expansion and policies.

[20]For background on American foreign policy toward Asia and Korea, see Frank Baldwin, ed., *Without Parallel: The American-Korean Relationship Since 1945* (New York: Pantheon, 1973).

was on the verge of removing American troops in 1977, the step was never taken and the United States is still directly tied to Korea's military security.

Historically, South Korea's own foreign policy has been simply a reaction to the initiatives taken by China, the Soviet Union, Japan, or the United States. However, in recent years, perhaps dating from its participation in the Vietnam War as an ally of the United States, and certainly because of its growing economic strength and the complexity of its economic problems, South Korea has begun to assert itself in foreign affairs. Security against North Korea (which is supported by the Soviet Union and the People's Republic of China) is still South Korea's primary concern. And its relations with the United States from which it receives military protection and economic and political support are still its number-one priority. But the Vietnam War also revealed the limits of American power. Korea also knows that the United States needs it if it is to project its power and presence into the Asian world. For these and other reasons, South Korea has become a more sophisticated negotiator with the United States. It has also broadened its contacts with the Association of Southeast Asian Nations (ASEAN) and the Third World in order to keep pace with the changing needs of its export economy. Its relations with Japan remain volatile and troublesome despite Japan's heavy investment in and considerable aid to Korea. And South Korea has been at pains to show that it is willing to talk about how the two halves of Korea can be united peacefully.[21]

South Korean governments have worked hard to promote national pride and have even begun to purge the Korean language of Chinese characters and of words borrowed from China, Japan, and the United States. But dependency is structured deep into the fabric of Korean life. Despite its highly centralized political tradition and its explicit intertwining of state and economy, Korea's radical dependence on world markets makes it extremely vulnerable to the vagaries of the world economy. The political turbulence of the late 1970s, climaxed by the assassination of President Park Chung Hee in 1979, is directly linked to the painful economic recession that accompanied the dramatic rise in oil prices after 1973 and the surge in world prices for raw materials. Efforts to intensify exports to pay for the higher cost of imports left Koreans with fewer consumer goods and high inflation. A government-promoted recession further violated domestic expectations. Korea's internal political instability is directly linked to its economic dependency.[22]

During the late 1970s, Korea's efforts to develop heavy industry did not work out as successfully as its earlier investments in light industry. By the

[21]For a valuable set of essays on all aspects of Korea foreign policy, see Youngnok Koo and Sung-joo Han, eds., *The Foreign Policy of the Republic of Korea* (New York: Columbia University Press, 1985).

[22]Chong-Sik Lee, "South Korea 1979: Confrontation, Assassination, and Transition," *Asian Survey* 20, no. 1 (January 1980):63–76.

1980s, things were back on track and Korea, somewhat chastened, was now a producer of steel, automobiles, ships, and other products that directly competed with even mighty Japan. Korea's main problem, however, is still political. Its internal political instability is unlikely to end as long as an authoritarian government is geared to the defense of an economy that does not benefit the Korean people directly and equitably. Authority is undermined when followers can no longer connect the actions of powerholders with their interests. The flow of benefits from economic expansion and the manner in which economic troubles and political protests have been handled have made it clear whose interests Korean society serves. The move toward representative government in 1987 was followed by considerable labor-union activity, including strikes, demanding better wages and working conditions. A new, more ideological anti-Americanism appeared among Korea's influential students. Whether these significant events will give the Korean people more influence over their society remains to be seen.

STRATIFICATION AMONG SOCIETIES: A SUMMARY

Relations among societies are characterized by domination, conquest, exploitation, and dependence—in short, by stratification and imperialism.

Leaving aside the discredited folk theories based on biology, theorists tend to agree that imperialism occurs for economic reasons. Liberal (capitalist) theorists argue that imperialism is unnecessary and should be curbed as a barrier to competition and efficiency. Marxists, following Lenin, argue that imperialism is a necessary stage of mature capitalism and will lead eventually to vigorous competition from colonies and the downfall of capitalism. Dependency theorists, similarly influenced by Marx, also argue that imperialism is necessary for capitalism to continue but say that it creates dependency among colonies and former colonies.

Empire imperialism is characteristic of agrarian society and consists of conquering other lands and peoples. *World market* imperialism is when *core* societies exploit their economic superiority toward *peripheral* societies. *Semiperipheral* societies, while economically backward, manage to avoid being turned into underdeveloped, dependent countries.

Nationalism in the West emerged as part of the surge to power by the middle class. Nationalism destroyed feudal particularism and resulted in central government (common currency, taxation, laws, transportation) and large domestic markets. Nationalism outside the West is often part of a liberation movement directed against imperialist powers.

The international system from 1450 to 1950 was marked by acute rivalry among the capitalist countries of the West and the dominance of these countries over most of the world. Since 1950, the *First World* (the developed capitalist societies) have united under American leadership because of challenges from the *Second World* (the developed socialist societies led by the Soviet Union) and the *Third World* (the developing nations).

The developed capitalist countries, with their advanced technologies, high energy consumption, and intricate division of labor, produce the bulk of the world's output and conduct most of its trade among themselves.

As opposed to the developed capitalist and socialist societies, the Third World of approximately 140 of the world's 165 nation-states, is economically weak and dependent.

Imperialist core societies tend to turn colonies and dependencies into exporters of food, labor, and raw materials while they diversify and upgrade their own economies. When developed societies collide with simple feudal or horticultural societies, the result is *underdevelopment* (a society's labor force and economy are geared to remain suppliers of food and raw materials). When advanced societies act on smaller feudal-authoritarian systems, the result is *dependent development* (a society develops a labor-intensive export-oriented manufacturing sector but is dependent on the outside world for markets, raw materials, and capital).

CHAPTER 4

Social Stratification and the Problem of a General Theory

The goal of every field of science is to develop a unified depiction of its subject matter and a comprehensive causal theory that explains how that subject matter behaves. The heart of such a unified or general theory in social stratification would consist of generalizations applicable to all systems of stratification. Our task in this chapter, therefore, is to review the progress that has been made toward a general theory of stratification and to identify some of the barriers standing in the way of its realization.

THE DIVERSITY OF STRATIFICATION: THE PROBLEM OF A GENERAL THEORY

Analyzing a particular system of stratification presents the usual scientific problems of identifying variables and demonstrating relationships between them; but these problems are minuscule compared to the difficulty of establishing generalizations applicable to all systems of stratification. Even the concepts of caste, estate, and class—our most advanced means of ordering the phenomena of stratification—tend to distort the historical richness of systems of inequality if they are not properly qualified. The same is true of the even more abstract distinction between agrarian and industrial systems of inequality, or among, for example, primitive, feudal, and bourgeois systems of inequality. And, of course, none of these is a unitary scheme; at least for the time being, there seems to be an irreducible diversity in the record of social stratification.

The idea of irreducible diversity does not sit well with scientists, and, of course, does not lend itself easily to the type of legitimation that most dominant strata seem to want and need. In approaching the construction of a general theory of stratification, it is first necessary to escape from the legitimating symbols of class stratification. (If we were living in caste or estate systems, we would have the underlying assumptions of those systems to worry about.) We have already warned against the simple functionalism that confuses differentiation and social stratification, and against the ideology of "nonegalitarian classlessness." We will now also warn against a premature adoption of unitary schemes by discussing two main types, evolutionary Marxism and evolutionary liberalism.

EVOLUTIONARY MARXISM

Marx's Vision of a Unitary Line of Historical Development

The great drama of secular salvation depicted by Marx is one of many monuments to human beings' ceaseless search for a way to escape from history. Marx's theory, and the assorted revisions and extensions undertaken by his disciples, represents a rich branch of social science and social philosophy, and it is not our wish to dismiss it out of hand. We have already acknowledged Marx's insight into economic causation as the most important contribution to nineteenth-century social science. Here we wish simply to raise some general objections to his theory of social evolution and to acknowledge his idea of a classless society as a moral ideal.

Briefly, the major objection to Marx's prediction of human progress through class struggle is that it has not been fulfilled. A dynamic economy is the exception, not the rule, in world history. All non-Western societies, including the great civilizations of China and India, reached a certain point of economic development and then stagnated. Even in the West, Marx's prediction of the future of capitalism has failed to materialize. Industrial society has not been split apart by polarized classes, and the working class has not risen to proclaim the end of private property and thus of social exploitation. What appears to have happened instead is that modern society has been diversified internally into a number of social classes, and has evolved a number of practices for adjusting (and even disguising) the relations between them. To refute Marx's metaphysics, however, is not to accept evolutionary liberalism or "nonegalitarian classlessness." Modern society is a class structure that is not easily related to any of the explanations offered on its behalf.

It is true that Marx foresaw future developments quite accurately in many respects. Modern society is characterized by a high concentration of economic power and a deep interpenetration of economic and political power. It is exploitative and wasteful, and its legitimating symbols contain much ideology (the symbolic justification of an outmoded status quo) and even hypocrisy. And there is also a considerable amount of "false consciousness," or acceptance by the lower classes of upper-class symbols that are not in their true interests. But modern society has not fulfilled Marx's prediction of class polarization and struggle. In all industrial countries, including those where class hostility was once pronounced, the forces of economic expansion and political reform have diversified and diffused the structure of social classes. As a result, class society is far more stable and adaptable than Marxists (and others) are wont to believe. Instead of a dynamic system containing the seeds of its own destruction, one must think of capitalism as a society that successfully reproduces itself generation after generation despite and often because of exploitation and misery. We will explore the various agencies by which this is accomplished in due course, but central to any study of social stability are the ascriptive processes inherent in the idea of social class itself.

The image of a classless society (about which Marx said very little) is surprisingly similar to the liberal idea of nonegalitarian classlessness. By positing a society based on the fulfillment of all individuals, it sets a high standard for human hopes and aspirations. But, as Marx himself understood only too well, moral values reflect the realities of economic life. As we examine the realities of class in the United States, we will find ample proof of the power of economic life over society and of the way in which it reflects and disguises itself in appealing moral terms, not the least of which is the belief that a classless society has already been achieved. As we examine another industrial society, the Soviet Union, one based on a Russianized Marxism, we will find a system of inequality and a legitimizing ideology that are strikingly similar to those in the United States.

Creative Marxian Currents

Marxist theorists have long since understood all of the above. As early as Edward Bernstein (a Marxist revisionist in the German Social Democratic Party at the turn of the last century) and Vladimir Lenin (the leader of the Communist party that seized power during the military defeat of Czarist Russia), Marxist scholars have grappled with the ambiguous legacy left by Marx.

The main thrust of creative Marxian thought has been twofold: one, to find a place for noneconomic forces, especially political action, in the promotion of socialism, and two, to extend Marxian analysis beyond the single nation-state and to make the relation among societies one of the variables explaining domestic inequality (and vice versa).

In the developed capitalist societies of Europe, Marxists from Bernstein to Louis Althusser,[1] Perry Anderson,[2] Nicos Poulantzas,[3] and Erik Olin Wright[4] have all found value in the capitalist political system, in effect, advocating the use of liberal political institutions, including alliances between workers and other classes, to bring about socialism. Orthodox Marxists have resisted this approach as a dilution and distraction from class struggle.

Marxists outside the developed West have also placed their faith in political action, but here politics has taken an aristocratic, elitist turn. The two main figures are Lenin in Russia, who saw the need for a vanguard to lead the proletariat, and Mao Tse-Tung in China.

The other current in creative Marxism is its theory of imperialism. Capitalism, argue Marxists in this tradition, has been able to forestall class polarization and the pauperization of its working class because of its profits from colonies and investments abroad.[5] Lenin, who was one of the founders of imperialist theory, argued that the development of colonies would soon lead to the demise of the mother countries. Contemporary dependency theorists argue that imperialism will postpone the demise of capitalism for the foreseeable future.

Creative Applications of Marxism to Understanding the United States

A number of Marxist scholars have produced new images of American history and social development. Gabriel Kolko has interpreted the rise of the regulatory state from the late nineteenth century on as a capitalist device to stabilize markets under corporate capitalism.[6] William Appleman Williams has interpreted American foreign policy in the nineteenth century as imperialist because of pressure from domestic groups, especially farmers, eager for foreign markets.[7] And Michael Harrington has produced a Marxian picture of American politics since the New Deal of the 1930s that ranks as high as any image produced by liberal thinkers.[8]

In an important test of Marx's idea that workers would be "proletarianized" under advanced capitalism, Wright and Martin subjected the overall

[1]*Reading Capital*, with Etienne Balibar (London: New Left Books, 1970), and *For Marx* (London: New Left Books, 1977).

[2]*Lineages of the Absolutist State* (London: New Left Books, 1974).

[3]*Political Power and Social Classes* (London: New Left Books, 1973).

[4]*Classes* (London: Verso, 1985).

[5]For an earlier discussion, see Chapter 3.

[6]Gabriel Kalko, *The Triumph of Conservatism: A Reinterpretation of American History* (New York: Free Press, 1963).

[7]William A. Williams, *The Tragedy of American Diplomacy*, 2nd rev. and enlarged ed. (New York: Dell, 1972).

[8]Michael Harrington, *The Twilight of Capitalism* (New York: Touchstone, 1976), pt. 2.

American occupational system between 1960 and 1980 to close empirical scrutiny. Contrary to Marx's belief that the labor force faced deskilling and declining income, Wright and Martin found evidence that white collar, supervisory (managerial) occupations have grown. Relying on Marxian economic causation theory (imperialism and technology), Wright and Martin argue that, one, American class relations were internationalized during this period and, two, that economic concentration (made possible by technology and bureaucracy) made more managerial jobs necessary.[9]

Wright has argued that Marx's concept of labor exploitation is still central to class analysis but that it must be elaborated to distinguish the different ways in which surplus value is extracted from the working class. The owners of the means of production along with managers get more income than is warranted even when education, occupational status, age, and job tenure are held constant.[10] There is also a second form of exploitation that results in undeserved income and the use of organizational assets. The larger the organization the more unwarranted income (big business and upper-level managers getting significantly more than small business and single-person enterprises). The third form of exploitation is through control of skills and credentials. Here better-educated and skilled people get more income than is warranted by their education (Wright says this form is not as clearly established or as important as the first two forms of exploitation).

These three forms of exploitation are obviously found in mixed and combined form in large corporations. But Wright's argument and empirical findings should also be seen as pertaining to hospitals, schools, voluntary groups, professions, and state officials. Wright's findings can also be seen in the large number of supervisory occupations in the United States (much larger than in capitalist Sweden), which act both as a buffer between the upper classes and the masses and which serve to produce America's large number of "working class" individuals and households with "contradictory class positions" (that is, they are both exploiter and exploited).

Despite many similarities in technology and standard of living, capitalist Sweden is different from the United States. It has a strong trade union and socialist movement and the capitalist segments of the society have not been able to depoliticize the polity the way they have in the United States. It has far fewer supervisory occupations and college graduates, and 40 percent of its labor force works for the state as opposed to 20 percent in the United States. Despite these differences, class consciousness is similar in both countries—the further up the three dimensions of exploitation one goes the more pro-capitalist the attitudes. Swedish workers are more likely to be polarized on

---

[9]Erik Olin Wright and Bill Martin, "The Transformation of the American Class Structure, 1960–1980," *American Journal of Sociology* 93 (July 1987): 1–29.

[10]For details, see the section "Social Class as Property Relations" in Chapter 5.

issues, largely because they have a supportive union and political environment.

Wright's fascinating empirical contrast between the United States and Sweden also allows him to develop a picture of historical development somewhat different from Marx's (and orthodox Marxists) but one that he feels is still fully consistent with Marx. Wright argues that the case of Sweden (and other evidence) shows that capitalism can have "multiple futures"—either statism or communism. Those who are interested in the democratization of capitalist society should try to use the state (as Sweden has done) to reduce the unwarranted income of those who own or control the three forms of exploitation. Not only can this be done through class alliances, taxation, and public services, but the policymaking positions of organizations can and should be democratized.[11]

The search within Marxism for a unified picture of social development continues, and we will come across further creative applications of Marx's ideas in later chapters.

EVOLUTIONARY LIBERALISM

The main metaphysical legitimation of capitalist society has also taken an evolutionary form—that of evolutionary liberalism.[12] This metaphysical orientation is composed of various elements: the doctrine of progress developed during the French Enlightenment, Utilitarianism, representative government, Social Darwinism, liberal reformism, and related phenomena. Though the evolutionary theory of social development was rejected by social science in the early decades of this century as teleologically biased and inconsonant with the facts, the idea was too firmly planted to be even partially erased from the public consciousness. It lives on in various guises: "nonegalitarian classlessness"; functionalism in sociology; the theory of convergence; faith in progress, especially through economic growth; and the denial that classes exist. In its simplest form, it is a belief that industrial capitalism is uniquely capable of carrying humanity toward a better future for all. Let us examine some of the variations of this position, beginning with the ideology of convergence.

The Ideology of Convergence

Liberal social theorists, in and out of stratification theory, tended to argue that a general process of convergence was taking place in all developed

---

[11]Wright, *Classes.*

[12]For this term, see the valuable critique of American stratification theory by John Pease, William H. Form, and Joan Huber Rytina, "Ideological Currents in American Stratification Literature," *The American Sociologist* 5 (May 1970): 127–137.

and developing societies. The main cause was the process of industrialization, which would standardize social development through three sub-processes:

1. differentiation based on achievement, accompanied by growing equality in all dimensions of stratification;
2. consistency, or the integration of class (economic position), status (prestige position), and power (political-legal position);
3. common patterns and increasing rates of social mobility.

In an early challenge the English sociologist John Goldthorpe said that there was a great deal of empirical evidence against these alleged trends.[13] Ever since Goldthorpe's analysis, evidence against convergence toward the ideals of liberal society has continued to grow. There may well be a convergence of industrial and developing systems, but, as we will see later, they seem more bent toward becoming oligarchies than classless achievement societies.

The Evolutionary Liberalism of Davis and Moore

In 1945 Kingsley Davis and Wilbert E. Moore published an essay on social stratification at the level of general theory; that is, they articulated what they claimed were the universal principles of stratification. Written in the spirit of functionalism and with only an implied evolutionary framework, this work, which is not characteristic of the work of these two eminent sociologists and which has since been modified by their other writings, stimulated a wide and valuable debate among stratification theorists.

In keeping with the basic strategy of sociology, which is to establish generalizations about human behavior, sociologists in the functional tradition argue that phenomena that occur universally must stem from the inherent needs of society itself. Thus, society is defined naturalistically, as having given structural features that can be identified despite empirical or historical variations and changes. Working in this tradition, and leaving aside "variable" or historical issues, Davis and Moore argue that the "main functional necessity explaining the universal presence of stratification is precisely the requirement faced by any society of placing and motivating individuals in the social structure."[14] Assuming that different positions in society require different incentives and rewards, they conclude that "social inequality is an unconsciously evolved device by which societies ensure that the most important positions are conscientiously filled by the most qualified persons." The

---

[13]"Social Stratification in Industrial Society" in Reinhard Bendix and Seymour Lipset, eds., *Class, Status, and Power: Social Stratification in Comparative Perspective*, 2ed. (New York: Free Press, 1966), pp. 643–659.

[14]Kingsley Davis and Wilbert E. Moore, "Some Principles of Social Stratification." *American Sociological Review* 10 (April 1945): 242–249.

thrust of their argument is that despite both historical variations in the way inequality manifests itself and the failure of given societies to live up to their own values and norms, inequality as such is generic to society, intrinsic to its nature. All societies, say Davis and Moore, simply must define some positions—in general, the leadership of major institutional areas—as more important than others and must structure the distribution of social, cultural, and personality benefits so as to ensure an adequate supply of personnel for these positions, which require various talents, arduous training, and heavy responsibility.

A number of general points should be made about the Davis-Moore position. First, whether palatable or not, their argument is a scientific effort and should not be attacked on the basis of value judgments. Second, they are in no way culpable for having overlooked the dysfunctions of inequality or the imperfections in given empirical systems of inequality; they deliberately separate such questions from their main concern, which is to determine in what way inequality is related to the universal nature of society.[15] Their position is simply that society, however variously organized to emphasize different abilities in individuals, must always—if it is to be a society—make human beings unequal.

A first criticism of this particular statement of the functional position is that it is really a discussion of differentiation, not stratification. Secondly, the critics of the Davis-Moore position, Tumin especially, have sensed the basic emptiness of their generalization. By and large, conflict theorists—those who see society and inequality as a means by which the strong can induce the weak to do more for less—tend to bypass the Davis-Moore analysis. It is one thing to argue that differentiation must take place—that individuals must be motivated and trained to occupy different statuses in the hierarchies of work, or leisure, or warfare, or whatever—and quite another to decide how all this is to be done. Invariably, the placement of individuals has been a result of social stratification, not individual achievement or natural social processes, which is to say that at some point in history families are ranked with regard to general economic, social, and political power and worth, and that this hierarchy of families then becomes the basis for the next generation's hierarchy of families. Equally important, the hierarchy of strata that emerges eventually controls the definition of functional positions and recruitment into them. It is, according to the critics of functionalism, the radical inequality of ascriptive conditions that lies at the heart of stratification analysis, regardless of the type of society. The fact that liberal democracy (or communist dictatorships, for that matter) demands high levels of achievement does not alter the fact that birth into the class hierarchy determines, by and large, who will be trained to succeed and who to fail.

[15]This paragraph recapitulates the general line Davis has taken in replying to criticism on both these counts by Melvin M. Tumin. "Some Principles of Stratification: A Critical Analysis." *American Sociological Review* 18 (August 1953): 387–397.

As opposed to the abstract analysis of differentiation, therefore, stratification theory must question whether there is any correspondence between social rewards and the performances of social functions, and even whether functional positions can be precisely defined as to value. The Davis-Moore view of inequality resembles the dominant lay tradition in the United States, "nonegalitarian classlessness," or the view that while Americans are unequal they deserve their positions because all have an equal chance to show their worth.[16] As our subsequent analysis will show, the United States has extensive ascriptive and exploitative elements that appear to be deeply institutionalized. The view that America has found a way to distribute rewards on the basis of individual achievement is thereby rendered problematic. We will encounter many obstacles to understanding stratification structures and processes in America, but none will rival the view that the United States is already an equal-opportunity achievement society or can become one given time and judicious reform.

The Evolutionary Liberalism of Gerhard Lenski

Gerhard Lenski has made a notable contribution to stratification analysis at the level of classification and description.[17] His attempt at a unified or general theory of inequality, however, has not succeeded. Indeed, his alleged synthesis of stratification phenomena is simply unabashed evolutionary liberalism. Lenski bases his theory almost exclusively on the concept of power, providing (in chapters 3 and 4 of his book) a number of penetrating and highly useful comments about its employment, consequences, and general nature. His comments, however, are quite *ad hoc,* and his definition of power eventually becomes a synonym for causation (or all the variables in stratification analysis).

Not surprisingly, Lenski makes no attempt to characterize systems of stratification; to recognize that caste, estate, and class systems are viable historical structures is not compatible with a unitary theory. Lenski constantly refers to the variety of ways in which various forces behave, depending on time and place, and then solves the problem of causation by imposing an evolutionary pattern on his wayward and unstructured historical materials. His analysis of power (or the materials of social stratification) is further vitiated by the introduction of certain constant human (nature) needs and propensities, most of which are suspiciously similar to the behavior characteristic of liberal society.

---

[16]Ralf Dahrendorf has criticized the functional approach, and all other approaches, only to propose something quite similar to Davis and Moore's argument. Society is always a moral community, he argues, and the very act of imposing norms and sanctions will make individuals unequal; see his *Essays in the Theory of Society* (Stanford, Calif.: Stanford University Press, 1968), pp. 151–178.

[17]Gerhard Lenski, *Power and Privilege: A Theory of Social Stratification* (New York: McGraw-Hill, 1966).

To fully appreciate Lenski's theory and obtain its many potential bene-fits, one must focus mainly on his fascinating description and classification of the ways in which inequality has manifested itself throughout history. Basi-cally, says Lenski, the variety of inequality a society exhibits depends upon how the "power" system distributes material surplus, especially food. Focus-ing his analysis on the basic techniques of subsistence, Lenski develops the typology of societies illustrated in Figure 4–1, each type having a distinguish-able degree of inequality. As production grows, says Lenski, so does inequal-ity, reaching its greatest height in agrarian society.

The emergence of an industrial technology represents a profound change in the "means of subsistence" available to society. As a consequence, sharp increases take place in production and in specialized economic activity. Lenski claims that the resulting material surplus does not lead, as in the past, to increases in inequality but to a reversal of this historic trend. While eco-nomic, prestige, and political inequality is still considerable, it is less marked than in agrarian societies. The top 2 percent of income units, for example, receive at most 15 to 20 percent of the total income, as opposed to 50 percent in agrarian societies, and the emergence of universal suffrage represents a diffusion and popularization of political power. The main reason for this reversal of the trend toward increased inequality is that industrial society is

Figure 4–1   Lenski's Societal Typology: Subsistence Techniques as the Basis of Society

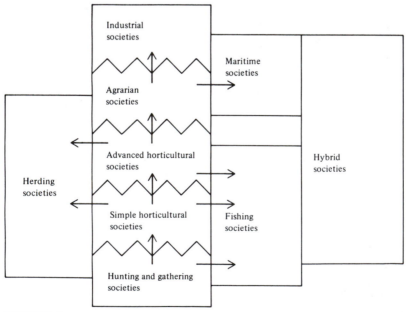

SOURCE: From *Power and Privilege: A Theory of Social Stratification* by Gerhard Lenski, p. 92. Copyright 1966 by Gerhard Lenski. Used with permission of Gerhard Lenski.

too complex to be run personally or arbitrarily. The upper groups tend to find it in their interests to involve the lower and intermediate groups in economic and political processes.

The foregoing is only a rough sketch of Lenski's rich portrayal of human inequality through the ages. Indeed, the materials he presents are so rich that they could easily be interpreted as irreducibly diverse and nondirectional. Lenski's description of human inequality and his classification of a wide variety of societies would have been perfectly acceptable scientific procedure had he limited himself to searching for their similarities. But locating his types in a scheme of evolutionary development begs all the important questions in social science. Above all, Lenski never addresses himself to the basic question of why one agrarian society—Western feudalism—transformed itself into industrial society while the rest "stagnated." What was to Max Weber and most of the classical theorists of sociology a great novelty in need of explanation presents no problem for Lenski, since he assumes that the basic ideas and values of capitalism are normal to human nature. Instead of trying to explain the unique historical phenomenon of liberal society, he unabashedly attributes liberal values and behavior to human nature. To assume that liberal society is natural to humans is also to assume that all other societies are distortions or pale reflections of that norm. One can then rest easy with an explanation of the emergence of industrial society consisting of casual references to constitutionalism as the result of "a peculiar combination of historical circumstances," the willingness of elites to delegate authority to markets, the rapidity and magnitude of increases in productivity (which encourages concessions by the elite), birth control, the great expansion of human knowledge, and the new democratic ideology.[18]

Most of these "explanatory" remarks are not intended as an explanation of the rise of capitalism, which never presents itself as a problem to Lenski, but occur as part of Lenski's assertion that industrial society represents a reversal of the historical trend in which increasing surplus is turned into increased inequality. The argument that industrial society is characterized by a decrease in economic and political inequality relative to agrarian society is a major theme in Lenski's work; it also deserves careful scrutiny since it occupies a central place in the American belief system.

Lenski's careful description of the reduction of certain forms of inequality by industrial society is useful and important. Who cannot be impressed with the fact that all individuals (of both sexes) have for the first time in human history been defined as moral entities with the legal right to engage in economic pursuits of their own choice, participate equally in political decision making, and be treated as legal equals by the state? And it is significant, as Lenski emphasizes, that the top economic elite in industrial society claims

---

[18]Ibid., pp. 60, 313–318.

a smaller portion of the economic pie than the economic elite of agrarian society. However, these are not important enough to warrant Lenski's central theme emphasizing the reduction of inequality as the salient feature of modern capitalism. The same transformation can also be interpreted as the displacement of one unique historical set of social inequalities by another. The unique inequalities of industrial society are steep, stable, and illegitimate enough to warrant caution in making overall judgments. Lenski, however, minimizes the problem of inequality in industrial society by framing his analysis primarily as a broad comparison with the past, and by stating that the full flowering of industrial society is yet to come, claiming that modern society will continue to reduce inequality.[19]

Comparisons among types of society are fraught with difficulties that distort reality. Feudal society is unequal in ways that are different from industrial society. To see how slippery such concepts in this area are, consider this: The vast majority of the inhabitants of ancient Egypt, Rome, Imperial China, and the Ottoman Empire were far more equal in their occupations, their material existence, and their life expectancy than the majority of present-day Europeans or inhabitants of the United States or the Soviet Union. True, the elite of feudal society received a larger percentage of the total income than today's industrial elites. And the elites of today's non-developed countries also receive a larger percentage of total income than the elites of the developed countries. But that is only a small part of the total inequality picture. Putting elite comparisons aside, the remaining population in contemporary industrial countries is more steeply graded than the mass of people in the agrarian societies of either the past or present. In addition, it is not clear that there is much difference in the nature of economic power (control over the use of material and human resources) between the elites of complex societies in the past and those of the present. When judged by economic concentration, all complex societies are heavily concentrated, whether they are agrarian, capitalist, socialist, developed, or nondeveloped.[20]

Lenski's work led to an important body of cross-national analyses during the 1970s.[21] None of the analyses compared inequality in feudal vs. industrial society, and judgments here must be made on the basis of other reasoning.[22] Instead, these studies focused on the relative importance of

---

[19]Ibid, pp. 344, 397, 400–402.

[20]All statements about trends in the distribution of income in developing countries are highly suspect because the data are either not available or not reliable; in this respect, see Albert Berry, "On Trends in the Gap Between Rich and Poor in Less Developed Countries: Why We Know So Little," *The Review of Income and Wealth* Series 31, no. 4 (December 1985): 337–354.

[21]The studies that appeared in the 1970s were based on data mostly from 1965 and earlier and have been superseded by the enormous economic changes that have occurred since then.

[22]Harold Lydall, *The Structure of Earnings* (London: Oxford University Press, 1968), stresses the difficulties, if not impossibility, of comparing economic inequality in agrarian and industrial societies.

economic and political variables. The results contradicted two more of Lenski's assertions: Using certain assumptions, one can find some reduction in economic inequality during the initial stages of modern economic growth. But the reduction is not large and inequality has remained high (using more recent data, inequality has remained high for a long period, and if anything, has increased). Second, Lenski also claimed that political democracy has played an important part in the dramatic reversal of the historic process in which economic growth is associated with a growth in inequality. Most studies found that once economic growth is accounted for, political democracy plays little or no role in reducing economic inequality. As part of this argument, Lenski also claimed that strong trade union and democratic socialist movements reduce economic inequality. This aspect of Lenski's argument has received some support.[23]

Lenski has rightly focused on economic variables as the movers of society. But by taking capitalism at face value he has missed its main stratificational outcome: the emergence of deep and persistent inequality on a new and unique set of economic dimensions. Indeed, Lenski has obscured stratification analysis by his idiomatic use of the terms *power, privilege, prestige,* and *class,* and by failing to provide an overall characterization of the modern system of stratification. Instead, he presents a long series of *ad hoc* statements about industrial societies' political class system; property class system; entrepreneurial class; class of party functionaries; managerial class; military class; professional class; unemployed and slave-labor classes; educational class system; racial, ethnic, and religious class systems; class system based on sex; and class system based on age. These are followed by a miscellany of statements about mobility, class struggle, prestige, stratification, and the like, and throughout, data are drawn first from one society and then from another.

Although Lenski presents many important and valid ideas and arguments, the result of his analysis is to hide the specific historical system of class stratification from our view. He does so by overemphasizing the contrast between the present and the past (which amounts to a teleological bias in favor of contemporary liberal society), implying a trend toward greater equality within liberal society, and obscuring sociology's hard-won advances in analytic concepts (for example, caste, estate, and class systems; class, prestige, and power variables), concepts that are still our most advanced tools for examining and interpreting the phenomena of inequality without ideological bias.

The Evolutionary Liberalism of Talcott Parsons

One of the most prominent variations on the theme of convergence is the evolutionary theory of Talcott Parsons, America's foremost sociological

---

[23]For a further discussion of these studies, see Chapter 6.

theorist from the end of World War II until his death in 1973.[24] Primarily a specialist in general theory, and the United States' leading exponent of the functional perspective, Parsons devoted considerable attention to social stratification.[25] Like Lenski, his depiction of the American system of stratification is also derived largely from an abstract contrast with feudal society. He emphasizes the decline of ascriptive forces and the rise of equality, choice, pluralism, and functional inequality based on achievement processes during the past few centuries. His depiction of stratification is also based on a refutation of Marx (he asserts that property is declining in importance); he sees social class, in the traditional sense, as a transitional phenomenon.

In his contribution to stratification analysis, Parsons stressed the importance of egalitarian forces, especially equality of opportunity, mass education, and civic rights in government and private associations. These forces, Parsons claims, tend to have real effectiveness in controlling and moderating inequality. The "competence gap" produced by achievement and competition is also modified by fiduciary mechanisms located most prominently in law, government, and the professions. Some ascriptive advantage accrues in the family, but Parsons does not see this as a great problem. Actually, he argues that the concept of social class should be divorced from kinship and property and that we should instead think in terms of hierarchical differentiation. A social class should now be thought of as an aggregate of people who "in their own estimation and those of others" occupy achievement positions of approximately equal status. Basically, social classes "represent a more or less successful resultant of mechanisms dealing with integrative problems of the society, notably those having to do with the balance between factors of equality and of inequality."[26]

The trouble with Parsons' stratification theory, of course, is that he is simply stating as fact or operative ideal what society itself claims to be. In short, beneath his elaborate language and conceptualizing lies an acceptance of liberal society as a valid, progressive, and natural structure and process. Everything that science should consider problematic is accepted at face value. As we will see later in more detail, much of what modern society (actually, its power-holders) says about itself is not true, highly dubious, or as yet incapable of being tested. Many favorable judgments about modern society are based on highly abstract and dubious comparisons with the

---

[24]Parsons' commitment to evolutionary social theory is explicitly articulated in *Societies: Evolutionary and Comparative Perspectives* (Englewood Cliffs, N.J.: Prentice-Hall, 1966) and *The System of Modern Societies* (Englewood Cliffs, N.J.: Prentice-Hall, 1971).

[25]"An Analytical Approach to the Theory of Social Stratification," *American Journal of Sociology* 45, no. 6 (May 1940): 841–862; "A Revised Analytical Approach to the Theory of Social Stratification," in Reinhard Bendix and Seymour M. Lipset, eds., *Class, Status and Power: A Reader in Social Stratification*, 1st ed. (New York: Free Press, 1953); and "Equality and Inequality in Modern Society, or Social Stratification Revisited," *Sociological Inquiry* 40 (Spring 1970): 13–72.

[26]"Equality and Inequality," p. 24.

feudal-monarchical past. But the contemporary United States still has many powerful ascriptive forces, including class ascription, and it is not even possible to say that their efficacy has been reduced during the course of American history.[27]

Nor is it defensible to equate existing inequalities with social functions as easily and neatly as Parsons (and others) is prone to do. As we will see, much of what passes for equality in America is empty formalism and rhetoric, and the "educational revolution" Parsons makes so much of is actually a facade masking middle-class dominance and privilege.[28] And, finally, Parsons' emphasis on the assumed competence and fiduciary nature of law, government, and the professions is an error of misplaced faith, an uncritical continuation of a technocratic strain in liberal thought that dates back to the sociology of Saint-Simon and Comte. And, in a wider context, Parsons' evolutionary liberalism is part and parcel of the pervasive American faith that the United States is simultaneously at the terminal stage of social development and busily engaged in perfecting itself. This faith, which found wide expression in early stratification theory, has now been seriously questioned.

Evolutionary Liberalism as Ideology

The ideology of evolutionary liberalism is so widespread that it is important to know where it comes from and why it persists. Pease, Form, and Rytina suggest three sources: the dominant ideology of individualism, the

---

[27]While such comparisons are difficult, there appears to have been no decrease in social class inequality since our colonial period; see Jackson T. Main, "The Class Structure of Revolutionary America," in Reinhard Bendix and Seymour M. Lipset, eds., *Class, Status, and Power: Social Stratification in Comparative Perspective*, 2nd ed. (New York: Free Press, 1966), pp. 111–121; Jackson T. Main, *The Social Structure of Revolutionary America* (Princeton, N.J.: Princeton University Press, 1965); and Gary B. Nash, ed., *Class and Society in Early America* (Englewood Cliffs, N.J.: Prentice-Hall, 1970). For an analysis of substantial social inequality during the second quarter of the nineteenth century, the so-called era of the common man, see Edward Pessen, *Riches, Class, and Power Before the Civil War* (Lexington, Mass.: D. C. Heath, 1973).

Robert S. and Helen M. Lynd's classic community studies, *Middletown* (New York: Harcourt, Brace, 1929) and *Middletown in Transition* (New York: Harcourt, Brace, 1937), provide valuable material suggesting a growth in inequality by comparing three years in the history of Muncie, Indiana: 1890, 1924, 1935. An extremely valuable historical analysis of social stratification in New Haven and Connecticut that traces the changing bases of what it depicts as an unchanged relative structure of inequality may be found in August B. Hollingshead and Frederick C. Redlich, *Social Class and Mental Illness* (New York: John Wiley & Sons, 1958), chap. 3. Stephan Thernstrom, *Poverty and Progress: Social Mobility in a Nineteenth Century City* (Cambridge, Mass.: Harvard University Press, 1964), argues that Newburyport, Massachusetts (the same city analyzed by Lloyd Warner in his Yankee City series—see the section, The Small Town Focus in Chapter 5) is a relatively good and our best example of a typical American community of the nineteenth century and challenges the conclusion reached by Warner and the Lynds that upward mobility is becoming more difficult. It has always been difficult, he argues, no more so today than in the past.

[28]For a full analysis, see Chapter 8 and sections titled "Government and Education: The Public as Partisan" and "Legislation, Government, and Minorities" in Chapter 15.

association of social and stratificational explanations with Marxism, and sociology's search for scientific status (which predisposed it toward quantitative methods and which, in turn, predisposed stratification analysts toward the concepts of status or prestige rather than class or power).[29] Our own explanation would acknowledge the ideological causes cited above but we would also ask: Where do these ideological phenomena themselves come from?˙ The answer, of course, is history, or, more specifically, American society and its class system. To understand how the American class system works, in other words, is to understand the consciousness of the American people and a good deal about the consciousness of American intellectuals. America's ahistorical seventeenth- and eighteenth-century rationalism, proclivity for biopsychological explanations, optimistic faith in progress, and moral struggle to overcome the disruptive forces of ascription all combine to distort Americans' insight into their system of inequality. The United States' symbolic culture is itself explicable as the product of a virgin and fabulously rich continent; the selective diffusion of European sociocultural elements; low population density; and high rates of social mobility, relative to agrarian societies, induced by an economic growth unprecedented in human history.

In a broader context, the ideology of progress satisfies an important need for the middle class: It legitimates industrial capitalism as a terminal society while allowing for technological and economic growth under private auspices. In other words, by employing the appealing terms of inevitable moral and material progress, the main beneficiaries of economic expansion can indefinitely postpone the solution of social problems and explain away the social system's failures.[30]

GENERAL THEORY IN STRATIFICATION ANALYSIS:
A SUMMARY

The goal of every field of science is to develop a unified picture of its subject matter and to derive a comprehensive causal theory that explains how that subject matter behaves.

In social stratification, a unified or general theory would consist of generalizations that are applicable to all systems of inequality.

The two major attempts to produce a general theory of social stratification are *evolutionary Marxism* and *evolutionary liberalism*.

Marx's identification of economic causation was the single greatest

---

[29]John Pease, William H. Form, and Joan Huber Rytina, "Ideological Currents in American Stratification Literature," *American Sociologist* 5 (May 1970): 127–137.

[30]The power of liberal ideology is obscured because it undergoes updating and reformulation. Examples are postindustrial theory (associated with Daniel Bell) and status attainment theory. These views will be analyzed later.

contribution to nineteenth-century social science. His theory of a linear development of society through class struggle (resulting in a classless society) has not stood the test of time and research. Capitalist society in the West has managed to raise living standards and to mitigate class struggle through reform.

Marxist theorists have struggled to find a place in Marx's general theory for noneconomic variables, especially political action. And they have argued that capitalism has managed to avoid class struggle only through imperialism, that is, by its ability to exploit colonies and the Third World.

Evolutionary liberalism also argues that history is a linear development toward a classless society, that is, a society based on achievement and knowledge, which will eliminate ascriptive and other nonrational forces. In the case of liberals, however, capitalist society represents the terminal stage of history. For liberals, capitalist society (usually referred to as industrial society) is based on achievement criteria, functional differentiation, and either has or is trying to eliminate nonrational vestiges from the past.

Variations among liberal thinkers are:

1. Some argue that the logic of industrialization is leading to or has led to a classless society.
2. Some argue that inequality based on functional need is inherent in society.
3. Some argue that industrial society is marked by institutions promoting equal opportunity, especially mass education, and by referee institutions, especially government, law, the professions, and voluntary groups. These institutions have greatly modified—some even say eliminated—the power of property.

Research has failed to confirm liberal theory. To the extent that such a comparison can be made, industrial society is not more equal than agrarian societies. Birth into economic classes as well as such birth factors as race, ethnicity, and sex are still enormously important in modern society. And few today are able to say that mass education, government, law, the professions, and voluntary groups counteract ascriptive (illegitimate) inequality or offset the power of property.

Liberal theory appears to be an ideology, which is the biased defense of a particular society. By claiming that capitalist society has either overcome the forces of ascription or can overcome them through the application of science, technology, and modest reforms, liberal theorists have asked us to take the capitalist economy and other institutions at face value, in short, to overlook the many ways in which modern society deviates from its stated ideals.

Consequently, general theory is still a distant goal. Theorists have been unable to escape the assumptions of their own time and place, and they have been unable to account for the radical diversity of social stratification through time and place. For the time being, theorists of stratification must confine themselves to understanding particular systems of inequality while keeping an eye on what these systems all have in common.

It is time now to abandon the high-level abstraction of general theory in order to discuss the concrete achievements of stratification analysts and some of the research problems they face as they struggle to understand a phenomenon that has long intrigued and baffled theorists.

CHAPTER 5

The Struggle
to Understand
Social Stratification

In the preceding chapters we discussed some of the broad theoretical concerns that have occupied stratification theorists. In this chapter we will concern ourselves with the basic concepts, methods, and problems of contemporary stratification analysis, with a special focus on American developments.

HISTORICAL BACKGROUND

The Monopoly of Liberalism

Though most of the pioneer American sociologists paid at least some attention to social stratification, interest in stratification was minimal in American sociology until the 1920s.[1] This relative lack of interest in class theory before the twentieth century reflects the unusual lack of class consciousness in American history. While Americans have always been much concerned with questions of equality and inequality, they have not until

[1]For an analysis of the class theories of many of the leading figures in early American sociology, see Charles H. Page, *Class and American Sociology: From Ward to Ross* (New York: Dial Press, 1940); for a critical review and analysis of class theory and research from the 1920s to the 1950s, see Milton M. Gordon, *Social Class in American Sociology* (Durham, N.C.: Duke University Press, 1958). Gordon's search for conceptual clarity in the field of social stratification, which resulted in an elaboration of the multidimensional approach, constitutes a valuable contribution to stratification analysis in its own right.

recent decades conducted their discussions and disputes in terms of class categories. From the 1920s on—perhaps especially since the 1930s as a result of the shock of the Great Depression—interest in social stratification has grown, and a veritable flood of material about stratification has developed. Today, even the general public analyzes behavior and social problems in the broad language of class (often in euphemisms and rarely in the language of class antagonism), which would have been inconceivable fifty years ago.

As we suggested earlier, and as we will see in abundant detail later, not only is the United States a deeply unequal society but its structure of class inequality differs little from those of other industrial societies. Given this general similarity, why did American thought, on the part of laypeople and experts alike, ignore European developments in class theory until recent decades? In Europe, and especially on the Continent, stratification theory tended to acknowledge the reality of social classes and to assume widespread economic, social, and political conflict among them. In the United States, however, theorists have tended to deny the existence of class conflict and even the reality of social classes. The reasons for this divergence lie in the nature of American social and cultural development. Of special importance is the absence in American history of a feudal or authoritarian past. The American middle class did not have to gird itself against either a deeply entrenched nobility and clergy or an authoritarian state as did its counterpart in Europe. This allowed liberal theorists in the United States to define American society in the universalistic terms of the French Enlightenment and the optimistic individualism of John Locke. As a consequence, American thought has concentrated on the problem of relating the interests of the individual with those of society rather than on the conflicting interests of classes.

From the beginnings of the American republic, American experience with conflict and inequality always involved functionally specific issues dividing functionally specific groups. The major subjects of conflict in American history have been highly specific and issue-oriented: for example, the national bank, tariffs, and canals in the early nineteenth century; railroads, silver, the Haymarket riot, the Pullman strike, monopolies, and pure food and drug acts in the late nineteenth century; Prohibition, sit-down strikes, collective bargaining, Social Security, the National Recovery Act, the Taft-Hartley Act, civil rights, and the war on poverty in the twentieth century. American thought divorced conflict from the idea of a confrontation between classes, and conflict as such was defined in such a way as to emphasize an ultimate harmony of interest between individuals and groups. Given the widespread uniformity of economic conditions and of religious and ethnic background in the early agrarian United States, it is no wonder that inequality and conflict were interpreted in a nonclass way. Given the social reality of individualism (small farms and businesses, local markets, local politics, the relative absence of external and internal military threats), it is not hard to understand why the United States accepted the Newtonian-inspired image of a natural economic and social system. And it is also easy to understand why the United States accounted for the increased conflicts and social evils of hectic industrialization by grafting Darwin's doctrine of evolution and natural selection (the survival of the fittest) to the doctrine of laissez-faire that had emerged in economics.[2]

During this period, when gross inequality in wealth and power had become commonplaces of private and public discourse, and conflicts between economic groups (class) and between status groups (prestige) and their various mixtures had become troublesome in the extreme, there was no pronounced tendency to view America's problems in class terms. There were too many factors preventing the growth of class consciousness; the United States was experiencing real economic expansion and unprecedented rates of upward social mobility; immigration not only enhanced mobility but tended also to make economic classes extremely heterogeneous in religious and ethnic composition; and, of course, the vitality of the American political process allowed for enough reform to channel discontent away from radicalism and to turn injustice and exploitation into political rather than class issues.

All in all, the American experience gave rise to a widespread consensus that social inequality is natural. If it is assumed that the United States is a free society, what could be more natural than to believe that inequality reflects the natural distribution of talent among human beings? And, being natural, inequality and the conflicts that resulted from it posed no threat to American society, although it did create problems of adjustment. If these adjustments could not be made by free economic markets, they could be undertaken by the nation's free political markets.

American sociology's new interest in social class was basically continuous with the evolution of America's symbolic culture. This evolution was essentially a shift from early to late liberalism. Late liberalism is characterized by a greater appreciation of the power of social variables over human behavior—in other words, by a shift from a biopsychological to a moderate sociocultural view.[3] But despite the emphasis on the social roots of behavior in the thought of late liberal theorists like Charles Horton Cooley, W.I. Thomas, John Dewey, and Charles Beard, and in late liberal reform movements like Progressivism, the New Freedom, the Square Deal, the New Deal, the Fair Deal, and the Great Society, late liberalism is continuous with the past.

The purpose of reforms, even when they involve extensive changes in the social environment, is not to change society but to make it more consistent with its basic principle—the emancipation of unequal individual talent through

[2] See Richard Hofstadter, *Social Darwinism in American Thought*, rev. ed. (Boston: Beacon Press, 1955).

[3] For intellectual histories of this relatively important shift, see Morton White, *Social Thought in America: The Revolt Against Formalism* (New York: Viking Press, 1949), and Henry Steele Commager, *The American Mind: An Interpretation of American Thought and Character Since the 1880's* (New Haven, Conn.: Yale University Press, 1950).

equality of opportunity—and thus produce a natural and just society (or system of "nonegalitarian classlessness"). To accomplish this, however, it is necessary to know how society promotes or retards personal achievement. Along with the other social sciences, sociology responded to this intellectual challenge, and the development of stratification research and theory represents an important part of its response.

During the twentieth century American sociologists have pursued some of Weber's ideas in developing stratification theory, though on the whole they have extracted only as much from him as suited the distinctive flavor of American sociology and American culture and society. Heeding Weber's admonition to see more than the economic dimension, they identified the three general dimensions of class, prestige, and power. During the formative years of stratification analysis, sociologists, while not unmindful of economic inequality, stressed prestige variables. Ever since World War II, there has been a shift toward treating economic status as the central focus of stratification. And recently there has been an emphasis on the role of the state in the stratification process.

Despite mistakes and errors of emphasis, there emerged from this richly creative period a clear recognition of the major problems of stratification analysis. How does one construct indices in the economic realm (income, wealth, occupation, education) that make for causally meaningful and valid economic classes? What does one do to relate agriculture, manufacturing, and service sectors to each other? How does one establish gradations of prestige and power that are causally meaningful and valid? Above all, how does one relate class, prestige, and power gradations? How, in other words, does one turn formal analytical categories into a synthesis in which the concept of social class expresses the behavioral reality of social stratification?

The Small-Town Focus

The American tradition of stratification research and theory emerged as a focus on the small town. From the 1920s on, American social scientists developed a complex set of skills for analyzing social class (and "caste") in small-town America. While an important aspect of this tradition was a search for the typical community, almost every kind of community and region was studied. From this effort emerged a rich and colorful picture of regional and other variations in inequality: from the well-established and differentiated class structure of the Northeast and South to the frontier communities of the Middle and Far West, from complex industrial communities to homogeneous farm and mining communities, from ethnically and racially homogeneous communities to those richly diversified by ethnicity and race, and from small towns to metropolitan centers and suburbs.[4]

---

[4]For a useful review of representative examples of this tradition between the 1920s and 1950s, see Milton M. Gordon, *Social Class in American Sociology* (Durham, N.C.: Duke University Press, 1958), chaps. 3–5.

Despite variations in the approaches of the pioneer analysts of class, certain common characteristics may be noted. Virtually all researchers chose communities of manageable size—small enough for the observer (often a team) to get to know it fairly well, and, even more importantly, for the inhabitants to identify each other in terms of stratification categories. The customary point of entry to the sociological reality of social classes was the classes themselves, namely, individuals' subjective evaluations of each other. Thus, community members evaluated families on a number of different bases (income, amount and type of wealth, occupation, club memberships, breeding, power, and so on), and the observers presumably allowed the reality of social class to emerge.

The main outlines of this tradition stemmed from the work of the social anthropologist W. Lloyd Warner, who with many collaborators investigated a number of communities, starting in 1930 with Yankee City (Newburyport, Massachusetts). In 1949 Warner and his associates published a manual[5] in which they formalized their method, presenting two different procedures for determining social classes: Evaluated Participation, or the subjective determination of social classes by community members, and an Index of Status Characteristics, or an average of weighted scores for occupation, source of income, and house type and location. The results obtained by using these two procedures were found to correlate quite well in the case of a small town; and presumably the Index of Status Characteristics could be substituted for the more cumbersome interview procedure to allow for the study of larger population complexes whose members do not know each other well enough to judge others' class positions.

Small-town stratification theory is characterized by many difficulties, notably its basic assumption that studying the small town is tantamount to investigating the nature of the United States.[6] This assumption was probably not justified even at the time such studies were being conducted, and their current relevance to the dynamics and structure of the American system of stratification is even more problematic. Aside from their diverse orientations and conclusions, these studies all focused on something that has since virtually disappeared, small-town America.[7] The great creative period of small-

[5]W. Lloyd Warner, Marcia Meeker, and Kenneth Eells, *Social Class and America: A Manual of Procedure for the Measurement of Social Status* (Chicago: Science Research Associates, 1949).

[6]W. Lloyd Warner, the leading researcher associated with small-town studies, states this explicitly in the foreword to *Democracy in Jonesville* (New York: Harper & Row, 1949), and implicitly in the titles of the first four volumes (of a total of five) of the Yankee City series: *The Social Life of a Modern Community* and *The Status System of a Modern Community*, both with Paul S. Lunt; *The Social System of American Ethnic Groups*, with Leo Srole; *The Social System of the Modern Factory*, with J.O. Low. The fifth volume is entitled *The Living and the Dead* (New Haven, Conn.: Yale University Press, 1941–1959).

[7]Small towns are still plentiful in the United States, but most are caught up in the dynamics of a national economy and state; for a pioneering study along these lines, see Arthur J. Vidich and Joseph Bensman, *Small Town in Mass Society: Class, Power, and Religion in a Rural Community* (Garden City, N.Y.: Doubleday Anchor Books, 1960).

town stratification research lasted from the mid-1920s to the early 1940s; it occurred, in other words, at the same time that the United States was rapidly becoming an urban society dominated by a national economy and governed by a national state. Today, even the concept of an autonomous nation-state is inadequate; one must think in terms of an international political economy that has important consequences for class structure.

Small-town studies have other shortcomings. Their emphasis on prestige distracted attention from the major determinant of stratification, the economy. And their subjective, or reputational, method and choice of subject matter tended to emphasize stability and homogeneity; to highlight prestige phenomena without tracing them to their historical roots, especially economic developments; and to substitute the judgments of lay individuals for those of social scientists.

These local studies were not without value, however. They gave rise to an extremely fruitful research methodology and revealed most of the problems basic to stratification analysis. The small-town studies were important for another reason: Despite differing methodologies and emphases, they all agreed that the United States is a deeply stratified society.

THE NATIONAL FOCUS: DEVELOPMENT OF CLASS INDICES AND CATEGORIES

The Shift from Subjective to Objective Data

The insufficiency of a narrow concentration on small communities was sensed by Warner, who eventually developed a more efficient procedure for analyzing stratification phenomena than the reputational approach he had used. However, credit for the transition, both theoretical and practical, from the study of the small town to the study of the metropolitan center belongs to August B. Hollingshead. Early in his career, Hollingshead had used the reputational approach to study the impact of social class on education in Morris, Illinois, a small midwestern town of 6,000 inhabitants.[8] But later when he wanted to tackle the relation between social class and mental illness in New Haven, Connecticut, a metropolitan center of 240,000, Hollingshead could not rely on subjective awareness of social class. Instead, he developed an "objective" substitute, the Index of Social Position.[9] After intensive interviews with a cross-sectional random sample of 552 households, Hollingshead and his associate Jerome K. Myers ranked the families. Work-

[8]August Hollingshead, *Elmstown's Youth* (New York: John Wiley & Sons, 1949).
[9]For a full explanation, see August B. Hollingshead and Frederick C. Redlich, *Social Class and Mental Illness: A Community Study* (New York: John Wiley & Sons, 1958), Appendix 2.

ing independently, they agreed, by and large, on the ranking of the families in a scheme of five classes. They then extracted the three basic criteria they had used to rank the families: (1) location of residence, (2) occupation, and (3) education (which was taken to indicate associational and cultural life). Each of these factors was scaled and weighted, and the resulting range of scores produced five distinct classes, the upper classes containing 2.7 percent, 9.8 percent, and 18.9 percent of the total number of families and the two lower classes containing 49.4 percent and 20.2 percent.

Stratification analysis has blossomed since the 1950s. The main tradition, including both sociology and federal data-gathering, has focused on income, occupation, and education with considerable interest in race, sex, and age. This focus coincided with the main tradition of American liberalism, the tendency to interpret all behavior in individualistic terms within the assumption that the United States is a meritocracy (or is on its way toward becoming one). However, in recent years a powerful conflict tradition has emerged that has sought to reorient stratification theory. The best way to introduce this tradition is to discuss the renewed interest in the economy as a structural force in its own right.

Social Class as Property Relations

Recently stratification theory (often inspired by Karl Marx) has given much more attention to the tiny upper class that owns so much of the basic economy. From this perspective, the initial need was to go beyond individual income and occupation and focus on wealth and economic power, and this has been done clearly and persuasively by E.O. Wright and Luca Perrone, who argue that empirical research in sociology has neglected Marxian categories, especially the fundamental concept of owner vs. nonowner. Arguing directly against sociology's preoccupation with occupation, Wright and Perrone set out to learn whether being an owner has any bearing on income. Defining class as a position in the social relations of production, they use four criteria to place people:

1. the ownership of the means of production;
2. the purchase of the labor power of others;
3. the control of other people's labor power;
4. the sale of one's own labor power.

The result is the four classes shown in Table 5-1. When income data are analyzed, owners (both capitalist and petite bourgeoisie) receive more income than do managers and workers *even when education, occupational status, age, and job tenure are held constant.* And managers, in turn, have more income than do workers even when education is held constant. Wright and Perrone

TABLE 5-1. Class as Property Relations

	CRITERIA FOR CLASS POSITION			
CLASS	OWNERSHIP OF THE MEANS OF PRODUCTION	PURCHASE OF THE LABOR OF OTHERS	CONTROL OF THE LABOR OF OTHERS	SALE OF ONE'S OWN LABOR
Capitalists	Yes	Yes	Yes	No
Managers	No	No	Yes	Yes
Workers	No	No	No	Yes
Petite bourgeoisie	Yes	No	No	No

Source: E. O. Wright and Luca Perrone, "Marxist Class Categories and Income Inequality," *American Sociological Review* 42 (February 1977), Table 1 (original title, "Expanded Marxist Criteria for Class"), p. 34. Used with permission.

The above authors use the term *Petty Bourgeoisie* but let's standardize here and elsewhere as Petite.

argue that the high income of managers is largely a function of social control—here higher rewards induce rising executives to operate within the assumptions of a capitalist society, thus also providing a buffer between the upper class and workers.[10] Wright and Perrone have heightened sociology's awareness of economic power, and in later chapters we will report on other ways that scholars in the conflict tradition have altered our image of American stratification.

Identifying Class Levels

The federal government provides continuous data about the distribution of income, occupation, education, and other factors pertinent to social stratification. In analyzing these hierarchies, how does one establish cutoff points that identify economic and social classes? For example, how does one dissect the income hierarchy to reveal stratification differences? Is it meaningful to distinguish between households in the $0–5,000 range from those in the $6,000–10,000 range? At what point is a household considered of "modest means" rather than poor, and how is the former distinguished from the well-off, and it in turn differentiated from affluent households? The only way to answer these questions is to determine empirically what happens to families and unrelated individuals with a given range of income. Better still, we want to know what the relation is between general economic status (income, occupation, education) and all other kinds of behavior.

In developing our portrayal, we will canvass what scholars have

[10]Erik Olin Wright and Luca Perrone, "Marxist Class Categories and Income Inequality," *American Sociological Review* 42 (February 1977):32–55.

learned about social class and be on the alert for knowledge gaps. To give an example of the latter, we can determine the number of people employed in thousands of occupations, but we do not know how many prostitutes there are. It is not unrealistic to guess that the United States has five hundred thousand prostitutes. This is a sizable number of human beings occupying a distinctive stratification position, and yet we know little about them because the Census Bureau does not recognize prostitution as an occupation. As a matter of fact, the total number of people in illegal occupations (drug dealers, pimps, bookies, pickpockets, confidence men and women, fences, and so on) is probably high. And the number of people who transact business in the underground economy (many of whom do not think of themselves as criminals) is also high. Estimates of the volume of business not captured by official figures (and on which no taxes are paid) put it at 15 to 25 percent of the gross national product.

In other words, researchers do not always use the total universe of human behavior when they formulate their research designs. In addition to overlooking illegal occupations, researchers often overlook unrelated individuals, inmates of mental and penal institutions, uncounted members of society (significant numbers are missed by the Census Bureau), illegal immigrants (estimated at 5 million to 10 million) and "immigrant" workers. Perhaps the best-known bias in stratification research is its systematic neglect of the very poor prior to the 1960s.

The area of subjectivity—how individuals feel about and apprise themselves and each other—will form an important part of our picture. There is little doubt that we need to know how and what individuals think and feel in order to understand the nature of inequality and equality. Stratification analysis has developed two different ways to obtain data in this area, the reputational and the "subjective" methods. The reputational approach was referred to earlier in our discussion of the small-town approach; it consists of asking individuals what they think of other individuals, and involves the evaluation of others on the basis of family, religion, race, occupation, income, wealth, and similar factors. Far more valuable to the study of metropolitan and national patterns of stratification is the subjective approach, which seeks to determine what people think and feel about themselves and about a variety of issues, such as education, politics, sense of power and ability to control one's life, work satisfaction, class self-identification, and the like.

In identifying class levels by probing the inner world of Americans we will be opening up the "prestige" dimension. And we will also focus on how class and political-legal behavior are related. Indeed, most of our strategy in future chapters will be to find systematic links among economic, prestige, and political-legal behavior. But we will also find that there are inconsistencies among these variables; for example, households with the same income will have more or less prestige because of skin color, religion, or style of life.

We will also find that members of the same income group may behave quite differently politically or be treated differently by those who exercise power. In addition, high income does not always bring more prestige than that given to those with less income; for example, a garbage collector or call girl compared with a minister or school teacher. Considerations of this sort lead us to questions of status consistency or the relation among class, prestige, and power.

Analyzing Relations Among Class, Prestige, and Power: Status Consistency

All caste and estate societies are marked by a high degree of consistency in the ways in which individuals and families are ranked across all dimensions. The same holds true for their behavior. Economic status leads to high prestige status, high prestige status leads to high power status, and high prestige-power leads to high class status, and so on. Caste and estate systems of stratification develop not only unified strata (consistency in class, prestige, and power) but also relations between strata that are rigid and stable over time. When status inconsistency appears in a caste or estate system (as in the case of the bourgeoisie in prerevolutionary France), one can speak of deviations from the normative sociocultural system.

Class societies also reveal considerable status consistency, though they are also marked by considerable inconsistency, especially among the lower classes. And, of course, status consistency (or class consolidation) leads to class perpetuation, since parents tend to pass on their high or low positions to their children. Broadly speaking, consistency analysis seeks to establish relations within and between each of the major hierarchies:

1. *Status Consistency or Crystallization.*[11] One employs this concept to describe families and unrelated individuals characterized by comparable or consistent benefits across the various hierarchies of inequalities. Examples are a white Presbyterian doctor, a white Methodist skilled worker, and a white Baptist farm laborer.
2. *Status Inconsistency.* This concept is used to describe families and unrelated individuals characterized by different or inconsistent levels of benefits in the various dimensions of stratification. Seen from a national standpoint, examples are a black Presbyterian doctor, an Italian Roman Catholic building contractor, and a Jewish lawyer.

One of the most advantageous features of the concept of status consistency is that it enables an analyst to demonstrate that class position is often

[11]The essence of the concept of status crystallization (or status consistency) is old, though its specific terms are associated with Gerhard Lenski, "Status Crystallization: A Non-Vertical Dimension of Social Status," *American Sociological Review* 19 (August 1954):405–413.

perpetuated without superior achievement.[12] Speaking more generally, status consistency reveals a great deal about the fundamental causal process in social stratification. This process occurs as follows: Those with high incomes, occupations, and education tend also to enjoy high prestige, stable families, more and varied opportunities for interaction, and greater political-legal power; and these factors in turn tend to protect and enhance high economic status. Such families also have the resources, motives, and skills to ensure a high social class position for their offspring, especially through the careful management of socialization.

The same causal process is discernible at the bottom of the class hierarchy. The poor have low income, educational, and occupational statuses, and thus have low prestige, unstable families, and deadening patterns of social interaction. These factors not only reinforce each other but also tend to give rise to a process of class "inheritance"; that is, the offspring of the poor tend to inherit the general class position of their parents.

Some of the more extreme incongruities in stratification status are found among minority groups: Middle-class blacks, for example, suffer serious status inconsistency, as do Jews of high economic or professional achievement. The same thing is probably true of well-to-do Irish, Italian, Japanese, and other ethnic-racial minority Americans, and also women. Exact comparisons between power and the other dimensions of inequality are difficult to make, but those who live in big cities and have fairly substantial incomes (middle management and skilled workers) are probably not enjoying political power consistent with their class positions.[13]

Analyzing the consistency of positions in the hierarchies of class, prestige, and power calls into play all the fundamental questions in social theory, questions involving social causation, mobility, pluralism, and integration, as well as the dynamics of personality. In a general way, the explanation of behavior by reference to social disjointedness and incoherence is central to the entire tradition of modern social science. Any number of social theorists have explained major social trends and stresses and breaks in the social structure as a result of internal contradictions. A good example of social breakdown because of internal contradictions is the French Revolution, which resulted because the middle class's prestige and power statuses were badly out of line with its class position. Obviously, the idea that there can emerge a class that contradicts the society it is a part of, and is thus revolutionary while other classes are reactionary, is central to the Marxian tradition. In sum, there is little doubt that consistency analysis is a valuable tool.

---

[12]For a discussion of how this takes place in and through education, see Chapter 8.

[13]On the basis of ideas from Max Weber and Karl Marx, Norbert Wiley has developed a more complex analysis of consistency and inconsistency within the class dimension and has related it to political behavior; see his "America's Unique Class Politics: The Interplay of Labor, Credit and Commodity Markets," *American Sociological Review* 32 (August 1967): 529–541. For a discussion of this essay, see the section "America's Unique Class Politics" in Chapter 13.

The concept of stratification consistency contains dangers, however. As a concept it is intriguing and seductive, and it suits intellectuals' professional predilections for logic and abstraction. However, serious questions have been raised about its empirical validity and about the ideological biases it might contain. When the idea first surfaced in American stratification theory in the 1950s, it led to a number of research projects. But, by and large, researchers found little evidence to support the idea. The question posed by attempts to explain behavior in terms of status consistency can be put more simply: Do all the inconsistencies in class, prestige, and power statuses that exist logically (or even statistically) actually affect the behavior of Americans? There is little question that the behavior of Americans is deeply affected by the ambiguities, conflicts, and contradictions in American society. However, individuals and aggregates do not behave in a specified manner simply because their social and stratificational statuses are illogical or incongruous. Lurking behind this mode of explanation, it would seem, is the early liberal assumption of the rational individual. Early liberals tended to assume that behavior results from a continuous series of pleasure-pain, profit-loss calculations. Basically, early liberalism explained behavior by reference to the alleged rationality of economic markets and to a primitive psychology of basic hunger and gain drives, and by assuming that the unity of statuses found among the successful classes must be psychologically normal. The consistency explanation in social science is probably best seen as a modern version of this assumption.

Sociocultural systems are often contradictory and ambiguous in the demands they place on individuals, and as a result personalities become contradictory and ambiguous. There is little evidence, though, that human beings have any psychological need to think things out or to introduce coherence into their lives. The simple fact remains that unless people are taught to integrate their values and thoughts they do not do so, and do not recognize or regret the lack of such integration. In short, the consistency explanation is in large part a product of social scientists' attribution of their own predilections to ordinary people (and thus to the alleged empirical nature of society).

ANALYSIS OF SOCIAL MOBILITY

Types of Mobility

In stratification analysis, *mobility* refers to movement (or lack of movement) between different social classes or strata. In the past, disproportionate attention has been paid to upward mobility, though, of course, reference to any type of vertical mobility logically implies downward mobility and lack of mobility.

The essence of the clumsy term *lack of mobility* is that individuals and families do not move from the stratum into which they are born. A number of distinctions should be kept in mind with reference to this idea. Static stratification positions based on ascription are characteristic, of course, of caste and estate systems (usully referred to as *closed systems of mobility*) as opposed to class societies (usually referred to as *open systems*).[14] Thus, one meaning of a lack of mobility in industrial society is that ascriptive barriers—such as racism, poverty, religious-ethnic discrimination, and, in a special sense, sexism—prevent people from rising on the social ladder. The degree of rigidity of such barriers is of interest because it is also a measure of *equal opportunity mobility*. (An important mobility analysis that contains a measure of equal opportunity mobility will be discussed shortly.) A lack of mobility also exists when an absolute increase in benefits is unaccompanied by a relative increase vis-à-vis other classes.

People can be stationary in a variety of other ways, however. *Horizontal mobility* (accompanied or not by geographic mobility)[15] is a change of occupation *within* a stratum. For example, a sales manager for a corporation becomes an advertising executive; a scientist for the Department of the Interior becomes a professor of geology; a milk-truck driver becomes a bus driver; and so on.

Mobility: Increasing or Declining?

The basic pattern of social mobility in the United States is the same as in other industrial countries (from the beginning of industrialization—insofar as data are available—right up to the 1970s).[16] The small variations toward more mobility (equality) are found in societies with strong labor and socialist movements.

Since the 1970s, mobility may have declined. The shift to service occupations, toward employment in large bureaucracies (public and private), the decline of skilled blue-collar workers and labor unions, the decline of public services, and the mobility of capital may have produced a more static American society. Data on income, wealth, occupation, and education strongly

---

[14]That *open* and *closed systems of mobility* are misleading terms will become apparent.

[15]Geographic mobility is of interest because it alerts us to some interesting consequences of the clustering and dispersion of class elements: Thus, the high concentration of particular class elements in political capitals, residential neighborhoods, research and development centers, and retirement areas all help to produce stratification-related phenomena of considerable importance.

[16]For a full analysis of British data and a comparison with the United States and other advanced capitalist societies, which concludes that mobility rates are similar and stable in all capitalist systems (they appear high when compared with static societies but come nowhere near approximating an equal opportunity system), see John H. Goldthorpe (in collaboration with Catriona Llewellyn and Clive Payne), *Social Mobility and Class Structure in Modern Britain*, 2nd ed. (New York: Oxford University Press, 1987).

indicate this.[17] The entire process has been masked by the rapid growth of female labor participation leading to double-breadwinner households and by debt. In later chapters we will also see that the United States appears no longer able to generate political coalitions that can protect the many victims of the contemporary economy.

Intragenerational, Intergenerational, and Social-Origins Mobility

Sociologists have focused on three distinct aspects of social mobility, usually emphasizing vertical mobility. The first is *intragenerational* or *career mobility*. Here the analyst follows individuals' careers to see what paths they follow, the barriers they face, how far they progress, and so on. The lives of successful people are of perennial interest, and much has been written about and by individuals who have struggled and prevailed against great obstacles. A good deal of fiction has also been written on this theme, most notably the novels of Horatio Alger, which were written during the latter third of the nineteenth century. Alger's books were not far from some important truths about social mobility.[18] His heroes were middle-class boys, carefully socialized to Protestant bourgeois ways, who began the ascent to success only through a lucky break. Despite their mechanical plots, wooden characters, and unabashed sentimentality, Alger's novels were phenomenally successful, perhaps mostly because they offered a detailed, colorful picture of city life in an age when America's rural migration to the city was in full swing.

The Horatio Alger myth, like all stories about virtuous, talented individuals who rise from humble beginnings, should be scrutinized carefully and even with suspicion. For one thing, such stories are far from typical; for another, the individual's "humble" beginnings are often staged apprenticeships for well-placed sons, such as the lad who begins his career by driving a truck in his father's factory and within a few years becomes a vice president of the company.

Too much attention is usually given to occupational mobility, diverting attention from the numerous other channels of mobility: marriage, political life, carefully planned consumption (on a number of fronts), crime, sports, friendship, family connections, and the operation of religious, ethnic, and racial organizations and networks. But occupation is undeniably central to mobility in industrial society, and increasingly such mobility (or lack of it)

---

[17]For a detailed analysis, see Chapter 6.

[18]Much of the following is based on R. Richard Wohl, "The Rags to Riches Story: An Episode in Secular Idealism," in Reinhard Bendix and Seymour M. Lipset, eds., *Class, Status, and Power: Social Stratification in Comparative Perspective*, 2nd. ed. (New York: Free Press, 1966), pp. 501–506.

occurs within the various bureaucracies that now dominate our institutional life.[19]

The growing importance of mobility in organizations is part and parcel of a major transformation in American society, the relative decline of small economic enterprises as channels of mobility, and the relative growth of mobility through formal and vocational-professional education.[20] The role played by education in mobility (which is much misunderstood, as we will see later) focuses attention on an individual's family-of-origin, since education takes place during the formative years of an individual's life. Thus we arrive at the second aspect of mobility: *intergenerational mobility*, which is the analysis of the relation between parents' class position and that of their children, especially their son(s). (Because studies in this area mostly involve father-to-son mobility, our report focuses on males and neglects females). The analysis of intergenerational mobility is attractive superficially because it appears to tell us how open or closed a social system is over time. Its study, however, is fraught with difficulties.

One need only realize, for example, that the son of a black postman has a better chance of upward mobility than the son of a white Protestant doctor to appreciate the conundrums in this area. Of first importance in tracing father-to-son mobility is the difficulty of matching occupations from one generation to the next. Second, it is hard to identify generations, as "fathers" and "sons" can range over a large age span. Third, the decision to focus on the father-to-son relation makes for the omission of fathers who had no sons and households run by divorced, unmarried, and widowed women, many of whom raise sons.

Other complications that stand in the way of a more precise prediction of a son's career in terms of his father's class can be mentioned in passing. Sons can skip college, for example, and inherit a business directly; they can enter college after spending a few years traveling or being self-employed; or they can voluntarily live, at least for a while, below their class level of origin, and thus be ignored by some methods of collecting data. And sons can obviously be affected differently by such social events as economic booms or

[19]The importance of occupational context, as well as the need to examine other channels and forms of mobility, is emphasized by Harold L. Wilensky, "Measures and Effects of Social Mobility," in Neil J. Smelser and Seymour M. Lipset, eds., *Social Structure and Mobility in Economic Development* (Chicago: Aldine, 1966), chap. 3. Some hints about the variety and nuances of mobility can be culled from Anselm L. Strauss, *The Contexts of Social Mobility* (Chicago: Aldine, 1971). For a case study of a large American corporation that advocates what is now known as the Japanese industrial model with a special focus on using reforms to enhance the mobility of minorities, see Rosabeth Moss Kanter, *Men and Women of the Corporation* (New York: Basic Books, 1977).

[20]Small business is still a powerful theme in American life, and large numbers of people continue to move into and out of the self-employed category. We are talking here, it should be emphasized, of a relative decline.

busts, war, governmental science policies, and the like, depending on their location in rural or urban areas, their age, and so on.

Despite difficulties, the analysis of father-to-son mobility tells us much about the openness or rigidity of a given system of social stratification. Father-to-son studies are also valuable when they are part of the third type of social mobility analysis, the focus on social origins. Here analysts want to find out from what social level the occupants of various occupations have been recruited. Whether school teachers, for example, are drawn primarily from the lower or upper segments of the middle class will make a big difference in the nature of that occupation. Similarly, if the officer ranks of the military or the senior officials of the State Department are drawn from a narrow class base, occupational performance can be expected to be different than if their class base were broad. Many key occupations have been studied, including business people, teachers, civil servants, legislators, and the military. We will have occasion to refer to such studies later.

Status Attainment Theory

The early research on father-to-son mobility reflected the broad acceptance in sociology of the basic tenets of American liberalism (capitalism). From its beginnings until the 1960s and 1970s, American sociology envisioned the United States as an open society based on and progressively realizing universalistic principles. Universalism meant that science and achievement statuses were displacing nonscientific beliefs and statuses derived from ascription. Society was gradually developing objective criteria for evaluating people and positions. In time, all particularistic evaluations based on family, religion, race, and sex would be displaced by achievement criteria. Science, efficiency, rationality, and achievement would eventually triumph over any religious, philosophical, or humanistically derived beliefs and values that could not be empirically verified.

From Cooley to Parsons, and from Sumner to Davis-Moore, American sociologists had an image of society as a functional division of labor headed by natural elites as determined by competition, science, and achievement criteria. The United States was an open society, and whatever barriers to achievement remained were being dismantled. The occupational system already embodied the principle of merit as established in open-market competition. The occupational hierarchy was esentially a functional differentiation based on a growing consensus of what each occupation was worth. Already the rational division of labor had produced a large and growing middle-level mass.

The causes of progress were technology, education, urbanization, industrialization, and the growth of specialization and formal organizations. In the above, education had perhaps a special importance because one could actually observe the meritocratic process in action and understand how individuals were attaining their status in society.

This is the context in which early mobility studies were conducted.[21] Now known as the *status attainment* perspective, early mobility studies assumed that American society had already become a meritocracy (the theorists rejected the local community studies that had discovered deep non-meritocratic class structures, claiming that they were not representative of the nation at large). Taking the United States at face value, status attainment theorists focused on individual characteristics, essentially asking: Who has the basic American values and how did they get them?

The pioneering and extremely influential study in this regard was by Duncan and Blau, who found that class background influences the mobility-achievement process with middle-class and above parents providing an impetus to occupational success. But, argued Duncan and Blau, the individual's personal characteristics also count and this is reflected in education.[22] Their analysis of this process was replicated by Featherman and Hauser with identical results.[23] Other studies in this vein expanded the variables to include educational aspirations, peer interaction, and the impact of significant others (The Wisconsin School).[24]

Status attainment analysts found a relation between class and success but did not evaluate this relation critically. They found personal characteristics and small-group experiences (related to class) that led to educational and occupational success but again they did not disapprove. They found school systems that fostered success by those who came from the better classes, but again status attainment theorists did not interpret their findings, in effect endorsing them. The reasons that the status attainment tradition did not raise questions about what they found is that they assumed that the middle (and above) class represented the valid march of history, or rather the forces of science, rationality, and individual achievement. Thus it is right and proper that the middle class (and above) should produce sons who have the personal attributes that lead to success and that educational institutions should embody the universalistic values that were progressively enveloping all of society. The role of the objective, value-neutral researcher is simply to lay bare this objective, historical process.

---

[21]For much of the above context, see J. David Knottnerus, "Status Attainment Research and Its Image of Society," *American Sociological Review* 52 (February 1987):113–121.

[22]Otis D. Duncan and Peter M. Blau, *The American Occupational Structure* (New York: John Wiley & Sons, 1967).

[23]David Featherman and Robert Hauser, *Opportunity and Change* (New York: Academic Press, 1978).

[24]William H. Sewell and Robert M. Hauser, *Education, Occupation, and Earnings.* (New York: Academic Press, 1975) and William H. Sewell and Robert M. Hauser, eds., *Schooling and Achievement in American Society* (New York: Academic Press, 1976).

Critics of the status attainment position appeared and, by and large, their view has prevailed. The easy optimism of not only status attainment theory but of mainstream sociology (probably from Condorcet and Comte down through the 1970s) has been overturned by conflict sociologists.

The Conflict Approach to Mobility

During the 1970s the main creative currents in stratification research came out of the conflict tradition. In regard to mobility, conflict theorists criticized the status attainment model as narrow and biased, narrow because of its focus on occupation, and biased because of its focus on personal characteristics. Status attainment analysis, argued critics, was directly in line with mainstream liberalism and functionalism.[25]

The status attainment model had failed to explain the overall process of mobility. Occupation is too broad a term; hence, one must include important distinctions such as occupational power and complexity of skills. And fundamental structural forces in the economy and society are central to mobility: Property relations are crucial in maintaining continuity among generations in the upper class and controlling the admission of new members. Property relations as economic concentration, and in static vs. dynamic sectors in the economy, are also central to mobility.[26] The actions of professional associations and trade unions in controlling labor flows, the actions of government, the behavior of foreign countries, and so on—all are important to how well each generation fares.[27] All in all, the conflict perspective has made *structural* mobility central to how sociologists think of mobility and stratification.

The conflict tradition has also produced a different picture of education from the one found in mainstream American thinking and in status attainment research. Far from being a progressive force reflecting progressive middle-class values, the school is basically a class phenomenon, ensuring the success of the established classes and the failure of the lower classes. And to make matters worse, success in school cannot be linked to functional achievement in the outer society.[28]

All in all, what has happened to status attainment theory and mainstream functional sociology is that their image of society, and the underlying presumptions on which they were based, have been rendered false by both history and other research. The United States was probably never the classless, progressive society that mainstream America and its social science took

[25] Patrick M. Horan, "Is Status Attainment Research Atheoretical?," *American Sociological Review* 43 (August 1978): 534–541.

[26] E. M. Beck, Patrick M. Horan, and Charles M. Tolbert II, "Stratification in a Dual Economy," *American Sociological Review* 43 (October 1978): 704–720.

[27] For more details, see the section titled "Power Over the Labor Market" in Chapter 6.

[28] For details on the new understandings that have developed about class and education, see Chapter 8.

for granted. Today, although belief in the ideal of classlessness and progress remains strong, most sociologists are now aware that the gap between social reality and ideals has widened.

Structural vs. Equal Opportunity Mobility

In assessing mobility phenomena, care should be taken to distinguish between structural or "forced" mobility and equal opportunity or "circulation" mobility.[29] A great deal of social mobility is due to causal processes that alter economic opportunities. Examples are technological innovation, war, public and private credit policies, depressions, and public tax and land-use policies. One of the most dramatic transformations in American society in the past century has been the radical decline of farming and the rise of factory and office occupations. A great deal of father-to-son upward mobility, therefore, should be seen as the "forced" departure from the land of millions of rural people, both white and black.

It is important to keep structural mobility in mind when trying to assess the relative roles played in the mobility process by human nature, talent, equal opportunity, individualism, and equal competition (roughly, equal opportunity or "circulation" mobility). It would seem, basically, that mobility is socially induced, but occurs so fitfully and selectively as to create the misleading impression of stemming from the capricious way in which nature distributes ability and ambition. In their valuable analysis comparing intergenerational mobility rates in Australia, Italy, and the United States, Broom and Jones conclude that, whereas the United States has the highest rate of overall mobility, Australia has a higher rate of equal opportunity mobility (a larger amount of the American rate being structural in nature).

Absolute vs. Relative Mobility

Of decisive importance in studying social mobility is the distinction between absolute and relative mobility. *By absolute mobility is meant the general upward absolute movement of the class system itself as measured by income (rising standard of living), occupation (more brainwork, less manual labor), and education (more literacy, more years of school completed).* Seen in this way, the entire American population has experienced upward mobility during the last century (see Figure 5–1), a phenomenon that resembles structural mobility (economic expansion). *Relative mobility, on the other hand, is movement by individuals and families (and various other collectivities and groups) up, down, or across the line(s) separating one social class or stratum from another.* Relative mobility also stems from economic expansion, which provides opportunities for some

[29]This distinction is derived from an important paper on mobility: Leonard Broom and F. Lancaster Jones, "Father-to-Son Mobility: Australia in Comparative Perspective," *American Journal of Sociology* 74 (January 1969): 333–342.

Figure 5-1   A Nonempirical Construct Depicting the Absolute Upward Movement of the American Class
Structure and the Absence of Change in the Relative Distribution of Social Values Despite
Upward, Downward, and Lack of Mobility

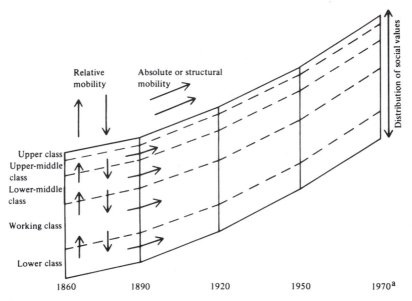

[a]The figure ends in 1970 because the upward movement of the American class may have ceased after that
point (this possibility is a major theme in later chapters).

individuals to rise above their class of origin; and, of course, economic
contraction can plummet individuals into the classes below. Relative mobility can also stem from noneconomic "equal" opportunity institutions, such as
education, and governmental efforts to subsidize training or combat discrimination, but it is very difficult to measure the impact of such institutions, and
their power must not be exaggerated. There is a strong tendency to assume
that equal opportunity leads to relative mobility, as well as to structural
mobility (economic expansion). Actually, the reverse is more accurate: Economic expansion leads to structural and relative mobility, as well as to efforts
to promote equal (and unequal) opportunities.

Keeping the foregoing distinctions in mind, it is easy to understand
how it is possible for a family to experience dramatic improvements in its
absolute class position over two or more generations but to remain in the
same social stratum. Much of this structural mobility is the result of the
growth of white-collar occupations, a process that should be interpreted
carefully. A great many white-collar jobs, for example, are difficult to distinguish from working-class jobs (the distinction between mental and manual
work notwithstanding). Also, most of the mobility into white-collar ranks

involves working-class individuals, which lends lower-level white-collar ranks a working-class outlook that matches their objective economic functions and income. And, finally, a large percentage of the increase in white-collar occupations is accounted for by women, who for the most part share the class levels of their fathers or husbands and therefore should not automatically be assumed to increase the number of white-collar families.

Of considerable importance in understanding absolute mobility is the knowledge that abundance does not eliminate or even reduce overall scarcity or overall inequality. Industrial society elaborates new forms of scarcity ("needs") to replace old ones, and one should not automatically assume that absolute increases in affluence, or in educational and occupational skills, reduce the relative distance between the various classes.[30] Confusion of absolute and relative mobility is perhaps the major source of errors about class stratification, and thus every effort should be made to keep this distinction clearly in mind.

A valuable contribution to understanding this distinction has been made by Norbert F. Wiley, who has identified a special variety of absolute movement unaccompanied by class mobility and aptly termed it a *mobility trap*.[31] The mobility trap is mobility *within* a stratum. Although Wiley focuses on the ethnic mobility trap, he lists four distinct types:

1. The "age-grade trap," or the tendency of age and sex groups to adopt prestige values that conflict with those of older age groups. Thus, popularity as a sports star or beauty queen in high school may well be a barrier to social mobility for those who cannot break into professional sports or the field of entertainment.
2. The "overspecialization trap," or lower-level, highly specialized administrative jobs from which one cannot be promoted.
3. The "localite trap," or the pursuit of local prestige at the expense of national standing. Certain occupations, such as social worker, planner, school superintendent, professor, and clergyman, increasingly allow for mobility only on a nationwide basis.
4. The "minority group trap," or advancement within a minority group in lieu of advancement into majority structures.

The general slowdown in the standard of living since 1970 may have ushered in a new environment for mobility. Instead of a growing pie fostering a nonzero-sum game (a game that does not require losers), a static pie leads to a zero-sum game (one gains something at the expense of others). Absolute and relative mobility may have changed their meaning—existing power groups may now be eager to keep competitors down.

[30]For a fuller discussion, see Chapter 6.

[31]"The Ethnic Mobility Trap and Stratification Theory," *Social Problems* 15 (Fall 1967): 147–159.

Absolute and Relative Ambition

LaMar Empey has made an important distinction in the area of ambition (or aspirations) that has significant bearing on a number of problems in stratification analysis, including social mobility. In his study of high school seniors in the State of Washington in 1954, Empey found that one must distinguish between absolute and relative occupational aspirations. If one asks the various classes about their aspirations in terms of a single hierarchy of occupations, it is clear that the upper classes aspire to upper occupations more frequently than do the lower classes. But if one examines the strength of aspirations in terms of starting point, it becomes clear that the lower classes want to move beyond their class positions at birth as much if not more than those in the classes above them. Testing further, Empey also found little difference between preferred and anticipated occupational goals.[32]

The implications of Empey's findings have been followed up by Ralph Turner in his sophisticated study of the social factors affecting ambition. To help us conceptualize mobility in an open class system of stratification, Turner uses the analogies of a race and a ladder. By studying high school seniors selected to represent as accurately as possible the nonethnic twelfth-grade population of Los Angeles, Turner also found strong educational and occupational mobility aspirations among all classes in both an absolute and a relative sense.[33] The implication is clear: One must envisage mobility in the United States as both a race to the top and a climb up a ladder. All classes, in other words, are motivated for success, either success through beating out competitors for the important upper positions or success in making deliberate moves up the occupational or business ladder. Beyond what people want, however, is a world where most mobility, especially for the lower classes, is decided by structural forces.

Mobility and Class Consistency

As we have noted, there is a tendency in all systems of stratification for families and individuals to receive consistent types of benefits in each of the major dimensions and subdimensions of stratification and for "hereditary" strata to appear. This tendency is more pronounced in caste and estate systems, but one must be careful in those cases, too, not to overestimate the amount of consistency or to assume an identity among class, prestige, and power. Maintaining a rigorous distinction among class, prestige, and power is even more important in the class system of stratification, for its various dimensions tend not only to interlock and merge but also to oppose and contradict each other in some respects. For example, two Americans with the

---

[32]LaMar T. Empey, "Social Class and Occupational Aspiration: A Comparison of Absolute and Relative Measurement," *American Sociological Review* 21 (December 1956): 703–709.

[33]Ralph H. Turner, *The Social Context of Ambition.* (San Francisco: Chandler, 1964), chap. 3.

same incomes may each have occupations that yield very different prestige. Even if they have the same income and occupation they can have different prestige because of race, religion, family lineage, taste, or other factors. Disparities between the various dimensions of inequality are made possible by the unique capacity of the human personality to harbor incongruities and contradictions and by the capacity of society to function not only despite such contradictions and incongruities, but often because of them. One general cause of such disparities is the rich complexity of values pursued by modern society—for example, the American population simultaneously pursues the values of success, equality, educational and professional achievement, self-discipline, high consumption levels, salvation, nationalism, internationalism, religion, ethnicity, religious and ethnic superiority, and racism. Another cause is the general absence of formal coordination of its various institutional sectors. Given well-established but incongruous values and beliefs, it is not surprising that individuals and groups may rise in one dimension without a corresponding rise in the others (for example, the *nouveau riche*, the economically successful Jew); or may descend in one dimension, such as the economy, without a corresponding decline in another dimension, such as political power (for example, farmers, small-business owners). It is important, in other words, to distinguish between mobility in one hierarchy and movement or lack of movement in the several hierarchies that constitute the full system of stratification.

Class Mobility and Rigidity

In thinking about class rigidity and class mobility, care must also be taken to avoid the obvious mistake of assuming that these two processes are mutually contradictory. A substantial rate of social mobility is perfectly compatible with a high degree of class rigidity. What this means in simple terms is that it is possible for individuals and families at the top of a class hierarchy to remain stationary even though other individuals and families are moving up. To understand this process one need only remember that the size of an upper-class compared to other classes may remain unchanging in terms of percentage, whereas its absolute numerical size increases greatly. Thus, if 10 percent of the American population is considered to be upper-middle class between 1900 and 1990, the absolute numbers in this class will be much larger in 1990 than in 1900. It is possible, therefore, for most of the families in the top 10 percent in 1900 to remain at the top because of class perpetuation and simultaneously for considerable social mobility into it to take place. What this means is that the original 10 percent (minus any that have succumbed to downward mobility) is joined by families that have risen with the expansion of the American economy and population.

This point can be stated differently by focusing on the fact that different social classes have different birthrates, the upper classes consistently producing fewer children than the lower classes. What happens, in other words, is that the upper classes produce only enough offspring to replace part of themselves, and vacancies at the top have to be filled from below (overwhelmingly from the ranks of the lower-middle class). (As daughters in the upper classes have become more important sources of recruitment into the upper reaches of our occupational system, they have probably deprived the lower classes of some mobility.) It is necessary to keep this overall compatibility in mind whenever we refer to these two salient features of class stratification: the tendency for benefits at various levels to congeal and reinforce each other, producing class rigidity, and the tendency in an expansive society for various elements to move up and down in the class system.

The Dysfunctions of Social Mobility

We are so accustomed to thinking of upward mobility as a good thing that a brief word of caution about this process is in order. Melvin Tumin has identified dysfunctional consequences of the tradition of achievement and success.[34] A high rate of social mobility gives rise to insecurity among the newly mobile, which interferes with performance of role responsibilities in their newly won positions. In addition, the general approval and encouragement of social mobility, as well as the reality of success, make role responsibility difficult at *all* levels as *all* think of rising above their present positions. (Analysts have argued, for example, that one of the reasons for Japan's phenomenal economic success is the fact that Japanese executives are far less likely to hop from job to job as do their American counterparts.)

This blurring of status and role responsibilities as a result of high rates and high expectations of mobility, Tumin claims, induces insecurity at the personal level and *anomie* at the social level. Another latent function—or, rather, dysfunction—of social mobility, according to Tumin, is the buying off of intellectuals and the stifling of social criticism. Surprisingly, Tumin fails to cite the tendency of social mobility to rob lower groups of their leadership through co-optation, a process of enormous consequence for, say, the black American. Perhaps this process is now known well enough and practiced consciously enough to qualify as a manifest function.[35]

Mobility: A Big Caution

Mobility is such a deeply planted American value that Americans rarely question the nature of the positions that they are aspiring to. However, if the position of doctor (whether acquired by Protestant, Catholic, or Jew)

---

[34]Melvin Tumin, "Some Unapplauded Consequences of Social Mobility in a Mass Society," *Social Forces* 36 (October 1957):32–37.

[35]For example, many public policies are designed to pacify the black American by providing employment or welfare.

requires the exploitation of nurses, orderlies, and patients, if corporate executives (male or female) exploit workers and consumers, if the owners of businesses (whether black, white, male, or female) receive income in excess of their own input, if college professors (whether Asian, Hispanic, or whatever) require the exploitation of secretaries, and so on through all upper-level positions, then it does not matter how mobility takes place or whether we improve opportunities for the lower classes or minorities. What matters is to focus on the nature of the prizes being held out and to remember that a class system should be evaluated and not merely lubricated.

Social Mobility: A Summary

Because the foregoing ideas about social mobility violate some common-sense understandings and accepted mores, it might be useful to summarize them. Perhaps the most important thing to keep in mind about stratification in America, and industrial countries in general, is that the class structure as a whole (up to the 1970s) has moved upward. Thus, there has been a consistent absolute rise in income, but there has been little relative equalization of income; there has been a consistent upgrading of occuptional skills, but little relative equalization of occupational statuses; there has occurred a consistent absolute rise in the number of years of school completed, but little relative equalization in education.[36] As a consequence, one must undertake any analysis of mobility with the image of a class structure that is static insofar as relative differences in income, occupation, and education (and other factors) are concerned, but that is moving up an inclined plane (see Figure 5–1). In employing this model, however, it is important to note that while the American class structure is static in terms of the abstract distribution of its central social values (aggregate income, wealth, occupational status, education), the families within any given class do not necessarily remain stationary throughout the lifetimes of a particular set of parents or over generations (relative mobility).

The salient features of social mobility can be listed succinctly: (1) mobility rates are composed of structural as well as equal opportunity segments; (2) aggregates of individuals are prepared for mobility, or the lack of it, by the existing class structure (that is, by their class or family of origin); and (3) upward mobility does not necessarily mean that families at any given level are displaced. Downward mobility, like upward mobility, should also be interpreted in social and intersocietal terms and not merely as the result of personal demerit. For example, an upper-class manufacturer of wooden office furniture is ruined by the advent of metal furniture; a farm family loses its farm because of a political decision not to sell food to the Soviet Union; a semiskilled worker, aged forty-five, is replaced by a machine and never

---

[36]For an empirical analysis of these areas, see Chapter 6.

works regularly again; an automobile or textile worker or middle manager is laid off because of imports from Japan or Hong Kong; cheap foreign oil devastates the oil industry of the Southwest, and also leads to economic ruin for people in banking and real estate.

Perhaps the greatest pitfall in the analysis of class dynamics is the confusion of apparent mobility (absolute upward movement) with real mobility (relative gains). It must be remembered that absolute gains in such class factors as income, occupation, and education do not necessarily represent movement from one class to another. To illustrate the latter point, one can cite a number of hypothetical family histories characterized by absolute gains in class factors unaccompanied by upward mobility. If, for example, the great-grandson of a blacksmith who earned $500 per year is an automobile worker earning $20,000 per year, one cannot speak of upward social mobility; in fact, this could be a case of downward mobility. If the grandson of an independent farmer with no formal education is a bank teller with a high school education, one again cannot speak of mobility from one class to another. (See Figure 5–2, which contrasts types of mobility.)

Another source of confusion about contemporary stratification is incompletely thought-out comparisons between modern and premodern societies. It cannot be overemphasized that the transition from agrarian estate

Figure 5–2   Absolute (or Structural) and Relative Intergenerational Mobility

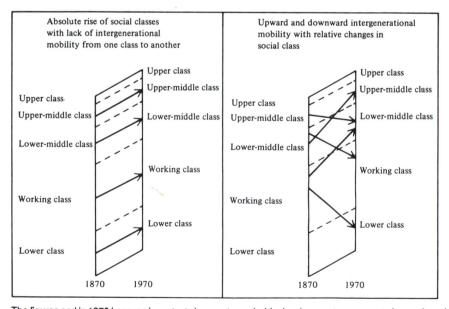

The figures end in 1970 because important changes toward a bipolar class system appear to have taken place after this date.

systems to industrial class systems is a movement not toward equality but toward a *new type* of inequality. Economic expansion has made most people wealthier, healthier, more skilled, better educated, and the like than their forebears, but modern populations are just as unequal, relative to their own societies, as people were in the past. The changing composition of human populations attributable to the impact of absolute or structural mobility and the unchanging degree of inequality are depicted graphically in Figure 5–3.

In analyzing social mobility, therefore, it is essential not to prejudge trends. It is especially important not to assume automatically that overall mobility is producing a society composed primarily of middle-class families and individuals, or that such mobility represents progress toward the abolition of ascriptive barriers to mobility. (This is the ideology of convergence.) To do so is to confuse affluence (absolute mobility) with equality of opportunity and substantive equality. The United States has been and remains a very unequal society, characterized by significant differentials in ascriptive advantage (birth into different classes), and there is as yet no way to tell whether these differences are increasing or decreasing. However, the American economy appears to have undergone structural changes. The sluggish economic growth over the past two decades has been unable to increase the standard of living. With declining productivity, rising national debt, declining economic competitiveness with other nations, and a stalemated political system, the United States may be facing a future different from its past (understanding this change is a major theme of future chapters).

Figure 5–3 Economic Expansion (Absolute or Structural Mobility), Changing Population Composition, and Unchanging Degree of Inequality

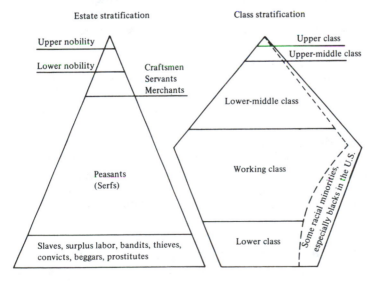

Finally, because upper-level positions are often acquired through class advantage rather than fair competition and are often exploitative, one should remember to *evaluate* the class system and not merely focus on what may well be impossible in a capitalist society—making mobility a fair contest to reveal natural inequalities.

It is now time to turn to a direct analysis of the American system of social stratification. We will begin with an analysis of the distribution of economic values.

THE STRUGGLE TO UNDERSTAND SOCIAL STRATIFICATION: A SUMMARY

American liberalism, which monopolizes how Americans think about society, explains inequality in terms of nonegalitarian classlessness (the United States is a free society with equal opportunity, and any inequality is natural to human beings.).

American sociology gradually overcame its belief in nonegalitarian classlessness, and from the 1920s on began its long struggle to understand social stratification.

The early study of stratification focused on small-town America. While small-town studies revealed deep inequality based on birth into economic classes and other ascriptive factors, the shift from entrepreneurial to corporate capitalism made it necessary to develop ways to understand the newly emerging national and international system of stratification.

By the 1950s sociology was analyzing income, occupational, and educational data about large aggregates. The essence of analyzing these data was to explore the relation between a given range of, say, income and behavior elsewhere, say, visits to the dentist or voting.

Two distinct emphases emerged in identifying social classes. Functional theorists, while aware of ascriptive class factors, still thought in terms of an open, fluid, meritocratic society (nonegalitarian classlessness). Conflict theorists tended to stress wealth rather than just income, occupation, and education, and they insisted that economic power as such shaped the distribution of basic values in all dimensions.

The relations among class, prestige, and power have been explored by both functional and conflict theorists using the concept of status consistency (or crystallization). While there is a long- term tendency for economic class to absorb and control the prestige and power dimensions, there are many inconsistencies in the short term. These inconsistencies do not necessarily disturb individuals or affect their behavior.

Social mobility refers to movement up or down between different class levels. Relative mobility of this kind must be distinguished from absolute mobility or an increase in standard of living without movement to another class.

Three different aspects of mobility have been distinguished:

1. intragenerational mobility, or how individuals make out in the pursuit of their careers over their life cycle;
2. intergenerational mobility, or the analysis of the relation between parents' class position and their children's class position;
3. social origins mobility, or determining from what social class the occupants of various occupations have been recruited.

Status attainment theorists tend to continue the emphasis on non-egalitarian classlessness and analyze mobility as a process of individual achievement. Conflict theorists stress structural mobility, the way economic power is exercised to produce economic expansion or contraction.

A zero-sum game of mobility and success (winners require losers) may have appeared in recent decades to make American society different from its past.

A capitalist society may be inherently unfair to the lower classes; thus, one should remember to evaluate it rather than to focus only on trying to make mobility a fair contest.

CHAPTER 6

The Changing Hierarchy of Economic Classes

Tonight, all over the United States, tens of thousands of Americans must find a place to sleep. These are not travelers or tourists but America's homeless. Tomorrow, they must somehow find food and again wonder where they will sleep. More fortunate than America's homeless are the 35 million Americans who are poor. Most have a place to live, much as it is, and they have enough to eat more or less for the better part of the month. Far above, a few hundred thousand families live in comfort, security, and splendor.

In between these distant extremes are further contrasts. Some Americans face an interesting workday but most labor at boring jobs. Millions more are not only bored at work but are subject to disease, disability, and death from it because their workplace is unsafe. Most working Americans find it hard to make ends meet and their spouses have to work. The number of such Americans seems to be growing (as a percent of the whole) while the relative number of Americans in interesting, well-paid jobs appears to be declining. Some Americans work steadily at something from the age of twelve on, while millions work irregularly and never have a steady job—some Americans who want and need work, for example, some black males, never even get a first job.

Analyzing the United States in terms of its contrasting social classes introduces us to a world not easily accessible through ordinary experience. Typically, Americans think of inequality as something that emerges from individual competition and equal opportunity. How can that image be squared with the fact that major portions of the American economy are inherited? Americans think that inequality comes directly from individuals and that it serves social needs. But don't humans acquire their personalities from their socialization experiences? Many argue that equality is opposed to efficiency. But how efficient is it to have an economy in which millions are idle? What right has government to take from some to give to others? How would Americans frame this question if they knew that government spending and taxation favored the upper classes?

Class analysis addresses these and other questions. Is equality increasing or decreasing? Is the United States still a land of opportunity? Is upward mobility through hard work a feasible dream for the majority of Americans? In short, we are back to our old question: Is the United States a meritocracy?

In the following chapters we will present data on inequality on a number of dimensions. The general distribution of economic values (class) is presented in this chapter. Later chapters will explain the relation between class and behavior outside the economy.

INCOME DISTRIBUTION

Absolute and Relative Economic Levels

Distribution of income and wealth is roughly uniform in all developed capitalist countries. Despite variations owing to historical circumstances, political ideology, tax, defense, and welfare policies, the outstanding characteristic of the material culture of capitalist society—aside from the dramatic increase in the standard of living—is its radically unequal distribution. Of perhaps equal importance is the fact that this sharp inequality in the distribution of goods and services has been remarkably stable over the entire period for which we have reliable data. The inequality of income in the United States, for example, seems to be fixed over time and not to be affected by rising productivity, taxation, or the rise of the welfare state. No understanding of class (economic) stratification is possible, therefore, unless one guards against the popular equation of rising productivity, progressive tax schedules, and the inauguration of the welfare state with a growing equality of material conditions. As we have suggested, one must distinguish clearly between criteria that determine absolute levels of goods and services and criteria designed to establish relative shares of these benefits. It is especially important not to succumb to the popular ideology that equates rising productivity and income with a more egalitarian distribution of life chances.

To appreciate fully the fact that a rise in the absolute standard of living has not significantly affected the *relative share* of national income enjoyed by various income classes, one may think of modern structures of stratification as a fleet of ships in a harbor: An incoming tide—rising productivity and a rising standard of living—does not diminish the differences between row-boats, cabin cruisers, cargo vessels, and giant ocean liners.[1]

Comparative Income Distribution: Preindustrial and Industrial Societies

Whether the focus is on the great feudal civilizations of the past or the developing countries of today, preindustrial societies are marked by deep economic inequality. But developed countries are also very unequal and one should be wary of assuming that today's developed societies are more equal than those of the past. First, such comparisons are extraordinarily difficult and succumb easily to ethnocentric bias.[2] From both comparative analyses (both at particular times and over time) and in-depth historical analyses of particular countries, one can neither say that modern society is more equal than agrarian society not that it is making progress in that direction. The most important thing that can be said about economic inequality is that it is very high in all complex societies whether they are feudal, capitalist, socialist, developed, or nondeveloped. There are some ups and downs, but by and large, there is no discernible long-term trend toward equality.

The mistaken idea that modern society is more equal than feudal society was given scholarly credence by Gerhard Lenski's *Power and Privilege* (1966) and ever since by his introductory text *Human Societies* (5th ed., 1987). Lenski's work (among others) led to a series of cross-national studies during the 1970s. Scholars found little support for Lenski's claim that modern society has reversed the historic association between economic growth and inequality. They also found little support for his claim that political democracy helps to curb economic inequality.[3] Support was found for Lenski's claim that

---

[1] Recent changes toward increased inequality are discussed below.

[2] For a technical analysis stressing the difficulty, if not the impossibility, of comparing economic inequality in agrarian and industrial societies, see Harold Lydall, *The Structure of Earnings* (London: Oxford University Press, 1968). Comparisons are also difficult because the data on developing countries are either not available or not reliable; see Albert Berry, "On Trends in the Gap Between Rich and Poor in Less Developed Countries: Why We Know So Little," *Review of Income and Wealth* 31, no. 4 (December 1985):337–354.

[3] For a pioneering study of all aspects of modernization (using 1960 data from sixty countries), which disputes the claim that political democracy has an independent role in reducing inequality, see Robert W. Jackman, *Politics and Social Equality: A Comparative Analysis* (New York: John Wiley & Sons, 1975). Richard Rubinson and Dan Quinlan, in their article "Democracy and Social Inequality: A Reanalysis," *American Sociological Review* 42 (August 1977):611–623, reaffirmed the lack of effect that political democracy has on income inequality (using personal income instead of economic-sector income as Jackman had done) and found instead that class inequality has a negative effect on political democracy.

strong trade unionism and strong democratic socialist movements help reduce inequality.[4]

The above studies were all based on data from 1965 (or earlier). While useful in confirming the importance of economic variables and making us wary of assuming that political democracy can exert an independent force against class inequality, these studies have been upstaged by historical developments. Many new nations have appeared since the 1960s, and the economies of the industrial nations and the world economy have all changed dramatically since then. The economies and living standards of all societies are no longer growing as robustly as they once did. And the distribution of income within a society seems to be importantly affected by its location in the world economy.[5] The importance of the world economy has grown dramatically since the 1960s, and we must assume that the world market is an important force in the shaping of the internal class structure of today's societies.[6]

Comparative Income Distribution: Developed Capitalist and Socialist Societies

All developed countries, capitalist and socialist alike, are very unequal and reveal no trend toward equality when looked at broadly. Under closer scrutiny, however, a number of variations appear. The developed capitalist countries that have had long-term socialist governments or sustained welfare states (for example, Sweden) have more income equality than the more market-oriented societies (for example, the United States). In addition, it is clear that capitalist countries with more income equality than the United States (because of their greater commitment to full employment and their more developed public-service sectors) have not suffered economically. On

[4]Christopher Hewitt, in "The Effect of Political Democracy and Social Democracy in Industrial Societies: A Cross-National Comparison," *American Sociological Review* 42 (June 1977): 450–464, found no power in political democracy by itself to reduce inequality but did find it when it contains a strong democratic socialist movement. Steven Stack in "The Effect of Direct Governmental Involvement in the Economy on the Degree of Income Inequality: A Cross-National Study," *American Sociological Review* 43 (December 1978):880–888, argues that one aspect of Keynesian political action does reduce income inequality. Stack has been criticized for including eight Soviet-bloc nations in his sample of thirty-two nations. In addition, a fuller use of Keynesian political action would have led to the conclusion that government action can also *increase* inequality (as we saw with the supply-side Keynesianism of the Reagan administration of the 1980s).

[5]Christopher Chase-Dunn, "The Effects of International Economic Dependence on Development and Inequality," *American Sociological Review* 40 (December 1975):720–738 and Richard Rubinson, "The World Economy and the Distribution of Income Within States: A Cross-National Study," *American Sociological Review* 41 (April 1976):638–659.

[6]The case studies of El Salvador and the Republic of Korea in Chapter 3 illustrate the important influence that the world market has on the internal development of class structure. Chapters 18 and 19 of this text, which discuss Soviet society and inequality, also emphasize that Soviet elites have been forced to make internal changes in response to developments abroad.

the contrary, the economies of West Germany, Norway, Sweden, the Netherlands, and Japan have outperformed the American economy.[7] The European capitalist countries also have a better record of curbing poverty.[8] Not only is it possible to reduce income inequality and alleviate the hardships of poverty without curtailing economic growth, but, on the contrary, the commitment to full employment seems to lead to a more productive economy!

One of the reasons for the steep inequality among capitalist countries and for higher and lower levels of inequality is income from property (rents, interest, dividends, profits). If one focuses on income from employment alone (setting aside income from the ownership of property), the distribution of income is remarkably similar, for example, in Denmark, the United Kingdom, Sweden, Yugoslavia, Poland, the Federal Republic of Germany, Canada, Belgium, the United States, and Austria, though there are variations in particulars. On the same basis, it appears that New Zealand, Australia, and most communist countries have less income inequality than the Western capitalist countries.[9]

By and large, the greater actual equality of income in the Soviet-bloc countries is because they have eliminated the significant income that goes to the capitalist upper class (and others) from the ownership of property.[10] Also important in producing greater income equality is the open promotion of full employment. Though this leads to some inefficiency in the use of labor, it curbs the surplus labor that is such a chronic condition in the capitalist countries.

Income Distribution in the United States

The American standard of living (as expressed in income) grew spectacularly after World War II, more or less doubling between the late 1940s and 1970. Since then the standard of living has grown more slowly and may even have stopped growing. Despite the spectacular economic growth in the early postwar period and the slower growth since, income distribution remained both very unequal and remarkably stable (for income distribution by fifths of families, see Figure 6–1). It should be noted that the Census Bureau's data are

[7]Malcom Sawyer, *Income Distribution in OECD Countries* (Paris: Organization for Economic Cooperation and Development, 1976). The data in this work are from the 1960s and early 1970s. There is little reason to assume that any changes have taken place in recent years.

[8]Vic George and Roger Lawson, eds., *Poverty and Inequality in Common Market Countries* (London: Routledge & Kegan Paul, 1980).

[9]Harold Lydall, *The Structure of Earnings* (London: Oxford University Press, 1968), pp. 156–162; Jerry Cromwell, "The Size Distribution of Income: An International Comparison," *Review of Income and Wealth* 23, no. 3 (Summer 1977):291–308; Gerhard Lenski, "Marxist Experiments in Destratification: An Appraisal," *Social Forces* 57 (December 1978):364–383.

[10]The importance of property ownership will become apparent in the following sections. For a more detailed comparison between communist and capitalist income distribution, see Chapter 19.

Figure 6–1   Percentage Share of Total Income by Fifths of Families 1987.

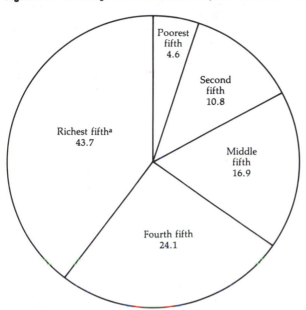

[a]The top 5 percent of families received 16.9 percent of total income. Income inequality among Unrelated Individuals is even more pronounced than among Families.

Source: U.S. Bureau of the Census, "Money Income of Households, Families, and Persons in the United States: 1987," *Current Population Reports*, P-60, no. 162 (Washington, D.C.: U.S. Government Printing Office, 1989), Table 12. Total equals 100.1 percent because of rounding.

not completely accurate because they fail to consider nonmoney income, realized capital gains, and retained corporate earnings, and suffer from underreporting, especially in the areas of interest, rents, and dividends. On the whole, underreporting and the omission of certain kinds of income tend to cause the Census Bureau to understate the degree of income inequality.

Despite the overall stability of income shares, an undeniable trend toward greater income inequality appears when the gap between richest fifth and poorest fifth is measured (see Table 6–1).

New Income Trends: The End of a Growing Standard of Living?

The United States experienced a much higher growth in living standards in the 1950s and 1960s than in the period after 1970. The slowdown in economic growth can be seen in declining real wages, productivity, and personal savings. The medium household (not family) income declined from its high of $28,167 in 1973 to $23,580 in 1984. Seen in another way, the average

TABLE 6-1.   Income Inequality Ratios, 1970–1985

YEAR	INCOME SHARE OF HIGHEST FIFTH	INCOME SHARE OF LOWEST FIFTH	RATIO HIGHEST FIFTH LOWEST FIFTH
1985	43.5%	4.6%	9.45
1984	42.9	4.7	9.13
1983	42.8	4.7	9.11
1982	42.7	4.7	9.09
1981	41.9	5.0	8.38
1980	41.6	5.1	8.16
1979	41.7	5.2	8.02
1978	41.5	5.2	7.98
1977	41.5	5.2	7.98
1976	41.1	5.4	7.61
1975	41.1	5.4	7.61
1974	41.0	5.5	7.45
1973	41.1	5.5	7.47
1972	41.4	5.4	7.67
1971	41.1	5.5	7.47
1970	40.9	5.4	7.57

Source: Bureau of the Census, "Money Income of Households, Families, and Persons in the United States: 1985," *Current Population Reports*, Series P-60, no. 156 (August 1987), Table 12.

30-year-old male earned $25,580 in 1973 compared to $17,520 in 1983. And the same male had to pay 44 percent of gross earnings to buy a median-priced house in 1983 compared to 21 percent in 1973.[11] The percent of national income derived from property (rents, dividends, interest) has risen since the 1960s and the share going for wages and salaries has declined. Understandably, the amount of personal debt (as well as public and corporate debt) has risen to an all-time high as Americans find it hard to adjust their expectations to economic realities.

Another way of measuring standard of living is by median family income (the point at which 50 percent of families are above and 50 percent are below). As Figure 6–2 shows, median family income grew strongly in the 1960s but remained fairly stationary after 1970. But different kinds of families fared quite differently. The Congressional Budget Office computed an Adjusted Family Income (using family size and a different inflation index) and found that elderly families and individuals had a strong growth (50 percent), families in general had a low growth of 14 percent, and single-mother families had an anemic 2 percent growth over the space of these sixteen years.

[11]Frank S. Levy and Richard C. Michel, "Economic Future of the Baby Boom," Report, Joint Economic Committee of Congress (Washington, D.C.: U.S. Government Printing Office, 1985).

Figure 6-2   Median Family Income: 1960 to 1986 (In 1986 dollars)

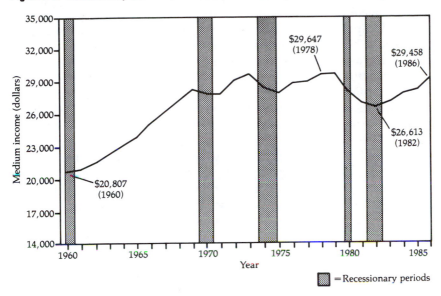

Source: Burea of the Census, "Money Income and Poverty Status of Families and Persons in the United States, 1986," *Current Population Reports*, P-60, no. 157 (Washington, D.C.: U.S. Government Printing Office, 1987), Figure 1.

Significantly, the Adjusted Family income of families varied by age. Families headed by 65-year-olds rose 54 percent while young families under age twenty-five had a *drop* of 18 percent.[12]

The American standard of living when computed in the above way exhibits growth, but a number of things should be noted. One, it grew at a much lower rate than previous decades. Two, it grew because some families had more workers as both spouses worked. Three, it grew because families got smaller as the birth rate declined. Four, it grew because the elderly received substantial sums of non-means-tested Social Security increases. And it grew because all sectors of the society (individuals, business, and the federal government) went deeply into debt.

New Income Trends: A Bipolar America?

The 1970s saw a new trend in income distribution. Reversing its previous history, the United States appears no longer able to provide an expanding number of middle-income households. The American economy has continued to generate jobs but interpreting the number and quality of jobs is

[12]"Trends in Family Income: 1970–1986," Congressional Budget Office, (Washington, D.C.: U.S. Government Printing Office, 1988).

not easy.[13] One analyst argues that the United States continued to generate good middle-income jobs between 1973 and 1982 and that the middle class was alive and well.[14] Rosenthal may be right about middle-income jobs holding steady, but he confuses middle income with middle class[15] and individual with family income.[16] Others have argued that the United States is no longer generating good-paying jobs.[17]

Looking at high- vs. low-growth sectors of the economy reveals some disturbing trends. Many argue that service occupations (which have been setting the pace of the American economy) pay significantly less than do skilled manufacturing jobs. Blackburn and Bloom point out that the twenty fastest-growing businesses paid $100 a week less than the twenty fastest-declining businesses. Tracing the growth of family income between 1969 and 1983, Blackburn and Bloom found faster growth among lower and upper families as opposed to lower-middle and upper-middle families.[18] And in 1988, the Senate Budget Committee issued a report showing that jobs with middle-level wages had shrunk considerably and that the majority of newly created jobs were paying poverty wages (for a family of four).[19]

The new household income structure is moving away from the big bulge in the middle that was once characteristic of the United States and toward a bipolar (hour glass, two-tier) shape (see Figure 6-3). The United States may or may not be generating as many good-paying jobs as in the past, but even assuming that it is, the crucial question to ask is: How are these jobs distributed by households? Double earners are now common at all levels, but better-paid individuals marry each other and this means that middle-income jobs are no longer held by single breadwinners (see Table 6-2). In addition, the lower classes have more single-income households largely because divorced mothers pile up at that level.

The structural reasons for the new distribution of household income are the surge toward service industries, the movement of capital to low-wage,

---

[13]It cannot be said too often that the unemployment rate is not a reliable indicator of how many people are out of work.

[14]Neal H. Rosenthal, "The Shrinking Middle Class: Myth or Reality?," *Monthly Labor Review 108 (March 1985):3–10.*

[15]For a fuller discussion of this distinction, see the section titled "Is The Middle Class Disappearing?" in this chapter.

[16]For the need to go beyond individual income and for the complexities of determining family income, see Judith Treas, "U.S. Income Stratification: Bringing Families Back In," *Social Science Research 66,* (April 1985):231–251.

[17]For two early warnings, see Paul Blumberg, *Inequality in an Age of Decline* (New York: Oxford University Press, 1980) and Lester Thurow, *The Zero-Sum Society* (New York: Basic Books, 1980).

[18]McKinley L. Blackburn and David E. Bloom, "What Is Happening to the Middle Class?," *American Demographics* (1985):18–25.

[19]Committee on the Budget, U.S. Senate, "Wages of American Workers in the 1980s" (Washington, D.C.: U.S. Government Printing Office, 1983).

Figure 6–3   The Trend Toward a Bipolar Distribution of Household Income, 1960s to the 1980s

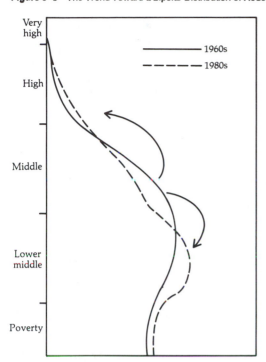

nonunionized sections of the United States and abroad, the decline of trade unions, and active support of these trends by government (deregulation, the large tax cuts of 1981–83, rapid depreciation for tax purposes, the curtailment of public services and benefits, and anti-union rulings by the National Labor Relations Board). The women's movement and the rising divorce rate also contributed to the new trend toward bipolar family incomes. The women's movement has opened up opportunities for the daughters and wives of the upper classes (see Box 9–2, "Is Women's Liberation a Middle-Class Movement?"). But the general surge of civil rights, individualism (laissez-faire American liberalism), easier including no-fault divorce laws, and an erratic economy have also led to a high divorce rate—the major casualties of divorce, even in no-fault divorces, are women and thus the swollen ranks of lower-level, one-parent female households.

THE DISTRIBUTION OF WEALTH

Knowledge about wealth is important because it tells us who makes the investment decisions that determine how material and human resources will be used. Scholars in this field are generally agreed that the basic pattern in the

TABLE 6-2.   Occupation of Wives by Occupation of Husband: March 1987. (Numbers in thousands).

SUBJECT	TOTAL	EMPLOYMENT STATUS AND OCCUPATION GROUP OF WIFE				
		EXECUTIVE, ADMINISTRATIVE, AND MANAGERIAL	PROFES-SIONAL SPECIALITY	TECHNICAL AND RELATED SUPPORT	SALES	ADMINISTRATIVE SUPPORT, INCLUDING CLERICAL
All races						
Total husbands	52,286	2,927	4,649	921	3,181	8,604
Executive, administrative, and managerial	6,227	760	902	147	486	1,281
Professional specialty	5,145	445	1,412	129	256	855
Technicians and related support	968	50	127	49	51	220
Sales	4,525	394	493	74	589	1,014
Administrative support, including clerical	1,988	116	220	49	148	489
Private household service	4	—	—	1	—	1
Service, excluding private household	2,730	142	182	61	165	510
Farming, forestry and fishing	1,573	66	103	21	66	210
Precision production, craft, and repair	8,223	403	448	176	544	1,680
Machine operators, assemblers, and inspectors	2,850	87	150	52	140	505
Transportation and material moving	2,708	100	112	53	177	540
Handlers, equipment cleaners, helpers, and laborers	1,554	56	64	16	129	296
Unemployed	1,867	81	100	28	140	262
Armed forces	820	38	45	11	61	151
Not in labor force	11,103	189	292	54	229	590

Source: U.S. Bureau of the Census, *Current Population Reports*, Series P-20, no. 424, "Household and Family Characteristics: March 1987" (Washington, D.C.: U.S. Government Printing Office, 1988), Table 6.

distribution of wealth is high and relatively steady concentration.[20] Whether analyzed and measured in terms of liquid assets, personal property, real estate, business assets, bonds, stock ownership, ability to save, or income from property, the distribution of wealth in the United States is characterized by the same pronounced pattern of concentration. As we shall see, the concentration of wealth is even more pronounced than that of income.

The concentration of wealth is apparent in Table 6–3. Far from being a people's capitalism, the American economy is owned by a tiny handful of households.[21] The super-rich (one-half of 1 percent or about 400,000 house-

[20]Jeffrey G. Williamson and Peter H. Lindert, *American Inequality: A Macroeconomic Analysis* (New York: Academic Press, 1979) and James D. Smith, ed., *Modeling the Distribution and Intergenerational Transmission of Wealth* (Chicago: University of Chicago Press, 1980).

[21]Remember we are talking of personal wealth. There is also wealth owned by pension funds, foundations, university endowments, and government.

TABLE 6–2. *continued.*

				EMPLOYMENT STATUS AND OCCUPATION GROUP OF WIFE				
PRIVATE HOUSEHOLD SERVICE	SERVICE EXCEPT HOUSEHOLD	FARMING, FORESTRY, AND FISHING	PRECISION PRODUCTION, CRAFTS AND REPAIR	MACHINE OPERATORS, ASSEMBLERS, AND INSPECTORS	TRANSPORTATION AND MATERIAL MOVING	HANDLERS, CLEANERS, HELPERS, AND LABORERS	UNEMPLOYED	NOT IN LABOR FORCE
284	3,911	334	626	1,782	254	360	1,325	23,127
16	294	26	66	83	20	18	103	2,025
6	179	12	44	52	3	12	78	1,663
4	65	6	14	19	6	9	23	325
7	287	10	28	66	16	25	86	1,435
15	164	3	25	72	16	10	48	614
—	—	—	—	—	—	—	—	1
23	492	4	33	86	12	19	70	931
12	128	158	18	53	8	10	47	674
43	756	41	176	390	49	109	271	3,140
27	303	11	39	340	30	45	101	1,020
31	296	22	37	174	51	30	76	1,008
10	173	10	31	113	9	20	74	554
17	215	4	30	119	14	14	180	662
11	103	—	6	11	3	1	53	325
62	457	28	79	206	18	38	113	8,749

holds) owned 35.1 percent of the total wealth (net worth or assets minus liabilities). The richest 1 percent owned 41.9 percent of the total personal wealth, and the richest 10 percent owned 71.8 percent of the total. This left the remaining 90 percent (about 72 million households) with 28.2 percent of the total wealth. Significantly, commercial real estate, corporate stock, bonds, and business assets are even more highly concentrated. Essentially, this means that investment decisions (where and when factories, offices, and stores will be built, and the amount and nature of jobs available to Americans) are in the hands of a small fraction of the total population.

As Table 6–4 indicates, a dramatic increase in the concentration of wealth took place between 1963 and 1983. The top 10 percent of the population had an 8.8 percent increase in their net worth, the top 1 percent had a 24.3 percent increase, and the top one-half of 1 percent saw their holdings swell by a whopping 34.5 percent. The bottom 90 percent obviously lost, falling 16.8

TABLE 6-3. Concentration of Personal Wealth, The United States, 1983 (Amounts in Billions of Dollars)

	ALL HOUSEHOLDS		RICHEST 10%		RICHEST 1%		RICHEST .5%	
	AMOUNT	%	AMOUNT	%	AMOUNT	%	AMOUNT	%
Real Estate	5362.3	100.0	2632.6	49.1	1048.4	19.6	821.8	15.3
Home (gross)	3585.5	100.0	1251.1	34.9	300.8	8.4	189.1	5.3
Other (gross)	1776.8	100.0	1381.5	77.8	747.6	42.1	632.7	35.7
Corporate Stock	981.7	100.0	876.5	89.3	588.8	60.0	456.6	46.5
Bonds	329.6	100.0	297.7	90.3	168.2	51.0	143.6	43.6
Savings Bonds	28.9	100.0	11.8	40.8	4.7	16.3	4.0	13.8
Other Federal Bonds	93.8	100.0	87.5	93.3	36.6	39.0	32.2	34.3
State and Local Bonds	163.7	100.0	159.8	97.6	114.8	70.1	101.6	62.1
Corporate Bonds	43.2	100.0	38.6	89.4	12.1	28.0	5.8	13.4
Checking Accounts	115.8	100.0	52.3	45.2	20.3	17.5	12.0	10.4
Saving Accounts	189.2	100.0	11.8	6.2	4.7	2.5	4.0	2.1
Certificates of Deposit	385.7	100.0	193.9	50.3	43.7	11.3	20.6	5.3
Money Market and Call Accounts	265.8	100.0	163.5	61.5	65.8	24.8	46.5	17.5
IRAs and Keogh	142.6	100.0	95.9	67.3	31.6	22.2	21.1	14.8
Trusts	491.6	100.0	467.8	95.2	402.9	82.0	378.4	77.0
Business Assets (net)	3272.0	100.0	3065.7	93.7	2168.1	66.3	1904.9	58.2
Management Interest	2903.1	100.0	2724.3	93.8	1977.5	68.1	1753.2	60.4
No Management Interest	368.9	100.0	341.4	92.5	190.6	51.7	151.7	41.1
Insurance Cash Surrender Value	260.8	100.0	80.2	30.8	26.0	10.0	16.9	6.5
Land Contracts	111.2	100.0	56.6	50.9	18.4	16.5	15.6	14.0
Miscellaneous	157.9	100.0	84.2	53.3	43.7	27.7	25.9	16.4
GROSS ASSETS	12066.2	100.0	8078.7	67.0	4630.6	38.4	3867.9	32.1
DEBT	1479.0	100.0	481.1	32.5	202.2	13.7	153.8	10.4
Consumer Debt	327.1	100.0	108.7	33.2	48.6	14.9	31.2	9.5
Real Estate Debt	1151.9	100.0	372.4	32.3	153.6	13.3	122.6	10.6
NET WORTH	10587.2	100.0	7597.6	71.8	4428.4	41.9	3714.1	35.1

Source: James D. Smith, *The Distribution of Wealth* (Ann Arbor: Survey Research Center, University of Michigan, 1986), Table 2. Used with permission.

TABLE 6–4. Trends in the Concentration of Personal Wealth, 1963–1983

	SHARE (%)		ABSOLUTE CHANGE	PERCENTAGE CHANGE
	1963	1983		
Richest				
10%	66.1	71.8	+5.8	+ 8.8
1%	33.7	41.9	+8.2	+24.3
0.5%	26.1	35.1	+9.0	+34.5
Lowest				
90%	33.9	28.2	−5.7	−16.8

Source: James D. Smith, *The Distribution of Wealth* (Ann Arbor: Survey Research Center, University of Michigan, 1986), Table 5. Used with permission.

percent. Much of the increase came from changes in the stock market value of holdings, but it was also caused by explicit government policies: tax laws favoring the upper classes, anti-labor policies, a relaxation of anti-trust law enforcement, and a sizable cut in social services. The trend toward a more concentrated economy undoubtedly continued during the 1980s since the same policies remained in effect.

The high concentration of wealth has persisted ever since colonial times. This does not mean that the same families have stayed rich since that time. It does mean, though, that the ownership of the American economy has remained in relatively few hands and that so far this pattern has been relatively immune to war, depressions, taxation, the expansion of suffrage, and the welfare state.

SOURCES OF INCOME AND WEALTH

To understand the causal processes that distribute material values one must go outside the American tradition, which attributes success and failure to personal attributes. Like everything else, the sources of income and wealth are social phenomena.

Concentration of Economic Power

Economic activity is not conducted by abstract capital or abstract individuals. The reality of economic behavior is *the group organized for economic action*. Profit-oriented groups, especially corporations, dominate the American economy. A corporation is a legal entity, administered bureaucratically, that allows large numbers of people to pool their resources and thus engage in a scale of economic behavior they could not do as solitary individuals. The result is a responsive chain of command that allows the owners or controllers of the corporation to amass and focus large amounts of capital to produce desired outcomes. The responsibilities and liabilities of corporations are spelled out in legal norms—one provision protects the owners' other property in case the corporation fails (law of bankruptcy). In addition, the corporation enjoys legal immortality and continues even though individual owners change hands or die.

The most striking feature of the American economy is the pronounced cleavage between dominant and weaker groups: A small number of corporations dominate all sectors of the economy and a small number of groups dominate economically related activities (professional associations, hospitals, universities, law firms, newspapers, and so on).

The size of dominant American corporations defies comprehension. A United States Senate study reports that the 122 largest corporations from all sectors of the American economy had 41 percent of the market value of all outstanding common stock in 1976.[22] The same study found that voting rights in large American corporations are concentrated among relatively few firms.[23]

A recent United states Senate study of 100 large corporations across the top of the business spectrum (banking and insurance, automotive industry, energy, telecommunications, information processing, office equipment, retailing, and twelve industry leaders) also found extensive economic concentration. The largest American companies each have concentrated ownerships and extensive participation in each other's governing boards (interlocking directorships).[24]

Concentration and the Ability to Save

Thrift is a virtue basic to capitalist society and is undoubtedly practiced by millions of Americans. Realistically speaking, however, the ability to save significant sums is restricted to relatively few people, basically those in high-income groups. To recognize this is to know a great deal about the basic class structure of American society. The fact that only high-income groups can save helps to explain the high concentration of wealth; conversely, the high concentration of wealth helps to explain high income. The ability of high-income groups to save creates extra income (dividends, interest, capital gains, stock appreciation), which in turn promotes the unequal ability to save, and so on. This has been called the Matthew Effect—"For to everyone who has will more be given" (Matthew 25:29, Revised Standard Version).

[22] U.S. Senate Committee on Governmental Affairs, *Voting Rights in Major Corporations* (Washington, D.C.: U.S. Government Printing Office, 1978), p. 1; derived from *Forbes* (May 15, 1977).

[23] Ibid., p. 1. As little as 5 to 10 percent ownership constitutes voting control since stockholders in general either do not vote or follow the lead of management.

[24] U.S. Senate Committee on Governmental Affairs, *Structure of Corporate Concentration: Institutional Shareholders and Interlocking Directorates Among Major U.S. Corporations* (Washington, D.C.: U.S. Government Printing Office, 1980).

Further, the large majority of those who are wealthy either inherited their money or used an inheritance to make money.[25] If we examine three factors—(1) the sources of income from property, (2) the ways in which such income is protected against taxation, and (3) the ways in which estate and inheritance taxes permit the transmission of wealth from one generation to the next—certain relationships become apparent that go far toward explaining the highly concentrated and highly stable distribution of America's material culture.[26] A focus on the 400 richest individuals (*Forbes*) or on the 100 largest corporations (*Fortune*) obscures a fundamental fact if one is not careful. Rich individuals are parts of interconnected families, corporations are connected parts of a concentrated economy, and rich families are owners and directors of the concentrated economy. And the fact that the individuals and families who make up the rich and powerful are not always the same because of upward and downward mobility should not be allowed to obscure the reality of the processes that produce a high, stable, and often illegitimate structure of wealth in the United States.[27]

Power groups are invariably surrounded by myths, and the corporation is no exception. In the nineteenth century there developed the legal fiction that the corporation was a person and that its rights were absolute under the Constitution. Endorsed by the United States Supreme Court between 1865 and the 1930s, this myth facilitated the rise of the large corporation and the oligarchic economy. More recently, other myths have developed to camouflage the power of corporations. One such fiction is that the rise of labor unions has provided workers an effective check on managerial power. There is no evidence of any equalization of either income or wealth since the rise of trade unions in the 1930s.

Another myth is that the power of property has declined in favor of managerial power, and that the corporation, under the guidance of well-educated executives, has become socially responsible. This idea, which is widespread in sociology and throughout the social sciences, is now being reexamined, for it implies that a basic change has taken place in capitalist society. Implicitly, and often explicitly, it is held that the prevailing elites

[25]"The Richest People in America," *Forbes* (October 1985), pp. 108–330.

[26]For a classic analysis of the basic economic, governmental, and educational forces that produce highly concentrated ascriptive wealth, and for some proposed remedies, see Howard P. Tuckman, *The Economics of the Rich* (New York: Random House, 1973). Because of the scarcity of data, Tuckman's definition of wealth is based on high income and ability to save (aided by favoritism in the tax laws and elsewhere).

[27]It is interesting to note that the concentration of power over material culture is a more or less standard feature of every industrial society, regardless of past history, type of culture, or the ascendancy of a capitalist (liberal or fascist), socialist, or communist government. The techniques of concentration and control—interlocking directorships; intercorporate stockholding; favorable tax laws; private corporate concentration; nationalized industries with private managerial control; public corporations; governmental ownership; supervision by monopolistic political parties—vary considerably, of course.

have won their positions in open competition and can exercise power objectively because they are not tied to special interests, such as property. Recent studies have cast doubt on the proposition that the power of property has declined and that occupation has supplanted it as the modal control force in the modern economy.[28] Actually, it is best to think of a mutuality of interests and motivations between property owners and managers. As Maurice Zeitlin reports,[29] there is no difference in profit orientation between family-controlled and manager-controlled businesses, and dollar profit and rate of return on equity are major determinants of executive compensation. Indeed, it is probably better to think of the ownership of corporate property as a chain linking many otherwise disparate groups to a capitalist order of society: Not only managers (who are important stockowners) but also labor unions, universities, churches, professional associations, and voluntary organizations of all kinds have their funds invested in corporate stocks.

The Changing Distribution of Occupations

The modern division of labor is highly specialized. For example, the latest *Dictionary of Occupational Titles*[30] lists approximately 20,000 occupations. The extensive specialization of industrial society is also attested to by the fact that no single occupation accounts for more than a tiny percentage of the total labor force. Occupations constantly change, and historic shifts in their distribution are worth noting.

The Census Bureau tracks the distribution of occupations in three different ways: (1) it keeps a "detailed occupation classification" of 479 categories, (2) it groups all occupations into twelve major categories, and (3) it makes intermediate groupings based on selected characteristics. To highlight gross historical trends, the twelve major categories are sometimes consolidated into three comprehensive categories:

1. Primary: Agriculture[31]
2. Secondary: Manufacturing, construction, mining
3. Tertiary: Trade, communication, transportation, and services (personal and professional)

---

[28]For a careful analysis of the data that find a significant degree of family control in big business, see Philip H. Burch, Jr., *The Managerial Revolution Reassessed* (Lexington, Mass.: D.C. Heath, 1972). For a case study of an alliance or "interest group" formed by a number of wealthy families, see James C. Knowles, "The Rockefeller Finanical Group" (Andover, Mass.: Warner Modular Publications, module 343, 1973, pp. 1–59). For a review of the literature in this area that finds the alleged divorce of ownership and control highly problematic, see Maurice Zeitlin, "Corporate Ownership and Control: The Large Corporation and the Capitalist Class," *American Journal of Sociology* 79, no. 5 (March 1974): 1073–1119.

[29]Zeitlin, "Corporate Ownership and Control," pp. 1094–1095.

[30]Fourth edition (U.S. Department of Labor, 1977).

[31]Fishing, forestry, and mining are sometimes considered primary and sometimes not. In any case, the number of people engaged in these pursuits is very small.

The transformation of occupational structure over the past century or so has been noted and commented on by many social scientists. When a society commences the process of industrialization, the initial occupational trend is from primary to secondary occupations. Eventually, however, a second trend occurs: Primary occupations continue to decline, secondary occupations become stabilized, and there is an enormous growth of tertiary occupations. In a few countries, such as the United States, Canada, and Australia, the majority of the labor force is now employed in tertiary occupations. The trend in this direction is clear in all other industrial countries.

It is of considerable importance that although America is now a society of employees, its basic values and beliefs originated in a period when Americans lived in an agrarian society of small independent farmers serviced by a small segment of independent business people and professionals. This intimate connection among property, work, family, and politics characteristic of small-town rural America has long since been lost. In its place, Americans now experience a world in which property and work are divorced and the relations among work, family, and politics have become increasingly tenuous, ambiguous, and complex. In other words, Americans now work, not as autonomous individuals whose endeavors and competitions are mediated by impersonal markets (commodity, credit, labor), but as employees of large bureaucratic organizations.[32]

Power Over the Labor Market

The image of an open, fluid, equal opportunity labor market composed of freely competing individuals is a major and damaging American myth. We came across this image earlier, especially in the guise of the functional school of stratification and the status attainment perspective. In opposition to it, theorists have pointed to a dual labor market that corresponds to the dual economy. One part of this economy is composed of dynamic companies riding the crest of new technology, products, and services. Here job opportunities abound, including opportunities for advancement. The other part of the economy is composed of firms in stagnant or declining industries—for example, textiles and shoemaking. Here jobs are low-paying, often unhealthy, and without prospects for advancement.

Job opportunities are also affected by the uncoordinated actions of governments and schools. In the 1980s law schools produced more lawyers than the country could use. But licensing and certification for dozens of occupations are based on unnecessary requirements imposed largely to curb entry into choice jobs.[33]

[32]For the classic and unsurpassed analysis of this all-important trend, see C.W. Mills, *White Collar: The American Middle Classes* (New York: Oxford University Press, 1953).

[33]For a detailed picture of how education (which also means government) structures educational opportunities in keeping with the class system, see Chapter 8.

Those who see the occupational system as reflecting personal ability as determined by equal opportunity and competition are wrong on all counts. It is an image that ignores power—the power of those who control capital investment and make decisions about where plants and office buildings will be located.[34] These decisions also determine the use of human resources. A focus on personal ability ignores the power of professional organizations and labor unions, which set up arbitrary, nonfunctional requirements for job entry. It ignores the power of governments to affect the economy through tax laws, spending, and regulations.

Those who hold this false image are aware of unemployment, poverty, and the plight of minorities. However, many assume that these phenomena are temporary, mere vestiges of the past that will disappear as the United States ends discrimination and fine-tunes its economy to yield sustained economic growth. But everything we know about the economy and polity tell us that, far from integrating the poor or minorities, it is the basic political economy that is generating poverty and unemployment (for a discussion, see the section "Myths About the Poor," later in this chapter).

THE ADVENT OF POSTINDUSTRIAL SOCIETY?

The trend toward white-collar occupations has led a number of commentators to conclude that we are experiencing the advent of a postindustrial society. This outlook is related to a theme we explored earlier, the mistaken belief that there has been a radical divorce between property and management. Given the rise of bureaucracy, some commentators have come to believe that society is no longer centered on an entrepreneurial class of property-owners, but on an educated set of elites, especially business executives and professionals.

The idea of a postindustrial society shares a basic kinship with status attainment theory (see Chapter 5) and is also an aspect of the liberal ideology of convergence, the belief that society is leaving behind the period of ascription, property, factory work, and centralized power and entering an era of achievement, administration, "strategic" elites, and a pluralist power structure.[35] One of the more sophisticated versions of this mistaken perspective is that of Ralf Dahrendorf, who believes we are in a postcapitalist era. Dahrendorf stakes much of his argument on the erroneous belief that industry and politics have been separated and mutually insulated and that indus-

[34]For a study showing that capital movement (plant closings and relocations) is related to the avoidance of labor unions, see David Jaffee, "The Political Economy of Job Loss in the United States, 1970–1980," *Social Problems* 33 (April 1986):297–318.

[35]See Chapter 4 for a discussion of the ideology of convergence and evolutionary liberalism, and Chapter 17 for an analysis of the ideology of pluralism.

trial conflict has been muted and self-contained. Industry, argues Dahrendorf, no longer supplies the model for the organization of the rest of society. Dahrendorf has also fallen prey to other liberal clichés. He claims that occupation is no longer a dominant force in a worker's life or personality, that there has occurred an equalization between strata, especially with regard to living conditions, and that these developments have helped to separate industrial and political conflict. However, Dahrendorf does not stress the idea of convergence, correctly emphasizing that modern society remains hierarchical. His main point is that society is now pluralist, a series of discrete "imperatively coordinated associations." In this new pluralist system, conflict has been localized and wealth and political authority have been separated. Indeed, governmental elites (the heads of governments, legislatures, and the judiciary) form the heart of the new ruling class.[36]

The main thrust of Dahrendorf's analysis is directed at Marx, especially at Marx's belief that industrial society is heading toward open conflict between two highly organized and self-conscious social classes. In pointing out that this has not occurred and that conflict is now managed (presumably) within institutional sectors on an issue-by-issue basis, Dahrendorf is undoubtedly right. And he is no doubt correct in pointing to the enhanced role of political authority. However, he is wrong to think that class and power, industry-wealth, and political authority have been separated. On the contrary, the modern state is still an adjunct of the market economy, and one must at all times think in terms of an imperatively coordinated social system in which the needs of the economy are the needs of the state and society.

One of the latest versions of the postindustrial perspective is Daniel Bell's.[37] Bell hedges his ideas—they are too *ad hoc* to be called a theory—by stipulating that he is talking about changes in the economy (which for some reason he refers to as "the social structure" or as "postindustrial society"). The essence of these changes, Bell claims, is a shift to a knowledge-centered economy, which is in turn creating unique problems for society to solve. The ultimate shape of the new society cannot be predicted because each industrial country (the United States, Germany, the Soviet Union, Japan) will handle its problems in terms of its own traditions and political institutions. Essentially, Bell is arguing that the economic system needs political direction; indeed, that the shift from an economy-centered to a politically centered society has already occurred and is a key aspect of the postindustrial age. Bell rejects both Marxian and functional (sociological) theories, claiming that both err by focusing on the total sociocultural system. It is best, he says, to think in terms of autonomous subsystems pulling in various directions, some known and some still unknown.

---

[36] Ralf Dahrendorf, *Class and Class Conflict in Industrial Society* (Stanford, Calif.: Stanford University Press, 1959), especially chaps. 7 and 8.

[37] *The Coming of Post-Industrial Society* (New York: Basic Books, 1973).

Bell's argument is also framed in terms of the decline of industrial workers relative to service workers, which is the equivalent of the growth of theoretical knowledge as the "axial" principle of society. The empirical support for Bell's views is derived from census data on the changing composition of the labor force. In 1947 goods-producing jobs accounted for 51 percent of the total; in 1968, 35.9 percent; and he predicts that in 1980 such jobs will account for only 31.7 percent of the total. The service-producing totals for the same years are 49, 64.1, 68.4 percent, respectively. Accordingly, argues Bell, "if industrial society is defined as a goods-producing society—if manufacture is central in shaping the character of its labor force—then the United States is no longer an industrial society.[38] Bell acknowledges that service work is not always white-collar work, including as it does transport workers and automobile mechanics (and, we might add, barbers and beauticians). Also, many blue-collar workers service machines. And Bell also recognizes that much of the increase in the white-collar category is accounted for by minor clerical and sales jobs (a significant portion of which are held by women). But, he argues, the male labor force has also been transformed in the direction of white-collar work. Whereas in 1900 only 15 percent of American men (mostly independent small businessmen) wore white collars, in 1970 almost 42 percent of the male labor force held white-collar jobs. Of these almost 60 percent were managerial, professional, or technical workers, "the heart of the upper middle class." (Blue-collar workers were 35 percent of the total labor force in 1900, 40 percent in 1920 and 1950, 36 percent in 1968, and will be only 32.7 percent in 1980.[39]

Bell's reference to managerial, professional, and technical workers as the heart of the American upper-middle class is both correct and misleading. While they include the upper-middle class, a very large percentage of these categories is composed of teachers, nurses, dental assistants, entertainers, and the like. But even if we focus exclusively on the upper-middle class, it is not easy to depict it as a revolutionary force. One has only to list some of its members—doctors, lawyers, engineers, business executives, scientists, college professors—to realize that it is anything but revolutionary.

The rise of white-collar jobs cannot be interpreted, therefore, as a break or qualitative change in the nature of liberal society. As we will see, lower-level white-collar workers are different from blue-collar workers in important respects, but the differences do not represent a break with industrial society: *white-collar workers are different from blue-collar workers because most of the former belong to industrial society at a higher level.* As for upper-level white-collar workers, they are hardly proponents of even a liberalizing, let alone a revolutionary, political ethic. All evidence points to a basic economic and

[38]Ibid., pp. 132–133.
[39]Ibid., pp. 134–135.

political conservatism among the upper-middle class, a conservatism often characterized by a pragmatic, reformist outlook and behavior.

Bell is mistaken in many of his assumptions. As we have noted, it is far from certain that property is divorced from management, that the property-owner has lost control of his property, or that there is any significant tension between property-owners and managers. Secondly, it cannot be said that the economy is declining vis-à-vis the state, but only that we are now more aware of the role of the state and the shortcomings of the economy. The economy and state have always served each other, and the former has always been the obvious pacesetter and beneficiary. Also, Bell implies that theoretical knowledge (a new intellectual technology) has come into play, but fails to cite any empirical evidence suggesting a consequent or eventual transformation of society. All in all, the new white-collar occupations appear to be firmly embedded in bureaucracies oriented toward private property and a market economy and society.

Bell's prophecy that a postindustrial society is upon us appears to be another variation on the technocratic theme in liberalism, which has its sources in the views of Condorcet, Saint-Simon, and Comte. To his credit, Bell avoids the easy optimism of early liberalism. Instead, he stresses the inchoate nature of social change and is willing to predict only that the future will pose unique problems to tax humanity's political and moral capabilities. Despite his caution, however, Bell endorses many liberal myths: He believes that equality of opportunity is a feasible ideal; that meritocracy is possible and is at odds with substantive equality; that prosperity has reduced inequality; and that the power of bureaucracies has been curtailed by committees and the popular demand for participation. These beliefs supplement his overriding belief that property and management have been divorced and that knowledge (embodied in upper-middle class managers and professionals) has replaced property and economic entrepreneurialism as the "axial" principle of society.

In sum, the best interpretation of the growth of white-collar occupations has been undertaken outside the liberal tradition. Though many questions are still unsettled, it seems best to think of the growth of white-collar occupations as a change *within* industrial (liberal) society. The classic analysis along these lines remains C. Wright Mills'. Leaving aside many of Mills' tendentious conclusions, the basic thrust of his argument is sound. The new service or white-collar or professional occupations represent a change *within* the middle class. Far from transcending class or industrial society, the new occupations are firmly embedded in economic, political, and social structures based on private property, managed markets, upper-level coordination, and bureaucratic administration. That significant portions of the new middle class are propertyless does not dilute their commitment (unconscious as well as conscious) to a property-oriented market society.

THE DISTRIBUTION OF FORMAL EDUCATION

Formal education is a jealously guarded prerogative of most dominant strata, and until the nineteenth century only a tiny fraction of any given population could read and write. With the advent of industrialization, whether or not it was accompanied by political democracy, the requirements of occupation and citizenship made literate populations necessary. In the United States, as in other industrializing nations, a dramatic surge in education brought mass literacy into being.

Between 1900 and the 1930s the United States put almost all teenagers in high school. From the 1950s on the number going to college rose until approximately 50 percent of high school graduates were entering some form of higher education. If one looks at the formal distribution of education there is a steady increase in the number of Americans with high school, college, and graduate school diplomas and degrees. Does this mean what it seems to mean, that we are a better-educated nation? If better educated means an improvement in the ability to perform economic, political, and social roles, the answer is no. Educational comparisons with the past based on years of schooling or degrees are meaningless. The essential criterion for judging education is whether it prepares one for performance in today's social statuses and for meeting today's problems. Seen from this perspective an illiterate frontiersperson may be better educated than today's typical college graduate. By and large, studies have failed to find any positive relation between schooling and what happens to people after school or how they perform in occupational or citizenship roles.

The United States has promoted literacy beyond what people prior to the nineteenth century thought possible. But it still has millions who cannot read and millions more who are functional illiterates (that is, who cannot read well enough to understand application forms for a driver's license). Even when the lower classes or minorities show educational gains, even relative gains, it does not mean that the class system has opened up or is basing itself on merit. For one thing, the lower classes attend different kinds of schools and take different programs. And even when minorities make relative gains in education, education does not pay off for them as it does for white males. But far more important is the possibility that narrow, specialized higher education has produced functional illiterates among America's upper classes (long years of unnecessaary and irrelevant formal education may succeed in certifying the masses as unworthy of elite positions but it also yields an elite mired in a taken-for-granted world).

And mass education has not equalized or homogenized Americans. Like the rise in income and occupational skill levels, therefore, it is best to think of the rise of educational attainment as resembling the rise of boats of unequal sizes on an incoming tide (for a fuller discussion of education, see Chapter 8).

CLASS AND THE INTERNATIONAL ECONOMY

Interrelations Between the Domestic and Foreign Economies

No economy or society stands alone; all are subject to the world market. The developing capitalist societies upgraded their occupational system by importing labor both unskilled and skilled (including professionals[40]) and by exporting machinery to have unskilled, dirty work done by foreign labor. Historically, human capital of both high- and low-level productivity was able to move freely. Today, only the more productive levels of human capital can move easily from one country to the next as countries exercise more and more control over immigration (and even migration). However, large numbers of unskilled workers still move from country to country either as temporary or illegal workers. It is estimated, for example, that the United States has anywhere from 5 million to 15 million illegal aliens, most of them from Mexico.

A dramatic example of the interdependence between the American economy and those of foreign countries is the automobile industry. To remain competitive, American automobile companies are now producing or buying many of their parts in foreign countries with cheap labor and raw materials. In the meantime, America's midwestern cities decay as parts factories close (see Box 6–1, "Is Ford's World Car Un-American?").

The United States' economy has relied heavily on foreign trade, investment, resources, and labor, and even territorial expansion throughout its history. Today, it is very dependent on overseas trade and investment to protect its internal markets and capital, to find outlets for surplus capital, and to ensure a steady supply of raw materials. An important reason for America's spectacular economic growth in the past was its abundant supply of cheap fossil fuels and other raw materials. Table 6–5 illustrates contemporary America's large dependence on foreign sources for most basic raw materials. Projections for the future indicate that by the year 2000 the United States will be dependent on foreign sources for more than half of all basic industrial minerals except phosphate.

The Outward Thrust of the American Economy

Social classes do not begin and end at national boundaries. In their organized forms as corporations, trade unions, governments, churches, universities, foundations, and so on, their reach extends beyond national borders into other societies.

The major economic units that carry on class relations beyond

---

[40]For data showing a substantial brain drain from less-developed countries into the United States, the United Kingdom, Canada, and Australia, see Jagdish Bahagwate, "The Brain Drain," *International Social Science Journal* 28, no. 4 (1976):691–729.

BOX 6–1. *IS FORD'S WORLD CAR UN-AMERICAN?*

The automobile is highly prized all over the world, and auto manufacturers have long hoped to build a car that is suitable for all countries. Standardization is one of the keys to successful manufacturing, and the ability to supply cars for the world market would be the ultimate in standardized manufacturing. In 1980 the Ford Motor Company announced its World Car, the Escort, which is not only designed to function all over the world but is made of parts that have been manufactured all over the world:

Taiwan—wiring
Mexico—door-lift assembly
Brazil—rear brake assembly
Japan—transaxles
Spain—shock absorber struts
Britain—steering gears
France—clutch assembly
West Germany—valve bushings
Italy—cylinder heads

The use of parts from abroad reflects the lower cost of labor and materials in other countries. It also reflects the emergence of a world automobile industry and dealer network. It is part of a world economy that makes it difficult for workers to control their economic lives. It also makes it difficult for societies and national governments to direct their affairs. The contradictions of all this are exemplified in the request by American automakers to restrict the import of foreign cars while they themselves were busy importing foreign car parts.

America's national boundaries are corporations engaged in manufacturing, agriculture, mining, timber, construction, and in various services such as banking, insurance, law, publishing, research, journalism, entertainment, and sports. Professional associations and labor unions also operate abroad in pursuit of class interests.

The United States was openly protectionist until the 1930s when the Great Depression forced it to liberalize its international trade in conjunction with other countries. At the end of World War II, from which it emerged with by far the world's strongest economy, the United States embarked on a philosophy of free trade. From the late 1950s on, American corporations began their spectacular surge of direct foreign investment. This unique historic process was part of the shift from empire imperialism to world-market imperialism: Instead of owning countries and then lending them money (the British Empire), the United States adopted the practice of direct foreign investment—the ownership and management of businesses in foreign countries.

Most international trade takes place among the developed capitalist

TABLE 6–5.   Percent of Minerals Imported by the
United States, 1950 and 1978

MINERALS	1950	1978
Columbium	100	100
Mica (sheet)	98	100
Strontium	100	100
Manganese	77	98
Cobalt	90	97
Tantalum	99	97
Platinum-group metals	74	91
Bauxite and alumina	55	93
Chromium	95	92
Tin	82	81
Asbestos	94	84
Fluorine	35	82
Nickel	90	77
Potassium	9	61
Gold	25	54
Zinc	41	62
Antimony	33	48
Cadmium	17	66
Selenium	53	61
Mercury	87	57
Silver	66	41
Barium	8	40
Tungsten	80	50
Titanium	33	39
Vanadium	4	27
Gypsum	28	34
Iron ore	11	29
Copper	31	19
Lead	40	11

Source: Department of the Interior, *Mining and Minerals Policy* (Washington, D.C.: U.S. Government Printing Office, 1979), Table 3–1.

countries and most of that is done by a small number of giant multinational corporations, many of them American. Significantly, the majority of American overseas trading has shifted to Asia in recent years. Another significant aspect of the growing internationalization of the United States' economy is an increase of direct investment in manufacturing in Third World countries. Still another significant development (representing movement away from entrepreneurial to corporate capitalism) is the gradual shift from ethnocentric and polycentric to geocentric organizations. Huge corporations, operating in as many as sixty nations, are each administered from a central command post thanks to advances in transportation and communication technology, espe-

TABLE 6-6.   Sales of Selected Geocentric
             Corporations Compared with
             the Gross Domestic Product of
             Selected Countries (in billions
             of dollars), 1985

	GDP	
United States	$3,275	
Japan	1,062	
France	519	
United Kingdom	455	
Italy	352	
GENERAL MOTORS	96	(Sales)
Sweden	91	
EXXON	86	(Sales)
Belgium	80	
Austria	66	
Denmark	56	
Norway	55	
MOBIL	55	(Sales)
FORD MOTOR	52	(Sales)
IBM	50	(Sales)
Finland	49	
Greece	31	
New Zealand	23	
Israel	21	
Ireland	18	

Source: "Fortune Directory of the 500 Largest
Industrial Corporations," *Fortune* (April 1986);
World Bank, *World Development Report, 1980–
1986* (New York: Oxford University Press, 1986).

cially the computer. These corporations are so large that their annual sales exceed the gross domestic product of major nation-states (see Table 6–6).

Two key patterns about the United States' international investment position should be noted. First, direct investments are mostly in developed countries ($157 billion in 1980) as opposed to developing countries ($52.6 billion), but the United States receives a much higher yield on its investments in underdeveloped countries. In 1980 it received $24.5 billion or 15.6 percent return from investment in developed countries and $11.7 billion or roughly 22 percent return from Third World Countries (See Table 6–7). The other pattern in the United States' international investment position does not bode well for the future. In 1976, net American international investment (American investment abroad minus foreign investment in the United States) was $82.5 billion yielding an annual profit of $15.93 billion.[41] But each year thereafter

[41]U.S. Bureau of the Census, *Statistical Abstract of the United States: 1978* (Washington, D.C.: U.S. Government Printing Office, 1978), Tables 1501, 1503.

TABLE 6-7.   U.S. Direct Investment Abroad and Income, 1980 (in billions of dollars)

	DIRECT INVESTMENT	INCOME	PROFIT RATE
Developed countries	$157.08	$24.58	15.6%
Developing Countries	52.68	$11.7	22.2%

Source: U.S. Bureau of the Census, *Statistical Abstract of the United States:* 1981 (Washington, D.C.: U.S. Government Printing Office, 1981), Table 1501.

the United States ran a large trade deficit and by 1985 had become a debtor nation, owing more to foreigners than they owed it.

Most international economic transactions are among the developed countries. However, underdeveloped nations attract considerable investment because they have important resources and cheap labor. The freedom of capital to move from Detroit, Cleveland, and other areas of the United States to utilize cheap labor in Taiwan, the Philippines, or South Korea is one of the reasons for unemployment and decay in America's midcentral and northeastern cities (and for a decline in good-paying, skilled jobs). Oftentimes capital movement is aided by tariff laws that allow American companies to send parts abroad for assembly, import the finished products to the United States, and pay a tariff on the "value added" overseas (which is very little when computed on the basis of the low wages paid abroad).

The 1980s witnessed new developments in America's international trading status. The ominous shift to a debtor nation has already been noted. The internal shift of the American economy to services has been matched by a growth in the service share of American exports, but America's advantages here have not borne fruit because of foreign protectionism and because Americans do not understand that many services must be modified to suit other cultures. The failure of the government to regulate domestic and international banking led to bank failures (and fraud) at home and huge bad loans to foreign countries. The giant federal deficit in the United States' domestic budget was matched by a huge balance of payments deficit, *both of which appear to be deeply rooted in how the American economy is organized.*

Clearly, the United States is living beyond its means. One reason is that the huge, untargeted tax cuts of 1981 had deprived Uncle Sam of revenues without making the United States more productive or competitive (large portions of the tax cuts went abroad, into luxury goods and services, or corporate mergers). The American deficit kept interest rates high because the federal government had to borrow huge sums, thus putting pressure on limited savings. High interest rates attracted large flows of capital from abroad, which helped to finance large portions of the American deficit but deprived other countries of needed capital. And the rise of interest rates aggravated the debt problem of Third World countries. During this time the

United States cut spending on social programs for the poor and working class, dramatically increased military spending, preached free trade, practiced selective protectionism, and refused to cooperate with other societies that were demanding that the United States live within its means.

America's position in the world economy had deteriorated so much under its free-trade philosophy that in the mid-1980s even the right-wing Reagan administration was forced to take action. In a new departure and as a way to forestall protectionist legislation, the American government began to make agreements with the major capitalist countries on coordinating tax, interest, and spending policies so that international supply and demand could be put in better balance. Here was Keynesianism at the international level. An important insight into the international context of the American class system is the fact that, while American exports have declined, the share of the total world market held by American multinational corporations has held steady at significant levels.[42]

IS THE MIDDLE CLASS DISAPPEARING?

The American middle class has long since disappeared if middle class is defined as a moderate-sized property owner of a business or autonomous professional. Today, property is highly concentrated, and Americans, including professionals, are largely employees of large bureaucratic corporations, government, hospitals, foundations, voluntary groups, and churches.

The disappearance of the middle class was hidden from view by economic growth, especially from the late nineteenth to mid-twentieth century. Economic growth created a new middle class of salaried professionals and high-income semiprofessionals and blue-collar skilled workers. The new economy of abundance also homogenized a great deal of consumption, creating both a real and fictitious mass of middle-class consumers. And labor segmentation, the creation of meaningless gradations among occupations, also misled Americans into thinking that things were getting better.[43]

However defined, the new middle class that appeared in the twentieth century seems to be shrinking. In assessing trends in household income, it is important to distinguish between middle income and middle class. A middle income can be acquired in a household in which husband and wife both work in blue-collar or working-class jobs. Thus middle income now requires two workers. And both the nature of the work and family background make this a working-class family despite its middle-level of income. Middle class, on

[42]Robert E. Lipsey and Irving B. Kravis, "Business Holds Its Own as America Slips," *The New York Times*, January 18, 1987, p. F3.

[43]David M. Gordon, Richard Edwards, and Michael Reich, *Segmented Work, Divided Workers: The Historical Transformation of Labor in the United States* (New York: Cambridge University Press, 1982).

the other hand, means a certain level of income but from a source that promotes an independent, self-directed personality. It means awareness about and a desire to live in a certain way: owning a home with enough space for family members to have private lives, and enough appliances, including a second car, to service it. It means vacations as well as saving for the future. It means expectations for future advancement at work. And it means proper socialization of the young for future middle-class (or upper-middle-class) status, especially through a four-year college education.

In the 1970s and 1980s there were laments for the skilled workers in so-called smokestack industries. What few realized then was that during the same period millions of middle-level managers were laid off by hard-pressed corporations (many were "hard-pressed" by their own subsidiaries in cheap labor countries). And all experts predict that layoffs will continue through the 1990s, thus effectively curbing opportunities for the formation of middle-class households. By the 1980s it was clear that high-tech industries and upper-level occupations were also being exported to Third World countries.[44]

Trends in the ownership of productive property, household income, and occupation indicate an erosion in the size and power of the historic American middle class. And by the 1980s another change had taken place in the middle class—diversification. The middle class is now made up of singles, married childless couples, double-earners with children, divorced and remarried individuals, and older couples and singles.

The decline of the middle class and its fragmentation into many different subtypes has serious implications for American society. The broad, politically moderate middle class was the mainstay of American representative government. As we will see later, American political life has changed for the worse and this may well be due to the change in the American middle class.

THE PERSISTENCE OF POVERTY

Despite spectacular economic growth the United States has been unable to make significant inroads into poverty. We do not know all the reasons, but what we do know requires rethinking our views on poverty and our policies to eliminate it.

Myths About The Poor

There are many persistent myths about the poor and programs to help them. Many Americans believe that the welfare rolls are filled with deadbeats

[44]For a fascinating picture of downward mobility in the American middle class (defined broadly to include managers and downward mobility by a blue-collar community), based on 150 in-depth interviews (not a random or representative sample), see Katherine S. Newman, *Falling From Grace: The Experience of Downward Mobility in the American Middle Class* (New York: Free Press, 1988).

and cheats, able-bodied individuals who don't want to work. They believe that welfare makes people dependent and that people don't want to get out of poverty. Many believe that welfare spending is the reason for their high taxes. Many Americans are afraid to provide help to the down-and-out because they think it will attract the poor to their city or state. The truth contradicts all these beliefs. People on welfare are mostly children, mothers, and the elderly. Most poor people are poor for a short time and most would work if work were available or possible. Able-bodied men cannot get welfare checks regardless of how poor they are (they can get food stamps). People do not move to get higher welfare. The amount of money spent on welfare for mothers with dependent children is very small and even the highest amounts represent a very low level of living. Food stamps make up a more sizable amount but this helps to dispose of surplus food that the federal government buys from farmers and which would rot if not given away. As for cheating and waste, experts agree that there is very little and that most of the waste and fraud is due to poorly researched laws, government confusion and incompetence, and corrupt administrators.

Leonard Beeghley, a leading expert on poverty, says we must distinguish between anti-poverty programs and public assistance. The antipoverty programs of the 1960s and 1970s were designed to help the poor become self-reliant, productive members of society. These were far more successful than people realize, but because they threatened powerful business and professional groups and right-wing Republicans and racist Democrats, they were largely abandoned. Assistance for the poor, on the other hand, is basically institutionalized pauperism—one has to be destitute to receive aid, and aid levels are set at subsistence and sub-subsistence levels. In addition, the overall amount for public assistance is far lower than people think (and far lower than government benefits given to the middle and upper classes).[45]

Structural Poverty and the New Poor

Structural poverty means that basic institutions and power relations are causing poverty. Specific causes are chronic unemployment, unnecessary qualifications for occupations, poor management, the cultural bias toward technology and against labor, the movement of capital abroad, anti-family bias in welfare programs, the lack of public programs fostering birth control, the separation of work and residence, the irrelevance of education to work, and in general the absence of socioeconomic planning.[46]

[45]For perhaps the best single book on poverty, see Leonard Beeghley, *Living Poorly in America* (New York: Praeger, 1983). For a valuable, more personal account of poverty, focused on how the world looks to a variety of poor teenagers, see Terry M. Williams and William Kornblum, *Growing Up Poor* (Lexington, Mass.: Lexington Books, 1985).

[46]Poverty in the United States tells us much about the nature of American society and is discussed further in a number of places; for details, see the Index.

These trends have generated a new mix of poor people in recent decades.[47] The poor are still disproportionately made up of racial and ethnic minorities. But poverty is now made up of female-headed households and this means that children are disproportionately poor.[48] Almost 25 percent of America's children live in poverty. There has also been a striking increase in full-time workers and their families that are poor (somewhere between 1 million to 2 million families). And there are large numbers of the nearly poor, families that must buy used clothing and cars, do without health insurance, live in substandard housing, and rarely travel. These working poor and nearly poor increased dramatically during the 1980s. And then there are the poor of the poor, the homeless.[49]

THE CHANGING HIERARCHY OF ECONOMIC CLASSES: A SUMMARY

It is clear from the data that economic values in the United States, and all industrial countries, are steeply and stably graded. Not only is the distribution of income, wealth, occupation, and education very unequal but there is no evidence that inequality has been reduced significantly either in comparison with past societies or since the inception of industrial society.

The functional view sees the United States as a society composed of voluntaristically propelled individuals competing for rewards in an open, fluid world of equal opportunity. Sociologists have increasingly abandoned this view for one that focuses on institutions and groups. This latter view reveals a power structure that shapes the world of rewards to suit itself.

The American economy is highly concentrated and provides the upper and upper middle classes with great power over how resources are invested and with a large and growing share of income.

After more than a century of economic growth *and* a rising standard of living, the United States has experienced what appears to be a historic reversal of momentous importance. There is increasing evidence that while slow economic growth has continued since 1970, it has more than been absorbed by a rising overhead of crime, pollution, military expenditure, support of idle people, and interest payments on debt (of which increasing amounts are going to foreigners).

The impact of economic slowdown on the American class system is significant:

[47]Michael Harrington, *The New American Poverty* (New York: Holt, Rinehart & Winston, 1984).

[48]Ruth Sidel, *Women and Children Last: The Plight of Poor Women in Affluent America* (New York: Viking Press, 1986).

[49]For a discussion of the homeless in the context of America's housing policies, see Chapter 15.

1. The capitalist class has undergone considerable turmoil but, by and large, capitalism has remained an accepted part of the American scheme of things even as capital flows to cheap labor areas in the United States and abroad were causing considerable trouble for ordinary Americans.

   The internationalization of the American economy has had a large impact on the American class system. Capital flows abroad have kept the American upper classes prosperous but have helped undermine the economic status of large portions of the rest of the population.

2. Economic slowdown and the exposure of the American economy to foreign competition have produced momentous changes in the American middle class. Defined as middle income, the American middle class in shrinking unless double-earners and smaller families are included. The middle class—defined as single-earner households or households headed by autonomous, self-propelled individuals who live in a certain way, who have hopes for advancement, and who raise their children to succeed—also appears to be shrinking. The middle class has been the mainstay of representative government, and its decline may help explain the declining performance of our political system.

3. Poverty appears to be a chronic outcome of American capitalism, perhaps a necessary feature. There are many kinds of poor people: working poor, one-parent female households, the destitute and homeless, a disproportionate number of racial and ethnic minorities, and young white males. Poverty and near poverty stem from sectors of the economy that are faltering, and many Americans are disconnected from the economy altogether. The United States appears to have a permanent underclass. Significantly, 25 percent of American children live in poverty.

The most important conclusion to emerge from the foregoing analysis of economic values is that private property, economic competition, and economic growth have not brought about, and do not necessarily, lead to economic equality. As we proceed with our empirical definition of social class, we will also see that the dynamic and expanding capitalist economy of the past did not bring about, and was not inherently related to, equality in other areas of class (family life, health, the education of children), and that the same is true of its relation to prestige and political-legal phenomena. The fundamental image that must be kept firmly in mind about liberal democracy, and industrial society in general, is of a deep, stable, and comprehensive system of stratification whose main differences with the past are not the degree, permanence, and extent of its inequality but rather its sources and forms. What will occur to inequality when the effects of economic slowdown unfold fully cannot be predicted but must be anticipated.

CHAPTER 7

Class, Family, Personality, and Health

In the preceding chapter we have seen a general statistical picture of the distribution of economic benefits and power in the United States currently and over time. We are now ready to examine the causal and behavioral structures that characterize the *overall* distribution of benefits and power in the United States. Our analysis will introduce a large number of sub-dimensions, each of which will refer to some concrete benefit or type of behavior (life expectancy, divorce, dropping out, and so on). Our subject is the national structure of statification, and we will pay relatively little attention to local stratification (the small-town focus) for reasons already advanced.

Almost every conceivable form of behavior has been related to class position: methods of rearing children, types and amounts of interaction, sexual behavior and tastes, levels of information, perception, consciousness, marital styles, consumption, beauty contests, language skills, survival of disasters, combat survival, tolerance, voting, justice, sainthood, the sending of Christmas cards, nudism,[1] and so on.

---

[1]The relationships between class and sainthood, class and the sending of Christmas cards, and class and nudism will not be touched on here. For those who are interested in the upper-class bias in the selection of saints, see Katherine George and Charles H. George, "Roman Catholic Sainthood and Social Status," in Reinhard Bendix and Seymour M. Lipset, eds., *Class, Status, and Power: Social Stratification in Comparative Perspective*, 2nd ed. (New York: Free Press, 1966), pp. 394–401; for those who want some shrewd ideas and insights into the middle-class (and upper-class) basis and the upward mobility aspirations behind the practice of sending Christmas cards, see Sheila K. Johnson, "Sociology of Christmas Cards," in William Feigelman, ed., *Sociology Full Circle* (New York: Praeger, 1972), pp. 158–164; for those who are interested in the middle-class basis of nudism, see Fred Ilfeld, Jr., and Roger Lauer, *Social Nudism in America* (New Haven, Conn.: College and University Press, 1964), pp. 69–73.

In canvassing the available research material, our general strategy will be to increase our understanding of social class (individuals or groups that share a common location across the dimensions of class, prestige, and power) by identifying its constituent parts gradually. The family is an obvious starting point for analyzing the behavioral consequences of class position. For one thing, the class position of a breadwinner is by definition shared with all members of his or her family. Second, the family is the conduit by which the class system is transmitted from one generation to the next. Third, the structure of the family and the fortunes of its members are intimately affected both by type of social stratification and by the family's overall stratum position in a given type of stratification.

CLASS AND FAMILY

It is popularly thought that falling in love, acquiring a wife or husband, begetting children, and weathering the tribulations of marital and family life are attributable to body chemistry or drives (romantic love, sexual energy) and/or moral fiber (innate moral traits). There is evidence, however, pointing to the central role of class in such phenomena as sexual values, beliefs, and behavior; choice of marriage partner; marriage and family styles; number of children; styles of raising children; and family stability.

Class and Sexual Values and Practices

All societies distinguish between legitimate and illegitimate sexual activity, and legitimate sex, by and large, is synonymous with family institutions. Once institutionalized, the answers to such questions as how one acquires a mate, what mates are suitable, which births are legitimate, and what ties of kinship and descent exist make up the structure of family life.

A nuclear family, which raises children to be individuals (independent, self-sufficient, adaptable), is obviously well suited to the needs of an economy that requires a mobile labor force—an economy, in other words, that is constantly generating new occupations. And with the emergence and institutionalization of the liberal political norms of liberty and equality, it is no wonder that arranged (instrumental) marriages were abandoned as fundamentally incompatible with the idea that all individuals are ends-in-themselves. It is the special function of romantic love to allow individuals to enter marriage as equals and to find their own class level irrespective of their family of origin.

Only in industrial society are love, marriage, reproduction, and child-raising combined into one basic relationship between a male and female. In the United States, this unique marital relationship is shaped by a fairly distinct definition of the nature and morality of human sexuality. The causes and legitimate forms and sexual behavior are defined by American society as follows (in general and without regard to such questions as who holds such views, with what degree of intensity, and with what consequences for behavior):

1. Sexual behavior springs from deep biological urges in human beings.
2. In some general way males are presumed to be more sexual than females.
3. Legitimate sexual relations are heterosexual in nature.
4. Sexual intercourse and reproduction are legitimate (normal and good) only within the confines of monogamous marriage based on love.
5. Certain individuals cannot marry each other, for reasons either of age or kinship.
6. Sexual relations are especially bad if one of the partners is a minor or if force is used.
7. Only certain sexual acts, out of the total range of possible sexual acts, are permissible.
8. The portrayal of nakedness and sexual intercourse in written and pictorial form for popular consumption is bad both morally and in terms of consequences.

The above code has undergone change in recent decades in the direction of greater permissiveness and a greater similarity of attitudes among men and women. This change in attitudes has occurred at all class levels.[2] However, actual sexual behavior deviates from the above code and varies considerably by class. In a comparison of data compiled by Kinsey and his associates mostly during the 1940s with data collected in 1969/70, Weinberg and Williams found that premarital sexual behavior still varies by social class (education). Less-educated males experienced sexual intercourse at an earlier age than better-educated males and had more sexual partners. The less-educated are now similar to the better-educated in the variety of sexual experiences but again engage in them earlier.

Kinsey found no difference among females by class in sexual behavior. Weinberg and Williams found a pronounced difference by class: Less-educated females were more likely to experience petting and especially coitus earlier and more frequently than better-educated females. Middle-class women also reported more positive feelings toward their various sexual experiences. On the whole, therefore, lower-class men and women had become more alike in their sexual behavior, the same was true of middle-class men and women, and the behavior of the two classes differed significantly from each other.[3]

[2]Ira L. Reiss, *The Family System in America*, 3rd ed. (Holt, Rinehart, & Winston, 1980), chap. 7.

[3]Martin S. Weinberg and Colin J. Williams, "Sexual Embourgeoisment? Social Class and Sexual Activity: 1938–1970," *American Sociological Review* 45 (February 1980):33–48.

Premarital sex is a violation of the American sexual code. Sex before marriage is partially sanctioned by the code itself, of course, in that men are presumed to be more sexual than women; it is accepted, therefore, for men in a partially acknowledged way. The double standard, however, seems to be on the decline within the middle class. The increase in premarital sex among college-educated females (starting past the age of twenty) is associated with courtship, affection, or love, eventual marriage, and a claim to equality. The growing sexual expressiveness of middle-class females is due, in part at least, to the increased education required for adult middle-class status, which has caused ever larger numbers of middle-class youth to attend coeducational colleges. Significantly, better-educated males engage in premarital sex with far fewer partners than do less-educated males, and presumably with females they intend to marry.

This deviation from the accepted sexual code on the part of the middle class is far more important than any deviation, however extreme, by the "lower class." As the custodian of American morals, the middle class is in a better position to legitimate its deviant practices. For example, pornography seems to be primarily a middle class (male) phenomenon, and the general relaxation of legal prohibitions on it has a class base.

However, "lower-class" men (and women, where the reference is applicable) tend to accept middle-class definitions of sexual respectability. They distinguish between women one does and does not marry, are more likely to condemn deviations from the legitimate sexual code, are less likely to vary their sexual techniques than the middle class, and tend to accept the definitions of sexual and physical attractiveness of the classes above them. The double standard—the belief that men are more sexual and therefore should have more sexual freedom—is also more prevalent among the "lower class." Despite the more matter-of-fact attitude toward sex characteristic of the "lower class," its members tend to derive less satisfaction from sexual relations than do middle-class couples. Research has revealed considerable differences in how the middle and lower (working) class view marital sex. James Henslin has summarized these differences (see Table 7–1), also asking us to note that middle-class males and females are more in agreement about sex than lower (working)-class males and females.

Robert Bell reports that rates of illegitimacy also vary inversely with class, a particularly high rate prevailing among lower-class blacks (even in contrast to lower-class whites).[4] Abortions were illegal until 1973, and data in this area are unreliable. Nothing definitive can be said, therefore, about how abortion rates vary among classes and how these rates affect our data about

[4]Robert R. Bell, *Marriage and Family Interaction*, 6th ed. (Homewood, Ill.: Dorsey Press, 1983). Illegitimacy has been used as an index of the malintegration of Indian and former slave populations into the dominant culture; see William J. Goode, "Illegitimacy, Anomie, and Cultural Penetration," *American Sociological Review* 26 (December 1961):910–925.

TABLE 7-1.   Orientation to Marital Sex on the Basis of Social Class and Gender

	FEMALES		MALES	
	LOWER CLASS	MIDDLE CLASS	LOWER CLASS	MIDDLE CLASS
Orientation				
Open to sexual experimentation	Low	Medium	High	High
Demands own satisfaction first	Low	Medium	High	Medium
Idea that sex is a woman's duty	High	Medium	High	Medium
Idea that sex is for pleasure	Medium	High	High	High
Expects the self to experience orgasm	Low	Medium	High	High
Expects the spouse to experience orgasm	High	High	Medium	High

Source: James M. Henslin, ed., *Marriage and Family in a Changing Society*, 2nd ed. (New York: Free Press, 1985), p. 346.

Reprinted with permission of the Free Press, a division of Macmillan, Inc., from *Marriage and Family in a Changing Society*, 2nd ed., James N. Henslin, ed. Copyright © 1980, 1985 by the Free Press.

illegitimacy. It would not be amiss, however, to assume that the further up the class ladder one goes, the more likely women are to abort unwanted pregnancies, especially since public funding of abortion gave rise to a determined anti-abortion (Right to Life) movement. The controversy over abortion is also a clue to deep social change—Kristin Luker has found that better-educated middle-class and above women support abortion while less-educated women, oriented toward traditional female roles, oppose it.[5]

Sexual attitudes, and possibly behavior, are influenced by the mass media and popular culture. Certainly, mass culture symbolizations reflect current norms, values, and practices. Magazines such as *Vogue*, *Harper's Bazaar*, and *Glamour* along with *Ms*, *Self*, and others obviously cater to women in the upper classes, providing much advice about beauty, sex, romance, marriage, and how to combine all these with a career. Women in the lower classes also have their outlets in soap operas and Harlequin romance novels.

Interpreting the mass media and popular culture is not easy. *Playboy* magazine is not merely what it appears to be—a gratification of and incitement to sexual passion. Commentators have argued that it is really anti-

---

[5]For a full background and an incisive, empirical study of the politics of abortion, which argues that the abortion issue is only part of a much deeper cleavage between working- and lower-middle-class forces that want to uphold a wide set of traditional values and middle- and middle- and upper-class forces that want new meanings about women and society, see Kristin Luker, *Abortion and the Politics of Motherhood* (Berkeley: University of California Press, 1984).

sensual, amounting to a rejection of commitment to enduring sexual relations. *Playboy* separates the sexes, making women appear to want men while the latter pick and choose like calculating consumers. Actually, *Playboy's* real function is as a guide to upper-middle-class consumption (see Chapter 11). Its importance in this context is that it also reflects the decline of the breadwinner ethic among young upwardly mobile males.[6]

Class and Marriage

From the beginning of the twentieth century until the 1960s, Americans married at increasingly earlier ages. Since the 1960s this trend has reversed itself, largely in keeping with the growth of college attendance and economic hardship. These two causes have affected the classes differently: Greater college attendance by the middle class has delayed marriage for its members and economic hardship has delayed marriage for the lower classes. Nonetheless, age at marriage varies directly with class, the children of the upper classes marrying later largely because of the education required for adult economic roles. Another class-related aspect of marital behavior is that Americans tend to marry within their own class (as measured by residential propinquity, education, or occupation of breadwinner in family of origin and occupation of spouses), and to marry within their own religion, ethnic group, and race. The belief that American men marry women from a lower class than their own, and that women do the opposite, was questioned long ago.[7] Nevertheless, it would appear that the upper class has the fewest unmarried men and the most unmarried women while the lower class has the most unmarried men and the fewest unmarried women.

The hoary belief (found in many sociology textbooks) that marriages between individuals of different class backgrounds tend to be unstable appears to be an old wives' tale. In any case, one study found no empirical basis for this belief; indeed, it found limited evidence that marriages between low-origin males and high-origin females were remarkably free of divorce.[8]

An interesting analysis of the college sorority identified a problem unique to middle- and upper-class parents of daughters.[9] In a male-dominated society, women tend to acquire their primary adult status in marriage; thus, middle-class females must marry someone of either superior

[6]Robert Jewett and J.S. Lawrence, "Playboy's Gospel: Better Wings Than Horns," in Robert Jewett and J.S. Lawrence, *The American Monomyth* (Garden City, N.Y.: Anchor, 1977), pp. 58–83, and Barbara Ehrenreich, "Playboy Joins the Battle of the Sexes," in her *The Hearts of Men: American Dreams and the Flight From Commitment* (Garden City, N.Y.: Anchor, 1983), chap. 4.

[7]Zick Rubin, "Do American Women Marry Up?," *American Sociological Review* 33 (October 1968): 750–760.

[8]Norval D. Glenn, Sue Keir Hoppe, and David Weirer, "Social Class Heterogamy and Marital Success: A Study of the Empirical Adequacy of a Textbook Generalization," *Social Problems* 24, no. 4 (April 1974):539–550.

[9]John Finley Scott, "The American College Sorority: Its Role in Class and Ethnic Endogamy," *American Sociological Review* 30 (August 1965):514–527.

or equal class status if they are to avoid downward mobility. In a caste society, marriage is carefully confined within caste boundaries, but in a class society marriage can (theoretically) take place across ethnic and class lines. Thus, education is a threat to upper- and middle-class families in that it mixes the sexes across ethnic and class lines and creates the possibility that a female will marry outside such boundaries. A college campus, however, serves as an opportunity for middle-class girls to meet middle-class or upwardly mobile boys. It provides a means, in other words, to solve what John Finley Scott calls the "Brahman problem": the shortage of suitable marriage partners for high-status females and the competition they face from those in the classes below them. The college sorority, Scott argues, is an ascriptive mechanism by means of which parents can channel their daughters' attention away from males in the lower classes and into paths that lead to marriages suitable on both ethnic and class grounds. Sororities have probably declined in influence since their early twentieth-century heyday, but their function is undoubtedly being fulfilled in various other ways.

Commentators on American marriage have identified several class-related variations in the basic structure of monogamous marriage:

1. The companion marriage—largely an upper-class phenomenon.
2. The partner marriage—largely a middle-class phenomenon.
3. The "husband-wife" or "working-class" marriage—largely a working- and lower-class phenomenon with a number of subvariations.

LeMasters and Rubin have provided rich (and disturbing) portraits of working-class marriages, ranging from those among higher-skilled, better-paid, and more work-satisfied construction workers to those among lower-level, blue-collar workers.[10] The lives of working-class spouses are differentiated by sex. Men lead their lives largely outside the home (at work and with male friends) while women lead their lives largely inside the home and with relatives. All this may be changing as more wives are forced into the labor market. Middle-class spouses may also lead differentiated lives, especially when only the husband works, but they have far more in common (about sex, raising children, planning for the future) than do working-class spouses. In another study, David Halle has provided a variation of working-class marriage. He too found much that Le Masters and Rubin had found. But because his study group consisted of well-paid workers at an automated chemical plant, the cleavage between the sexes and differences with white-collar workers were not as extreme as those found by Le Masters and Rubin.[11]

[10]E.E. LeMasters, *Blue-Collar Aristocrats* (Madison: University of Wisconsin Press, 1975), and Lillian Breslow Rubin, *Worlds of Pain: Life in the Working Class Family* (New York: Basic Books, 1976).

[11]David Halle, *America's Working Mass: Work, Home, and Politics Among Blue-Collar Property-Home-Owners* (Chicago: University of Chicago Press, 1984), chap. 3.

These class-based models are general in nature and one must be careful in using them. For example, the middle-class male has been found to be dominant vis-à-vis his wife in the selection of friends.[12] Males in the lower classes, though believing in and claiming authoritarian marital and family statuses, exercise less effective authority over their wives and children than men in the classes above them. According to Blood and Wolfe, the dominance of a working-class husband is drastically curtailed if his wife works— an increasingly prevalent pattern.[13] By and large, it appears that the higher a man's position in the class system, the greater his dominance of the family (though a working wife curtails her husband's dominance at all class levels).

The influx of women into the labor force has changed marital relations. The breadwinner ethic has declined and a number of class-based variations have appeared. Among the broad working classes, double breadwinners are an economic necessity. Marital stress here is still high because of sex-segregated lives and because women, in addition to working, are still saddled with housework and the raising of children. Working wives among the middle and upper middle classes have produced changes in the pattern found among early researchers. At one time middle-class wives were often "gainfully unemployed"—that is, the wife was often an adjunct to the husband's career. In a classic analysis, William H. Whyte outlined how the wives of business executives were incorporated into their husbands' companies. Wives were often interviewed when their husbands were being hired; they were expected to get along and to accept their spouses' long hours and frequent moves; and they were integrated into the company by such means as prizes, company socials, and norms governing breeding, deportment and consumption, including place of residence. In effect, the wife became an "extra employee."[14] Women were also prominent in voluntary activities of all kinds, activities that closely correlated with class background.[15] The women's

---

[12]Nicholas Babchuk and Alan B. Bates, "The Primary Relations of Middle-Class Couples: A Study in Male Dominance," *American Sociological Review* 28 (June 1963):377–384.

[13]Robert O. Blood, Jr., and Donald M. Wolfe, *Husbands and Wives: The Dynamics of Married Living* (New York: Free Press, 1960), pp. 40–41, reprinted 1978; Hyman Rodman, "Marital Power and the Theory of Resources in Cultural Context," *Journal of Comparative Family Studies* 3 (Spring 1972):50–69; Bertram H. Raven, Richard Centers, and Aroldo Rodriques, "The Bases of Conjugal Power," in Ronald E. Cromwell and David Olson, eds., *Power in Families* (New York: Halstead, 1975).

[14]William H. Whyte, Jr., "The Wives of Management," *Fortune* 44 (October 1951):86ff., and "The Corporation and the Wife," *Fortune* 44 (November 1951):109ff. Rosabeth Moss Kanter's case study of a large corporation, *Men and Women of the Corporation* (New York: Basic Books, 1977), reports (pp. 116–122) that the practice of making the wife a member of the corporation team is still prevalent. A claim that this practice has been curtailed by the women's movement may be found in *Fortune* (August 20, 1984), "The Uneasy Life of the Corporate Spouse," pp. 26–32.

[15]For an analysis of the voluntary behavior of upper-class women, see G. William Domhoff, *The Higher Circles: The Governing Class in America* (New York: Random House, 1970), chap. 2, and Susan S. Ostrander, *Women of the Upper Class* (Philadelphia: Temple University Press, 1984).

movement has brought important changes in this pattern. This movement, overwhelmingly middle and upper class in its goals and achievements, has produced the two-career marriage (for the middle-class nature of the women's movement, see Chapter 9).

Satisfaction from marriage is a complex subject because it takes different forms and is affected by many factors. However, studies tend to show that marital satisfaction rises with class (with education and occupation more than with income), and that it is higher if the class positions of husband and wife are similar (class in this class is determined by education and religion).[16]

Evidence shows that at all class levels the roles of husband and wife are deeply differentiated,[17] in effect making man-women and husband-wife relationships difficult. What data exist indicate that role segregation is deepest in working- and lower-class marriages, and suggest less strongly that there is significant role segregation by sex in upper-class families. By contrast, middle-class families tend toward the partnership type of marriage. And as more women work, especially among the middle and upper classes, the tendency toward partnership marriages will probably increase.

Class, Birthrates, and Birth Control

Birthrates are related inversely to social class (using family income and woman's education).[18] Class differentials also appear among black and Spanish-origin Americans.[19] There appears to be no deviation from national class-related patterns in fertility among religious groups.[20]

Class, Family, Socialization, and Personality

In 1958 Urie Bronfenbrenner published a paper that reconciled the serious contradictions that had appeared in research into class child-raising practices

[16]Robert O. Blood, Jr., and Donald M. Wolfe, *Husbands and Wives: The Dynamics of Married Living* (New York: Free Press, 1960), pp. 253–257, and Ira L. Reiss, *Family Systems in America*, 3rd ed. (New York: Holt, Rinehart, & Winston, 1980), p. 253.

[17]For differences between the sexes in upper-middle-class American marriages (based on informal conversations), see John F. Cuber and Peggy B. Harrof, *The Significant Americans: A Study of Sexual Behavior Among the Affluent* (New York: Appleton-Century, 1965). The sharp separation between masculine and feminine roles among the working and lower class has been documented by, among others, E. E. LeMasters, *Blue Collar Aristocrats* (Madison: University of Wisconsin, 1975), and Lillian Breslow Rubin, *Worlds of Pain: Life in the Working Class Family* (New York: Basic Books, 1976).

[18]*Statistical Abstract of the United States, 1986*, Table 91.

[19]Donald J. Bogue, assisted by George W. Rumsey, Odalia Ho, David Hartmann, and Albert Woolbright, *The Population of the United States: Historical Trends and Future Projections* (New York: Free Press, 1985), Table 6–23A.

[20]Ibid., p. 659–662.

over a period of twenty-five years.[21] Bronfenbrenner showed that working-class mothers had been more permissive than middle-class mothers in the 1930s, but that after World War II this relationship was reversed: Middle-class mothers became progressively more permissive, surpassing working-class mothers in this regard. The greater leniency of middle-class parents toward the expressed needs and desires of their children is accompanied by higher expectations of their children and the consistent use of reasoning and "love-oriented" techniques of discipline, techniques research has shown to be more effective than physical punishment in controlling and orienting children. Greater permissiveness, in other words, has not lessened the greater amount of normative social control exercised by middle-class parents.[22]

One way to illustrate the difference in "home atmosphere" between middle- and working-class families is to contrast their value orientations. Using a representative national sample of all men employed in civilian occupations (that is, compared with samples drawn from Washington, D.C., and Turin, Italy), Melvin Kohn established the preeminent role of class (education and occupation) in developing the strikingly different value orientations of middle-class parents (independence) and working-class parents (conformity).[23] The single most important factor in this difference, according to Kohn, is that higher occupations (higher in the sense that they allow for greater independence) tend to emphasize self-direction whereas lower occupations tend to emphasize conformity to external authority. Kohn's findings, it should be emphasized, hold true regardless of age of children, sex, religion, race, region, or urban-rural location.

Class, Family, and the Transmission of Abilities and Values to Children

Studies have shown that parents socialize children differently by class. Do these differences result in different personalities and behaviors among

[21] "Socialization and Social Class Through Time and Space," in E. E. Maccoby, T. M. Newcomb, and E. L. Hartley, eds., *Readings in Social Psychology*, 3rd ed. (New York: Henry Holt, 1958); reprinted in Reinhard Bendix and Seymour M. Lipset, eds., *Class, Status and Power: Social Stratification in Comparative Perspective*, 2nd ed. (New York: Free Press, 1966), pp. 362–377.

[22] E. E. LeMasters, *Blue-Collar Aristocrats* (Madison: University of Wisconsin Press, 1975), chap. 7, and L. B. Rubin, *Worlds of Pain* (New York: Basic Books, 1976), chap. 7 and *passim*, give rich details of parenting among both skilled and unskilled workers. For a review of the literature on socialization, see Viktor Gecas, "The Influence of Class on Socialization," in Wesley R. Burr, Reuben Hill, P. Ivan Nye, and Ira L. Reiss, eds., *Contemporary Theories About the Family* (New York: Free Press, 1979), pp. 365–404.

[23] Melvin L. Kohn, *Class and Conformity: A Study in Values* (Homewood, Ill.: Dorsey Press, 1969). Kohn and his associates have reaffirmed the power of occupation, especially its complexity, over personality and cognitive outlook; for a variety of essays in this area, see Melvin L. Kohn and Carmi Schooler with the collaboration of Joanne Miller, Karen A. Miller, Carrie Schoenbach, and Ronald Schoenberg, *Work and Personality: An Inquiry Into the Impact of Social Stratification* (Norwood, N.J.: Ablex, 1983). For a further discussion of Kohn's work into the relation between work and personality, see "Class, Personality, and World View" in Chapter 10 of this text.

children? In an early search for an answer to this question, Schneider and Lysgaard developed the concept of *deferred gratification pattern*, the tendency to postpone satisfactions and renounce impulses in favor of long-range benefits.[24] Youngsters who exhibit the deferred gratification pattern (or the Protestant-bourgeois ethic) would be less prone than others to physical violence, free sexual expression through intercourse, and free spending; they would be more likely to stay in school than go to work and to remain dependent on parents. In their analysis of a national sample of high school students, Schneider and Lysgaard found a strong relationship between student acceptance of the deferred gratification pattern and class origin—those further up the class ladder being more likely to accept it than those further down. Of special interest is a study done in Detroit, undertaken in the early 1950s, which suggested strongly that as the United States transforms itself from an entrepreneurial to a welfare bureaucratic society, a shift was taking place in its general pattern of child training. Evidence showed that those in "entrepreneurial" occupations continue to raise their children according to the deferred gratification pattern, but that families in "bureaucratic" occupations place less stress on strict impulse management. Because the American occupational structure was undergoing a shift toward bureaucratic forms of work, the authors concluded that this trend would be increasingly reflected in child training patterns.[25]

Basil Bernstein has provided an important analysis of personality differentials by studying ways in which the children of different classes develop linguistic skills. Bernstein distinguishes between *formal* (or elaborated) and *public* (or restricted) languages. Middle-class children acquire a language (less vocabulary than sentence organization) that facilitates comprehension of a wide range of symbolic and social relationships. The lower-class child, on the other hand, acquires a language with a lower order of conceptualization and causality and a greater emphasis on affective responses to immediate stimuli. Consequently, concludes Bernstein, the middle-class youngster who knows both languages is able to respond to and master a wider variety of symbolic and social situations than the youngster whose personality is environed, indeed constituted, by a public language.[26]

A follow-up of Bernstein's theory lends support to his supposition that the various classes impart different language codes to their children.[27] Using

[24]Louis Schneider and Sverre Lysgaard, "The Deferred Gratification Pattern: A Preliminary Study," *American Sociological Review* 18 (April 1953):142–149.

[25]Daniel R. Miller and Guy E. Swanson, *The Changing American Parent* (New York: John Wiley & Sons, 1958).

[26]Basil Bernstein, "Social Class and Linguistic Development: A Theory of Social Learning," in A. H. Halsey, Jean Floud, and C. Arnold Anderson, eds., *Education, Economy, and Society* (New York: Free Press, 1961), pp. 288–314.

[27]Robert D. Hess and Virginia C. Shipman, "Early Experience and the Socialization of Cognitive Modes in Children," *Child Development* 36 (December 1965):869–886.

a sample of 163 black mothers and their four-year-old children drawn from four different class levels, this analysis focused on the communication process between mother and child. Judged in a number of different ways, the communication process was distinctly different in the various classes, the top classes providing their children with a greater range of linguistic skills than the lower classes. The relevance of this research to learning and education is obvious, and we will touch on it again later when we explore the relationship between class and education. Indeed, we will find class influence on personality reflected in a wide variety of phenomena: marital stability, mental health, IQ, values and beliefs in general, and political orientation.

In an important extension of his work on the relation between occupation and personality, Kohn and his collaborators have shown that occupational stratification not only affects parents' values and socialization practices, but that these are also clearly related to the personality and self-direction of children, especially as they pertain to education.[28] As we will see in Chapter 8, the ability of the upper classes to socialize their children for success in school is an important aspect of class power and perpetuation.

Class and Family Values

The extended family is a group of related nuclear families living and working together as a single structure in the performance of most social functions. It does not exist in this form in the United States, except in isolated instances. Cooperation among related nuclear families does exist, however. Within the upper class, for example, a "voluntary" sense of kinship among related nuclear families persists and is focused around the common ownership of large and varied forms of productive property. Among working- and lower-class families, it is often necessary for parents and young married couples, or aged parents and married couples, to live together. There is also a strong patriarchal preference among working-class males and among some Roman Catholic ethnic groups, although this tradition is not effective in practice. The matriarchal family common among poor blacks lacks normative support but has in practice helped blacks to prevail in slavery and postslavery class society. And, to further qualify the notion that the United States is made up of autonomous, isolated nuclear families, research has found considerable financial and other help, socializing, recreational and ceremonial activities, and positive kin feelings among related nuclear families.[29]

---

[28]Melvin L. Kohn, Kazimierz M. Slomczynski, and Carrie Schoenbach, "Social Stratification and the Transmission of Values in the Family: A Cross-National Assessment," *Sociological Forum* 1, no. 1 (Winter 1986):73–102.

[29]For a review of the literature, see Ira L. Reiss, *Family Systems in America*, 3rd ed. (New York: Holt, Rinehart, & Winston, 1980), pp. 413–431.

Our knowledge of the upper-class family is limited, but the partial studies that exist all point in the same direction.[30] Some upper-class families place value on the longevity of their family line, their accomplishments as a family line, and loyalty and cooperation among the various nuclear families that constitute a stem or general family line. Such families (old wealth, old family) must be distinguished from other upper-class families that have as much or even more money but lack a family tradition (*nouveau riche, parvenu* families). This distinction is expressed by the terms *upper-upper* and *lower-upper*, used by Warner. Upper-upper-class families have been found in one community after another, and the existence of an urban upper-upper class is attested to by *The Social Register*.[31] Such families enjoy financial security because of family trust funds, high income because of their occupations and savings, and high standards of consumption; they exercise close supervision over their children by means of servants, summer homes, private schools, and controlled socializing.

Middle-class and working-class families all exhibit significant amounts of interaction between relatives: visits, communication on ceremonial occasions, help with children, stabilization of broken families, and economic aid either bilaterally or between generations. The reasons for extended kin relations in an achievement society and for a possible increase in such relations have been advanced by Ira Reiss: About twenty years have been added to life expectancy during this century, increasing the number of families in which three generations are living simultaneously; the increased length of required education makes more young couples dependent on their parents; the undisputed primacy of the independent nuclear family makes it possible for kin (and related religious-ethnic) ties to exist without posing a threat to achievement-individualist values; and it may be that the nuclear family (the main focus of the individual's emotional life) yields such sparse psychic satisfaction that emotional need tends to enforce extended family relations. And a point made by Sussman and Burchinal should not be overlooked: Modern means of transport and communications make it relatively easy for geographically separated nuclear families to maintain kinship relations.

The significance of extended kinship ties for class analysis has to be approached by means of indirect evidence. Extended family relations account for a much larger proportion of the total interaction of working-class families than other families. Or, in other words, the classes above the working class have significantly higher rates of participation in friendship groups and

---

[30]For an invaluable summary of what we know about upper-class families, see Frederic Cople Jaher, *The Urban Establishment: Upper Strata in Boston, New York, Charleston, Chicago, and Los Angeles* (Urbana: University of Illinois Press, 1982).

[31]Susan A. Ostrander's book, *Women of the Upper Class* (Philadelphia: Temple University Press, 1984), shows that the women of the upper class spend much time and energy in maintaining family tradition.

in formal voluntary associations.[32] The extended kin pattern in the working class has been documented in a number of studies and forms the basis for the belief in the existence of a distinct working-class subculture.

Class and Family Stability

Class is a good predictor of family stability. The disruption of family takes different forms: premature death of the breadwinner, separation or divorce of the spouses, unemployment, and so on. The lower a person is in the class system, the greater the chances of disruption.[33] Note should be taken of the fact that men and women in the lower classes have divergent views on sex, raising children, and marital-family relations in general, which, combined with economic deprivation, puts such marriages at great risk.

One of the more interesting attempts at a general explanation of marital failure, with important implications for class society, is Kirkpatrick's concept of *ethical inconsistency*.[34] Kirkpatrick argues that the United States has three general marital models, defined in terms of the wife's role: the wife-mother, partner, and companion types. Each is related to a specific class and each specifies a different set of rights and duties for the wife. But because all three types are well known beyond the confines of their classes of origin (and because of the society's general encouragement of self-interest), women tend to adopt aspects of each that are in their interest, whereas men select aspects in the interest of the husband. The result is that marriage at all levels is heavily burdened by contradictory role expectations. Men expect their wives to be hardworking drudges who are also responsible, efficient, pleasant to be with, and glamorous, while women expect credit and respect for household work, economic security, a say in family decisions, and certain forms of indulgence because they are women (romance, luxuries, courtesy). Too much should not be made of Kirkpatrick's limited study, but its theme is reminiscent of Merton's explanation of deviance, which helps to place marital instability in a broad social context and to bring it within the orbit of anomie theory.[35] In any case, America's universal encouragement of self-interest, together with its multiple class-related marriage models (widely known through the mass media), makes it highly unlikely that many married indi-

[32]See Chapter 12.

[33]For a discussion of class and divorce, which sees growing marital stability through college-educated men and women, but growing divorce rates for women with graduate degrees, see Ira L. Reiss, *The Family System in America*, 3rd ed. (New York: Holt, Rinehart, & Winston, 1980), chap. 12.

[34]Clifford Kirkpatrick, "The Measurement of Ethical Consistency in Marriage," *International Journal of Ethics* 46 (July 1935):444–460.

[35]For Merton's theory of anomie, see "Class, Universal Goals, and Deviant Behavior" in Chapter 16.

viduals at any class level will experience the stability and satisfactions of role complementarity in marriage.

Actually, a society based on competitive individualism is not conducive to a stable family life at any class level. The deeper reality of American individualism is the relative scarcity of prizes and rewards even in the best of times. Competition hides the fact that few win, most stand still, and many lose. These outcomes occur from the way in which economic activity is structured. When the economy slows down, as it did from the late 1960s on, the negative impact on the family increases.

The overall experience with the American economy during the post–World War II period has transformed the American family. Given our laissez-faire society (no economic planning, toleration of high unemployment, the absolute right of capital to move, and poor public services), the United States now has a highly stratified set of households diversified into stable and unstable families, two-parent and one-parent families, unrelated individuals, and the homeless. Along with these changes has come the feminization of poverty—the large increase in one-parent households run by women with inadequate income.

Seen from a different perspective, little evidence exists that the lower classes have adopted middle-class values and behaviors in marriage and family, any more than they have in other areas of life. In other words, the theory of convergence, the alleged movement toward classlessness, and the embourgeoisment thesis are wrong.

CLASS AND DIFFERENTIALS IN HEALTH AND LIFE EXPECTANCY

The American Health-Care System

The United States has an abnormal health-care system compared to all other capitalist societies. The American health-care system began as and has remained a private-profit system providing different health care to the various classes and costing far more than any other developed capitalist society for health results that at best are the same.

The United States spends huge amounts of public money (and a larger percentage of its GNP than any other developed capitalist society) on its health-care system, but because there is no effective counterweight to the providers of services and products, prices, incomes, and profits are pretty much set by those who receive these funds. All in all, the medical establishment has succeeded in obtaining public financing without public supervision, direction, or control (actually, it decides on how public authorities behave). And to make matters worse there is no direct positive relation between money spent on curative medicine and better health.[36]

All other developed capitalist countries have national health insurance (private health care financed by comprehensive public insurance) or socialized medicine (free public health care), and costs are contained and standards maintained because the government acts as a monitor and negotiator on behalf of the public.[37]

Class, Health, and Life Expectancy

Many studies over the past decades have shown a relation between social class, on the one hand, and health and life expectancy on the other. Studies tend to refer to upper and lower classes, but all agree that the lower classes suffer more from all diseases (and have much higher rates of infant mortality). And the lower classes, whether judged by income, occupation, or education (or all together), live significantly fewer years than do the upper classes.[38]

The lower classes are also more likely to be uninsured (out of a total of between 25 million and 34 million uninsured in 1977) and the uninsured do not utilize health services. By and large, the lower classes have poorer health and life expectancy because of their class status and not because they are not getting medical services (the absence of or inadequate health care merely aggravates their problems). The lower classes are more subject to work-related diseases, disabilities, and deaths. Their lives are more stressful, including the health-debilitating stress of unemployment.[39] And they know less about how to maintain health, and they suffer both from deprivation

[36]Thomas McKeown, *The Modern Rise of Population* (London: Edward Arnold, 1976); John Powles, "On the Limitations of Modern Medicine," in David Mechanic, ed., *Readings in Medical Sociology* (New York: Free Press, 1980). For a summary of research in this area, see John B. McKinlay and Sonja M. McKinlay, "Medical Measures and the Decline of Mortality" (1977), in Peter Conrad and Rochelle Kern, eds., *The Sociology of Health and Illness*, 2nd ed. (New York: St. Martin's Press, 1986), pp. 10–23.

[37]For an analysis of Canada's health care system, which provides health outcomes equal to the United States at considerably less cost, see Theodore R. Marmor, "Canada's Path, America's Choices: Lessons from the Canadian Experience with National Health Insurance," in Peter Conrad and Rochelle Kern, eds., *The Sociology of Health and Illness: Critical Perspectives*, 2nd ed. (New York: St. Martin's Press, 1986), Selection 38.

[38]Some narrowing in the gap between the upper and lower classes occurred over much of the twentieth century but has now started to grow again, at least based on British data. See Richard G. Wilkinson, ed., *Class and Health: Research and Longitudinal Data* (London: Tavistock, 1986).

[39]For a valuable analysis (by a leading authority on the blue-collar world) of stress at work among white blue-collar males, along with a picture of their physical and mental health and their fears about employment loss because of environmental protection, see Arthur B. Shostak, *Blue-Collar Stress* (Reading, Mass.: Addison-Wesley, 1980).

(hunger affects millions) and from the wrong foods and other style-of-life habits.[40]

Over and above all these factors is another factor that shapes the health-care system by social class—the health-care delivery system itself. As Dutton points out, the health-care delivery system is oriented toward the middle and upper classes, and barriers to using health-care facilities are an important part of the low use of health services by the poor.[41]

The Female Patient: Double Jeopardy of Class and Sexism

Well-to-do women probably receive the best medical care possible. But the large majority of women are subject to the negative consequences of class and sexism. Working- and lower-class women, like their male counterparts, do not receive the same medical care received by the middle class and above. But in addition to deprivation by class, broad segments of the female population, including women above the working classes, are treated differently by the medical profession (see Box 7–1, "The Female Patient"). The different and damaging treatment of female patients is no doubt a result of the pervasive sexism of American society. But it is also due to the fact that women are excluded from the upper reaches of the health-care professions.

Class and Mental Retardation

Researchers have established a link between class and mental retardation (organic impairment). Presumably, the extremely few naturally defective babies are randomly distributed on the class ladder. However, the bulk of all other defective human beings are products of an environment of poverty: The fetus is injured because the mother is in poor health, received an unskilled abortion, or is not under a doctor's care; or the child is organically impaired by illness, malnutrition, ingestion of lead paint, rat bites, and the like. Of some significance in understanding the class nature of mental retardation is the fact that its incidence in the United States is much higher than in England, Denmark, and Sweden, which have national maternal and child care programs.[42]

---

[40]For a summary of the literature and a discussion, see S. Leonard Syme and Lisa F. Berkman, "Social Class, Susceptibility, and Sickness," and Karen David and Diane Rowland, "Uninsured and Underserved: Inequalities in Health Care in the United States," both in Peter Conrad and Rochelle Kern, eds., *The Sociology of Health and Illness: Critical Perspectives* (2nd ed.; New York: St. Martin's Press, 1986), Selections 2 and 22.

[41]Diana B. Sutton, "Explaining the Low Use of Health Services by the Poor: Costs, Attitudes, or Delivery System?," *American Sociological Review* 43 (June 1978):348–368.

[42]Rodger L. Hurley, ed., *Poverty and Mental Retardation: A Causal Relationship* (Trenton: New Jersey Department of Institutions and Agencies, 1968), especially chap. 2, Ronald Marlowe, "Poverty and Organic Impairment."

BOX 7–1.   *THE FEMALE PATIENT*

Mary Healthy goes to the doctor (the chances are high that the doctor will be a male).[43] Mary is getting a checkup—the doctor examines her heart, lungs, blood pressure, but not her breasts and does not give her a pelvic examination (general reproductive organs). Mary has had no problems with these over-looked regions of her body and is just as happy to leave them unexamined. What has happened? Why should a doctor overlook obvious, distinguishing, and potentially troublesome parts of the female anatomy? The reason, however ludicrous it may seem, is that medical schools locate these parts of the body in a gynecology course—it follows, therefore, that if patients want those parts of the body checked they must go to a specialist. A few years later Mary enrolls in a prepaid group health plan. Her doctor sees her through some discomfort, advising against a hysterectomy. Mary is fortunate—if she had been in a program like Blue Cross, where doctors get paid only if they do something, her chances of having a hysterectomy (needed or not) would be 50 percent higher.

Mary's luck changes and her marriage sours. She begins to drink. Her self-esteem, not high to start with given the lower value accorded to women by American culture, suffers a double blow. Mary has internalized the double standard for alcoholics and thinks that women who drink are morally reprehensible (men who drink, on the other hand, are considered to be victims of the job, comic figures, and so on). And she believes herself a failure for not succeeding at marriage. Mary does not feel tip-top and begins to go to the doctor with vague symptoms (confirming his stereotype of women as complainers). Her doctor never spots her alcoholism (he was not trained in this area though he does tend to spot male alcoholics more often than women). It's just as well, perhaps, because there are few treatment centers for women.

Doctors tend to have different images of health for males and females. Healthy women are "more submissive, less independent, less adventurous, less competitive, more excitable in minor crises, more easily hurt, and more emotional than a mature healthy man." Their conception of a healthy adult closely parallels that of a healthy man (for sources, see Marian Sandmaier, "Alcoholics Invisible," p. 28). It is no accident, therefore, that her doctor uses drugs to cure (sedate) Mary since submissiveness is part of his definition of a healthy female. Women are not only far more likely to be given drugs than men but far more likely to become cross-addicted. It is not long before Mary becomes addicted to drink *and* pills.

Mary's luck changes for the better. A 1970 federal law requires provision for female alcoholics in centers receiving federal money. She is one of the few to get a place but the treatment doesn't work. The center has no program for job training, no provision to care for her children, no follow-up program once she is released, and the image used by the male staff to rehabilitate her is the same one

[43]Much of the following discussion is based on Susan Schiefelbein, "The Female Patient: Heeded? Hustled? Healed?," *Saturday Review* 7 (March 29, 1980):12–16; and Marian Sandmaier, "Alcoholics Invisible: The Ordeal of the Female Alcoholic," *Social Policy* 10 (January/February, 1980):25–30.

that led her to drink in the first place. They want to give her a feminine personality, which she also wants deeply but which conflicts with a deep urge to be her own person (married women are much more likely than married men to become mentally ill—never-married women tend to have much lower rates).[44] Her troubles will appear all over again after leaving the treatment center since she will either be very poor, or, if she marries again, subject to unhealthy sex roles.

Both men and women in need of medical care benefit from the miracles of modern medicine but they are also mistreated. Mistreatment varies by age, class, and sex. The female as female is subject to all that befell Mary: excessive specialization in medical school by students, the profit motive, medical myths, popular myths in medicine, double standards, and poor public health-care policies. And by having her deviance (alcohol, mental illness, other behavior) "medicalized," she is being mistreated even when she receives the best of care since only her symptoms are being treated.

[44]Walter R. Gove, "Sex, Marital Status, and Psychiatric Treatment: A Research Note," *Social Forces* 58 (September 1979):89–93.

Of perhaps greater significance is the growing suspicion that many of the mentally retarded are not organically impaired at all. Hurley has argued that at least 85 percent of those designated mentally retarded are simply poor people who have been damaged by their experience in a society with a strong propensity for using the middle class as the yardstick of normality and for labeling those who deviate from its norms as genetic defectives.[45]

In an interesting analysis, Farber has argued that modern society has restricted access to valuable social positions by progressively raising standards in all fields, thereby creating a surplus population (the mentally retarded, the unemployed, the mentally ill, the disabled, the criminal, the functionally illiterate, and so on), which he estimates at as high as 20 to 25 percent of the total population. Farber reports that the best estimate of the proportion of mentally retarded in the United States is between 2 and 3 percent (between 4 million and 6 million people).[46] Despite the vitality of the biopsychological tradition, which tends to stress a natural distribution of intelligence and ability in general, it appears that our mentally retarded are victims of the American class system.

[45]Ibid., introductory essay. *The New York Times,* July 18, 1983, p. 1, reports that the number of newborn suffering from physical and mental disability doubled from the late 1950s to 1983.

[46]Bernard Farber, *Mental Retardation: Its Social Context and Social Consequences* (Boston: Houghton Mifflin, 1968), chap. 1.

The social creation of mental retardation has also been argued by Mercer in her analysis of the relation between mental retardation and education. Mercer suggests that her analysis is applicable to other social systems besides education: the family, the neighborhood, law enforcement, welfare, churches, and public institutions for the retarded.[47] Mercer reports that empirical studies in California show that Spanish-speaking and black students tend to be assigned to special classes (thus beginning the process of becoming mental retardates) at significantly higher rates than English-speaking white students, *even white students with similar scores on intelligence tests.*[48] And in a full-scale study of Riverside, California, a city of 85,000, Mercer again documents the class-ethnic-racial basis of mental retardation. Of further value in this study is Mercer's argument that there is a sociocultural (middle class) bias in the evaluation of what is considered normal intelligence, and that this bias is deeply institutionalized in the individualistic clinical approach of professional diagnosticians and in the interlocking network of organizations that allegedly uncover and treat mental retardation—especially the public schools, public-welfare-vocational rehabilitation agencies, law enforcement agencies, medical facilities, the Department of Mental Hygiene, and private organizations concerned with mental retardation.[49]

Class and Mental Illness

Research has discovered a direct correlation between class and amounts of mental illness, certain kinds of mental illness, and the type and effectiveness of professional treatment received. And it is also clear that the higher the class, the more sympathetic, positive, and tolerant the attitude toward mental disturbance and the greater the likelihood that deviant behavior will be attributed to mental illness.[50] The relation between social class and mental illness received little attention from social scientists until the pioneering community analysis undertaken by August B. Hollingshead and Frederick C. Redlich during the 1950s.[51] In their highly sophisticated empirical study of greater New Haven, Connecticut (at that time a metropolitan center of approximately 240,000), the authors posed five hypotheses:

[47]The social creation of incompetents in general is analyzed more fully in Chapter 8, on the relation between class and education.

[48]Jane R. Mercer, "Sociological Perspectives on Mild Mental Retardation," in H. Carl Haywood, ed., *Socio-Cultural Aspects of Mental Retardation* (New York: Appleton-Century-Crofts, 1970), pp. 378–391. This publication is an indispensable reference on mental retardation. The concluding summary by H. Carl Haywood is especially valuable.

[49]Jane R. Mercer, *Labelling the Mentally Retarded* (Berkeley: University of California Press, 1973).

[50]With regard to the latter point, see Judith Rabkin, "Public Attitudes Toward Mental Illness: A Review of the Literature," *Schizophrenia Bulletin* 10 (Fall 1974):21–22.

[51]*Social Class and Mental Illness: A Community Study* (New York: John Wiley & Sons, 1958).

1. The prevalence of treated mental illness is related significantly to an individual's position in the class structure.
2. The types of diagnosed psychiatric disorders are connected significantly to the class structure.
3. The kind of psychiatric treatment administered by psychiatrists is associated with the patient's position in the class structure.
4. Social and psychodynamic factors in the development of psychiatric disorders are correlative to an individual's position in the class structure.
5. Mobility in the class structure is associated with the development of psychiatric difficulties.

The data supported a clear affirmative answer to each hypothesis.[52] A follow-up study of the same patients ten years later showed that class is significantly related to the long-term outcome of treatment and to the adjustment of former patients in the community: The higher the class, the less likelihood that a patient would receive custodial hospital care and the greater likelihood that his or her adjustment to the community would be successful.[53]

The most ambitious investigation of mental health in American social science, a study of a midtown Manhattan residential area of 175,000 inhabitants, offers important corroborating evidence of an inverse relation between class and mental illness.[54] A number of other aspects of this study are of special interest: The authors suggest strongly that midtown Manhattan is typical of segments of other highly urbanized centers across the United States and that therefore their findings are not germane only to that locality. Second, the study attempts (by means of a questionnaire evaluated by psychiatrists) to diagnose the mental health of the entire population (and not to base its analysis on treated patients, as the New Haven study did). Third, the Midtown Manhattan Study distinguished between the class of the individuals studied and that of their parents, so that the impact of each on mental health could be studied.

While emphasizing that they are in no way implying that sociocultural processes account for all mental illnesses, the authors conclude (1) that class-of-origin and one's own class are both significantly related directly to mental health or, conversely, that both are inversely related to mental illness, with an especially high rate at the bottom levels; (2) that social mobility is associated with a higher level of mental health (which is directly at odds with the general belief that the opposite is true); (3) that there are no differences in the frequency of some forms of mental illness (schizophrenia, anxiety-tension,

---

[52]Data supporting the last two hypotheses are presented in Jerome K. Myers and Bertram H. Roberts, *Family and Class Dynamics in Mental Illness* (New York: John Wiley & Sons, 1959).

[53]Jerome K. Myers and Lee L. Bean, *A Decade Later: A Follow-up of Social Class and Mental Illness* (New York: John Wiley & Sons, 1968).

[54]Leo Srole, Thomas S. Langner, Stanley T. Michael, Marvin K. Opler, and Thomas A. C. Rennie, *Mental Health in the Metropolis: The Midtown Manhattan Study* (New York: McGraw-Hill, 1962), chaps. 11–13.

excessive intake) and intellectual, affective, somatic, characterological, and interpersonal disturbances; and (4) that the lower the class the less likely that those suffering from mental illness will receive treatment.[55]

Kessler compared eight mental studies from 1967 to 1976 and found a relation between socioeconomic status and psychological distress. Kessler made fine distinctions among such variables as income, occupational status, education, and job conditions, and concluded that we need to know more about these and other factors before we can decide between the selection explanation (individuals with psychological problems are selected out by the society and drift downward) and the social causation model (experiences at various class levels cause mental illness).[56] Kessler's distinction between individual and social factors is misleading. All human behavior is social, including "individuals with psychological problems."

In a study of Anglos, Mexican-Americans, and Mexicans living in the companion cities of El Paso, Texas, and Juarez, Mexico, Mirowsky and Ross found paranoia clearly associated with low socioeconomic status (and Mexican heritage, and being female). A sense of having enemies who are plotting against you is related to a sense of being powerless. The association of paranoia with low-class position confirms previous studies.[57]

Analysts of schizophrenia (inability to select relevant stimuli or to focus sustained attention on the important stimuli in given situations) have directly challenged the claim that the relation between low class status and schizophrenia (and mental illness in general) is because defective individuals sink in the class hierarchy. Though they caution that more work remains, these analysts found clear evidence that significant numbers of normal individuals in jobs characterized by noise, heat, cold, fumes, or physical hazards became schizophrenic.[58]

Mental health experts were disheartened by the failure to cure mental patients through hospitalization and were encouraged by evidence that what patients needed were structured social experiences. During the 1960s and 1970s hundreds of thousands of mental patients were released, presumably to go to community homes where they could learn to live productive lives.

---

[55]Our understanding of the nature of alcoholism and its relation to class is limited. We do know, however, that the diagnosis and treatment of alcoholism vary with class position and that this variation favors the upper classes (males); see Wolfgang Schmidt, Reginald G. Smart, and Marcia K. Moss, *Social Class and the Treatment of Alcoholism* (Toronto: University of Toronto Press, 1968).

[56]Ronald C. Kessler, "A Disaggregation of the Relationship Between Socioeconomic Status and Psychological Distress," *American Sociological Review* 47 (December 1982):752–764..

[57]John Mirowsky and Catherine E. Ross, "Paranoia and the Structure of Powerlessness," *American Sociological Review* 48 (April 1983):228–239.

[58]Bruce G. Link, Bruce P. Dohrenwend, and Andrew E. Skodol, "Socioeconomic Status and Schizophrenia: Noisome Occupational Characteristics as a Risk Factor," *American Sociological Review* 51 (April 1986):242–258.

As these homes were never built, many of these patients ended up as America's homeless.

Class and Learning Disability

The general class bias of American society applies to learning disability. James Carrier has shown that biased professional and political judgments create much of what is called *learning disability*. But Carrier goes much further. In a brilliant synthesis of existing research, he connects class bias about learning disability to similarly biased naturalistic arguments about a wide range of alleged deviations from normality: IQ, educational potential, mental retardation, mental illness, physical disabilities, sexual deviation, being gifted, and crime. And he also shows how professional judgments by psychologists, guidance counselors, medical researchers, teachers, and educators combine with economic and family interests to produce political pressure that results in the legalization of the alleged deviation from the normal. The overall result, Carrier argues, is class society, not nature, creating inequality and then reproducing itself.[59]

CLASS, FAMILY, PERSONALITY, AND HEALTH: A SUMMARY

The hierarchy of economic classes correlates with the distribution of family, personality, and health benefits.

Attitudes toward sex have grown more permissive in recent decades and do not vary much by class. However, sexual behavior does vary by class. Men and women in the middle classes (and above) are behaving similarly, but their first sexual experiences occur later than do those of working class males and females (who are also becoming more alike in their sexual behavior). Premarital sex among the middle (and upper) classes is more clearly associated with romance, commitment, and intention to marry than is true among the lower classes. Both upper and lower classes also have different orientations toward marital sex.

Lower classes have higher rates of illegitimacy than do the upper classes. The abortion controversy is related to class, with those opposed defending traditional marital family values while those in favor are women (and men) in the middle and upper classes who want to combine career and motherhood.

Popular culture provides class-oriented views of sex, marriage, and family.

[59]James G. Carrier, *Learning Disability: Social Class and the Construction of Inequality in American Education* (Westport, Conn.: Greenwood Press, 1986).

Americans are marrying later, but age of marriage varies by social class, with the middle and upper classes marrying later because of the need for longer years of schooling.

Americans marry within their own class, ethnic and religious group, and by race.

American marriages are sex-segregated at all class levels but more so at the lower levels.

Males in the upper classes are more effectively dominant in their marriages than males in the lower classes, but all power relations are equalized significantly if wives work.

Birthrates vary inversely by class but not as much as in the past.

The upper classes socialize their children for independence and provide them with the personality-cognitive skills that ensure success in school.

Family values are important to Americans at all class levels, but the realization of these values varies somewhat by class. Important differences exist by class in marital stability, with the lower classes more unstable.

Economic change and the high divorce rate have diversified the American household.

All in all there is no convergence in sexual or family behavior among the various classes.

Physical health and life expectancy vary by social class, with the upper classes enjoying better health and longer life spans. Economic stress, dangerous workplaces, and poorer living styles are the main reasons for these differences.

Working- and lower-class women receive poorer health care and are also subject to sexist (inferior) medical care.

Mental retardation, mental illness, and learning disability are also related to class. The lower classes are physically impaired by poverty and they also suffer from being falsely defined as subnormal by the upper classes, who have a stake in keeping valued statuses scarce.

As with physical illness or disability, health-care treatment for those with personality problems varies by social class.

The pronounced relation between the hierarchy of economic class and the family, personality, and health benefits of households at each level is clear. This relation also means that parents in the upper classes are able to give their children important advantages in the struggle to join tomorrow's class system. The implications of this causal process for class power and perpetuation over the generations will become even clearer as we trace the relation between class and education.

CHAPTER 8

Class
and Education

AMERICA'S FAITH IN EDUCATION

Thomas Jefferson wanted a society that allowed human nature's best to emerge and rise to the top as leaders. In Jefferson's time this idea was revolutionary just as a similar idea in Plato's *Republic* had been revolutionary. Both Jefferson and Plato thought of a society led by high-ability individuals recruited from all class levels. And both stressed the importance of education in developing a natural elite and thus a well-ordered society. Jefferson was as proud of his part in establishing the University of Virginia as he was of writing the Declaration of Independence.

Jefferson's faith in education as a way to reveal who was qualified to occupy positions in the division of labor was combined with a faith in free markets and free elections to become America's social philosophy of "non-egalitarian classlessness." For Americans, it is axiomatic that there should be no arbitrariness in the relation between social rewards and personal worth. Since the founding of their new Jerusalem, Americans have believed that they at last had found the way to realize nature's hierarchy of talent and to put unequal rewards on a just and natural basis. For Americans, the key to overcoming the artificial barriers of social condition, religion, ethnicity, and race and to revealing the true universe of individuals is equal opportunity and competition in the spheres of economics, politics, and education.

In this trinity of free markets, education holds a special place in American hearts. It is alleged to have great power to improve people and solve problems; nothing is more characteristic of an American faced with a problem than to attribute it to a lack of education. The power of education is thought to be enormous, largely because Americans attribute great power to ideas and knowledge. This faith in ideological causation—in the power of truth over ignorance and evil—along with the difficulty of running a regionally, racially, economically, and ethnically diverse society, has led the United States to assign a heavy burden of functions to education. And given their belief in biopsychological causation, Americans find it easy to equate the absence of formal barriers to education and the existence of free public schools with equality of opportunity.[1] For an American, an opportunity is something one seizes or makes use of; inequality in any field is simply the record of those who did and did not have it in them to profit from opportunities available to all.

The reality of education is far different from our beliefs about it. Education has been studied extensively by sociologists since the 1920s, and these studies have revealed that education is a thoroughgoing class phenomenon and that its power to improve society is quite limited. No matter what type of behavior was investigated, research revealed the power of class: expenditure per pupil, attendance, educational aspirations, IQ and achievement tests, years completed, grades, diplomas, and degrees. The upper classes even benefit more from remedial courses. Of great importance was the finding that class determines who goes to college and to what type of college. By and large, attendance and completion of four-year colleges is a monopoly of the upper classes.

During the 1960s two distinct strands of sociological research on education appeared. One adopted a functional position more or less in line with Davis-Moore and the mainstream American tradition derived from Thomas Jefferson (this is the status-attainment perspective that we encountered earlier).

The other strand was a many-sided conflict perspective (both liberal and Marxist) that focused on class and the power of the economy to explain success in school and after (the result was to downplay the causal importance of both biogenic-personal factors and the school itself in explaining educational and occupational success).

THE STATUS-ATTAINMENT POSITION

Earlier we reported that Duncan and Blau developed a model to explain social mobility (see Chapter 5). Their focus was on the relation between father's occupation and son's occupation. Their finding was that class origin was important in success but so were individual attributes as mediated by education. All in all, there was no tendency to decry the role of class because

---

[1] Equality of opportunity as an equal chance at the starting gate should not be confused with equal access to education of some sort or with proposals to provide different or more effective educational opportunities for diverse social classes.

status attainment theorists assumed that the influence of the middle (and upper) classes reflected the long-range march of American society toward universalism (an achievement society based on objective evaluations of persons and positions).

The original Duncan and Blau study left much about the son's economic status unexplained. Others in this tradition (the Wisconsin school) added some other factors in the achievement process such as aspirations, and the influence of significant others (peers and adults), but still a gap remained in the overall causal process. In 1972, Jencks argued that luck explained a great deal of what happened to sons, claiming that there was no strong relation between class origin, education, and son's economic status (including income).[2]

The net result of status attainment theory did more than merely endorse the idea that the upper classes, the individual, and education were central to achievement and the idea of meritocracy. It also endorsed the idea that American society was essentially meritocratic and progressive. Ironically, Jencks (otherwise a critic of American society) supported mainstream complacency with his idea of luck. Luck, long a mainstay of American culture, and in particular of the Horatio Alger tradition, has no part in science. Luck merely means that there is more to be known and this is exactly what the conflict tradition set out to do.

THE CONFLICT POSITION

Most sociologists who analyze education differ profoundly from not only the status-attainment theorists (who themselves have begun to modify their position) but from the basic beliefs of most educators, public officials, national leaders, and the lay public. Sociologists in the conflict tradition have reinterpreted past findings, and by using new assumptions they have come up with a radically different view of education.

In fashioning their perspective, conflict sociologists built on the main tradition in stratification analysis. Earlier research going back to the Lynds' *Middletown* study of 1927 and Hollingshead's *Elmtown* study in the 1940s had established the class basis of education. Conflict sociologists were also inspired by an insight in the Coleman Report, namely, that education appears to have little independent power in its own right (this report will be discussed shortly). Running counter to basic American beliefs, conflict sociologists argue that education is merely a way to transmit class position from one generation to the next and to hide the fact that the basic power over occupation and income lies in the economy itself.

[2]Christopher Jencks and others, *Inequality* (New York: Basic Books, 1972).

Early Research

The small-town focus of early stratification research (1925 to 1945) gave us a good portrayal of the mixed-class educational system that prevailed under the sway of this tradition of educational equality.[3] With some modifications, which will be noted, this system was probably characteristic of the United States from the advent of mass public education in the middle of the nineteenth century until close to the middle of the twentieth. Under this system the various classes throughout rural, small-town, and small-city America (probably) attended the same schools at every educational level through high school. Most of America's educational norms date from this period: free tax-supported compulsory education; a curriculum stressing literacy, abstract knowledge, patriotism, and the Protestant-bourgeois virtues; and a testing and grading system that supposedly revealed the hierarchy of talent ordained by nature. The fact that rich and poor often attended the same school, in combination with heavy educational expenditures, rising overall levels of education, and the great normative appeal of education, gave a semblance of reality to the norm of equal educational opportunity. However, Hollingshead's finding that Elmtown's schools were deeply biased in favor of its upper classes is much closer to the reality of American education, then and now.

Awareness of the relation between class and education has grown consistently in the twentieth century. In the early part of the century, progressive educators began to question the wisdom of imposing a uniform education on a student body composed of a mixture of social classes.[4] Though it took massive effort and caused deep controversy (and still does, for that matter), progressive educators managed somewhat to diversify the school to make it more suitable for a diverse student body. Accordingly, students were grouped into classes on the basis of their speed of learning; various types of programs (vocational, commercial, academic) were offered; and special schools (music and art, science, vocational) were made available for special students. The early efforts to adjust education to students' differing values and skills were motivated by a desire to overcome class differences, including ethnic and linguistic differences, and thereby to make equal education a reality. But progressive educators in the 1920s and 1930s, even when they advocated special programs and special schools, did not (and could not)

[3]The classic example is August Hollingshead, *Elmtown's Youth* (New York: John Wiley & Sons, 1949). This pattern, which suited the class system of rural–small-town and small-city America, did not prevail in the "caste" system of the South, which, after it began to provide education for black Americans, had a legally segregated system based on the doctrine of "separate but equal facilities" accepted as constitutional until 1954.

[4]For an excellent history of Progressivism in education, see Lawrence A. Cremin, *The Transformation of the School* (New York: Alfred A. Knopf, 1961).

envisage the trend that developed in the decades after World War II. The booming economy of the post-1945 period accelerated the process of urbanization and suburbanization, in effect segregating residential and political districts by social class throughout the United States. The inner city became blighted and black, and layers of white working, middle, and upper-middle-class suburbs grew up around the decaying core city. What makes this overall process important, of course, is that residential areas are also the economic and political units on which America's schools are based. Given the United States' powerful tradition of political decentralization, this class-structured hierarchy of local communities deeply affects its educational system; indeed, it particularizes education by class so deeply that it is probably a mistake to speak of an American *system* of education at all.

Class and Expenditure per Pupil

The amount of money spent on education in the United States varies enormously from state to state, and from one school district to another within any given state. The basic reason for these differences is that school expenditures are the responsibility of local communities: since there are enormous variations in the wealth of localities, there is enormous variation in the amount of money expended per pupil.

As part of the Civil Rights Act of 1964, Congress created a commission to study the "lack of availability of equal educational opportunities for individuals by reason of race, color, religion, or national origin in public educational institutions at all levels in the United States, its territories and possessions, and the District of Columbia."[5]

The Coleman Report found considerably variation in the nature of schools as measured by such factors as age of building, average number of pupils per classroom, textbooks, library, science and language laboratories, accreditation, specialized academic programs, teacher tenure, principal's salary, extracurricular activities, and the like. With due regard for the dangers inherent in the use of averages and for the marked regional disparities in the United States, it was found that blacks have access to fewer of some of the facilities that seem to be related to academic achievement.[6] All in all, how-

---

[5]The formal title of the resulting study is *Equality of Educational Opportunity* (Washington, D.C.: U.S. Government Printing Office, 1966); its informal title is the Coleman Report. It should not go unnoticed that educational opportunity was placed in the context of civil rights and that while many of the factors that enter into social stratification were cited, class as such was ignored in the commission's terms of reference. The research team itself, though not ignoring class, consistently uses the euphemism "family background."

[6]Ibid., pp. 8–15.

ever, the report did not find as much disparity along these lines as many thought existed.[7]

The Coleman Report also found distinct differences in academic achievement between majority (white) students and ethnic-racial groups (Puerto Ricans, Indian Americans, Mexican Americans, and blacks), and by implication between social classes. Variations in academic achievement by class will concern us again shortly, but are of particular interest here in connection with unequal educational expenditures. By holding socioeconomic status constant, the Coleman Report concluded that the quality of a school (library, curriculum, building, teachers' qualifications, and so on) has very little independent effect on the academic performance of students. (Minority students are affected somewhat more by the quality of a school than majority, or white, students.) The Coleman Report (p. 302) did find that students' aspirations and performance are strongly affected by the social composition of a school's student body; but this variable, it should be noted, is a function of class factors.[8]

The Coleman Report (p. 325) summarizes its major finding in these words:

> *Taking all these results together, one implication stands out above all: that schools bring little influence to bear on a child's achievement that is independent of his background and general social context; and that this very lack of an independent effect means that the inequalities imposed on children by their home, neighborhood, and peer environment are carried along to become the inequalities with which they confront adult life at the end of school. For equality of educational opportunity through the schools must imply a strong effect of schools that is independent of the child's immediate social environment, and that strong independent effect is not present in American schools.*

The approach that emphasizes equalization of expenditures per pupil in order to equalize educational opportunity would appear to be futile. The difficulty of equalizing expenditures per pupil would itself be overwhelming, affecting as it would the deeply entrenched tradition of decentralized political control of schools. In any case, the strategy of focusing on educational expenditure as the key to equal opportunity is rendered suspect by the Coleman Report. One should not be surprised at this finding, since it is consonant with what is known about socialization. People learn from social relationships, not from buildings, libraries, cafeterias, or contact with curricula and teachers remote from and irrelevant to their previous (class) socialization. A well-educated teacher with middle-class beliefs and values in a

---

[7]The Coleman Report is a broad abstract study of national and regional data, and caution should be exercised when its findings are cited. Shocking disparities between individual, black urban schools and upper-class suburban schools, for example, obviously exist.

[8]This is discussed further in the next section, "Class and Educational Aspirations."

plush school is likely to be ineffectual if the pupils come from lower-class families; indeed, such ineffectualness has a cumulative effect, making relations between the student and the school increasingly difficult. The same teacher in a run-down, ill-equipped school attended mostly by middle-class youngsters would probably be far more effective; the social environment of the school would mesh with and complement the values and beliefs acquired by the students at home. On any objective test the latter students would in all likelihood score higher than the former.

The error of relating equality of educational opportunity with equality of educational expenditure has a practical component: Virtually insurmountable political barriers confront those who want to equalize (or make more equitable) educational expenditures. But even if these barriers were overcome and an equal amount of money spent on each child in America, there would still be wide differentials in academic achievement—differentials best accounted for by the class structure.

Class and Educational Aspirations

The American commitment to education is well known: Masses of people attend and service schools, great sums of money are spent on them, and the numbers rise every year. The high value Americans place on education must be qualified carefully, however, if we are to understand its social meaning. For one thing, Americans do not value education as an end in itself. Always, and often explicitly, it is a means to other ends. And of special significance is the fact that Americans value education unequally by class. Discussing the relation between class and personality, we pointed to sharp differences in the values of parents in the higher classes and those of parents in the lower classes. The relevance of these differences to education is apparent. Speaking broadly, families in the higher classes prepare and motivate their children for success in school, while families in the lower classes prepare and motivate their children for average academic performance or even failure.

Two things about aspirations should be kept in mind. One, the aspirations of the lower classes rise if they attend predominantly middle-class schools. Two, given the phenomenal growth of junior colleges, vocational training, and open admissions, aspirations to certain kinds of education appear to be strong at the lower levels of American society.

Class and Academic Achievement

Decades of research have yielded the same results again and again—namely, achievement in school correlates strongly with class origin. In addition to studies of small-town America, national and urban-studies conducted from the 1960s on all reached a similar conclusion: Children's class origin is directly and strongly related to all forms of academic achievement, including IQ.[9]

Differentials in expenditure per pupil, educational aspirations, and academic achievement are not the only ways in which class influences education. While almost every aspect of education is implicitly embraced by these three categories, it should also be noted that pupil and teacher turnover, emotional health, regularity of attendance, regular promotion in grade, school-leaving rates, enrollment in college preparatory programs, participation in clubs, receipt of scholarships, parent participation in school activities, and school board composition are all directly related to class level. Surprisingly enough, even enriched and remedial classes and subsidized milk and food programs benefit middle- and upper-class youngsters more than those who come from the lower classes.[10]

Of no small importance in assessing the relation between class and education is the class position of the public school teacher. Recruited largely from middle-class backgrounds, teachers absorb the ethos of middle-class America, including the hunger for professional status, regardless of background.[11] As a result, they develop an image of the ideal student and an ideology of education highly inappropriate to many of the actual students and situations they face.[12] It has even been argued that teachers behave in such a way as to elicit from lower-class pupils the low achievement they expect.[13]

The class explanation of success or failure in school is part of the overall sociocultural approach to behavior. Though modern scholarship has tended

[9]In addition to the Coleman Report (1966), see Robert E. Herriott and Nancy Hoyt St. John, *Social Class and the Urban School* (New York: John Wiley & Sons, 1966); Patricia Cayo Sexton, *Education and Income* (New York: Viking Press, 1961); Robert J. Havighurst, Paul H. Bowman, Gordon P. Hiddle, Charles V. Matthews, and James V. Pierce, *Growing Up in River City* (New York: John Wiley & Sons, 1962); and Robert J. Havighurst, *The Public Schools of Chicago: A Survey Report* (Chicago: Board of Education, 1964). For general summaries, see Caroline Hodges Persell, *Education Inequality: A Theoretical and Empirical Synthesis* (New York: Free Press, 1977) and Richard H. de Lone, *Small Futures: Children, Inequality, and the Limits of Liberal Reform*, Report for the Carnegie Council on Children (New York: Harcourt Brace Jovanovich, 1979).

[10]For a lucid and comprehensive presentation of data on all these areas from "Big City" (and from other studies), see Patricia Cayo Sexton, *Education and Income* (New York: Viking Press, 1961). For the first of a long line of research linking poverty, poor health, poor nutrition, and poor learning, see Herbert G. Birch and Joan Dye Gussow, *Disadvantaged Children: Health, Nutrition and School Failure* (New York: Harcourt Brace Jovanovich, 1970).

[11]Robert E. Doherty, "Attitudes Toward Labor: When Blue Collar Children Become Teachers," *School Review* 71 (Spring 1963):87–96.

[12]Howard S. Becker, "Social Class Variations in the Teacher-Pupil Relationship," *Journal of Educational Sociology* 25 (April 1952):451–465.

[13]Ray C. Rist, "Student Social Class and Teacher Expectations: The Self-Fulfilling Prophecy in Ghetto Education," *Harvard Educational Review* 40 (August 1970):411–451. For the research supporting the general argument that all forms of alleged deviance, including mental retardation, mental illness, learning disability, crime, being gifted or sexually different, and so on are creations of an arbitrary American power structure legitimated by professionalism, see Chapter 7.

in this direction, there persists a pronounced tendency to include biopsychic factors in explanations of educational and other behavior. And there is still vitality in the tradition that places the burden of explanation on biopsychic variables, especially on the alleged existence of significant differences in inborn intelligence.[14]

LIFE IN CLASSROOMS: THE HIDDEN CURRICULUM

The classroom as a structure of interaction and power has been largely neglected by educators. But thanks to a pioneering work by Philip W. Jackson[15] we have begun to understand more about the classroom.

The typical classroom is affected by a number of factors that are not given much thought. Teachers routinely face classes that are too big even for the room let alone for the personal attention that each student needs. Often there are shortages of texts, other materials, and equipment. Students spend much time lining up to use facilities. The typical solution to crowding and scarce materials creates the classroom's basic power relation. Students are anchored at their desks and all proceed according to the same lesson plan. Teachers spend a great deal of time talking. Students must receive permission to talk or participate. Students are called on at random, producing fear and anxiety for students can never be sure they are prepared. Comments on their written or oral work are made by teachers and other students, thus exposing them to evaluation by others and often to humiliation and embarrassment. Many evaluations such as IQ scores remain secret.

The typical classroom wastes a great deal of time—students sit isolated and silent, and even when they try to listen their attention spans are short while teachers are long on wind. It is common practice for teachers to have students help them manage their classes. Standards for selecting students (and for evaluating class behavior) are arbitrary and lack balance. Teachers tend to favor character traits that suit the needs of managing large numbers: passivity, docility, conformity, silence until called on, and so on. There is a heavy reliance on textbooks, many of which are incomplete and biased (high school history texts, for example, were biased against labor and omitted two-thirds of what actually happened in American history, usually the disagreeable parts).[16] And typical texts have been found to be of little value to

---

[14]For the radical genetic explanation, see Richard Herrnstein, *I.Q. in the Meritocracy* (Boston: Little, Brown, 1973). For a radical indictment of the IQ as a weapon of class domination, see Samuel Bowles and Herbert Gintis, "I.Q. in the U.S. Class Structure," *Social Policy* 3, nos. 4 and 5 (1972/1973): 65–96; reprinted in Jerome Karabel and A.H. Halsey, edited with introduction by, *Power and Ideology in Education* (New York: Oxford University Press, 1977), pp. 215–232.

[15]*Life in Classrooms* (New York: Holt, Rinehart & Winston, 1968).

[16]Jean Anyon, "Ideology and United States History Textbooks," *Harvard Educational Review* 49 (August 1979):361–386, and Frances Fitzgerald, *America Revised: History Textbooks in America* (Boston: Little, Brown, 1979).

students.[17] The teacher also imparts nonideological skills that prepare students to fit in. The great emphasis on abstract reading and writing skills and on abstract science and mathematics shortchanges most of the middle classes as well as the lower classes.[18] In most respects education's stress on discipline, the passive learning of routine skills, and standardized testing all resemble the corporate economy and society that surround the school.

The school and the classroom have many of the characteristics of a total institution (prison, military, monastery). The school and classroom prepare students for life but not as we normally think of it. What the school most resembles is the factory and office, and it is preparation for subordinate roles in the economic division of labor that makes up the hidden curriculum for most students.

The average classroom does not awaken or nourish citizen skills—students are not introduced to the conflicts and shortfalls of American society, but are given, by and large, a bland, consensus picture of national achievement and progress. Instead of raising policy issues that bring national assumptions into question, the schools reinforce the ready-made world that students experience elsewhere. And the school fails to produce informed consumers—quite the contrary, the teacher tends to reinforce and extend the nonideological consumerism that students acquire at home and through the mass media.[19]

All in all, the power structure of the school and the hidden curriculum are part of the way in which schools reproduce the class system. Many studies have shown that schools have a pronounced bias in favor of the values, norms, and skills of the upper classes and that they either overlook or discriminate against the values and skills of the lower classes. Schools require character and cognitive skills (for example, punctuality, self-discipline, the ability to manipulate symbols) that are found in the middle and upper classes and are absent or lacking in the lower classes. Subject matter also favors the upper classes, and teachers and textbooks rarely discuss the world in conflict terms or from the standpoint of the lower classes. Instead, schools teach a complacent nonideological subject matter that suits children from the upper

[17]*The New York Times*, April 8, 1980, p. C 4.

[18]For insight into how schools shortchange the middle classes, see Eleanor Smollett, "Schools and the Illusion of Choice: The Middle Class and the 'Open' Classroom," in George Mardell, ed., *The Politics of the Canadian Public School* (Toronto: James, Leurs, and Samuel, 1974). For a pioneering participant observation analysis of a community college, which reports that it fails to serve its lower-middle and working-class students, see Howard B. London, *The Culture of a Community College* (New York: Praeger, 1978). For the adverse effects of segregated all-black schools, see Ray C. Rist, *The Urban School: A Factory for Failure* (Cambridge, Mass.: MIT Press, 1973), and Helen Gouldner, with the assistance of Mary Symons Strong, *Teachers' Pet, Troublemakers, and Nobodies: Black Children in Elementary School* (Westport, Conn.: Greenwood Press, 1978).

[19]For a long catalogue of abuses, see Sheila Harty, *Hucksters in the Classroom: A Review of Industry Propaganda in the Schools* (Washington, D.C.: Center for the Study of Responsive Law, 1979). For examples of reforms and industry restraint, see chap. 8 of the Harty text.

classes and ignores the conflicts and deficiencies in American life that children from the lower classes could relate to. Teachers also overlook assets and skills associated with the lower classes and frown on behavior and values that would be easy to include in the educational process. Students from the upper classes arrive in school already housebroken, and teachers can concentrate on academic work. In schools populated by the children of the lower classes much of the time is spent on fostering obedience to rules.

TRACKING AND CLASS REPRODUCTION

Most societies have explicit systems for separating students into academic and nonacademic groups to determine who will go on to higher education. In Great Britain children take tests at the age of eleven that decide who will go on to university training. Ralph Turner has called this *sponsored* mobility, a system in which students are selected from above (by the people who believe in the validity of tests) for sponsorship into higher achievement status. The United States, says Turner, relies on *contest* mobility, a system in which individuals compete to determine who goes on and who doesn't.[20]

The two systems, however, are not so different in their basic causes and outcomes. Education in both reflects social class and acts as a gatekeeper to elite positions. The ability to do well in school and on IQ and other tests correlates strongly with social class. The quality of schooling also varies by social class. One way to see education as a gatekeeper protecting class advantage is through the system of *tracking*.

The tracking system takes place in various ways. The tradition of community-based schools means that students often go to schools composed of similar income groups (this also leads to racial and ethnic segregation). Thus one form of tracking is when the lower classes do poorly in their own schools and the upper classes do well in their schools. Another form takes place *inside* a school. This occurs when students from various economic classes attend the same school. Here separate academic, business, and general streams or tracks emerge, a process affecting 85 percent of American students.

Explicit tracking would be sponsored mobility and would violate American norms and values. Rosenbaum has found that tracking takes place deceptively and that decisions by the school are made to appear as contest mobility and student choice.[21] Using class-based academic achievement from

[20]Ralph Turner, "Sponsored and Contest Mobility and the School System," *American Sociological Review* 25 (December 1960):855–867.

[21]The following discussion relies on James E. Rosenbaum, "The Structure of Opportunity in School," *Social Forces* 57 (September 1978):236–256; "Track Misperceptions and Frustrated College Plans: An Analysis of the Effects of Tracks and Track Perceptions in the National Longitudinal Survey," *Sociology of Education* 53 (April 1980):74–88.

earlier grades, the high school separates students into two tracks, one for college and one for noncollege students. School records indicate a rigid tracking system in which students never attend mixed classes and the only crossover among programs is from college to noncollege tracks. A follow-up of the graduating class revealed that most college-track students attended four-year colleges and virtually all students in the noncollege track did not.

The school's grading system also made it virtually impossible for students in the noncollege track to shine. Teachers were stingier with good grades in the noncollege as opposed to the college track and the school discounted noncollege grades significantly when it came time to record them—an A in a noncollege course was considered a D. The net result was that noncollege students were not taking courses that prepared them for college admission and the grading system discriminated against them arbitrarily. Almost as if to make sure that these students would be refused admission to college, the school made it part of their record that they were in noncollege programs.

Throughout all this, noncollege students knew what track they were in but had no idea that they were in dead-end programs. Most of them in their senior year believed they were preparing for college. Throughout, the school and guidance counselors gave almost no information about the implications of choosing one course or program over another. Actually, there is evidence that the school encouraged misinformed choices. When asked, principals denied that their school had tracks.

Still another variation is gender segregation among the lower classes. While males and females among the lower classes are in nonacademic programs, they typically take gender-stereotyped courses—the males in industrial courses, the females in business courses.[22] It would be interesting to know how much change has occurred in gender segregation among the middle and upper classes.

Whatever the form, tracking in elementary and secondary schools means that higher education is closed to large numbers of students who could profit from it. Those who don't go on are overwhelmingly from the lower classes, often despite good grades (the upper classes go on to college often despite poor grades and test scores). But even in higher education class-based tracking continues. Here it takes the form of offering students a wide variety of "choice" with most working- and lower-middle-class students going to community colleges while students from the middle and upper classes attend four-year colleges.

[22]For this overlooked aspect of tracking, see Jane Gaskell, "Course Enrollment in High School: The Perspective of Working-Class Females," *Sociology of Education* 58 (January 1985):48–59.

TRACKING AND ELITE PRIVATE SCHOOLS

Tracking also takes place through private schools. Elite private schools are of special importance because they provide the socialization necessary for wielding upper-class power and of course, for access to elite colleges. These schools arose originally as ways for old wealth to protect itself against the new rich, but as Levine points out, the elite private schools eventually assumed their true function—to blend old and new wealth into a cohesive national upper class.[23]

HIGHER EDUCATION: THE CAPSTONE
OF CLASS EDUCATION

Throughout much of its history (approximately from 1500 to 1850) the nascent class society of the West required little formal training or education in the socialization process. By the mid-nineteenth century the social need for literacy had enforced the inauguration of mass public education, and by the end of the nineteenth century the free high school was becoming a standard feature of American education. Between 1900 and 1940 enrollment in America's high schools rose from about 5 percent to over 90 percent of the relevant age group. But in the post-1945 period the terminal high school systems were asked to expand their college preparatory programs as the United States inaugurated a system of mass higher education. In 1940 only 15 percent of eighteen- to twenty-one-year-olds were enrolled in institutions of higher education; by 1970 this figure exceeded 50 percent.[24] Since the 1960s both graduate training and professional training have increasingly become the gateway to upper-level occupations.

Americans institutions of higher education developed in a decentralized fashion during the nineteenth century. As a result, a vast variety of what Jencks and Reisman[25] call "special-interest" colleges emerged: colleges for each of the many Protestant denominations; for Roman Catholics and for Jews; for men or women only; for whites or blacks; for farmers, engineers, or teachers; for

---

[23]Steven B. Levine, "The Rise of American Boarding Schools and the Development of a National Upper Class," *Social Problems* 28 (October 1980):63–94. For a full-scale study of elite private schools, see Peter W. Cookson, Jr., and Caroline Hodges Persell, *Preparing for Power: America's Elite Boarding Schools* (New York: Basic Books, 1985).

[24]For these developments, see Martin Trow, "The Second Transformation of American Secondary Education," *International Journal of Comparative Sociology* 2 (1961):144–165; reprinted in Jerome Karabel and A. H. Halsey, ed. and intro, *Power and Ideology in Education* (New York: Oxford University Press, 1977), pp. 108–118.

[25]Christopher Jencks and David Reisman, *The Academic Revolution* (Garden CIty, N.Y.: Doubleday, 1968).

inhabitants of a given town, city, or state; for adolescents or adults; and for the rich and not-so-rich. While the composition of the governing boards of institutions of higher education was necessarily affected by this diversity, analysts have agreed that by and large such boards exhibit a common trend: a decline in the power of clergymen and a corresponding rise in the power of businesspeople and professionals. Though there are variations among institutions, it is clear that farmers, manual workers, lower white-collar workers, ethnic and "racial" groups, intellectuals, scientists, labor union officials, and artists (as well as women and young adults) are not represented on governing boards in proportion to their numbers or importance.[26]

It is of considerable interest that higher education can no longer claim to be an interconnected, multilevel meritocracy. It is what it has probably always been, a fragmented set of unrelated, noncompetitive clusters. High-quality, high-prestige institutions, especially private ones, continue to emphasize elitist goals (pure research, liberal arts, preservation of the cultural heritage, an intellectual atmosphere of free inquiry). Such goals also further faculty members' professional careers and assign a low priority to teaching, especially at the undergraduate level. Lower-quality, lower-prestige institutions, usually public, appear to have given up trying to compete with the front-ranking universities and have come to be characterized by different goals: vocational programs, applied research, teaching, service to the immediate community, and equality of opportunity.[27]

It should surprise no one to learn that higher education is deeply implicated in our class system. It is important at the outset, however, to insist on viewing higher education as a class phenomenon and to resist the notions that colleges are attended exclusively by an elite of personal merit, and that such extraneous factors as race, ethnicity, religion, or class, though perhaps influential at the lower levels of schooling, have somehow been overcome or neutralized by the time students enter college. As we will see, the student bodies of our colleges and universities not only do not include all the available academic talent, but also are havens of class privilege.

Class influence over entry to higher education takes a number of forms. First, local school districts are often homogeneous by income and are thus class-based. This means a vast difference in the amount of money spent on

---

[26]For a review of previous studies and a corroborating analysis of a sample of private and public universities, see Hubert Park Beck, *Men Who Control Our Universities: The Economic and Social Composition of Governing Boards of Thirty Leading American Universities* (Morningside Heights, N.Y.: King's Crown Press, 1947). For the most comprehsnsive body of empirical data on the composition and attitudes of governing boards, see Morton A. Rauh, *The Trusteeship of Colleges and Universities* (New York: McGraw-Hill, 1969). Though not intended as a representative sample of all American colleges and universities, the survey includes 654 selectively chosen institutions in a number of basic categories.

[27]Edward Gross and Paul W. Grambsch, *Changes in University Organization, 1964–1971* (New York: McGraw-Hill, 1974).

education from one district to another. But more important it means that students entering school are already programmed either for success, mediocrity, or failure. This process is institutionalized by the high school tracking system in which students are assigned to programs by IQ or previous academic achievement.

All this leads to differential access to higher education with large numbers of youngsters with academic ability dropping out of high school or not going on (for the relation between family income and college attendance see Figure 8–1). And tracking continues in higher education because class again determines what quality of four-year school one attends and whether or not one attends a junior college.[28] In addition, class is also related to type of programs selected once in college.

THE COOLING-OUT FUNCTION OF EDUCATION

Social mobility in the United States is thought to be, to use Ralph Turner's term, a contest between equals. Unlike the English system of "sponsored" mobility, in which members of the elite identify likely elite prospects in the classes below and consciously recruit them into the higher levels of society, American society regards upper status as a prize to be won by the worthiest individuals.[29]

The American contest system, says Turner, helps to solve a problem all societies face—maintaining loyalty to the system despite evident deficiencies. American education makes sense if seen in this light. American educational institutions avoid the formal separation (or *tracking*) of students, and the avenues from one program to another are kept open. Education is overtly viewed as a means to get ahead; it is avowedly vocational or practical; a great deal of effort is expended on keeping students in school as long as possible to insure a fair contest; much attention is paid to skills of "social adjustment," since the upward aspirant has no homogeneous elite on which to model his or her behavior and must not lose contact with the masses; and failure is due to individual deficiencies.

As we noted earlier, however, behind the rhetoric and attempts to provide for equal opportunity and competition, the United States has a

---

[28]The increase in college attendance by the lower classes should not be misinterpreted. Postsecondary education for the lower classes takes place overwhelmingly at junior colleges, which now account for 36 percent of higher education enrollments. For a careful compilation of evidence showing the pronounced separation by class that exists at this level, see Jerome Karabel, "Community Colleges and Social Stratification: Submerged Class Conflict in American Higher Education," *Harvard Educational Review* 42 (November 1972):521–562; reprinted in part in Jerome Karabel and A. H. Halsey, ed. and intro., *Power and Ideology in Education* (New York: Basic Books, 1977), pp. 232–254.

[29]Ralph H. Turner, "Sponsored and Contest Mobility and the School System," *American Sociological Review* 25 (December 1960):859.

Figure 8–1. College Enrollment of Dependent Family Members 18 to 24 Years Old by Family Income, 1986.[a]

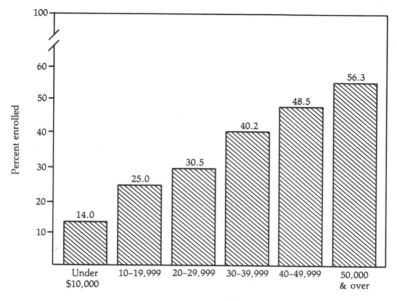

a. College enrollment refers to junior as well as four-year colleges, and family income includes households with more than one wage earner. Class differences in college attendance would be far more pronounced if only four-year colleges were included.

Source: U.S. Bureau of the Census, Current Population Report, Series P-20, no. 429, "School Enrollment—Social and Economic Characteristics of Students, October, 1986" (Washington, D.C.: U.S. Government Printing Office, 1988), Table 12.

well-developed class-based tracking system. Actually, it appears that there is very little difference between the United States and England in continuity of social level from father to son, or in the relative importance of social origin and ability in the son's educational attainment. And while the two nations' educational systems differ greatly, the tracking of students into academic and nonacademic streams reflects class origin and ability almost identically. It appears, in other words, that the two countries use different mechanisms to produce the same results.[30]

Turner's classic analysis concentrates on the way in which education is used to institutionalize and legitimate upward mobility, or success. It ignores, except by implication, the way in which failure (or relative failure or only moderate success) is institutionalized. Addressing himself to the latter problem, Burton R. Clark has suggested that the junior college performs a "cool-

[30]For this comparison, see Alan C. Kerckoff, "Stratification Processes and Outcomes in England and the United States," *American Sociological Review* 39 (December 1974):789–801.

ing-out" function.[31] The United States, says Clark, must somehow solve the problem created by the contradiction between its encouragement of all to succeed and the ability of the social structure to provide success only for a few—and a deeply graded structure of relative success and failure for the rest. Deliberately structured to diminish the enrollment pressure on colleges and universities, the junior college charges either low or no tuition and provides considerable choice among technical, commercial, and academic programs. But, says Clark, those who enroll in academic programs in the hope of eventually transferring to four-year colleges cannot all succeed, and a need exists to shift potential transfer students into terminal programs. Rather than allow for outright failure, says Clark, the junior college has developed an elaborate but disguised process for easing students into terminal programs and allowing all to save face. Among the features of this process are pre-entrance achievement tests, regular counseling interviews, a mandatory orientation course devoted to "realistic" vocational goals, an elaborate system of supervision in courses, and the routine use of probationary status.

It is important to recognize that standards of academic achievement (in all fields) are norms derived from the behavior in school of middle- and upper-class students. Departures from established academic norms are then labeled C or F students, low-IQ, "two years behind in reading," culturally deprived, dropouts, A+ students, brilliant, "college material," and so on. Conformity to such upper- and middle-class norms is, by definition, harder for working- and lower-class youngsters, rendering the concept of equal educational opportunity (no matter how defined) highly problematic. What exists, in other words, is an unacknowledged tracking system or, actually, nonsystem, made up of noncompeting clusters heavily related to class. Any assumption or argument that the hierarchy of achievement produced by this interplay of class and education coincides with (or approximates) the structure of ability ordained by nature is thoroughly suspect. And, finally, it means that we have no way of knowing how good our best really are.

The nature of education is seen in quite a different light, of course, by lay persons and, I suspect, many professional educators and social scientists. IQ, achievement and aptitude tests, grades, prizes, diplomas, degrees, and the like are all commonly viewed as reflecting native ability and motivation. The wide diversity of types of education (the class-based tracking system) is seen both as a wise provision for tapping and developing differences in native ability and as a moral universe allowing choice and providing a redemptory process for "late bloomers." Scholarships, graduate school

---

[31]"The 'Cooling-Out' Function in Higher Education," *American Journal of Sociology* 65, no. 6 (May 1960):569–576. The term *cooling-out* is taken from the work of Erving Goffman and refers to the management of disappointment. Goffman illustrates his argument by reference to the confidence game, which often features a means to mollify the victim and thus prevent him from alerting the police.

grants, and low or no tuition charges at quality colleges (which in reality represent a vast subsidy for middle and upper class students, since it is primarily they who meet admission requirements) are viewed as a contribution to equal educational opportunity.[32] And low or no tuition and low admission standards at good or poor institutions are also seen in this light, despite the fact that such opportunities are often accompanied by deliberately created high failure rates.

American education is through and through a class phenomenon, complete with mechanisms for mollifying average and marginal students. What the United States offers is educational opportunity, not equal opportunity; to fail to recognize this simple distinction, as well as the class nature of American education, is not to understand why and how American society produces shortage, waste, and privilege in the development of its woman- and manpower. But to understand all this fully, one must first examine education as a "great training robbery."

EDUCATION: THE GREAT TRAINING ROBBERY

It is almost universally accepted that the two chief goals of education are to prepare (sift, train, and sort) the young for an ever-more demanding occupational hierarchy and to prepare them for citizenship. The value placed on education and the powers attributed to it are apparent in many ways: Education is used to reward demobilized soldiers; it is considered responsible for the success or failure of the nation's science; it is thought of as a bulwark of defense; it is a basis for exempting citizens (college students) from military obligations; it allegedly reduces delinquency, unemployment, underemployment, and unemployability; it is associated with economic progress, and is thus used by employers who require more and more formal education all the time as a criterion for hiring in almost every line and level of work; and it is alleged to raise the income of the poor, and thus to make them viable citizens.

As education was assigned ever more explicit economic and social functions, Americans came to think of it as a natural or objective process for sorting out and training the talent manifested in each generation. In this sense, education has come to resemble the United States' central institutional system, its economy. But because education has been so deeply imbued with sacred social purposes, it has not been possible for Americans to ask fundamental questions about its actual social role. Of course, Americans have been quite critical of their educational institutions. They have spent and will no

---

[32]See Chapter 15 for an analysis of how public higher education redistributes income from the lower classes to the middle and upper classes.

doubt continue to spend enormous amounts of time and energy debating their performance. What the empirical record suggests, however, is that America's fundamental premises about education are wrong; that is, a sizable amount of evidence indicates that formal education bears no positive relation to economic behavior. If anything, education is associated with negative economic consequences!

Perhaps the simplest way to look at this evidence is to examine Ivar Berg's indictment of education as a "great training robbery."[33] Summarizing the considerable evidence on the relation between formal education and work performance and satisfaction, as well as a study of his own, Berg found no relation between formal education and work productivity, low absenteeism, low turnover, work satisfaction, or promotion. If anything, he found an inverse relation between amount of formal education and occupational performance. While the studies reported by Berg varied with regard to the type and reliability of their data, the impression gained from reviewing data on blue-collar, white-collar, and engineer-scientist workers is that formal education plays one single role: It determines where one enters the occupational system. What is crucial, in other words, is that employers believe that formal education makes better workers and therefore use it as a criterion for hiring. But once hired, workers with more and less formal education exhibit no significant difference in work performance. The only apparent difference is in income, because workers with more formal education enter the labor force at higher levels and change jobs more often.

Berg also found no relation between formal education and success in the military or the civil service. In one highly demanding occupation (air controller) for which the Federal Aviation Administration was forced to train its own employees quickly, no difference in performance was found between high school and college graduates. And, interestingly enough, the demand that teachers have undergraduate and even graduate degrees is associated with high turnover and departure from the profession. Thus Berg and others suggest that formal education is mostly a means of assigning credentials that control the supply of labor, and thus access to jobs and income. Given the close relationship between class and the acquisition of educational credentials, the American system of education is thus, as much as anything else, a way of transmitting class position from one generation to the next.

The suspicion that formal education has little economic significance (in a conventional positive sense) is corroborated by Randall Collins' sophisticated and intensive analysis of this overall question. Reviewing the literature and the data on the increased schooling required for employment in the

---

[33]Ivar Berg, assisted by Sherry Gorelick, *Education and Jobs: The Great Training Robbery* (New York: Praeger, 1970).

United States, Collins found that education is better understood as a status-conferring process by means of which dominant groups seek to control occupations by imposing irrelevant cultural requirements than as a reflection of the greater skills needed on the job due to technological change.[34]

But what about class mobility? Do not significant numbers of young people climb the economic ladder after having climbed the ladder of education? Of course, but mobility (or the lack of it) looks quite different if one thinks of it as a function of economic, political, or military need (structural mobility) rather than as a result of education and personal ability (equal opportunity mobility). At great psychic cost, the United States compels all youngsters in the lower classes to compete for a relatively small number of vacancies in the classes above them. The conclusion that should be drawn is that education is among other things a way of controlling the supply of labor, without acknowledging that this is being done, and of incorporating youth—those who fail as well as those who succeed—into American society. And education performs these functions without presenting a challenge to the principle of class (the ideology of nonegalitarian classlessness) or to the incumbents of favored class levels.

School achievement does lead to higher occupations and income. But one need only look at the difference between one to three years of college and four years to realize that employers honor credentials, not knowledge. (See Table 8–1.)

The process by which families perpetuate themselves at given class levels can be better understood if we remember that parents' class position is a heavy determinant of children's performance in school. Parents at the upper levels of the class system provide their children with the motives and skills that ensure academic success. In turn, success in school means high income and occupation, and thus high class position, a process that is then recapitulated in the next generation. At lower class levels, parents provide their children with lower levels of academically relevant interests and skills, and fewer opportunities for personal enrichment, all of which is reflected in a lower level of school performance. In turn, poorer school performance leads to poorer jobs and lower income. Since job markets are increasingly controlled by educational credentials, here again class achievement is tightly circumscribed by class ascription. Of the many functions of American educa-

---

[34]Randall Collins, *The Credential Society* (New York: Academic Press, 1979). It also appears that the high-quality colleges have relatively little impact on the future occupations of their students, since the type of student they recruit more adequately explains future success. See Duane F. Alwin, "College Effects on Educational and Occupational Attainment," *American Sociological Review* 39 (April 1974):210–223.

For the lack of positive results from professional programs for doctors, lawyers, and business executives, see Andrew Hacker, "The Shame of Professional Schools," *Harper's* 263 (October 1981):22–28. For the way in which the distribution of jobs and income is best explained by economic and political forces, see the section "Power Over the Labor Market" in Chapter 6.

tion, the legitimation of this process of inheritance is surely one of the least understood.

EDUCATION AND CITIZENSHIP

In the nineteenth century, Americans believed that education in a common school could provide moral and intellectual cement to bind the nation together. Children would acquire a shared outlook and spirit, it was thought, by growing up together under adult supervision. The common curriculum in the common school was no doubt inspired by, or at least congruent with, the social experience of most Americans in the early nineteenth century. Most Americans shared the experience and values of Protestantism, Newtonian cosmology, farming, and small-town life, which no doubt made it natural for them to think in terms of a common school. Later, the common school was also seen as a corrective to the increased diversity brought about by urbanization and immigration. Even when the school was diversified at the high school level, there persisted the faith (among whom and how strongly is difficult to say) that educational homogenization was gradually taking place and/or that ever higher levels of education were good for society.

A century and a quarter after the advent of mass public education, Americans are probably no more united by common values and beliefs acquired through education than they were before public education. The public also displays ignorance about a large range of public matters as well as a lack of interest in politics.

Why Americans persist in thinking of education as a mechanism for promoting social integration through homogeneity cannot be explained with precision. Whatever its source, however, the ideology of homogeneity in education (equality of opportunity, objective-national norms, professional standards, accreditation, national programs) helps to conceal an unfair contest for social position. In fact, beneath the rhetoric of homogeneity and universalism, American society has created wide diversification: It has diversified its high school system so that even students who attend the same school receive different educations; it has created a highly diversified hierarchy of colleges, universities, and junior colleges; it has diversified its entire elementary and high school systems by class, as a result of residential segregation and the tradition of the neighborhood school; and it has taken class diversification one step further to create severe racial isolation in all parts of the nation. But educational diversification disguised by the rhetoric of equality and competition serves important latent functions. The truth of the matter is that the American educational nonsystem does create social stability, but in a manner extremely incongruous with normative ideology: The class-based tracking system protects those with power and legitimates the failure of those without power.

TABLE 8-1. Total Annual Money Income of Males, 25 Years Old and Over, By Years of School Completed, United States, 1982

SEX, INCOME, AND AGE	TOTAL	ELEMENTARY SCHOOL			YEAR OF SCHOOL COMPLETED								MEDIAN SCHOOL YEARS COMPLETED
					HIGH SCHOOL			COLLEGE					
			LESS THAN 8	8						4 OR MORE			
		TOTAL			TOTAL	1 TO 3	4	TOTAL	1 TO 3	TOTAL	4	5 OR MORE	
1	2	3	4	5	6	7	8	9	10	11	12	13	14
					NUMBER, IN THOUSANDS								
Men:													
Total 25 and over	65,004	9,853	5,505	4,348	29,915	7,867	22,048	25,236	10,310	14,925	7,930	6,996	12.7
With income	63,725	9,546	5,297	4,249	29,182	7,592	21,590	24,997	10,170	14,827	7,871	6,956	12.7

Table 8-1, continued.

PERCENTAGE DISTRIBUTION OF MEN WITH INCOME

Total	100.0	100.0	100.0	100.0	100.0	100.0	100.0	100.0	100.0	100.0	100.0	100.0	—
$1 to $1,999 or loss	3.7	4.7	5.2	4.2	4.0	5.5	3.5	2.9	3.4	2.5	2.8	2.1	12.4
$2,000 to $2,999	1.8	4.4	5.5	3.1	1.8	2.4	1.5	0.8	1.1	0.7	0.7	0.6	11.5
$3,000 to $3,999	2.8	8.6	11.1	5.5	2.4	3.5	2.0	1.1	1.5	0.8	0.7	0.9	9.8
$4,000 to 4,999	2.9	8.5	10.2	6.4	2.5	4.0	1.9	1.3	1.6	1.1	1.2	1.0	10.1
$5,000 to 5,999	3.5	8.8	9.6	7.9	3.4	5.0	2.8	1.5	1.9	1.2	1.3	1.1	11.1
$6,000 to $6,999	3.4	7.4	7.0	7.8	3.6	5.7	2.9	1.6	2.2	1.1	1.2	1.1	11.6
$7,000 to $8,499	5.0	10.6	10.4	10.8	5.4	7.7	4.5	2.5	3.1	2.2	2.2	2.1	12.0
$8,500 to $9,999	4.2	7.0	7.4	6.4	4.7	6.2	4.2	2.6	3.3	2.2	2.6	1.7	12.2
$10,000 to $12,499	9.3	13.0	12.5	13.6	10.7	12.0	10.3	6.3	9.1	4.4	5.0	3.7	12.4
$12,500 to $14,999	7.1	6.7	6.3	7.2	8.5	9.3	8.3	5.7	7.1	4.8	5.4	4.0	12.5
$15,000 to $17,499	8.1	5.9	5.1	6.9	9.7	9.0	9.9	7.2	8.6	6.2	7.4	4.8	12.6
$17,500 to 19,999	6.4	3.4	2.6	4.3	7.3	5.8	7.8	6.5	7.3	5.9	6.4	5.4	12.8
$20,000 to $24,999	12.7	5.4	3.6	7.7	13.8	11.3	14.7	14.2	15.9	13.1	14.0	12.1	12.8
$25,000 to $29,999	9.6	2.9	1.9	4.1	9.7	6.4	10.8	12.0	12.6	11.6	11.6	11.7	13.0
30,000 to $34,999	6.6	1.4	1.0	1.9	5.9	3.2	6.9	9.5	9.0	9.8	9.6	10.1	13.8
$35,000 to $49,999	7.9	1.0	0.6	1.5	5.1	2.5	6.0	13.7	8.9	17.0	16.1	18.0	16.0
$50,000 to $74,999	3.3	0.3	0.1	0.4	1.1	0.4	1.4	7.0	2.7	9.9	8.7	11.3	16.6
$75,000 and over	1.6	0.1	0.1	0.1	0.4	0.2	0.5	3.6	0.9	5.5	3.2	8.1	17+

Source: U.S. Department of Education, *Digest of Educational Statistics* (Washington, D.C.: U.S. Government Printing Office, 1986), Table 178.

KNEE-JERK FORMALISM: THE EDUCATIONAL REPORTS OF THE 1980s

The United States experienced a number of setbacks from the 1960s on: defeat in Vietnam, political scandals, relative loss of power on the international scene, sluggish economic growth, stagnant living standards, and chronic deficits in both domestic and foreign accounts. Instead of focusing on its economic and political institutions and its elites as the cause of its problems, the United States (actually its leaders) seem to place most of the blame on education. Certainly they looked to education as the way to solve our economic, political, and social failures. Starting in 1983 and running through 1987, over a dozen national reports on lower and higher education appeared. Every report accepted blame for social failures on behalf of education, and, ignoring over fifty years of research, every report acted as if education could reform and thus improve American society.

The various commission reports all dealt with secondary problems, thus their proposed solutions were wide of the mark. Research has established that the best way to improve the functioning of American schools is to stabilize the homes from which students who do not do well come from. Beyond this, the critics of American schools have failed to identify the real problem—our elite high schools and colleges, which cannot show that they are producing better citizens or better professionals and leaders. And yet the heart of the commission reports stressed doing more of the same.

The surge of concern about education starting in 1983 has produced many proposals to strengthen academic programs. But the sociology of education prevents optimism. The large sums of money that are needed will not be forthcoming unless national priorities are reordered at the federal level. Unless drastic changes are made, large segments of the working and lower classes will continue to flounder in middle-class schools. Above all, schools will continue to avoid political controversy and teach a consensus curriculum that favors the status quo. Bland, biased school texts will continue to be used. And the apolitical, politically conservative emphasis on abstract reading and writing skills will continue. Even if reform succeeds, the only result will be better scores on life-removed subjects and skills.

The fewest changes will take place where they are needed most—in our elite high schools and colleges. Abstract liberal arts will continue to dominate the curriculum and narrow and ineffective specialization will dominate the curriculum of graduate and professional schools. Since few realize that there is even a problem, there is little hope that American elites will give up the irrelevant education that favors them and their offspring. More science and mathematics will be taught but little will be said about the purposes of science or the threat to the environment posed by technology. Little will be said about the failure of economics to provide a better way to handle our economy. No realistic analysis of our stalemated political system will be forthcoming.[35]

CLASS AND EDUCATION: A SUMMARY

As the evidence amply demonstrates, class exerts a heavy influence, even control, over all aspects of education. Class is related strongly and directly to the amount of money spent per pupil; educational aspirations; IQ, grades, prizes, diplomas, and degrees; rate of attendance and years of school completed; choice of school and program of study; income and occupation; and success in school without superior academic achievement.

Academic education does not seem to be related to occupational performance, and it does not produce social integration by developing homogeneous citizens.

The main (latent) function of education appears to be control of the flow of woman- and manpower into the economy; or, more exactly, its main function appears to be to insure that the elite occupations are not oversupplied with qualified people. Academic education, in short, is primarily a means of maintaining and transmitting the existing class structure. But since it is not genuinely related to economic performance, academic education is really a prestige phenomenon masquerading as a personal achievement process, thus concealing the fact that entry into the valued levels of American society is primarily due to class birth. In addition, education serves as a convenient scapegoat for the power groups whose mistakes are the cause of social problems.

Our definition of social class to this point can be stated thus: The American population is composed of a hierarchy of families and unrelated individuals separated into levels on the basis of worth in various economic markets. Different levels are characterized by significant differences in family values and stability, life expectancy, and mental health, and by pronounced differences in the ability to put children through school successfully, an overall structure and process that tends to produce a static class system over time (as measured by the distribution of the above class values) and a considerable amount of class perpetuation (ascriptively based achievement and nonachievement).

So far we have paid only occasional attention to minorities. We now turn to an analysis of the class position of America's minorities.

---

[35]For a more detailed indictment of the higher education reports, see Daniel W. Rossides, "Knee-Jerk Formalism: The Higher Education Reports," *The Journal of Higher Education* 58, no. 4 (July/August 1987):404–429.

CHAPTER 9

The Class Position of America's Minorities

The term *minority* was first used in the peace treaties of World War I to refer to ethnic groups in Eastern Europe that needed protection against dominant ethnic groups. Today the term refers to a wide variety of groups and aggregates that want a change in power relations: ethnic, racial, and religious groups as well as such aggregates as women, the aged, youth, the handicapped, the overweight, and those with different life-styles, especially homosexuals (who prefer to be called gays).

ETHNICITY AND RACE IN COMPARATIVE PERSPECTIVE

Science tells us that human beings have the same mental and moral capacity regardless of skin color, sex, or other physical features. The fact that all must learn to behave is of the greatest importance in establishing human equality. Most observable differences among human beings are due to *what* they experience (learn), and differences become pronounced if human beings in different cultures are compared.

In the great agrarian empires of the past, different ethnic groups lived together as separate societies within a larger imperial whole. The relations of these groups were sometimes peaceful, sometimes turbulent, but there was no effort to mingle or assimilate the various ethnic or racial groups in a greater whole. All this was changed by the rise of capitalism. The dynamic capitalist economy moves people around to suit the needs of commerce and industry, and this tends to bring ethnic groups into contact with each other. The capitalist economy is powered by cheap labor, and capitalist societies import labor often diversifying their ethnic and racial makeup. The United States imported a large number of slaves to toil on the cash-crop plantations of the American South. It imported 40 million immigrants during the nineteenth century to work in its cities and factories. Also important in the development of the United States is the wide use of female labor outside the home. One consequence of all this was the emergence of themes of ethnic, racial, and sexual inequality. Often these themes took on the force of law and well-established practice.

Capitalism also had a counter current. As it developed in England, France, and the United States, it declared all people eligible for participation in the main benefits and positions in society. The rising middle classes argued that all human beings had the right and the duty to develop their brains, morals, and tastes. This could best be done by participating in a free and rational division of labor. In keeping with this argument, capitalist society transformed its members into a legally free, all-purpose labor force (possessive individualism, or the doctrine that individuals own themselves and are free to work for themselves or sell their labor to others). All this runs counter to racial and ethnic beliefs and practices that keep people ignorant, idle, and apart.

The clash of these two traditions is the heart of America's majority-minority relations. To state the conflict concretely: Early (entrepreneurial) capitalism developed racist-ethnic-sexist norms and values to justify the cheap labor it needed, but it also established values declaring all humans eligible for full membership and participation in the life of society. When beliefs that ethnic newcomers, nonwhites, females, and others were innately inferior crumbled in the face of experience and science, and when economic need required a more fluid, flexible (efficient) use of labor, a later (corporate) capitalism changed the legal and political statuses of minorities in an effort to create an abstract labor force, that is, a labor force made up of all members of society.

ETHNIC AND RACIAL MINORITIES IN THE UNITED STATES

The United States has had a continuous wave of newcomers from different ethnic and racial backgrounds.[1] Though some came willingly and others by force, newcomers were largely thought of and treated as inferiors. Over time,

---

[1] For a comprehensive reference book with good thematic essays on American ethnic and racial groups, see Stephen Thernstrom, ed., *Harvard Encyclopedia of American Ethnic Groups* (Cambridge, Mass.: Harvard University Press, 1980).

some newcomers managed to attain full membership in American society. By and large, Roman Catholics (from Europe and Canada but not Latin America) have been culturally assimilated (though not in terms of associational patterns) and are well represented at all income, occupational, and educational levels. Roman Catholics from Spanish-speaking countries (with the exception of Cubans), however, are still minorities and differ markedly from mainstream Americans on all counts. Greek-Americans have also assimilated and can no longer be considered a minority. Japanese, Chinese, and Jewish Americans have enjoyed notable success in educational and occupational achievement but are still minorities in some important respects.

The groups that have fared the worst are racial groups. Race, as such, has no scientific standing since no causal relation between behavior and skin color (or hair texture, eyelids, or other such physical attributes) has ever been established. But to its enduring shame, white America has been openly racist in its treatment of all nonwhites and, at one time or another, has made black Americans, native American Indians, Hawaiians, Aleutians, Chinese, Japanese, and Filipinos into distinctly depressed racial minorities.[2]

ETHNIC AND RACIAL DEMOGRAPHICS

Minority groups vary considerably in size (see Table 9–1). Black Americans are the largest minority group, forming 11 percent of the total population. Latin or Hispanics, most of whom are Mexican American, are the next largest. Excluding Jewish Americans, approximately 17 percent of the American population is made up of deeply disadvantaged minorities. Ethnic and racial minorities are younger than dominant groups. Their birthrates are higher and they have a shorter life expectancy than majority Americans. And they have a higher dependency ratio (the number of those not likely to work in relation to those that are).

MAJORITY MALES VERSUS ALL OTHERS

The federal government did not collect meaningful and useful data about American minorities until well after World War II. Its growth in data-gathering capability about minorities was climaxed by the 1978 publication of the United States Commission on Civil Rights, *Social Indicators of Equality*

---

[2]Prentice-Hall's Ethnic Groups in American Life Series, edited by Milton M. Gordon, provides excellent case studies of major ethnic and racial minorities, including a study of white Protestant Americans. Harry H. L. Kitano and Roger Daniels, *Asian Americans: Emerging Minorities* (Englewood Cliffs, N.J.: Prentice-Hall, 1988) updates our picture of Chinese and Japanese Americans and provides a valuable picture of other Asian Americans as well as Pacific Islanders.

TABLE 9-1. Racial and Cultural Minorities in the United
            States

Total American Population	245,807,000 (1988)
Blacks	28,802,000
Hispanic Origin (Total)	19,431,000 (1988)
Mexican	12,110,000
Puerto Rican	2,471,000
Cuban	1,035,000
Central or South American	2,242,000
Other Hispanic	1,573,000
Jews	5,814,000 1986 est.
Native Americans	800,000 est.
Asian Americans (Total)	5,147,900 1985 est.
Chinese	1,079,400
Filipino	1,051,600
Japanese	766,300
Vietnamese	634,200
Korean	543,400
Asian Indian	525,600
Laotian	218,400
Kampuchean	160,800
All other	169,200
Pacific Islanders (Total)	259,566 (1985)

Source: *Statistical Abstract of the United States, 1989* (Washington, D.C.: U.S. Government Printing Office, 1988), Tables 5,
78; U.S. Bureau of the Census, *Current Population Reports*, Series P-20, no. 431; "The Hispanic Population in the United
States, March 1988" (Washington, D.C.: U.S. Government Printing Office, 1988), Table A; and Robert W. Gardner, Bryant Ro-
bey, and Peter C. Smith, "Asian Americans: Growth, Change,
and Diversity," *Population Bulletin* 40, no. 4 (October 1985), Table 1.

for Minorities and Women.[3] The commission's report is particularly valuable
because it contains data on both large and small minorities: women, blacks,
American Indians, Alaskan natives, Mexican Americans, Japanese Americans, Chinese Americans, Filipino Americans, and Puerto Ricans.

The commission addresses the following concerns of minorities and
women:

1. underdevelopment of human skills through delayed enrollment, nonenroll-
   ment in secondary education, and nonparticipation in higher education;
2. lack of equivalent returns for educational achievement in terms of occupational
   opportunities and earnings;

[3]United States Civil Rights Commission, Washington, D.C. 20425.

3. discrepancies in access to jobs, particularly those having greater-than-average stability, prestige, and monetary returns;
4. inequality of income, relatively lower earnings for equal work, and diminished chances for salary and wage increases;
5. a high likelihood of being in poverty;
6. a proportionately higher expenditure for housing, less desirable housing conditions, restricted freedom of choice in selecting locations in which to live, and greater difficulty in attaining homeownership.[4]

The thrust of its analysis is to establish equality ratios between majority males and minorities over time. Assembling data from 1960, 1970, and 1976, the Commission's findings are clear and unequivocal—minorities and women are grossly unequal (even when achievement is held constant!) in twenty-one measures in the above areas. Even more important, their position has not improved since 1960, and in some areas has not even kept pace with majority males!

BLACK AMERICANS

The class position (income, occupation, education) of black Americans changed dramatically for the better between the late nineteenth century and the 1950s as a result of migration from southern farms to northern and western cities.[5] Thanks largely to technological displacement from agriculture, a burgeoning industrial economy, and wartime labor shortages, the black American also made class gains relative to whites during this period. Most of these gains came from the quickened economic pace and subsequent boom produced by World War II. Between 1939 and 1954, black median annual income jumped from 37 to 56 percent of white income. The movement out of agriculture and into the lower reaches of the urban industrial labor force also represented a significant upgrading of occupational status for black Americans. And gains both absolute and relative were made in education.

The 1950s on tell a different story. Despite the greatest and longest period of prosperity in American history, the economic status of black

[4]*Social Indicators of Equality for Minorities and Women 1978*, p. 3. The commission notes that a lack of data prevents it from inquiring into such areas as the working order of housing facilities, criminal victimization, health service utilization, and hidden unemployment.

[5]Good general sources of information about black Americans are W. Augustus Low and Vergil A. Clift, eds., *Encyclopedia of Black America* (New York: McGraw-Hill, 1981), the National Urban League's annual report *The State of Black America*, and the U.S. Bureau of the Census, *Current Population Reports*, "The Social and Economic Status of the Black Population in the United States, 1970–1978," Series P- 23, no. 80 (Washington, D.C.: U.S. Government Printing Office, 1979). Two books with background on the class position of blacks, which also include a refreshing emphasis on policy analysis, are Harrell R. Rodger, Jr., ed., *Racism and Inequality: The Policy Alternatives* (San Francisco: W. H. Freeman, 1975) and Douglas G. Glascow, *The Black Underclass: Poverty, Unemployment, and Entrapment of Ghetto Youth* (San Francisco: Jossey-Bass, 1980).

Americans grew more slowly after the 1950s and in some ways stagnated and even worsened. Though blacks made steady gains, their gains came mostly from continued migration out of agriculture, the Vietnam War, and because black families tend to have multiple wage earners more often than whites. Thus, black *family* income improved during the 1960s and 1970s in relation to white family income. But the economic slowdown of the 1970s and the recession of the early 1980s hit blacks harder than whites and black gains have receded. The same period saw a large increase in one-parent black families, and black poverty levels today are higher than they were in the 1960s. In addition, while the percentage of well-to-do black households has increased, so has the gap between white and black median income.

Black employment status has also remained highly unequal to that of whites. Black unemployment has been double that of whites for the entire postwar period (regardless of education or occupation). Among black teenagers, unemployment is chronically of crisis proportions and more than twice the rate for white teenagers. Despite gains, blacks are still heavily underrepresented in top occupations. Whether blacks can consolidate and extend their small relative gains remains to be seen.

By and large, black gains in occupational status reflect structural changes in the American economy. The rise in the overall economic status of blacks (and whites) is largely due to the drastic displacement of agriculture from the center of the American economy and the emergence of a manufacturing and white-collar economy. Situated in marginal occupations, and thus subject to technological change and cutbacks during recessions, black Americans are displaced more often than whites, which goes far toward explaining their higher level of unemployment. However, they also find jobs at higher skill levels, thus their occupational upgrading, however slow. All in all, black Americans have not made any breakthrough into the white-collar ranks despite their presence in the urban-industrial scene for at least two generations. Not only are they heavily overrepresented in blue-collar occupations but perhaps chronically so. A closer look at white-collar data also reveals that black Americans are concentrated at the lower reaches of the white-collar world, especially with regard to managerial positions, and they tend to practice their professions in a segregated context. Among blue-collar workers, black Americans are highly underrepresented in elite trade unions and have had little success in expanding their representation. And in recent years blacks have faced considerable competition from the influx of white women into the labor force.

Empirical studies confirm the difficulties that black males have had in recent years. Ernest R. House and William Madura argue that structural changes in the economy have been especially harmful to black males and the major cause of their plight (they also cite competition from women). Marshal Pomer found little upward mobility among prime-age men (white or black) in low-paying occupations from 1962 to 1973, a period of economic expansion. But black mobility was far less than white mobility, and black males who advanced did not go nearly as far as did whites.[6] And Daniel Lichter found that while underemployment (a more important indicator of economic status than unemployment alone) increased among both white and black urban males between 1970 and 1982, black underemployment increased far more.[7]

In an important study of wealth, the Census Bureau found a surprisingly large disparity of 10 to 1 in the holdings of white households compared to black. Not only do blacks find it hard to save, but the absence of assets means psychological insecurity and, of course, lack of economic power.[8]

In education, black Americans have made significant absolute and relative gains against formidable odds. These gains extend to higher education, even though the overall ratio of black and white college graduates has remained stationary—black absolute increases being offset by white increases. It is significant that a majority of black college students are now enrolled in predominantly white institutions. However, black gains in higher education peaked in the 1970s, and since 1976 there has been an ominous decline in black male college attendance. By 1986, 60 percent of blacks in higher education were women, and experts say that the decline among black males has continued. The reason is tuition costs and the distorting, dangerous, deviant world that many black males are forced to grow up in.[9] And in any case, education does not benefit blacks in the same way it does whites. Black unemployment remains higher than white regardless of occupation (and, by implication, regardless of education), and black income is lower regardless of occupation.

One of the reasons why blacks in the aggregate have not been able to make significant class gains is the extent of black poverty. Not only does a much higher percentage of the black population live in poverty as opposed to whites, but a higher percentage of poor blacks are children under eighteen, and a higher percentage of black children are growing up in single-parent families headed by females. Ominously, the number of female-headed black families with children under eighteen has continued to grow, and the percentage of female-headed families with children under eighteen increased significantly between 1960 and the 1980s.

[6]Ernest R. House and William Madura, "Race, Gender, and Jobs: Losing Ground on Employment", *Policy Sciences* 21 (1988):351–382; Marshall J. Pomer, "Labor Market Structure, Intragenerational Mobility, and Discrimination: Black Male Advancement Out of Low-Paying Occupations, 1962–1973," *American Sociological Review* 51 (October 1986): 650–659.

[7]Daniel T. Lichter, "Racial Differences in Underemployment in American Cities," *American Journal of Sociology* 93 (January 1988): 771–792.

[8]U. S. Census Bureau, Current Population Reports, Series P-70, no. 7, "Household Wealth and Asset Ownership: 1984" (Washington, D.C.: U.S. Government Printing Office, 1986), Table G.

[9]Lee A. Daniels, "Ranks of Black Men Shrink on U.S. Campuses," *The New York Times*, February 5, 1989, p. 1.

Black families are significantly less stable than majority families:

1. Black males are more passive at home than whites and share tasks less with their wives.
2. The male is absent more in black homes than in white homes.
3. There is deeper estrangement between the sexes both before and after marriage among blacks than among whites.
4. Lower income and greater size place greater financial strains on the black family.
5. Rates of family disruption due to desertion, separation, divorce, and death are much higher among blacks than among whites.[10]

All these data are characterized by marked variations by class. Black family life ranges from matriarchal-extended forms among poor blacks in both rural and urban areas to the nuclear family among working- and middle-class blacks.[11] While much attention has been given to the pathology of the lower-class black family, the adaptive mechanisms developed by blacks to cope with a hostile social environment have been neglected. Given the harsh reality of slavery and segregation, migration and economic marginality, it is not surprising that the black family has experienced severe instability and malfunctioning. The industrial nuclear family needs considerable support: steady employment for the breadwinner(s); a congenial neighborhood of stable families; a compatible, supportive school system, and so on. All these supports were denied large portions of the black population as it struggled to overcome the legacy of slavery and segregation.

Black family instability occurs even when class is held constant. While both white and black marriages become more stable with a rise in class position (education, occupation, income), black marriage disruption rates are uniformly far higher than those for white marriages at all class levels. (Black and white rates are parallel for occupation, converge slightly with increased education, and diverge more than slightly with increased income).[12] Today, and at an increasing rate, there is a far larger percentage of female-headed families among blacks (47 percent) than among majority families (13.9 per-

[10]For an excellent collection of readings on the black male, see Doris Y. Wilkinson and Ronald L. Taylor, eds., *The Black Male in America* (Chicago: Nelson-Hall, 1977).

[11]For a wide-ranging theoretical and historical analysis of the black family, see Andrew Billingsley, assisted by Amy Tate Billingsley, *Black Families in White America* (Englewood Cliffs, N.J.: Prentice-Hall, 1968). For a comprehensive contemporary picture, see Robert Staples, ed., *The Black Family*, 3rd ed. (Belmont, Calif.: Wadsworth, 1986).

[12]J. Richard Udry, "Marital Instability by Race, Sex, Education, and Occupation Using 1960 Census Data," *American Journal of Sociology* 72, no.2 (September 1966): 203–209, and "Marital Instability by Race and Income Based on 1960 Census Data," *American Journal of Sociology*. 72, no 6 (May 1967): 673–674; reprinted as one essay in Charles V. Willie, ed., *The Family Life of Black People* (Columbus, Ohio: Charles E. Merrill, 1970), pp. 143–155. For current divorce and separation rates, see U.S. Bureau of the Census, *Statistical Abstract of the United States, 1982–83* (Washington, D.C.: U.S. Government Printing Office, 1982), Tables 50, 51.

cent), which also means a large and growing number of black children growing up in marginal one-parent homes.[13]

Poverty is associated with greater health problems, and blacks, because they are disproportionately poor, have serious health problems. Despite these problems, they also have less health care than Americans above them in wealth and income and much less than they need.[14] Higher black infant mortality rates and other health problems are well known. But perhaps the most telling statistic is that black Americans live six years less than white Americans and that black males did not reach an average life expectancy of sixty-five until 1985 (approximately fifty years after the passage of the Social Security Act, which set retirement at sixty-five).

Black Americans, who make up about 11 percent of the American population, account for about 30 percent of arrests and 34 percent of all prison inmates. But black crime rates are identical to white *once class is held constant.*[15] Blacks are also mistreated by law enforcement groups: They are punished more severely than whites for similar crimes and are more likely to be executed. Blacks are mistreated by the police and black neighborhoods are subject to open, heavy patrol. But again it is probably best to think in terms of class rather than race—law enforcement agencies deal illegally and harshly, and are more openly antagonistic to all members of the lower classes regardless of race, religion, or ethnicity.

Blacks' prospects for improving their overall position in American society can also be analyzed in terms of the strengths and weaknesses of the black middle class. The black professional-managerial class has been and continues to be small relative to whites. Within it there is a lopsided emphasis on medicine, law, the ministry, and teaching, at the expense of business administration and the natural sciences. The situation is similar with regard to black business people: They are few in number relative to whites and their number has been shrinking as desegregation has undermined their protected markets. And within black business there is a significant pattern of specialization in small business. Of the few black-owned businesses, most tend to be eating and drinking establishments, grocery stores, personal services (barbershops, beauty salons), and insurance companies.[16]

The American systems of racial and class stratification have produced

[13]U. S. Department of Commerce, *Statistical Abstract of the United States: 1982–83* (Washington, D.C.: U. S. Government Printing Office, 1982), Table 73.

[14]For background, see John C. Norman, ed., *Medicine in the Ghetto* (New York: Appleton-Century-Crofts, 1969) and Harold S. Luft, *Poverty and Health: Economic Causes and Consequences of Health Problems.* (Cambridge, Mass.: Ballinger, 1978).

[15]Edward Green, "Race, Social Status, and Criminal Arrest," *American Sociological Review* 35 (June 1970): 476–490.

[16]Andrew F. Brimmer, "The Negro in the National Economy," in John F. Kain, ed., *Race and Poverty: The Economics of Discrimination* (Englewood Cliffs, N.J.: Prentice-Hall, 1969), pp. 88–89. For current data showing that the vast majority of black businesses are firms without paid employees, see the *Statistical Abstract of the United States, 1982–83*, Table 882.

what appears to be a deeply institutionalized pattern of inequality for black Americans. Improvement in blacks' legal status, income, occupation, and education since their migration to the North are best interpreted as a change in position from bottom "racial caste" to the bottom levels of class society. Of course, their concurrent rise in absolute social benefits, especially since World War II, is real and has no doubt eased the physical hardships of many black Americans. But the *relative* position of blacks in American society has not changed. When blacks and whites are compared in the aggregate, blacks are still concentrated at the bottom of every index used to measure the benefits of American life.

The reforms of recent years do not appear to have produced much change in blacks' overall position. *In other words, black gains (with some minor exceptions) are offset by corresponding white gains.* Without attributing any conscious design to the overall process that has transformed blacks from a rural to an urban labor group, we must acknowledge that the result has not been the gradual integration of blacks into white society. (We are defining *integration* to mean the random distribution of black Americans throughout the occupational, income, educational, residential,[17] and associational structures of the country, in effect producing a salt-and-pepper society.) The history of blacks since the Civil War—including the reforms of recent years—is best seen as the incorporation of a black (and white) rural labor force into the lower reaches of an urban-industrial system.

Black Americans are not predominantly situated in the lower class, although they make up a disproportionate percentage of that class. The large majority of blacks are members of fairly stable working-class families. But the improvement in blacks' class position should not be misinterpreted: Black entry into skilled occupations has been very slow; the black middle class (defined in terms of the income of one earner) is still small and vulnerable; and black income and employment rates are distinctly lower than white rates, regardless of education.[18] And given their economic weakness, even

[17]Nancy A. Denton and Douglas S. Massey, in their "Residential Segregation of Blacks, Hispanics, and Asians By Socioeconomic Status and Generation," *Social Science Quarterly* 69 (December 1988): 797–817, argue that blacks are still heavily segregated residentially through all socioeconomic levels and that they are the only minority that has been unable to integrate with a rise in class status. Marta Tienda and Ding-Tzann Lii, in their "Minority Concentration and Earnings Inequality: Blacks, Hispanics, and Asians Compared," *American Journal of Sociology* 93 (July 1987): 141–165, argue that the three minorities they studied all suffered earnings losses because of residential and labor market concentration, but blacks, and especially college-educated blacks, suffered the greatest losses (thus benefiting white college graduates).

[18]For an analysis of black family income that finds no change between 1960 and 1982 and continuing income and occupational inequalities at all levels and regardless of education, see Henry E. Felder, *The Changing Patterns of Black Family Income, 1960–1982* (Washington, D.C.: Joint Center for Political Studies, 1984). For an analysis that sees mixed results in black progress, see Reynolds Farley, *Blacks and Whites: Narrowing the Gap?* (Cambridge, Mass.: Harvard University Press, 1984). Farley's conclusion that blacks have made progress would have been more negative had he clearly distinguished between absolute and relative benefits, not relied on misleading Census Bureau categories, and not overestimated the importance of education.

black gains are not secure. Many black advances, including entry into the middle class, are due to public employment and public service programs. The Reagan administration's cutbacks in public services hit blacks especially hard.[19] Given the recession between 1979 and 1983 and the cutbacks in public services and employment, blacks are now as far behind whites as they were in the 1950s.[20]

During the 1960s the persistence of black poverty gave rise to the "culture of poverty" explanation. Blacks were poor, said this theory, because once the middle and working classes left the city, the way of life (culture) of poor blacks led to assorted forms of pathology and failure. Essentially, black traits, perhaps those brought to the North from sharecropper experience in the South, were to blame for black poverty and immobility. This theory is still strong and should be resisted because it blames the victim rather than structural forces and the actions of power groups. The economy moved out of the older industrial cities during the 1960s and 1970s aided and abetted by public policies (taxes, highways, FHA mortgages). Given this process, cities were emptied of working-class and middle-class families, leaving the poor behind. Poor blacks no longer had role models on how to behave and aspire and, perhaps more important, they had no local job or other opportunities. By the 1980s, large portions of the American population (white and black) had been disconnected from the mainstream economy by structural forces in the economy and polity.[21]

THE DECLINING SIGNIFICANCE OF RACE?

William Julius Wilson has argued that race has given way to class as the major determinant of the life chances of blacks. The United States, argues Wilson, has gone through three stages of race relations: the plantation economy of racial-caste oppression in the pre–Civil War South; the period of industrial expansion, class conflict, and racial oppression between 1875 and the 1930s; and the period of progressive transition from race inequalities to class inequalities after 1945. Race relations, says Wilson, have been shaped by the systems of production characteristic of each period and by the laws and policies of the state.

---

[19] Sharon M. Collins, "The Making of the Black Middle Class," *Social Problems* 30 (April 1983): 369–382.

[20] For a full-length treatment of the black middle class, which agrees largely with the above (but which defines the black middle class as households that include white-collar workers, firefighters, police officers, and which therefore has a rosier picture of black success), see Bart Landry, *The New Black Middle Class* (Berkeley: University of California Press, 1987).

[21] For a structural explanation of the underclass (the routine operations of capitalist investment aided by government) as opposed to racial discrimination or the characteristics of blacks, see William Julius Wilson, *The Truly Disadvantaged: The Inner City, The Underclass, and Public Policy* (Chicago: University of Chicago Press, 1987).

Today, says Wilson, blacks are more differentiated and somewhat resemble the white class structure. Young educated blacks, especially males, are entering the middle classes at rates exceeding those of whites. Blacks are going to college in huge numbers, their percent of college students even exceeding their percent of the population (and most are going to white colleges). But, says Wilson, there is a huge black underclass that is subject to "class subordination" and unable to enter the American mainstream. The dislocations of the modern industrial society affect many whites and other minorities as well. What are needed, Wilson concludes, are broad public policy programs to attack inequality on a broad class front.

Charles V. Willie has criticized Wilson for using social class theory, a theory preferred by the affluent because they can argue that poverty is a function of individual capacities, not institutions. But after this promising beginning, Willie argues that blacks have not progressed as far as Wilson claims and that the reason is still discrimination by race (and sex). Black income, education, occupational status, and residence are still far less satisfactory than whites, show no great improvement, and still lend themselves to racist rather than achievement explanations. And, concludes Willie, the black middle class today is still very much concerned, even obsessed, by race.[22]

Perhaps Wilson and Willie are both wide of the mark. Combining Wilson's focus on class and Willie's realism about race, a conflict sociologist might argue as follows: Wilson's class explanation is on the right track but incomplete. To understand the present position and prospects of black Americans, Wilson must realize that racism has been a function of class interest throughout American history, first as slavery, then as racist segregation and discrimination to favor both the white property and working classes, and now as a theory of equal opportunity and competition through civil rights, busing, and affirmative action. In the present period, blacks are still subordinated by the system of production. The black middle class is very small and has made its gains through employment, not business ownership. And a substantial part of the gains in black employment has been in the public sector. Here again there is status without power—the Reagan administration's cutback on services and its anti-urban policies have hurt the black middle class as well as the black poor. Wilson must be asked, therefore, whether abstract talk about economic growth and the abandonment of concrete policies to help the underclass is really the answer. The corporate

[22]Wilson's argument may be found in William Julius Wilson, *The Declining Significance of Race: Blacks and Changing American Institutions* (Chicago: University of Chicago Press, 1978) and *The Truly Disadvantaged: The Inner City, The Underclass, and Public Policy.* (Chicago: University of Chicago Press, 1987). An exchange between Wilson and Willie may be found in W.J. Wilson, "The Declining Significance of Race," *Society* 15 (January/February 1978):56–62; Charles V. Willie, "The Inclining Significance of Race," *Society* 15 (July/August 1978):10ff.; and W.J. Wilson, "The Declining Significance of Race—Revisited but Not Revised," *Society* 15 (July/August 1978): 11ff. For another argument that racism is more important than class in blocking black progress, see Alphonso Pinkney, *The Myth of Black Progress* (New York: Cambridge University Press, 1984).

capitalist society that he identifies is highly concentrated, generates large amounts of unskilled jobs, and appears inherently unable to achieve full employment. But even economic growth is unlikely to trickle down to those bypassed by mainstream society. If Willie cannot use the overt racism of the pre–World War II era to characterize black-white relations, then neither can Wilson use mainstream optimism and incrementalism.

Class standing measured by wealth, income, occupation, and education is fundamental to other behavior. In an interesting analysis that tends to favor the Willie thesis, Thomas and Hughes argue that black Americans are consistently lower than whites in the general social survey on six items designed to determine psychological well-being and quality of life, discounting class, age, and marital status.[23] As Thomas and Hughes note, the period of 1972 to 1985 may be too short a time for black subjectivity to change and, further, black expectations about what the civil rights movement would accomplish may have been far too high. They conclude that blacks are still aware of real disparities in life chances between them and whites, and their unhappiness may continue until real parity with whites is reached.

MEXICAN AMERICANS

Mexican Americans are the largest ethnic minority in the United States, but reliable data about them have appeared only in recent years.[24] The Census Bureau has also changed its way of counting Mexican Americans, making comparisons over time difficult. Further, Mexicans make up the bulk of the millions of illegal aliens in the United States, thus further clouding our picture of the Mexican-American population.

Mexican Americans make up 62.3 percent or 12.1 million of the 19.4 million Americans of Hispanic descent (see Table 9–1). Their history is unique in a number of ways. Some are from families that have been living in what is now the United States from before the Pilgrims landed at Plymouth Rock. When the United States expanded into the Southwest, the native inhabitants, both Mexicans and Indians, were treated as subject peoples.[25] Mexican

---

[23]Melvin E. Thomas and Michael Hughes, "The Continuing Significance of Race: A Study of Race, Class, and Quality of Life in America, 1972–1985," *American Sociological Review* 51 (December 1986): 830–841.

[24]For a comprehensive summary of what we know, see Joan Moore, with Harry Pachon, *Mexican Americans*, 2nd ed. (Englewood Cliffs, N.J.: Prentice-Hall, 1976). For the latest data on Mexican Americans as well as data on Puerto Rican and Cuban Americans, see Joan Moore and Harry Pachon, *Hispanics in the United States* (Englewood Cliffs, N.J.: Prentice-Hall, 1985).

[25]For a careful, detailed Marxist analysis of the history and sociology of Mexican Americans with valuable comparisons with black Americans, see Mario Barrera, *Race and Class in the Southwest: A Theory of Racial Inequality* (Notre Dame, Indiana: University of Notre Dame Press, 1979).

TABLE 9–2.   Employment Status and Major Occupation Group of the Total and Mexican-American Population: March 1987.

EMPLOYMENT STATUS AND OCCUPATION	TOTAL POPULATION	MEXICAN
Both sexes		
Persons 16 years old and over (thousands)	183 093	7 642
In civilian labor force (thousands)	118 134	5 072
Percent unemployed	7.0	11.7
Employed (thousands)	109 854	4 476
Percent	100.0	100.0
Executive, Administrative, and Managerial Occupations	11.8	5.1
Professional Specialty Occupations	13.3	5.3
Technicians and Related Support	2.9	1.5
Sales Occupations	11.9	7.9
Administrative, Including Clerical	16.5	13.3
Private Household Occupations	0.8	1.4
Service Occupations, Exc Pvt HH	12.7	15.9
Farming, Forestry, and Fishing	2.9	10.0
Precision, Craft and Repair	12.0	15.4
Mach. Oprs. Asmblrs., and Inspectors	7.0	12.1
Transportation and Material Moving	4.1	4.7
Handlers, Equipment Cleaners, Helpers, and Laborers	4.1	7.4

Source: U.S. Bureau of the Census, *Current Population Reports*, Series P-20, no. 434, "The Hispanic Population in the United States: March 1986 and 1987" (Washington, D.C.: U.S. Government Printing Office, 1988), Table 12.

Americans are also unique in that they are the only minority in American history (excepting the American Indian) that failed to make significant economic and other gains from one generation to the other prior to 1950.[26]

Mexican Americans were handicapped by rural isolation and deliberate segregation. They were openly exploited and mistreated by private citizens and law enforcement officials. Government policies have gone against them. And always present was the crushing weight of poverty. Mexican Americans have made gains since 1950, especially in urban areas, but gains have been slow and their income, occupational, and educational levels are still low. Table 9–2. shows the distribution of Mexican Americans in the occupational structure of the United States. Note the difference when compared to the Total Population column. A difference in occupation means a difference in income. But, as Table 9–3 shows, this is not the whole story.

[26]Though the time periods are different, Hawaiians and Puerto Ricans have also been unable to enter mainstream America.

TABLE 9-3. Median Income of Spanish Origin and Not of Spanish Origin By Occupation and Sex, March 1987.

OCCUPATION AND CLASS OF WORKER	MALE		FEMALE	
	SPANISH ORIGIN	NOT OF SPANISH ORIGIN	SPANISH ORIGIN	NOT OF SPANISH ORIGIN
Total with earnings	11 958	19 588	8 258	10 110
Occupation				
Managerial and Professional Specialty	26 093	32 092	18 261	18 570
Professional Specialty Occupations	27 291	31 771	17 417	18 221
Health Technologists and Technicians	(B)	21 143	(B)	14 891
Engineering and Science Technicians	(B)	24 035	(B)	16 861
Technicians, Excluding Health, Engineering and Science	(B)	28 609	(B)	20 159
Sales Occupations	15 258	21 419	5 432	5 477
Administrative, Including Clerical	14 058	18 067	11 607	11 580
Private Household Occupations	(B)	(B)	3 369	1 474
Protective Service Occupations	18 236	20 292	(B)	6 858
Other Service Occupations	8 100	6 754	5 343	5 088
Farming, Forestry and Fishing	6 677	4 394	(B)	2 107
Mechanics and Repairers	16 988	20 853	(B)	21 052
Construction Trades and Extractive	14 352	19 103	(B)	(B)
Precision Production	16 077	24 107	10 561	11 163
Machine Operators, Assemblers, and Inspectors	12 118	17 794	7 995	9 703
Transportation Occupations	15 459	17 378	(B)	7 611
Material Moving Equipment Operators	13 659	18 519	(B)	(B)
Handlers, Equipment Cleaners, Helpers, and Laborers	7 987	7 853	4 519	6 044

Source: U.S. Bureau of the Census, Current Population Reports, Series P-20, no. 434, "The Hispanic Population in the United States: March 1986 and 1987" (Washington, D.C.: U.S. Government Printing Office, 1988), Table 13.

Table 9-3 shows the median income of Spanish Origin (no data for Mexican Americans are given) and Not-of-Spanish-Origin Americans by occupation and sex. Holding occupation constant, it is apparent that males and females of Spanish origin earn considerably less than do Americans who are not of Spanish origin.

Mexican Americans had an unemployment rate of 11.7 percent in 1987 (the unemployment rate for the general population was 7 percent). Their poverty rate of 24.7 percent in 1986 had actually increased from 1981 (the

TABLE 9-4. Educational Achievement of Mexican Americans Contrasted with Majority Whites (Anglos), Selected Years 1969 Through 1980

Percent who:		
Graduate from high school	Anglos	85
	Mexican Americans	55
Enter college	Anglos	38
	Mexican Americans	22
Complete college	Anglos	23
	Mexican Americans	7
Enter graduate or professional school	Anglos	14
	Mexican Americans	4
Complete graduate or professional school	Anglos	8
	Mexican Americans	2

Source: *Final Report of the Commission on the Higher Education of Minorities* (Los Angeles: Higher Education Research Institute, 1982), Figure 1. Used with permission.

general poverty rate in 1986 was 10.9 percent).[27] All in all, Mexican Americans show every sign of being firmly planted in the secondary labor market where economic benefits are low and uncertain. In addition, as a sizeable portion of other Hispanics (except perhaps Cubans) along with black Americans, Native Americans and Hawaiians, they make up a large portion of what appears to be a permanent underclass.

The educational status of Mexican Americans is also quite different from the general population. In 1986 only 43.3 percent of Mexican Americans had 4 years of high school or more and only 5.4 percent had 4 years of college or more, compared to 74.7 percent and 19.4 percent, respectively, of the general population.[28] A special study (see Table 9-4) focused on educational attrition) shows why educational gains for Mexican Americans are slow: They enter educational levels at lower rates and complete their programs at lower rates.

Mexican Americans' high birth rate has changed their population composition from that of the wider American population. The Mexican-American family is large, even larger than the black or Puerto Rican family. Given their marginal economic status, their high birth rate has created an unfavorable dependency ratio (those of working age in relation to those not likely to work).

[27]U.S. Bureau of the Census, *Current Population Reports*, Series P-20, no. 434, "The Hispanic Population in the United States: March 1986 and 1987," (Washington, D.C.: U.S. Government Printing Office, 1988), Table 2. The comparison would be even more negative for Mexican Americans if the rates for the general population did not include the higher rates of unemployment and poverty among other minorities (for example, black Americans and most other Hispanic groups).

[28]U.S. Bureau of the Census, *Current Population Reports*, Series P-20, no. 434, "The Hispanic Population in the United States: March 1986 and 1987," Table 33.

Mexican Americans also are unusual in that there are more males than females (except among the old).

Though Mexican-American family troubles are not as severe as those of black Americans, Mexican Americans have more family problems than majority Americans. The image of the warm, caring, extended Mexican-American family directed by male authority is a romantic myth. Mexican Americans clearly prefer the nuclear family. Many Mexican-American children lack two parents (especially fathers) and the percent of such families increased between 1982 and 1988 from 26 to 30 percent. While the norm of male dominance is maintained in theory, in practice women exercise considerable power. The use of contraceptives is high, especially among women, attesting both to their independence and to their lack of desire for large families (the acceptance of birth control is higher among higher income groups). And Mexican-American families exhibit high rates of pathology in all areas: divorce and separation, domestic violence, trouble between parents and children, and so on.[29]

Like black Americans and poor people in general, Mexican Americans have had an unhappy relation with law enforcement agencies.[30] They have been mistreated by federal customs and immigration officials and by local and state police throughout the Southwest. Mexican-American organizations have been harassed illegally. Mexican Americans have found it almost impossible to stop such abuse, and they suffer police retaliation if they complain. Mexican Americans have been grossly underrepresented on law enforcement agencies and juries, inadequately represented by counsel, and subject to bail when Anglos are not.[31] There are signs that better organization and a growing political consciousness by Mexican Americans are bringing about significant changes in their relation to law enforcement agencies.

Mexican Americans have become significantly more aware politically in recent decades, and their political power, based on numbers and organization, has increased. By and large, Mexican Americans (and Hispanics in general) are now a significant force in American politics.[32]

---

[29]In addition to Moore and Pachon (see footnote 24), see the empirical study of Mexican-American families in San Antonio and Los Angeles by Leo Grebler, Joan W. Moore, and Ralph Guzman, *The Mexican-American People: The Nation's Second Largest Minority* (New York: Free Press, 1970), Chap. 15.

[30]Ibid., Chap. 21.

[31]U.S. Commission on Civil Rights, *Mexican Americans and the Administration of Justice in the Southwest* (Washington, D.C.: U.S. Government Printing Office, 1970).

[32]For the growth of Mexican American and Hispanic political consciousness and power, see Joan Moore with Harry Pachon, *Mexican-Americans* (Englewood Cliffs, N.J.: Prentice-Hall, 1976), chap. 8, and Joan Moore and Harry Pachon, *Hispanics in the United States* (Englewood Cliffs, N.J.: Prentice-Hall, 1985), chap. 10. For a valuable contrast among pluralist, elitist, and internal colonialism interpretations of the political (power) relations of Mexican Americans to their outer society, see F. Chris Garcia and Rudolph O. de la Garza, *The Chicano Political Experience* (Belmont, Calif.: Wadsworth, 1977). For a valuable collection of essays in a more conventional political science mode focused on the politics of Mexican Americans, Cuban Americans, and Puerto Ricans, see F. Chris Garcia, ed., *Latinos and the Political System* (Notre Dame, Ind.: University of Notre Dame Press, 1988).

THE NEW IMMIGRANTS, LEGAL AND ILLEGAL

The United States has always had mixed motives about immigrants. Americans are proud that their country is a refuge for the oppressed and the poor of the world. American business has always welcomed the influx of cheap labor, legal and illegal. But Americans have also worried about what the influx of newcomers would do to the cultural unity of their country. And, of course, working Americans and trade unions have always been apprehensive about the competition posed by immigrant labor.

The United States restricted immigration in the 1920s, using a national origins quota system. Based on racial and ethnic grounds, the quota system barred Asians and favored Northern and Western European peoples over the peoples of Mediterranean Europe. The McCarran-Walter Act of 1952 continued the basic quota system, but explicit racist criteria were dropped and token numbers of Asians were admitted. The Immigration Act of 1965 and amendments thereafter saw the abandonment of all national origins and racial criteria. The United States adopted a policy of putting a general ceiling on immigration from the Western Hemisphere and the rest of the world. Nonrelatives and nonrefugees who were admitted had to obtain a labor clearance certifying that American workers were not available for the jobs and that the immigrants would not depress wages or working conditions. The net result of the laws was to favor Southern Europe, Asia, and Latin America. However, the overall application process is very complex and favors the educated and monied, in effect, fostering a "brain drain" from the Third World to the United States.

One result has been an increase of Asian Americans (Chinese, Japanese, Filipinos, Asian Indians, Koreans, Southeast Asians, especially Vietnamese, and Pacific Islanders).[33] The U.S. Census Bureau now keeps track of seventeen Asian-American groups and nineteen Pacific Islander groups. The total Asian-Pacific American population reached 5.1 million in 1985 (2.1 percent of the total population) and with all Asian groups increasing (except the Japanese) this figure may reach 9.8 million in the year 2000 (4.0 percent of the total U.S. population).

Chinese, Japanese, and Asian-Indians have reached parity more or less with white Americans in general income, occupation, and education. They have succeeded more than blacks and Hispanics because they had intact families and more capital to start with. They are not well represented at the top of the American power structure and still suffer from negative media images.[34]

---

[33]For a superb account, see Harry H. L. Kitano and Roger Daniels, *Asian Americans: The Emerging Minority* (Englewood Cliffs, N.J.: Prentice-Hall, 1988).

[34]The data compiled by Kitano and Daniels paint a better picture of the relative position of Asian Americans than that found in the report by the U.S. Commission on Civil Rights, *Social Indicators of Equality for Minorities and Women* (1978).

After 1970, it became apparent that the United States had a sizable number of illegal immigrants, especially from Mexico. Illegal immigration raises several distinct questions:

1. *Numbers*—the best estimate is that the United States has between 3.5 and 6 million illegal immigrants.
2. *Labor force impacts*—the net result of all impacts by illegal workers on the labor force or economy cannot be judged conclusively. Illegal immigrants undoubtedly hold down wages and depress working conditions but they also help to revitalize some sectors of the economy—for example, the garment and restaurant businesses. On the other hand, some workers, mostly minorities, suffer from the influx of "illegals."
3. *Social services*—numerous studies have concluded that illegal workers pay more into the system than they take out. But again, the impact is not uniform; the Social Security system benefits because "illegals" pay in but receive few benefits, while local school and hospital systems are net losers since they provide services but receive little in the way of taxes or payments.[35]
4. *An underclass outside the law*—little is known about the overall consequences of having a large number of people living outside the law.

Another major development in American immigration (besides the changes in legal and illegal immigration) is the large influx of refugees. The United States has 1 million Cubans (who are a potent political force in the Miami area), hundreds of thousands of Indo-Chinese, and a steady stream of refugees from Eastern Europe and the Soviet Union, Haiti, and Central America.

Legal immigration provides about 25 percent of the United States' annual population growth (it is not that the numbers of immigrants are so high, but rather that the United States' birthrate is so low). The impact on population is higher if one considers illegal and refugee immigration. By the late 1970s and the early 1980s, many Americans felt that immigration had gotten out of control.[36] In 1986 a bill to hold employers responsible for hiring "illegals" (while granting amnesty to most present illegals) became law.

THE ECONOMIC POSITION OF WOMEN

Comparative Sex Statuses

Racial and ethnic groups can be radically stratified because they are composed of households. Female inequality (along with age inequality) must

---

[35]In 1982, the United States Supreme Court ruled that the children of illegal aliens are entitled to free public education.

[36]For a good survey of immigration history, laws, and present impact, see Charles B. Keely, "Immigration and the American Future," in The American Assembly Series, *Ethnic Relations in America* (Englewood Cliffs, N.J.: Prentice-Hall, 1982), Chap. 2.

be conceptualized differently since females (and different ages) are found in most households high or low in the ladder of social class.

Men and women seem to be unequal in almost all societies. Even among the Arapesh peoples, in which men and women both have nurturing personalities, men have more privileges and authority.[37] But the inequality of females, even though universal, varies considerably depending on the type of society. One need only compare women among the Tiwi[38] (where they are essentially the property of older men) to middle-class and upper-class women in the United States (who have considerable independence and who have achievements in a variety of fields) to appreciate the sociocultural basis of gender identity. Women and men are unequal in hunting and gathering societies but, on the whole, are far more equal than in any of the complex societies. The most sexual inequality occurs in agrarian societies where most of the ideology about women's innate inferiority was developed as part of the great universal, patriarchal religions. The basic variable associated with more equality for women, argues Blumberg (on the basis of the anthropological-historical evidence), is not work or economic participation but control over productive property and its surplus.[39] Marvin Harris argues that male supremacy stems from warfare and the male monopoly over weapons.[40] Though social scientists continue to disagree about causes, most have discarded human-nature explanations as the reasons for sexual inequality.

Comparisons among contemporary countries (developed and developing) do not reveal any real break with the pervasive pattern of sexual inequality. Developing socialist societies bring about dramatic changes in the position of women but seem only to incorporate them into a more up-to-date, male-dominated family, educational, and political-economic institutions. Women in some countries are better off in some ways because of local policies (for example, better maternity or child-care facilities) or they may be more equal to men because the entire society is more equal (for example, Sweden, a highly unequal capitalist society, has more overall equality for all people, including women, than does the United States). On the whole, however, women in industrial societies are very unequal to men regardless of the ideology of their respective societies and regardless of whether they live in capitalist or socialist societies.[41]

[37]Margaret Mead, *Sex and Temperament in Three Primitive Societies* (New York: Dell, 1935).

[38]C.W.M. Hart and Arnold R. Pilling, *The Tiwi of North Australia* (New York: Holt, Rinehart & Winston, 1979).

[39]Rae Lesser Blumberg, *Stratification: Socioeconomic and Sexual Inequality.* (Dubuque, Iowa: Wm. C. Brown, 1978).

[40]Marvin Harris, *Cannibals and King: The Origins of Culture* (New York: Random House, 1977), Chap. 6.

[41]For a superb comparative-historical analysis of gender inequality in terms of specific types of society (forager, horticultural, pastoral, agrarian, and developed and developing capitalist and socialist), see Charlotte G. O'Kelly and Larry S. Carney, *Women and Men in Society: Cross-Cultural Perspectives on Gender Stratification,* 2nd ed. (Belmont, Calif.: Wadsworth, 1986).

Changing Patterns of Economic Participation

Women have always performed economic tasks. Their economic participation in recent times (as measured by the percent of women in the labor
force) is not so much an increase in the amount of economic work done by
women but a change in type of work. In America's rural past, women made
their primary economic contribution on the family farm and at home.[42]
Changes in how women participate in the economy correspond somewhat to
that of men—from the nineteenth century on, more and more economic work
by both men and women has been done off the farm and in factories, offices,
and stores.

Two major patterns stand out in the economic participation of females
since the nineteenth century: The number of working women has increased
greatly (more than half of all women between the ages of eighteen and
sixty-four are working, making up almost half of the work force), and women
are working before and *after* marriage and before and *after* having children.

The major reason why women work is to support their families. Some
work to find fulfillment in careers. Significantly, even working-class women
find low-paying, unfulfilling jobs preferable to housework because they offer
clear-cut responsibilities and escape from isolation.[43]

The Occupations and Incomes of Women

Women tend to be in lower-skilled jobs and are underrepresented in the
professions.[44] Often, their jobs are identified as belonging to the female sex
(for example, clerks, saleswomen, waitresses, hairdressers, nurses, elementary school teachers). These jobs are associated with less responsibility, authority, and education, yield low income, and therefore have less prestige.
They also seem to have less prestige because they are associated with women.

In recent years, women have made considerable relative increases in
college enrollment, graduate and professional education, and in acquiring

---

[42]Robert W. Smuts, *Women and Work in America* (New York: Schocken, 1971), originally
published in 1959.

[43]Myra M. Ferree, "The Confused American Housewife," *Psychology Today* 10 (September
1976): 76–80.

[44]Some basic sources on the economic and other troubles of women through the hierarchy
of class are: Athena Theodore, ed. and intro., *The Professional Woman* (Cambridge, Mass.: Schenk-
man, 1971); Constantina Safilios- Rothschild, ed., *Toward a Sociology of Women* (Lexington, Mass.:
Xerox Publishing, 1972); Louise Kapp Howe, *Pink Collar Workers: Inside the World of Women's Work*
(New York: Avon paperback, 1977); Rae Lesser Blumberg, *Stratification: Socioeconomic and Sexual
Inequality* (Dubuque, Iowa: Wm. C. Brown, 1978). For two Marxist analyses, see Dorothy E.
Smith, *Feminism and Marxism: A Place to Begin, A Way to Go* (Vancouver: New Star Books, 1977)
and (from a Latin American perspective) Heleieth I. B. Safioti, *Women in Class Society* (New York:
Monthly Review Press, 1978).

professional occupations. But these advances have not paid off in full professional rewards. Women receive considerably less income *regardless of education or general occupational category* and tend to be channeled into female-related specialties even within the professions. For example, in medicine women doctors tend to specialize in the medical problems of children and women.

There are also distinct patterns in the careers of women—almost all the jobs they hold have ceilings beyond which women cannot go. Particularly striking is elementary and high school teaching—despite the large number of female teachers in this area, the majority of authority positions, principals and superintendents, especially in high schools, are occupied by males.

Women also make considerably less money than men, averaging only about 65 percent of what men make. The basic reason for this is not sex discrimination but the fact that women hold low-paying jobs. Men in similar jobs also earn less than men in higher-level jobs (unjustifiable income differences between types of work is a class phenomenon and affects both women and men). A serious problem of equity arises when comparisons are made between women and men holding *comparable* jobs—whenever women hold comparable jobs they earn significantly less than men (see Table 9–5). For a discussion see Box 9–1.

In his study of young people entering the labor force (which held education and productivity factors constant), Gordon W. Green (of the Census Bureau) found that white women actually lost ground between 1970 and 1980. This came about despite increases in their education and affirmative action programs.[45] By and large, women do not appear to have made any relative gains in their economic status. It is clear that women are unequal participants in the economy and that their economic position has not improved relative to dominant males despite new laws, programs, and attitudes.

The Feminization of Poverty

The capitalist economy of recent decades (along with other factors) has altered the American household and the composition of the poor. Today, women make up approximately two-thirds of poor people, and approximately half of all poor households are headed by women (a significant number of elderly widows are also poor). All this has occurred during and despite the women's movement.

The feminization of poverty appears to be a trend in other industrial societies although capitalist Sweden with its advanced welfare state, and socialist Poland and the USSR appear to have offset the trend much better than the United States, France, or Canada.

[45]*The New York Times*, January 16, 1984, p. 1.

BOX 9–1.   *IS IT POSSIBLE TO DETERMINE THE COMPARABLE WORTH OF OCCUPATIONS?*

The Equal Pay Act of 1963 and Title VII of the 1964 Civil Rights Act declared it illegal to pay women less than men when both do the same or similar work. Yet after more than twenty years, women as a whole still earn roughly 60 percent of what men earn—not only has there been no narrowing of the gap but if anything it has widened. Little of this gap remains that is due to unequal pay for the *same* work. Experts agree that the major reason for the disparity in pay between men and women is that the latter are massively segregated into low-paying jobs.

In recent years efforts have been made to expand on Title VII of the Civil Rights Act to include equal pay for *comparable* jobs. Why, say critics, should nurses be paid less than streetcleaners or parking meter repairmen? Why should librarians and teachers make less than janitors, truck drivers, or construction workers? There is no reason why clerks and secretaries should receive less than workers doing comparable work outdoors or in factories.

Comparable worth cannot be legislated or established by the courts, say opponents, because there is no scientific way to judge the worth of occupations. Occupations are based on value judgments found in our culture, and the best way to determine the hierarchy of job values is through the free labor market and the law of supply and demand. Only the market can determine who have the skills, the diligence, and the sense of responsibility that are the core attributes of occupations.

A more radical approach argues that comparable worth, even if successful, cannot do much to change the basic structure of labor in the United States. Far from having a free labor market, the United States' occupational system is a result of historical accidents and arbitrary power (slavery, immigration, and the general ebb and flow of cheap labor, the brain drain, excessive professional credentials, control of labor entry by trade unions, excessive qualifications for occupations established by licensing and certification boards, the flow of capital overseas, and so on). Women, no more than men, cannot get a fair shake in the employment market until the organized public structures the economy to prevent monopolies over good jobs (and thus excessive income and benefits) and outlaws exploitation and degradation in the lower reaches of the economy.[46]

---

[46]For a good review of the issues on comparable worth by the Committee on Occupational Classification and Analysis of the National Research Council, including a conservative disclaimer and a radical minority report, see Donald J. Treiman and Heidi I. Hartmann, eds., *Women, Work, and Wages: Equal Pay for Jobs of Equal Value* (Washington, D.C.: National Academy Press, 1981). For a report on current reform efforts, comparable worth legislation at the state level, and court decisions, see *Pay Equity and Comparable Worth*, The Bureau of National Affairs (Washington, D.C., 1984).

TABLE 9–5.   Median Income of All Persons and Year-Round, Full-Time Workers By Occupation and Sex, 1987

ALL MALES AND FEMALES	ALL PERSONS		YEAR-ROUND, FULL-TIME WORKERS	
	M	F	M	F
	MEDIAN INCOME (DOLLARS)	MEDIAN INCOME (DOLLARS)	MEDIAN INCOME (DOLLARS)	MEDIAN INCOME (DOLLARS)
Occupation Group of Long-est Job (Earnings)	17 752	8 101	26 722	17 504
Total with earnings	19 878	10 618	26 008	16 909
Executive, administrators, and managerial	33 408	19 134	36 155	21 874
Professional specialty	32 891	19 643	36 096	24 565
Technical and related sup-port	25 670	16 242	29 170	19 559
Sales	21 624	6 268	27 880	14 277
Administrative support, including clerical	18 512	12 220	23 896	16 346
Precision production, craft and repair	20 737	11 758	24 931	17 190
Machine operators, assemb-lers, and inspectors	17 363	10 050	20 821	13 028
Transportation and material moving	18 047	7 669	22 472	12 770
Handlers, equipment cleaners, helpers, and laborers	8 046	6 209	16 730	13 118
Service workers	8 523	4 714	17 320	11 000
Private household	(B)	1 614	(B)	7 053
Service, except private household	8 654	5 256	17 336	11 214
Farming, forestry, and fishing	6 479	2 574	12 389	7 034

B = Base less than 75,000

Source: U.S. Bureau of the Census, *Current Population Reports,* Series P-60, no. 162, "Money Income of Households, Families, and Persons in the United States: 1987" (Washington, D.C.: U.S. Government Printing Office, 1989), Table 27.

Factors and policies relevant to female poverty and to poverty in general are:

1. economic markets for labor;
2. government policies such as commitment to full employment, equal pay, and affirmative action;
3. government policies in regard to economic support for families such as money, housing, health care;

4. demographic factors such as teenage pregnancy, age of marriage, divorce, and life expectancy.[47]

Women as a Minority

Women are a unique minority in a number of ways. One, they comprise about 52 percent of the American population, which means that a minority does not have to be a numerical minority (a point made in an earlier reference to the position of blacks in South Africa). Second, despite a large change in attitudes, women are still subject to class—thus women in the upper classes have a very different level of existence than do women in the lower classes. And quite apart from class, women have fewer benefits and opportunities than do men, holding class constant.

Minority Women

Women are a minority but there are also minorities *within* the female minority. Women as a whole have unequal economic statuses (occupations and earnings) in relation to majority males, but inequality *among* females is also significant. In education, American Indian, Alaskan Native, black-American, Mexican-American, and Puerto Rican females do less well than majority females, Japanese-American, Chinese-American, and Filipino-American females, and they are much more likely to be poor.[48] There are other minorities within the minority. Homosexual women face a double burden. Handicapped, deformed, or disfigured women probably suffer more than men in similar straits. And the same is probably true of women who are overweight, mentally ill, or "over aged." It goes without saying that all of the above burdens can be made heavier or lighter by adding race, ethnicity, social class, or age to any given category.

THE POLITICS OF GENDER STRATIFICATION

Two distinct periods of struggle by women against sexual inequality stand out. In the nineteenth and early twentieth century, women fought to get the vote and succeeded with the nineteenth amendment to the U.S. Constitution (1919). Since the 1960s the women's movement has broadened its struggle to

[47]For a valuable analysis of female poverty in five capitalist and two socialist societies, see Gertrude S. Goldberg and Eleanor Kremen, "The Feminization of Poverty: Only in America," *Social Policy* 17 (Spring 1987): 3–14.

[48]United States Commission on Civil Rights, *Social Indicators of Equality for Minorities and Women* (Washington, D.C.: United States Commission on Civil Rights, 1978). For background on the largest minority within a minority, see La Frances Rodgers-Rose, ed., *The Black Woman* (Beverly Hills, Calif.: Sage, 1980) and Phyllis A. Wallace, with Linda Datcher and Julianne Malveaux, *Black Women in the Labor Force* (Cambridge, Mass.: MIT Press, 1980).

include equality in other areas, especially the economy, education, the law, and marriage.

Changing Attitudes By and Toward Women

A revolution in attitudes about women (on the part of both men and women) has occurred in recent times. Both men and women have largely abandoned the idea that women are innately different and inferior to men. The long-held myth that women should confine themselves to being wives and mothers and develop passive, pious personalities has been abandoned by the majority of both male and female Americans.

Surveys over the last two decades have shown a large shift in attitudes among women at all age and educational levels toward a more liberal, equalitarian stance toward sex roles. In 1977, for example, only a third of women agreed that "most of the important decisions in the life of the family should be made by the man of the house," whereas in 1962 two-thirds agreed.[49] Surveys also show that most women now want to be wives, mothers, *and workers*, and most now expect to realize values in all three areas.

Though a clear majority of males and females now favors equality, changes in attitudes are not the same as changes in behavior. The same holds for new laws—a change in law does not automatically lead to a change of behavior. Remember, new attitudes and laws can be a burden to the extent that they shift responsibility from the power groups who control the distribution of opportunities and rewards to the individual (see the section titled "The Burden of Moral Equality," in Chapter 10).

Other forces also help explain why the relative position of women has not changed. In an interesting study of college women, Laurie Cummings found that feminist students projected a "Horatia Alger" image of success (the Protestant-bourgeois achiever plus luck). In addition, they resolved possible conflicts among marriage, motherhood, and career with the concept of *superwoman*. On the other hand, college women who were not feminists saw few difficulties in combining new work roles with old "female" roles. The study concludes that both types of women were conservative in that they saw progress for women within American society as presently constituted.[50]

Attitudes toward and about women in achievement (professional) positions are also relevant in explaining why women have not made more progress. Philip Goldberg found evidence that college women are prejudiced

[49]For a report of a study using data from 1962, 1963, 1966, and 1977 by Arland Thornton and Deborah Freedman, see *ISR Newsletter*, Institute for Social Research, University of Michigan (Winter 1980), 3. Similar shifts in attitudes have been found by the Roper Organization in its survey for the 1980 Virginia Slims American Women's Opinion Poll—see *The New York Times* (March 13, 1980), C1.

[50]Laurie Davidson Cummings, "Value Stretch in Definitions of Career Among College Women: Horatia Alger as Feminist Model," *Social Problems* 25 (October 1977): 65–74.

against female professionals even in traditional female occupations.[51] In a similar study (though too different to support their criticism of Goldberg), Ferber and Huber found bias by college males against women professionals and no special bias by women students against women professionals.[52]

In a study of a large sample of high school students in northern Georgia, Ward and Balswick found that female and male students shared sex-role stereotypes both of their own as well as the opposite sex. Actually the consensus was stronger in regard to same-sex stereotypes. All agreed that men were strong-dominant and women were weak-submissive.[53]

These are some of the facts about sex-role attitudes. But how do distinct power groups see women? What are the expressed political perspectives on women? Three such perspectives, the right liberal, left liberal, and the radical are the subject of the next three sections.

Right Liberals and Women

Right liberals give women's equality low priority—indeed, they oppose it, though not always openly. The right liberal position is found in the Republican party, especially in its conservative wing. The main thrust of the Republican party is to protect and enhance the interests of propertied and professional groups. The Republican party is relatively indifferent to women's issues because resolving them threatens the interests of its main supporters. Republicans (and conservatives in general) argue that all will be well if the private economy is given first priority. Women and other minorities will benefit most, argue right liberals, if existing economic forces are left alone to produce wealth and opportunities for all (the trickle-down theory).

Extreme right-wing liberals oppose many things that the majority of women want or that reform and radical groups want for them. They oppose the Equal Rights Amendment, abortion (whether paid for privately or with public funds), and non-traditional family practices or sexual preferences. In 1981, federal tax-supported abortions for women were eliminated (unless the mother's life was in danger but not for rape[54] or incest), largely at the insistence of conservative forces. Conservatives were also influential in the defeat of the Equal Rights Amendment in 1982. The Reagan administration openly relaxed enforcement of all civil rights law. In 1983 it succeeded in getting the

---

[51]Philip Goldberg, "Are Women Prejudiced Against Women?," *Transaction* 5 (April 1968): 28–30.

[52]Marianne Abeles Ferber and Joan Althaus Huber, "Sex of Student and Instructor: A Study of Student Bias," *American Journal of Sociology* 80 (January 1975): 949–963.

[53]Dawn Ward and Jack Balswick, "Strong Men and Virtuous Women," *Pacific Sociological Review* 21 (January 1978): 45–52; reprinted in Richard F. Larson and Ronald J. Knapp, eds., *Readings for Introductory Sociology* (New York: Oxford University Press, 1982).

[54]Newspaper accounts of the abortion controversy cite estimates from an undisclosed source that place the number of pregnancies from rape at 15,000 per year. Neither side of the abortion controversy dispute this estimate, which may or may not be accurate.

courts to agree that colleges receiving federal money could only be held accountable to civil rights laws for programs specifically funded. It also supported the state of Washington's appeal of a federal court decision upholding equal pay in a comparable worth case. The basic economic policy of the Reagan administration and its cuts in public programs for the poor, children, the elderly, and pregnant women all hit women, especially working, lower-class, and minority women very hard.

In a departure from the conservative position, the Reagan administration openly advocated continued public funds for family planning services.[55] The reason probably is that unwanted pregnancies by the poor and by unmarried women and teenagers represent a heavy burden on the taxpayer. The matter is far from resolved, however, because many conservatives still oppose family planning, especially sex education and access to contraceptives by teenagers.[56] Conservatives and the Reagan administration also pressed hard for regulations requiring family planning agencies to inform parents when unmarried teenagers came in for advice, something experts say will effectively curtail the spread of birth control among young women (and men). By and large, the courts have struck down this attempt to improve morals through regulatory fiat.

Left Liberals and Women

Female leaders, with help from men and other minority groups, have pushed for a full complement of rights for women and for an enhancement of their opportunities. Mainstream feminist groups such as the National Organization for Women (NOW) and the Women's Equity Action League (WEAL) engage in traditional political action and tend to be reformist in spirit. By and large, left liberals, including mainstream feminism, put their faith in new laws and in political reform to achieve their goals.

Right and left liberals do not question America's ability to absorb its minorities, including women. Given time and enough political and moral effort, the United States will realize all its ideals.

Radicals and Women

The radical position on women tends to be ambiguous; but by and large, women's issues are usually subordinated to economic questions. Radicals, including radical feminists, view the subjugation of women as merely part of the more general subjugation of working men and women to property groups. One difference among radical feminists is that some of them are

[55]*The New York Times*, June 24, 1981, p. C12.

[56]In a study of thirty-seven developed countries, the Alan Guttmacher Institute found that the United States had by far the highest rate of teenage pregnancy. The reason seemed to be that the United States is alone in not publicly promoting sex education and birth control; *The New York Times*, March 13, 1985, p. 1.

opposed to masculine forms of domination, and they have taken a stance against what they feel is the uncritical acceptance by many liberals and radicals of competitive, achievement values. Feminine values of cooperation, sharing, and caring are seen as running counter to Protestant-bourgeois values and as the only basis for a nonsexist society.

Radical feminist groups are organized on a highly decentralized basis. Individuals are encouraged to exercise choice as to amount and type of participation and are given opportunities to change their life-styles in an atmosphere of mutual support. Though small in number, radical feminist groups have had considerable influence on mainstream feminism especially through their research and study reports.

The Women's Movement: Any Net Gains?

Since the 1960s, new laws have been passed to outlaw sex discrimination and guarantee equal pay; affirmative action programs have been mounted; social science research on women has grown dramatically; and women are now more visible in the world of business, the media, sports, the professions, government, and in elected offices. In 1981 President Ronald Reagan nominated and the Senate confirmed the first female United States Supreme Court Justice. In 1984 Geraldine Ferraro became the first woman to run for vice-president of the United States.

Appearance aside, a basic question remains: Has the overall women's movement resulted in any *net* gains? The same question can be asked differently: Is the latent function of the women's movement to strengthen the status quo by permitting handfuls of upper- and middle-class women to achieve some gains while dooming the vast majority of women to illegitimate inequalities? (see Box 9–2, "Is Women's Liberation a Middle-Class Movement?"). Most (including almost all introductory sociology textbooks and all books on sex roles) exaggerated the gains made by women, not least by overlooking negative evidence. What the facts show is that political and civil rights, favorable laws, and more education have not changed the relative position of women over the past twenty years (if anything, that position has deteriorated). Nor is the undoubted increase in participation by women in the general life of society an unmixed blessing. Women, for example, have rising rates of lung cancer. Women are also increasing their criminal behavior and becoming adept at more specialized types of crime as their opportunities become more varied.[57] And companies report that they are having problems with (and thus developing a negative attitude toward) over-thirty pregnancies by women executives and professionals, something that indicates that it is still difficult for women to combine career and motherhood.[58]

---

[57]*The New York Times*, January 21, 1980, p. A18; for general background, see Freda Adler and Rita James Simon, eds., *The Criminology of Deviant Women* (Boston: Houghton Mifflin, 1979).

[58]*The Wall Street Journal*, July 20, 1981, p. 1.

BOX 9–2. *IS WOMEN'S LIBERATION A MIDDLE-CLASS MOVEMENT?*

The thrust of mainstream feminism has been to seek justice and progress for women through a redefinition of their political and legal rights. By and large, mainstream feminism has asked that women be accorded full and equal rights with men. The women's movement has also focused on issues that are of special importance to women: abortion, rape laws, maternity leaves with pay or coverage by insurance, tax subsidies for child-care centers, and enhanced educational opportunities.

These are certainly valuable reforms, but why not other reforms? Mainstream feminism has not focused on the problems of working women except to support the efforts of women to enter previously all-male occupations. It has not asked for a national system of child-care services. Little has been said of the exploitation of women by businesses that violate labor laws (there are now as many sweatshops in the United States as in the scandalous era of the early industrial period). Nothing has been said about the need for labor unions to protect workers, changes in the minimum wage, control of runaway plants, public housing, and comprehensive medical services for ordinary people. Mainstream feminism wants a fair share of the good jobs for women but has said nothing about the need to break down the artificial and wasteful barriers that keep such jobs scarce (and its occupants far less competent then they could be).

The single most important thing that would benefit women is a national commitment to full employment. But nothing is heard on this score.

As the wives and daughters of the middle and upper classes get an increasing share of good jobs, as their daughters marry men in the middle and upper classes, and as the structure of family income resembles a bell shape (a shrinkage of middle-level households has already begun—see Chapter 6), there will be less and less heard about the reforms women need most.

Women's liberation has little to do with the interests of the bulk of women. It is primarily a class phenomenon. The American upper classes treat their sons and daughters equally. From roughly 1875 to 1960, the American middle and upper classes built up a large backlog of educated daughters with no outlets for their abilities (aside from nursing, teaching, or library work). From the 1960s on, the upper classes (remember that educated men have given strong support to the women's movement) have worked hard to make it possible for the women of the upper classes to enter the world of business and the professions. By calling these actions a *women's* movement, the historic middle class (propertied and professional groups) continues (falsely) to associate its own interests with humanity at large.

Assessing changes in the position of women is complicated. Women who work have more equality at home. Part of the low economic position of women stems from the breakup of marriages—here women may be losing economically but gaining in another sense because they are freed from unhappy marriages. No-fault divorce has not turned out to be the blessing that feminists once thought, because women are not getting a fair share of economic rewards from divorce settlements. On the positive side, some evidence indicates that the greater participation by women in formal work roles has reduced their incidence of mental illness (which up to now has appeared to be higher than the rates for men).

Nonetheless, progress in the crucial economic realm appears to be minimal. The main thrust of the women's movement has assumed that increased opportunity and favorable laws can bring about economic change. As such, women are still being subordinated by the basic norms that promote inequality in America. Achieving political and legal equality and formal equality of opportunity can only serve to legitimate sexual inequality in much the same way that formal equality legitimates the inequality of black and other minority Americans (the first to be victimized by this ideology were white Anglo-Saxon males). On balance, the evidence points to one conclusion—the basic outcome of the women's movement has been *to modernize the terms under which women will be dominated.* Until women reform groups commit themselves to full employment and question the artificial scarcity of good jobs, the only result of their reforms will be to replace white and minority males with middle- and upper-class females. Once the upper classes have enough women in visible economic and professional positions, it will become harder for the vast bulk of women to argue that they are being victimized. Perhaps better said, the women's movement will become more effective on behalf of women when upwardly mobile females realize that they will continue to be exploited even as members of the upper classes.

INEQUALITY THROUGH DISABILITY

Legitimate and Illegitimate Discrimination

The United States has about 35 million disabled people who cannot behave as the physically and mentally normal can, and they are treated differently. To discriminate against those who are unable to perform social roles is not totally wrong. However, the treatment of the handicapped far exceeds legitimate discrimination. The handicapped are looked down upon, ridiculed, and shunned. Some of the worst problems they encounter stem from indifference and lack of sensitivity on the part of architects and builders, those who design mass-transit systems, and those who make articles for daily living, including recreation. Above all, the handicapped can *do* many things, including a day's work, but they are not given the chance. For a nation dedicated to fostering the full development of its citizens, the United States has treated its disabled citizens shamefully.[59]

[59]For background and data, see United States Commission on Civil Rights, *Accommodating the Spectrum of Individual Abilities* (Washington, D.C.: U.S. Commission on Civil Rights, 1983), and Frank Bowe, *Handicapping America: Barriers to Disabled People* (New York: Harper & Row, 1978).

Half-Way Measures: Laws Without Enforcement

Congress passed the Rehabilitation Act of 1973 prohibiting recipients of federal aid from discriminating against the handicapped either by denying them access to buildings or through economic means. A Special Education Act of 1975 required education for handicapped students, including an effort to "mainstream" them whenever possible. The disabled gained from these acts but not much. Congress did not supply the needed funds, and the Reagan administration actually tried to abolish the enforcement board (it failed and had to be content with merely weakening the law's enforcement). The Reagan administration arbitrarily and, as it turned out, illegally eliminated hundreds of thousands of disabled people from the rolls of the Social Security system.

Given deeply seated prejudices and discriminatory behavior by the American people, and hypocrisy on the part of government, the main burden of obtaining legal rights and a fair shake for the disabled has fallen on the disabled themselves. Ironically, spending money to turn the disabled into productive citizens is a wise investment as opposed to the costly waste of present practices.[60]

Preventing Disability

Helping the disabled to lead productive and satisfying lives is one thing. Quite another is to prevent disability in the first place. America's disabled come from all classes, races, ethnic groups, sexes, and age groups (though the lower classes probably provide the largest numbers both in absolute numbers and per capita). Disability, however, is not from nature or God—it is a *social* phenomenon: babies born to malnourished poor women; babies born to women who smoke and drink; victims of industrial accidents, noxious fumes, and harmful substances; victims of highway accidents; those disabled by combat; children who eat lead-based paint; casualties of the ski slopes and other sports; and those who lead unhealthy life-styles. Here again the government has failed to implement environmental protection and occupational health and safety laws. The one law that government implements, workers' compensation, provides workers (and widows) with low compensation for injury and death while depriving them of the right to sue employers (in effect, providing American business with legal protection for operating unsafe workplaces).

---

[60]Gary L. Albrecht, ed., *The Sociology of Physical Disability and Rehabilitation* (Pittsburgh: University of Pittsburgh Press, 1976), and Frank Bowe, *Rehabilitating America: Toward Independence for Disabled and Elderly People* (New York: Harper & Row, 1980). For a fascinating portrait of a successful struggle to mainstream retarded individuals and establish this as a feasible ideal as opposed to warehousing, see David J. Rothman and Sheila M. Rothman, *The Willowdale Wars* (New York: Harper & Row, 1984).

In Chapter 7 we came across considerable evidence that large amounts of deviant behavior (mental retardation, learning disability, high or low IQ, crime, and so on) are the creation of liberal institutions. The way to prevent such deviance is to change the power of those who make the professional and political decisions that doom millions to unnecessary and socially costly inequality.

The Mentally Ill

Data on the mentally ill are not easy to assemble, but the best estimate is that United States has 32 million individuals who suffer from some form of mental illness.[61] This number is larger than the number of mentally ill included in the total number of handicapped because of differing definitions. Keeping in mind the difficulty of finding precise data, the number of mentally ill is still quite large.[62]

The conventional approach to mental illness has been to think of it as a personal disorder to be cured by one-on-one treatment by a trained specialist. However, the sociology of mental illness is much closer to the view expressed by Thomas Szasz (mental illness results from difficulties in coping with life in society).[63] In short, sociologists actively seek the *social* causes of mental illness. As we saw in Chapter 7, research has discovered a distinct relation between social class and mental illness—the lower classes suffer from it more than the upper classes.[64] The lower classes also receive poorer treatment than do the upper classes.

Historically, the basic treatment of the mentally ill was to isolate them in hospitals. The success with drugs in calming patients led to a change from the 1950s on—the release of patients into the community. In 1963 Congress passed the Community Mental Health Centers Construction Act to provide mental patients with a way to make the transition to normal life. Failure to provide adequate funding and deep resistance to the centers by the American people led to a complete failure of the program.[65] By the 1980s, America's streets were filled with homeless people (estimates of their numbers ranged from 250,000 to 2.5 million), most of them former mental patients.

---

[61]*The New York Times,* October 3, 1984, pp. A1, D27.

[62]If one added all the Americans who for one reason or another (physical-mental impairment, illiteracy, unemployment, unwanted idleness because of old age) are not productive citizens, the total could easily add up to 30 to 40 percent of the population.

[63]Thomas Szasz, *The Myth of Mental Illness* (New York: Harper & Row, 1971).

[64]Leo Srole, Thomas S. Langner, Stanley T. Michael, Marvin K. Opler, and Thomas A.C. Rennie, *Mental Health in the Metropolis: The Midtown Manhattan Study* (New York: New York University Press, 1978). For an excellent source book, see Oscar Grusky and Melvin Pollner, eds., *The Sociology of Mental Illness: Basic Studies* (New York: Holt, Rinehart & Winston, 1981).

[65]*The New York Times,* September 13, 1984, pp. A1, B12.

Preventing Mental Illness

The treatment of the mentally ill has not been marked by much success—indeed, suspicion has been cast on the basic ability of professionals to even identify the mentally ill. The most promising lead on how to treat the mentally ill and on how to prevent it in the first place is to construct a livable society. Instead of focusing on the best way to treat victims, research suggests that we should instead concentrate on eliminating social stress, false expectations, false promises, denied opportunities, and anomic groups and institutions.

STRATIFICATION BY SEXUAL LIFE-STYLE

Males and females who prefer member of their own sex for purposes of companionship, affection, and sex have long had to hide their homosexual orientation (homosexual females are usually referred to as *lesbians;* many homosexuals now prefer to be called *gays*). The heterosexual majority long considered homosexuals deviants and characterized them as sick or sinful, or both. In recent decades homosexuals are more and more being considered by others and by themselves as a minority.[66]

The main reason for thinking of homosexuals as a minority is because they are excluded from valued rights and forms of social participation on irrelevant grounds. A sexual preference is not a disqualification for citizenship or for an occupation any more than skin color, ethnicity, sex or age. In recent years the gay rights movement has struggled to promote the civil rights of gays and to make it easier for homosexuals to come out of hiding. A large number of local organizations have appeared, and many colleges have acknowledged the right of students to form campus organizations for gays. Because male gays are often conservative in regard to matters affecting women, female gays (lesbians) have struggled independently to promote their own rights. Lesbians have also not received explicit support by the larger women's movement, and this too has prompted them to act on their own behalf.[67]

[66]For two valuable discussions, see Franklin E. Kameny, "Homosexuals as a Minority Group" and Helen Mayer Hacker, "Homosexuals: Deviant or Minority Group?," in Edward Sagarin, ed., *The Other Minorities: Nonethnic Collectivities Conceptualized as Minority Groups* (Waltham, Mass.: Ginn., 1971), 50–65, 65–92.

[67]For general background, especially on the politics of heterosexual vs. homosexual life-styles, see Laud Humphreys, *Tearoom Trade: Impersonal Sex in Public Places* (enlarged ed. with a retrospect on ethical issues; Chicago: Aldine, 1975), originally published in 1970; Joseph Harry and William B. De Vall, *The Social Organization of Gay Males* (New York: Praeger, 1978); Deborah G. Wolf, *The Lesbian Community* (Berkeley: University of California Press, 1979); Sasha G. Lewis, *Sunday's Women: A Report on Lesbian Life Today* (Boston: Beacon Press, 1979); and Toby Marotta, *The Politics of Homosexuality* (Boston: Houghton Mifflin, 1981).

The number of gays in the United States is not known, but most estimates put it at about 5 to 10 percent of the adult population. The reasons for homosexuality are also not known, some pointing to genetic and unconscious factors, others to childhood conditioning, and still others to willful preference.

The gay movement is not homogeneous. A sharp cleavage exists between male and female gays, and gays are further divided by class, race, and ethnicity. Many gays in the upper classes lead otherwise straight lives and merely want a full measure of civil rights. Others are more radical and want to dismantle the entire system of sex roles imposed by society.

Gays made some progress in achieving a measure of civil rights during the 1970s and 1980s. Wisconsin has made discrimination against homosexuals illegal, and New York City passed an important gay rights measure in 1986 after turning it down numerous times. Gays have even been elected to office in a number of states. But the gay movement received a setback in the early 1980s when the dread disease AIDS became associated with homosexual sex. AIDS, together with strong opposition by right-wing Christian groups and general prejudice by the American people, has slowed progress for gays.

AMERICA'S MINORITIES: RUNNING HARD AND STANDING STILL

The foregoing analysis of black Americans, Mexican Americans, other ethnic-racial minorities, women, the handicapped, and gays raises disturbing questions about the nature of minority inequality and what to do about it. Of the greatest importance is the fact that minorities in America have made no relative advance toward equality despite considerable legal and political help during the greatest and longest period of economic expansion in American history.[68] The highly stable and unequal position of ethnic and racial minorities (and women) raises the following questions.

Do civil rights laws and other minority-oriented legislation have any effect on economic inequality? The answer appears to be no. Should minorities make a greater effort in education? The answer appears to be no. Are the civil rights laws and programs mostly a way for corporate capitalism to modernize its labor force? The answer appears to be yes. Over the past 500 years capitalism has developed a labor force composed of legally free indi-

---

[68]L. Paul Metzger argues that the traditional assimilationist perspective of sociology (and of left and right liberals) was shattered by the events of the 1960s—see his article "American Sociology and Black Assimilation: Conflicting Perspectives," *American Journal of Sociology* vol. 76 (January 1971): 627–647. Events of the 1970s and 1980s have done little to restore faith in it and, if anything, have undermined it further.

viduals. In the United States it also developed first a slave and then a segregated labor force. Are the civil rights laws merely a way to turn minorities into legally free individuals who can then be held responsible for failure? The answer appears to be yes.

All evidence points to systematic and stable injustice for large portions of the American population. The evidence again underscores not only the failure of American society to live up to its norms and values but what appears to be an inherent inability to do so. Evidence suggests that American society cannot hope to achieve its values as long as the nature of its economy remains unproblematic. Giving minorities their civil rights may actually be more a process of legitimating their exploitation than a real improvement in their relative social position.

CLASS AND MINORITIES: A SUMMARY

Approximately 17 percent of the American population is made up of deeply disadvantaged racial, ethnic, and female minorities. The number increases considerably if the large number of handicapped are included along with those who are discriminated against because of their sexual preferences.

The largest (defining minority to exclude women) and most oppressed minority are black Americans (11 percent of the population), along with smaller "racial" groups, especially American Indians.

Mexican Americans and other ethnic groups from Latin America (excluding Cubans) have a long history of oppression at the hands of majority America.

Women are the largest minority, but unlike racial and ethnic groups, they cannot all be put in the lower classes. Thus, women are members of the upper classes although they are unequal at those levels too. The mainstream women's movement has opened up opportunities for women but, by and large, the main beneficiaries have been the wives and daughters of the upper classes.

Handicapped people are a large and varied group who have been disabled largely through membership in American society.

Homosexuals (gays) are yet another minority making up anywhere from 5 to 10 percent of the population.

All in all, no relative advances have been made by any of these minorities despite nearly a half century of economic expansion and the passage of laws and programs to help minorities.

Evidence suggests that if no changes are made in the basic capitalist economy and its supporting polity, America will have a fairly large and permanent underclass of poor people and minorities.

CHAPTER 10

The Prestige Dimension and How Americans Regard Themselves

The class order is a hierarchy of families and unrelated individuals (embedded in economic groups such as business enterprises, professional and trade associations, public service occupations and associations, and labor unions) ranked on the basis of ability to prevail in various economic markets. In our discussions of income distribution, wealth, occupation, education, family stability, family values, basic personality structure, mental and physical health, education, and minorities, we have identified the salient features of the United States' class hierarchy. Our task now is to consider the class dimension as a hierarchy of families and unrelated individuals who not only face economic markets but also behave as moral agents, acting to maintain and enjoy various levels of psychic and social existence (the prestige dimension).

In analyzing prestige, we will again deal with some of the phenomena we encountered in the analysis of class. This time, however, we will use a finer analytical framework, and will focus more explicitly on group formation and structure and on the development and distribution of psychic resources and satisfactions.

Prestige phenomena have been put into three major categories: how Americans regard themselves (discussed later in this chapter), how Americans consume "material" and "symbolic" culture (Chapter 11), and how Americans associate, or the structure of prestige groups (Chapter 12).

THE REALM OF EVALUATION

The classis analysis of prestige is Max Weber's. Weber identified status or prestige stratification as a realm separate from, though related to, class stratification. Stratification by status, he argued, is based on the distribution of honor (or prestige) and can take a number of forms:

> *The term of "social status" is applied to a typically effective claim to positive or negative privilege with respect to social prestige so far as it rests on one or more of the following bases:*
>
> *a. mode of living,*
> *b. a formal process of education which may consist in empirical or rational training and the acquisition of the corresponding modes of life, or*
> *c. on the prestige of birth, or of an occupation.*[1]

According to Weber, prestige differentials stem from usurpation, but their long-range stability and effectiveness require successful conventionalization and often require added support from the legal order (privilege). Though the bases of prestige can be as varied as birth (into a religious, family, ethnic, or racial status), breeding, property, occupation, education, or some mixture of these, the prestige hierarchy is always opposed to the free play of market (class) forces. Prestige stratification thrives, says Weber, when the distribution of economic power is stable. It reaches its highest development when a prestige group(s) succeeds both in embedding property and occupations in a hierarchy of prestige values, thus making them immune to the play of economic forces, and monopolizing education and other opportunities for subjective development. Impersonal economic forces threaten prestige stratification because they cannot be relied on to honor the special prestige status of persons, property, or occupations. Dynamic economies undermine and transform prestige hierarchies beyond recognition. In short, Weber argued that class and prestige inequality were different though related and that, in a broad sense, classes stemmed from the production of goods and services, while prestige groups were derived from the consumption of ideal and material values.

Weber directed his analysis of prestige against Marx's argument that class is the universal basis of social stratification. But Weber never meant to replace class with prestige as the universal source of stratification; he was simply against the use of metaphysical generalizations. And he would no doubt have interpreted prestige phenomena *within* class society in economic

[1]*Max Weber: The Theory of Social and Economic Organization*, tr. A. M. Henderson and Talcott Parsons, ed. with an intro. by Talcott Parsons (New York: Oxford University Press, 1947), p. 428. For Weber's major discussion of prestige, see Max Weber, "Class, Status, Party," *From Max Weber: Essays in Sociology*, tr., ed. and with an into. by H. H. Gerth and C. Wright Mills (New York: Oxford University Press, 1946), chap. 7.

terms. Today, the economic basis of prestige is commonly acknowledged. But it is still necessary to distinguish between the economic and evaluative realms. Perhaps the best way to understand this distinction is to cite some examples. When an individual buys a house to shelter his or her family, we can associate this event with class by calling it a real estate transaction, relating it to income distribution, using it to determine whether the demand for housing is elastic or nonelastic, and so on. But when an individual buys a house (especially one he or she cannot quite afford) because it or the neighborhood has prestige, or when someone acts to prevent those who can afford the same house from buying it because they are black or *nouveau riche*, the event involves the special moral realm of prestige (style of life, status evaluation, snobbery, deference, exclusiveness, social etiquette, values, consciousness, honor, breeding, taste, racism, and the like).

Other examples of prestige-related behavior come readily to mind. When an employer hires a less qualified individual for a position in preference to a better qualified Jew, Roman Catholic, black, or Protestant, this act also inhabits the realm of moral appraisal (prestige). If we assume that there are ten, twenty, or fifty colleges that provide educations equivalent or even superior to that of, say, Harvard College, the higher cash or occupational value of a Harvard degree is attributable to an unwarranted academic reputation (prestige). Prestige (or status) considerations are paramount when an upper-class woman cannot be seen shopping for food or carrying packages, or when a widow cannot work because work is considered demeaning in her "class." Every culture has its own peculiar prestige-related associations and taboos. There is an interesting story of an African student at a midwestern American university who reported a faculty member as an impostor because he saw the man washing his car, something no faculty member would ever do in the student's country.

The relationship between class and prestige is not one-directional, however. In the history of social stratification, free economic markets are scarce; in fact, free markets are analytical fictions created by economists. Whatever their origin, prestige groups exert moral pressure on economic behavior and on the uses to which economic goods and resources are put. In some societies, families withdraw homes, land, and labor from economic markets—by means, for example, of entail and primogeniture or of family trust funds—in effect lodging these "economic" values in a structure of familistic values.[2] In preindustrial societies occupations tend to be assigned on the basis of family or religious status at birth. Even today a prestige order can deeply affect the operation of economic markets by defining a labor force in racial, religious, ethnic, sexual, and/or family terms, often making occupations hereditary.

---

[2]Chekhov's *The Cherry Orchard* is the story of an aristocratic family that keeps its cherry orchard off the real estate market despite the fact that it is facing economic ruin.

High prestige groups can bias the uses to which a society's economic re-sources are put by monopolizing the use of some goods and benefits (for example, forbidding lower prestige groups to own land, hunt, or wear fur); by creating and supporting a demand for luxuries; by demanding abstention from work on the Sabbath and/or holidays; or by abstaining from work in favor of conspicuous leisure. The prestige order can also affect consumption-related behavior by, for example, requiring segregated facilities on railroads or segregated barbershops and restaurants. It can also—and this is of consid-erable importance in the United States—promote the value of residence in one-family houses in the suburbs, a phenomenon that entails a specific pat-tern of allocating economic resources (land, labor, building materials, auto-mobiles, highways).

The prestige order is composed, therefore, of standards considered to be moral, decent, civilized, and/or in good taste. What is considered honor-able or civilized obviously entails an enormous range of behavior, and the beneficiaries (or, to use Max Weber's term, usurpers) of prestige differentials are, by definition, those who have social power. Clearly, therefore, no analy-sis of social stratification can overlook the prestige groups that exercise power over the evaluative or moral realm.

ACHIEVED AND ASCRIBED PRESTIGE

The distinction between ascribed and achieved prestige is crucial to the understanding of stratification. The decisive difference between achievement and ascriptive prestige is not the difference between equality and inequality; both ascriptive and achievement standards lead to pronounced and lasting hierarchies of inequality. Its nature may instead be defined by asking whether a given prestige status is achievable or not—that is, by asking whether it is accessible to individuals and their families on the basis of training and competition or is assigned to them by criteria deemed important and unalterable.

The major source of achieved prestige in industrial society is occupa-tion. Given its ultimate value-idea that mastery of the world is possible through science and human effort, industrial society accords the major share of prestige to occupations directly related to control of the social and natural environments. Ascriptive barriers to occupational achievement, therefore, not only deny individuals and groups the benefits of class but prevent them from acquiring prestige as well. Achieved prestige can also be found outside of occupation among students, in the realms of taste and consumption, and among members and participants in nonprofit, professional, fraternal, phil-anthropic, civic, sports, and cultural groups. Achieved rankings in these areas again presume individuals or families to be qualified (or unqualified) for inclusion according to an achievable criterion: for example, achieving an

A average or good grooming; being an architect, a manager of a bank, or a college alumnus; being interested in opera or heart research; and the like. When a fixed attribute such as race, religion, ethnicity, family, or sex is used to withhold prestige or to deny membership in prestige-giving organizations or activities, regardless of an individual's performance vis-à-vis the relevant achievement standards, one is dealing with an ascribed form of prestige.

Like all other societies, the United States uses age, sex, and family to determine an important range of social statuses. American society far exceeds the elementary use of ascription by also ascribing statuses on the basis of religion, ethnicity, family lineage, and race.

The areas of ascriptive evaluation in the United States that are fully contradictory of the achievement ethic are sex and race: Women, Indians, Chinese, Japanese, dark-skinned groups, and especially blacks have at one time or another all been categorized as permanent outsiders unfit to participate in the full range of available social statuses. Sexual ranking does not figure directly in social stratification, since females who are wives (or daughters) generally receive the class position of their husbands (or fathers). It is germane to the case of many working females, who are subject to deep ascriptive discrimination in pay and employment. However, the tradition of sexual inequality in America has never had the sustained ideological and political-legal base of racist inequality, and while women have not always been treated well they have never suffered the overt systematic degradation visited on nonwhite racial groups, especially blacks.

MORAL (OR PRESTIGE) EQUALITY

Stratification analysis does not always give due recognition to America's deep commitment to moral equality. Many of the definitive components of moral equality have been standard features of Western society since the ancient Greeks and Hebrews. Until the modern liberal period, however, moral equality in the West simply meant that all individuals were subject to universalistic moral norms, such as the Ten Commandments, and that all should aspire to certain universalistic ethical goals, such as love and brotherhood. While this tradition helped to prevent the development of a caste system in the West, it was perfectly compatible with an estate system of inequality (feudal Christendom). With the rise of liberal society, this moral tradition blended with the economic and political needs of capitalism to give rise to a more comprehensive definition of moral equality. It is not sufficiently understood that moral equality is an indispensable feature of industrialization. Prestige differentials based on birth invariably subsume and ultimately rigidify economic behavior, and are therefore the deadly enemy of economic expansion. The modern tradition of moral equality should also be understood, in other words, as a means of inviting all to participate in the new economy of capitalism or, in effect, as a moral sanction for dissolving feudal ties and developing an abstract labor force. Though the principle of moral equality emerged differently in countries, it has come to mean, speaking ideally, that all individuals either are or have the right to become persons—that is, self-propelled, responsible actors in and of the society in which they live. As a result, the state and society are defined in such a way as to confirm and promote (at least as an ideal and often in practice) the equal right of all citizens to influence the state and to participate in social life.

The American version of moral equality is unique, given the absence of a feudal tradition. The American state is unrivaled, except by France, in its formal acceptance of the almost absolute reality and rights of individuals. This atomistic-egalitarian definition of political-legal relations is matched by a widespread egalitarianism in social matters. Speaking broadly, Americans expect their leaders to be folksy, and they resent titles, uniforms, and badges denoting supersubordination.

On the whole, prestige forces tend to make populations unequal. Indeed, in the Indian caste system prestige forces were at one time so radically inegalitarian that they ruled out even token notions of equality. In the West, however, an important prestige force stemming from the Judaic-Christian tradition, democratic ideology, and secular humanism emphasizes the equal worth of individuals as moral-spiritual entities. At one level, in the United States, this realm underlies the widespread institutionalization (outside of occupation) of peer relations and "democratic manners"; at another level, it undergirds the egalitarianism that pervades the ideology (but not the practice) of American political-legal institutions. Americans resent attempts to translate occupational superiority into personal superiority. The deep streak of egalitarianism in the United States has been a constant theme in the work of commentators since the time of Tocqueville.

THE NEW "FREE" TIME (LEISURE)

Many of the most important forms of prestige behavior take place outside of work. For this reason, a full discussion of prestige must include a picture of noneconomic or "free" time. There is a widespread tendency to think that people today have more "free" time than their forebears, and that modern populations are being gradually emancipated from the compulsions of work. It is widely believed that as an economy grows it relaxes its grip on the personality and allows people to develop and elaborate morally valuable prestige pursuits. It is a central tenet of liberal democracy that economic growth leads to an increase in goods and services (discretionary income) and an increase in freedom from work (discretionary time), which in turn lead to an enhanced morality, higher culture, and personal fulfillment. That industrialization has brought about a growth in goods and services and an increase in time spent away from work since industrialization cannot be denied. But as we shall see in examining consumption (of both "material" and "symbolic" culture), it is not at all clear that there have been increases in discretionary income and time, if by *discretion* one means the capacity to choose freely from a meaningful set of alternatives.

It is undeniable that industrial society has brought about changes in the amount of "free" time as well as in the way in which time away from work is spent. Preindustrial societies are characterized by aristocracies with little interest in economic activities and a penchant for lavish consumption. Industrial society has obviously foreclosed the possibility of the dominant stratum being a leisured, nonworking group of this sort. Indeed, as we will emphasize, to understand contemporary society it is necessary to explore the fact that the powerful middle classes, and probably the upper class as well, are work-oriented.

Exactly what developments have taken place, then, in "free" time? Our contemporary economy has reduced the percentage of the labor force engaged in hard physical labor and produced a dramatic increase in the standard of living, changes that are obviously germane to understanding how people feel and behave off the job. There has also been a well-known decrease in the average work week. But the consequences of these changes have been badly misinterpreted. Many have come to the erroneous conclusion that affluence and the reduced work week have produced a style of life (consumption, use of time) that reflects a dissolution of classes. Just as we saw little evidence of the growth of a middle class mass in our analyses of income, wealth, occupation, education, and family and related behavior, we will find little evidence that the classes are converging in the area of prestige. It is important, therefore, that the deeply ingrained belief that economic growth leads inexorably and directly to moral growth (the dissolution of classes, growing participation in and harmony between groups, a rise in the levels of personal fulfillment and social service) must be carefully qualified if we are to understand prestige phenomena. For one thing, it is not at all certain that modern society has made more free time available. In a pioneering analysis, Wilensky has pointed out that the work week lengthened from the Middle Ages through the nineteenth century.[3] Preindustrial societies are characterized by a great deal of what in modern terms we would call unemployment and underemployment, and in this sense burden their populations with enforced idleness. Modern society, in other words, employs its population far more fully and effectively than do preindustrial systems. In an insightful

---

[3]Harold L. Wilensky, "The Uneven Distribution of Leisure: The Impact of Economic Growth on 'Free' Time," *Social Problems* 9 (Summer 1961): 32–56.

analysis, Linder has argued that it makes more sense to say that time has become increasingly scarce.[4] In addition to a more fully employed work force, one must also consider housewives (whose work week does not necessarily decline as a result of labor-saving devices—they simply become more productive); work and time devoted to personal maintenance; and work and time devoted to using and maintaining consumption goods.

Thus, idleness has declined since the preindustrial period (and is now an attribute of despised categories of people) and "cultural time" (time devoted to cultivation of the mind and spirit) since full industrialization may not be rising as much as we think. Linder argues that people experience the modern shortage of time in many ways: as a sense of being endlessly busy, a hectic tempo, compulsive punctuality, a yearning for simpler times, and a constant need to calculate the highest yield for any unit of time (either at work or during "free" time). This shortage of time stems from a class-based definition of time. In thinking about this and other aspects of "free" time in industrial society, a number of considerations should be kept in mind. First, the reduction of the work week appears to have ended during the post-1945 period; second, "free" time is distributed very unevenly; third, the use of "free" time differs qualitatively by class; and fourth, the basic uses of "free" time (prestige) are deeply embedded in and difficult to distinguish from "unfree" time (economic behavior and values).

More will be said about these various aspects of "free" time in subsequent chapters on prestige. At this point, we need clarify only one of the many misconceptions in this area, the tendency to assume that the work week has declined significantly for all and that it will continue to do so. It is undeniable that the work week itself has declined: During the nineteenth century it was well over sixty hours, in 1909 fifty-one hours, and by 1929 it had declined to forty-four hours. Since 1945, however, the work week has remained at about forty hours, which represents not only no decrease but also not much of a change since 1929. Averages (which include part-time work) are misleading and so are comparisons with the past, when more people worked in agriculture. Also, the legal work week should not be confused with the actual work week, since many workers put in overtime (much of it compulsory) and approximately 5 percent of the employed labor force holds two or more jobs. Though data in this area tend to be crude, one general conclusion seems justified: The reduction in the work week ceased after 1945.[5]

Wilensky has also argued against the popular notion of increasing leisure, claiming that the decline in the work week during the last century or so is vastly misunderstood. Basically, he argues, upper occupational groups work very long hours, and much of the apparent new leisure is actually

---

[4]Staffan Burenstam Linder, *The Harried Leisure Class* (New York: Columbia University Press, 1970), chaps. 1–5.

[5]Ibid., pp. 135–137.

involuntary under- or unemployment among the lower classes. The more favored occupations and classes, concludes Wilensky, "have what they have always had—the right to choose work as well as leisure."[6]

Wilensky's general theme is borne out by retirement studies showing that the upper classes tend to retire later than the lower classes, but that they also anticipate and plan more for retirement and experience less of a loss in self-esteem and, of course, income than the lower classes.[7]

THE PRIMACY OF CLASS

The distinction between class evaluation and prestige evaluation is an analytic convention, not always easy to substantiate empirically. To complicate matters, the distinction between class and prestige belies an underlying unity. Nevertheless, even when prestige phenomena can be explained in economic terms, they often take on lives of their own and become causes in their own right. As a rule, however, the two spheres are not often distinct entities. In the long run the "social order" and the class hierarchy are brought into harmony—but prestige always appears as a separate realm. Sheer property is never accepted as an absolute credential for social honor or admittance to valued forms of social interaction. In consequence, there is always a tension between these two spheres of inequality, though it is often concealed by the dominance of one over the other. In this there appears to be no set pattern: sometimes class dominates prestige (the class system associated with industrial society), but more often prestige has subsumed the class order (the caste and estate systems of stratification associated with agrarian society).

The power of prestige vis-à-vis class (or power) in industrial society must not be exaggerated. Weber reminds us that the market is no respecter of persons. Once unleashed, economic forces can upset even the most deeply rooted prestige structures, such as when colonial powers promote extraction, commerce, and industry and thereby undermine the authority of tribal elders and the family; or when considerations of efficiency hasten the absorption of blacks into the labor force and weaken commitment to racially segregated waiting rooms and toilets; or when businesspeople endow universities, receive honorary degrees, and eventually come to dominate their governing boards.

The rise of capitalism represents a major transformation in the relationship between prestige and class (and power). The basic thrust of liberalism in the past five hundred years has been to free land, labor, and prices—and

---

[6]Wilensky, "The Uneven Distribution of Leisure," p. 56.

[7]Frances M. Carp, ed., *Retirement* (New York: Behavioral Publications. 1972), pp. 176f.; 251f., and Malcolm H. Morrison, ed., *Economics of Aging: The Future of Retirement* (New York: Van Nostrand Reinhold, 1982), pp. 120–122.

values and beliefs in general—from their subordination to moral, religious, and ascriptive-feudal standards. For this reason one must not exaggerate the autonomy of prestige within liberal society.[8]

In the rest of this chapter and the two that follow we will explore a large and diverse body of prestige data. In exploring this highly complex material, our basic orientation will be to view the dimension of prestige in terms of the logic of a class system of stratification, being careful, however, not to assume that economic institutions are always at odds with ascription or that prestige phenomena are always easy to relate to class.

CLASS AND HOW AMERICANS REGARD THEMSELVES

In the remainder of this chapter we will examine how Americans regard themselves and explore some of their basic attitudes about the world they live in. This aspect of stratification analysis has a rich history and has yielded important data not only about inequality, but also about the congruities and incongruities between economic life (class) and the world of subjectivity (prestige). Perhaps the most important form of prestige inequality is that attributed to occupational status, a subjective hierarchy that correlates highly with income and education (though there are some exceptions).

THE HIERARCHY OF OCCUPATIONAL PRESTIGE

The first scientifically reliable national study of the prestige of occupations was conducted by the National Opinion Research Center (NORC) in 1947.[9] Americans were asked to rate ninety occupations as "excellent," "good," "average," "somewhat below average," "poor," or "don't know where to place." Their answers, though they contained few surprises, composed a valuable profile of occupational prestige in the United States. Highest prestige was consistently accorded to occupations characterized by highly specialized training and high responsibility for the public welfare. The occupations of United States Supreme Court justice, physician, state governor,

[8]On the other hand, it is of some significance that Christianity provided much of the moral lubrication needed to bring about the free interaction of entire populations, a freedom indispensable to a dynamic economy. Thus, Christians (unlike Hindus, for example) regarded themselves as well as non-Christians as human beings capable of having social relations; in this connection see, for example, St. Paul's *Epistle to the Romans*. In recent American history, Christianity has played a similar role in bringing blacks into American life. Though framed in terms of morality and civil rights, the drive for black equality (often spearheaded by black churches) can also be seen as an effort to incorporate a despised rural labor force ("caste") into America's abstract, mobile, industrial labor force (class).

[9]C.C. North and P. K. Hatt, "Jobs and Occupations: A Popular Evaluation," *Opinion News* 9 (1 September 1947): 3–13.

member of the federal cabinet, diplomat in the United States Foreign Service, mayor of a large city, college professor, and scientist headed the list, and were followed by other professions. Then came skilled and unskilled workers, with garbage collector, street sweeper, and shoe shiner at the bottom of the list.

In 1963 the NORC conducted another study of occupational prestige, reproducing its original study as closely as possible in order to see what changes, if any, had occurred in the intervening period. The results revealed a remarkable overall stability in Americans' views of occupations. Though there was some shifting of ranks, the hierarchy of occupational prestige scores in 1963 remained essentially the same as in the earlier study.[10]

Later surveys have confirmed this hierarchy in public opinion (see Table 10–1). Of perhaps greater importance than the stability of occupational prestige is the striking consensus Americans display about the relative worth of occupations. The fact that a sample representing the American population are in substantial agreement time and again on how to rate occupations is of enormous significance primarily because it means that those in low-rated occupations voted that their own occupations deserved low prestige. This finding dramatically illustrates why social inequality is rarely a matter of physical coercion, resting instead on "moral coercion," or, put more politely, socialization. The significance of the American social achievement in this regard is enhanced if one remembers that work is the central source of identity in modern society and that the United States also has a deep commitment to egalitarian values. Perhaps nothing in the annals of functional role specialization equals the way in which Americans combine a commitment to moral and political-legal equality with a consensus on the radically unequal worth of occupations.

The stability and consensus about occupational ratings in the United States should not be interpreted as a fundamental of social structure or that we live in a meritocracy. This mistaken view of occupation can be found in a comparative study of occupational prestige in sixty countries by Donald Treiman, who argues that occupational prestige is similar in countries representing complex feudal and industrial societies. This similarity means that we are dealing with a fixed feature of social organization and that functional imperatives see to it that similar occupational hierarchies arise everywhere. These hierarchies reflect ability and training and result in differentials in income and authority.[11]

---

[10]For this study and for additional materials showing stability in the distribution of occupational prestige between 1925 and 1963, see R. W. Hodge, P. M. Siegel, and P. H. Rossi, "Occupational Prestige in the United States, 1925–63," *American Journal of Sociology* 70, no. 3 (November 1964): 286–302.

[11]Donald J. Treiman, *Occupational Prestige in Comparative Perspective* (New York: Academic Press, 1977).

TABLE 10-1.   The Relative Occupational Prestige of Fifty Occupations in the United States

OCCUPATION	PRESTIGE SCORE	OCCUPATION	PRESTIGE SCORE
Physician	82	Secretary	46
Professor	78	Air traffic controller	43
Lawyer/judges	76	Firefighter	44
Dentist	74	Mail carrier	42
Bank officer	72	Restaurant manager	39
Airplane pilot	70	Building superintendent/	
Clergy	69	manager	38
Engineer	67	Automobile mechanic	37
Registered nurse	62	Airline steward	36
Dental hygenist	61	Brick/stone mason	36
Officials, administrators,		TV repairperson	35
public administration	61	Hairdresser	33
Elementary school teacher	60	Bulldozer operator	33
Union official	58	Bus driver	32
Accountant	57	Truck driver	32
Actors	55	Cashier	31
Dietician	52	Retail sales clerks	29
Funeral director	52	Gas station attendant	22
Social worker	52	Taxi driver/chauffeur	22
Editor/reporter	51	Bartender	20
Locomotive engineer	51	Waiter	20
Sales manager	50	Farm laborer	18
Electrician	49	Household servant/maid	18
Machinist	48	Garbage collector	17
Police and detectives	48	Janitor	16
Insurance agent	47	Bootblacks	09

Source: Adapted from James A. Davis and Tom W. Smith, *General Social Surveys, 1972–1986: Cumulative Codebook* (Chicago: National Opinion Research Center, 1986), Appendix F. Missing from the general social survey are titles such as U.S. Supreme Court Justice, Federal Cabinet Member, U.S. Representative in Congress, Mayor of large city, and State Governor which had appeared in earlier surveys and received high prestige scores. Used by permission.

Conflict theories have rejected this argument. Occupational prestige and differentials in income and authority all result from social power—they do not reflect either human ability or functional necessity. Analysts have discovered distinctly different prestige ratings in Marxist societies with working-class occupations accorded both higher prestige and more income that those found in capitalist societies.[12]

[12]Roger Penn, "Occupational Prestige Hierarchies. A Great Empirical Invariant?," *Social Forces* 54 (December 1975): 352–364. This study shows that Czechoslovakia and Poland have distinctively different prestige hierarchies that accord skilled workers higher prestige and utility to society than do studies in the United States. For differences in the USSR, see Murray Yanowitch, *Social and Economic Inequality in the Soviet Union* (White Plains, N.Y.: M.E. Sharpe, 1977).

Nothing in American (or any class) society matches the importance of occupation for influencing the images people have of themselves and each other. Changing their position in the occupational structure is vital, for example, to enhancing the image and power of minority groups. But for minority and majority groups alike, there is a problem that transcends discrimination and prejudice: the problem posed by an economy that not only cannot provide jobs for all, but also contains a great many jobs with negative prestige.

Occupational Structure and the Lack of Prestige

The United States (its powerful corporations and its property- oriented legislatures) tolerates significant amounts of unemployment. America's insensitivity to unemployment not only causes physical but also psychic hardship for millions of Americans. In addition, there are many occupations (out of a total of approximately 20,000 job titles in the United States) that afford little if any prestige and often burden their occupants with negative prestige. Thus, while there is a hierarchy of occupational prestige, it must be visualized as characterized by sharp breaks: an upper range of high-prestige occupations that coincide, by and large, with high position in all other hierarchies; a middle range of heterogeneous occupations difficult to define easily; a lower middle range of occupations with little or no prestige; a still lower group of negatively evaluated jobs, and beneath them the underemployed and unemployed. Those who occupy these lower occupations, or are chronically out of work or only partially employed, also occupy the lower rungs of other stratification ladders.

The importance of the occupational prestige dimension for unifying and legitimizing the hierarchies of class, prestige, and power is difficult to exaggerate. Those at the top receive the moral blessing of society by virtue of their occupations, which helps to legitimate their activities, benefits, and leadership in other areas; those at the bottom are morally evaluated in a negative way, which tends to legitimate both their economic failure and their overall position at the bottom of society.

The difficulties involving occupational prestige that many experience in industrial society elicit a variety of responses and solutions. Occupations that provide little prestige are invariably associated with close supervision, confining routines, punching a time-clock, and wearing a uniform (though some upper-level occupations, such as admirals and archbishops, also involve uniforms). Perhaps the ultimate prestige difficulty is to be without work. Because the problem of job prestige shades off into other problems, such as work satisfaction, pay, and personal identity, the following remarks have been framed in general terms. There are, first of all, the well-known disastrous consequences to personality and family life of unemployment.[13] There is the tendency to invent ego-inflating occupational titles (such as "sanitary engineer" for janitor) and to provide name plates and other prestige associated items in the work situation. Workers set informal production quotas to prevent their identities from merging with the incentiveoriented, impersonalized factory system. The "protection of the inept" appears to be widespread as society struggles to find places for average people and noneconomic values.[14] Featherbedding occurs as workers violate achievement norms rather than face the humiliation of unemployment. Low-level and dissatisfied workers retire early when given the choice, and massproduction automobile workers, responding overwhelmingly to early retirement plans, expressed great enjoyment of the freedom of retirement.[15] The demand for high wages is probably largely understandable as a compensation for psychologically unrewarding occupations and, in some cases, an overt substitute for social mobility. Some workers with good jobs have a prestige problem because their work is difficult to describe and understand, and is therefore not readily converted into prestige; examples are legislative committee staffers and systems analysts. And some jobs present particularly onerous prestige problems—for example, servant, garbage collector, and so forth.

Stratification Within Classes and Occupations

Social classes tend to be roughly uniform in prestige, income, occupation, and power. But a social class can also contain economic statuses that differ in significant ways. For example, within the upper-middle class, doctors and professors enjoy comparable prestige but have very different incomes. The same thing is true of ministers, psychologists, and airline pilots.

A similar form of hierarchy is the hierarchy within a given occupation. Thus, some doctors earn more and are accorded more prestige than other doctors, and a similar pattern is apparent in many other occupations. With a few exceptions, stratification within occupations is not well documented.[16] We do know, in a general way, that the world of the corporate executive is

---

[13]The classic pioneering empirical study in this area is Mirra Komarovsky, *The Unemployed Man and His Family* (New York: Octagon Books, 1971; originally published in 1940).

[14]See William J. Goode, "The Protection of the Inept," *American Sociological Review* 32 (February 1967): 5–19.

[15]Richard Barfield and James N. Morgan, *Early Retirement: The Decision and the Experience* (Ann Arbor, Mich.: Institute for Social Research, 1970), pp. 1–7.

[16]An interesting and unexplored avenue to information in this area is analysis of the proliferating Halls of Fame in such areas as sports, aviation, agriculture, the franchise industry, and the like, and among songwriters, actors, cowboys, ethnic groups, and the like, and of the wide variety of achievement awards in such fields as moviemaking, the recording industry, the theater, writing, sports, industry, government, and so on.

permeated with prestige gradations and distinctions. The executive washroom is a well-known example and symbol of the numerous occupationally based benefits that have prestige significance; size and location of office, type of desk, furnishings, and the like make for deep prestige differentiation among members of the same occupation.

The world of government (the legislature, the judiciary, and the executive, including the civil service and the military) also contains obvious hierarchies within occupations. For example, a member of the United States Senate has far more prestige than a senator in the Maine legislature. A judge is only an abstraction until we know whether he or she works at the municipal, state, or federal level.

The growth of professionalism has undoubtedly led to greater internal stratification in business, government, and other occupations, including the world of sports. Perhaps the best way to conceptualize stratification within occupations is to note two characteristics of occupations: (1) occupations (especially organized occupations) try to maintain and promote the overall social class level of their members, and (2) occupations tend to be stratified internally. Perhaps the best-known example of stratification within an occupation involves lawyers. We know that lawyers enjoy high national prestige when ranked in the abstract. They also have high incomes and exercise great power. In fact, one of the interesting features of the legal profession is its close alliance with the modern corporation as well as with the exercise of political power. No other profession enjoys such enviable access to high stratification benefits in both the class and power dimensions. Straddling the upper reaches of all three dimensions of stratification, lawyers are a strategic link in the structure of social power. However, despite their high abstract class position, lawyers are not a narrowly homogeneous group. Jerome Carlin's empirical study[17] of a substantial number of the lawyers in New York City (who are probably representative of lawyers in most urban areas of the nation) reveals a distinct hierarchy *within* the legal profession. According to Carlin's evidence, the bar of New York City is "a highly stratified professional community" based on a hierarchy of law firms (or business enterprises). The large firms tend to have more respectable clients and to deal with the upper levels of the court and governmental systems. Their members come from the established classes and the more prestigious colleges and law schools, and tend to be Protestant. The cleavage between the elite firms and those below them tends to maintain itself over time, suggesting an organized pattern of recruitment and retention. Mobility between the various levels is rare and tends to favor those with elite backgrounds. Contact between the levels is also rare, and their separation is formalized by the existence of two

---

[17]*Lawyers' Ethics: A Survey of the New York City Bar* (New York: Russell Sage Foundation, 1966). For similar results in Chicago, see John Heinz and Edward Laumann, *Chicago Lawyers* (New York: Russell Sage Foundation, 1982).

separate bar associations. Violations of professional norms occur mostly at the lower levels of this hierarchy. And, finally, the overall organization of the profession results in a decided pattern of distribution of legal services according to social class. The upper classes are well served by the elite firms, the poor are not served at all, and the rest are served by the nonelite firms.[18]

The distribution of occupational prestige appears to conform to a number of well-known cultural and social themes and trends. Within an occupation, prestige tends to be highest among those who work for national and international enterprises (corporations, governments), size tending to reflect importance and competence. A similar set of standards operates in other occupations: colleges, universities, and professional schools, for example, are ranked according to national (and international) standards, and professors' prestige in the academic world as well as among the general public is a function of the prestige of the school they work for. Occupations also derive prestige from the clients they serve. Federal politicians and civil servants work for "the people," while local politicians work for the town, city, or state. Research doctors work for humanity, while medical practitioners work for individual patients; doctors with rich patients have more prestige than doctors with poor patients. Professors with well-to-do students gain prestige, while professors at plebian schools lose prestige. Prostitutes with upper-middle class clients enjoy more prestige than streetwalkers. And lawyers associated with corporate or public power enjoy more prestige than those whose activities are confined to divorce and criminal cases.

These well-structured hierarchies of prestige within occupations may forestall a number of prestige problems. (We have no direct evidence on this question.) To the extent that people are oriented toward prestige within occupations, for example, the social system is spared the task of judging the absolute or relative worth of the various occupations. Secondly, the focus on prestige *within* occupations probably leads to absorption with the economic issues pertinent to specific occupations, which may in turn reduce concern about differences in the economic worth of occupations. And, finally, preoccupation with prestige (and economic) status within occupations may make it possible for a social system to avoid having to make precise correlations between standings in the realms of class and prestige (and power). Though this is all mostly conjecture, it is probably no exaggeration to say that "status communities" based on occupation can reveal a great deal about how modern society remains stable and integrated. And they can probably tell us a lot about the unethical conduct, incompetence, and outright exploitation that are such significant and chronic features of our economic system.

---

[18]The latter point is also made by Leon Mayhew and Albert J. Reiss, Jr., "The Social Organization of Legal Contacts." *American Sociological Review* 34 (June 1969): 309–318; reprinted in Donald Black and Maureen Mileski, eds., *The Social Organization of Law* (New York: Seminar Press, 1973), chap. 11.

The existence of stratification within various economic statuses raises an important problem for class analysis. Because many economic enterprises and occupations are internally stratified, one cannot automatically assign all members of a given economic status to the same class. This is of special importance when analyzing the middle classes. In other words, individual farmers, businesspeople, lawyers, doctors, professors, and so on do not have uniform economic statuses; by and large, it appears that some are upper, some upper-middle, and some lower-middle class.

CLASS SELF-IDENTIFICATION

If Americans are asked what class they belong to, or whether they are upper, middle, or lower class, their overwhelming response is to select the middle class. In his pioneering study based on 1945 data, Richard Centers gave white Americans the choice of these three classes and the working class. As a result of the extra option, he elicited a different response than did previous surveys; 40 percent of his respondents identified with the middle class and slightly more than half identified with the working class.[19]

Drawing on a 1964 NORC study, Robert W. Hodge and Donald J. Treiman[20] found that 16.6 percent of the American population identified with the upper middle class, 44 percent with the middle class, and 34.3 percent with the working class. Thus, between 1945 and 1964 there occurred a significant decline in the number of Americans who considered themselves working class.

In a recent study, Mary and Robert Jackman found that Americans are very much aware of classes. Americans, argue the Jackmans, perceive classes as a graded series of social communities that they define in economic and cultural terms. In a national sample, Americans were asked to place themselves in the following hierarchy of five classes: upper class, upper middle, middle, working, and poor. Out of 100 respondents, 97 indicated that they knew which class they belonged to and they used the basic components of class such as income, occupation, and education in defining class. The results can be seen in Table 10–2.

Americans' awareness of class contained no cleavage between blue- and white-collar workers or between the propertied and nonpropertied. Americans also failed to carry their awareness of class into the arena of politics. This is not surprising, say the Jackmans, because American political

---

[19]Richard Centers, *The Psychology of Social Classes* (Princeton, N.J.: Princeton University Press, 1949), Table 18, p. 77.

[20]"Class Identification in the United States," *American Journal of Sociology* 73 (March 1968): 535–547; reprinted in Joseph Lopreato and Lionel S. Lewis, eds., *Social Stratification: A Reader* (New York: Harper & Row, 1974), pp. 182–192.

TABLE 10-2.   Class Self-Identification by Americans, 1975

CLASS	PERCENT
Upper	1
Upper middle	8
Middle	43
Working	37
Poor	8
Other (don't know, don't exist)	3

Source: Mary R. Jackman and Robert W. Jackman, *Class Awareness in The United States* (Berkeley: University of California Press, 1983), Table 2.1. Used with permission.

institutions, including our political parties, consistently deny the existence of class-based interests.

PREJUDICE AND DISCRIMINATION

The belief that some people are unalterably different from and inferior to others is a widespread feature of both the internal and external histories of societies. Essentially, such views are promoted by dominant power groups to support their economic exploitation and political control of their own or subject peoples. This relationship is somewhat obscured in the United States, where the dominant ethos proclaims the moral equality of all human beings and the upper classes tend to voice more tolerant views than the lower classes. Attitude studies, however, should probably be discounted somewhat: The upper groups have greater verbal facility and are conscious of the bad publicity that attends expressed prejudices; in other words, their more tolerant views may contain a certain measure of hypocrisy and rationalization. And perhaps more importantly, attitudes are not the same as behavior. Upper, intermediate, and even lower (nonminority) groups can voice egalitarian views while practicing and benefitting from discrimination. *Formally expressed opinions, in other words, do not necessarily represent people's actual behavior in other contexts.* Therefore, while attitudes are important indices of stratification, they should not be confused or equated with actual behavior. Lofty thoughts and noble emotions expressed in the abstract are often ineffective when they conflict with contradictory thoughts and values in concrete situations.[21] And lofty thoughts and sentiments often serve to camouflage

[21]For example, individuals who sincerely believe in human equality may, because they also believe in protecting or enhancing their own property, resist low-income housing in their community.

power relations and important social processes.[22] In the following analyses of attitudes toward black, Jewish, and Mexican Americans, we will see two patterns: The expression of prejudice is related to class, and the growing tolerance and acceptance of these minorities does not mean that they are entering an era of achievement, equality of opportunity, and nondiscrimination.

Changing Attitudes Toward Minorities

White Americans developed a dramatically more favorable view of the capabilities and rights of black Americans from the 1930s to the 1980s. White Americans expressed a clear acceptance of the idea that blacks have the same intelligence as whites; of the black Americans' formal right to equality of opportunity in education, employment, and housing; and of the need to desegregate schools and transportation. Nonetheless, Americans continued to be prejudiced about black Americans, though less so among the young and the better educated.[23]

In 1964 the Survey Research Center of the University of California at Berkeley, in cooperation with the National Opinion Research Center of the University of Chicago, conducted the first extensive analysis of anti-Semitism in the United States, using a representative national sample.[24] One of its important findings is that one-third of the American population holds anti-Semitic prejudices in some form or another. The most recent studies suggest, however, that there has been a decline in Americans' negative evaluation of Jews. Majority Americans also developed a more positive view of Hispanics between 1948 and 1987.[25]

These trends, it should be repeated, indicate nothing more than a change in attitudes, which cannot necessarily be equated with other forms of behavior. Nevertheless, while majority Americans are still capable of discrimination (and prejudice), they are less and less willing to justify their actions with words.

The Burden of Moral Equality

The modern belief in the moral (including political-legal) equality of human beings is not an unmixed blessing, and it should not be assumed that this tradition rejects all forms of social inequality. It is unquestionable that the

---

[22]For example, the civil rights movement is as much a class process (a way of transforming rural labor into an urban-industrial labor force) as it is a political-legal-moral movement.

[23]Howard Schuman, Charlotte Steeh, and Lawrence Bobo, *Racial Attitudes in America: Trends and Interpretations* (Cambridge, Mass.: Harvard University Press, 1985), and *Public Opinion* 10 (July/August 1987), Special Issue on Prejudice.

[24]For an extended analysis of this data, see Gertrude J. Selznick and Stephen Steinberg, *The Tenacity of Prejudice: Anti-Semitism in Contemporary America* (New York: Harper & Row, 1969).

[25]*Public Opinion* 10 (July/August 1987), Special Issue on Prejudice.

concept of moral equality is deeply incompatible with caste and estate forms of stratification. But it is wrong to say that moral equality is necessarily in conflict with class stratification; it actually meshes with and reinforces the class hierarchy. One need only remember that the liberal tradition of moral equality is often posited on the assumption that individuals as individuals are responsible actors to appreciate the way in which this tradition harmonizes with the liberal explanation of social stratification, "nonegalitarian classlessness." Given equality of opportunity, according to this explanation, all social inequality is natural and just since it reflects the innate capabilities of the individual.

One of the best illustrations of the irony contained in the American tradition of moral equality is apparent in the pattern of white attitudes toward blacks. Remember that a comparison of public opinion polls from 1939 on found a dramatic decrease in the percentage of white Americans who believe that whites are racially (morally and intellectually) superior to blacks. But when asked in the late 1960s the cause of the depressed social position of Negroes, a majority of whites answered "Negroes themselves." In other words, acceptance of the black American as an equal entails acceptance of the liberal belief that human beings are free to determine their own destinies and therefore responsible for their own lives.[26] Americans, in other words, have little understanding of behavior as a function of institutions, and the fact that white Americans are discarding racist beliefs does not mean that they have adopted a sociocultural explanation of inequality. What they have done in discarding racist views, it appears, is to explain black behavior in the same way that they explain white behavior, as emanating from forces in individuals themselves.

The ability of the class system to protect itself is enhanced, therefore, by the widespread prestige phenomenon called moral equality. Obviously, the tradition of moral equality is also helpful to minorities in combating inequality; indeed, it is a continuing source of tension in American society. Our purpose here, however, is to stress the latent consequences of this tradition: to point out that insofar as it rests on the assumption that individuals are free to determine their own destinies, the tradition of moral equality is a burden to those who seek redress for inequities through the reform or restructuring of society.

When the tradition of moral equality is manifested in public policy as equal treatment and equal opportunity, the results are just as mixed. Obviously, it is a gain for minority groups no longer to be discriminated against, but to be treated uniformly does not have the positive consequences our tradition of equality implies. When blacks, Mexican Americans, Puerto

[26]For the development of this point by means of a comparison of these two sets of data, see the article by Howard Schuman, "Free Will and Determinism in Public Beliefs About Race," *Transaction 7* (December 1969): 44–48.

Ricans, or Indians in the aggregate are allowed to compete in school and for jobs, fellowships, and so on, the outcome is predictable: They will lose because their social experience has shaped them for failure. Special efforts to offer realistic opportunities to minorities are another matter. But even here no change in the relative position of minorities in the aggregate (as opposed to individuals) should be expected to follow automatically.

THE CULTURE HERO AS AN INDEX TO PRESTIGE

The Culture Hero in America

Culture heroes personify some of the core values and beliefs of a society, and therefore illustrate the processes that elevate some individuals above others. In the United States, the culture hero *par excellence* is the individual who is his or her own person and who overcomes adversity by drawing on his or her own resources. American culture heroes are easy to name: George Washington is an obvious choice, as are some of our other presidents, most notably, Thomas Jefferson, Abraham Lincoln, Theodore Roosevelt, and Franklin Roosevelt. Of all our culture heroes perhaps none has achieved the stature of Lincoln, a man who personified all the most vigorous American values: humble origins, hard work amid adversity, intellectual striving, moral strength, and a common touch. Probably the only figure to rival Lincoln as a culture hero is Dwight Eisenhower; in terms of popularity in one's lifetime, no American in our history has enjoyed more popular esteem than this general-turned-politician.

The United States, like most nations, has a rich complement of heroic figures, real and mythical, who serve as models or reference "groups" for its population. As Dixon Wector[27] has pointed out, Americans love character more than brains; earthy secular personalities more than saints; lowbrow more than highbrow types; and men of simple, decent, and honorable traits who are forgiven bad means if the cause is noble. It is noteworthy that our major heroes are Anglo-Saxon and Protestant; that women have rarely been chosen as heroic models; that artists, doctors, and lawyers are bypassed; and that invariably the soldier, the explorer, and especially the wartime leader has been cast as a hero.[28]

Our understanding of the relation between heroes and social stratification has been furthered by Theodore P. Greene's use of magazine biographies to gauge changes in America's images of its heroes.[29] Greene distinguishes

[27] *The Hero in America* (New York: Charles Scribner's Sons, 1941), chap. 18.

[28] Religious-ethnic and racial groups have their own heroes (Malcolm X and Martin Luther King, for example, among blacks). It would be interesting to know more about the heroes who serve as models for minority groups, and to know whether there is variation in hero worship by class among both majority and minority groups.

three periods in American history, each characterized by a distinctive type of popular hero, as judged by magazine biographies. Between 1787 and 1820 America worshipped "The Idols of Order"; in Greene's terms, the "hero emerges as a Patriot, a Gentleman, and a Scholar in magazines of gentlemen, by gentlemen, and for gentlemen." Between 1894 and 1913 America worshipped "The Idols of Power and of Justice"; according to Greene, the "hero has become the Master of His Environment and gains national stature in new magazines of the people, by business entrepreneurs, for profit." During the latter part of this period the "hero dons some social garments to protect his individualistic frame in magazines at the peak of their power." And finally, from 1914 to 1918 (and presumably since), America worshipped "The Idols of Organization"; as Greene says, the "hero becomes a Manager of Massive Organizations portrayed in magazines for the masses."

The Celebrity

Twentieth-century communications technology has produced a new type of culture hero, the celebrity. What is the significance of celebrities and what images of life are portrayed through them by the mass media? Does their advent represent a significant change in the models held up for Americans to emulate? In the absence of rigorous empirical research, one can only speculate about these and other questions. Does the cult of the celebrity provide vicarious meaning and satisfaction to millions of otherwise drab lives? As C. Wright Mills has suggested, the phenomenon of the celebrity may serve as a distraction from other problems and is probably influential in diverting attention from the shortcomings of society.[30] Exactly how "mass culture" works to distract the masses and distort their image of the world cannot as yet be said scientifically. But questions are easily raised. What is the significance of the theme of violence and aggression in America mass media (the cowboy, the gangster, the private detective, the football star and team)? Does violence, for example, help the audience to discharge in fantasy its resentment of bosses, or competitors, or economic forces? Do the mass media portray a world of clean-cut morality and easy solutions, thus disguising the role of power groups and compounding the ambiguities and conflicts in the workday world? What is the significance of the heroes who use unsavory or illegal means to achieve their ends?

It is possible that the rise of the celebrity signifies a shift from a world of achievement to a world of ascription. Celebrity status is difficult to achieve—after all, an unusual voice, face, figure, height, or agility is inborn. And the cult of the celebrity tends to associate success with luck and inborn traits

---

[29] *America's Heroes: The Changing Models of Success in American Magazines* (New York: Oxford University Press, 1970).

[30] For these points and for a valuable general discussion of prestige, see C. Wright Mills, *The Power Elite* (New York: Oxford University Press. 1956), Chapter 4.

rather than with hard methodical work. The rags-to-riches theme is prevalent in the world of the celebrity, like the hero, but the celebrity's success is often attributed to good fortune rather than intelligence, frugality, or work. Nonetheless, the phenomenon of the celebrity may serve to keep the American Dream alive among the disadvantaged and oppressed: Black youth may derive vicarious satisfaction from seeing Bill Cosby, "Magic" Johnson, or Whitney Houston make it big. There are many analogues for other minorities and for whites as well.

The celebrity may also signify a shift from a production-oriented society to one in which consumption must be stimulated and managed. Celebrities are often connoisseurs of consumption, and are used extensively in advertising to encourage and guide others in their consumption. In so doing, celebrities lend their prestige to the world of business and help to develop and legitimate the ethic of consumption. And one must not forget that the various spheres of entertainment in which celebrities perform are big business in their own right. Celebrities also involve themselves in politics and in the sphere of voluntary action. They support various political parties, run for office, and are occasionally elected. And celebrities lend the magic of their names and presences to many forms of moral uplift (boys' clubs, neighborhood programs, ghetto youth activities). And, finally, the celebrity signifies the professionalization and commercialization of sports and entertainment, processes related to basic developments in other areas of modern society. Indeed, the realms of sports and entertainment may reveal more clearly than other areas the emergence of a spectator society, a basic cleavage between elite and mass, and the failure of the early liberal ideal of the versatile individual in a participatory society.

The relationship between public and celebrity is a national phenomenon, a true nationwide prestige currency. But, as C. Wright Mills reminds us, prestige relationships based on worship, admiration, and envy of celebrities are difficult to institutionalize, and thus provide no easy way for the economic, political, and "social" elites to legitimate themselves. The celebrity's fame is too personal and ephemeral to serve as a basis for the long-range legitimation of positions acquired by other means. For that reason, says Mills, the cult of the celebrity is primarily a distraction and only an indirect way of enhancing and sanctioning high class and high political power.

CLASS, PERSONALITY, AND WORLD VIEW

The most influential and best-known analysis of class and personality is in the work of Karl Marx. Marx had a profound influence on social science by treating not only conventional behavior but also thoughts and emotions (personality) as reflections of class position. Marx, as we have said, held that the key to the nature of classes is the modal technology of the period, and that ownership and nonownership of the means of production is the basic factor in the composition of social classes. However, classes can also be identified by their thoughts and values, according to Marx. Each class, he argued, has a distinctive subjective existence that emanates from its relation to the means of production. Marx's sociology of knowledge—the relation between social experience on the one hand, and values and ideas, subjective existence, and personality on the other—was capped by his concept of ideology. According to Marx, when a class is riding the crest of a new mode of technology, its thoughts and values are rational, valid, and progressive. In time, however, technological change renders these ideas and values obsolete, thereby turning them into ideology, or the symbolic defense of an outmoded social system.

While enormously influential, Marx's ideas about the relation between class and personality are not easy to verify empirically. For one thing, the means of production are now enormously complex. For another, it is difficult to establish a relation between the ownership of productive property and the occupational system. Despite these difficulties, however, the fundamental thrust of Marx's thought was sound: classes emerge from economic institutions and can be identified by their distinctive world views.

In his pioneering cross-national study, Melvin L. Kohn found a profound cleavage in the basic perception of self and reality between higher and lower classes, as distinguished by occupation. Analyzing data from Turin, Italy; Washington, D.C.; and a national sample of the United States representing all men in civilian occupations, Kohn concludes that the intrinsic nature of work is the most important determinant of a worker's values. A self-directed personality and the feeling that one lives in a "benign" society are associated with jobs that are not closely supervised; entail complex work involving data or people, rather than things; and are intricately organized. Workers whose jobs are closely supervised, simply organized, and involve things are likely to be conformists and feel that they live in an "indifferent or threatening" society.

The variable of occupational self-direction was found to be more important in determining world view than family structure, race, religion, national background, income, or subjective class identification. Other variables of occupation, such as bureaucratic or entrepreneurial settings; governmental, profit-making, or nonprofit employers; degree of time pressure; job satisfaction; ownership of the means of production; and job rights and protections (union contracts, seniority, grievance procedures, tenure, civil service, and such) were also less consequential. The self-directed personality, says Kohn—though related to education, which is itself closely related to occupation—is basically a function of occupational self-direction.[31]

[31]Melvin L. Kohn, *Class and Conformity: A Study in Values* (Homewood, Ill.: Dorsey Press, 1969). For follow-up studies in the same vein, see Melvin L. Kohn and Carmi Schooler with Joanne Miller, *Work and Personality: An Inquiry into the Impact of Social Stratification* (Norwood, N.J.: Ablex, 1983).

Evidence from other sources indicates that class tends to override other allegiances. For example, it is known that Protestants, Roman Catholics, and Jews, as well as whites and nonwhites, who are members of the same class, share similar values and beliefs and develop similar personalities. Indeed, the cultural assimilation of immigrants and acculturation across religious-ethnic-racial lines by class is fairly complete.[32]

Another national survey has given us a more detailed picture of the distribution of values in the American population. In 1968 the National Opinion Research Center administered the Value Survey to a national sample of Americans over twenty-one. Developed by Milton Rokeach, the Value Survey consists of two lists of eighteen terminal and instrumental values, arranged alphabetically. Respondents were asked to rank each list "in order of importance to YOU, as guiding principles in YOUR life." One of the clear findings of the 1968 survey was that values vary considerably by class (income, education), especially between the bottom and top levels.[33]

CLASS AND CLASS CONSCIOUSNESS

Are Americans Conscious of Stratification by Class?

Karl Marx saw class consciousness as the awakening of the working classes (the great majority of the population) to their exploitation by a small group of big property owners. Marx felt that class consciousness was a natural by-product of class struggle in which first the middle class rises against the feudal lord (in the name of liberty, equality, and representative government) and then the working class rises against the now obsolete middle class (in the name of humanity and the classless society).

Are Americans class conscious in the Marxian sense? Are they conscious of social classes and class exploitation in any sense? Are they aware that the American class system has many illegitimate elements? Are they aware that their society has a deeply rooted system of advantage and disadvantage based on family birth?

By and large, the answer to these questions is no. Americans are not very conscious of class and do not consciously frame their lives in class terms. Invariably, they interpret differential striving and differential success in individual terms (as functional competition between individuals of different innate ability). Of course, Americans are aware of the existence of inequality, even radical inequality, but they do not characteristically think of it in class terms—that is, they do not explain inequality in terms of economic and social

---

[32]For a fuller discussion of cultural and social assimilation in relation to social stratification, see Chapter 12.

[33]Milton Rokeach. *The Nature of Human Values* (New York: Free Press, 1973), pp. 59–66.

variables. Class consciousness, in other words, is awareness that one's social level derives from an economic and social environment one shares with those in similar circumstances and that social level has little to do with natural forces, human or otherwise.

Class consciousness, in other words, is awareness that basic forms of inequality are historical in nature—that is, changeable, with those at the top of society usually interested in preventing change and those at the bottom (who are class conscious) wanting a restructuring of economy and social power.

Americans are aware, naturally, that some people are rich and others are not rich, that some are advantaged and others disadvantaged, that some have easy jobs while others have difficult jobs, and that some individuals inherit considerable sums of money while others inherit little or nothing. By and large, though, Americans believe that a person's position in society is the result of work, brains, drive, or even luck or connections; only rarely do they see the distribution of benefits as the reflection of a class system. What consciousness of class does exist is found mostly among the upper classes. Probably the closest approximation of class thinking among Americans is the view that the lower classes face barriers to achievement because of inadequate opportunity. They have little awareness, however, of a comprehensive social system that determines the distribution of opportunities and other social benefits. They are not aware, in other words, of the highly organized system of social power connecting the economy, the professions, education, family, health, consumption, interaction in primary and secondary groups, politics, government, and law.

Americans are conscious of inequities in their society, but they regard them as correctable defects of a fundamentally sound society—sound because it works the way people say it works and because it is flexible and reformable. Invariably, reform is directed at making functional competition between individuals more equal. Despite persistent criticism and occasional denunciations of middle-class society, very few have questioned the ability of middle-class society to reform itself and become what it is supposed to be: a system based on equality of opportunity leading to "nonegalitarian classlessness."

Why the Lack of Awareness About Class Stratification?

Marxists argue that the lack of class consciousness and the belief that capitalist society is either already classless or can become so are manifestations of "false consciousness." But one need not be a Marxist to understand the social processes that have prevented Americans from becoming class conscious:

1. Economic expansion has diversified the economic interests of Americans, often giving them contradictory and cross-cutting interests. Economic growth has

provided economic mobility for many and has raised living standards (remember that a general rise of living standards is not the same thing as social mobility or movement across class lines, but it can easily be misinterpreted as such).

2. Immigration and migration (along with the aftermath of racial slavery) have diversified economic classes on ethnic, religious, and racial grounds, making it difficult for those in similar economic positions to develop an awareness of their common class identity.

3. Sexual inequality has also contributed to diversity among those in similar economic statuses and has also made it difficult to think in terms of common class interests and grievances.

4. The steady extension of legal and political rights encouraged Americans to feel that equal, individual competition was either a reality or could become one. However, American political institutions have always reflected the interests of property and professional groups—not surprisingly, political parties and the politically powerful rarely present the problems of American society in class terms.

5. American popular and intellectual culture, including the social sciences and religion, have a pronounced tendency to formulate goals and to explain success and failure in individualistic (biopsychological) terms and to assume that social problems are temporary and correctable (evolutionary liberalism). By and large, the American ethos of individualism prevents Americans from seeing their world as an organized structure of institutions and power groups. By and large, American popular culture, religion, social science, and intellectual culture have depoliticized American society by claiming that it derives from supernature, nature, and human nature.[34]

CLASS AND SUBJECTIVITY: A SUMMARY

In this chapter we examined the vast and complex world of prestige (subjectivity) and looked at one aspect of this world—how Americans regard themselves and each other. The inner world of human beings is not always easy to characterize or interpret. It seems clear, however, that class position is the controlling variable in explaining how people think about themselves and the world in which they live. Two extremely important subjective phenomena, occupational prestige and basic personality (self-direction versus conformism), are directly related to class.

In their attitudes toward minority groups, majority Americans have become more tolerant. But majority Americans are also saddling minorities with the burden of moral equality, the liberal belief that human beings—high or low, rich or poor, strong or weak—are responsible for their own success or failure.

We also found that class self-identification and class consciousness are not sharply delineated or directly related to class. Nevertheless, it is justifi-

---

[34]For a full discussion of why the American system of inequality works and does not produce mass disaffection, see Chapter 17.

able to explain our findings in class terms: The class dimension and related areas are so complex and inconsistent that they have diffused and blurred subjective awareness of class. In addition, a general process of legitimation (social science, religion, and popular culture) also makes it difficult for Americans to think in terms of social class.

CHAPTER 11

Class and Style of Life: Consumption

Economic classes invariably spend their money differently, which tends to result in varying types and levels of prestige. In this chapter, therefore, we are interested in understanding another of the ways in which "economic income" is turned into "psychic income." While we will distinguish between material and symbolic culture in the following section, this distinction is adopted for expository purposes only. All human activities, including consumption, are infused with symbols or meanings of the most varied sort. The purchase of clothing or a dwelling is no mere material or objective act; it has important symbolic-value overtones—overtones relevant in the present context to prestige stratification.

Analysis of the noneconomic or honorific aspects of economic behavior was pioneered by Thorstein Veblen (1857–1929),[1] whose penetrating insights into the ways in which honor is acquired through material accumulation and consumption are the source of much of our present-day understanding of prestige behavior (though, as we will see, his ideas have to be updated somewhat). It was Veblen who focused attention on the fact that men and

---

[1]Much of the following is indebted to Veblen's classic, *The Theory of the Leisure Class* (New York: New American Library, 1953; originally published in 1899).

women above the level of subsistence engage in what he called *pecuniary emulation.* In the past, according to Veblen, men and women created invidious distinctions by accumulating more property than they could use, because to do so gave them prestige and thus made them morally worthier than their neighbors. Modern society makes pecuniary emulation difficult, however: Property must be conspicuous if it is to enhance prestige, and much of modern property is inconspicuous because of residential segregation, or because it takes the form of factories, office buildings, and the like, or has no tangible form other than pieces of paper.

Veblen also pointed to conspicuous leisure—careful avoidance of work and cultivation of noneconomic activities and skills—as a way in which high economic position is advertised. Acquiring prestige in this way is difficult in industrial society because of its high valuation of work and utilitarian activity. A final means Veblen identified of translating economic or class position into prestige is conspicuous consumption. It is this phenomenon that has particular relevance to prestige stratification in industrial society, especially if one defines it in combination with pecuniary emulation and conspicuous leisure as the display of all manner of economic assets on a scale and with a flair that has known prestige meaning.

HONORIFIC POSSESSIONS, CONSUMPTION, AND ACTIVITIES

The concept of conspicuous consumption is probably best introduced by noting Veblen's synonym for it, conspicuous waste. Perhaps the most dramatic example of this form of prestige is provided by Ruth Benedict's portrayal of the value system of the Kwakiutl Indians.[2] Native to the northwest coast of North America, the Kwakiutl enjoyed an economy of abundance. The sea provided ample food for slight labor, which allowed for their absorption in self-glorification at the expense of rivals. The specific form their ego rivalry took was the potlatch, a social convention based on the distribution and/or destruction of property. Noneconomic, nonmaterial property such as names, titles, myths, songs, privileges, and pieces of copper were combined with other forms of property such as fish oil, blankets, and canoes to serve as the means of personal rivalry. The object of the potlatch was to enhance personal prestige by shaming a rival, either by giving him property he could not return with the required heavy interest or by detroying one's property in amounts he could not match.

Veblen employed the term *waste* neutrally to signify economic behavior with no immediate or obvious economic utility. Something is done or used

[2]*Patterns of Culture* (Boston: Houghton Mifflin, 1959; originally published in 1934), chap. 6.

because it is expensive either of material or of time; because it is aesthetically novel, moral, or true; or because it combines certain of these features. The individual engaged in conspicuous waste can be either aware or unaware of what he or she is doing. Quite often, the compulsions of class position make conspicuous consumption (waste) a necessary aspect of one's standard of living, part of the minimum level of decency in dress, housing, equipment, and services required to maintain class standing.

Veblen provided an enormous catalogue of prestige pursuits whose consequences, intended or not, were to create invidious distinctions between economic classes: acquired wealth; inherited wealth; abstention from productive labor (by a man, by his wife, and sometimes by both, often accompanied by the employment of slaves, servants, or mechanical devices); the cultivation of nonutilitarian pursuits and skills such as (in Veblen's words) quasi-scholarly, quasi-artistic accomplishments like languages, correct spelling and syntax, domestic music; the latest proprieties of dress, furniture, and equipage; games, sports, and fancy-bred animals; and manners and breeding, polite usage, decorum, and formal and ceremonial observances in general.[3]

NONUTILITARIAN BEHAVIOR IN INDUSTRIAL SOCIETY

While Veblen's work contains many insights into the manifest and latent functions of consumption, his analysis is not a complete guide to present-day consumption. Veblen was primarily concerned with identifying vestiges of feudal and barbarian prestige in an emerging industrial civilization. To analyze the prestige patterns developed by a maturing industrial class system, therefore, requires an updating and refocusing of Veblen's ideas. His insights into preindustrial forms of prestige (property accumulation, leisure as avoidance of work, waste, canons of taste that emphasize expense over utility, and the cultivation of a wide assortment of nonutilitarian values and skills) are still pertinent, since consumption is still linked strongly to class, but must be supplemented.

Probably the most important single fact about the American system of stratification is that the upper classes are gainfully employed. This appears to be true even of the very rich, though there are no exact studies of how members of this class are employed by sex and age. Members of the upper class of industrial society are undoubtedly different from other classes in their ability to choose not to work and to choose their work from a wide variety of options (though in this respect they are probably similar to the upper middle class). Nevertheless, the upper class of industrial society ap-

---

[3]Veblen, *The Theory of the Leisure Class*, p. 47.

pears to be neither a leisure nor a *rentier* class, and it certainly does not specialize in religious, governmental, and military occupations. All available indications are that the upper class is actively engaged in a wide variety of (economic) occupations, chief among which, undoubtedly, is the management and supervision of property interests. The significance of all this is that it is work, not property, that legitimates consumption in industrial society, a phenomenon that makes it difficult to uphold cultivated idleness as a prime social value.[4] In the United States, free time is the mark of the half-citizen: the young, the old, the retired, women, the infirm and disabled, and the unemployed. One enjoys leisure in a positively valued sense only after one's work is done: after five o'clock, after fifty weeks, or after age sixty-five. Given the heavy emphasis on work and on such related values as thrift, economic growth, and technical efficiency, it is also difficult both to uphold waste as a positive value and to place supreme or even high value on nonutilitarian activities such as art, music, classical learning, religion, and exotic hobbies. Activities of this sort exist and even flourish, but by and large run counter to the main thrust of American culture.[5]

The United States never developed deep ascriptive limitations on consumption. The black American, of course, was forced to consume in segregated stores and to use segregated facilities, a tradition that represents the most serious contradiction of pure class consumption in American history. And women have been segregated with regard to certain forms of consumption; examples are the need to have an escort in order to use certain facilities, and moral strictures against smoking and drinking. By and large, however, such ascriptive forces have been overcome by the power of class. The central point about consumption in the United States is that it is legitimate for all to be interested—indeed, very interested—in material consumption. One of the major changes in twentieth-century life is the growing respectability of consumption and the apparent decline of Protestant-bourgeois asceticism. The major reason for this development, of course, is the emergence of a mass-production economy and the consequent economic need to make consumption a major public virtue. In the process, consumption has become a semiofficial way of establishing prestige and, from a broader standpoint, of establishing and maintaining class position.

The ways in which consumption is promoted are also of considerable importance. Our mass media, for example, do much to support and inculcate consumption values, in terms of both program content and advertising. The

---

[4]Though the rich undoubtedly enjoy their property and its income as much as they do their income from work, it cannot be said that the ownership of property as such has ever established itself in the normative culture of America in the same way that work has.

[5]Nonetheless, prestige skills and values in these areas are acquired only after considerable nonutilitarian effort, and Veblen's central concept of waste behavior is still relevant in this respect.

mass media cater both to class and prestige mobility aspirations and undoubtedly contribute heavily to creating them in the first place.[6] Consumption prestige is also promoted by the power dimension. The rise of the Keynesian state parallels the rise of a mass-production economy. Under Keynesianism, government acts to maintain effective economic demand either by acting as a consumer itself or by cutting taxes or interest rates.[7] Tax laws favoring the upper classes permit a wide range of luxury consumption. By declaring holidays, the power dimension specifies the values to be celebrated and preserved; and the legal fiction that the birthdays of some of our national heroes take place on Mondays is partly due to the fact that three-day weekends are good for tourist and recreational businesses and thus of more prestige value to those with the money to travel on such mini-vacations.[8] The state also regulates the work week and vacations; subsidizes postal rates for magazines, newspapers, and books, publications which help to promote many other prestige activities; and grants tax deductions for expense accounts (more stringent under the Tax Reform Act of 1986 but still a large source of differential prestige through club membership, dining, entertainment, and travel).

The federal government also subsidizes the arts, humanities, and public television, following the lead of municipal and state governments. The power dimension also supports professional sports in a number of ways: by not holding them strictly accountable to the antitrust laws: by granting money to build sports facilities or by backing their bond issues with public credit; and by building the highways that make it possible to locate such facilities in the suburbs (thus making them accessible to some income groups and not to others). The government also subsidizes differential recreation through its system of national parks, which are used mostly by the middle and upper classes, and it has even paid for public works which have resulted in lakes and recreation areas becoming the preserves of private residential communities.

The blurring of the private (prestige) and public (power) spheres of behavior has occurred on another front as well. Public regulation of the airways lends an aura of legitimacy to private enterprises in radio and televi-

---

[6]The phenomenal success of *Playboy* magazine, for example, can no doubt be explained in part by the fact that it provides a guide to upper-middle-class consumption patterns for upwardly mobile males.

[7]For a fuller discussion of Keynesianism, see Chapter 15.

[8]Travel, both in general and in terms of specific categories (visits to friends and relations, business trips and conventions, outdoor recreation, sightseeing and entertainment, weekend travel, and vacation travel), is distinctly class-related. (The relation between class and visits to friends and relatives is not pronounced.) For the way in which higher income, occupation, and education are related to more travel, see U.S. Bureau of the Census, Census of Transportation, 1982, *National Travel Survey: Travel During 1982* TC72-N3 (Washington, D.C.: U.S. Government Printing Office, 1983), chart 4.

sion, though the public's control over program content and advertising is minimal. Public regulations on land use, building materials, house and plot size, and the like (zoning) are often tantamount to class and racial segregation; and, of course, public highways make it possible for certain income and racial groups to enjoy the prestige of nonurban living.

In studying the oftentimes bewildering array of consumption behaviors and analyzing the relation of prestige consumption to class, there is a general pattern that helps to structure understanding: Some consumption behaviors are based on differences while others, especially in industrial society, result in broad and significant similarities.

DIFFERENTIAL CONSUMPTION: INDUSTRIAL POTLATCHING

Despite the existence of a great many ideas about the relation between class and consumption, little research has been undertaken in this area. To organize what is known about the distribution of consumption prestige, we will examine in turn five areas of consumption: residence, dress, commodities, the consumption of time and "symbolic" culture, and the donation of money and time.[9]

Residence

The importance of residence for identifying and certifying class position needs little emphasis. The significance of residence is apparent in the vividness of such stratification-related images as "the wrong side of the tracks," the Gold Coast, a slum, Nob Hill, the East Side, and so on. Type of house and dwelling area are so important to class position that one school of stratification analysis has used both to construct an index of class position.[10] Prestige stems from one's residence in a number of ways: for example, from its size, architectural style, location, size of plot, and exterior decoration and maintenance. Obviously, one's residence, especially a single-family house, is an important way to display income and/or wealth. But it is also a way to advertise lineage and good taste. Thus, the Early American style in the Northeast suggests continuity of descent as well as good taste; its counterparts are Greek Revival in the South; Spanish in the Southwest and Califor-

---

[9]Even death does not end the search for prestige. One need only think of the tombs of the Pharoahs, the state funerals of the mighty, segregated cemeteries, and the class-oriented appeals of undertakers and cemeteries to appreciate the varied ways in which the lower classes are denied even the democracy of death. For a marvelously insightful analysis and critique of funeral practices in America and the economic groups behind them, see Jessica Mitford, *The American Way of Death* (New York: Simon & Schuster, 1963).

[10]See W. Lloyd Warner, Marcia Meeker, and Kenneth Eells, *Social Class in America* (New York: Harper & Row, 1960; first published in 1949), pp. 39–42.

nia; and Victorian in the Midwest. Actually, a house affords many ways of displaying values (furnishings, a separate dining room, a private bedroom for each child, a music room). Geographical location (high ground, distance from commerce and industry), size of plot, and landscaping are all important to the prestige (as well as economic) value of a house. In other words, one's address is often a quick and easy way to know who one is.

A rise in class position usually calls for a change of residence. In fact, it is one of the functions of differential consumption in general to help to establish people who have moved up (or down) in the class hierarchy. Residence is also an index of low prestige (and power) and low class position. Many black Americans, for example, are badly housed because they are poor, subject to racist evaluations, and unable to protect themselves politically. Even when black Americans rise in class, they have great difficulty acquiring the type of residence their new economic position calls for.[11]

Residential segregation by race does not come about by accident, due to the play of impersonal market forces, or as a result of attitudes. The people and organizations that create and perpetuate residential racial segregation are identifiable: real estate brokers, real estate firms, real estate boards, banking and other lending agencies, and local residential communities themselves, including property and tenant organizations and local governments.[12]

Residential segregation does not affect black Americans alone. Many other minorities are segregated residentially (though none with such thoroughness and seeming permanence). American Indians on reservations and in urban enclaves; Chinese Americans restricted to Chinatowns and widely excluded from suburban housing developments; white ethnic groups; and Mexican Americans in *barrios* and in rural isolation[13] have all been hemmed in by geographical boundaries. And, of course, geographical boundaries mean social boundaries. The effects of residential segregation, in addition to the loss of comfort and convenience, are to deny some members of minority groups the prestige their class position calls for and to make it difficult for the rest to change their class position (for example, by restricting educational and employment opportunities).

Though we have emphasized the roles of private forces in producing

[11]For an analysis that shows that black Americans have significantly less home ownership than whites even when income is held constant, see Mary R. Jackman and Robert W. Jackman, "Racial Inequality in Home Ownership," *Social Forces* 58(June 1980):1221–1234.

[12]Rose Helper, *Racial Policies and Practices of Real Estate Brokers* (Minneapolis: University of Minnesota Press, 1969), p. 144.

[13]For an analysis of the high residential segregation of Mexican Americans (and blacks) in thirty-five southwestern cities, see Leo Grebler, Joan W. Moore, Ralph C. Guzman and others, *The Mexican-American People: The Nation's Second Largest Minority* (New York: Free Press, 1970), chap. 12. For an analysis showing that Mexican Americans have a significantly lower level of home ownership than majority whites even when income is held constant, see Lauren J. Krivo, "Home Ownership Differences Between Hispanics and Anglos in the United States," *Social Problems* 33 (April 1986): 319–334.

residential segregation, the power of the state is used to the same effect. Though discrimination in most housing sales and rentals is now illegal, an extremely important form of legal protection for property is the widespread use of zoning, a device that serves to segregate minority groups and the poor in general and to make housing scarce for both groups and for others further up the social ladder. In addition, government credit, mortgage, tax, transportation, and general housing policies all work to perpetuate the class-prestige hierarchy of housing (also see the section on housing in Chapter 15).[14]

To move from the palatial residences of the rich to the comfortable homes and apartments of the upper middle class to the modest homes of the lower middle and working classes on to the squalid dwellings of the lower class is to take a quick trip through the American class system. Residence does not signify social class in a mechanical fashion, of course. There is evidence that working-class people are not overly conscious of residence as a mark of class, and people are not always as mobile as they might be because of ethnic and other ties to their old neighborhoods. A further complication is the shortage of housing: Many people who might have moved have not done so because of the almost chronic undersupply of housing in the United States. In recent years the gap between income distribution and the affordability of housing has widened because of slow economic growth. During the 1980s this gap produced a significant number of homeless people, including large numbers of homeless families (including many with full-time workers). One interesting pattern in American housing is the significant number of second homes. In 1970 there were 2,890,000 second homes,[15] and it is reasonable to assume that the number has grown steadily since then (the Census Bureau has stopped compiling data on this subject. For a fuller discussion of housing, see the section "Housing" in Chapter 15).

Dress

In addition to providing warmth and helping to promote and uphold the sense of modesty, clothing is an important advertisement of class status. The terms *white-collar* and *blue-collar*, for example, signify distinct stratification worlds. Many occupations entail special costumes, the function of which is to identify those who wield authority and to provide for the mutual recognition necessary to efficient work, communication, and exchange of services—for example, judges, soldiers, prostitutes, police officers, airline attendants, doctors, and clergy.

---

[14]The pattern of residential segregation by class (and by minority status) has far-reaching political implications, which we will have occasion to discuss later; see "Class-Prestige and Political Representation" in Chapter 14. Essentially, it makes possible the neutralization of the numerical strength of the lower classes through the gerrymander (employed in a variety of ways).

[15]U.S. Bureau of the Census, *Statistical Abstract, 1974* (Washington, D.C.: U.S. Government Printing Office, 1974), Table 1201.

A discerning observer can usually identify a man's class by looking at his clothing, even when he is not wearing a conventional occupational uniform. This may be even truer of his wife, since women are strongly encouraged to advertise class status through dress. (And women are used in other ways to manifest status; in some countries, for example, the number of a man's wives is a measure of his ability to support extraneous personnel.) All in all, the norms of dress, or fashion, are widely used to identify those with good taste, money, and exemptions from labor.

Another aspect of the world of fashion should also be noted. According to Barber and Lobel, women's clothes in contemporary society manifest two contrasting principles: First, all are invited to be fashionable along lines that are decreed for all by the fashion industry; second, differences in dress are also allowed for by variations in, for example, cut, type of fabric, and tailoring. Such differences tend to be associated with class levels. These contrary emphases on difference and sameness would tend to cause strain were it not for the "trickle-down" process, whereby upper-class fashions are eventually copied and made available to the classes below. The overall effect is to allow some women to stress their class position or to aspire upward, and other women to feel equal to the women in higher class positions.[16]

Commodities

There are many types of goods associated with class that lend prestige to their owners. At the advent of the automobile age, only the wealthy could afford to own cars. Mass production caused car ownership to spread, but until recently the type of car one owned was still an indicator of one's class. Now that the same car is owned by members of many different income groups, mere ownership is no longer an easy guide to class. Ownership of two or more cars, however, still indicates the class to which the owner belongs as does ownership of extremely expensive or exotic cars.

Many other types of commodities are still strongly associated with class. Though ownership of some commodities, such as black-and-white television sets, loses its strong association with class over time, possession of many major appliances, such as clothes dryers and dishwashers, is still a class phenomenon.

The Consumption of Time and "Symbolic" Culture

The expenditure of "free" time can be thought of as a form of consumption, and there are evident differences in the ways in which the various classes spend their time away from work. A great many studies have shown that blue-collar workers differ from middle-class individuals in that they

---

[16]Bernard Barber and Lyle S. Lobel, "'Fashion' in Women's Clothes and the American Social System," *Social Forces* 31 (December 1952):124–131. This trickle-down effect is widely used in American society and is discussed again later in this chapter.

read less; attend fewer movies, concerts, lectures, and theaters; travel less; display less interest in artistic and musical pusuits; and participate far less in formal associations. Working-class individuals spend more time than their middle-class counterparts working around the house, watching television, working on their automobiles, taking automobile rides, playing cards, fishing, informally interacting with relatives and friends, and tavern-visiting.[17] There is also little doubt that significant differences in the use of "free" time characterize the poor and the middle class.

Differences in the use of time can also be represented as differences in modes of consuming "symbolic" culture. The term *symbolic culture* is a roomy construct into which we can deposit whatever evidence we have about differential participation in the moral, aesthetic, and intellectual life of society. We have already analyzed the most important form of symbolic consumption in modern society, formal schooling. No conclusion in the realm of education is more important for understanding contemporary inequality and differentials in subjective development and enjoyment than the fact that formal schooling and professional training are largely middle class monopolies. An important variation on this theme is that rising levels of education have led neither to greater homogeneity nor to a greater consensus of values and outlooks. Actually, effective participation in American society is severely limited for many people by functional illiteracy.

Participation in "symbolic" culture can also take the form of participation in voluntary groups, especially those devoted to religion, reform, and politics. We discuss this form of participation further in Chapter 12 but here again there is little doubt that the stimulation and prestige afforded by associational activity correspond to a general pattern of middle- and upper-class dominance.

Participation in "symbolic" culture can also be analyzed in terms of differential class consumption (and production) in the aesthetic and intellectual-moral sphere.[18] The main American pattern in this area is clear: Americans consume aesthetic, intellectual, and moral values in class-structured

---

[17]For an interpretive study that identifies various levels of "culture" in America and their relations to class, see Herbert J. Gans, *Popular Culture and High Culture: An Analysis and Evaluation of Taste* (New York: Basic Books, 1974). For dominance by the upper classes in the consumption of high art, see Paul DiMaggio and Michael Useem, "Cultural Democracy in a Period of Cultural Expansion: The Social Composition of Arts Audiences in the United States," *Social Problems* 26 (December 1978):179–197. For a general survey of research in this area with considerable reference to the United States, see Stanley Parker, *Leisure and Work* (London: George Allen and Unwin, 1983).

[18]Two Marxist scholars who have achieved fame exploring the general relation between society (class) and aesthetic life are Georg Lukacs, especially his *The Historical Novel* (London: Merlin Press, 1962) and *Studies in European Realism* (New York: Grosset & Dunlap, 1964), available in paperback, and Arnold Hauser, *The Social History of Art*, 4 vols. (London: Routledge and Kegan Paul, 1962; originally published in 1951). For a valuable historical analysis of the class basis of various forms of art, see Vytautas Kavolis, *Artistic Expression: A Sociological Analysis* (Ithaca, N.Y.: Cornell University Press, 1968).

ways. The corollary to this pattern is the significant fact that the production of "symbolic" culture is also geared to class audiences. And perhaps of even greater significance is the fact that "symbolic" culture is now in an advanced industrial stage of production and consumption. In other words, organizations engaged in creating and distributing aesthetic, intellectual, and moral values are managed in much the same way as is the economy; they are characterized by narrow upper class "ownership" and control, professional staffs who manage day-to-day operations, and benefits bestowed according to class.

A case in point is Edward Arian's analysis of the Philadelphia (Symphony) Orchestra.[19] Suggesting that the forces at work in Philadelphia are found throughout the United States, Arian argues that the Philadelphia Orchestra Association is dominated through its board of directors by upper class (old-rich) families, and that they and the upper classes are its chief beneficiaries. To combat mounting costs, the board has instituted a rigidly bureaucractic, efficiency-minded mode of operations; this innovation has enabled the board to retain control, since the orchestra's budget can still be financed by private wealth. One of the interesting by-products of this process is that the orchestra does not play before a wide spectrum of community audiences and performs little modern or experimental music.

Middle- and upper-class dominance in the general area of aesthetic-intellectual-moral values makes for differences in the amount and type of enjoyment available to the various classes. Furthermore, control of prestigious forms of cultural activity by the upper classes strengthens and supports the general system of stratification by class. To the extent that high culture is thought to bear a special relationship to the integrity of society, the upper and middle classes are seen as its patrons and preservers. To the extent that the aesthetic-intellectual-moral realm has a bearing on social problems and issues, it is the upper classes that control its operations and compose its audiences, thereby deeply influencing the way in which issues and problems are formulated and solved. And, finally, it is the upper and middle classes whose sensibilities are stimulated and wits sharpened by offerings in the worlds of music, theater, painting, dance, sculpture, and quality publications, outcomes that are valuable in their own right and that have applications in the areas of class and power.

The relation between voluntary organizations in the field of "symbolic" culture and government (power) is of growing importance and deserves much greater study. In addition to its growing influence on higher education, the federal government now supports an extensive television network (the Corporation for Public Broadcasting and Public Broadcasting System) and has

---

[19]Edward Arian, *Bach, Beethoven, and Bureaucracy: The Case of the Philadelphia Orchestra* (University, Ala.: University of Alabama Press, 1971).

made large sums of money available to the arts and humanities (through the National Arts Endowment and the National Humanities Endowment). Framed in the image of the independent regulatory commissions, these public bodies resemble their predecessors: Ostensibly nonpartisan, objective and aloof from politics in practice, they dispense public monies and public prestige in a manner that coincides with the basic structure of class and political power.

An interesting review of some empirical findings on the mass media suggests that because the logic of economic life, and especially its technology, impels the mass media to try to attract mass audiences, very little of their content is specialized according to class.[20] While blue-collar and white-collar families clearly tend to have different tastes and preferences in broadcast programs and print media (the former preferring more entertainment and less information), the interesting thing, according to Bogart, is that the differences are so small. What the mass media represent, Bogart suggests, is a powerful instrument for inducing working-class conformity to a middle-class society.[21]

Pressure to conform is one thing; actual homogeneity of outlook and values is another. Despite the mass media, significant differences exist between the symbolic interests and skills of white- and blue-collar Americans. This is not surprising given differences in the amount and type of reading (books, magazines, newspapers), formal education, socialization, travel, community participation, and occupational experience engaged in by the two groups.

The Donation of Money and Time

One the ways to convert money into prestige is to give it away. Donating money enhances one's reputation among those who benefit from such generosity and among those who are impressed that one can afford to give money away. It also helps to make people forget how one earned one's money. (The classic case is the Rockefeller family, which has succeeded in living down the image of John D. Rockefeller as a robber baron.) Thus, individuals give money to hospitals, settlement houses, adoption agencies, colleges, museums, symphony orchestras, and the like, and in return often gain fame and social immortality through the buildings, scholarships, or endowed chairs that memorialize their names.

Another way to gain prestige is to give time to community service. Despite constant complaints that they are overly busy, upper- and middle-

[20] The growth of publicly supported television has produced significant diversification of television programming. As is true of the other subsidized arts, public educational television represents stimulation for the middle and upper classes.

[21] Leo Bogart, "The Mass Media and the Blue-Collar Worker," in Arthur B. Shostak and William Gomberg, eds., *Blue-Collar World: Studies of the American Worker* (Englewood Cliffs, N.J.: Prentice-Hall, 1964), pp. 416–428.

class men often serve on committees or boards associated with the full range of voluntary organizations.[22] Their high class status and skills are useful to voluntary organizations (even if they merely lend their names) and, in turn, the moral prestige of such groups rubs off on volunteers. The wives of such men are also deeply involved in community work, the donation of time in their case also signifying freedom from the need to work.[23] Such women are so secure economically that they can afford to give their time away. They too lend their prestige (actually, the prestige of their families and/or husbands), time, skills, and money to such enterprises, and in return they and their families gain prestige by being associated with projects and organizations dedicated to moral and civic betterment.

The linkage between the upper classes and voluntary organizations probably involves far more than prestige. In a study of the board of trustees of a nonprofit hospital, it was found that economically dominant individuals maintained a steady representation on the board and were influential in controlling the hospital's not inconsiderable economic resources.[24] The economic nature of much of the voluntary world was more openly recognized during the 1980s when business groups mounted challenges to the tax exemptions given to the economic activities of schools, churches, and hospitals.

Interestingly enough, membership on the boards that control voluntary associations appears to be remarkably homogeneous.[25] Arian's analysis of the Philadelphia Orchestra, cited above, found its board to be not only upper class but predominantly *Social Register* upper class. Further, the board rejected a consulting firm's suggestion that it diversify its membership, arguing that to do so would jeopardize its standards. One can assume that charitable and social service agencies are hampered in their purposes by the exclusion from membership of the people they serve. And, obviously, the absence and exclusion of many professions, ordinary workers, lower-level businesspeople, the semiprofessions, and minorities from the governing boards of voluntary associations also hamper their operation and represents a serious loss of prestige and power for such groups.

An important means of acquiring prestige through the sacrifice of eco-

---

[22]Participation in voluntary organizations is in general a middle- and upper-class phenomenon; see "Primary Prestige Groups" and "Secondary Prestige Groups" in Chapter 12.

[23]This has changed since the late 1970s and voluntary groups are experiencing a shortage of volunteers at all levels since many women in the middle and upper middle classes are now working.

[24]Robert G. Holloway, Jay W. Artis, and Walter E. Freeman, "The Participation Patterns of 'Economic Influentials' and Their Control of a Hospital Board of Trustees," *Journal of Health and Human Behavior* 4 (Summer 1963):88–99; reprinted in E. Gartley Jaco, ed., *Patients, Physicians and Illness: A Sourcebook in Behavioral Science and Health*, 2nd ed. (New York: Free Press, 1972), pp. 313–324.

[25]The basic analogue is corporate ownership and control. The reader should also remember the homogeneity found to characterize the boards of institutions of higher education, especially private ones.

nomic assets is public service. Upper-class individuals contribute their time to public commissions of all kinds and accept public positions at considerable sacrifice of income. Ambassadors are perhaps the best examples of the latter, but there are many high-income businesspeople and professionals who accept government positions or run for public office at some (temporary) economic sacrifice. Obviously, the prestige of such individuals is enhanced, and so is that of upper occupational and income-wealth groups in general. Above all, this process helps to create and maintain the impression that middle- and upper-class interests and values are identical with the public interest, an impression fostered by the entire range of voluntary behavior.

COMMON CONSUMPTION

The Logic of Mass Production

An outstanding and unique feature of consumption in the United States is that large portions of the American population consume the same items and services. The inherent tendency of an industrial economy is to create a national (and international) market for products and services and to transform all citizens into equivalent consumers. A mass-production economy is obviously at odds with norms and values that seek to restrict or differentiate consumption according to social position. Unlike industrial social systems, agrarian societies often develop *sumptuary laws,* or laws that lend the power of the "state" to moral and religious norms governing consumption. Such laws establish differential consumption by, for example, stipulating that only aristocrats can wear fur or silk. In caste, multireligious, or multiethnic societies, there develop strong normative traditions that define appropriate forms of consumption for each level or segment of society, especially in the areas of food, drink, and clothing. But the United States, like other industrial societies, has successfully established the primacy of class position with regard to consumption. One's income, and thus one's relation to the commodity market, is the main legitimate restriction on consumption.[26]

Common consumption does not, it should be noted, mean equivalent expenditures. The various classes obviously spend different amounts in their overall consumption. What is of interest here is that sharp differences in consumption, and resulting sharp differences in prestige, do not exist in the United States in an easily recognizable way. The major reason for this is that the majority of the population consumes a wide range of similar products, often brand-name goods with national prestige: food (staples as well as nonstaples); beverages (milk, soft drinks, beer); household products (soap,

---

[26]There are, of course, laws prohibiting certain kinds of consumption (such as consumption of drugs), but these laws are applicable to all.

polishes, waxes, detergents); household appliances (refrigerators, vacuum cleaners, television); clothing (quality ready-made clothing of all sorts, such as suits, dresses, shoes, underwear); and such other items as cigarettes, entertainment products, and sporting goods. The crucial point is that vast portions of the public consume these goods in common regardless of income. In addition, sizable segments of various classes can afford to consume in common even such expensive goods as automobiles, washing machines, air conditioners, and color television sets.

The meaning of common consumption, and other common behavior, is not self-evident. As Handel and Rainwater have emphasized, there is only a superficial similarity between the working and middle classes even when they seem to be saying or doing identical things. For example, both classes have positive attitudes toward education and home ownership, but the meanings they attach to these values are quite different. The working class views education quite instrumentally, while the middle class also sees it as a process of refinement, a foundation for later learning, a means to enjoy life more, and a way to learn how to get along with people. Similarly, the working class sees home ownership as a way to escape from the landlord while the middle class tends to see it as a "validation of status." In addition, the working class tends to purchase durable goods in common with the middle class, but not such services as meals in restaurants, vacations, home and automobile repairs, clothing, and education.[27]

In his empirical test of the thesis of the *embourgeoisement* of the working class, Gavin Mackenzie also found that the various classes (in Providence, Rhode Island) do not attach the same meanings to similar consumption. It is clear, for example, that skilled blue-collar workers attach a different meaning to home ownership than do white-collar workers, especially managers. Mackenzie's conclusion is the same as Handel's and Rainwater's finding about stable working class families: Basically, skilled workers see home ownership as a way to escape accountability to landlords, an urge analogous to their desire to escape their bosses. For their part, members of the lower and especially the upper middle classes, though they also stress privacy and freedom, cite the economic advantages and prestige of owning a home.[28]

Public Accommodations and Facilities

Another category of common consumption is "public" accommodations and facilities, both those that are privately owned—such as restaurants, housing, hotels, movie theaters, and stadiums—and those that are usually

---

[27]Gerald Handel and Lee Rainwater, "Persistence and Change in Working-Class Life Style," in Arthur B. Shostak and William Gomberg, eds., *Blue-Collar World: Studies of the American Worker* (Englewood Cliffs, N.J.: Prentice-Hall, 1964), pp. 36–41.

[28]Gavin Mackenzie, *The Aristocracy of Labor: The Position of Skilled Craftsmen in the American Class Structure* (London and New York: Cambridge University Press, 1973), pp. 74–77.

run by government—national, state, and local parks, transit systems, highways, beaches, swimming pools, recreation centers, golf courses, hospitals, colleges, libraries, theaters, stadiums, and museums. The United States has a long history of regarding such services and facilities as less than totally public; their use, for example, was deeply affected by racial segregation in the American south.[29] This situation was changed by law during the 1960s. The Civil Rights Act of 1964 forbade discrimination on the basis of race, religion, or national origin in such "public" facilities as private hotels, motels, restaurants, lunch counters, movie houses, gasoline stations, theaters, stadiums, barbershops and taverns located in hotels, restaurants located in department stores, and facilities that receive federal funds (hospitals, schools for the deaf and blind, colleges and universities). A fundamental feature of this act is that it voids on constitutional grounds state laws requiring segregation in private facilities not engaged in interstate commerce, but cannot forbid private discrimination in them.[30] The Housing Act of 1965 also asserted the public nature of most privately owned housing and forbade discrimination in the sale or rental of most of the nation's housing stock.

On the whole, there is now full formal access to most such facilities and accommodations. Speaking broadly, use and nonuse is now based on class rather than "caste" for all Americans. In practice, however, there are glaring exceptions to pure class consumption, the most important of which is housing. It appears that, in relative terms, no significant progress has been made in providing black Americans with more, better, or integrated housing. Though systematic data are lacking, the same is probably true of hospital use and a host of public services such as police and fire protection, garbage removal, and the like. And, of course, the ghettoization of black Americans and other minorities means that effective access to many free or low-cost public facilities is severely reduced.[31]

The amount and type of use made of "public" accommodations and facilities is also related to class, but no exact picture can be drawn due to lack of research. Many "public" accommodations (hotels, restaurants, lunch counters, housing) are geared to income, and often psychologically deter people who could otherwise afford them. Many rich and many poor people do not use low-cost public facilities such as subways, buslines, and golf courses, or use them less than do the middle-rich and near-poor. The poor probably do not use public facilities such as highways, libraries, and museums much, speaking both in absolute terms and in relation to higher income

---

[29] At one time, Oklahoma even had segregated telephone booths.

[30] Many states outside the South have their own laws prohibiting discrimination.

[31] Minority groups have in recent years asked for access to the public airwaves (radio and television channels). While this demand has not been met as often or as fully as minority groups would like, it has served to raise the question of how such public facilities denigrate or neglect minorities.

groups. And while hospitals are ostensibly open to all, their use depends on money. They are thus segregated internally by class—the poor who use hospitals are identified as charity cases—and little common consumption can be said to take place in this area.

Both the rich and the poor, therefore, are exceptions to the pattern of common consumption of public accommodations and facilities. But while the rich consume privately and out of the public eye (though aided extensively by the power dimension which, for example, protects their privacy, property, and income through favorable and discriminatory zoning and taxation), the poor face important prestige disabilities because they consume minimally and are objects of private and public charity. The prestige implications of poverty in the midst of plenty are difficult to gauge. Earlier in our history, the poor were subject to private charity, which allowed the upper classes to acquire prestige by displaying their concern and generosity. During the twentieth century responsibility for solving the problems of the poor has shifted from private markets and private organizations to government. In any case, the poor continue to suffer from low prestige because of low consumption, but in new ways, and perhaps more severely, now that they are acknowledged to be wards of the state.

In sum, the impact of "public" accommodations and "public" facilities on the American class system cannot be gauged with precision. It is clear that such accommodations and facilities could not exist under caste or estate systems of stratification. It is also clear that in a society oriented toward private life, many undoubtedly take governmental services for granted, others resent them as unearned gifts to the poor, still others do not use them, and many lack access because rights are not enforced or because equal services are not provided. On the whole, it cannot be said that the common consumption of class society is as egalitarian as a cursory comparison with caste and estate systems might suggest, nor that any significant reduction of inequality can be said to result from it. The formal right to use "public" accommodations and facilities does, however, create the illusion that an important form of common (and thus equal) consumption is taking place. And, like the illusion of equality of opportunity to consume education, this illusion serves to legitimate and stabilize the American class system.

THE ROLE OF CONSUMPTION IN CLASS STRATIFICATION

All the evidence about consumption indicates that rising absolute income (and a shorter work week) has not led to the homogenization of the American population into one great middle class (or mass) bounded at the top by the very rich and at the bottom by the very poor. The American working class, including highly skilled workers and their families, has not translated its rising income into middle-class levels of prestige. Even if the idea of cultural consumption is broadened to subsume any use of time or money, or to refer to the intake of intellectual, aesthetic, and civic values in general, no middle-class homogenization of the American population is discernible.

Consumption patterns undoubtedly play a role in reducing social stress and producing social stability. Large amounts of common consumption (and the illusion of still more) are undeniable. Patterns of common consumption have a moral effect: They tend to create and uphold belief in moral (prestige) equality. It is not unimportant in this respect that various income groups, Protestants, Roman Catholics, Jews, Republicans, Democrats, whites, blacks, and other "racial" groups all use or are free to use the "same" soap, drink the "same" water, eat the "same" food, and wear the "same" clothes.

Perhaps more important to social integration than common consumption is differential consumption. To understand the American class system fully, it is essential to recognize that, by and large, the culture of capitalism has successfully established the legitimacy of differential styles of class consumption and resulting styles of differential prestige. Americans at all levels accept the principle of a hierarchy of consumption, which is in keeping with their acceptance of the differential worth of occupations and the legitimacy of a hierarchy of income and wealth. Those who consume well or even lavishly deserve to do so, it is thought, because of their economic accomplishments. As long as differential consumption does not lead to rigid categories of prestige affecting the moral or political-legal worth of individuals, there is little public resentment of differential income classes and differential prestige through consumption.[32] In other words, American society has successfully compartmentalized the forces of liberty and success (inequality) and the forces of equality. Nothing signifies the stability of American society so completely as the fact that its economic groups invariably make demands on each other based on a desire to maintain their present share of the national product. In other words, they do not draw on the tradition of equality to question the principle of class inequality. Normally, Americans discuss the problems created by class within the context of a class system of society. For example, they draw on the tradition of equality to identify lack of equal opportunity in the general system, not to question whether the system is capable of providing it. Similarly, Americans accept differential consumption because it is believed that consumption is related to what individuals earn and thus to what they are worth. But they also expect the economy to provide for continuous increases in consumption, and strains occur whenever the economy falters. Therefore, the health of the system depends on continuous economic expansion and on the relative balance of differential and common consumption—and (as we will now see) on special processes at work within each of these areas.

---

[32]This does not mean that Americans do not complain about inequities and inadequacies in living standards and public services.

Consumption and Absolute and Relative Prestige Levels

In an interesting essay, Fallers has suggested that the "trickle-down" effect identified by Barber and Loebel in the world of fashions characterizes the entire range of consumption, and that in addition to reconciling the contrary emphases on difference and equality, the trickle-down effect has consequences for society-at-large insofar as it reconciles the emphasis on success and the fact that most must fail.[33] Basically, the trickle-down effect helps to create the illusion of success, and thus to motivate people to continue striving against unfavorable odds. A wide range of products is trickled down—that is, gradually made available to the masses for common consumption.

This form of trickling down is somewhat different from that of the world of women's fashions, and Fallers discusses it in terms of how individuals experience a rising hierarchy of consumption. Of central importance is the fact that many individuals have come to regard an absolute rise in the standard of living as normal. As all incomes rise, an absolute rise in consumption does not lead to a relative change for most people. Thus, while their relative consumption position may not change, there is a realistic payoff for most people (and thus for society) as the economy expands: Relative to their own past experience, they are consuming at a higher level, and there is no threat to their prestige in the fact that others are consuming more. As a consequence, their motivation to work and strive continues unabated even though they are not achieving success in relative terms. Some individuals experience unchanged levels of consumption during an upward shift in real income, and are aware or unaware of a relative loss depending on their consumption level and social location (for example, small town or big city). Others drop in the consumption hierarchy, but the blow is softened by the facts that total consumption is rising and that their slippage in consumption is more moderate than their decline in the prestige hierarchy. And, of course, other individuals can realize relative gains in their prestige status by consuming more, differently, or both.

This fundamental process of motivating people to continue working and striving in order to modify or overcome consumption gradations in prestige obviously depends on the continued expansion of the economy. Failure to develop more (and, probably, new) goods and services could lead to serious strain in the relations between classes. Much of the tension created by the black movement in the 1960s may be attributable to the fact that some black advances were made at the expense of the white working class—at the

---

[33]Lloyd A. Fallers, "A Note on the 'Trickle Effect'," *Public Opinion Quarterly* 18 (Fall 1954):314–321; reprinted in Reinhard Bendix and Seymour M. Lipset, eds., *Class, Status and Power: Social Stratification in Comparative Perspective*, 2nd ed. (New York: Free Press, 1966), pp. 402–405.

same time that the Vietnam War and inflation hampered the steady growth in real income expected by the American public and required by the American system of society. Decreases in investment in public services also contribute, no doubt, to the feeling that the standard of living is not rising. And, finally, unknown amounts of the gross national product (as well as many undesirable economic by-products) do not constitute real improvements or are difficult to perceive as such: airport noise, the cost of commuting by automobile, tobacco consumption and the medical technology and facilities needed to combat the cancer caused by tobacco; deterioration of products because of pollution; police officers; and, of course, the growth of what is now a large and important segment of our economy, military production and space exploration.

Counterfeit and Compensatory Consumption

C. Wright Mills has suggested that white-collar people in lower-middle class occupations engage in a "status cycle" to alleviate "status panic."[34] The secretary who skips lunches to save money for a wardrobe and a two-week vacation in a plush resort is one example. Many other means of enjoying prestige above one's class level are available to Americans because of the anonymity of modern life: after-hour clothing, a splurge on theater tickets, a new hairdo, inexpensive travel tours, and the like. Again, as is true of so much consumption behavior, we have little data and can only speculate on the extent to which Americans rely on a "status cycle" to alleviate prestige anxieties.

Another way of counterfeiting prestige is to live beyond one's income, either by endangering one's economic position (by, for example, failing to save for retirement, or to own life or medical insurance) or through credit. Installment credit and mortgages do allow an unknown number of Americans to live on future earnings, a practice that often entails serious psychic and family costs. The role of the state in making credit and mortgage money available (and allowing the interest paid as an income tax deduction) is an indispensable aspect of our prestige system. Expense-account living, also subsidized by the state, is another form of counterfeit consumption; how many engage in it cannot be said with certainty. The role of the state in enforcing one-sided contracts and credit terms also allows for a form of high-cost "compensatory consumption" among the poor. The function of this type of consumption is to provide consumer goods to high-risk customers and thus promote self-respect among the poor.[35] As we have suggested, the

---

[34]C. Wright Mills, *White Collar: The American Middle Classes* (New York: Oxford University Press, 1953), chap. 11.

[35]David Caplovitz, *The Poor Pay More: Consumer Practices of Low Income Families* (New York: Free Press, 1963), chap. 2.

integrative function performed by consumption at this level—maintaining loyalty to the system among the poor—is performed by various forms of consumption (common, differential, counterfeit) at various class levels.

Consumption Extremes

Commentators on American society have tended to stress the decline of ostentatious display by the rich, in terms both of the long-term historical transition from feudal society and of developments within industrial society during the twentieth century. (The White House, says Talcott Parsons, is not the Palace of Versailles.) This overall perspective on consumption is sound enough, though some of the conclusions drawn from it are not.[36] Comparisons between modern society and feudal systems, as we have pointed out, are monumentally difficult to make and a source of endless confusion and distortion. For example, most of the French aristocracy during the heyday of Versailles led lives of relatively deep impoverishment and were incapable of flaunting luxurious consumption. It is also true that there has been a decline of splendor in private residences—in the use of gold plumbing, large servant staffs, and the like—simultaneous with the decline of "High Society." The reasons generally adduced for this decline are the income tax (a much-exaggerated cause), the competition for and cost of servant labor, the growth of a democratic spirit, and the decline of a leisure class of nonworking very rich.

Of central significance in understanding consumption extremes is the phenomenon of relative deprivation. Industrial populations are now highly urbanized and subject to high levels of stimulation—for example, through the mass media—which among other things make known to them higher and often unattainable levels of consumption. And it is no longer possible to comfort most Americans with the promise of a better life in the next world, or to persuade them that their poverty is due to original sin. The fact remains that an upper-class man or woman may routinely spend on clothing an amount that millions of Americans must live on for an entire year. In short, large numbers at the upper levels enjoy multiple dwellings, expensive hobbies, and private boats and planes while significant numbers go hungry, lack plumbing, and suffer from lack of medical care.

CLASS AND CONSUMPTION: A SUMMARY

The use of property, money, and time has prestige implications, and a wide variety of prestige differences has appeared in industrial society. The hierarchy of class is accompanied by a hierarchy of differential consumption

---

[36]Actually, the American presidency is embellished by impressive facilities, ceremonies, and protocols, and has been referred to as the imperial presidency.

that leads to sharp and enduring differences in prestige. Unlike agrarian societies, however, industrial society is characterized by a sphere of common consumption and promotes expectations of increased consumption at all levels. Given an expanding economy, and thus rising consumption, Americans accept prestige differences in consumption despite the fact that such differences are at odds with their moral egalitarianism. There is little evidence of the development of a great middle mass of consumers. (If anything the middle-income sector has shrunk in recent years). In sum, the area of consumption prestige reflects the nature of the capitalist economy and its steeply and stably graded class system.

CHAPTER 12

Class and the Structure of Prestige Groups

The analysis of prestige groups is central to understanding the American class system. In analyzing prestige groups, we will maintain our society-wide focus, making few references to prestige structures in local communities (despite the fact that small-town America is still a stronghold of mutually accepted prestige claims). As the nation has urbanized and suburbanized, there has been a pronounced trend toward the segregation of class and prestige groups by residence and political community, and the small-town hierarchy of prestige groups is not an accurate model of contemporary national prestige behavior.

Many of the terms traditionally used to differentiate prestige from class behavior are ambiguous and misleading. The distinction between private and public is not overly useful, since class behavior, for example, can stem from occupations that cut across the economic, social, and political spheres. Much the same problem characterizes the prestige realm; for example, private clubs are prestige groups, but so are publicly supported museums, schools and universities, and charity organizations. Some prefer to think of the area of prestige as social space particularly amenable to individual choice; indeed, it is often referred to as the *voluntary sector.*

Voluntary behavior can be both primary and secondary in nature: Its focus can be intimate, as is true of love, family, friendship, and some clubs, or it can be reformist, humanitarian, or charitable, like the League of Women Voters, political parties, the Red Cross, and the Salvation Army. We speak of this realm in terms of the rights of free speech, free association, and petition. But despite such traditional phrases and the appearance of behavior in this area as natural and spontaneous, it would be a mistake to think of prestige as the domain of human nature and of freely chosen behavior. Choices in the realm of prestige are still social choices tied closely to class (and power), and the alternatives that are considered normal effectively rule out many other feasible courses of action.

There are two perspectives that can guide us through the maze of American prestige phenomena as they express themselves in prestige groups. First, voluntary behavior exerts an influence beyond itself to counteract or modify the inequalities and inequities of class and power. A vital tradition of moral egalitarianism, derived largely from Christianity and secular humanism, and especially from the liberal democratic tradition, permeates the voluntary sector and supports its autonomy from the rigid frameworks and compulsions of work and law. It is in this realm that Americans relax and rest, undertake new activities, pursue old interests and values, criticize themselves and their institutions, and launch movements of reform and regeneration. The voluntary realm has seen a significant historical increase in the number of people eligible to participate in important institutional sectors and to consume hitherto restricted goods and symbols. And it is in the voluntary realm that commentators from Tocqueville on have found the essential explanation of America's freedom, equality, and democracy: Here, theorists argue, we find a pluralistic, decentralized group structure responsive to both personal and public need.

The other perspective that will guide us through the sector of prestige or voluntary groups is equally important, if not more so. As we will see, all the available evidence points to a steeply graded, sharply segregated, and highly stable stratification of benefits derived from memberships in prestige groups. Not only are such benefits distributed unevenly, but there is also a far-reaching interpenetration of class and prestige (and power) structures. The prestige realm, for example, is subject to the same inexorable growth of rational organization (bureaucracy) as the realms of class and power. The United States has an incredible number of formally organized, private associations.[1] Beneath this multiform associational life there is a basic trend toward bigness and

---

[1]*Encyclopedia of Associations*, 21st ed. (Detroit: Gale Research Company, 1987) Volume 1, "National Organizations of the United States," lists more than 20,000 trade associations, professional societies, labor unions, fraternal and patriotic organizations, and other types of groups consisting of voluntary members.

concentration. Churches; universities and colleges; fraternal and charitable groups; research institutes; foundations; the mass media and entertainment businesses (radio, movies, television, recording, sports); businesses devoted to hobbies and recreation; publishers of magazines, newspapers, and books; and the world of "high" culture (symphony orchestras, ballet groups, museums) are all characterized by large-scale organization and increased concentration. A shift from preindustrial to industrial modes of operation is clearly discernible in the fields of entertainment, religion, "high" culture, philanthropy, education, medicine, and the professions in general. Services formerly provided on the basis of individual need are beginning to be offered in large-scale standardized ways to families, neighborhoods, cities, states, regions, the nation, and even other countries. In other words, private organizations in these areas are in step with the major trend evident in our economy and government.

PRESTIGE PROCESSES

Prestige Diversity and Struggle

American history is filled with rivalries between prestige-seeking groups: whites have oppressed nonwhites; the well-bred have struggled to maintain ascendancy over those they consider their social inferiors; native-born American whites have looked down on immigrants and native nonwhites alike; people of property and/or education have expected deference from the poor; unlettered rural people have railed against the city; and so on. The winners of these various struggles are not always easy to determine. It is, however, of no little importance to the development of American prestige patterns that the United States has never had to dislodge a powerful set of feudal families from the upper levels of its economic, religious, educational, and political life. But while it was spared this problem, the United States has witnessed many attempts to translate old wealth and lengthy pedigrees into a prestige (and even power) factor.

Analysts of social stratification in the United States have found deep prestige divisions based on "family lineage" in every community they have studied. This is not to say that Americans assert the superiority of particular family bloodlines (except when families are differentiated according to "race"). Americans believe in biopsychic differences between individuals, which is quite different from the feudal principle of a hierarchy of hereditary families. Where families come to believe themselves superior (or inferior), their prestige claims (or shame) are based on achievable factors such as income, wealth, expensive residence, breeding and good taste, philanthropy, leisure pursuits, or some mixture of these.[2] The American social system encourages and accords achievement prestige in a wide variety of areas: business, science, education, the arts, charity, reform movements, and in such areas of taste as dress, speech, home furnishings, music, and art. By and large, therefore, when prestige distinctions seem at odds with class, they are really at odds with *newly acquired* class position; thus the distinction between the old rich and the new rich.

The identification of prestige differentials as the basis of social stratification is best exemplified by the Warner school. Their own research and that of others led Warner and his associates to identify six class levels in the more established regions of the country (New England and the Deep South) and five levels in the Midwest and Far West.[3] The essence of Warner's scheme is to assert the independent force of prestige differences based on old wealth, tasteful consumption, superior breeding, and public service. Critics have pointed out, however, that while these hierarchical prestige differences exist, they are not only lodged in economic status (as Warner is not unaware) but must be seen in historical context: prestige phenomena are not the essence of social class but manifestations of economic positions consolidated over generations.

The Upper Class as a Prestige Group

It is an extremely important feature of the American class system that no prestige group has ever been able to establish itself on a nationwide basis. For such a thing to happen one group would need to combine prestige assets with either class or power assets, or both, to form a dominant stratum. On a regional basis, the plantation aristocracy of the old South can be considered such a stratum. And one can interpret the prestige aspirations of the "Four Hundred" at the end of the nineteenth century as an abortive attempt to become a national prestige group. But while that attempt to establish a high society failed, the American upper class—composed essentially of families of old wealth—has developed a unique and powerful prestige position. Though it lacks public acceptance, the upper class' prestige pursuits and achieve-

---

[2]For a history of prestige phenomena in the United States, such as democratic politics, books of etiquette, blue books and *The Social Register*, clubs, the society page, the American search for feudal splendor, and prestige sports, see Dixon Wecter, *The Saga of American Society: A Record of Social Aspiration, 1607–1937* (New York: Charles Schribner's Sons, 1937). Other accounts of the American plutocracy's concern with establishing "society" are Cleveland Amory, *The Last Resorts* (New York: Harper and Brothers, 1948), and *Who Killed Society?* (New York: Harper and Brothers, 1960); and Lucy Kavaler, *The Private World of High Society* (New York: David McKay, 1960).

[3]W. Lloyd Warner, Marchia Meeker, and Kenneth Eells, *Social Class in America: The Evaluation of Status* (New York: Harper & Row, 1960), pp. 11–24; originally published in 1949 without chaps. 16 and 17, which have been substituted for the original appendix.

ments are in keeping with its high class and power position and serve many important functions.

The identification of this class through its prestige practices is primarily the work of E. Digby Baltzell. In his study of the upper class in Philadelphia[4] and subsequent historical study of the upper class on a national scale,[5] Baltzell has traced the parallel fortunes of an emerging national political economy and a national upper class, defined as possessing a common cultural tradition, a sense of solidarity resulting from regular interaction, and a consciousness of itself as a distinct social class.

Though his account of the upper class is badly marred by the assumption that the United States has (and has always had) open class and power dimensions that allow individuals of ability to rise in the economic and political-legal systems, and though he fails to understand that prestige exclusiveness buttresses class and power interests and privileges, Baltzell nevertheless draws a fascinating and insightful picture of what he calls America's "caste-ridden" prestige dimension. Primarily as a response to large-scale immigration but also, Baltzell suggests, as patrician protective devices against populism, progressivism, urban blight, and trust-busting, the WASP upper class began in the 1880s to develop a series of exclusive prestige groups and practices:[6]

1. The trend toward exclusive summer resort communities was ratified when President Eliot of Harvard built a summer cottage at Northeast Harbor, Maine, in 1881.

2. The trend toward exclusive country clubs was initiated by the founding of The Country Club at Brookline, Massachusetts, in 1882.

3. The patrician search for family roots and the craze for genealogy gave rise to the founding of the Sons of the Revolution in 1883, followed by the Colonial Dames in 1890, the Daughters of the American Revolution in 1890, and the Society of Mayflower Descendants in 1894.

4. That important institution for socialization, the exclusive country day school and boarding school, experienced its most rapid growth in the last two decades of the nineteenth century. Andover and Exeter, established in the eighteenth century, and St. Paul's, established before the Civil War, experienced their greatest growth in these decades. They were joined by Groton in 1884, Taft in 1890, Hotchkiss in 1892, Choate in 1896, and approximately seventy other similar schools. Among the exclusive suburban day schools established at the same time are Browne and Nichols (1883) in Cambridge, Massachusetts, and Haverford (1884) and Chestnut Hill (1895) in Philadelphia.

---

[4]E. Digby Baltzell, *Philadelphia Gentlemen: The Making of a National Upper Class* (New York: Free Press, 1958).

[5]E. Digby Baltzell, *The Protestant Establishment: Aristocracy and Caste in America* (New York: Random House, 1964).

[6]Ibid., chap. 5.

5. The development of exclusive suburban residential areas, initiated by the open-ing of Tuxedo Park, New York, in 1886, ushered in a flight from the city on the part of the upper class.

6. Graduates of the exclusive lower schools attended high-prestige universities (Yale, Princeton, and Harvard) of, in those decades, somewhat indifferent qual-ity. We must add that there is now a circuit of high (and medium) quality liberal arts colleges and universities, primarily in the northeastern United States, to complete the educational careers of upper class men and women.

7. *The Social Register*, first published in 1887 in New York City, soon added listings for many of America's major cities. This widely imitated register, sold by a profit-making publisher, adheres to no established rules for rejection or ejection. It simply lists details about old wealthy families who stay out of trouble and receive no adverse publicity.[7] *The Social Register* probably contributes consider-ably to facilitating social events and intercity mobility on the part of the upper class.

8. The metropolitan men's club emerged as a potent adjunct to corporate power during the latter part of the nineteenth century. Baltzell, who makes much of the anti-Semitism and anti-Catholicism of all upper-class prestige activities, points out that Jews were excluded from clubs (and some Jewish members expelled) at this time. He fails to note, though, that this was probably necessary because Jews were also being systematically excluded from the upper reaches of the business world.

The development of these prestige groups and practices, says Baltzell, helped to unify the upper class both locally and throughout the metropolitan United States, and in time produced a national upper class. The unity of this upper class results from common socialization; intermarriage; frequent inter-action in clubs and resorts, and at parties; and trusteeships of such prestige organizations as schools, clubs, resort associations, and the like. The possibil-ity that the upper class is or could become a dominant stratum does not concern Baltzell, who believes that every society needs a "representative establishment," or an elite that is also an aristocracy—that is, an establish-ment that represents talent in the spheres of class and power, and expresses a society's highest values in the prestige realm. Assuming that class and power are open elite systems, Baltzell's main concern is that the upper class prac-tices ethnic-religious and racial exclusion and therefore violates in the pres-tige dimension the moral universalism that should accompany the open merit system of the class and power dimensions. Baltzell is hopeful, given leadership by elite elements of the upper class, that these practices will be abandoned, the upper class will again become a representative establish-ment, and the United States will cease being a "caste-ridden, open class" system.

---

[7]Baltzell's analysis of *The Social Register* and comparison of it with *Who's Who in America* may be found in his *Philadelphia Gentlemen*, chap. 2.

Baltzell's evolutionary liberalism pervades his work, and is particularly evident in his failure to see deep connections between the castelike nature of upper class prestige patterns and the protection of class and power interests and privileges. This is not the case with two theorists who have benefited from Baltzell's analysis of upper class prestige practices and have incorporated it into their radical analyses of the American class system. C. Wright Mills treats the foregoing prestige practices as devices to unify the elites who control the apexes of the economic, political, and military orders. As such, these prestige practices are integral features of the United States' power elite, the tiny group of men and families Mills believes to control the nation's basic decisions.[8]

G. William Domhoff, pursuing the approach established by Mills and others, developed a set of social indicators to more positively identify members of the upper class (and has thereby helped to update Baltzell's prestige analysis). According to Domhoff, a male can be considered to belong to the upper class:

1. if he is listed in an edition of *The Social Register* or one of its counterparts.
2. if he, his father, brothers, or father-in-law attended an exclusive prep school.
3. if he, his father, brothers, or father-in-law belongs to an exclusive club.
4. if his sister, wife, mother, or mother-in-law attended an exclusive school or belongs to an exclusive club.
5. if his or his wife's father was a millionaire entrepreneur or $100,000-a-year corporation executive or corporation lawyer *and* if he or she attended any of several private schools or belongs to certain clubs.[9]

Domhoff also offers an interesting analysis of the socialization of upper-class women and their leadership of voluntary and reform groups—groups that help to stabilize society and enhance the prestige of the upper class.[10] In addition, he analyzes upper-class control of prestigious research and public-interest organizations and their impact on foreign and domestic policymaking.[11]

Mills' view that the United States is dominated by a power elite (and Domhoff's view that we are dominated by a ruling class) will concern us again later. The evidence, however, makes one thing certain: The various elites at the apex of a centralized economy and state have developed prestige

[8]This is the theme of Mills' discussion of prestige in *The Power Elite* (New York: Oxford University Press, 1956), chap. 3.

[9]G. William Domhoff, *The Higher Circles: The Governing Class in America* (New York: Random House, 1970), chap. 1.

[10]Ibid., chap. 2.

[11]Ibid., chaps. 5 and 6. This aspect of Domhoff's analysis has been updated in his *Who Rules America Now? A View for the '80s* (Englewood Cliffs, N.J.: Prentice-Hall, 1983).

groups that provide them with a common psychology and a means to coordinate and protect their interests, values, and privileges. In sum, while the American upper class has not been able to elicit national consensus on its prestige superiority, it has managed in practice to establish formidable prestige barriers between itself and the general public. These barriers support a set of benefits that are enjoyed in their own right, are aped by and thus help to divide and co-opt the classes below them, and above all, protect the economic and political power of this class from being diluted by the free play of economic and political forces. Whether or not the upper class is the dominant stratum in America, these prestige values and practices are essential to the formation and maintenance of its extraordinary wealth and power.

Associational Segregation by Race, Religion, and Ethnicity

Americans from all ethnic and racial backgrounds have, by and large, been acculturated—that is, they accept America's economic and political beliefs, its diet, dress, manners, and language (Spanish-speaking groups are an important exception to the latter). But the various racial, ethnic, and religious groups do not associate freely. The United States is characterized by multiple associational systems divided by race, ethnicity, and religion. In turn, class divisions are found among the various racial, ethnic, and religious groups to create what Milton Gordon calls *ethclasses.*[12]

At first, prestige differentiation and discrimination in the United States, along with the facts of economic and political life, created clusters of "ethnic communities": separate churches, social clubs, philanthropic organizations, residential areas, and schools; ethnic cultural activities; foreign-language newspapers; and specialized forms of economic life were salient characteristics of first-generation ethnic groups. But the virtual institutional self-sufficiency of ethnic communities gradually disintegrated. In response to the impact of public education and economic mobility, ethnic groups severed ties with the past (illustrated by the decline of foreign-language newspapers), and began to exhibit class differentials among themselves. Thus, to the extent that Irish Americans are rich, middle rich, and poor, and high, middle, and low on the occupational and educational ladders (class differences), they are less likely than before to live together, intermarry, and belong to the same clubs or other voluntary organizations.

---

[12]Milton M. Gordon, *Assimilation in American Life: The Role of Race, Religion, and National Origin* (New York: Oxford University Press, 1964).

PRIMARY PRESTIGE GROUPS

Class and Primary Behavior

Primary relations (groups) are forms of interaction that usually occur face-to-face, have diffused emotional-moral content, and involve the entire personality in an enduring web of obligations and rights. Friendship, love, marriage, family, neighborhood interaction, as well as dining and certain other forms of socializing, all belong in this category. The fact that primary relations seem normal and spontaneous should not mislead us about their social nature or their relation to the prevailing system of stratification. Class society, no less than estate and caste societies, is characterized by class-related prestige groups that control the basic forms of primary interaction.[13] We know that class factors play an important role in determining marriage and eating partners, as well as place of residence and membership in clubs.

Though many stratification analysts have long been intrigued by the role of clubs in stratification inequality, no systematic study has been undertaken. Of all the classic empirical studies, perhaps the most systematic, and certainly the most informative, is August B. Hollingshead's *Elmtown's Youth.* Hollingshead found distinctive types of clubs and club affiliations for each of Elmtown's five classes.[14] For their part, E. Digby Baltzell and G. William Domhoff have examined upper class clubs.[15] Though a good deal is known about clubs, much has to be conjectured. It would not be amiss, however, to assume that the exclusive urban men's clubs offer basic psychic benefits in their own right and are important adjuncts of the business world as well. The simplest and most direct clue to the latter relation is that it appears to be common practice for businesses to pay the club dues of their executives. High-prestige clubs of all types often have annual fees and dues that amount to thousands of dollars, and as such obviously represent an exclusiveness based on price (class).[16] There is also an obvious and fairly specific class factor (old wealth) in the membership of exclusive men's clubs: Duquesne (Pittsburgh), Detroit (Detroit), Union, Knickerbocker, Brook, Racquet and Tennis, Century, Union League, Metropolitan, and University (New York), and so on. There are also elite women's clubs such as Colony (New York), Friday

---

[13]The classic analyses of social stratification in small-town America contain a wealth of information about the class basis of primary behavior.

[14]August B. Hollingshead, *Elmtown's Youth: The Impact of Social Classes on Adolescents* (New York: Wiley & Sons, 1949), chap. 5.

[15]E. Digby Baltzell, *The Protestant Establishment: Aristocracy and Caste in America* (New York: Random House, 1964), chap. 16; G. William Domhoff, *Who Rules America?* (Englewood Cliffs, N.J.: Prentice-Hall, 1967), chap. 1; *The Higher Circles: The Governing Class in America* (New York: Random House, 1970), chaps. 1 and 4; and *Bohemian Grove and Other Retreats: A Study in Ruling Class Cohesiveness* (New York: Harper & Row, 1974).

[16]Courts have begun to recognize this and have begun to enforce civil rights laws against single-sex clubs and service organizations.

(Chicago), Chilton (Boston), and Acorn (Philadelphia). Patriotic-historical-genealogical societies are by definition limited to members of old families (often possessing old wealth).

Class content is also obvious in the membership of country clubs and resorts, some of which are restricted to old wealth, some to wealth, and others of which cater to the middle classes at large. Service clubs such as the Kiwanis and Rotary are anchored in the world of business and the professions, while fraternal orders and lodges and veterans' groups, such as the Elks, Shriners, and American Legion, appear to be largely lower-middle and working class in composition. An interesting new form of primary interaction (in a commercial setting) is the singles club and bar, and the singles weekend at resorts. Though little researched, it is highly likely that this is a primarily middle class activity. In sum, primary relations have a pronounced class basis: Fundamentally, only class peers engage in primary or intimate forms of interaction.

One must add that there also exists a relatively sharp qualitative discontinuity by class in the *kind* of primary relations Americans enter into. Working-class Americans tend to have fewer friends, entertain less, and belong less to clubs and other organizations devoted to entertainment and companionship than the classes above.[17] And working-class marriages and family life provide fewer and lower-quality satisfactions than characterize those of the classes above. And below the working class is an underclass that experiences deep social isolation, since members of this class do not engage much in either primary or secondary behavior.

Primary relations are also affected by forms of consumption: Since consumption skills and interests can vary within a given class, individuals and families having similar class positions may enjoy different levels and types of primary interaction. The best-known distinction is between the old rich and the new rich, but such distinctions are applicable at all class levels. However, while style of life (consumption) can be independent of class, it invariably succumbs to class; in other words, given time, an economic position can and does acquire the prestige credentials needed for inclusion in

[17]For an old but excellent review of the literature in this area within the context of role theory, see the article by Alan F. Blum, "Social Structure, Social Class and Participation in Primary Relationships," in Arthur B. Shostak and William Gomberg, eds., *Blue-Collar World: Studies of the American Worker* (Englewood Cliffs, N.J.: Prentice-Hall, 1964), pp. 195–207.

For a valuable start toward understanding primary associational structures in our urban-suburban life, see Edward O. Laumann, *Prestige and Association in an Urban Community: An Analysis of an Urban Stratification System* (Indianapolis: Bobbs-Merrill, 1966). Laumann, who used both old and new empirical techniques to study Cambridge and Belmont in the Boston metropolitan area, found a considerable relation between occupation and intimate (primary) relationships, especially friendship, and a more pronounced relation at the top and bottom levels. The world of the upper and lower working classes has been studied more recently by, respectively, E. E. LeMasters, *Blue-Collar Aristocrats: Life Styles at a Working Class Tavern* (Madison: University of Wisconsin Press, 1975) and Lillian B. Rubin, *Worlds of Pain: Life in Working Class Families* (New York: Basic Books, 1976).

primary prestige groups. It was inevitably, in other words, that Mrs. Astor (old real estate wealth) would call on Mrs. Vanderbilt (new railroad wealth). And, of course, primary relations between families and individuals with similar class positions are strongly differentiated by religion, ethnicity, and "race"—but this issue is best discussed separately.

Class and Religious-Ethnic Primary Behavior

Religious groups in the United States—Protestants, Roman Catholics, Jews, Greek Orthodox, adherents of Oriental religions, Muslims—are characterized by unique forms of primary interaction, which (where applicable) are further differentiated by ethnicity. Thus, residence, friendship, marriage, forms and functions of family life, socializing at home and in clubs, and worship all tend to take place within the boundaries of religious-ethnic identification. But each of these religious-ethnic groups is also differentiated internally by class-structured forms of primary relations. As already stated, Milton Gordon has suggested the term *ethclass* to refer to this behavioral reality:

> *The ethnic group is the locus of a sense of historical identification, while the ethclass is the locus of a sense of participational identification. With a person of the same social class but of a different ethnic group, one shares behavioral similarities but not a sense of peoplehood. With those of the same ethnic group but of a different social class, one shares the sense of peoplehood but not behavior similarities. The only group which meets both of these criteria are people of the same ethnic group and the same social class.*[18]

Accordingly, there is an upper, middle, and (broadly speaking) lower class type of club and pattern of friendship, marriage, and "church" orientation within each broad religious category.

Class and "Racial" Primary Behavior

It seems best to treat class and "racial" forms of primary behavior separately. Despite the strength of religious-ethnic values and beliefs among whites, there is still enough social and moral elbow-room for members of various religious-ethnic groups to mix (or even to "pass") to make it necessary to distinguish this form of segregation from racial segregation. In the aggregate, American whites and blacks (and Indians, Orientals, and other groups whose skin color is not white) simply do not mix on a primary, or even a secondary, basis.[19] Thus residence, intermarriage, friendship, and socializing at home, in clubs, or at church (even within a given religion) are all sharply bounded by lines based on color and impervious to equality in class.[20] Primary relations

---

[18]Gordon, *Assimilation in American Life*, p. 53.

[19]Even death does not unit the "races"—cemeteries have traditionally been segregated, though the practice is now being modified by legislation and court decisions.

[20]Upper-class blacks and other "races" tend to mix more with whites than their counterparts lower on the class ladder.

among black Americans do not compare favorably with the primary relations of the rest of the population, primarily because of the historic disorganization of the black family. As we have pointed out, the economically marginal black male has historically played a passive role in his family; he is often entirely estranged. There also appears to be a sharper estrangement between the sexes among blacks, though this is not uncommon in American, and especially in working class, life. The relation between parents and children in economically marginal or depressed black families differs markedly from that of stable families. The absence of adult role models makes for a different form of socialization and means that black children at this level are highly subject to peer control, often in the form of street gangs. And because of their historically depressed economic position, blacks have been unable to develop kinship networks or communal groups to help them face their problems or to provide capital for economic needs and endeavors.[21]

Black American primary relations are also differentiated internally by class. As is true of whites, upper-level blacks enjoy more stable family lives (though not as stable as those of whites at similar class levels), belong to more clubs, and participate in a greater variety of social events than lower-level blacks.[22]

SECONDARY PRESTIGE GROUPS

Class and Power and Secondary (Voluntary) Behavior

Secondary interaction involves only a portion of an individual's personality and tends to be functionally specific and emotionally neutral: seeing a doctor, getting on a bus, going to school, working in an office or factory, going to church, voting, being on trial, serving on a committee, joining an interest group, going to the park or a ball game or a restaurant or a movie, and joining a trade union or professional association are all examples of secondary interaction.

Research has revealed a pronounced class-related pattern to participation in secondary (voluntary) organizations. The upper classes, identified by occu-

[21]For an analysis of the weak primary group development of blacks relative to economic development contrasted with the strong development of economically relevant primary behavior among Japanese and Chinese immigrants, see Ivan H. Light, *Ethnic Enterprise in America: Business and Welfare Among Chinese, Japanese, and Blacks* (Berkeley; University of California Press, 1972).

[22]The primary relations of upper-level blacks depicted in E. Franklin Frazier, *Black Bourgeoisie* (New York: Free Press, 1957), chap. 9 can be contrasted fruitfully with the primary relations among lower-level blacks depicted in Elliot Liebow, *Tally's Corner: A Study of Negro Streetcorner Men* (Boston: Little, Brown, 1967).

pation, income, and education (either separately or combined), have higher rates of membership, active participation, and leadership in secondary groups, especially in general-interest, career-related business and professional, community-and-service-oriented, educational, cultural, and political-pressure groups. (The working class tends to concentrate its membership in churches, unions, fraternal groups, and sports clubs.) By and large, the overall rate of participation in important power groups is low among the working class and almost nonexistent among the lower class.[23]

The low rate of participation by ordinary citizens in voluntary organizations is far from the full story. Participation in policy-making and in the management of voluntary organizations is restricted to very small numbers drawn almost exclusively from the upper middle and upper classes. No effective or meaningful popular participation takes place in such groups as hospitals, colleges and universities, charities, public-policy research institutes and foundations, and cultural groups. An analysis of Scouting and the Young Men's Christian Association (YMCA) has shown biases derived from the upper classes in even these seemingly nonpartisan groups.[24]

Indeed, the working and lower classes engage in so little voluntary secondary behavior that one must conclude that qualitatively different life experiences divide these two segments of American society. Not only is the United States not a nation of joiners—excluding trade unions and churches, it is doubtful that even half of the adult American population belongs to a secondary organization—but the evidence clearly indicates that the American social system tends to restrict and routinize the experience of its working and lower classes.[25]

The Functions and Dysfunctions of Voluntarism

Foreign commentators—for example, Tocqueville and Bryce—were impressed by how much American society relies on voluntary behavior to handle social functions. European societies also experienced a growth of voluntarism but less so than the United States. The reasons are relatively clear—Europe had established churches and governments to perform many of the functions and to tackle many of the problems that arose with industri-

[23]For a comprehensive guide to voluntary behavior, see David Horton Smith and Jacqueline Macauley, eds., *Participation in Social and Political Activities: A Comprehensive Analysis of Political Involvement, Expressive Leisure Time, and Helping Behavior* (San Francisco: Jossey-Bass, 1980).

[24]David I. MacLeod, *Building Character in the American Boy: The Boy Scouts, YMCA, and Their Forerunners, 1870–1920* (Madison: University of Wisconsin Press, 1983).

[25]There is also evidence that, in addition to relying on family and friends for most of its interaction experience, the working class does not travel as widely as the classes above it, and that its participation in the thought-life of the nation is qualitatively lower than the classes above it. The amount and quality of moral, intellectual, and artistic enrichment is even lower among the lower class.

alization. Given the conditions of the New World, Americans were forced to do for themselves. Today, organized as private groups, Americans initiate reforms across a wide front and take on social problems such as disease, homelessness, distressed families, alcoholism, battered wives, and unmarried pregnant women. The voluntary sector is also responsible for a good deal of American education (and private schools provide a model for much of public education). It also conducts a great deal of American research and is responsible for much of what goes on in the world of the arts.

Right liberals favor a voluntary solution to most social problems. The Reagan administration of the 1980s stressed a return to voluntarism to justify cuts in public services. Left liberals support voluntarism but are much more likely to view it as a way to test ideas so that the good ones can be implemented by government. Radicals argue that voluntarism is an ideology to keep social problems out of the political arena and thus prevent the public from evaluating how property and professional groups behave. In addition, voluntarism protects income and wealth groups from paying taxes (the United States, remember, is the least taxed of all industrial nations except Japan).

Radical critics specifically charge that:

1. The absence of public participation in cultural groups means that only the art of the upper classes is available.
2. The boards of hospitals and universities are effectively dominated by business and professional interests and many alternatives to present-day health and educational policies are ruled out.
3. The United Way tends to support only traditional, respectable charities and discriminates against consumer advocacy, political reform, tenants, feminist, gay rights, and other groups.
4. The voluntary approach to research and development means that many dubious projects are undertaken and that the interests of power groups are served under the cover of academic freedom and objective research (for an example of bias in research that favors the upper classes, see Box 15–1, "The Tomato Harvester: How Education Serves the Corporate Economy").

Participation in secondary prestige groups is a well-known way in which the upper classes exert influence over important activities (outside of class and power) and an important source of moral, intellectual, and aesthetic prestige. It is also a way in which upwardly mobile families establish their claims to full inclusion in a higher social stratum. Large business firms routinely use fund drives to test the abilities of young executives; and they are quite aware that their participation in such drives is a means to acquire a favorable public image. The ties between the upper levels of the business and professional worlds and institutions of higher education are well documented. We also have considerable documentation of the upper and upper-middle class base of foundations, prestigious research institutes, hospitals, cultural groups, and voluntary organizations in general.

While secondary organizations are primarily middle and upper class groups, the class composition of particular organizations varies. Though data are scarce and often impressionistic, it is clear, for example, that cultural groups like museum or symphony orchestra boards have different class memberships than parent-teachers associations, and that various shades of upper and middle class membership characterize the Rotary, the Kiwanis, the Elks, the Masons, the Young Men's Christian Association, the Democratic and Republican parties, the Red Cross, the American Cancer Society, the American Bar Association, the American Sociological Association, and so on. There is also wide variation by class in type of church and church membership; this matter is best discussed separately, since it touches on differences based on religion and ethnicity.

Any sharp distinction between the dimensions of prestige and power must be fallacious, for the traditional distinction between the private and public sectors has been badly blurred by the dynamics of mature industrialization. Actually, the separation of these spheres was never as complete as we sometimes imagine. For example, the property and income of religious, charitable, and educational organizations have traditionally been exempt from taxation. This practice indicates a broad consensus on the value of such activities, and the exemption from taxation of our churches, foundations, and institutions of higher education is contingent on their political neutrality.

One of the more portentous aspects of the relation between government and the private sector of voluntary organizations is the growth of government by grant and contract.[26] In recent decades, the federal government and lesser governments have sought to achieve a host of purposes by contracting with established private groups such as the National Urban League or the Young Men's Christian Association or financing new organizations to render intellectual and scientific services at home and abroad. ("Not-for-profit corporations" provide advisory and technical services to the military, the Atomic Energy Commission, the Department of State, the Central Intelligence Agency, and so on.) This trend has made many traditional voluntary organizations dependent on government for financing, creating a new type of quasi-voluntary group. As Alan Pifer points out, the trend toward government by contract and grant has important implications for the autonomy of private bodies and poses problems of accountability.[27]

---

[26]The significance of this development was first noted by Alan Pifer, president of the Carnegie Corporation, in two essays, "The Nongovernmental Organization at Bay" (New York: Carnegie Corporation *Annual Report*, 1966), and "The Quasi-Nongovernmental Organization" (New York: Carnegie Corporation *Annual Report*, 1967).

[27]For an indictment of the federal government's use of advisory bodies and private consultants, see Daniel Guttman and Barry Willner, *The Shadow Government: The Government's Multi-Billion-Dollar Giveaway of Its Decision-Making Powers to Private Management Consultants, 'Experts,' and Think Tanks* (New York: Pantheon, 1976).

In addition, the federal government has begun large-scale funding of medical, scientific, and educational undertakings, often funneling public monies through "nonpolitical" conduits like the National Science Foundation. In the case of education, institutions of higher education (including private and religious schools) have received direct governmental grants for construction, special programs, research, and (since the Higher Education Act of 1972) normal operation.

The trend toward public institutions of higher education also represents a way in which power is explicitly engaged in serving class values in the realm of prestige.[28] This process also characterizes the many areas in which power endorses the right of private or "public" organizations to certify individuals for high-level occupations and to enforce regulations controlling the behavior of their members (for example, the American Medical Association, the National Association of Securities Dealers, the American Bar Association).

Still another way to examine the interrelatedness of our class-prestige-power systems is to trace the pattern of overlapping personnel and policies in the areas of research, reform, and public policy formation. Presidential and congressional commissions are composed of high-level representatives of various segments of the economy and the professions; and private foundations, associations, and institutes (such as the Committee on Economic Development, the Rockefeller and Ford Foundations, the Brookings Institution, the Council on Foreign Relations, and the Twentieth Century Fund) cultivate images of public disinterestedness and develop highly influential policy proposals in the realms of business, education, population, foreign policy, medicine, the arts, race relations, and the like.[29]

One of the more interesting examples of a partisan political stance with partisan consequences by an ostensibly nonpartisan research-charitable group is the American Cancer Society. With very little input from the public, the American Cancer Society helps to channel huge resources (far more than can be efficiently or honestly absorbed) into a search for a cancer cure while diverting resources and attention away from the most promising way to curb cancer—direct public action to create healthy natural and social environments. Unable to ignore a rising tide of knowledge connecting cancer to unhealthy habits (for example, smoking, sunbathing), unhealthy diet (for example, the excessive intake of animal fat), and unhealthy air, water, and workplaces, threatened business and professional groups now advocate prevention—not prevention through direct public action but through *voluntary* changes in personal life style (see Box 12–1, "The Cancer Establishment"). Here is an example of how high-minded reform is mostly a way to depoliti-

---

[28]For a discussion of the way in which public institutions of higher education subsidize the middle and upper classes, see Chapter 15.

[29]For further discussion, see the section "Political Parties and Interest Groups" in Chapter 14.

BOX 12–1.   *THE CANCER ESTABLISHMENT[30]*

The powerful and rich have a large stake in finding a cure for cancer. For one thing, no matter how much money they have they can't buy a cure. But more important, they have an economy to protect.

For over fifty years powerful individuals and groups have defined cancer as a medical problem that is somehow in the genes of individuals (individual human nature at fault). Though we know that there are many different kinds of cancer and that there is no magic bullet to cure it, the basic approach remains the same as in dealing with other diseases. Some medical progress has been made in treating cancer through surgery, drugs, and radiation. Survival rates have risen. But the limits of a medical-scientific approach are also known and yet not acted on. Why? The fear of cancer (its unpredictable and mysterious nature) gives power and rewards to those who have any knowledge about it (medical specialists, biology researchers, drug companies, medical technology manufacturers). Given the dominance of professionalism (only experts should be allowed to solve problems), what could be more plausible than medicalizing cancer?

However, the basic causes of cancer are in the American economy and this makes it more of a political than a medical problem. Research has established that tobacco, asbestos, and certain chemicals, industrial processes, foods, drugs, and energy sources (including the sun) are cancer causing. Prevention requires that Americans be protected from exposure to these agents. But cancer prevention is a direct threat to much of the American economy. It is no accident that a cancer establishment, linking the basic economy, voluntary groups, the mass media,* cancer treatment and research centers in hospitals and universities, and the federal government (National Cancer Institute, Federal Drug Administration) has developed across the apex of American society to promote *one* approach to cancer. For many years this approach was narrowly medical—treat cancer patients and find a cure. In recent years this medical approach has been widened to include advice to the public to adopt voluntarily healthier lifestyles. What the voluntary approach does, of course, is to undercut efforts to reap the large gains in health that would result if the natural and social environments were directly cleansed of disease-causing agents. Whether the problem of cancer (and all the other problems affecting the health of the American people) can be kept depoliticized by a glamourized, high-technology medical approach combined with voluntaristic ideology remains to be seen.

---

[30]For much of the following discussion, see Ralph W. Moss, "The Cancer Establishment: Whose Side Are They On?" *The Progressive* 44 (February 14, 1980):14–18.

*Juanne N. Clarke reports that between 1961 and 1980 six general-interest magazines discussed cancer in images of war and combat and only 5 percent of the articles referred to social causes (such as industrial pollution) in a political context; reported in *The Chronicle of Higher Education* (September 4, 1985), p. 20.

cize a problem and to protect the status quo (the capitalist economy that is causing the problem).

In sum, it is clear that the entire realm of secondary prestige groups (along with consumption and primary group behavior) represents an adjunct to economic and political power. It is through various secondary prestige activities that a vital moral and intellectual cement is applied to the overall structure of American inequality. And secondary prestige groups are as narrowly based, unresponsive, and backward in their procedures and policies as corporate and governmental bureaucracies. The function, largely latent, of secondary prestige groups can perhaps be stated more simply: By deflecting attention away from the class (and power) basis of America's social problems, such groups help to preserve the status quo.

Class and Religious-Ethnic Secondary Behavior

A great deal of secondary behavior is marked by religious-ethnic segregation, some forced and some self-imposed. By and large, religion and ethnicity are ascriptive forces; children inherit the religion and ethnic identity of their parents, as well as a wide range of interactional experience: worship, the discussion of moral and public issues within a sacred context, and opportunities to participate in charity drives, parochial school education, church-based or related youth groups, men's and women's auxiliaries, hospitals, nursing and retirement homes, credit unions, and intellectual-reform groups.

The concept of ethclass also encompasses this form of group behavior, since religious-ethnic secondary behavior is also differentiated by class. A classic analysis pointing to the dual nature of voluntary behavior is Hollingshead's study of the Junior League in New Haven. Hollingshead found no less than eight Junior Leagues, all "upper" class but differentiated by religion, ethnicity, and race.[31]

The three worlds of Protestantism, Roman Catholicism, and Judaism are a stable feature of associational behavior in the United States. But churches are not immune to the dynamics of class stratification. Each of the three major religions in the United States is differentiated by class. Among Protestants, the upper classes tend to prefer Episcopalian, Congregational, Presbyterian, and Unitarian forms of worship, while the lower classes tend to be Baptist or members of one of the many fundamentalist sects.[32] Roman Catholicism has been associated with the working class for much of American history, but is now evenly divided among all classes. Also characteristic of Roman Catholicism is the "national parish," or differentiation by ethnic

---

[31] August B. Hollingshead, "Trends in Social Stratification: A Case Study," *American Sociological Review* 17 (December 1952):679–686.

[32] Churches in the South have traditionally practiced open segregation by race as well.

group: Irish, French Canadian, Italian, Spanish-speaking, and so on. However, there is some evidence that the "national parish" is slowly declining in prevalence. Jewish Americans are more likely to be in the middle and upper classes.[33]

Religiously based organizations have helped many of America's minorities adapt to American society. Religious organizations helped immigrant Irish, Italian, Swedes, Germans, French-Canadians, Jews, Greeks, and so on adapt to an alien social environment. However, the Roman Catholic Church, which has played a vital role in helping a variety of ethnic groups to adapt to American life, has not performed that function for Mexican Americans. Short of resources and clergy, lacking an English-speaking clergy, and dispersed over vast rural areas, the Roman Catholic Church in the Southwest was markedly dissimilar to the English-speaking, Irish-led, and politically skilled Church in other parts of the country.[34]

The same contrast is apparent in other areas of secondary voluntary life. Because of their urban concentration and rise in class position, Jewish Americans have had the human and material resources to develop a large and vital network of groups to support Jewish and community values: charity and service groups of all kinds, groups supporting Zionism, civil rights groups like B'nai B'rith, and the like. In addition, Jews have been active in political life and in the trade union movement. Given the lower and working class status and rural isolation of Mexican Americans, it is not surprising that they have developed few voluntary groups. In this respect, they are worse off than black Americans, who, for various reasons (including help from whites), have had a more viable network of voluntary organizations to help them cope with a hostile environment.

Sentiments of ethnic solidarity are still strong among Mexican Americans. Their political participation is low, though not abnormally so given their aggregate class position, and they favor the Democratic party by an overwhelming percentage. Mexican Americans have increased their political activities in recent years but they still reject allying themselves in common cause with black Americans. This attitude, together with Mexican American prejudice against blacks, forestalls cooperation between the two, though they are members of essentially the same classes. Even the Chicano movement, which represents a more militant Mexican American stance against economic and political domination by Anglos, has been unable or unwilling to build bridges to the black community.[35]

---

[33]For a carefully compiled and comprehensive picture and analysis of religion and social stratification and of the relation among religion, race, and ethnicity, see H. Paul Chalfant, Robert E. Beckley, and C. Eddie Palmer, *Religion in Contemporary Society*, 2nd ed. (Palo Alto, Calif: Mayfield, 1987), chaps. 13 and 14.

[34]Leo Grebler *et al, The Mexican-American People* (New York: Free Press, 1970), chap. 19.

[35]For a fuller discussion, see Chapter 14.

The historic power of religious-ethnic institutions in the United States is clear. Less clear is how closely Americans still adhere to patterns associated with their religious-ethnic groups of birth. Much of the data is tangential, and much of it is old and focused on small communities. An important study comparing three generations of Jewish Americans in Providence, Rhode Island, indicates that the present generation is less likely than its forebears to belong to Jewish organizations and more likely to belong to non-Jewish organizations (especially among college-educated Jews living in the suburbs).[36] More recent evidence indicates that Jews who make it into the upper class have largely given up their ethnic identity.[37]

Class and "Racial" Secondary Behavior

Despite some weakening of the rigid barriers between the white and nonwhite "races," it is still best to discuss racial segregation in secondary groups separately from religious-ethnic segregation. Black Americans do not as a rule belong to white secondary organizations, largely because of class factors—membership in secondary organizations is a middle-and upper-class phenomenon, and few blacks enjoy such class status (due, it must always be remembered, to centuries of oppression). Racist exclusion has also prevailed in many areas, forcing black Americans to found their own organizations. Furthermore, blacks have probably believed that their interests would be submerged and their power dissipated if they joined white organizations. Thus, parallel to white secondary organizations there exist all-black clubs, charities, veterans groups, labor unions, and associations of manufacturers, lawyers, doctors, psychiatrists, ministers, bridge players, cowboys, businesspeople, executives, and the like. Of great importance in the history of black Americans is the all-black religious organization. The racially segregated church is as much a part of the history of blacks and whites as the segregated school or waiting room. So too, the all-black college has played a considerable role in the ability of blacks to survive, though all indications point to its relative decline in the near future.

The best-known black organizations are those dedicated to civil rights and politics: the National Association for the Advancement of Colored People (founded in 1909 as an interracial group but now predominantly black), the Southern Christian Leadership Conference, the Student Nonviolent Coordinating Committee, and the Congress of Racial Equality (founded in 1942 as an interracial group but soon thereafter predominantly black). Also well-known is the National Urban League (1910), which works mostly to advance the cause of blacks in the economy and in the field of housing.

[36]Sidney Goldstein and Calvin Goldscheider, *Jewish Americans: Three Generations in a Jewish Community* (Englewood Cliffs, N.J.: Prentice-Hall, 1968), chap. 10.

[37]Richard L. Zweigenhaft and G. William Domhoff, *Jews in the Protestant Establishment* (New York: Praeger, 1982).

The secondary behavior of black Americans is not too well researched, though the class basis of black business and occupational groups is obvious. Class is also associated with residential distinctions among blacks, and there are black upper class "society" organizations and events and magazines devoted to reporting black class achievements (for example, *Ebony*). In short, the concept of ethclass encompasses both primary and secondary behavior among blacks.

THE RELATION BETWEEN CLASS (AND POWER) AND PRESTIGE: A GENERAL SUMMARY

The United States has an enormously varied array of both primary and secondary prestige groups. There is a distinct class basis to both types of prestige behavior, and a distinct segregation of prestige behavior by ethnicity, religion, and "race." The major function of prestige behavior appears to be to maintain existing class and ethnic-religious-"racial" (and political-legal) inequalities.

The major patterns in prestige group activity (which can be defined broadly to include forms of consumption, education, and use of leisure in general) appear to be:

1. Strong integration and reciprocal support between class, prestige, and power for the upper, upper-middle, and lower-middle classes, and a general pattern of less prestige and support from prestige activities in the working and lower classes.
2. A general pattern of ethnic-religious-"racial" segregation in prestige groups, and a distinct differential within each religious-ethinic and "racial" group by class (ethclass). Minorities have distinctly different records of prestige group behavior. Given their strong religious-ethnic identification and urban middle-class status, Jewish Americans have developed strong, supportive prestige groups; they differ from the majority middle class, however, in that their political orientation is strongly toward the Democratic party. Black Americans have had poor family primary relations but their voluntary organizations have been surprisingly active and somewhat effective, even though blacks lack a large middle class from which to draw funds and personnel. Mexican Americans have also had poor primary relations (though not as poor as those of blacks). The much-vaunted familism of Mexican Americans is only a partially operative ideal—as we have said, there is evidence that the Mexican American family has suffered considerably from poverty. Furthermore, Mexican Americans were unable to develop a network of supportive voluntary organizations due to their poverty and rural isolation. This pattern has changed somewhat since the 1960s, when Mexican Americans began to shed the apathy induced by poverty and oppression and to take steps toward determining their own future.

The wide diversity in types of prestige that is such a salient feature of prestige in a class society, as opposed to the tightly meshed and all-encompassing ascriptive prestige systems of caste and estate societies, has important consequences for the functioning of American society. On the one hand, it leads to struggle and conflict, since those with low ascribed prestige, such as blacks and other racial minorities, can combat their prestige "superiors" with prestige values the latter accept, like accomplishments in science or warfare, the Bill of Rights, and Christian brotherhood.

But prestige diversity can also prevent struggle, since individuals and families have access to a wide variety of traditional and new opportunities to acquire prestige. In this sense, prestige phenomena can be likened to the American economy: both undergo continuous expansion and diversification, thereby avoiding to a considerable extent the *subzero* type of competition in which one person's or group's gain is another's loss.

Despite their functional importance, the autonomy and power of prestige processes and structures should not be exaggerated. The evidence points overwhelmingly to the power of class and power over prestige. Class and power forces determine the boundaries and cleavages in prestige differentiation, and more often than not prestige phenomena are blatantly economic or political-legal in nature. Direct links between class and prestige are abundantly evident, as are the links between power and prestige. For one thing, many prestige activities—including music, art, sports, books, magazines, and consumption in general—are now dominated by profit-making organizations. For another, the staffs of profit and nonprofit organizations in the realm of prestige have similar qualifications, which also makes them interchangeable with personnel in the realms of class and power. It is also well known that many voluntary organizations, such as museums, hospitals, symphony orchestras, universities, and charities, rely heavily on business and professional people and their spouses for policymaking and financial support. An additional link between class and prestige is the investment of the endowment funds of churches, universities, foundations, and other voluntary organizations in the major corporations of our economy. Studies of university and hospital boards reveal that the upper classes exercise strong control over the budgets of voluntary-prestige groups, and thus over the allocation of community resources.

The dependence of prestige groups on the power dimension is also pronounced. Government supports prestige groups in many ways, and thereby endorses private solutions to public problems: It charters private education and allocates tax money to an enormous range of class-oriented educational services. It subsidizes cultural activities and research, and its tax laws exempt a wide range of charitable, religious, and educational groups. Government also has enormous impact, often inadvertent, on the prestige realm through postal rates, highway and recreational programs, mortgage policies, and the celebration of holidays.

As we have said, the consolidation of the existing class system appears to be the major function of the prestige dimension. Perhaps this point can be stated differently. The possibility that class, prestige, and power differentials will lead to social friction is ever-present in a formally egalitarian society, and the specific prestige processes that serve to minimize this danger are of more than passing interest.

Thus is it not unimportant that primary prestige groups exist in relative isolation from each other (or are insulated from each other). By and large, each class level develops distinctive primary prestige groups, and the various classes do not participate in each other's primary forms of interaction. Just as important is the fact that membership in secondary prestige groups, while formally open to all according to achievement criteria, tends to be relatively homogeneous by class. And where membership is heterogeneous, prestige problems are minimized by the segmentalization of interaction; that is, people do not interact as members of a class but as individuals with a common specialized interest, such as birdwatching, stamp collecting, retarded children, and the like. There is also specialized prestige interaction on both primary and secondary levels by religion-ethnicity and "race," though here too each religious-ethnic and "racial" aggregate is differentiated by class. (That is, there is a class hierarchy among Irish Roman Catholics, Mexican Americans, Chinese Americans, Protestants, Jews, blacks, and so on.)

Because of these processes, there is no need for class society to develop a society-wide concensus about all prestige values. The isolation and insulation of primary prestige groups makes it possible for people who would not dream of eating together, let alone intermarrying, to regard themselves as moral, political, and legal equals. Class society avoids, in other words, the general supersubordination by an upper prestige stratum (aristocrat) of a lower prestige stratum (serf). When Americans of different prestige interact, it is invariably in a functionally specific situation (such as at work, in a voluntary group, in a court of law, as a patient).

Thus, the American prestige system avoids the spread of one form of prestige into other areas (diffused, categorical-ascriptive prestige) and inhibits the development of behavior that expresses and continuously reinforces the general superiority of one collection of families over another, a prestige system characteristic of caste and estate societies. The operation of these prestige processes allows the United States to avoid tension between its universalistic moral (and political-legal) system and the requirements of a class structure of stratification. And these isolating and insulating prestige processes help to moderate the deep tension between, on the one hand, the tradition of moral equality and achievement and, on the other, the United States' ascriptive values in ethnicity, religion, and especially race relations.

CHAPTER 13

The Dimension of Power (Politics, Government, and Law)

Power is one of the most ambiguous terms in social science. Using it in stratification analysis, care should be taken, first of all, to distinguish between *social* power (the combined effects of class, prestige, and power) and *political-legal* power alone. The conceptualization of political-legal power is the least developed aspect of stratification theory, though a rough definition is easy to provide. Following Max Weber's usage, *political-legal power* refers to only one form of social power, the state, or the political-legal forces that promote or reduce social inequality.[1] Max Weber's classic article on social stratification, "Class, Status, Party," contains only a fragmentary discussion of party, or the realm of power. Just as class and prestige do not ordinarily separate or come into conflict in an agrarian (estate or caste) society, Weber tells us, no autonomous political realm emerges unless a movement away from "community" and toward "societalization" takes place. Only when a certain level of rationality is reached does the state emerge. That is, only when conflicting potential courses of action dictate conscious choices and the evaluation of consequences does there appear a specialized, full-time staff to make and enforce the norms called law in the name of social adjustment, integration, and other ideals.

[1]For Weber's discussion of law and politics in relation to social stratification, see his "Class, Status, Party," in H. H. Gerth and C. Wright Mills, ed. and tr., *From Max Weber: Essays in Sociology* (New York: Oxford University Press, 1946), chap. 7, Sections 1, 10.

All societies, and particularly the more complex, develop some form of politics to handle conflicts, exact norms, and legitimate the general structure of supersubordination. Political institutions, Weber says, can reflect their class or status (prestige) groups, or a mixture of both. The purpose of political action is to influence or control a specific category of norms, law. Law is said to exist, according to Weber, when a staff can obtain conformity to norms (or punish those who violate them) by either physical or psychic means. When such a staff and such a body of norms are accompanied by accepted procedures for controlling the staff and for legislating law, one can speak of the state (power). Politics, in other words, means access to and influence over the state—that is, the tax collector, the courts, the police, the military, and so on. *Stratified politics* means that the various levels of society have differential access to and differential control over the state.

Our major purpose in this and the following three chapters is to analyze the stratification of politics in America, or, in other words, to find out how the hierarchy of class (and prestige) is related to the hierarchy of power (politics, government, and law). Our strategy will be to relate class (the hierarchy of individuals and families defined in terms of economic market assets and liabilities) and prestige (the hierarchy of individuals and families defined in terms of psychic and interactional or, roughly, moral assets and liabilities) on the one hand, to the structure of power (the hierarchy of individuals and families defined in terms of political-legal assets and liabilities) on the other. For convenience, *class* and *prestige* can be treated as a single entity (*class-prestige*), or referred to (with caution) as *socioeconomic class*. To portray a full-fledged social class, in other words, one must examine political-legal power in combination with economic and prestige power. *Formally defined, a social class (or social stratum) is the composite of assets and liabilities that characterizes aggregates of individuals and families (and other groups and collectivities) in the economic realm, the social (or prestige) realm, and in the realm of politics, government, and law.*

In broadening our concept of social class, we will also be accomplishing another purpose: As we discover how class-prestige affects power and vice-versa, we will also be laying bare the overall structure of *social* power. In stratification analysis, the overall structure of social power is synonymous with the hierarchy of social classes.

THE FORMAL MATERIALS OF POLITICAL-LEGAL (POWER) STRATIFICATION

Much of our thinking about politics (and society) is formal in nature—that is, concerned with appearance, words, and ideals, rather than substance and operational reality. Indeed, so prevalent is formal thinking in American life that it seems best to begin by articulating the conventional or formal view of politics, so that we can devote ourselves fully to examining its validity. To put the matter bluntly, whenever the word *formal* is encountered, the reader should be on notice that the reality of the phenomenon being discussed will be challenged.

The Formal Separation of State and Society

During the seventeenth and eighteenth centuries, and even into the ninteenth, the leading liberal societies (England, France, and the United States), each in its own time and way, struggled to separate the state from society. Liberal theorists assisted this process by asserting individual rights that the state could not violate and by claiming that citizens deserved equal access to and equal treatment by the state. The process of distinguishing the state from society reached its climax in the characteristic liberal separation of law (the state) from morality (freedom of speech, association, worship, and so on), a separation that seeks to limit the discretionary power of the state by specifying in precise legal norms what it is authorized to do and what it cannot do.

The attempt to separate state and society and to define their relations in legal terms is the essence of liberal democracy. As we will see, there is a considerable amount of formality in this formulation: common access to politics and equal treatment by government are far from being operational realities. And laissez-faire theory, one of the main devices with which liberal theorists have tried to separate state and society, is also an empty formality. As we will see in abundant detail, it is far more realistic to think in terms of the *intertwining* of state and society—an intertwining that represents a coordination, if not a merger, of the hierarchies of class, prestige, and power. In contradiction to the alleged existence of common rights and equality before the law and the alleged separation of state and society, therefore, we will speak of a corporate state or a political economy. This does not mean, of course, that the formalities of American life have no force or reality; it simply means that they should not be allowed to monopolize our thinking.

The Logic of a Class System
of Political-Legal Power

The interplay between power and the forces of class and prestige has had varied and complex manifestations in American history. The sanctity of the person, which is such a prominent feature of the liberal tradition, led early to the abolition of imprisonment for debt and the development of the law of bankruptcy. Today, the law of bankruptcy, which even includes a specific prohibition denying the right of individuals to sell themselves into slavery, gives the individual political-legal protection against disastrous economic (class) reversals. The abolition by Thomas Jefferson, as governor of Virginia, of *primogeniture*—the legal requirement that the first-born, usually the first-born male, must inherit the entire family estate—and *entail*—legal prohibition of the owner's right to sell his or her property either in part or as a whole—are other examples of the class logic of power. When primogeniture and entail are in effect, economic and familistic values have blended and been lent added force and legitimacy by the state. Thus, the abolition of primogeniture and entail signified the egalitarianism of the United States and its need to free economic assets from familistic and legal controls.

Until well into the nineteenth century, American political institutions were explicitly tied to economic status through the imposition of property qualifications for voting or for holding public office.[2] The official sale of exemptions from military service during the Civil War is a well-known example of the connection between class and power. And until the Fourteenth and Fifteenth Amendments (1868 and 1870), the power dimension was formally tied to class (and prestige) forces in other ways, though practices differed in the North[3] and in the South.[4]

The Formal Tension Between Class-Prestige and Power

It is not difficult, on a formal level at least, to illustrate the tension between class and prestige on the one hand, and power on the other, and to demonstrate the relative autonomy of the power dimension. Political and legal privileges based on ascriptive criteria are incongruent with both the achievement ethic and industrialization, and have been gradually undermined. Today, formally speaking, all American citizens have extensive political and legal rights, and American political-legal institutions are autonomous from class and prestige forces.[5] And, formally, the egalitarian norm of

---

[2]Chilton Williams, *American Suffrage: From Property to Democracy, 1760–1860* (Princeton, N.J.: Princeton University Press, 1960); Margaret Chute, *The First Liberty: A History of the Right to Vote in America, 1619–1850* (New York: E. P. Dutton, 1969). White male suffrage was achieved unevenly after the American Revolution. General elimination of the property qualification and extension of the vote to white adult males was not completed until the 1850s.

[3]In extending suffrage, most northern states specifically exempted blacks. Before the Civil War only five northern states (accounting for 6 percent of the blacks in the North) extended the right to vote to black males (Chute, *The First Liberty*, p. 313).

[4]The black American's formal right to vote was virtually meaningless in the South, however, until the 1960s. Another ascribed status, which is not directly germane to stratification analysis but which also qualified the full autonomy of political-legal institutions from ascription, was denial of the vote to women until 1919.

[5]The United States Supreme Court has clearly separated religion and the state in a number of decisions; court decisions requiring legal counsel and other legal rights for the poor and the "despised" (lower class criminal defendants) and evidence of the continued vitality of political-legal rights against the forces of class and prestige. The Supreme Court decision voiding state laws that prohibit marriage between members of different "races" (miscegenation) is also evidence of continued pressure to undermine "caste" forms of prestige inequality. And legislation and governmental pressure to extent the rights of women signify the autonomous role of power vis-à-vis ascriptive sexual inequality in the areas of both prestige and class.

"one person, one vote" is at odds with inequalities based on income or wealth and with inequalities based on prestige, whether derived from occupation, education, sex, family lineage, religion, ethnicity, race, or taste. The corollaries of this norm, majority rule and compromise, mean that in order to win majorities, political parties cannot appeal to narrow class and/or prestige interests, but must evolve programs that cut across class and prestige rankings (provided that constituencies are relatively heterogeneous in composition). And a party that obtains political power must continue to placate and serve interests transcending any single social class if it hopes to remain in power. Given these pressures, groups striving for political power have created and are forced to maintain the concepts of a *public* and of an ideal realm lying above the passions and particularities of the moment.

The formal tension between class-prestige and power can also be illustrated on another level. The existence of a system of public taxation means that certain functions are accepted as public responsibilities and that all class and prestige groups must make material contributions to the common good. In other words, such phenomena as the progressive income tax, estate and inheritance taxes, and eminent domain promote the presumption that class and prestige forces cannot expect to be left alone when they conflict with public need or the public interest.

There is further formal evidence of the autonomy of political institutions vis-à-vis the forces of class and prestige. A merit-based career civil service is at odds with the idea that one is equipped to serve the many simply by virtue of high class or prestige qualifications. Conflict-of-interest norms (such as the requirement that cabinet members and even the president sell stocks or put them in blind trust funds) also presuppose the differing functions of political status and class or prestige status.[6] And, finally, one can point to the norm of equal justice under law, dispensed by an independent judiciary, as a way in which legal institutions resist the tendency of the class and prestige dimensions to make justice subject to privilege. Justice, in other words, is tax-supported and public in nature and, at least ostensibly, the same for all.[7]

Our analysis has to this point stressed the *logic* of a class system of power and the *formal* tension between class-prestige and power. As we explore the actual relation between class-prestige and power, however, we will uncover a very different picture. Unfortunately, the confusion of rhetoric with empirical reality is widespread. In general, our rhetoric reflects our faith in the efficacy of political-legal institutions to solve social problems and realize social ideals, in effect, a belief in progress, an assertion that liberal

[6]Conflict-of-interest norms are relatively undeveloped (almost to the point of scandal) for legislators and, excluding the federal judiciary, for judges as well.

[7]United States Supreme Court decisions guaranteeing due process to paupers illustrate both of these aspects of justice.

democracy is an ultimate social system capable of improving itself without changing (evolutionary liberalism). Speaking factually, however, there is little question that political-legal institutions are under heavy pressure to conform to class and prestige values. As we will see, for example, both the frequency and nature of voting and other forms of political participation are heavily influenced by class and prestige factors. And in many ways the small but powerful upper classes use the political and legal system to further their own interests. While the use of political-legal institutions to realize, buttress, and legitimize class and prestige interests considerably modifies their expression and impact, we must not assume that either our public institutions or our public policies are in the public's interest.

LATE LIBERAL (CORPORATE CAPITALIST) SOCIETY: SOME BASIC TRENDS

The Bureaucratization of Politics

Bureaucratization in one form or another has come to characterize all spheres of life. Though the tendency to associate bureaucratization only with governmental administration is unfortunate, there is little doubt that the power and effectiveness of public bureaucracies have grown steadily. The growth of government in general is related to social complexity and its attendant frictions and conflicts. And in a related way, the relative growth in power of governmental bureaucracies vis-à-vis legislatures is largely due to the political stalemates generated by mature industrialization. Given the highly decentralized structure of American political life (federalism, states' rights) and the complex issues and interests that arise routinely in an advanced industrial system, it is difficult for political parties to forge detailed, coherent programs of action. As a result, the United States' two national parties are loose coalitions of diverse interest groups and classes held together by vague rhetoric and improvised policies. Thus, legislatures are not controlled by disciplined parties with coherent mandates; instead, they tend to reflect rather accurately the enormous variety of articulate social interests and thus tend toward stalemate, inaction, or inappropriate action. For this reason, legislatures have declined vis-à-vis governmental bureaucracies and elected executives. In other words, interest groups that want concessions from the state tend to place less stress on influencing the traditional political arena (the political party, the politician, the legislature) than on dealing directly with governmental bureaucracies.

One of the significant effects of the professionalization of political life is the relative decline of the political entrepreneur, or political boss. The decline of the political entrepreneur, like that of the economic entrepreneur, should not be interpreted as a radical break with the past. In his classic discussion of the power dimension,[8] Max Weber referred to the boss as a central figure at the advent of representative government—that is, during the initial stage of politics based on mass suffrage. The traditional political boss had no personal economic base and enjoyed little prestige. His strength was derived from his ability to mobilize and control voters, and thus candidates and legislators—or, in effect, his ability to dispense public jobs, and to pass legislation and obtain state concessions for clients. The rise of a merit-based civil service, municipal reform, and the welfare state combined to undermine his power (and, of course, that of political machines and the masses in general).[9]

This development is in full harmony with the process of rationalization that has transformed other sectors of contemporary society. Those who want to use the state to secure or protect their economic or other interests no longer need to make deals with party bosses. The rise of the regulatory state after the 1890s and increases in explicit legislative lobbying and official and semiofficial contacts with political figures and governmental administrators represent a deep intertwining of economic and political institutions. Recourse to boss politics has been left to those who remain outside the corporate economy: small businesses, and blacks and other minorities. Just as boss politics was an outcome of early industrial society, so are the rise of a merit-based civil service, the welfare state, and an administered, expert, "nonpolitical" politics and government in keeping with the rise of a bureaucratic socioeconomic system.

Bureaucratization in politics has also given rise to professional party managers and staffs, professional image-makers, and professional intellectuals. Perhaps the most significant such change in American political life is the demise of the political party and the decline of creative politics.[10]

The Welfare State as a Middle-Class Phenomenon

Perhaps no expression in the lexicon of modern politics is an ambiguous and misleading as the term *welfare state*. This term is sometimes used in the abstract to refer to the interventionist state that developed in the United States after 1890. The growth of the welfare state was significantly advanced in the 1930s when the United States Supreme Court abandoned its tenacious sixty-year-old opposition to governmental intervention in economic matters and allowed the federal government to take measures against the worst depression in the nation's history. The term *welfare state*, however, is ren-

---

[8]"Politics as a Vocation," in H. H. Gerth and C. Wright Mills, tr. and ed., *From Max Weber: Essays in Sociology*, (New York: Oxford University Press, 1946), chap. 6.

[9]It was already clear to Max Weber that civil service reform meant a curtailment of the power of the masses in favor of the educated (and thus the propertied); see his essay "Bureaucracy," chap. 8, Section 14.

[10]For a discussion, see Chapter 14.

dered ambiguous by its use in a narrower and derogatory sense to mean state action to serve the needs of workers (the legal recognition of trade unions, unemployment insurance, social security, minimum wage, and the improvement of working conditions), and of the working and dependent poor (broken families with dependent children, the aged, the blind, and the disabled and sick).

The nineteenth-century liberal denunciation of state activity, in the name of self-reliance, individual responsibility, and competition, has reverberated to stigmatize efforts to do for workers and the poor what has been done on a much larger scale for other segments of American society. Antigovernmental rhetoric, which stems primarily from small business but also suits the interests of big business and professional groups, should not be allowed to obscure the fundamental reality of American political history: the state has been used actively and extensively by the upper and middle classes to serve their many and varied interests. Actually, the main impetus to an enlarged sphere of activity on the part of government has come from business and upper occupational groups of various kinds: bankers, farmers, transportation businesses, large and small manufacturers, retailers, doctors, and so on. Only during the Great Depression did workers and the needy come to be acknowledged as legitimate recipients of state support (largely because there existed a depressed and badly hurt middle class). It is important to recognize that, by and large, the lower classes have had things done to them and for them (paternalism). Unlike the classes above them, the poor and even the working class (labor unions notwithstanding) neither set the pace nor prevail in American politics.

There is little doubt that *in practice* Americans do not believe in the theory of laissez-faire; and if one judges beliefs by behavior, they have never believed in it. American economic and other interest groups have never hesitated to use political means, including organized violence, to obtain their ends. American history is filled with examples of state action on behalf of interest groups: bank charters, laws protecting slavery, subsidies for canals, land grants for railroads, policies on Indians, territorial annexation, land grants for education, tariffs, gunboat diplomacy, cheap credit, aid to farmers, subsidies for industry, the use of troops to break strikes, antitrust legislation, collective bargaining legislation, the protection of consumers, and so on. And, judging from contemporary public opinion polls, the majority of the American people believes the government should be more active with regard to practical bread-and-butter issues. American politics and American government must be considered in the context of a complex, dynamic industrial economy. Beneath the formalities of political life, it is clear that the main functions of political-legal institutions are to reduce economic and other conflicts, to stabilize or restore economic relations, and to enhance and promote opportunities within an expanding industrial society.

Our understanding of government in the United States is enhanced by viewing it from still another vantage-point. It is popularly thought that the federal government has grown bigger and stronger during the twentieth century, and in absolute terms the activities of the federal government have undoubtedly grown, whether measured in terms of expenditures, revenues, number of employees, or functions. But measured in more meaningful terms—such as relative to the growth of the American economy, the labor force, or state and local governments—a very different picture emerges. Using a constant dollar and excepting the special military and international obligations of the federal government and such unusual domestic crises as the Great Depression, there has been an amazing stability in federal domestic expenditures, tax revenues, and numbers of civilian employees, and a steady and sizable decline in the national debt when computed as a fraction of the gross national product.[11] Finally, it is not always appreciated that federal programs and funds in the area of social welfare are largely administered by local governments, which goes a long way toward explaining why the purposes of federal legislation are so often thwarted.

Exaggeration of the benefits bestowed by government on the poor and on workers and the use of the derogatory term *welfare state* to characterize such assistance probably serves a number of functions. For one thing, it permits middle and upper class Americans to think of the enormous range of money benefits they receive from government in nonwelfare terms, and thus to legitimate state activity on their behalf.[12] Similarly, it helps them to legitimate the enormous range of benefits they receive from governmental regulation (and, often, nonregulation) of such activities as transportation, communications, banking, brokering, and the manufacture of food and drugs; antitrust action, or inaction; tax policies; fair trade laws; price supports; professional certification practices; zoning laws; school policies; and the distribution of franchises and licenses. We can conjecture that these benefits prevent the upper classes from seeing that the problems of workers and the needy are often attributable to governmental policies that aid the middle and upper classes. For example, lavish governmental aid for research leads to technological displacement; urban renewal and highway grants deprive the poor of homes and isolate them from jobs and public services. And such

---

[11]The national debt grew enormously from 1980 on largely because of tax cuts and large military expenditures initiated by the Reagan administration. However, it remains low as a percentage of GNP because of economic growth.

[12]Cash benefits to middle- and upper-class Americans are rarely called subsidies, let alone "public assistance." They are invariably defined as ways to make the economy, science, or society work more effectively for the common good. Most middle-and upper-class benefits are obscured by being linked to tax policy, disaster aid, defense needs, public safety, or public convenience, and by the fact that they take the form of "public interest" franchises, licenses, contracts, regulations, quotas, research grants, and Social Security, Medicare, and guaranteed student loan programs.

benefits are sufficiently indirect to allow many to avoid recognizing that the natural economy and society posited by laissez-faire liberalism is a myth, and that modern society not only needs political supports, but has received them throughout American history.

The Welfare State as an Upper- and/or Upper-Middle-Class Phenomenon

To see that the middle class is the main beneficiary of the welfare state is by no means sufficient. It may well be that the real force behind and main beneficiary of liberal political reform since the late nineteenth century is the upper and/or upper middle class, rather than the middle class (or lower classes). This is a difficult question, and caution should be exercised in confronting it. The middle-class imagery of early capitalism (small-town America) is still a vital intellectual tradition with wide support among the lay public, especially small farmers, small businesspeople, and independent professionals. But even though one can be fairly certain that the middle class as a whole dominates American society, there is some justification for thinking in terms of upper and upper middle class (as opposed to power elite) dominance. Historians have come to question the traditional view that the Progressive Era represents a struggle to tame the power of big corporations and corrupt politicians. For one thing, the Progressives accomplished very little by way of concrete reform, rhetoric notwithstanding. And, for another, the upper class (large business interests) was far more active in promoting political reforms that complemented its interests in the developing nationwide and even worldwide economy than people realize.[13]

AMERICA'S UNIQUE CLASS POLITICS

Before addressing the intricacies of political behavior, we need a more explicit framework for understanding the class basis of politics. Specifically, we must look beyond the fairly well-established idea that economic interests are

[13]For an analysis of municipal reform during the Progressive Era as a curtailment of the power of both the masses and the middle class by an upper class of businesspeople, professionals, and old families (in our terms, the upper and upper middle class), see Samuel P. Hays, "The Politics of Reform in Municipal Government in the Progressive Era," *Pacific Northwest Quarterly* 55 (October 1964); reprinted in B. A. Brownell and W. E. Stickle, eds., *Bosses and Reformers* (Boston: Houghton Mifflin, 1973), pp. 137–161. For an analysis of national politics during the same period as the consolidation of "political capitalism," see Gabriel Kolko, *The Triumph of Conservatism: A Reinterpretation of American History, 1900–1916* (New York: Free Press, 1963). For an analysis of American foreign policy during the post–Civil War period as a search for a world order favorable to liberal capitalism, see William A. Williams, *The Tragedy of American Diplomacy*, 2nd rev. and enl. ed. (New York: Dell, 1972). For the view that the upper middle class is the main power-holder in the United States, and consistently thwarts the political aspirations of the majority, see Richard F. Hamilton, *Class and Politics in the United States* (New York: John Wiley & Sons, 1972).

the basis of most political behavior. We need to see economic interests in class terms, which is, ironically enough, difficult to do if we rely exclusively on Marx's conception of politics and government. Marx's conception of class focuses on just one form of class action: the labor market, or the struggle between the buyers and sellers of labor. While this class relationship (which became prominent during the nineteenth century) is of great importance, it is but one of a number of forms of class action.

For Weber, a class is any group sharing a "class situation," a "typical chance for a supply of goods, external living conditions, and personal life experiences, in so far as this chance is determined by the amount and kind of power, or lack of such, to dispose of goods or skills for the sake of income in a given economic order." For Weber, as for Marx, the basic polar determinants of class situation are "property" and "lack of property"—but between these poles a great many class situations must be distinguished. Class situations, says Weber, lead to class protest or struggle only when it is widely recognized that the distribution of life chances is due to a given distribution of property or to the structure of a concrete economic order. Such recognition depends on the general nature of society but especially on "communalization," a process that takes place, according to Weber, when there is interaction between members of *different* classes (and not, as Marx said, when there is interaction between members of the *same* class). The history of class struggle, Weber suggests, is roughly a sequence of the three basic forms of class action and rivalry: the credit market, the commodity market, and the labor market.

The "transparency" of class interest is obscured by general sociocultural conditions, and a number of unusual political consequences flow from the vagaries of class experience. Direct competition between buyers and sellers of labor, for example, is usually bitter while the "unearned" income of the *rentier*, shareholder, and banker go unchallenged. Politically, this situation can lead to varieties of "patriarchical socialism," such as Tory socialism and upper-class reformism, or to attempts by threatened prestige groups, such as clergymen and intellectuals, to form alliances with the proletariat against the "bourgeosie."[14]

Thus, a full understanding of American political life in class terms is impossible if one relies on Marx's exclusive emphasis on the struggle over the price of labor. Even Weber's suggestion that an evolution has taken place in the modal type of class action is somewhat misleading. But, as Norbert Wiley points out, Weber's theory of class does contain the conceptual elements needed for framing American political behavior in class terms. The United States should be thought of, Wiley says, as characteristically a rich mixture of

[14]Max Weber, "Class, Status, Party" in H. H. Gerth and C. Wright Mills, tr. and ed, *From Max Weber: Essays in Sociology* (New York: Oxford University Press, 1946), chap. 7. sections 2–4; the above quotation is from p. 181.

all three basic forms of class situations, a mixture that gives it a unique class politics. The three basic market relationships are:

1. the labor market (occupational versus property-owning groups)
2. the credit or money market (debtors versus creditors)
3. the commodity market (buyers versus sellers; tenants versus landlords).

One can distinguish, says Wiley, groups that have consistent, inconsistent, and highly inconsistent class interests in their total market or class relationships. An individual with consistent class attributes is one who is an employer-creditor-seller (propertied) or is an employee-debtor-buyer (non-propertied). But many have inconsistent and contradictory class attributes, making it difficult for them to unite with groups holding similar class interests in some respects.[15]

An examination, provided by Wiley, of class-related political behavior in American history is instructive. The most radical political group in American history has been the farmers, whose economic class interests focus on the prices they pay for money (credit), equipment and services (such as railroad transport) on the one hand, and the prices of the products they sell (basically, food), on the other. When the allegedly rational markets in these areas did not perform as expected, American farmers turned to politics to protect and enhance their class interests—interests they defined as cheap money and manufactured goods and high price supports for farm products. In their political and economic struggles, farmers could not readily identify with labor, another class underdog, whose class interests lay in the high price of labor, the high price of manufactured commodities, and the low price of food.

Class analysis is also revealing when applied to other economic groups. Small businesspeople are both buyers and sellers of products; they are often in debt and are small-scale buyers of labor. Thus they are of a classic mixed type who find it difficult to identify with either big business or labor. As an economic group whose class interests are highly inconsistent, small businesspeople are also radical politically, though on the right wing. Others who suffer from high inconsistency in their class positions are workers with property or side income, retired people on small incomes, and white-collar workers. The difficulties experienced by individuals with high (class) inconsistency stem from ambivalence, or, in other words, from the inability to identify a coherent class enemy. Those who are subject to such cross-pressures see the world as capricious and arbitrary and feel psychological pressure to escape into a world of simple certainties. And when class inconsistency is associated with prestige inconsistency, the political situation be-

[15]Norbert Wiley, "America's Unique Class Politics: The Interplay of the Labor, Credit and Commodity Markets," *American Sociological Review* 32 (August 1967):529–541.

comes even more highly charged. All in all, Wiley concludes, the United States has not experienced generalized class warfare because of its rich and inconsistent class structure. Throughout our history, in other words, there has been a different subordinate class in each subdimension of class conflict, and the various subordinate classes have been too diverse to unite; in other words, they have never had a common enemy to rise against.

CLASS-PRESTIGE AND POWER: A SUMMARY

We have warned against the uncritical acceptance of a formal definition of political behavior. Over the centuries, a heady mixture of liberal rhetoric has created the impression that invoking the ideas of equal rights and equal treatment by government is the same thing as actually realizing these ideals. In reality, politics and government have a class base. While class forces in the United States are exceedingly complex and lead to a unique form of class politics, there is little doubt that the upper levels of the class structure have more direct access to, exert more influence over, and receive more benefits from the state than their fellow citizens in the classes below.

In the following chapters, we will study this process in a more detailed way. Chapter 14 examines political participation, including voting, lobbying, political careers, political attitudes, and political extremism. In Chapter 15, we will try to determine who benefits most from legislation and governmental action in such areas as taxation, Social Security, housing, education, and public economic policies. And Chapter 16 investigates the American legal system to see how the distribution of justice is related to the hierarchies of class and prestige.

CHAPTER 14

Class-Prestige and Political Participation

In this chapter we will inquire into the relation between the many forms of political participation and class-prestige standing. Thought of in broad historical terms, we want to find out if the growth of representative government marks an increase in the power of the general populace. To put the matter bluntly, has formal political equality resulted in any appreciable measure of actual political equality and has it reduced economic and social inequality?

THE SEGREGATION OF CLASSES
BY POLITICAL JURISDICTION

The pattern of governmental levels and jurisdiction in the United States can be analyzed quite fruitfully in terms of social stratification. One basic and increasingly prevalent pattern is the segregation of class-prestige groups by political jurisdiction. This is perhaps the most ominous political development of the twentieth century, amounting as it does to a decline in political jurisdictions with mixed constituencies. Much of the vigor of liberal democracy—indeed, perhaps, its very existence as a form of government—is attributable to the fact that it has forced those who would exercise political power to persuade a majority of a mixed group of articulate interests (either groups or voters) to support them. The need to search for common interests stimulates and develops the political creativity of candidates and parties. And, once elected, officials and parties are more likely to be independent and broad in their outlooks when their mandates are from mixed rather than homogeneous constituencies.

The pattern of class-related political constituencies implicit in the growth of homogeneous suburban and urban areas poses enormous problems for the United States, since it implies that legislators and governments will eventually come merely to reflect the class-prestige structure and no longer perform the normal political function of solving the problems created by the forces of class and prestige.

The problem of political jurisdiction segregated by class and prestige is compounded by a further problem, the lags and imbalances that characterize the American system of political representation.

CLASS-PRESTIGE AND POLITICAL REPRESENTATION

The American population has been badly represented in state and national legislatures, in terms of both numbers and social composition (economic, ethnic, and racial differences), during the entire period for which we have reliable records. Until the 1960s, this malrepresentation was steadily worsening, to the point that it is not amiss to characterize it as a "rotten borough" system. Numerically smaller portions of the population enjoyed significantly more political power than larger portions, and rural–small-town populations (often synonymous with the smaller portions) were more heavily represented in legislatures than urban populations.

Aside from the dynamics of industrialization and urbanization, two basic processes created these imbalances: (1) legislatures that had the power and often the constitutional obligation to reapportion did not do so (or did not reapportion strictly on the basis of numbers); and (2) legislatures practiced gerrymandering. The first of these causes of representational imbalance was struck down by the United States Supreme Court in a series of decisions between 1962 and 1964. After having declined jurisdiction in this area, the Supreme Court changed its mind and in a landmark decision[1] gave individuals the right to sue to protect their voting rights, thus making voting rights a constitutional rather than a political issue. The Court did not define the kind of representation required by the Constitution in this decision, but in a later case it held that "the fundamental principle of representative government in this country is one of equal representation for equal numbers of people,

[1]*Baker* v. *Carr*, 363 U.S. 186 (1962).

without regard to race, sex, economic status, or place of residence within a state."[2] As a result of this and other cases, the basic doctrine of "one person, one vote" was upheld for primaries, and for elections to the House of Representatives and to both houses of state legislatures.

But while the Supreme Court has clearly spelled out the doctrine of equal representation, even full application of the principle of "one person, one vote" will not correct imbalance in the American system of representation as long as legislators are free to gerrymander—that is, to concentrate voters for the opposing party (usually identified in terms of class-prestige factors) in selected constituencies where votes will be wasted in overwhelming victories, and to allot supporters so as to achieve narrow victories in as many constituencies as possible. Since congressional districts (which are reapportioned on the basis of census figures) are drawn by state legislatures, the national House of Representatives is also gerrymandered, and thus represents neither quantitatively nor qualitatively the nature of the American population. The significance of the gerrymander for the student of social stratification is that it allows obsolete or declining class and prestige groups (racists, farmers, small town businesspeople, and professionals) to entrench themselves politically. The United States Supreme Court dodged a gerrymander case in 1986, in effect endorsing the practice.

The segregation of classes and ethnic-racial groups by political jurisdiction goes a long way in explaining the politics of recent decades. The freedom of capital to move as it pleases, the failure to integrate minorities, the decline of public services, the failure to keep up public investment in highways, bridges, and the like, the decay of cities and many suburbs, and the persistence of poverty can be attributed in part to this interplay of class, prestige, and power forces. It is of special interest that the process of suburbanization, which has done so much to segregate the United States' political jurisdictions by class and prestige, has become an important component of this broad alignment of political forces. High-income suburbs, which pay heavy local taxes to support high-quality schools and other public services for their own families, are reluctant to pay taxes to support similar public services in the big cities and in working class suburbs. The fact that high income groups often earn their livings in these cities does not prevent them from taking advantage of their political power.[3] In any case, the *ad hoc* growth of local governments (towns, cities, suburbs) characterized by a tangle of overlapping jurisdictions, duplication of services, and unresponsiveness to public complaint and need signifies the power over political life exercised by the hierarchies of class and prestige.

---

[2]*Reynolds* v. *Sims*, 377 U.S. 533 (1964).

[3]The suburbs are very diverse and have grown so much (while big cities have stagnated or even declined in size) that they are now underrepresented in state and national legislatures.

CLASS-PRESTIGE AND POLITICAL CAREERS

Elected and Appointed Officials

Considerable evidence shows that individuals elected to public office at the federal level come largely from the middle and upper classes: Professionals, proprietors and officials, and farmers tend to account for the overwhelming majority of those elected to the presidency, vice-presidency, the Senate, and the House of Representatives. The upper levels of prestige hierarchies based on race, ethnic origin, and religion are also overrepresented among elected federal officials.[4] Those elected to state legislatures are considerably higher in class position (as measured by income, education, and occupation) than their constituents.[5] And delegates to both Democratic and Republican presidential conventions had incomes far in excess of the average American's.

The influence of socioeconomic status in the recruitment of high federal civilian and military officials is pronounced throughout American history. In an analysis of intellectuals who served the Roosevelt administration during the Great Depression, it was found that most of them came from the middle and upper classes, especially the upper middle class. A study of the occupations of fathers of high federal civilian and military personnel found that the offspring of business executives, owners of large businesses, and professionals were heavily overrepresented, especially in the military.[6] A study of high civil servants in California revealed an overrepresentation of the middle and upper middle class at the state level, which is almost identical with Lloyd Warner's findings at the federal level.[7]

In his study of military leaders, Morris Janowitz found that while they have become more representative of the general population over the years, military leaders are still drawn largely from white Protestant professional

[4]John Nagle, *Systems and Succession: The Social Bases of Political Elite Recruitment* (Austin: University of Texas Press, 1977).

[5]Harmon Zeigler and Michael A. Baer, "The Recruitment of Lobbyists and Legislators," *Midwest Journal of Political Science* 12, no. 4 (November 1968):493–513; reprinted in Donald P. Sprengel, ed., *Comparative State Politics: A Reader* (Columbus, Ohio: Charles E. Merrill, 1971), pp. 187–206.

[6]For evidence concerning the social origins of New Deal intellectuals, see Thomas A. Krueger and William Glidden, "The New Deal Intellectual Elite: A Collective Portrait," in Frederic C. Jaher, ed., *The Rich, the Well Born, and the Powerful: Elites and Upper Classes in History* (Urbana: University of Illinois Press, 1973), pp. 338–374. For the social origins of high federal and military personnel, see W. Lloyd Warner, Paul P. Van Riper, Norman H. Martin, and Orvis F. Collins, *The American Federal Executive: A Study of Social and Personal Characteristics of the Civilian and Military Leaders of the United States Federal Government* (New Haven: Yale University Press, 1963), chap 2; Beth Mintz, "The President's Cabinet, 1897–1972," *Insurgent Sociologist* 5, no. 3 (1975):131–149; and Philip H. Burch, *Elites in American History: The New Deal to the Carter Administration* (New York: Holmes & Meier, 1980).

[7]Bruce M. Hackett, *Higher Civil Servants in California: A Social and Political Portrait* (Berkeley: University of California Press, 1967), chap. 2.

and business backgrounds.[8] It is also important to note that schoolteachers, a large and influential group of public employees, appear to come from the upper third of the socioeconomic scale (and not primarily from lower-middle-class backgrounds, as is popularly thought).[9]

Interchangeable Careers

It is clear from the foregoing evidence that there is a pronounced trend for the male children of men in high class-prestige positions to move horizontally into high elected and appointed offices. There are many well-known examples of upper-class individuals and families who engage in public service careers either full- or part-time. Such people—who enjoy secure, often old, wealth, who have respected family names and connections and high-quality prestigious educations—serve both the Republican and Democratic parties. Some are national figures well known to the public, such as the Cabots, Lodges, Roosevelts, Averell Harriman, Adlai Stevenson, and the Kennedys; others, such as William Bullitt, Francis Biddle, Robert McNamara, C. Douglas Dillon, Robert Lovett, McGeorge Bundy serve in appointed, less publicized positions. There are a number of interesting observations to be made about this general practice. Many political leaders on the federal level, both elected and appointed, do not rise through the ranks of state and local politics and thus must learn their jobs after acquiring them. The practice of ignoring experience and proven worth is perhaps most conspicuous in appointments to ambassadorships (many of which are actually sold), but it is common practice to appoint amateurs at the apex of the federal government. One of the more damaging results of the practice of filling the more than two thousand high administrative positions at the federal level on a patronage basis is that it has helped to prevent the development of a strong civil service tradition at the upper levels of the federal bureaucracy. One can even conjecture that the prevalence of amateurs at the upper levels of the federal government makes it easier for their predecessors in office, who are now pursuing business and professional careers, to outmaneuver them. And, of course, this practice helps to insure the general control of public policy by the upper classes.

What exactly are the trends in the relation between careers in the upper echelons of industry, finance, commerce, law, medicine, university teaching, research, natural science, and the upper reaches of government? Though we do not have sufficient data to answer this question conclusively, there is

[8]Morris Janowitz, *The Professional Soldier: A Social and Political Portrait* (New York: Free Press, 1960), chap. 5.

[9]For data to this effect from Wisconsin, see Ronald M. Pavalko, "Recruitment to Teaching: Patterns of Selection and Retention," in Ronald M. Pavalko, ed., *Sociological Perspectives on Occupations* (Itasca, Ill.: F. E. Peacock, 1972), pp. 239–249; reprinted from *Sociology of Education* 43 (Summer 1970):340–353.

sizable if unsystematic evidence of considerable traffic among, on the one hand, banks, law firms, universities, and businesses (especially large corporations) engaged in agriculture, transportation, mining, communication, military manufacturing, and the like, and on the other, the various departments (civilian and military) and regulatory commissions of the federal government.[10] Career interchangeability is limited, however, by professional ethics, conflict-of-interest laws, and technical occupational requirements.

That elected and appointed officials are drawn from the upper levels of the class-prestige structure and that there is considerable interchange between the upper echelons of the "private" and "public" sectors means nothing in itself. As is common in social science, these facts lend themselves to varied interpretations. For some, they raise the specter that the state is a "committee of the ruling class"—that it is subservient to the interests of the rich and economically powerful. Some believe in the existence of a "power elite" (C. Wright Mills), others in a WASP establishment, and still others in "an iron triangle" sapping democracy and national strength (see Box 14–1, "The Iron Triangle, or Blurring the Lines Between Public and Private," and Figure 14–1, "Defense Expenditures and Lagging Productivity, 1960–1979").

At a slightly lower level of disgust and alarm, the same facts suggest to some the image of a "middle class" society impervious to reform. Generally speaking, those who are morally discontented with society or who adopt a conflict model of social stratification tend to interpret such facts in one of the foregoing ways.

But the same facts can be interpreted positively. It can be argued, for example, that the United States needs even more and better coordination between its various (social) power structures. Whatever coordination now exists can only help American society to identify problems more quickly and reach solutions more intelligently. It can be argued, further, that it is desirable for those in the command-posts of society to come from common backgrounds and share a common value-belief system; otherwise communication between them would be difficult. And, some might ask, what better way is there to enhance the social imaginations of specialists than for businesspeople and professionals to spend time in Washington gaining experience in public affairs? It can also be argued—and frequently is, given the American tendency to explain behavior in biopsychological, social-Darwinist terms— that individuals with talent and drive can always succeed, and that those at

---

[10]The interchangeability of careers leads to conflicts of interest; thus there are extensive tie-ins between members of Congress and professional (especially law) firms and businesses of all kinds. Some tightening up to prevent conflict of interest among legislators has appeared in recent years but whether abuses will stop remains to be seen.

Though not strictly their careers, note should be made of the middle- and upper-class individuals who serve on presidential or congressional commissions and advisory groups or as special appointees to the United Nations and other bodies. This general type of activity is now so widespread and routine that it should be considered "public office"; and some individuals serve in these capacities so often that such service should be considered part of their careers.

BOX 14–1.   *THE IRON TRIANGLE, OR BLURRING THE LINES BETWEEN PUBLIC AND PRIVATE*

The interrelations among the Department of Defense, Congress, and giant defense contractors has been called an *iron triangle.*[11] Gordon Adams' case study of eight of these contractors reveals a world in which the federal government and Congress enjoy a tight, often secretive relation with each other and with military contractors in violation of basic American norms and values. Defense contracts are noncompetitive, and in addition to their wasteful cost-plus basis, they include many hidden subsidies. There is a revolving door of personnel from the Pentagon to defense contractors and vice-versa. There is a questionable emphasis on high-technology weapon systems and a neglect of conventional weapons and combat readiness. And the general public is excluded from participation in the formulation of defense policy.

Not only does this concentration of power not yield adequate defense but it is a huge drain on national resources and a contributor to America's declining productivity (see Figure 14–1). And, of course, declining productivity further weakens the United States' ability to defend its interests.

[11]Gordon Adams, *The Iron Triangle: The Politics of Defense Contracting* (New York: Council on Economic Priorities, 1981).

the apex of all our occupational ladders deserve their prominence. In short, career interchangeability can be interpreted as signifying the existence not of a ruling class, but of legitimate intelligent government by the most talented. By and large, those who are satisfied with society, and especially those who see society as a functional process of "natural" equilibrium, would probably interpret evidence of elite interchangeability in this way.

POLITICAL PARTIES AND INTEREST GROUPS

While agrarian societies obviously have internal conflicts, they are on the whole characterized by widespread communilization—that is, by virtually universal acceptance of specific ways of believing and acting. In stratification terms, agrarian societies tend to congeal into static hierarchies of estates or castes. Industrial society, on the other hand, is characterized by a complex and changing social division of labor, and the motivation to perform its myriad activities took the form of "individualism" in the development of Western industrial states. An intricate division of labor means that disputes and conflicts are almost routine occurrences. As a result, modern society have developed specialized groups—especially the state—to keep order and resolve conflict. This trend away from communalization toward "societaliza-

Figure 14-1. Defense Expenditures and Lagging Productivity, 1960-1979

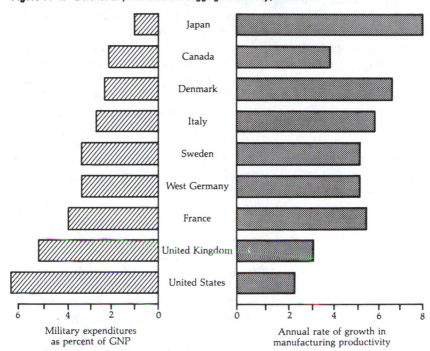

Source: U.S. Congressional Budget office, *Defense Spending and the Economy* (Washington, D.C.: U.S. Government Printing Office, 1983), p. 40. The burden of defense spending has, if anything, increased during the 1980s.

tion" (or associational or class society) is everywhere accompanied by the growth of political parties and interest groups.

Political parties' financial and voting support, as well as their staff recruitment (both professional and volunteer), are deeply related to class and prestige. And the major interest groups in contemporary society are also related to the hierarchies of class and prestige and tend to develop ideologies in keeping with their location in the class system. Politically relevant interest groups include learned societies, civic betterment associations, reform movements, groups concerned with particular problems (such as taxation, foreign affairs, or veterans' affairs), professional associations, and, of course, the entire range of pressure groups. Most pressure groups emanate from the American economy, but they also include governmental units themselves, associations of civil service employees, and even associations of elected officials.

Despite the highly visible organizations that represent workers, racial and ethnic minorities, and even welfare recipients, interest groups with direct relevance for political life are overwhelmingly middle and upper class in character. Whether measured in terms of rates of participation by members, the credentials of staff members, mode of operation, or consequences for society, pressure groups basically reflect the interests and power of the middle and upper classes (as do almost all voluntary groups).

Americans have traditionally been uneasy about concentrated power, whether public or private. The early liberal tradition tended to derogate collective action of any kind, and the existence of large private power blocs has been sensed as a threat to individualism throughout American history. This orientation has changed in recent years, and Americans (as we shall see) have come to accept large private groups as permanent, respectable, and even constituent features of social life. Helping to minimize uneasiness about the political and social impact of private interest groups are various laws, regulations, and ethical codes that seek to limit the influence of those with too much money or too few scruples, or both.

Thus various laws (especially the Corrupt Practices Act of 1925, the Hatch Act of 1940, and the Taft-Hartley Act of 1947) have been passed to prevent the financing (and thus control) of political parties by private wealth and private groups. These acts forbid corporations and labor unions to contribute to political parties, and limits have been set on the amounts that individuals can contribute to political parties and the amounts that can be spent on political campaigns. Lobbyists are required by the Federal Regulation of Lobbying Act of 1946 to register and to list their employers, salaries, and activities, and there are conflict-of-interest codes for political appointees and civil servants. In 1972 another effort was made to limit campaign spending and political contributions but to no avail. In 1974 the Federal Elections Campaign Act was passed, strengthening the effort to control the power of private wealth in public elections. Contributions by individuals and groups have been limited, matching tax funds are available for campaigns for presidential nominations, tax funds help pay for presidential elections, strict limits have been placed on presidential and congressional campaign spending and enforcement machinery has been created. But apparently through an oversight no real control over the political power of wealth appeared because political action committees (PACs), or direct contributions to individual candidates, are legal. Lobbies still flourish and continue to pressure legislators, parties, and public opinion,[12] but now also deal directly and on a large scale

---

[12]Actually, legislators do not have to be pressured to abandon independence and objectivity. Legislators are elected because they agree with the views of this or that constellation of pressure or interest groups. Pressure on legislators should thus be regarded as a means of reinforcing prior commitments. Two general discussions of lobbying are Ronald J. Hrebener and Ruth K. Scott, *Interest Group Politics in America* (Englewood Cliffs, N.J.: Prentice-Hall, 1982) and Congressional Research Service, "Congress and Pressure Groups: Lobbying in a Modern Democracy" (Washington, D.C.: U.S. Government Printing Office, 1986). Other important books in this area are Mark Green, *Who Runs Congress?*, 3rd ed. (New York: Bantam Books, 1979); Gordon Adams, *The Iron Triangle: The Politics of Defense Contracting* (New York: Council on Economic Priorities, 1981); and Sar A. Levitan and Martha R. Cooper, *Business Lobbies: The Public Good and the Bottom Line* (Baltimore: The Johns Hopkins University Press, 1984).

with governmental bureaucracies. The result is a massive intertwining of interest groups and government, or, more exactly, of particular interest groups and particular governmental agencies, bureaus, and commissions.[13] One of the interesting and not necessarily beneficial consequences of direct interest group involvement in government is that it has probably strengthened the trend toward objective, expert, and nonpolitical government. As we have pointed out, the professionalization of our class-prestige system has a parallel in the professionalization of our political institutions. Though it is difficult to be certain, the trend toward nonpolitical boards, commissions, and authorities, and the direct cooperation of interest groups and governmental bodies of all kinds appears to be a significant corollary of the modernization of our class system. However, both the neutrality and the accountability of these bodies are highly questionable. Furthermore, the legal status of many such bodies is hazy, and the scope and volume of their economic activities are very great. Of considerable interest are the "nonpolitical" councils, committees, institutes, corporations, advisory boards, and foundations (such as the Council on Foreign Relations, the Rand Corporation, the Committee for Economic Development, the Twentieth Century Fund, and the Brookings Institution), which are characterized by a narrow class composition, direct ties to specific business and professional interests, and great influence over domestic and foreign policies.[14]

VOTING AND OTHER FORMS OF POLITICAL PARTICIPATION

Though there are many forms of political involvement by individuals, all have one thing in common: The upper classes tend to monopolize political participation and to receive more from government than do the lower classes.

Voting Participation

The act of voting *per se* is clearly related to class position (and, as we will see, to such prestige factors as race and ethnicity). Those at the upper levels of the class system vote at far higher rates than do those lowest in the class hierarchy. Measured in terms of education, it is clear that those with four or more years of college vote at significantly higher rates even than high-school graduates (see Figure 14–2). The same pattern holds true for major occupa-

[13]All books on lobbying emphasize this point. For a general survey, see Samuel Krislov and David H. Rosenbloom, *Representative Bureaucracy and the American Political System* (New York: Praeger, 1981).

[14]G. William Domhoff has studied the latter phenomenon closely as part of his argument that the United States is ruled by a small upper class; see his *The Higher Circles: The Governing Class in America* (New York: Vintage, 1971), especially chaps. 5 and 6, available in paperback. Also see Thomas R. Dye, "Oligarchic Tendencies in National Policy-Making: The Role of the Private Policy-Planning Organizations," *Journal of Politics* 40 (1978):309–331.

Figure 14–2. Voting Participation by Years of School Completed, 1984

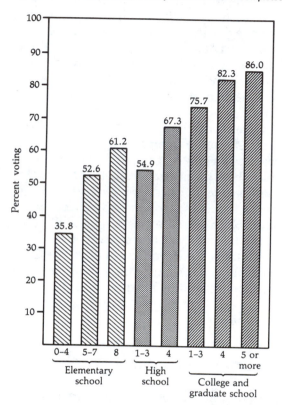

Source: U.S. Bureau of the Census, Current Population Reports, Series P-20, No. 405, "Voting and Registration in the Election of November 1984" (Washington, D.C.: U.S. Government Printing Office, 1987), Table 8.

tional groups, as shown in Table 14–1. White-collar workers of all kinds vote at significantly higher rates than do blue-collar, service, and farm workers. Not surprisingly, income differences are also related to differences in voting participation. As Figure 14–3 dictates, there is a substantial difference between the 37.5 percent rate of those with incomes under $5,000 per year and the 76 percent rate of those with incomes of $50,000 or more.

Historically, American citizens, especially the poor and minority groups, have faced numerous barriers to voting, including requirements that one register, satisfy literacy and residence qualifications, and pay a poll tax. Though the courts have struck down most of these qualifications, the need to register still seems to curtail voting participation. However, electoral apathy among the lower classes is by no means attributable solely to the need to register. Electoral apathy must be considered an outcome of class experience:

TABLE 14-1. Reported Voting and Registration of Employed Persons by Major Occupation Group, 1984

NUMBERS IN THOUSANDS

		REPORTED REGISTERED		REPORTED VOTED	
	ALL PERSONS	NUMBER	PERCENT	NUMBER	PERCENT
All Races					
Both sexes					
Total employed	104,173	72,322	69.4	64,213	61.6
Managerial and professional	25,309	20,640	81.6	19,307	76.3
Technical, sales and administrative support	32,081	23,704	73.9	21,313	56.4
Service occupations	13,481	8,270	61.3	7,132	52.9
Farming, forestry, and fishing	3,349	2,056	61.4	1,755	52.4
Precision prod., craft, and repair	13,155	8,126	61.8	6,931	52.7
Operators, fabricators, and laborers	16,798	9,526	56.7	7,774	46.3

Source: U.S. Bureau of the Census, *Current Population Reports,* Series P-20, No. 405, "Voting and Registration in the Election of November 1984" (Washington, D.C.: U.S. Government Printing Office, 1987), Table 12.

Those low on the class structure tend not to lead lives that emphasize active self-direction, and nonvoting is consistent with such experience.

To focus on the upper end of the class hierarchy, the upper classes enjoy a socioeconomic experience that prepares them for and predisposes them toward political involvement. Typically, members of the upper classes (especially the upper and upper-middle classes) have had considerable formal education and are therefore familiar with certain relevant information and with the concepts and skills needed to organize such information. They work in occupations that are, on the whole, more mental than manual. They participate in voluntary-interest groups that focus and reinforce their class-prestige interests, and their participation in voluntary groups in general gives them experience in the verbal and written analysis of public issues. They absorb "higher" levels of stimuli through reading, viewing, listening, and traveling. They are more secure in their finances and in their personalities. And they are quick to perceive political threats to their interests, and to counter them with both symbolic and overt political action. In other words, the typical member of the upper classes (again, especially of the upper and upper middle classes)

Figure 14–3. Reported Voting by Income, 1984

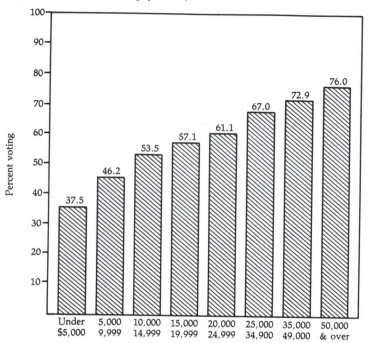

Source: U.S. Bureau of the Census, *Current Population Reports* Series P-20, No 405, "Voting and Registration in the Election of November 1984" (Washington, D.C.: U.S. Government Printing Office, 1987), Table 13.

is, in contrast to a typical member of the working and lower classes, much more of a self-propelled, conscious decision-maker across a broad range of activities. Thus, higher rates of voting participation reflect and reinforce higher rates of involvement in the upper reaches of the hierarchies of class and prestige. And, as we will see, the upper classes are also more active in other forms of political participation.

Voting Preference

The relation between class and voting preference has become a staple subject of political analysis. Like voting participation in general, voting preference correlates with the hierarchy of class-prestige (though there is little class consciousness in this regard in the United States). High and middle class-prestige individuals (professionals, managers, proprietors and other white-collar workers, college graduates, and individuals with high incomes) largely support the Republican party, while members of the working class and those with low prestige status regardless of class (manual workers, laborers, blacks, Roman Catholics, Jews) have tended to support the Democratic party, a division that corresponds roughly to the difference between laissez-faire and interventionist views on the economic responsibilities of government.

It has long been taken for granted that the upper classes are more liberal on social issues: the rights of women and blacks, personal freedom (abortion, birth control, divorce, premarital sex, homosexuality), and law and order (wiretapping, capital punishment, gun control). John Zipp, however, has found no differences on such issues when economic classes are compared by only economic status (owner, income, type of occupation). What differences appear are due to education (which Zipp prefers to call a *nonclass* variable), with the better educated exhibiting more liberalism in their attitudes.[15] If education is included in the definition of class, then class and attitudes toward social issues are directly related—the higher the class, the more liberal one's attitudes. Remember, however, that attitudes and behavior are not the same.

The amount of class voting in the United States appears low in comparison to other countries—for example, Great Britain and Australia. However, this should not obscure the class basis of racial, ethnic, and regional factors in American politics. "Racial" divisions stem from plantation capitalism; ethnic and religious diversity stem from immigration promoted by industry in order to acquire cheap labor. All in all, the American economy has grown so fast, and become so large and so diversified, that it is not surprising that its various elements do not fit readily into static homogeneous class categories. But one need only recall Wiley's argument about the unique class basis of American politics to see that American political behavior is not as unrelated to class as it appears. Americans, in other words, are subject to cross-pressures and inconsistencies *within* the class dimension unparalleled in other societies. There are also the effects of economic mobility: Many white-collar persons who do not vote for the Republican party are not violating the class behavior expected of them, since many white-collar workers are really working class both by origin and by function. And when a blue-collar voter fails to vote for the Democratic party, it may be that his wife works and that their combined income has led to property and rental income; or his wife and daughter may be working in white-collar jobs, thus introducing diversity and cross-pressures into an otherwise blue-collar family. At both the apex and the bottom of the various class hierarchies (commodity, credit, and labor) cross-pressures make it difficult for those in similar economic circumstances to develop a common consciousness (something that is much more difficult to achieve at the bottom). And, of course, differences *within* the class dimension are magnified by ethnic, religious, and "racial" differences.

All in all, the class interests of the mass of the American people appear

[15]John F. Zipp, "Social Class and Social Liberalism," *Sociological Forum* 1 (Spring 1986):301–329.

to be distorted and deflected from political expression by a number of factors from the past, including the pervasive ideology of individualism that stems from early capitalist experience. Fundamentally, it appears that both the upper classes and the upper middle classes dominate American politics and provide little political choice for the remainder of the American people. William Gamson has proposed an alternative to the pluralist model of political participation. Though pluralist theory tends to emphasize the openness of the American political system and its responsiveness to public need and changing times, Gamson argues that a model he calls *stable unrepresentation* may be more accurate. He hypothesizes that

> *the American political system normally functions to (1) keep unrepresented groups from developing solidarity and politically organizing, and (2) discourage their effective entry into the competitive establishment if and as they become organized. The competitive establishment is boundary-maintaining and the boundary-maintaining process involves various kinds of social control.*[16]

In terms of social stratification, stable unrepresentation appears to be deeply embedded in the political dynamics of social class.

WHY DOES THE UNITED STATES HAVE SUCH LOW POLITICAL PARTICIPATION?

Low and Declining Levels of Political Participation

Creative politics requires high levels of political participation by diverse groups. Creative politics derives from a many-sided interaction in which participants have to juggle and reconcile many points of view other than their own, in effect forcing them to recognize the many conflicts and gaps between self and public interest. It is obvious, therefore, that the structure of political participation is fundamental to society. Any exclusion of the mass of the population from meaningful political participation means that the upper classes will have that much less trouble equating their interests with the social interest. Research reveals that the United States has low levels of political participation and that its political system is marked by widespread apathy (and alienation). The rate of electoral participation in America is among the lowest in the liberal democracies and has been declining steadily in the post–World War II period; see Table 14–2, "Voter Turnout in 19 Industrial (Capitalist) Democracies, 1960–1980."

In a comparison of nineteen industrial (capitalist) democracies, Robert Jackman found that political institutions and electoral laws influence voter

---

[16]William Gamson, "Stable Unrepresentation in American Society," *American Behavioral Scientist* 12 (November-December 1968): 19f.

TABLE 14-2.   Voter Turnout in 19 Industrial
[Capitalist] Democracies, 1960-1980

COUNTRY	TURNOUT 1960-70	TURNOUT 1971-80
Australia	83.91	84.48
Austria	90.10	87.76
Belgium	86.87	87.83
Canada	70.75	67.15
Denmark	86.53	86.77
Finland	84.12	82.18
France	70.80	76.84
West Germany	82.74	84.22
Ireland	73.65	76.56
Israel	81.79	82.15
Italy	93.42	93.47
Japan	70.02	72.91
Netherlands	89.60	81.54
New Zealand	81.82	83.61
Norway	81.65	81.32
Sweden	83.96	87.46
Switzerland	25.08	43.29
United Kingdom	74.84	74.99
United States	61.73	54.22

Source: Adapted from Robert W. Jackman, "Political Institutions and Voter Turnout in the Industrial Democracies," *American Political Science Review* 81 (June 1987),
Table A-1. Used with permission.

turnout. His study of voter participation between 1960 and 1980 revealed that such political variables as national competitive districts, compulsory voting, system of apportioning seats by voter strength, a two-party vs. multiparty system, and unicameralism (one legislative chamber) each affect voter turn-out (particularly the first two). The United States is not particularly strong on these variables but that is not enough to explain its unusually low voter turnout. Jackman suggests that America's unique thirty-day residency requirement is one cause of its lower voter turnout but that the explanation requires further study.[17]

The general explanation of why the United States has such low political participation (including other areas besides voting as we will now see) is relatively easy. Despite the fact (as Jackman reports) that Americans have probably the strongest inclination to participate, they are subject to a comprehensive process of depoliticization. Elites across the apexes of institutional areas (economics, journalism, law, politics, religion, education, and popular

[17]Robert W. Jackman, "Political Institutions and Voter Turnout in the Industrial Democracies," *American Political Science Review* 81 (June 1987):405–423. Jackman says Switzerland's low turnout is largely due to the fact that national elections are not important in its decentralized polity.

culture) insist that the United States is a society based on human nature, nature, and the supernatural and that, therefore, politics and collective action are somehow against the national consensus.

The American population appears to be uniquely negative—even cynical—about politics. This attitude is found at all levels and reflects the overall depolitization process. By and large, Americans affirm their faith in democracy even as they withdraw their faith in politicians.[18]

Knowledge about politics and public issues is extremely limited among the American people. From 60 to 80 percent of the American people do not know the name of their representative in Congress (and state legislature), what their representatives think about issues, including burning issues of the day, or how they vote on them. More than a third do not even know if their representative is a Democrat or Republican. Females tend to have less knowledge about politics than males, younger people less knowledge than older ones, and residents of small towns, rural areas, and larger urban centers less than intermediate cities. Of even greater interest is the fact that there appears to be *no increase in political knowledge during the period when surveys have been conducted, the 1940s to the 1970s.* And this occurred during a period when the American people became better educated, had more money, more leisure from work, and when politics became more explicitly connected with all other aspects of American life.[19]

According to Norval Glenn, education does not produce more political knowledge among the young. Women know less because their lives (during this period at least) were more restricted than males. Young people and those in large urban centers, suggests Glenn, are "distracted" from politics. Young adulthood is a busy period filled with life-crisis events—personal identity formation, marriage, family, and career concerns. And those who live in fast-paced urban centers are distracted by work and by urban leisure opportunities.

Earlier we analyzed one form of political participation, voting. There we found that voting is affected by education, occupation, and income. However, political participation takes other forms besides voting: campaigning, contacting government officials, contributing money, attending rallies, and the like. In an early survey, Verba and Nie found that upper socioeconomic status levels (based on an average of income, occupation, and educa-

---

[18]For a valuable empirical study of negative political attitudes, combined with faith in American democracy, among well-paid blue-collar workers, see David Halle, *America's Working Man: Work, Home, and Politics Among Blue-Collar Property/Home/Owners* (Chicago: University of Chicago Press, 1984), pts. 4 and 5.

[19]For a perceptive analysis, see Norval D. Glenn, "The Distribution of Political Knowledge in the United States," in Dan D. Vimmo and Charles M. Bonjean, eds., *Political Attitudes and Public Opinion* (New York: Longman, 1972). There has been no follow-up of this important topic since Glenn's pioneering analysis.

tion scores) dominate all forms of political participation.[20] These two researchers also found that the policy preferences of both Democratic and Republican participants were much more conservative than those of the general population. They conclude that

> *the relationship of social status to participation as well as the relationship of political ideology to participation push in the same direction: the creation of a participant population different from the population as a whole. Our data show that participants are less aware of serious welfare problems than the population as a whole, less concerned about the income gap between rich and poor, less interested in government support for welfare programs, and less concerned with equal opportunities for black Americans.[21]*

In a later cross-national analysis, Verba, Nie, and Kim found low participation in all countries. Interestingly enough, the United States' rate of political participation was the lowest in the industrial West (that is, the one which offered least obstacles to political domination by a small number of affluent political activists).[22]

Not surprisingly, the American polity does not reflect the wishes of the American people.[23] Political parties and politically relevant elite groups that control the definition of issues and the forms of participation consistently thwart policies that the majority of the population endorse. Specifically, the will of the population is thwarted by gerrymandering, by high-level foundation reports that co-opt policy discussion, by the mass media, by the trend toward professionalized objective, expert government, and by the tradition of nonpartisanship.[24]

Political participation is also hampered by the antigovernment ideology that is peculiar to right-wing American liberalism. The decline of the political party has severed an important link between elites and masses. Political participation is hamstrung by a chaotic tangle of political jurisdictions (the federal system) and by a jungle of regulatory agencies, advisory and executive committees and boards, commissions, and special government districts and authorities. In comparing their 1967 survey of political participation with American electoral behavior compiled by the Survey Research Center at the University of Michigan, Verba and Nie concluded that low participation rates had been stable for two decades. More recent data suggest a decline. In

[20]Sidney Verba and Norman H. Nie, *Participation in America: Political Democracy and Social Equality* (New York: Harper & Row, 1972).

[21]Ibid., p. 298.

[22]Sidney Verba, Norman H. Nie, and Jae-On Kim, *Participation and Political Equality: A Seven Nation Comparison* (New York: Cambridge University Press, 1978).

[23]For a summary analysis of the cleavage in a wide variety of policy matters between American elites and ordinary people, see the section "Declining Legitimacy?" below.

[24]For a comprehensive study that concludes that nonpartisan elections at the municipal level favor the upper classes, see Willis D. Hawley, *Nonpartisan Elections and the Case for Party Politics* (New York: John Wiley & Sons, 1973).

addition, the alienation of the American people from politics and government is fairly large and appears to be growing.

Low political participation by broad segments of the American citizenry has important implications. In the 1980 and 1984 presidential elections only 53 percent of eligible voters participated. It is clear that the legitimacy of the American political system is seriously threatened—the authority of legislatures and government (that is, the felt sense that those in power are looking after the interests of those not in power) becomes questionable.[25]

Analysts have noted a rise in the political organization and effectiveness of American business, especially the corporate elite. Their profits threatened by the stagflation of the 1970s and by foreign competition, America's upper classes mobilized during the 1970s and succeeded in getting the public policy they wanted with the Reagan administration of 1980 to 1988. Essentially, this policy consisted of an attack on public spending (except for defense), a relaxation of environmental and other public regulation, and an anti-labor stance by government. The strong leadership by business was essentially an attempt to return society to the laissez-faire philosophy of the nineteenth century.[26]

The present pattern will be difficult to break: A weak and fragmented public leads to a cry for strong leadership. Strong leadership cannot solve social problems but comes up with half-solutions (often those that are causing the weak community in the first place). The lack of solutions perpetuates the weak community, fosters apathy, and the pattern continues. The American political process and its assorted professionals (candidates, party officials, party jobholders, pollsters, media and advertising specialists) are part of the broad separation of material and human capital from social functions that appears to be taking place across the apex of all institutional sectors.

Our Alienated Electorate

Most analysts agree that significant portions of the American electorate find the political realm alien and beyond control. One response is mass political apathy both at the ballot box and in civic organizations. Another is to use the vote to punish political figures who look as if they are agents of the status quo. Much of the difficulty that political experts and pollsters have had in recent years in predicting political behavior is due to their failure to take into account the alienation of many sectors of the electorate.

---

[25]For a fuller discussion, see the section "Declining Legitimacy?" later in this chapter.

[26]For one analysis showing the mobilization of American business under the leadership of the corporate elite, see Michael Useem, *The Inner Circle: Large Corporations and the Rise of Political Activity in the U.S. and U.K.* (New York: Oxford University Press, 1984). The emerging structure of social power in the United States will be discussed more fully in Chapter 17; the power of the upper classes across the capitalist world of nation states will be discussed in Chapters 20 and 21.

Functional theorists explain alienation in terms of the decline of intermediate organizations such as local political parties, neighborhood associations, newspapers, racial and ethnic associations, and reform groups. These groups are needed, say functionalists, becuase they involve and inform citizens and create the feeling and the reality of power for ordinary citizens.

Conflict theorists tend to agree with all this but point to the growth of corporate capitalism as the problem. Economic and political concentration (engendered by technology, rationalization, and bureaucratization), they argue, is the main reason why local groups have declined. If we are to understand our alienated electorate, we must see its roots in remote national and multinational corporations, national business and professional associations, large-scale churches, charities, foundations, research, and reform groups, and nationwide film, publishing, newspaper, and television corporations.

Declining Legitimacy?

A society rests on faith that its norms are fair and effective. There is considerable evidence that this faith has eroded in the United States. The United States has a huge underground economy made up of many respectable people. In this chapter we found considerable political apathy. Ominously, tax evasion is on the rise and seems to be feeding on itself.

In 1979 a Peter D. Hart and Associates poll revealed that half of the American people did not believe that they would ever collect their Social Security benefits. A Yankelovich poll in 1981 revealed that 83 percent of Americans agreed that rule breakers are rewarded while rule observers go empty-handed. The use of deception by the F.B.I., local police, journalists, and a wide variety of government agencies is often in a good cause but, nonetheless, the sense of trust that underlies authority relations is eroded.

Why all this public apathy and cynicism? Let's take one example that may provide a clue to an answer. In 1983 banks across the nation mounted a campaign against a law to enforce an *old tax* by withholding taxes on interest and dividends (large tax revenues are lost because the well-to-do and rich do not voluntarily report such income). The banks printed cards for their customers to mail to Congress and ran advertisements against the new law making it appear that it was a *new* tax. They also argued it would be a hardship on the poor and the elderly knowing full well that these groups were exempt from the new enforcement provision. Congress knew that the effort to repeal the law was based on deception but repealed it anyway. Is it any wonder that the public is apathetic and cynical?

The trend toward an *alienated* public appears to be paralleling the rise of a stalemated society. Public opinion polls have shown a steady loss of confidence by the American people in their leaders. Americans from all income levels and in all other social categories are disenchanted with the elites who serve them. On a scale measuring powerlessness, cynicism, and alienation (disenchantment), Americans registered 55 percent in 1973, up from 29 percent in 1966. Americans felt that the quality of life in the United States had declined and, on the average, only 33 percent of the American people expressed confidence in its leadership (only two functional areas still enjoy majority support: medicine and local trash collection). All areas fell in public confidence except for television news and the press.

The American elite (as represented by public officials) disagreed sharply with these views and expressed considerable satisfaction in American achievements as well as confidence in the future. Particularly striking was the cleavage between the people and public officials over television news and the press—public officials were far more critical of the news media than the general public.

The Survey Research Center and the Center for Political Studies (of the Institute for Social Research at the University of Michigan) have studied the attitude of trust in government for over two decades. Significant declines in trust in government began in the early 1960s and plunged during the 1970s. In tracing this development, Arthur N. Miller points out that "analysis conclusively demonstrates that the current, widespread political distrust of government is rooted in attitudes that are more generic than evaluations of the incumbents."[27] In short, American distrust of leaders is so profound that it seems to be undermining their faith in *institutions.* Widespread apathy toward elections can certainly be interpreted in this way. Trends in confidence toward institutional leadership rise slightly from time to time as presidents are elected or if the economy improves. But the long-term trend from the 1960s to 1982 clearly indicates a decline in confidence by the American people in its leadership. As such, this poses a distinct threat to the legitimacy of American institutions.[28]

The cleavage between elite and people extends to policy matters. The American people clearly want a strong federal government to solve the problems of war and peace, the economy, and quality of life. Nine out of ten Americans believe that the federal government is responsible for seeing to it that no one goes hungry and that every person achieves a minimum standard of living. Americans clearly express a preference for wage and price controls to fight inflation, and they support a woman's right to an abortion and favor a curb on handguns. Seventy-five percent of the American people express a clear preference for jobs as the best way to curb crime, a preference that runs

<hr/>

[27]Arthur H. Miller, "The Institutional Focus of Political Distrust" (paper delivered at the 1979 Annual Meeting of the American Political Science Association), p. 46.

[28]For a comprehensive review of the many polls tapping public confidence, and an analysis of the relation between declining confidence and the legitimacy of American society, see Seymour Martin Lipset and William Schneider, *The Confidence Gap: Business, Labor, and Government in the Public Mind* (New York: Free Press, 1983).

counter to elite beliefs.[29] Moreover, the American people express clear support for national health insurance.[30] Their attitudes toward nuclear arms and foreign policy are also at variance with those of American elites, most preferring a nuclear freeze and a less belligerent foreign policy.

The elites of the United States, with some minor exceptions, tend to ignore the public's wishes. There is a tendency among elites, including public officials, to regard the ordinary citizen as uninformed and self-contradictory. American elites, including sociologists, have a longstanding tendency of blaming and ignoring the masses, largely by regarding them as uneducated, selfish, and undisciplined.

Another index into disenchantment with public authority is the growth of direct-action groups, not only self-help programs, neighborhood organizations, communes, public-interest firms, and malpractice suits (by individuals) against a wide range of professionals, but direct-action groups aimed at corporations and other private groups. Many of these direct-action groups are political, but there appears to be less of a trust in government and legislature than in the past and more emphasis on self-reliance and direct action.

The decline in legitimacy appears real. By and large, it stems from the deep cleavage between the interests and values of American elites and those of the American people. In another sense, it reflects a decline in the adaptive ability of American elites. Again, the master problem seems to be a social system whose basic institutions separate elites from direct experience with the problems of ordinary people. Elites are separated from ordinary people because institutions allow them to solve their own problems under the false faith that by doing so they are also serving the public.

POLITICAL PARTICIPATION OF AMERICA'S MINORITIES

Black, Mexican, and Jewish Americans are all strong supporters of the Democratic party. On the whole, 90 percent of the voters in these minority groups tend to support liberal programs and the liberal wing of the Democratic party. Black and Mexican Americans have long been at the bottom levels of the class, prestige, and power hierarchies, and support for a reform party (in the absence of a radical party) is understandable as an effort to improve their positions. Jewish Americans, however, are middle class and above, and while their heavy commitment to the Democratic party is not necessarily surprising, it represents a deviation from the normal middle-class political pattern. However, as members of a religious minority in insecure

[29] As reported by Elliott Currie, "Fighting Crime," *Working Papers* 9 (July-August 1982):22.
[30] *Public Opinion Quarterly* 45, pp. 179–198.

economic positions, Jews too have a stake in economic reform and in public measures to ensure civil rights.

Jewish Americans have a high rate of political participation, but it appears to be almost completely a class phenomenon rather than a result of ethnic or relligous factors. Efforts to protect and enhance black voting rights in the South have been significantly successful. Thanks largely to a series of civil rights acts, especially the Voting Rights Act of 1965, and to the rise in absolute class level among southern blacks, the black voting rate in the South has climbed significantly. Nationally, black voting rates remained stable between the 1960s and 1980 at about 12 percent less than white rates. In 1984, thanks to the candidacy of Jesse Jackson, black voting rose to within 6 points of white rates.[31] Whether black Americans can continue their high rate of political participation remains to be seen.[32]

Mexican Americans have a low rate of voting and political participation. Their unusually low voting rates are attributable to such barriers as the requirement to register, often in unaccessible places; literacy tests, conducted in English; poll taxes; a low rate of naturalization; gerrymandering; and the co-optation of Mexican American leaders by Anglo groups. However, when Mexican Americans in San Antonio are compared with their ethnic counterparts in Los Angeles, it is apparent that Mexican American political behavior begins to approach that of other Americans in the freer and more inviting political atmosphere of Los Angeles: Their rate of participation is higher, and upper-level Mexican Americans participate more than do those in lower levels.

On the whole, Mexican Americans are quite ambivalent about politics, tend to have little confidence in government, and overwhelmingly reject any alliance with black Americans. Viewed nationally, the Mexican American voting rate is unusually low. Using the more general term, Spanish-Origin Americans (of whom Mexican Americans are the overwhelming majority), their voting rate in 1984 presidential and congressional elections was 40 and 35 percent, respectively, 15 points below both white and black voting.[33]

---

[31] U.S. Bureau of the Census, *Current Population Reports*, Series P-20, No. 405 "Voting and Registration in the Election of November, 1984" (Washington, D.C.: U.S. Government Office, 1987), Table A.

[32] Black electoral power is still diluted by gerrymandering, multimember districting, at-large elections, and in other ways; for an analysis, see Chandler Davidson, ed., *Minority Vote Dilution* (Washington, DC: Howard University Press, 1984).

[33] U.S. Bureau of the Census, *Current Population Reports*, Series P-20, No. 405 "Voting and Registration in the Election of November, 1984" (Washington, D.C.: U.S. Government Printing Office, 1987), Table B. For general background on the political experience of Mexican (and Spanish-Origin) Americans, see Leo Grebler *et al.*, *The Mexican-American People: The Nation's Second Largest Minority* (New York: Free Press, 1970), chap. 23; F. Chris Garcia and Rudolph O. de la Garza, *The Chicano Political Experience: Three Perspectives* (North Scituate, Mass.: Duxbury Press, 1977); and Joan Moore and Harry Pachon, *Hispanics in the United States* (Englewood Cliffs, N.J.: Prentice-Hall, 1985), Chaps. 8–12.

It goes without saying that most American minorities are not represented in political positions in proportion to their numbers, especially if one focuses on upper-echelon decision-making positions. Despite gains, women are still vastly underrepresented, and, though exact studies are lacking, the same is probably true of other minorities. Black Americans are employed in federal civil service occupations at higher rates than whites, and they have made significant gains in winning elective office in recent years, especially at the local level. However, black Americans are still far from holding a proportionate share of important public positions, at either the elected or the appointed level. The same is true for Mexican Americans.

CLASS-PRESTIGE AND POLITICAL PARTICIPATION: A SUMMARY

It is widely believed that the emergence of representative government marks a significant advance in equality, but the realities of political participation require this view to be heavily qualified. It is probably more accurate to say that elections and other forms of political participation are means to translate economic and prestige power into political power. It is clear from the evidence, in other words, that class and prestige control all forms of political participation and that the middle and upper classes dominate political life.

The dominance of the upper classes has made the solution of social problems difficult. As a result, there is a clear trend toward an alienated public and loss of faith in the legitimacy of America's leaders (and to some extent of American institutions).

Black and Mexican Americans are at last able to exercise the franchise, though both still manifest low rates of voting and other forms of political participation. This phenomenon is attributable to their class standing: By and large, black and Mexican American participation is comparable to that of other groups in a similar class position, though blacks have somewhat higher rates of political and other forms of voluntary behavior than their class warrants. Jewish Americans are traditionally active in politics owing to their concentration in urban areas and gradual acquisition of middle-class status. All three minority groups strongly support the Democratic party.

CHAPTER 15

The Class-Prestige Nature of Legislation and Government

THE CLASS-PRESTIGE NATURE OF LEGISLATION

There are many classic examples of class-prestige legislation. Every school-child knows that the repeal of the Corn Laws signified the rise of industry in the English economy. In the United States during the nineteenth century, industry and labor erected high tariff walls to protect manufacturing, and farmers tried to pull them down. Banking legislation and governmental credit and monetary policy also reflect the struggle between debtor groups—such as farmers—and creditors—such as bankers. It was governmental policy (the Homestead Act) that encouraged freeholding (capitalist) farming, as well as the private exploitation of minerals, timber, and waterways.

Many stereotypes prevent an accurate perception of political facts and keep observers from seeing the structure of power and the real and often ironic consequences of political-legal action. For example, it is well known that public authorities evict tenants whose incomes have risen above the maximum level of eligibility for public housing. Initially, one is likely to assume that this is a means of protecting the class interests of the poor. However, such an assumption overlooks the fact that public housing legislation was explicitly formulated to ensure that public housing would not compete with private housing. In other words, the eviction requirement is intended to protect the private housing market by guaranteeing that the nonpoor buy their housing from private owners! The net result is that the moral, economic, and political power of the state is used to make housing a private-profit field. Indeed, one of the latent functions of public housing itself is to divert attention from the failure of our economic institutions to house our population adequately, and from the possibility that this is a condition chronic to American-style capitalism.[1]

The latent consequences of legislation are obscured because political action is invariably framed in the rhetoric of public interest and moral rectitude. Among the most dramatic examples is our policy of military conscription. The administration of this system was in the best tradition of grassroots democracy: It relied on thousands of local draft boards, "little groups of neighbors," who allegedly represented their communities and were able to render fair judgments on who should serve. During the Vietnam War, however, there emerged a manpower surplus—that is, only a small percentage of the relevant age group was needed to fight a war that, while a major military effort, was something less than a national struggle. Thus, one of the main functions of the Selective Service System was to *defer* men from military service. Subject to scrutiny for the first time, the Selective Service System was shown to be a hodgepodge of varying and contradictory policies, administered by unrepresentative draft boards drawn from the upper socioeconomic levels and deeply discriminatory against the lower classes even when the high rejection rates associated with poverty are taken into account. In other words, the power dimension, in the guise of "little groups of neighbors," brought about the differential distribution of a burdensome civic duty and a differential death rate in war along the lines of class.[2]

As we examine the intricacies of public policy in the realms of taxation, Social Security, housing, education, and the economy, the foregoing examples should serve as a warning that things are not always what they seem.[3]

Taxation

Despite a strong verbal tradition affirming "ability to pay" as the underlying principle of taxation, and despite an equally strong commitment to reward work and achievement—and, by implication, not to reward idleness

[1]Public housing projects (our "penthouse prisons") also have the well-known effects of segregating the residences of white and black Americans and keeping the poor of both races out of the neighborhoods of the nonpoor.

[2]James W. Davis, Jr., and Kenneth M. Dolbeare, *Little Groups of Neighbors: The Selective Service System* (Chicago: Markham, 1968); M. Zeitlin, K.A. Lutterman, and J.W. Russell, "Death in Vietnam: Class, Poverty, and the Risks of War," *Politics and Society* 3 (Spring 1973): 313–328.

[3]For a good overview similar to the analysis that follows, see Benjamin I. Page, *Who Gets What from Government* (Berkeley: University of California Press, 1983).

FIGURE 15–1. Distribution of Before-Tax and After-Tax Household Income, United States, 1986

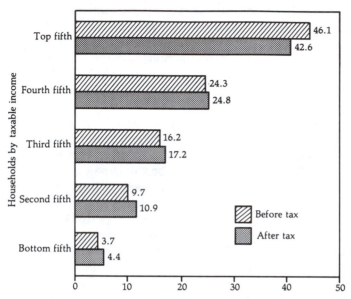

Source: U.S. Census Bureau, "After-Tax Money Income Estimates of Households: 1986," *Current Population Reports*, Series P-23, No. 157 (Washington, D.C.: U.S. Government Printing Office, 1988), Table C.

or inherited wealth—the American tax structure at all levels seriously violates these honored American values and beliefs.

The first noteworthy feature of income taxation is that it brings about relatively little change in income distribution (see Figure 15–1). Furthermore, there is not much difference in wealth before and after estate and inheritance taxes.[4] The reasons for this phenomenon are now fairly well known:

1. The federal income tax structure, while ostensibly progressive, is not very progressive in effect. The net effect of "tax loopholes" is to produce effective rates of taxation far different from the formal rates. The minimal progressive impact of federal income taxation is reduced, moreover, by regressive federal Social Security taxes and state and local property and sales taxes. The higher rates of taxes paid by the very rich and very poor affect less than 10 percent of total national income. It is noteworthy that the progressive income tax has little negative effect on work incentives, popular mythology not withstanding.[5]

[4]Joseph A. Pechman, *The Rich, the Poor, and the Taxes They Pay* (Boulder, Colo.: Westview Press, 1986).

[5]For our only full-scale study, see Robin Barlow, Harvey E. Brazer, and James N. Morgan, *Economic Behavior of the Affluent* (Washington, D.C.: Brookings Institution, 1966).

2. The federal tax structure favored property and nonwork income up to the Tax Reform Act of 1986. The capital gains tax, which is a low rate of taxation on profits received from the sale of property; rapid initial real estate depreciation, which means that the depreciation of property is assumed for tax purposes to occur at a rapid rate while the property is new; tax-free municipal and state bonds; and oil and mineral depletion and investment allowances all protected income resulting from the investment of money. In light of the fact that individuals on straight salaries or wages are taxed at full rates, it would seem that the federal tax code discriminated against those who worked for a living. This is especially true when salaried and wage workers are compared with those who can take advantage of two tax loopholes, such as the oil depletion allowance and capital gains, or rapid depreciation and capital gains.

3. The United States has ineffective death and inheritance taxes, judged in terms of the much-vaunted American ideal of providing each generation equal opportunity within a framework of equal competition. Again, the key word is *effective*, for the impression is widespread that it is pointless to work hard to build an estate since the government will confiscate it when one dies. On the contrary, the American system of taxation promotes a considerable level of familism, since it permits the bulk of one generation's wealth to be passed on to the next.

4. The United States gives strong support to *rentiers* and consumers of leisure. The rentier, or individual who lives off property, profits from the benefits described in (2) above, along with hardworking businesspeople and professionals. The expense account is a device with which the state (Internal Revenue Code) differentiates the American population on the basis of prestige (consumption). While tax regulations on expense account deductions have been tightened, this practice still supports high-consumption groups, mainly businesspeople and professionals, at public expense.

By not taxing income and property, Congress and state legislatures are making what analysts call *tax expenditures*. It is doubtful if the thousand and one tax loopholes could stand scrutiny as a direct expenditure in the budget. Accordingly, property and professional groups receive favored treatment, most of it unwarranted by standards of public interest and often obtained secretly, through the tax code. The welfare for the well-to-do and rich represented by tax expenditures exceeds many times over the direct expenditures for the poor.

Tax legislation, whether to raise, lower, or reform taxes, does little to change relative positions either of income or wealth. Over the years the poor have occasionally been favored by having their taxes reduced. The federal Tax Act of 1986 was especially valuable to the poor since it relieved them from some of the heavy tax burden that had resulted from the Reagan tax cuts of 1981. Despite this reduction, the poor will be paying significantly more in taxes in 1988 than in 1977, and the well-to-do and rich will pay significantly less. During the same period income in constant dollars will have declined for the bottom 80 percent of families and increased for the top 20 percent, with extremely large increases for the top 5 percent and 1 percent of families.[6]

[6]Congressional Budget Office, *The Changing Distribution of Federal Taxes: 1975–1990* (Congressional Budget Office: Washington, D.C.: 1987), Tables 6 and 12.

In sum, it is fairly clear from an analysis of taxation that a power dimension based on universal suffrage, which ignores income and wealth by giving each individual one vote, does not lead to a redistribution of income and wealth despite the fact that lower income-wealth groups (the lower middle class and below) form a numerical majority. The immunity of concentrated income and wealth to majority rule also characterizes the other liberal democracies. Nowhere is the contradiction between the ideal of equal opportunity and the class system so vividly apparent as in taxation: The American tax code not only reflects the power and privilege of the class-prestige structure, but also facilitates and legitimates the accumulation of power and privilege over time. Or perhaps the contradiction should be expressed differently: Is it reasonable to motivate people to work hard and save on an individual basis and then expect to tax their income and savings to promote social values?

Social Security

The historic Social Security bill of 1935 was denounced by many, especially the representatives of business, as a "giveaway" socialistic measure that would promote sloth and social decay. But the actual Social Security Act, including changes enacted since 1935, is quite different from what the ideological debates would suggest. Basically, it is a contributory insurance system to assist the retired and a public assistance program for those who cannot help themselves. Its components are as follows:

1. Old Age, Survivors' and Disability Insurance (OASDI), a system of benefits financed by a tax paid by workers and employers. Benefits go to retired individuals, disabled workers, and the widows and orphans of employees.
2. Old Age Assistance (OAA) and Aid to Families with Dependent Children (AFDC), a system of welfare benefits paid to the needy aged and to families with dependent children. This is a noncontributory program paid for largely through general federal revenues and administered by the states.
3. Health insurance for the elderly (Medicare), financed by employees' and employers' compulsory contributions.

The social insurance portion of this legislation, enacted quite haphazardly during the Great Depression,[7] has a number of features that need to be much better understood. Financed by a flat tax rate on only a portion of individual income, with no allowances for dependents or for deductions, it is a highly regressive tax. The funds collected under this system are then paid

---

[7]Theodore J. Lowi, in his book *The End of Liberalism: Ideology, Policy and the Crisis of Public Authority* (New York: W. W. Norton, 1969), uses Social Security legislation to illustrate the vagueness of legislation passed by the United States Congress.

out to retirees in terms of the amounts they have paid in, rather than on the basis of need. Actually, lowest-income retirees receive proportionately more than they paid in than do higher-income retirees, but the minimum pensions are extremely small; it cannot be said that income is significantly redistributed, or that this feature alters the regressive nature of the social insurance system. Actually, one-third of all Social Security payments in the early 1980s went to retirees who already had $30,000 or more in income, and there were 254,000 millionaires receiving free medical care under Medicare.

Furthermore, the amounts collected represent very large sums, amounting in effect to a major tax (running a close second to the personal income tax) and a considerable burden on most white-collar and almost all working-class incomes. Also, many jobs held by the lower classes were not covered between roughly 1936 and the late 1960s and early 1970s, and the retirement age of sixty-five discriminates against the lower classes; whole-life expectancy only began to reach that level in the 1980s (the average black male was still not living to age sixty-five as of 1985 when the retirement age began to rise). The lower classes do benefit most from the provisions for widows and for disability, since they die earlier and are disabled more frequently, but child support through college favors middle-class families. Incidentally, the original Social Security tax was based on extremely conservative actuarial estimates, and from the beginning the monies collected have been put in trust funds earning minimum interest (that is, the federal government lends the money to itself at interest rates lower than when it borrows from private sources). Unlike other countries, Social Security funds cannot be used as instruments of governmental fiscal and monetary policy or to provide capital for housing and other needs. If Social Security funds had been invested in the American economy like the pension systems of state government, their size would have grown enormously, making it possible to keep the Social Security tax much less burdensome than it now is. But investing Social Security funds in concrete areas of public interest or in a balanced portfolio of stocks and bonds would have made the federal government an owner of the American economy, a competitor of private capital, and presumably given it power to influence directly the direction of capital investment. For government to play a direct role in the economy is common in all other capitalist societies but fiercely resisted in the United States.

Payments to the needy from general tax revenues are designed to alleviate hardship, and they are ostensibly distributed according to need. But welfare programs are administered by the states, and there is wide variation in levels of payment, criteria used to establish need, and methods of administration. This portion of the Social Security system is still considered a "handout," an attitude that, along with a mode of administering payments that humiliates and stigmatizes recipients, tends to create a pariah group of public dependents. Not only does the administration of this program tend to invade the rights and privacy of the poor, but its latent function is to support and legitimize the social system that creates this form of poverty.[8]

Housing

The history of housing legislation in the United States is a preeminent illustration of class politics.[9] Various stages of public concern about and action on housing can be distinguished from the beginning of the century to the present. But all such legislation and action failed to provide housing for the poor: Every piece of legislation and every form of implementation has been heavily biased in favor of those that Lawrence Friedman calls "the submerged and potential middle class" and against the poor. What Friedman does not stress, because of his focus on the poor, is that housing is in chronically short supply for many who are not poor.[10]

Over the years the federal government has developed a variety of ad hoc housing programs but has never developed a coherent housing policy. The many piecemeal programs, however, manifest a rather distinct pattern, the trickle-down strategy—concentration on quality construction and subsidies, by far the largest of which is income tax deductions for homeowners (which of course favors the middle, upper middle, and upper income brackets), a strategy that benefits the poor only in that older homes eventually become available to them.[11]

The federal government acted to protect homeowners during the 1930s and it fostered low-income housing largely as an economic stimulus. During the 1950s and 1960s, the federal government undertook a gigantic support program for middle- and upper-class housing (through credit, tax, and highway programs). Throughout the 1930-to-1960s period the federal government actually cooperated with local governments to create a racially dual housing market. Little changed after the Fair Housing Law of 1968 because the federal government failed to develop a set of implementing regulations. After 1980 things actually got worse as the Reagan administration actively curtailed legal safeguards for minorities and curbed the already inadequate funds for low-

---

[8]For an argument that the two central functions of welfare are to quell civil disorder and to enforce work norms among the marginal labor force, see Frances Fox Piven and Richard H. Cloward, *Regulating the Poor: The Functions of Public Welfare* (New York: Random House, 1971).

[9]For a brilliant summary and analysis of housing legislation and action in American history, with valuable insights into the politics of class, see Lawrence M. Friedman, *Government and Slum Housing* (Chicago: Rand McNally, 1968).

[10]As Friedman points out, housing for the elderly has received substantial support, partly because the middle class nuclear family is not geared to accommodate aged parents.

[11]Henry J. Aaron, *Shelter and Subsidies: Who Benefits from Federal Housing Policies* (Washington, D.C.: Brookings Institution, 1972). The use of the tax code to subsidize housing favors the upper classes because they can reduce their property tax and interest payments by 70 percent (50 percent after 1981 and only 28 percent after 1989), whereas the lower classes can reduce theirs only by their much lower rates.

income housing.[12] During the 1980s a new housing phenomenon appeared: homelessness. Throughout the United States, to its disgrace, anywhere from a few hundred thousand to 3 million Americans are presently forced to sleep in alleyways, bus stations, huddled over gratings, or in their automobiles. The homeless are a diverse lot, consisting of the mentally ill who were released from mental institutions but who did not get the community-based shelters that were to serve as transition homes on the way back to normal life; the poor who used to find shelter in single-room occupancy hotels now torn down to make room for office buildings and other alleged improvements; the alcoholic; and the new poor made up of families either unemployed or whose income does not buy housing.

America's chronic housing shortage results from a disparity between the price of housing and the American income structure. This disparity grew worse between 1970 and the 1980s. A thirty-year-old person in 1970 paid 21 percent of gross earnings to buy a medium-priced house—by 1983 that same individual had to pay 44 percent. A full explanation of this disparity must acknowledge the formidable class-prestige-power forces that stand between Americans and adequate housing. Private credit policies; monopolistic craft unions; outmoded building codes; snob zoning; local tax policies; planning practices; the compliance of real estate boards with snob and racial practices; and the transportation, credit, tax, and housing policies of the federal government[13] all function to mesh the availability, type, and location of housing with the income-wealth and prestige structure of the United States. In sum, there is little doubt that the power dimension at the federal, state, and local levels is deeply implicated in the processes that keep housing scarce and segregated along class-prestige lines.[14]

GOVERNMENT AND EDUCATION: THE PUBLIC AS PARTISAN

Elementary and High School Education

Given both a "rotten borough" and gerrymandered system of political representation at the state and federal levels and our tradition of political decentralization, it is easy to understand why the distribution of educational

---

[12]For full background, see Citizens' Commission on Civil Rights, *A Decent Home: A Report on the Continuing Failure of the Federal Government to Provide Equal Housing Opportunity* (Washington, D.C.: Center for National Policy Review, Catholic University, 1983).

[13]The Reagan administration made drastic cuts between 1981 and 1987 in the federal government's already inadequate housing programs.

[14]For a radical indictment of American housing presenting valuable data and insights from successful policies abroad, see Rachel G. Bratt, Chester Hartman, and Ann Meyerson, eds., *Critical Perspectives on Housing* (Philadelphia: Temple University Press, 1986).

resources in local political districts conforms to class lines. The *Serrano-Priest* decision (1971), in which the California Supreme Court ruled unequal expenditures on education unconstitutional, stimulated an effort to make school expenditures more equal. However, in 1973 the United States Supreme Court ruled that unequal educational expenditures are not unconstitutional and spending more on the education of the well-to-do is now a taken-for-granted fact of American life. But even equal expenditures will do little to equalize educational opportunity, since astonishingly (as we saw in Chapter 8) the school itself has negligible impact on differentials in academic achievement.

Historically, Congress and the federal government have exerted considerable influence on education, largely through deliberate neglect. Though fought for in the name of equal opportunity, the flow of federal money to the schools, which began in 1958, has not changed the class character of American education. All that can be said is that federal aid may have provided better education for all, but without changing relative differences. Even when federal money is earmarked for the poor it does not reach them because states spend the money on all, leaving relative differences intact.

Government and Higher Education

Public policy in the realm of higher education also reflects and reinforces the American class system. As we have seen, higher education conforms to the basic pattern of class-structured education.[15] None of this is surprising, given (1) colleges' and universities' ideals of detachment from society (objective scholarship, political neutrality, and cloistered campuses); (2) their actual deep dependence on and involvement in society (control of their governing boards by businesspeople, professionals, churches, and state legislatures, the involvement of universities and professors in governmental research and consulting, and the dispensation of knowledge in terms of unconsciously held cultural postulates); (3) the fact that presidents, deans, and faculty enjoy upper- and upper-middle-class status; (4) and the fact that faculty and administrators are almost without exception innocent of any systematic training in education and up-to-date social science.

Basically, neither the infusion of public money into higher education nor the establishment and expansion of public institutions of higher education have equalized educational opportunity. For example, the free education made available to all veterans of World War II and subsequent wars represents an unparalleled educational opportunity for Americans—but making education available to all is not to make it equal. For one thing, not all veterans availed themselves of their educational rights. While precise data do not exist, it is safe to assume that a larger percentage of the well-to-do than of the poor did so. Second, one can assume that rich and poor attend different

---

[15]See "Higher Education: The Capstone of Class Education" in Chapter 8.

colleges and schools and pursue different academic programs. And third, the rich are thus enabled to invest the money they would otherwise have spent on education. The net result of the United States' generous support of education for veterans, therefore, was probably to widen the gap between rich and poor (as well as to help many individuals from the lower classes to succeed via education).[16]

The federal low-cost insured loan program for college students (a provision of the Higher Education Act of 1965) is a more recent example of the differential impact of allegedly nonpartisan equal opportunity programs. Designed to lower economic barriers to higher education, this program provides low-cost loans to college students. Students can borrow money with no interest during four years or more of school and then pay it back over ten years at subsidized rates. Though income limits were set in the early 1980s, effectively only the very wealthy are ineligible. Thus, the middle and upper classes can invest the money they would otherwise have paid for their children's education. By the mid-1980s it was costing the federal government $3 billion annually to generate $9 billion worth of guaranteed student loans.[17] That this program theoretically covers the poor and the general working class is of very little practical consequence. The children of the various classes acquire the motivation and skills necessary for college at different rates, attend college at unequal rates, choose different types of colleges, take different programs, earn different academic records, and complete different amounts of higher education. Thus, a formally equal opportunity is far from constituting equality of opportunity or equality of competition in practice. Nor do such programs even necessarily promote a higher level of ability among college populations. It is well known, for example, that there is class bias in the distribution of financial aid by institutions of higher education.[18] Students who can profit from higher education are turned down while students of equal ability who can afford to pay are given public aid, all in the name of equal opportunity (not to mention the unaccomplished well-to-do who feed at the public trough).

Colleges and universities are demonstrably subject to business, religious, and local political control, and one finds higher education explicitly implicated in serving social ends other than detached scholarship and the preservation and transmission of high culture. Higher education is part of a far-flung, intertwined network of economic, professional, and political inter-

[16]Veterans of the Vietnam War were treated less well than their predecessors for a number of reasons, not the least of which is the pronounced class bias in the system of drafting men to fight in Vietnam. In contrast to veterans of previous wars, Vietnam veterans include proportionately far more of the poor and minorities, and thus had less appeal for Congress and other public officials than did veterans of former wars.

[17]*The Chronicle of Higher Education* 33 (April 15, 1987), p. 1.

[18]George A. Schlekat, "Do Financial Aid Programs Have a Conscience?," *College Board Review* 69 (Fall 1968): 15–20.

ests. It engages in research for the military, for industry, and for government. This is not necessarily bad, but there are many suspicions that partisan interests are being served (for an example, see Box 15–1, "The Tomato Harvester: How Education Serves the Corporate Economy").

Our awareness of the class nature of public higher education is based on more than insight and hypothesis. Thanks to a study of the California system of public higher education,[19] we are now on firm ground when talking about the educational role played by the power dimension. As is well known, California has an extensive system of post–high-school public education, financed by public funds and characterized by low tuition and entrance and retention on academic merit. In their analysis of this system and its relation to class, Hansen and Weistrod conclude that public higher education in California is a system for redistributing income from lower to higher income groups. The authors add that California's reinforcement and aggravation of existing inequality by means of substantial subsidies to middle-class and upper-class students through "public" higher education is probably even more characteristic of the other forty-nine states.[20] Given what we know about public education at all levels, these findings are not surprising.[21] It is difficult not to conclude that the power dimension (local, state, and federal governments and political institutions), as it focuses on education, is an integral and dependent aspect of the American system of stratification. In performing its role in the American system of class, the power structure does more than certify the existing class system; it actually widens differential advantages while labeling its efforts "equality of opportunity," thus creating the impression that it is a neutral promoter of classlessness.

ECONOMIC POLICIES OF THE FEDERAL GOVERNMENT

Each branch of the federal government (legislature, executive, judiciary) has a basic posture with regard to economic issues. Thus, it is not easy to characterize the federal government's posture toward economic affairs, or to measure its independence or difference from the class-prestige forces it is acting upon. Some tentative answers can be posited, however, in three general

---

[19]W. Lee Hansen and Burton A. Weistrod, *Benefits, Cost, and Finance of Public Higher Education* (Chicago: Markham, 1969).

[20]The authors demonstrate that this is the case for Wisconsin, a state famous for its system of public higher education; see W. Lee Hansen and Burton A. Weistrod, *A New Approach to Higher Education Finance* (Madison: Institute for Research on Poverty, University of Wisconsin, 1970). For a study of public higher education in Florida, which corroborates the above findings, see Douglas M. Windham, *Education, Equality, and Income Redistribution: A Study of Public Higher Education* (Lexington, Mass.: D.C. Heath, 1970).

[21]It should be noted that public institutions enroll 75 percent of all college students.

BOX 15–1. *THE TOMATO HARVESTER: HOW EDUCATION SERVES THE CORPORATE ECONOMY*

The University of California at Davis is the biggest agricultural research station in the country. Out of its efforts has come a large-wheeled vehicle that can pick tomatoes. The picker is ungainly and unattractive, but it works. As a result, the backbreaking work of picking tomatoes is now done by a nonsweating, nonsuffering machine. Not only is an undesirable type of work being replaced but presumably productivity will increase. Seen from this perspective, all is to the good. But critics charge that there is far more to the story.

What happens to farm workers? Predictably, the introduction of machinery was accelerated after the victory of the Cesar Chávez-led farm workers union in getting better wages and working conditions. Jobs picking tomatoes have shrunk drastically in recent years. And this is not a question of the right of private property owners to manage their businesses any way they want. The tomato harvester was developed at a tax-supported state institution that also uses federal tax dollars for research. Critics charge that the University of California looks favorably on research that favors large agribusiness and chemical companies. This bias is furthered by private research grants to the university, which however small a fraction of the total, set the general direction of research. The bias is also explained by the fact that the university's governing boards have members with direct ties to farm, chemical, and other economic interests. In addition, say critics, the university neglects nutrition research, research that would benefit small farmers, and does little research into nonchemical ways to control pests. Characteristically, no provisions are made in research grants that would require its beneficiaries to help displaced workers develop new skills and find new jobs.

The tomato harvester cost $80,000 when it was introduced in the late 1970s. As only large farms could afford it or found it economical to use, it benefitted them most. Its use gave them a competitive edge over the small farmer and thus helped to accelerate the trend in farming in which more and more land goes into fewer hands. To make matters worse, big farm owners pay for the harvester with money borrowed from federal agencies (which were originally set up to help needy small farmers) and they used publicly-paid-for irrigation water illegally (the open violation for fifty years of a law restricting such water to small farmers of 600 acres or less was rectified by changing the law!).

To compound the injury a tomato must be bred to withstand mechanical picking—again, the University of California helped by developing a thick-skinned tomato. And the price of tomatoes has risen disproportionally, argue critics, despite claims that science and technology increase productivity. All in all, the deep bias toward technology, energy-intensive, chemically dependent, cash-crop farming in the United States causes human suffering, threatens the soil, and leads to concentration in farming and interlocks between agribusiness, concentrated industry, scientists, and educators.

In 1988 a California court decreed that the University of California had to evaluate the consequences of its research and to give small farmers and labor more attention. The university announced it would appeal.

areas: antitrust policy, regulatory policies toward various aspects of the economy, and public economic policies.

Antitrust Policy

The United States has a long history of concern about monopolistic economic power, much of it framed in terms of a theoretical ideal of free market competition. Free markets have probably never existed, except in the minds of theorists and in aspects of some areas such as labor and agriculture. Why this utopian image of economic competition persists is unclear: It may relieve anxiety about failure for some; it may serve others as a rationalization for easy success; and it may be a convenient facade behind which powerful groups can hide. In any case, the American public and the federal government have accepted bigness—or, perhaps more precisely, they tend to assume that the trend toward bigness is compatible with competition, efficiency, individualism, and democracy.

Americans see no contradiction in valuing both competition and bigness, perhaps because they believe that each promotes efficiency. One thing is certain, however: In the United States competition is honored more in ideology than in actual behavior, especially if behavior is measured against the classic ideal of competition among a large number of equals. In the name of this imaginary world, the Reagan administration noticeably relaxed the weak restraints on monopoly that had persisted up to 1980.

The role of the power dimension in promoting concentrated market power or oligarchic competition is apparent. The federal government is not, on the whole, a trust-busting agency. Its regulatory policies; its granting of patents, franchises, and licenses to engage in various businesses, including the production of atomic energy; and its import and production quotas clearly promote bigness and noncompetition.

The government's policies with regard to its own purchases of goods and services also contribute heavily to economic concentration, and thus to the redistribution of income and wealth through oligarchic control of markets. The Defense Department, the Nuclear Regulatory Commission, and the National Aeronautics and Space Administration clearly prefer to purchase goods and services from a small number of large contractors.

Regulatory Policy

Beginning in the late nineteenth century, Congress began to pass legislation to regulate certain forms of economic activity in the public interest: Almost all observers are agreed that government's various regulations and programs are biased in favor of the industry or profession being regulated. Workman's compensation, for example, was hailed as a gain for workers but what it did was to safeguard the unsafe world of work—workers got something for being injured on the job but they gave up the right to sue the employer. In the meantime, occupational health and safety laws go unenforced. Other regulations help to rationalize markets for those in them, thus providing a legal facade for oligarchic markets. We Americans are such innocents about government that during the crucial formative decades of nuclear energy policy we put both its promotion and regulation in the hands of the same agency. And despite much posturing in the health-care field there is little effective monitoring of either its costs or results. Deregulation was the watchword from the late 1970s on, and by the 1980s deregulation has led to new forms of concentration (the airline and railroad industries are prime examples).

Public Economic Policies

From the early nineteenth century until 1929, Americans developed a great faith that theirs was an economy based on natural principles. They believed that if left alone (laissez-faire economic theory), an economy inherently seeks equilibrium and brings about the most rational use of human and material resources. This faith was shattered by the Great Depression of the 1930s, which left 25 percent of the American labor force unemployed and devastated farmers and businesses. It also broke the consensus among property owners and professionals about the existence of a natural economy.

During the 1930s Americans looked to government to help them. Much of what government did was hit-and-miss, for government had had no direct experience in managing the economy. Gradually, however, a theory developed by the English economist John Maynard Keynes was adopted. Keynes argued that the economy is not governed by an inherent process of equilibrium. The economy contains no principles that will produce full employment (the full use of material and human resources). Economic groups, especially business firms but also labor unions, professions, and so on, seek security and control, not competition. Thus, the economy as a whole lacks the flexibility (markets) that ensures adaptation to new conditions. Over time, there is disequilibrium; for example, savings do not all go into productive investment, demand can falter and snowball into recession and depression as business cuts back production. Thus, argued Keynes, the government has a continuous and legitimate role to play in directing the economy. Though never clear on how the government was to do this, Keynes suggested three policy options—government can keep the economy growing in a balanced manner (full employment with price stability) by acting as a consumer itself (government spending for housing or public works, etc.), by cutting taxes to give private consumers or producers more money to spend (even if it means a public deficit), and by adjusting interest rates (the price of credit) to either stimulate or slow down consumption and investment.

The Democratic and the Republican parties have both adopted Keynesianism but interpret it differently. Democrats emphasize government spending and the giving of tax cuts to individual consumers to stimulate the economy (demand-side economics) whereas Republicans reject government spending and emphasize giving tax cuts to business to stimulate economic growth (supply-side economics). However, our experience with a *mixed economy* (a private economy dependent in important ways on government activity) is not overly positive. Democratic administrations have had some success in stimulating the economy by enhancing consumer demand but have been unable to control inflation.[22] The Reagan administration of the 1980s inaugurated an approach emphasizing tax cuts for producers. Almost all analysts agree that Reagonomics did not succeed in producing more capital investment and that economic growth in the 1980s resulted from private and public debt.

Actually, investment declined during the early 1980s because the tax cuts were not targeted to produce productive investment. In 1981, the industrial sector of the American economy (for example, the steel industry) showed evidence of decay and decline, and home construction was far below needed levels. Deep tax cuts had been made to stimulate investment, but the United States Steel Company, rather than modernize its plants, bought an oil company, Coca-Cola purchased a movie studio, and Holiday Inn announced a program to build luxury hotels. The improved economy after 1982 was led by consumers (who went heavily into debt), by cheap imports (which led to trade deficits and debt to foreigners), and by government buoyed by debt.

Public economic policies tolerate a large amount of unused economic capacity. America's powerful groups fear inflation more than idle capacity. And governmental economic policies can be judged from still another perspective. An enormous backlog of needs has developed in the public sector: hospitals, sewers and sewage treatment plants, garbage disposal facilities, schools, housing, park and recreational facilities, and mass transportation. So far federal tax and credit policies and direct governmental expenditures can be characterized as *reactionary Keynesianism*—the lopsided emphasis in public economic policy on stimulating private consumption and economic activity in the early liberal faith that "free" private markets rationalize an economy and promote the general well-being. The net result has been to starve public programs and encourage, in John Kenneth Galbraith's words, "private luxury and public squalor."

Finally, despite a highly unsatisfactory employment record, little progress has been made in rationalizing our labor market (such as through job training programs). Ironically, unemployment and underemployment caused by recession, bankruptcies, technological displacement, foreign competition, and the flow of capital overseas eventually create an underclass of

---

[22]John E. Schwarz, *America's Hidden Success* (New York: W.W. Norton, 1983), argues that the Democratic party's consumer-targeted Keynesianism (during the 1960s and into the 1970s) was far more successful than we have been allowed to believe.

welfare recipients who are denounced as shiftless and made dependent wards of the state. Thus, it is apparent that federal economic policies do not run counter to the general structure of economic power, and that federal tax, spending, and monetary policies simply reflect and reinforce the American class-prestige hierarchy.

LEGISLATION, GOVERNMENT, AND MINORITIES

Government and Black Americans

The liberal universe is obviously deeply at odds with American traditions that categorize human beings in ascriptive terms (race, sex, religion, ethnicity, and age). It is undeniable that the tradition of class (liberalism) has made inroads into the "caste" structure of the United States. And there is little doubt that its primary victim, the black American, has at least begun a transition from ascriptive inequality to achievement inequality. The explicit use of power to deny blacks the vote or to segregate them socially is now illegal and in growing disuse. The basic landmarks in the abolition of "caste" boundaries are well known: armed forces integration, fair employment laws, school desegregation, and civil rights acts, especially those relating to voting and the use of public accommodations and facilities. Implementation of these decisions has, however, lagged badly. Regardless of political party, all national administrations up to the 1960s failed to carry out their clear statutory and constitutional obligation to eradicate "caste" inequality. The inaccuracy of the popular belief that the federal government is an equalizing force is readily apparent if one examines the historic role of the federal government in fostering "caste" stratification in the United States. Of course, it was state governments, reflecting the values and wishes of white power groups, that institutionalized racial segregation as a way of life in the American South. State electoral laws systematically disenfranchised black Americans, and state and local laws decreed and enforced segregation in social life.[23] But Congress and the federal government looked the other way; indeed, the federal government actually fostered segregation in the armed forces and in federally assisted housing. Meanwhile, the U.S. Supreme Court accepted and legitimized racial segregation in one decision after the other, not merely before the Civil War but also between 1865 and the 1930s. (The Court issued no major attack on segregation until *Brown* vs. *Board of Education* in 1954).

The class bias that characterizes even the most high-minded legislation, ensuring that the upper classes gain more from political life than the lower

[23]Among the prime stereotypes that distort our perception of power is the belief that "local" government is more democratic, more personal, and more responsive than the national government.

classes, is readily apparent if one examines the impact of legislation on blacks. To use an example we have already discussed, the military conscription laws and practices in effect during the Vietnam War discriminated against those who were not in college—that is, against blacks, the poor, and the working class in general. Social Security taxes and minimum ages of eligibility burden blacks unequally because they start work earlier than whites, receive incomes mostly from wages (the only taxable income) and mostly within the taxable maximum, and have larger families (thus being burdened more by the Social Security tax's lack of exemptions). Also, the life spans of blacks are shorter than the classes above them, and thus they do not collect Social Security for as long a time or, in the case of the average black male, not at all (until 1986).

The federal and state trickle-down policy in housing tends to provide housing for blacks only when it is overage; subsidized housing tends to segregate blacks (often far from jobs); and urban renewal is often tantamount to black removal. Governmental policies to stimulate the economy through subsidies, tax depreciation, and low interest rates are another version of the trickle-down philosophy, which can be expressed as "what's good for the upper classes is bound eventually to be good for the lower classes." However, such policies never seem to have much impact on black unemployment. Furthermore, governmental policies that tolerate inflation burden the poor hardest, as do policies to fight inflation, which invariably amount to socially created increases in unemployment. And the substitute for meaningful employment, the welfare system, has provided only an inadequate level of goods and services and a heavy dose of social stigma.

Fair employment laws have never contained provisions for enforcement, and their ability to create a wider range of opportunities for blacks has thus been minimal. In the 1970s, however, as an aftermath (along with sexual equality laws) of the strong civil rights laws of the mid-1960s, the government and the courts began to strike down discriminatory hiring, retention, promotion, and pay practices. The impact of these initiatives has been small, but it represents a significant departure from the hypocrisy of the past.

And, finally, to explore one area in a little more depth, governmental efforts to desegregate schools have had very mixed results. Essentially, the causes of unequal education for blacks are increasingly located beyond the jurisdiction of explicit public policy and in the realm of private life (class position). The pattern of segregation by residence (class) is quite pronounced and no changes are in sight. Black children are just as effectively segregated in public schools, despite equality before the law and equality of opportunity, as they were in the segregated schools of the southern "caste" system. And it is unlikely that the pervasive pattern of class segregation will be modified by the power dimension at the federal, state, or local levels. Not surprisingly, there is evidence that while *de jure* segregation (the overt use of power to segregate schools) has declined in the South, *de facto* educational segregation (based on class forces that segregate the races by income, occupation, and residence) has become well entrenched.

It is interesting that education is the only sector of the class dimension in which black Americans seem to have made gains relative to whites during the post-1950 period.[24] But because education seems not to be related to economic advancement for blacks in the way it is for whites, black Americans are probably expending a disproportionate amount of effort in this area. It is clear, for example, that a given amount of schooling benefits blacks much less than whites: It affords significantly less income and is no protection against the greater unemployment rates prevalent among blacks, even for college graduates. It is also significant that relative gains in education by blacks have been confined mostly to the level of high school. Ironically, the worth of a high school diploma began to decline in 1945 (about the same time that blacks began to achieve in this area) with the advent of mass higher education. And, to compound the irony, blacks are now exerting themselves against great odds at the level of undergraduate education just as the bachelor's degree is undergoing a relative decline in value and postgraduate degrees have begun to be the educational credential for acquiring positions in the upper classes.

Government and Mexican Americans

Much of what has been said about black Americans' relations to legislation and government also holds true for Mexican Americans.[25] Therefore, after briefly noting these similarities, we will turn our attention to novel features in the Mexican American's relation to public law and authority.

Mexican Americans, like all others at the lower levels of society, are not affected equitably by laws passed and administered by those who dominate the political process. Laws passed for the benefit of typical Americans (such as the Social Security Act) affect those who are below typical levels differently, and usually unequally. National economic policies designed either to stimulate or restrain the economy affect Mexican Americans adversely since they, like all working and lower class people, bear the brunt of economic stagnation and inflation.

Furthermore, Mexican Americans have borne (and still bear) a series of hardships, ranging from minor embarrassment to physical brutality, peculiar to their unique status in American society.[26] As an aggregate, Mexican

---

[24]Relative gains *within* the class system should not be confused with progress in overcoming "caste" barriers blocking blacks' entry *into* the class system.

[25]For the class position of Mexican Americans, see Chapter 9.

[26]For much of the following, see Leo Grebler, et al., *The Mexican-American People: The Nation's Second Largest Minority* (New York: Free Press, 1970), chap. 21; Joan Moore with Harry Pachon, 2nd ed., *Mexican-Americans* (Englewood Cliffs, N.J.: Prentice-Hall, 1976), chap. 8; and Joan Moore and Harry Pachon, *Hispanics in the United States* (Englewood Cliffs, N.J.: Prentice-Hall, 1985), chap. 10.

Americans' legal status as citizens has been continuously challenged and/or ignored by the federal government (Border Patrol), local law enforcement agencies, and even welfare departments. American citizens of Mexican descent are indiscriminately lumped together with Mexicans who have entered the United States illegally, and they are constantly required to prove their legal status. During the 1930s, welfare departments throughout the country even helped to "repatriate" thousands of American citizens of Mexican origin who were on welfare, making no attempt to distinguish between citizen and noncitizen.

Governmental agencies tend to have poor relations with working-class and lower-class people because of the incompatibility of the impersonality and better education of civil servants and the greater personalism and ignorance of the lower classes. This relation is aggravated in the case of Mexican Americans because of a language barrier and because government in general, never having helped them—indeed, having mistreated them—is viewed with suspicion, hostility, and withdrawal.

Mexican Americans have a great deal of trouble with government, partly because laws are passed that ignore them, partly because laws are not enforced, and partly because laws designed to protect American citizens are broken or ignored in their case. To take an important example, some Mexican Americans earn their living grazing sheep; when laws are passed establishing national parks and regulating the use of park land, recreation and aesthetic pleasure for the upper classes are purchased at the expense of Mexican Americans. State employment bureaus typically think of themselves as agents of employers, and even break laws regulating minimum wages. And local law enforcement agencies, from vigilante groups to the Texas Rangers to the Los Angeles Police Department, have long histories of unconstitutional behavior toward Mexican Americans, including violence and brutality. The relation between law enforcement agencies and minorities will be touched upon again in Chapter 16; it is sufficient here to indicate that law enforcement officials have a long history of siding in economic matters with property owners against Mexican American workers, even when it means breaking or ignoring the law.

The United States Commission on Civil Rights has documented the United States' drastically unequal and discriminatory educational policies toward Mexican American children. Mexican American children go to schools that are ethnically unbalanced, and do less well in their studies and drop out more than do majority students. Schools not only do not welcome or reinforce the language and culture of Mexican Americans but Spanish is actively suppressed, and little effort is made to recognize the language barrier in dealing with children or parents. Indeed, the Mexican American community is ignored by the schools when involving parents in education, setting up advisory boards, and hiring consultants. And Mexican Americans are deeply discriminated against in the financing of schools; much less is spent on Mexican American children; Mexican American communities bear a heavier tax burden for education, and Mexican Americans are not represented on school boards in proportion to their numbers, even in predominantly Mexican American communities.[27]

Some modifications in Mexican American education have occurred in recent years, mostly bilingual pilot projects (the attempt to use Spanish in school in order to facilitate the learning of English). But so far no great improvements can be noted. And given a dismal record at the lower levels, American higher education is also remarkably unattended or understaffed by Mexican Americans.

The Mexican American has been virtually ignored by the federal government (except the Border Patrol). During the unrest of the 1960s, Mexican Americans came to the attention of Congress and the executive branch for the first time. (So ignorant was Congress that an early report on "Mexican American Affairs" was sent to the Foreign Affairs Committee.) The Mexican American's difficulty in gaining attention and help from government was changed somewhat by the antipoverty efforts of the 1960s. Under the Community Action Program, federal money was granted directly to Mexican American organizations—that is, to groups aware of the special needs of a distinct linguistic-ethnic group. For the first time, Mexican Americans had the opportunity to act on their own behalf and to develop the skills to help themselves and to deal with government. For the first time, they had become a constituency for federal legislators and administrators, which is an important prerequisite to acquiring political power and thus governmental attention and assistance. The political consciousness and power of Mexican Americans has grown, and by the late 1980s they had become a force to be reckoned with in both local and national politics (for current developments in the politics of Mexican Americans, Cuban Americans, and Puerto Ricans, see F. Chris Garcia, ed., *Latinos and the Political System*, Notre Dame, Ind.: University of Notre Dame Press, 1988).

Women

The enhancement of civil rights has benefitted women but not equally. The main beneficiaries of the women's movement have been women in the

---

[27]U.S. Civil Rights Commission, *Mexican American Educational Series*, "Report I. Ethnic Isolation of Mexican Americans in the Public Schools of the Southwest" (April 1971); "Report II. The Unfinished Education: Outcomes for Minorities in Five Southwestern States" (October 1971); "Report III. The Excluded Student: Educational Practices Affecting Mexican Americans in the Southwest" (May 1972); "Report IV. Mexican American Education in Texas—A Function of Wealth" (August 1972). All are available from the U.S. Government Printing Office, Washington, D.C.

upper classes. The issue of abortion (legalized in 1973) illustrates this class basis of public policy in regard to women—public funds for abortion are no longer available, which means that abortion is subject to class forces—those with money can get abortions, those without can't (for a fuller discussion of the middle-class nature of the women's movement, see Chapter 9).

Legislation to help women in the working and lower classes has faltered (for example, paid maternity leave, child-care). Even the inadequate health care for the lower classes has declined with cutbacks in Medicare, Medicaid, and programs to help low-income pregnant women.

The Handicapped

The handicapped received public support with the passage of the Rehabilitation Act in 1973 and the Special Education Act of 1975. However, these laws have neither been enforced nor fully funded and progress has been slow. And failure to enforce the occupational health and safety laws and in general provide a safer social environment mean that the number of handicapped will continue to increase.

CLASS AND FOREIGN ECONOMIC POLICY

By and large, post–World War II American governments have pursued a policy of free trade in international economic affairs. This philosophy is identical to domestic laissez-faire ideology—all should compete by doing what they do best (the doctrine of comparative advantage) and the result will be a rational domestic and international division of labor. This no more works on the international level than it does on the domestic. The doctrine of free enterprise hides a great many class-related phenomena. First, a huge amount of American capital went overseas from 1945 on, thus contributing to enormous problems for American workers, small farmers, small businesspeople, and older cities. By and large, American multinational corporations have prospered on a global basis even though the American economy has suffered in terms of job losses, loss of good jobs, and declining competitiveness.[28] Second, there is a vast network of protectionism beneath the rhetoric of free trade. Corporations and workers have benefitted from protectionism depending on the strength of the affected industries—textiles, shoes, steel, automobiles, computer chips, and so on. The voluntary agreement by Japan to limit its exports of automobiles was really a way for American manufacturers to raise the price of their cars by roughly $1,000 to $1,500 each.

[28]Robert E. Lipsey and Irving B. Kravis, "Business Holds Its Own as America Slips," *The New York Times*, January 18, 1987, p. F3.

CLASS AND FOREIGN POLITICAL AND MILITARY POLICY

The United States government maintains a vast military establishment both at home and around the globe to protect and further American interests (by latest count, it has 389 military bases abroad). Often framed in moral terms, the display of military might and alliances such as NATO, SEATO, and the Organization of American States are essentially ways to protect and enhance the United States' position in the world-market economy. The United States is massively dependent upon foreign resources to run its industrial economy, and it needs overseas markets for its goods, capital, services, and surplus food and staples. Like all modern societies, the United States cannot exist without relatively continuous economic growth, and economic growth is not possible unless its access to world markets is unhampered. In short, it is vital to American society that international trade is unhampered, that sea lanes are kept open, and that many diverse societies remain friendly and compliant to its wishes.

The most dramatic examples of the class basis of the policies of the United States government are its efforts (often secretive and illegal) to influence the internal politics of friendly countries (for example, the U.S. Central Intelligence Agency has a long history of contributing money to Italy's capitalist political parties), or to prevent the establishment of socialist and communist societies, as witness its actions in Russia (1917), China, Cuba, and Chile.[29] Less well known and often misunderstood are the elaborate tax and tariff laws that facilitate the penetration of American capital abroad, and the foreign aid programs that tie other countries to American technology and services. Very little of American foreign aid is given away as a gift, though there is a widespread impression that this is so. American foreign aid is primarily a subsidy to American business and professions (the impact on labor is mixed because jobs are won and lost through foreign aid) and a way for American capital to trade and invest abroad. Foreign aid invariably stipulates that foreign countries must buy American products and use American services such as engineering firms. This not only promotes sales on a long-term basis, since replacement parts must come from the United States, but prevents recipient countries from developing their own engineering and other skills.

Foreign aid also consists of providing money for various international lending agencies. The United States government participates in and is a preponderant influence in a number of international agencies such as the World Bank, the International Monetary Fund, and the Asian Development

[29]For the actions of the United States government (in conjunction with major American corporations) that helped to overthrow socialism in Chile, see James Petras and Morris Moreley, *The United States and Chile: Imperialism and the Allende Government* (New York: Monthly Review Press, 1975).

Bank. Essentially capitalist institutions, these agencies promote development along capitalist lines in Third-World nations by lending money primarily to finance the construction of ports, electric power plants, highways, and other facilities essential to trade and investment.

American immigration policies also reflect class interests. The United States imported approximately 40 million people during the period between its War of Independence and World War I to labor in its developing industrial economy. The large flow of illegal aliens since World War II may be curbed by the Immigration Act of 1986, which will penalize employers who use them. The United States also imports large numbers of professionals, relying, for example, on doctors trained abroad to make up significant portions of its hospital staffs.[30]

The United States also encourages exports—for example, through low-cost government loans (Export-Import Bank), government insurance against investment loss, and through its tax laws. Aid to investment abroad is explicit American policy. An empirical analysis has largely substantiated the radical claim that private investment by American companies and economic and military aid by the American government have a common feature: The recipient countries have compliant right-wing governments.[31] The United States has also developed some (small) payment and retraining programs to cushion American workers against the loss of jobs due to foreign competition. It also protects a large number of American industries not so much through tariffs but through voluntary agreements, in effect, allowing private corporations in foreign countries and the United States to divide up markets, raise prices, and keep the gains at the expense of American consumers.

American Leadership in Linking Class Interests Within the Capitalist World

From the beginning of the century to the 1970s, the United States gradually assumed the leadership of the capitalist world. Foremost among its objectives was to further the interests of American banks and manufacturers. The Marshall Plan, which brought Europe to its feet after World War II, was part of this process. By the 1960s the European powers were able to assert some independence, and the United States began to lose its clear dominance.[32]

---

[30]For data showing a substantial brain drain from less-developed countries into the United States, the United Kingdom, Canada, and Australia, see Jagdish Bhagwate, "The Brain Drain," *International Social Science Journal* 28, no. 4 (1976): 691–729.

[31]Steven J. Rosen, "The Open Door Imperative and U.S. Foreign Policy," in Steven J. Rosen and James R. Kurth, eds., *Testing Theories of Economic Imperialism* (Lexington, Mass.: Lexington Books, 1974), chap. 6.

[32]For background details on this overall process, see Kees Van der Pijl, *The Making of an Atlantic Ruling Class* (London: Verso, 1984).

In a related analysis, Michael Useem has shown the extensive cooperation that exists between core elements in American and British capitalism and their successful efforts to maintain profit margins against the demands of their respective populations for greater public spending on mass welfare (the Thatcher and Reagan governments of the 1980s).[33]

The Relative Decline of American Capitalism

A basic theme in American foreign policy since World War II is its unwavering support for Great Britain, France, and Portugal as these nations struggled in vain to suppress independence movements in their colonies. To a considerable extent the United States has succeeded in replacing British power in Canada, Egypt, and Saudi Arabia. It is struggling with only mixed results to replace British power in Greece, Turkey, and Palestine. It has failed in Iran, has been relatively unsuccessful in Africa, and suffered a heavy defeat trying to replace France in Vietnam. In addition to its huge military establishment, the United States conducts elaborate programs both at home and abroad to train the military and police forces of compliant and friendly countries. The United States also participates in the United Nations but no longer finds it the compliant instrument of Western interests that it was before the 1960s. By the 1980s, the United States was casting far more single negative votes on UN resolutions than any other nation.[34]

The basic dilemmas of American economic and foreign policy stem largely from its own actions (and from those of other Western countries). The instability of most Third-World countries stems from economic change induced by the impact of Western capital. The development of a cash-crop export economy dispossesses people from the land and leaves them easy prey for radicals. When landed and other oligarchies refuse to institute political and economic reforms, regimes become unstable and the United States rushes in (claiming that Soviet communism is to blame). To soothe public opinion and to keep American aid coming, regimes promise reforms but few are delivered (for a classic case, see the section on El Salvador in Chapter 3).

America's problems in foreign policy are also aggravated by its relative decline in power. In 1950 the United States had 40 percent of the total world production. By the 1980s, while its economy had continued to grow in absolute terms, its share of world production had dropped to 20 percent. Many of its problems stem from the inability of the American upper classes to under-

---

[33]Michael Useem, *The Inner Circle: Large Corporations and the Rise of Business Political Activity in the U.S. and U.K.* (New York: Oxford University Press, 1984).

[34]For the deep isolation of the United States in the United Nations, see Miguel Marin-Bosch, "How Nations Vote in the General Assembly of the United Nations," *International Organization* 41 (Autumn 1987): 705–724.

stand and adjust to this relative decline, which, in effect, means that it must share power with Europe, Japan, the Soviet Union, and others.

American foreign policy in the 1980s veered to the right. The Reagan administration began a massive military buildup, which, combined with large tax cuts, caused an abnormal and what appears to be a chronic federal deficit. The military buildup had no coherent policy behind it and consists of buying and developing every conceivable weapon system to cope with every contingency (this is a policy, of course, but not very practical since no nation is wealthy enough to afford it). America's military buildup also means a reduction in the use of economic and political means to bolster our allies and sway the uncommitted. In addition to its refusal to cooperate with our friends, the Reagan administration conducted economic warfare against the Soviet Union, in effect escalating the economic warfare against Cuba and Vietnam. This served only to harm American businesses and to outrage our European allies, which were especially incensed by our efforts to force the European subsidaries of American corporations not to trade with the USSR.

The ineptness of the Reagan administration led to a major political defeat in the Middle East when the United States acquiesced in Israel's invasion of Lebanon in 1982. Our isolation in the world increased because of our policies in Central America, the Middle East, and our failure to sign the Law of the Sea Treaty. The United States' success in placing first-strike missiles in Europe was a defeat for the Soviet Union, but it only highlighted our reliance on military force, our reluctance to negotiate arms control, and the American government's disregard for the majority of the American people who wanted a nuclear freeze. The Reagan administration's open policy of trying to overthrow the government of Nicaragua (as well as its illegal continuation of that policy) was a continuing source of embarrassment to the United States. In 1984 the Reagan administration announced that it would restrict population planning funds to private international organizations that perform or promote abortion (all this was done without congressional approval and contradicted American public opinion). The Reagan administration argued that economic growth through private enterprise was the solution to population problems. All population experts agreed that this policy would be disastrous and would undo years of effort to bring world population under control.

CLASS AND CULTURAL IMPERIALISM: EDUCATION, CHURCHES, FOUNDATIONS, AND MASS AND ELITE MEDIA

Class action is rarely suspected in the activities of educational groups, churches, foundations, philanthropies, news media, and so on because such groups are generally regarded as nonpartisan. Critics have argued, however, that the extension of American (or Western) educational principles to other societies amounts to neocolonialism.[35] Colonial nations such as England and France have a long tradition of educating at home the leaders of their colonies. Today the United States educates large numbers of foreigners: In 1985/1986 it had 343,780 foreign students, approximately 80 percent of the total coming from developing countries.[36] The major suppliers of foreign students in the United States are Iran, Taiwan, Malaysia, South Korea, India, Canada, Iraq, China, Nigeria, Japan, and Hong Kong.

Cultural imperialism takes many forms. The role of missionaries, technical-aid teams, exchange programs, foundations, philanthropies, and the news, publishing, and entertainment media are undoubtedly supportive of class values but their impact has not been studied systematically. There is little question that the United States has a large impact abroad through its entertainers, films and other mass-media materials, novelists, and athletes, and that it dominates global trade (outside the socialist countries) in television programs, films, books, magazines, and scholarly journals.[37] The content of American books, films, and television programs is often nationalistic and racist but such biases have declined as foreign sales have become more important to media producers. American publishers, however, continue to print books in languages and about subjects that correspond to the interests of privileged native elites.[38]

Cultural imperialism takes place in unsuspected ways. Textbooks and the media distort our image of foreign nations and people. Western literature has promoted ethnocentrism in the West and has created myths about the white man's burden.[39] American best-sellers about Asia in the twentieth century have given Americans a twisted view of all Asian peoples and societies.[40] The Western scholarly tradition has also biased the West's perception of other peoples, and, in turn, its perception of itself. Anthropology

---

[35]For general background, see Martin Carnoy, *Education as Cultural Imperialism* (New York: David McKay, 1974), and Ali A. Mazrin, "The African University as a Multinational Corporation: Problems of Penetration and Dependency," *Harvard Educational Review* 45 (May 1975): 191–210. For a history of the Ford, Rockefeller, and Carnegie foundations' educational policies toward Africa and a charge that they furthered American corporate rather than African interests, see Edward H. Berman, "Foundations, United States Foreign Policy, and African Education, 1945–1975," *Harvard Educational Review* 49 (May 1979): 145–179 (with brief but vigorous responses from foundation officials—pp. 180–184).

[36]*The Chronicle of Higher Education*, 30 (October 22, 1986), p. 34.

[37]Richard P. Nielsen, "International Trade and Policy in Mass Media Materials: Television Programs, Films, Books, and Magazines," *Culture* 3, No. 3, pp. 196–205 (UNESCO, 1976).

[38]Philip G. Altbach, "Literary Colonialism: Books in the Third World," *Harvard Educational Review* 45 (May 1975): 226–236.

[39]Jonah Raskin, *The Mythology of Imperialism: Kipling, Conrad, Forster, Lawrence, Carey* (New York: Random House, 1971).

[40]Daniel B. Ramsdell, "Asia Askew: U.S. Best-Sellers on Asia, 1931–1980," *Bulletin of Concerned Asia Scholars* 15 (October-December 1983): 2–25.

supplied information that furthered the ends of colonial administrators.[41] The West's main scholarly tradition, especially in England, France, and the United States (claims Edward Said), also created a fictitious Oriental world (encompassing the Middle East, parts of Africa, and all of Asia), which served largely to further the ends of colonialism.[42] The late nineteenth century also witnessed the spread of ethnocentrism to the general public through the medium of ethnographic exhibits,[43] the spread of mass education, and the rise of the yellow press. Even today, argues Edward Said, the mass media have a narrow and biased view of the world, as witness their handling of the Iranian crisis, especially from 1979 to 1981.[44]

The Rockefeller Foundation's sponsorship of agricultural research to spur food production in Third-World countries illustrates how "objective" research sponsored by "public interest" foundations can create more problems than it solves. The Rockefeller Foundation's agricultural research centers developed high-yield hybrid plants, the basis of the Green Revolution in the developing countries. High-yield plants require fertilizer, irrigation, and considerable technology; as a result the Green Revolution has everywhere led to high land concentration, the displacement of millions of families, massive Third-World unemployment, hunger, and dependence.[45]

As noted earlier (Chapter 12), a number of private voluntary groups exercise considerable influence in foreign affairs: the Council on Foreign Relations, The Committee for Economic Development, and a number of research corporations and institutes. All are basically financed by large corporations, their membership is drawn exclusively from the world of big business along with a few lawyers and university presidents, their members have often served in government foreign policy posts, they recruit candidates for government service, and their research reports and research grants play an important role in shaping public policy.[46]

---

[41]Talal Asad, ed., *Anthropology and the Colonial Encounter* (New York: Humanities Press, 1973); Roy F. Ellen, "The Development of Anthropology and Colonial Policy in the Netherlands: 1800–1960," *Journal of the History of the Behavioral Sciences* 12 (1976): 303–324; and Gerrit Huizer and Bruce Mannheim, eds., *The Politics of Anthropology: From Colonialism and Sexism Toward a View from Below* (The Hague: Mouton, 1979).

[42]Edward W. Said, *Orientalism* (New York: Pantheon, 1978).

[43]William Schneider, "Race and Empire: The Rise of Popular Ethnography in the Late Nineteenth Century," *Journal of Popular Culture* 11 (Summer 1977): 98–109 and "Colonies at the 1900 World Fair," *History Today* 31 (May 1981): 31–36.

[44]Edward W. Said, *Covering Islam,* (New York: Pantheon, 1981).

[45]For background on the widespread misery produced by Western, especially American, agricultural aid, and for a critical analysis of the rationalizations that cover American policies, see Susan George, *How the Other Half Dies* (Montclair, N.J.: Allan Held and Osmun, 1977). George shrewdly notes the connection between fertilizer and the Rockefeller oil interests. For a radical but balanced critique of the Green Revolution and for alternative strategies, see Bernhard Glaeser, ed., *The Green Revolution Revised* (London: Allen and Unwin, 1987).

[46]For an analysis from a conflict perspective, see G. William Domhoff, *Who Rules America Now?* (Englewood Cliffs, N.J.: Prentice-Hall, 1983), Chap. 4.

THE CLASS-PRESTIGE NATURE OF LEGISLATION AND GOVERNMENT: A SUMMARY

In *The Federalist Papers*, number 10, James Madison argued that individuals are unequal by nature, that natural inequality leads to economic inequality, that economic inequality leads to conflict, and that the proper province of government is to mediate and regulate (not change or eliminate) economic differences and disputes. Our own view is that explaining inequality by invoking human nature is a dubious enterprise. Nonetheless, American society is not only based on this view but has institutionalized Madison's political prescription for coping with inequality. Our analysis of federal legislation and its administration indicates that Madison's view, however dubious from the standpoint of science, accurately describes the performance of American political institutions. Government acts to soften and update inequality, not to curtail it and certainly not to eradicate it. In a sense, of course, government can only reflect the society that spawned it. But the American power dimension is charged with high moral purpose, often expressed in dynamic language. We are constantly led to believe, in other words, that government can and does change things; thus, it is important to note that it does not and probably cannot do this unless major changes are made in the American political system.

In assessing the relation between class-prestige forces and legislation, therefore, we must be careful not to overestimate the independence or power of the power dimension. This subject is exceedingly complex, and generalizations must be made with extreme caution. One conclusion, however, seems to have at least a tentative validity: During the course of American history, political institutions appear to have done little to change the positions of the various groups in the hierarchies of class and prestige. Basic changes and displacements have come about largely as results of economic expansion and inadvertent governmental action. (For example, the government helped to open up the West by subsidizing canals and railroads and by granting homesteads.) In point of fact, our political institutions either register changes in class or prestige or operate to forestall change. (For example, the economic decline of farmers has been arrested by their political strength.) Thus, it is especially important to exercise caution with regard to the role of the federal government vis-à-vis class and prestige forces.

In examining federal legislation in the areas of taxation, Social Security, housing, education, and economic policy, the conclusions are inescapable that government changes very little and that politics, legislation, and government are the handmaidens of the class-prestige hierarchy. Actually, an examination of other areas can only support the conclusion that the power dimension is an auxiliary of the American class and prestige hierarchies. Highway legislation, urban renewal, support for the humanities and arts, funds for pre- and postdoctoral faculty research in science, funds for medicine and mental

health, disaster aid,[47] small business loans, the enforcement of safety regulations, antipollution standards, labor legislation, and minimum wage laws are
all heavily slanted in favor of the upper classes. And nothing at the local and
state levels runs counter to this pattern; if anything, the class-prestige nature
of government is even more pronounced and apparent at these lower levels.

Thus far, political action has not changed the relative position of
America's minorities except to reduce racism and sexism. By and large, the
civil rights movement has merely brought racial and ethnic groups and
women into the capitalist labor force.

America's foreign economic, political-military, and cultural policies
have all furthered the interests and values of the American upper classes.

---

[47]Both public and private agencies give help to disaster victims in amounts in keeping
with the latter's class-prestige standings.

CHAPTER 16

The Class-Prestige Nature of Law and Deviance

In exploring the relation between law and the hierarchies of class and prestige, our main concern is to see whether the law affects the American population uniformly. More specifically, we want to determine whether obedience and disobedience to the law have anything to do with social class. In enforcing the law and administering justice, does the state—represented by police officers, prosecutors, juries, defense attorneys, judges, court officials and professional auxiliaries, and prison officials—treat individuals equally or in keeping with their positions in the class and prestige hierarchies? In other words, are the agencies of power that specialize in maintaining the law impartial in their treatment of the American people? Or, in short, is there equality before the law?

The law has always been an instrument for upholding the established order, and the modern legal system is no exception. Law in capitalist society is deeply slanted in favor of political authority, middle- and upper-class morality, and established economic interests and rights. We will begin our analysis of the relation between law and class society with a brief depiction of the American legal system and a discussion of both the functional and the conflict views of the law.

THE AMERICAN LEGAL SYSTEM

Americans have great respect for the law and associate it with fundamental values such as personal liberty and social unity. They also associate it with orderly change and social adaptation. To serve these important values the American legal system rests on a number of basic premises. One, Americans distinguish between ordinary laws and constitutional law with the former subject to the latter. Two, all laws can be changed should the need arise. And three, conscience and intellect are respected against law in that individuals can speak against laws they don't like and are protected against self-incrimination or arbitrary acts by the state.

The American legal system has a number of other distinguishing features. The United States has far more lawyers per capita and far more of them employed in private practice than in other countries. American law is subject to the power of money probably far more than any other developed society. Private groups with money exert a powerful influence on the creation of law by legislatures and government officials. The services of lawyers must be purchased, which means that those with money get more and better legal services. And while Americans respect the law in the abstract, they are also great lawbreakers and dispute the law in great numbers both in and out of courtrooms.

All of the above is understandable given the main thrust of America's social development:

1. an unprecedented commitment to individual rights;
2. an unprecedented incitement to material gain through competition;
3. a dynamic economic development that quickly outgrew custom and religion as sources of dispute resolution;
4. slavery and immigration, which diversified the American population and further undermined customary sources of social control and conflict resolution;
5. the inexpensiveness of law (the loser pays nothing in court or legal fees);
6. lofty, expansive constitutional ideals and a difficult and expensive-to-influence political system have prompted Americans to turn economic and political grievances into legal issues.

FUNCTIONAL AND CONFLICT IMAGES OF LAW

Elites uniformly regard law as the product of a society based on consensus. Law, they argue, reflects the considered judgment of the community and is thus binding on the community. Functionalist sociologists tend to agree, emphasizing the contribution of law to social stability, justice, and adjustment. Despite faults, law embodies our highest moral values and seeks goals that most agree on. Law as a set of procedures guarantees everyone a fair hearing and protects us against arbitrary state action. When law breaks new ground it does so in terms of values that people accept. True, there are many conflicting opinions about laws and the judicial process, but this is because law is in the thick of things busy solving problems and helping individuals, groups, and society adapt to new conditions. The law may lag behind society but that is not necessarily bad since it forces people to think before they act. The established classes and most lawyers accept this view of law.

Conflict theorists agree that the law is a stabilizing, integrative force, but, they argue, this serves to protect both the good and the bad in the status quo. Law is always and everywhere primarily an instrument for legitimating and supporting existing power groups be they priesthoods, landed aristocracies, businesspeople and professionals, or dictatorships. The development of American law during the late colonial and early republican period (to cite one conflict legal theorist) clearly reflected the interests and needs of America's emerging commercial and industrial classes. American law has been intimately associated with their interests ever since (see Box 16–1, "The Partisan Nature of Objective Law").

Americans break the law in large numbers and engage in litigation far more than other people, argue conflict theorists, precisely because the law does *not* rest on consensus. Legislatures enact ambiguous, vague, and contradictory laws, not because legislatures cannot write clearly but because legislatures themselves do not rest on consensus. Law, argue conflict theorists, is an expression of power. While it may sometimes express the common interest, law mostly expresses the interests of the strong and neglects the interests of the weak.

All this leads to poor law enforcement. Laws expressing a consensus often lack enforcement teeth (for example, fair employment and occupational safety laws). Though there is consensus on the need for law and order, the most important forms of criminal behavior cannot be controlled because they are being done by powerful business and professional groups often in conjunction with public officials.

Many of the deficiencies of the American legal system have been summarized by Derek C. Bok.[1] Bok charges that American law (for example, labor law, antitrust law, workplace safety regulations) cannot be related to the public interest (to verifiable results in each specific area). Legal scholars do little research into the legal system as such. The legal field, like medicine, is succumbing to bigness. The United States, says Bok, has far more lawyers than any other industrialized society, not only channelling huge numbers of able people away from fields in which they are needed, but once in place these lawyers (like surplus surgeons) create work whether needed or not. The legal

---

[1]Derek C. Bok, "A Flawed System," *Harvard Magazine* (May-June 1983): 38 ff. Bok, president of Harvard University, is a former dean of Harvard Law School.

BOX 16–1.   *THE PARTISAN NATURE OF OBJECTIVE LAW*

Legal historians and philosophers have portrayed American law as an objective, apolitical, and autonomous code of norms. Despite disagreements, say between Roscoe Pound and Oliver Wendell Holmes, American jurisprudence has argued that the development of American law is marked by consensus and that its outcome serves the common good. Even when legal analysts have seen the law in relation to economic and political developments, they have tended to adopt a functional and consensus approach in their interpretations. However, a minority of legal historians has argued that law is better seen from a conflict perspective. M. J. Horwitz,[2] for example, argues that American law was drastically altered during the formative years of the Republic primarily through judicial interpretations. The eighteenth century regarded law as stemming from community customs derived from natural law. Property meant the absolute right to enjoy something and to be able to prevent others from interfering with that enjoyment. From 1780 to 1860, argues Horwitz, the legal conception of property was drastically altered to mean that one had the right to develop and use property *regardless of injuries to others.*

Not surprisingly, argues Horwitz, the changed meaning of property was accompanied by a change in the meaning of a contract. In the eighteenth century a contract had to be fair and could be set aside if it wasn't. By the mid-nineteenth century, a contract was enforceable *even if its provisions were patently unfair.* The law was simply reflecting a fact of economic life: Strong commercial and industrial interests were using their competitive advantages to exploit smaller businesses, consumers, and workers, and they legalized their exploitation by putting it in the form of a contract. They also protected their economic power by getting the courts to reduce their responsibility for damages (in keeping with the new dictum that the central meaning of property was the right to develop it), and juries gradually had the power to make judgments and award damages on the basis of fairness curtailed. Once all this had been accomplished, legal philosophers who earlier had argued in the name of utility and progress then obscured the resulting changes by arguing that law is neutral, objective, and apolitical.

Why was all this permitted by a people who thought of themselves as living in a democracy? For one thing, the United States did not introduce universal male suffrage until the 1850s, that is, until *after* the new legal structures had been established. But perhaps the best explanation lies in the fact that the law was being shaped to benefit the dynamic property groups in the American economy. It suited the needs of an industrial capitalism and it was difficult to argue against the seemingly plausible assumption that economic growth was good for everyone. And those for whom it wasn't good—small manufacturers, small retailers, small farmers, consumers, and workers—were too weak and disorganized to do much about it.

---

[2]*The Transformation of American Law, 1780–1860* (Cambridge, Mass.: Harvard University Press, 1977).

system caters to the rich and powerful and neglects the interests of the middle class and the poor. Law schools have done little to counter all this—legal education, or learning how to think like a lawyer, means memorizing unique cases and knowing how to find variations in detail. Teaching students to think like lawyers, argues Bok, "has helped to produce a legal system that is among the most expensive and least efficient in the world." Ironically, concludes Bok, "the blunt inexcusable fact is that this nation, which prides itself on its efficiency and justice, has developed a legal system that is the most expensive in the world, yet cannot manage to protect the rights of most its citizens."

Though one must be careful to balance conflict and functional perspectives when assessing the law, it is probably best to assume that the main consequence of law is to uphold the status quo. This is especially important for Americans to remember because their legal tradition tends to depict law as the cutting edge of freedom, progress, and reform. Most Americans and certainly most upper-level Americans have an image of American society as an arena of free behavior bounded by a framework of impartial, commonly accepted legal rules. However, in recent years the most creative work in the sociology of law has been to view law and legal behavior from a conflict rather than a functional perspective. Perhaps the best way to understand the conflict perspective is to assume that legal rights are often empty formalities and that legal reform is more likely to modernize power relations than to change them.

MIDDLE-CLASS VALUES AND DEVIANCE

Class, Universal Goals, and Deviant Behavior

Sociologists have long recognized that a great deal, if not most, of deviant (abnormal) behavior is caused by the normal demands society places on its members. Conforming or trying to conform to social norms is, in other words, the prime cause of nonconformity. Perhaps the most ironic characteristic of American society is the way in which its rationalistic culture produces nonrational and irrational behavior. The American achievement ethic monopolizes the definition of identity (economic success) and stipulates the means to achieve it (the Protestant-bourgeois virtues).[3] When this moral universalism is promulgated within a deeply structured class system, which by definition cannot allow all to be successful, there are generated social pressures for individuals to acquire success illegitimately (innovation, basically crime) or to compensate for the lack of success (ritualism and retreatism). Robert Merton's depiction of the five ways in which people can respond

---

[3]This is a reference, of course, to Robert K. Merton's classic analysis, "Social Structure and Anomie," *American Sociological Review* 3 (October 1938): 672–682.

TABLE 16-1.   The Five Modes of Adjustment in a Class-Stratified Society to a
Universal Success Goal[a]

		UNIVERSAL GOAL OF SUCCESS	ACCEPTABLE METHODS OF ACHIEVING SUCCESS	PREDICTABLE RESPONSES IN A STRATIFIED SOCIETY
I	Conformity	+	+	Diligent, law-abiding citizens, dynamic Protestant-bourgeois achievers
II	Innovation	+	−	White- & blue-collar criminals
III	Ritualist	−	+	Formalism among elites, uncreative majority
IV	Retreatist	−	−	Dropping out, alcoholism, mental illness, suicide
V	Rebellion	±	±	Revolutionary middle class in past, socialist today

[a]Symbol equivalents are: (+ signifies acceptance, (−) signifies elimination, and (±) signifies rejection and substitution of new goals and standards.

Source: Adapted from Robert K. Merton, "Social Structure and Anomie," *American Sociological Review* 3 (October 1938): 676. Examples of predictable responses are mine.

to cultural goals and the institutional means for achieving them is illustrated in Table 16–1.

Society's response to deviant behavior (categories II–V in Table 16–1) is to pass laws, often of a type that make the deviance criminal. Innovation and rebellion are heavily criminalized, and if one thinks of some forms of vagrancy, gambling, and drugtaking as retreatism, it too has been criminalized. (Ritualism is heavily stigmatized and ridiculed morally by means of such epithets as *parasite, hack, bureaucrat, pencil-pusher*, and the like.) In sum, the deviant American is no aberration of human nature but an outcome of identifiable social variables.

Middle-Class Morality and the Creation of Crime

As we have suggested, middle-class morality and its legalization is a prime source of crime. To understand this process, one must view crime as a socially defined act, rather than as an intrinsic thing-in-itself. Illustrations of the socio-cultural context of crime are easy to cite. In ancient Athens, Socrates' free thinking was judged criminal; in the United States freedom of thought is a constitutional right. A prime example of the creation of crime through the legalization of a moral position is Prohibition. A rural-religious middle-class movement, whose morality differed from that of the urban middle class, the lower classes, and even the upper class, succeeded in out-lawing the use of alcoholic beverages, and during the 1920s the United States experienced a great deal of crime as Americans in large numbers circumvented Prohibition.

Middle-class morality—heavily influenced by biopsychic explanations, agrarian values, nationalism, and religion—has at one time or another come to view a large assortment of behavior as immoral, and consequently made it illegal. Middle-class sexual morality, for example, has in combination with other forces made abortion, birth control, and various sexual values and practices (homosexuality, pornography, prostitution) criminal offenses. Middleclass morality's emphasis on work and productivity also gave rise to vagrancy laws, which defined certain forms of idleness and poverty as criminal offenses. The liberal emphasis on self-control and belief in a rational, predictable universe led to laws that treat gambling, alcoholism, and drug use as criminal offenses.

The need to lengthen the period of youth and to keep the statuses of young people abstract, so that they can be kept abreast of new knowledge and prepared for new and more demanding occupations, has enhanced the potential for deviant behavior among the male young in industrial society. Anthony M. Platt has charged that upper-middle-class reformers (mostly women) invented the concept of *juvenile delinquency* and the judicial process that regulates it largely to protect their own values. According to Platt, many forms of youthful behavior have been labeled delinquent that are innocent enough and unindictable when engaged in by adults. Furthermore, this reform movement helped to consolidate the paternalistic and dependent legal status from which youth still suffer.[4]

Thus, it is difficult to escape the conclusion that crime is largely a product of society and its power groups, a view attested to by the history of criminal law. A good example of the way in which power groups translate their interests and values into law is the English law of vagrancy. In 1349 the first vagrancy statute made it a crime for any citizen to give charity to the unemployed and for an unemployed person to refuse to work for anyone who requested his labor. Quite clearly, this law was passed on behalf of landowners who were losing their supply of cheap labor to competition from a growing commercial and manufacturing town economy; in short, it was intended as a substitute for serfdom. When no longer needed, the law became dormant, only to be revived after 1500 in an effort to control the growing crime problem. The association of idleness (lack of employment) with crime persisted into modern times in both Great Britain and the United States.[5]

[4]Anthony M. Platt, *The Child Savers: The Invention of Delinquency* (Chicago: University of Chicago Press, 1969).

[5]William J. Chambliss, "A Sociological Analysis of the Law of Vagrancy," *Social Problems* 12 (Summer 1964): 67–77; reprinted in Delos H. Kelly, ed., *Deviant Behavior*, 2nd ed. (New York: St. Martin's Press, 1984), pp. 163–177.

The image of society as an arena of free behavior bounded by a static framework of impartial legal rules is a serious error. The law is always biased in favor of power groups, and all behavior is bounded, molded, and defined by law. A society that encourages self-interest, defines identity in terms of middle-class ideals, stigmatizes old ways of doing things, and constantly creates new opportunities to get ahead, often at the expense of others—in short, a dynamic industrial-urban society that separates the individual from control by the family, neighborhood, church, or work group—must rely increasingly on explicit legal norms and specialized structures (police, courts, prisons, regulatory commissions, schools) to ensure social control. And this reliance on law results in overcriminalization, which enhances the power of law-related professions and organizations, both public and private, and creates vested interests in legal solutions to social problems.

CLASS-PRESTIGE, CRIME, AND THE LAW

Sociologically, it is impossible to classify legal norms as criminal or civil, constitutional or legislative, public or private, and so on, just as it is unfeasible to distinguish precisely between deviant and conformist behavior or legal and criminal behavior. There is, in other words, no way to define crime precisely, though working definitions are easy enough to provide. Sociologically speaking, a crime is any violation of a legal norm punishable by the state. But such a definition raises numerous problems. Why are some violations of law not punished? Why is it that some violations of the law are punished but not considered crimes by the lawbreaker, his or her peers, or the general public? Why are various types of crime and of lawbreakers dealt with quite differently by law enforcement agencies? As we will see, the answers to these questions require an understanding of social class.

Class and the Definition of Crime

In a classic study, Edwin H. Sutherland drew attention to a major form of crime that had escaped the label of crime. Sutherland called this form of illegal behavior "white-collar crime," and defined it approximately "as a crime committed by a person of respectability and high social status in the course of his occupation."[6] He focused his discussion of overlooked crime on corporate business, saying little about the professions. Though the concept of white-collar crime initially evoked considerable controversy, it has achieved widespread general acceptance among criminologists and related profes-

[6] Edwin H. Sutherland, *White Collar Crime* (New York: Holt, Rinehart & Winston, 1949), p. 9.

sions.[7] Sutherland's conclusions (paraphrased below) about the nature of big business criminality—which is only one aspect of white-collar crime—are quite interesting:

1. Criminality among corporations is persistent; repeaters are as common here as in ordinary crime.
2. Illegal behavior at this level is much more extensive than is indicated by complaints and prosecutions.
3. Businesspersons who violate the law do not lose status among their associates, since a violation of the legal code is not a violation of the business code.[8]
4. Crime by businesspeople is organized crime, entered into deliberately and in skillful cooperation with others. Criminal businesspeople are also like other criminals (for example, the professional thief) in that they are contemptuous of law, government, and government personnel. Such businesspeople, however, do not look upon themselves as criminals (here they differ from the professional thief), nor are they looked upon as such by the general public. Businesspeople accept the designation "law violator" but on the whole their policy is to profess adherence to law publicly and to make defections from it in secret. While the professional thief must hide his identity, the white-collar criminal must hide the fact of crime. Secrecy is possible under the umbrella provided by lawyers, deceptive corporate structures and practices (especially against a divided, weak public) and public relations experts.[9]

Sutherland's insights can help us to answer the questions we raised earlier, which can now be rephrased as follows: Why are there such variations in the views on crime of members of the same society? Or, in other words, why was it possible for Sutherland to make a genuinely creative contribution to criminology by pointing out that members of the upper classes who break the law should be called criminals?

Ordinary or lower-class crime is more visible and more easily translated into personal terms than white-collar crime. It involves personal loss and violence, which makes it memorable and emotionally evocative. But ordinary crime does not cost as much as white-collar crime; in fact, the money costs of white-collar crime are infinitely higher. And the differential in moral costs is just as large: White-collar crime invariably involves a violation of trust, and if prestige is bestowed on crime by middle-class individuals (and eventually on

---

[7]There are obvious difficulties inherent in the term *white-collar crime* if one restricts its use to crimes by those of high social status, and primarily to the crimes of big businesspeople. The term *white-collar crime* should be also used (or refined or dropped) to account for the crimes of professionals and semiprofessionals, such as doctors, lawyers, advertising people, police officers, and inspectors; skilled workers in television repair, watch repair, automobile repair, and plumbing; and assorted small and intermediate businesspeople, such as slumlords, manufacturers of misrepresented or misgraded products, butchers who shortweight, fuel companies and gas stations that shortcount, and sales personnel who pilfer ("inventory shrinkage"). From the standpoint of class analysis, it is probably best to think of a hierarchy of types of crime associated with basic class attributes (income, property, education, occupation).

[8]There is an interesting parallel here with youth gangs.

[9]Sutherland,*White Collar Crime*, chap. 13.

lawbreaking in general), the bases of social respectability and authority could be undermined.

Conceivably, the illegal behavior of people in positions of prestige and authority could be defined as crime, and their reputations and positions could become tarnished. The reasons why this has not happened should be clear. While Sutherland's demand that lawbreaking by the high and mighty be called crime has been heeded by criminologists and some related professions, society-at-large has ignored his commonsense judgment. The illegal behavior of people in high social positions is still not seen as identical to the illegal behavior of those in inferior social positions. Robert K. Merton has outlined the nature of this moral hypocrisy in his essay "The Self-Fulfilling Prophecy,"[10] and one of his illustrations is particularly apt: A Jew who studies hard is labeled a grind and a grade-grubber, but a non-Jew who exhibits the same behavior is regarded as intelligent, studious, and ambitious. Similarly, when doctors control the supply of people who go into medicine, they are a professional association; when manual workers do the same thing, they are engaged in a restrictive labor practice. When wealthy, politically influential, and respectable people receive public money, it takes the forms of price supports, grants, tax benefits, or low-cost interest rates; when the lowly and despised receive public money it is called welfare, a handout, or something for nothing. The relevance of this point to the definition of criminal behavior is clear. Behavior has no meaning until society (its power groups) defines it. It is clear that our class-prestige structure, while not strong enough to prevent the passage of laws detrimental to the interests of the upper classes, has managed to keep the lawbreaking of the upper classes from being associated with that of the lower classes. Crime, in other words, has been successfully defined as something the lower classes do. There is no more dramatic example of the pervasive and powerful influence of the American class system.[11]

The association of crime with the lower classes is most striking in the case of blacks. Everyone knows that blacks have a high crime rate, which undoubtedly serves to reinforce a racist explanation of behavior. But if, instead of comparing the crime rates of blacks and whites (two meaningless causal variables), one compares the crime rates of various classes, the members of any given class seem to commit crime at similar rates regardless of skin color.[12]

---

[10]*The Antioch Review* 8 (June 1948): 193–210; reprinted in Robert K. Merton, *Social Theory and Social Structure*, rev. ed. (New York: Free Press, 1968), chap. 13.

[11]For a fact-filled, radical indictment of our criminal justice system, which argues that its failure to control crime is a mark of success because it diverts attention from the crimes of the upper to those of the lower classes, see Jeffrey H. Reiman, *The Rich Get Richer and the Poor Get Prison*, 2nd ed. (New York: John Wiley & Sons, 1984).

[12]Edward Green "Race, Social Status, and Criminal Arrest," *American Sociological Review* 35 (June 1970): 476–490. The author also specifically challenges the view that higher black crime rates are due to racist discrimination on the part of the general public or the police.

The double standard is no doubt partly attributable to the fact that the various classes commit different types of crime. Compared to middle-class youth, for example, youngsters from the lower classes seem to engage more in gainful crime and to be more violent and destructive.[13] Similarly, working-class and lower-class adult criminals commit different types of crime and use different techniques than do their middle-class counterparts. But neither these differences nor differences in the rates of crime and arrest at various class levels are sufficient to explain why we do not equate lawbreaking behavior with criminal behavior at all levels of society. They do not explain why we tend to define the teenage middle-class lawbreaker as a "problem child" and the teenage lower-class lawbreaker as a delinquent. The only satisfactory explanation is the power of class over our perception of reality, a power to which the universality and majesty of both reason and law are subject.[14]

Depoliticizing Crime

Crime is depoliticized when it is blamed on human nature (rotten apples) and divorced from the overall socioeconomic system that is its cause (the barrel). The prevalence of crime at all levels of society gives this false separation credibility. In addition, American power groups depoliticize crime by exaggerating the amount of crime likely to affect ordinary citizens and by turning the crime of powerful individuals and groups into acts of rotten apples.

Ordinary crime or crime by the lower classes has grown in the United States over the past decades and exceeds crime rates in other countries. However, public concern and fear about crime are much higher than they should be. One of the reasons for this is the artificially created crime wave. Crime rates are real and undesirable but crime waves do not exist. The belief that a crime wave is occurring and mass concern about it are both artifacts of organized interest groups: the press, television, the police, and politicians.[15] As a result, people turn defensive and vent their anger at individuals.

Entertainment stories in print and on television also depoliticize crime—this time, white-collar crime or crimes by the upper classes. Some

[13]For a comprehensive review of what we know about the class background of juvenile delinquents, see Don C. Gibbons and Marvin Krohn, *Delinquent Behavior*, 4th ed. (Englewood Cliffs, N.J.: Prentice-Hall, 1986), chapters 4, 8, and 9.

[14]It has been suggested by an experiment that unskilled workers who have criminal records are punished further by loss of employment opportunities, and that unskilled workers who have been *acquitted* of criminal charges are also discriminated against by prospective employers. By contrast, doctors who have been either convicted or acquitted of malpractice suffer almost no ill effects in their subsequent careers; see Richard D. Schwartz and Jerome H. Skolnick, "Two Studies of Legal Stigma," *Social Problems* 10 (Fall 1962): 133–142; reprinted in Delos H. Kelley, ed., *Deviant Behavior*, 2nd ed. (New York: St. Martin's Press, 1984), pp. 497–509.

[15]Mark Fishman, "Crime Wave as Ideology," *Social Problems* 25 (June 1978): 531–543. For a fuller discussion, see Kevin N. Wright, *The Great American Crime Myth* (Westport, Conn.: Greenwood Press, 1985).

conservatives have complained that television writers are acting politically and in a biased fashion because most of the evildoers on crime shows are businesspeople and professionals. This may be but the political bias is in favor of the status quo: These shows invariably focus on the rotten apple, in effect endorsing the soundness of the barrel, namely capitalism. (For a fuller discussion, see Box 16–2, "Are Crime Shows Political and, if so, Are They Biased?")

Class and Type of Law Enforcement

There is a vast difference between the ways in which the law is enforced against the white-collar criminal and against the ordinary criminal.[16] One need only compare the treatment of antitrust violators with the way in which law is enforced in a black ghetto to appreciate this point. White-collar criminals have fewer dealings with the police than do ordinary criminals; they are arrested less often; and, if arrested, they are rarely subject to pretrial detention.

Another such variation is the selective manner in which laws are enforced, which seems to be related to class. A classic example is urban renewal legislation, all the provisions of which are eagerly obeyed save the requirement that dispossessed families be relocated. Strenuous efforts are made to combat ordinary crime, but the development and enforcement of laws to protect the consumer and to stimulate competition are less than enthusiastic. It is well known that better police protection and public services are usually available in middle- and upper-class neighborhoods than in working- and lower-class areas. But the strong are protected in other ways too. Embezzlement laws, which protect the powerful against the weak, were quickly and easily passed when this form of theft first made its appearance. And the Securities and Exchange Commission is, despite its many failings, perhaps the most effective fiduciary structure among the various regulatory commissions. Also striking is the lack of enthusiasm with which the constitutional rights of black Americans are enforced against lawbreaking southern officials and safety laws are enforced against industries and business.[17]

Until recently, public programs of consumer protection were largely ineffective.[18] Consumer problems obviously vary with class level: The lower classes are affected more by the price of food than by the prices of swimming pools or single-family residences. Similarly, the lower classes are affected less

---

[16]It should be noted that many white-collar criminals, such as small retailers, small service businesses, and landlords, are subject to conventional treatment by law enforcement officials.

[17]Public protection measures in such areas as civil rights, fair employment, consumer protection, and factory safety are framed in terms of much-publicized goals, but invariably lack the provisions for enforcement necessary to make them effective. Thus, goals are not met and the authority of law and government is diluted.

[18]For an early but still useful analysis of the consumer problems of the poor, which refers to the way in which law is used to exploit poor consumers, see David Caplovitz, *The Poor Pay More: Consumer Practices of Low-Income Families* (New York: Free Press, 1963).

BOX 16–2. *ARE CRIME SHOWS POLITICAL AND, IF SO, ARE THEY BIASED?*

The Lichters found that television shows depict business people and professionals as criminals far more frequently than individuals from the lower classes. They also depict most crime-solving in terms of private detectives and private citizens. Interviews with television writers, producers, and executives reveal that they call themselves reform liberals, vote for the Democratic party, and are politically alienated. They also believe that business people have too much power, that the government should substantially redistribute income, and that television should be a "major force in social reform." The Lichters conclude that television's creators and their anti-authority perspective are not merely in it for the money but "seek to move the mass audience toward their own vision of the good society."[19]

A different perspective on all this is possible. The Lichters imply that television is biased in favor of liberal reform. But regardless of what television creators want, their anti-authority perspective is common to a great number of Americans including right-wing liberals ("conservatives"). Americans believe in the private individual, in voluntary behavior as a solution to problems, in vigilante heroes. This populist approach against authority is profoundly anti-political and antigovernment even as it espouses the need for government to do something. Far from being a political bias, what the Lichters really found is the pervasive American focus on evil and good individuals (human nature) and the protection of American society (elites and institutions) from scrutiny. What better way to protect the status quo than to focus on evil individual business people and professionals while leaving the institutions of the capitalist economy out of the equation. What better way to depoliticize social problems than to depict law enforcement officials as inept and unimaginative.

[19]Linda S. Lichter and S. Robert Lichter, *Prime Time Crime* (Washington, D.C.: The Media Institute, 1983); Linda and Robert Lichter, "Prime-Time Crime: Who and Why," *The Wall Street Journal*, January 6, 1984, p. 20.

by laws designed to protect the environment or establish national parks than the classes above them. Even the routine operation of our courts tends to be biased against the lower classes. For example, members of the lower classes are systematically cheated by an assortment of white-collar criminals and subjected to deceptive advertising, defective goods, tricky contracts, and shoddy services. Not only do they have little chance of legal redress, but the law is actually used against them to enforce tricky contracts, garnishee wages, and collect debts.[20]

[20]Small claims courts, which are now used as collection agencies, were originally established to allow ordinary individuals to adjudicate small disputes with a minimum of fuss and expense.

The Obsolete Disputes About the Causes of Crime

The social causation of crime (and deviance in general) is now accepted by most sociologists.[21] But some sociologists have argued that there is no relation between class and crime because it is widespread at all levels of society.[22] The denial of class-based behavior is widespread in the United States and must be confronted here as elsewhere. The lay public is also aware of lawlessness at all levels of society. Particularly striking are mass media accounts that report that the middle classes (both adults and juveniles) break the law and deviate in other ways in large numbers.

In a careful examination of the literature, John Braithwaite has shown that the empirical evidence clearly establishes a relation between class and crime. The "lower" class (essentially the marginal blue-collar class) commit considerably more juvenile and adult (blue-collar) crime than do the upper classes. One source of confusion in analyzing the class-crime relationship is the failure to distinguish between the crimes of the lower and upper classes. When crimes involving abuse of power and trust (price-fixing, embezzlement, consumer fraud, violation of professional norms, and so on) are analyzed, the class-crime relation also appears in a different form: The upper classes are clearly more criminal than the lower classes.[23]

The denial of a relation between class and crime extends to a denial of unemployment as a cause of crime. In a careful analysis of the data, Theodore Chiricos found a positive relation.[24] And in a finely textured analysis, Allan and Steffensmier found a heavy relation between property-crime arrest rates among male juveniles and young adults and labor market conditions (unemployment, underemployment, and poor job quality).[25]

Comparative Crime Rates

No comparative data on crime by the upper classes exist, and most intersocietal comparisons have been about blue-collar crime. It is clear that the "lower" class (not poverty class) commits more direct property crime and

---

[21]For a well-known political scientist and a psychologist who still think crime comes from human nature (psychological predispositions mediated by social factors), see James Q. Wilson and Richard J. Herrnstein, *Crime and Human Nature* (New York: Touchstone, 1985).

[22]C. R. Tittle, W.J. Villemez, and D.A. Smith, "The Myth of Social Class and Criminality: An Empirical Assessment of the Empirical Evidence," *American Sociological Review* 43 (October 1978): 643–656.

[23]John Braithwaite, "The Myth of Social Class and Criminality Reconsidered," *American Sociological Review* 46 (February 1981): 36–57.

[24]Theodore G. Chiricos, "Rates of Crime and Unemployment: An Analysis of the Aggregate Research Evidence," *Social Problems* 34 (April 1987): 187–212.

[25]Emilie Andersen Allan and Darrell J. Steffensmier, "Youth, Underemployment, and Property Crime: Differential Effects of Job Availability and Job Quality on Juvenile and Young Adult Arrest Rates," *American Sociological Review* 54 (February, 1989): 107–112.

more violent crime (murder, rape, robbery, assault).[26] As Braithwaite reports, the higher crime rate for these offenses among the lower class also holds for developing and for developed countries outside the United States.

Our most important comparative analysis of crime reveals that the United States has a much higher overall crime rate (2.8 times as high) than do all industrialized countries in the period 1970 to 1975. On a per capita basis, individual crimes are committed approximately three times more frequently in the United States than in other industrialized countries with robbery committed 5.7 times as much. While robbery (an amalgam of property and violent crime) is much more frequent, the overall amount of violent crime is not higher in the United States than elsewhere. The higher crime rate in the United States is largely a post-1945 phenomenon. The United States and other industrializing countries experienced an initial rise in crime, especially violent crime, during the early phase of industrialization and then crime, including violent crime, declined for all. But after following the pattern of other countries for a century, the United States experienced a rapid growth of crime after 1945 to become an international anomaly.[27]

The Obsolete Disputes About Controlling Blue-Collar Crime

Almost all the disputes about how to deal with crime tend to be about blue-collar crime. Conservatives (right liberals) argue that criminals deserve to be punished, and that swift and stern punishment will deter people from crime. Left liberals argue that punishment has always failed both to deter crime and to reform criminals. During the 1960s significant efforts were made to rehabilitate inmates through job training and other activities. There was also a focus on school and community programs to help the disadvantaged. The judicial system was put on notice to respect the rights of suspects and defendants. But all this failed miserably—the tide of crime rose ever higher. During the 1970s, right liberals dominated the discussion of crime. The federal government supplied huge amounts of money for crime-fighting technology and for the development of national and even international cooperation among law enforcement officials. The cry for "law and order" meant more people in jail for longer periods. Various neighborhood watch programs were instituted. Police and schools cracked down on trouble spots and repeat offenders. But stern law-and-order methods also failed—crime continued to rise. The slowdown and reversal of the crime rate in the early 1980s was due primarily to the decline of young males, the chief source of criminals.

[26]For the latter, see Judith R. Blau and Peter M. Blau, "The Cost of Inequality: Metropolitan Structure and Violent Crime," *American Sociological Review* 47 (February 1982): 114–129. Both whites and blacks who suffer from economic inequality (not poverty) commit significantly more violent crime. Ascriptive inequality (racist inequality) adds somewhat to the black rate.

[27]Louise I. Shelley, "American Crime: An International Anomaly?," *Comparative Social Research* 8 (1985): 81–95.

Law enforcement is a complex of many activities, none very successful. As a penal system the failure is well-nigh absolute.[28] Prison doesn't just brutalize inmates (or make them skillful, hardened criminals), it also brutalizes the guards.[29] In its other forms, law enforcement is badly hampered by institutions and socioeconomic policies that create resentment, frustration, and suffering. Law enforcement doesn't work because it is expensive and taxpayers don't want to pay for prisons, prison guards, or even police and the judicial system. One result of the conflict between wanting criminals caught and the refusal to pay for law enforcement is the widespread use of plea-bargaining (reduced sentences to save the expense of trials and imprisonment). Law enforcement doesn't work because many law enforcement officials are corrupt and are themselves criminals, often in collaboration with other criminals. Law enforcement doesn't work because it represents a threat to the affluent—strict law enforcement would quickly turn many among the well-to-do and powerful into defendants.[30] And it doesn't work, argues Reiman, because its very design protects not only the criminals in the upper classes but the basic system of capitalism.[31]

Sociologists vary in how they would deal with the fact of crime. Their approaches range from those who advocate prison reform, better-trained police, and an attack on poverty and slums to those who argue that crime can be controlled only by changing the fundamental capitalist system. Most sociologists, however, agree that crime by the lower classes stems from recession, poverty, unemployment, and broken homes, and most would agree that the best approach to controlling crime would be economic policies oriented toward providing meaningful jobs for all.[32] But public leaders resist despite an awareness that all other developed countries have far less crime than the United States. Conservatives argue that human nature needs restraints and that the breakdown of traditional morality has led to crime (as well as other social problems). Conservatives oppose government intervention in the economy by arguing that government cannot succeed and should focus on curbing crime by dealing firmly and directly with criminals. For some reason conservatives are oblivious to government intervention in the

---

[28]For an unsurpassed discussion, see Jessica Mitford, *Kind and Usual Punishment: The Prison Business* (New York: Random House, 1974).

[29]For a classic experiment in which college students played at being guards and then became guards with a vengeance, see Philip G. Zimbardo, "Pathology of Imprisonment," *Society* 9 (April 1972): 4–8.

[30]Richard Neeley, "The Politics of Crime," *Atlantic Monthly* 250 (August 1982): 27–31.

[31]Reiman, *The Rich Get Richer and the Poor Get Prison*.

[32]We do know that public assistance has a significant negative effect on crime rates; see James DeFronzo, "Economic Assistance to Impoverished Americans: Relation to Incidence of Crime," *Criminology* 21 (February 1983): 119–136. We also know that modest transfer payments to ex-prisoners can reduce arrests for both property and nonproperty crime; see Richard A. Berk and Kenneth J. Leniham, "Crime and Poverty: Some Experimental Evidence from Ex-offenders," *American Sociological Review* 45 (October 1980): 766–786.

form of taxation, transportation, energy, and other policies, which support an economy that disrupts communities and contains, on average, more unemployment than is present in other industrial countries (judging by the official rate, which counts part-time workers as employed and which does not count the large number who have been out of work for one year or more).

Left-wing reformers are once again talking of the need to go beyond law and prison reform. Other countries intervene directly to provide better levels of employment, family support, and more stable communities. These are known ways to bring down the crime rate—but power groups resist and (blue-collar) crime in America flourishes.[33]

White-Collar Crime: Deviance by Middle- and Upper-Level Individuals and Organizations

Blue-collar crime, however important, is not the main form of crime. By far the most important form of crime, both in terms of money and impact on society, is white-collar crime. For much of its history sociology concentrated its attention on deviance by individuals in the lower classes. Why did it fail to see deviance by the upper classes and by organized groups? The general reason is that early sociology had its roots in rural, small-town, Protestant (entrepreneurial) America. In recent decades its perspective has changed because, for one thing, most sociologists now have their origins and experiences squarely in corporate America.

W.E. Mann and Alan Listrak have suggested another reason for sociology's biased view of deviance. Sociology eagerly accepted the claims of professional groups such as lawyers, doctors, and economists, that their norms and values were inherently functional and provided automatic self-regulation, because sociology shared many professional values and interests with them.[34] For this reason, sociology neglected deviance by the professions and focused on deviance by the powerless. In effect, sociology helped insulate the professions from scrutiny and evaluation.

Individuals in the professions and the professions themselves, argue Mann and Listrak, break legal and professional norms on a widespread and systematic basis. They conclude by saying that professional claims for autonomy are not strong and that the public can (and should) set forth and enforce high-quality standards for all the professions.

Crime by the middle and upper classes refers to pilferage by employees of retail stores. It refers to crimes by small businesses, including arson to

---

[33]For a brilliant summary of what is known about crime, for a judicious presentation of the flaws in the positions and practices of both left and right reformers, and for a focus on full employment and integrated communities as the best way to tackle (blue-collar) crime, see Elliott Currie, *Confronting Crime: An American Challenge* (New York: Pantheon, 1985).

[34]W.E. Mann and Alan Listrak, "Deviance and the Professions," in W.E. Mann and Les Wheatcroft, eds., *Canada: A Sociological Profile*, 3rd ed. (Toronto: Copp Clark, 1976), pp. 296–308.

collect insurance. But it mostly refers to crime by highly placed executives and professionals who steal from their business (embezzlement), use business to defraud the public (price-fixing, adulterated, or counterfeited products), steal from clients (securities fraud), defraud the government (doctors and Medicare-Medicaid, the Pentagon, and defense contractors), steal from other businesses (industrial espionage, patent fraud, co-opting fashion designs; kickbacks, bribes, and payoffs in the construction business), or accept bribes or other rewards to violate the duties of public office. White-collar crime involves cooperation among different businesses, occupations, and class levels. Kickbacks, bribes, and payoffs in the construction business often involve the architect, the contractor, labor unions, workers, government inspectors, and the owners of the property. White-collar crime connects with street crime as banks launder ill-gotten gains from drug sales and other criminal activities. It means keeping abreast of the latest technology—for example, using the computer to steal money from banks or information from whoever has it. It involves the failure to enforce antitrust, environmental, or civil rights laws. It means government officials biasing decisions in favor of companies for whom they will eventually work. It means criminal networks involving city and state officials, businesses, and police and law enforcement officials.

The focus on deviance by middle- and upper-level individuals and organizations is the most important development in criminology in recent years and it tells us a great deal about the American class system.[35]

CLASS, LEGAL SERVICES, AND THE ADMINISTRATION OF JUSTICE

The Anglo-American legal system reflects the core values of society-at-large. The liberal presumption of the inherent validity of individual action is paralleled by the legal assumption that an individual is innocent until the state proves otherwise. The liberal dichotomy between the individual and society is echoed throughout the judicial process, most dramatically in the standard phrase "The People v. the Defendant." That court proceedings are competi-

[35]For a valuable collection of essays on white-collar crime, with cross-national comparisons, see Gilbert Geis and Ezra Stotland, eds., *White-Collar Crime: Theory and Research* (Beverly Hills, Calif.: Sage, 1980). For a comprehensive analysis of corporate crime, see Marshall B. Clinard and Peter C. Yeager, *Corporate Crime* (New York: Free Press, 1980). For a comprehensive analysis of deviance by powerful individuals and organizations, see David R. Simon and D. Stanley Eitzen, *Elite Deviance* (Boston: Allyn & Bacon, 1982). For a focus on organizational deviance, see M. David Ermann and Richard J. Lundman, eds., *Corporate and Governmental Deviance*, 3rd ed. (New York: Oxford University Press, 1987). For a clear, wide-ranging focus on upper-level crime, which stresses the structural cause of crime, see James W. Coleman, *The Criminal Elite: The Sociology of White Collar Crime* (New York: St. Martin's Press, 1985).

tive is obviously related to the liberal belief that competition is good for society. Under the Anglo-Saxon adversary system, it is assumed that justice (like better mousetraps and cheaper pig iron) will result if lawyers engage in combat under the eye of a referee, the judge. Another parallel is that justice must be purchased in much the same way as are food and clothing; thus, lawyers must be hired and court expenses and fees paid for before justice is done.[36] The reliability of the accused is also gauged by money (the bail system), and punishment is quite often monetary (the payment of a fine). And the law still assumes, despite modifications, that individuals cause their own behavior. The law is also still centered on the pleasure-pain principle of early liberal psychology in which it is assumed that clear-cut rewards (probation, parole, trustee positions, TV and exercise privileges) and punishments (imprisonment, execution, withdrawal of privileges, solitary confinement) serve as effective incentives and deterrents.

It is not surprising that the parallel between our judicial system and liberal society extends to the relation between law and the class system as well. Indeed, the emphasis on money produces a deep class bias throughout the judicial system. Legal services are performed primarily on behalf of the middle and upper classes, and especially of their most wealthy and powerful elements.[37] Many types of contract favor the rich and powerful, the myth of voluntary equal bargaining notwithstanding.[38] Those with money do not, as we have said, suffer pretrial detention, and if convicted are often given the option of sacrificing money rather than freedom. Class also determines what a life is worth legally (see Box 16–3). And even the jury system reflects class forces—for one thing, the jury system is shunned by defendants from the lower classes, suggesting that they regard a trial by their peers as unobtainable. We know very little about the class composition of juries, but prodding by the United States Supreme Court has prompted efforts to curtail the use of flagrantly unrepresentative juries. However, even juries chosen at random and representing a cross-section of the class structure do not guarantee that deliberations will be conducted by equals. One of the rare studies of a jury system that has relevance for class analysis found that jurors of higher occupational status were selected more as foremen, participated more in discus-

[36]Of course, the salaries of police officers, prosecutors, judges, court officials and, where clients are indigent, defense lawyers and court fees are paid out of public funds. In spite of this, the judicial process has a pronounced market flavor—the most important cases are handled by private law firms organized as profit-making businesses. And, as we will see, the provision of free justice for the poor has cheapened rather than guaranteed it.

[37]Jerome E. Carlin, *Lawyers' Ethics: A Study of the New York City Bar* (New York: Russell Sage Foundation, 1966). Leon Mayhew and Albert J. Reiss, Jr., "The Social Organization of Legal Contacts," *American Sociological Review* 34 (June 1969): 309–318; reprinted in Donald Black and Maureen Mileski, eds., *The Social Organization of Law* (New York: Seminar Press, 1973), chap. 11.

[38]Friedrich Kessler, "Contracts and Power in America," in Donald Black and Maureen Mileski, eds., *The Social Organization of Law* (New York: Seminar Press, 1973), chap. 10; reprinted from *Columbia Law Review* 43 (1943): 629–642.

BOX 16–3.   *WHAT IS A LIFE WORTH? IT DEPENDS ON WHO YOU WORK FOR*

The lawyers for Philip D. Estridge want Delta Air Lines to pay his estate $25 million for an accident that took his life. Delta acknowledged responsibility but disputed the amount of compensation. Lawyers produced witnesses saying that Mr. Estridge, forty-seven, had many productive and lucrative years ahead of him as a high-ranking executive for IBM. The chances are that the Estridge estate will get a sum somewhere in the vicinity of $25 million while most of the other victims in the plane crash will get less than 5 percent of that sum. Incidentally, the Estridge lawyers also wanted $5 million for Mrs. Estridge's estate, but it was not clear why her life was worth that amount.

sion, had more influence, derived more satisfaction, and were perceived as more qualified for jury duty than jurors from lower occupations.[39]

In general, acquittals, favorable sentences, and commutations of sentence are contingent on the skill of one's lawyer, which is in turn contingent on money. Mere representation by a lawyer does not ensure equal justice. One study has shown that among those convicted of murder, especially blacks, defendants with court-appointed counsel were less likely to have their executions commuted. Among blacks, those with private counsel were more likely to have their executions commuted. And sentencing itself varies in regard to identical offenses: Drunkenness is a classic instance where social position is a strong determinant of differential sentencing.[40] Where upper- and lower-class juveniles commit identical offenses, differential treatment and sentencing also appear. And restitution for a wrongful death is explicitly based on the decedent's class position; damages are computed on the basis of his or her projected lifetime income. But type of crime in general is so geared to class that it is difficult to establish class bias in sentencing. Data showing that the indigent plead guilty more, are convicted more often, receive probation less often, and so on, while suggestive, do not automatically add up to class bias; the various classes commit different crimes, are involved in crime at different rates, and present a different problem for sentencing and rehabilitation.

The Supreme Court's guarantee of due process to all, especially its

---

[39]Fred L. Strodtbeck, Rita M. James, and Charles Hawkins, "Social Status in Jury Deliberations," *American Sociological Review* 22 (December 1957): 713–719.

[40]For differences in commutation of execution sentences, see Marvin E. Wolfgang, Arlene Kelly, and Hans C. Nolde, "Comparisons of the Executed and the Commuted Among Admissions to Death Row," in Richard Quinney, ed., *Crime and Justice in Society* (Boston: Little, Brown, 1969). For different sentencing among those convicted of drunkenness, see Jacqueline P. Wiseman, *Stations of the Lost: The Treatment of Skid Row Alcoholics* (Englewood Cliffs, N.J.: Prentice-Hall 1970), pp. 90–94. For sentences to execution by race, see David Bruck "Decisions of Death," *The New Republic* 189 (December 12, 1983): 18–25; reprinted in J. H. Skolnick and Elliott Currie, eds., *Crisis in American Institutions* (Boston: Little, Brown, 1985), pp. 450–462.

controversial *Gideon, Escobedo,* and *Miranda* decisions, has done little to change the class character of justice.[41] Formally, due process means among other things that accused individuals are entitled to free lawyers, trials, and appeals if they are too poor to pay their own expenses, and to the right to remain silent and have a lawyer present at all stages of their dealings with the state. This new interpretation of due process, and the Court's determination to invalidate confessions and other evidence obtained illegally, has been hailed by some as rebalancing the relation between the individual and the state and condemned by others as contributing to the breakdown of law and order. But the real significance of these rulings seems to be to affirm the validity of our traditional adversary system of justice and reassert the traditional liberal view that the individual and the government are enemies. The general power of class over justice is not curtailed; an economic floor has simply been placed under the class system of justice to prevent the poor from being bypassed altogether. There is no doubt that these rulings will curtail shoddy and illegal behavior on the part of some law enforcement officials. But the administration of criminal justice differs markedly from the images conjured by these rulings and by those who applaud or condemn them. Despite these rulings, most crime in the United States will continue to go undetected and unpunished, rates of arrests will not change, rates of confession will continue at previous levels, and the overwhelming majority of defendants (mostly individuals from the lower classes) will continue to plead guilty. (And when they accept trial, they will continue to shun jury trials.) In other words, the reality of criminal justice is not the adversary system (or competition between legal entrepreneurs), abstract rights, or solemn pronouncements. The key to understanding criminal justice is the expression "the administration of justice." There exists a vast system of "bargain justice" in which judges, prosecutors, and private and public defense attorneys negotiate punishment to avoid trials. As Donald J. Newman argues, the idea of bargaining is at odds with a legal process based on facts and rules of evidence, favors the experienced criminal over the first offender, and promotes a general disrespect for law.[42] This assembly-line system of justice is a jerry-built construct created by judges, court officials, probation officers, court psychiatrists, prosecutors, and defense lawyers. As Abraham S. Blumberg points out, the Supreme Court's rulings upholding the rights of the accused have had the ironic result of enriching the resources of this existing organiza-

---

[41]The definition of due process has evolved slowly through a considerable number of Supreme Court decisions. The basic elements of due process are specified in three famous decisions: *Gideon* v. *Wainwright,* 372 U.S. 335 (1963); *Escobedo* v. *Illinois,* 378 U.S. 478 (1964); and *Miranda* v. *Arizona* 384 U.S. 436 (1966).

[42]Donald J. Newman, "Pleading Guilty for Considerations: A Study of Bargain Justice," *Journal of Criminal Law, Criminology and Police Science* 46 (March–April 1956): 780–790; reprinted in William J. Chambliss, ed., *Crime and the Legal Process* (New York: McGraw-Hill, 1969), pp. 209–220.

tional and professional arrangement by providing for a more efficient way of eliciting guilty pleas from defendants.[43]

The administration of justice in the realm of civil law is also heavily weighted against the lower classes. In general, members of the lower classes rarely use the machinery of the law on their own behalf, though they have many legal problems (and legal rights). Our legal institutions assume middle-class status: To benefit from the law in practice, one must be educated, informed about one's rights, comfortable in a world of specialization and impersonality, able to take initiative, and, of course, affluent. Members of the lower classes are thus by definition beyond the scope of law as an operational right.

But the law by no means ignores the lower classes, and its impact is not limited to differential treatment by the police and courts in criminal cases. It would not be inaccurate to say that the power dimension supplies one set of legal procedures and even of laws for the lower classes and another set of procedures and laws for the upper classes. Three distinct types of differential treatment of the upper and lower classes in substantive and procedural law have been identified: favored parties, dual law (*de jure* denial of equal protection), and *de facto* denial of equal protection.[44] The law favors landlords over tenants and lenders over borrowers; of course, the favored parties in such cases tend to enjoy higher class status than their adversaries. Dual law for the lower and upper classes characterizes the realms of family law and welfare law.[45] When they concern the lower classes, divorce, property settlements, and support relations are handled as public matters to ensure the smallest cost to the public; when they concern the upper classes, such cases are treated as civil matters pertaining to private individuals. Law and legal philosophy also differ with regard to government benefits for the lower classes (public assistance, unemployment insurance, public housing) and the upper classes (licenses, loans, subsidies, contracts). *De facto* bias means that equal application of law works to the detriment of the lower classes. Impartially applied restrictive abortion and divorce laws actually favor the upper classes; acceptance of common law market precepts ("let the buyer beware") works to the disadvantage of the lower classes in economic transactions. The draft law burdens the lower classes inequitably, since they are less likely to have exempt occupations or to be college students. In general, Carlin, Howard,

---

[43]Abraham S. Blumberg, "The Practice of Law as Confidence Game: Organizational Cooptation of a Profession," *Law and Society Review* 1 (June 1967): 15–39; reprinted in William J. Chambliss, ed., *Crime and the Legal Process* (New York: McGraw-Hill, 1969), pp. 220–237.

[44]Jerome E. Carlin, Jan Howard, and Sheldon L. Messinger, *Civil Justice and the Poor: Issues for Sociological Research* (New York: Russell Sage Foundation, 1967). Though the authors use the terms *rich* and *poor* throughout, it is clear that they are referring broadly to the upper and lower classes.

[45]Jacobus tenBroek, *Family Law and the Poor* (Westport, Conn.: Greenwood Press, 1971), and "The Two Nations: Differential Values in Welfare Law and Administration," in M. Levitt and B. Rubenstein eds., *Orthopsychiatry and the Law* (Detroit: Wayne State University Press, 1968); reprinted in Jerome H. Skolnick and Elliott Currie, eds., *Crisis in American Institutions*, (Boston: Little, Brown, 1970), pp. 350–361.

and Messinger observe, "the law itself serves to define and maintain the position of the poor.[46]

Implicit in these substantive differences between the law of the upper classes and the law of the lower classes are sharp differences in legal procedure. The assembly-line system of justice routinizes, standardizes, and processes a vast percentage of all legal cases involving the lower classes. There is a pronounced tendency to employ criminal proceedings in welfare and family cases involving the lower classes. And the lower classes are treated as wards of the state on the presumption that they are incompetent and that the interests of the state are in harmony with their interests.

The courts that deal with the lower classes tend to dispense with procedural safeguards: They do not give notice; they fail to observe rules of evidence; they are characterized by a lack of genuine adversariness; and they tend to delegate decisions to such nonlegal personnel as probation officers, psychiatrists, and social workers, which results in confusion and diffusion of responsibility. Carlin, Howard, and Messinger also note that the courts for the lower classes are characterized by grossly inadequate resources and least adequately trained and experienced judges and other personnel.

Of course, the net result of this system of mass-production justice is to help create the type of individual the law presumes. The law of the lower classes, in other words, is a self-fulfilling prophecy to the extent that it assumes that people in the lower classes are untrustworthy and incompetent and treats them as such. It is not surprising that, under a regime that deprives them of the opportunity to act as persons, the lower classes see the state and the law as remote and alien phenomena, are suspicious and cynical of its justice, and seem childish and confused. Their experience with the law is consistent with their dealings with authority at home, in schools, at the doctor's or dentist's office, in church, at work, at the unemployment or welfare bureau, and at the employment agency.

The intentions of the state are not in question. That the state "individualizes" justice for juvenile delinquents and the lower classes in an effort to treat all fairly can be taken for granted.[47] But the treatment of some (the upper classes) according to what they do and have and of others (the lower classes) according to who they are is a flagrant violation of the legal theory of the liberal state and contributes heavily of the serious identity problem of the lower classes. According to Carlin, Howard, and Messinger, the ultimate denial of identity by the legal system is that the lower classes are not allowed to mean what they say. Thus, if there is only one possible legal identity—broadly speaking, middle class in nature—those who cannot achieve it must do without a legal identity. (This status rounds out their nonidentity in other areas.) Or, perhaps, to pursue a suggestion by Garfinkel, the successful deg-

---

[46]Carlin and others, *Civil Justice and the Poor*, p. 21.

[47]In fact, however, true individualized justice is restricted to the nonpoor, who can hire good lawyers to particularize and devote attention to their unique legal problems.

radation of the deviant requires the treatment we now give defendants from the lower classes.[48] Whatever the reason for their present treatment, the American legal system would be far different were there equal treatment under law for the upper and lower classes.

LAW AND REPRESENTATIVE MINORITIES

Black Americans and the Law

The mistreatment of black people by law enforcement agencies is widely recognized, as is the high black crime rate. Though blacks make up about 11 percent of the American population, they account for about 30 percent of all arrests and 34 percent of all prison inmates. Blacks are victimized by crime more than whites, even holding income constant, and there is a tendency for offenders to victimize members of their own race.[49] Blacks are also punished more severely than whites accused of similar crimes, and are more likely to be executed. Blacks are often treated illegally by the police, and there is open and explicit police surveillance of black neighborhoods. And blacks are underrepresented throughout the apparatus of law enforcement. What is not known, however, is how much of the mistreatment of blacks by law enforcement agencies is due to race and how much to other factors.

In the South, where blacks have systematically been treated differently by the law, it was generally expected that they would be so treated. Given racist state and local governments, it is not surprising that law enforcement in the South was openly racist in character. But on a national scale, it is not at all clear whether race is any longer a significant factor in the mistreatment of black people. One of the most important findings about black criminal behavior is Edward Green's report, cited earlier, that black and white crime rates are identical once class is held constant. Though we have no data, it would not be implausible to argue that class is a far more important factor than race in criminal behavior by blacks and in their relation to law enforcement agencies in general. Basically, law enforcement agencies deal illegally with, and display excessive zeal and force against, all members of the lower classes, whether white, black, yellow, red, Anglo, Mexican American, Protestant, Jewish, or Roman Catholic. In short, the main purpose of law enforce-

---

[48]Harold Garfinkel, "Conditions of Successful Degradation Ceremonies," *American Journal of Sociology* 61, no. 5 (March 1956): 420–424.

[49]Philip H. Ennis, *Criminal Victimization in the United States: A Report of a National Study* (Washington, D.C.: U.S. Government Printing Office, 1967), pp. 32–36. This is a National Opinion Research Center study designed to develop a means of determining the amount of crime more accurate than the Uniform Crime Rate. (Survey data indicate far more crime than the UCR accounts for). The greater victimization by crime of the lower classes and of blacks and Spanish-origin Americans revealed by this survey is also demonstrated in the *Statistical Abstract of the United States*, 1987 (Washington, D.C.: United States Government Printing Office, 1986), Tables 270 and 271.

ment agencies, like all branches of government, is to defend the existing system of stratification.

Upper-income groups consistently express higher evaluations of the police than do lower-income groups (though support in general is high). However, blacks are negative toward the police regardless of income.[50] Generally speaking, blacks dislike the police and suspect them of singling out blacks for mistreatment. Thus, one of the (largely latent) ways in which the police defend the existing order of things is to displace the lower classes' resentments toward themselves and away from the class system. In other words, to the extent that blacks interpret their relation to the police and the law in racial terms, they are overlooking the class system, which is the prime source of American behavior.

Mexican Americans and the Law

Mexican Americans' relation to law enforcement agencies, as to government in general, has been thoroughly unsatisfactory.[51] In 1970, the United States Commission on Civil Rights found considerable discrimination against Mexican Americans on the part of law enforcement agencies. The police used excessive zeal and force against American citizens of Mexican descent, were disrespectful of their persons and their rights, and interfered illegally with Mexican American organizations. Adequate remedies against such abuse did not exist and the police retaliated against complainants. Furthermore, Mexican Americans were vastly underrepresented on juries, subject to bail when Anglos are not, inadequately represented by counsel, and greatly underrepresented in law enforcement agencies in general.[52]

Moore and Pachon report that some efforts have been made to improve the relation between Mexican Americans and law enforcement, but progress has been very slow. Our own view is that this should be viewed as a stratification phenomenon, a legacy partly of "caste" status and partly of class. Of course, law enforcement officials find it relatively easy to treat distinctive groups such as blacks and Mexican Americans differently. But it is crucial to keep in mind that all types of groupings in the lower classes are mistreated by law enforcement officials. The fact that mistreatment takes on a racial or ethnic flavor helps to divide groups with common grievances and interests. In other words, one of the latent functions of the mistreatment of blacks and Mexican Americans by law enforcement agencies is to foster racial and ethnic

---

[50]Philip H. Ennis, *Criminal Victimization in the United States* (Washington, D.C.: U.S. Government Printing Office, 1967), pp. 52–56.

[51]For a good review, see Leo Grebler, Joan W. Moore, Ralph C. Guzman and others, *The Mexican-American People: The Nation's Second Largest Minority* (New York: Free Press, 1970), chap. 21, and Joan Moore and Harry Pachon, *Hispanics in the United States* (Englewood Cliffs, N.J.: Prentice-Hall, 1985), pp. 164–168.

[52]U.S. Commission on Civil Rights, *Mexican Americans and the Administration of Justice in the Southwest* (Washington, D.C.: U.S. Government Printing Office, 1970).

defensiveness among those mistreated. To the extent that it does so, the affected parties are unlikely to recognize the class factor common to their shared mistreatment.

NEW DEPARTURES IN LAW: REFORM WITHOUT CHANGE

The law is not a static structure. Thanks to an active legislative process and to judicial interpretation, it is extended and reformed on a continuous basis. To speak of reform without change is not to minimize the impact of legal reform (or pending reform) in the United States; it is only to emphasize that such reforms represent neither change in nor departure from the fundamental principles of class stratification. What legal reform amounts to, in other words, is the modernization of class society.

The Redefinition of Deviance and Crime

The legal code of the United States is being purged of laws defining various kinds of behavior as criminal. Over the years a number of state legislatures have liberalized their abortion laws, in effect making the termination of pregnancy a private matter between a woman and her doctor; and in 1973 the Supreme Court ruled most antiabortion laws unconstitutional. The incentives for abortion reform have been many and varied: concern over population growth, women's rights, the performance of an enormous number of unsafe abortions every year under criminal auspices, and the fact that the chief victims of antiabortion laws are the lower classes.[53]

Laws against the sale of birth control devices have also crumbled, and public programs have augmented the efforts of private groups to extend the benefits of birth control to the general public. Here too, the lower classes are the chief beneficiaries of a reform for which solid middle class support was necessary.

The Supreme Court has extended the protection of the First Amendment to much of what was once defined as criminal pornography. It is of some interest that the chief users of pornography are middle-class males, and the successful liberalization of the law in this area is undoubtedly due to middle-class support.

Gambling has traditionally been designated a crime in the United States, though some changes in this position can be discerned. The fact that it enjoys widespread public support and is a lucrative source of revenue has prompted many states to legalize certain forms of gambling. Regardless of its

---

[53]For a full background and an incisive, empirical study of the politics of abortion, which argues that the abortion issue is only part of a much deeper class cleavage between the less educated, who want to uphold a wide set of traditional values, and the better educated, who want new meanings about women and society, see Kristin Luker, *Abortion and the Politics of Motherhood* (Berkeley: University of California Press, 1984).

disposition by the law, gambling will probably continue for some time to serve as recreation for the successful and as a substitute for success for the lower classes. Whereas these functions were once performed illegally by private business people, they are now increasingly being performed by public agencies (lotteries and betting parlors). In addition, challenges have been made to the state's right to enforce vagrancy laws.

Consumer Protection

Consumers are a diverse lot of people, and thus difficult to organize. But because of determined leadership, some notorious scandals, and growing public (especially middle class) apprehension about the quality and safety of a large number of products, a consumer movement strong enough to achieve significant legal reform emerged in the 1960s.

Safety and quality in automobiles, color television sets, appliances, boats, and other heavy durable goods are obviously more germane to certain classes than to others. In fact, all such issues, from the protection of children from lead poisoning to the effort to protect the natural environment, are related to class. The ways in which government regulates and stimulates industries—by distributing franchises, establishing depreciation rates, setting import and production quotas, and the like—and the way in which it treats oligarchic competition affect the distribution of income (and thus class) because they affect the prices consumers pay for products and services. Standardized packaging, the development of a pricing system based on unit cost, and truth-in-lending will probably be more beneficial to the working class and the poor than to the classes above them.

Programs to aid the poor and minority groups in overcoming consumption disabilities and to make their legal rights effective have had moderate success. The Economic Opportunity Act of 1964, for example, led to the provision of free legal services for the poor. Such help is not limited to the provision of defense in criminal matters; much more importantly, it allows the poor to initiate judicial proceedings to protect their interests and their rights.[54] Of some significance here is the growing use of legal class action

---

[54]Federal funding allows lawyers to be much more independent and to pursue more types of cases on behalf of the poor than the older Legal Aid system. Under the old system, lawyers were dependent for support on local business people, professionals, and, of course, other lawyers; thus, the Legal Aid system was a captive of the very people who were causing trouble for the poor. Local and state governments, having themselves been pressured by federally funded legal aid programs to adhere to their own laws, have applied pressure to curtail such programs. President Nixon started and President Reagan largely accomplished the emasculation of publicly supported legal aid to the poor. Ironically, President Reagan's actions against the Legal Aid system were illegal and his argument that tax money should not be used for such purposes was not accompanied by a request that the legal expenses incurred by the upper classes be disallowed as deductions by the tax code. For a comprehensive review, including case studies showing which local conditions foster reform as opposed to helping clients, see Mark Kessler, *Legal Services for the Poor* (Westport, Conn.: Greenwood Press, 1987).

(action on behalf of all individuals affected by the practice in question, not of a social class). At present, class actions are much easier to initiate in the federal courts than at the state level. While *class action* is a legal term, some such litigation may be undertaken on behalf of a social class; an example is legal action to protect the interests of all welfare recipients or all dispossessed and unrelocated families. The ability of the poor and working poor to fight back legally may bring about fresh appraisals of a number of social practices that now affect them adversely. The Uniform Commercial Code makes it harder to enforce "tricky contracts," and the use of the garnishee as a way of enforcing consumer payment is now subject to a prior hearing and may be on the decline; indeed, it has already been banned in a number of states.

The Civil Rights Acts of 1964 and 1965 also touched on the area of consumption by making it illegal to discriminate in public accommodations. But legislation outlawing "caste" and ethnic-religious discrimination have minimal effect on the poor as such. It should not go unnoticed that such legislation helps to legitimate the class system by incorporating into our legal understanding and sense of justice the assumption that the law protects only the equal right of poor and rich to consume according to class standing.

The Rights of Citizens

In the past few decades significant changes have taken place in the definition of the individual's rights, especially in relation to the state. We have already mentioned the provision of free legal services for the poor as a result of the Economic Opportunity Act of 1964. These services have been used in civil actions and in a wide variety of criminal proceedings. Of some importance in enhancing the value of free legal services are the Supreme Court decisions affirming the constitutional right of accused persons, including paupers, to due process. The Supreme Court has also ruled that welfare residency requirements are an infringement of the right to travel and that recipients have a right to formal hearings (due process) before their benefits (property) can be abridged. The courts are also being petitioned to hear cases involving burdensome court fees for divorce, such fees allegedly precluding equal treatment under the law for the poor. The large and thorny issue of housing, especially zoning and the use of public referendums to curtail low-income housing, is also before the courts, as is the problem of unequal public services.

Reform Without Change

However substantial and important American legal reform has been, its extent should not be exaggerated. The reform of the law should be seen as one aspect of the modernization of the American class system, and not as the growth of equal justice or as an attack on the basic structure of our class and prestige hierarchies. The law will continue to be a main support of the status quo, but in new ways. While the lower classes will enjoy more legal rights, they will continue to participate in a legal system structured to assume the validity of property rights and authority relations. Though new property rights (such as the right to welfare benefits) may be acknowledged, they will simply join the existing body of property rights and become subject to the assumption that unequal property is socially desirable and thus socially legitimate. Similarly, welfare recipients' right to due process before their benefits are curtailed also serves to enhance the validity of welfare as an effective and legitimate way to handle the problems of unemployment, racial discrimination, broken homes, illegitimacy, and the like. Welfare recipients will be treated on a national basis: local residency requirements have already been abolished, a national minimum income may someday be established, and national standards for welfare may be adopted. But the real meaning of such changes will be to legitimate class inequality and to incorporate the economically worthless into a nationwide structure of legalized and moralized destitution. Indeed, ironically, it may be that the United States Constitution, middle-class efficiency, and Christian compassion are being used to transform welfare recipients into noncitizens. In recent years reformers have enacted provisions that require welfare recipients to work ("workfare") but this too is meaningless without economic planning to provide jobs (and because most welfare recipients are mothers with dependent children).

Publicly supported legal services have improved the legal rights of the lower classes somewhat. But here again, efforts to improve their legal rights may serve to distract attention from the hard political decisions necessary if there are to be solutions to the major problems faced by those at the bottom of the American class systems: inadequate employment, housing, medical care, schooling, and general life experience. Nor should the value of these new legal services be exaggerated. The inadequacy of the newly created legal services and the exaggerated significance attributed to the new legal rights of American citizens (largely the poor) are most dramatically apparent in the case of the new rights of defendants in criminal cases. Remember that the Supreme Court has ruled that all defendants are entitled to full exercise of their constitutional rights: the right not to incriminate oneself, the right to legal counsel, and the right to a full measure of adjudication. This new definition of *due process* seems to sever these legal rights from economic (class) status by making them free if the defendant cannot afford to pay for them. Just as political status was divorced from economic status in the nineteenth century when property qualifications for voting were abolished, the power dimension appears to be freeing itself from economic status when it provides free legal services for the poor. Certainly the impact of these newly established rights would appear to be considerable, judging by the vigorous approval and outraged condemnation they elicited from various quarters.

The general controversy over whether or not these rulings leave the public adequately protected against crime appears to be largely irrelevant.

Ideally speaking, the *Gideon, Escobedo,* and *Miranda* rulings are the glory of liberal civilization. But, practically speaking, they change very little about the United States' basic legal institutions or their relation to the American class structure. Crime will persist at high and perhaps growing rates because of the *anomie* inherent in liberal society. *Law and order* will continue to mean the expenditure of large sums to enforce the law against ordinary criminals while less attention and money are devoted to curtailing far more serious white-collar crime. And, perhaps worst of all, controversy over these rulings and calls for law and order will divert attention from the main question: Why is there crime in the first place?

The law's distinctness, alleged separation from society, formality and prestige, and recent reforms do not prevent it from embodying many other features of liberal society. The basic stance of the American penal code is still to assume that potential and actual criminals respond to rewards and punishments much as business people and workers allegedly respond to pleasure-pain stimuli and cost-profit calculations. It assumes that competitive judicial proceedings will produce justice just as competition in economic markets allegedly produces true prices and better products. And it is taken for granted that justice will be available to all because it can be bought much as one buys food, clothing, and housing.

Nevertheless, the bail system will continue to victimize the lower classes. Police officers, lawyers, judges, jurors, and jailers will continue to employ class-based stereotypes in dealing with clients, defendants, and different types of crimes. Police protection will continue to be inadequate where it is most needed, and middle class efficiency in law enforcement will continue to make the relation between the law and the poor (and some minority groups) tenuous and a source of alienation. Juries will no doubt be chosen more carefully in the future, but the poor will continue to shun trial by jury; thus, the chief beneficiaries of jury trials will be white-collar defendants. And our prisons will continue to turn out hardened and more skillful repeat offenders.

Opposition to legal reforms on the part of vested interests in the legal profession, some police departments, small business people, landlords, and many citizens and politicians may be overcome in the years ahead. But the struggle over legal reform is largely a competition between the rearguard action of an old middle class and the modernizing pressures of the new middle class. The chief beneficiaries of legal reform will not be the poor but the middle and upper middle classes. Politicians will have more patronage to dispense, civil servants will have more money to spend, police forces will become professionalized, lawyers will enjoy more secure employment, more judges will be needed, and more and better-trained and better-paid court officials and auxiliary professionals will assist them. And the middle and upper classes will complacently conclude that equality under the law is viable in practice.

CLASS-PRESTIGE, LAW, AND DEVIANCE: A SUMMARY

The nature of law is directly related to the American class system. In general, law follows the interests of powerful property and professional groups.

Deviance, especially criminal deviance, is also directly related to the class-prestige system. Though the lower classes commit the most numerous and easily understood forms of crime, the main criminals in the United States are middle- and upper-level individuals and organizations, both private and public.

Our perception of crime also reflects the class system. For a long time the upper classes succeeded in associating crime with the lower classes. However, white-collar crime is now so prevalent that this may be changing.

Law enforcement also reflects the class-prestige system. Crime is defined differently depending on the class of the lawbreaker; law enforcement agencies treat lawbreakers from the various classes differently; legal services are more readily available to the upper classes than the lower classes; and legal reform rarely affects the essential inequality before the law characteristic of class society.

By and large, the working and lower classes enjoy substantially fewer legal rights, inferior legal services, and less justice than the classes above them. It is not clear that blacks and Mexican Americans, who are mistreated by the law, are abused more than other groups in the working and lower classes.

The main way to curb blue-collar crime is through full employment and integrated communities. Adopting such a social program would also mean harnessing the upper classes to social functions and thus would curb our most important form of crime, that committed by the upper classes.

CHAPTER 17

The American Class System: A Summary

The most important scientific question that can be asked in stratification analysis is: Does the concept of *social class* organize empirical phenomena so that the causes of behavior can be predicted at higher levels of abstraction? Based on our findings, our answer is emphatically yes.

THE REALITY OF CLASS AND CLASS ANALYSIS

Our analysis of the three major dimensions and numerous subdimensions of stratification indicates that the distribution of American social and cultural values (material comfort and convenience, psychic development and satisfaction, political-legal power and every conceivable subcategory of behavior and benefit) can be subsumed by the concept of *social class*, now understood to mean the location of families and individuals across the three major dimensions of inequality. The essence of social stratification is the existence of a hierarchy of valued things, traits, and behaviors, which, lodged in families, are transmitted by means of social processes to children.

The existence of mobility, inconsistency, lack of class consciousness, and such universal values and norms as the Bill of Rights, equality of opportunity, and universal suffrage should not obscure this fundamental structure and process. Liberal society has developed these phenomena as integral parts of a legitimated system of class inequality. To take an example, significant rates of social mobility are necessary to a class system, which is by definition derived from an expansive economy and requires extensive support and justification—thus, the emphasis on success, equality of opportunity, achievement, and the like. But high rates of upward mobility are fully compatible with a high rate of ascriptive transmission of class position from one generation to the next. That the latter is not compatible with American ideals should remind us that class society, like past forms of society, is also a system of illegitimate inequality.

THE GENERAL STRUCTURE OF AMERICAN CLASSES

A social class is made up of families and unrelated individuals who share similar benefits across the three dimensions of class, prestige, and power. The criterion for distinguishing among the several social classes is relative to the level of social benefits; that is, as a given social unit moves from one social class to another, it should experience a noticeable rise or drop in the overall amount and quality of social values available to it. This is not to say that important differences do not exist, say, between the bottom and the top of the working class, or that class boundaries (such as between the working and the lower middle class) are clear-cut. Furthermore, there are no easy equations among the three major dimensions, and changes are taking place at all levels that are difficult to interpret. But, as Table 17–1 indicates, existing research points to five relatively distinct strata in the United States, and to a fairly pronounced integration of the three dimensions, whose center of gravity is the class dimension.

Looked at broadly, America's social stratification by class is continuous with the past. It has legitimate elements (things work the way norms say they should) and illegitimate elements (behavioral phenomena that contradict basic norms and values: hereditary wealth, class advantages, oligarchic competition, racial-ethnic-sexual discrimination). Changes have taken place, of course, in the various elements that make up a class. The occupational skill levels of the various classes have risen consistently, and the nature of the family—the means by which the class system is transmitted from one generation to the next—has been modified by various factors. Also, new forms of upward and downward mobility have emerged, though overall mobility rates seem not to have changed much. For example, the shift from entrepreneurial to corporate capitalism means that the drama of social class is now played out largely within giant corporate structures. Recent data suggest that the first break in America's system of social stratification may have occurred:

TABLE 17-1. The American Class System in the Twentieth Century: A Composite Estimate[a]

CLASS (AND PERCENTAGE OF TOTAL POPULATION)	INCOME	PROPERTY	OCCUPATION	EDUCATION	PERSONAL AND FAMILY LIFE	EDUCATION OF CHILDREN
Upper class (1–3%)	Very high income most of it from wealth	Great wealth, old wealth, control over investment	Managers,	Liberal arts	Stable family life	College education
Upper middle class (10–15%)	High income	Accumulation of property through savings	professionals, high civil and military officials Lowest unemployment	education at elite schools Graduate training	Autonomous personality Better physical and mental health and health care	by right for both sexes Educational system biased in their favor
Lower middle class (30–35%)	Modest	Few assets Some savings	Small business people and farmers, lower professionals, semiprofessionals, sales and clerical workers	Some college High school	Longer life expectancy	Greater chance of college than working class children
Working class (40–45%)	Low income	Few to no assets No	Skilled labor Unskilled labor Highest unemployment	Some high school Grade school Illiteracy,	Unstable family life One parent homes Conformist	Educational system biased against them Tendency toward vocational programs
Lower class (20–25%)	Poverty income (destitution)	savings	Surplus labor	especially functional illiteracy	personality Poorer physical and mental health Lower life expectancy	Little interest in education, high dropout rates

406

TABLE 17-1. Continued

CLASS (AND PERCENTAGE OF TOTAL POPULATION)	PRESTIGE			
	OCCUPATIONAL PRESTIGE	SUBJECTIVE DEVELOPMENT	CONSUMPTION	PARTICIPATION IN GROUP LIFE
Upper class (1–3%	High occupational prestige	Consistent attitudes	Tasteful consumption	High participation in groups segregated by breeding, religion, ethnicity, race, and function
Upper-middle class (10–15%)		Integrated self-perception	Affluence and comfort	
Lower-middle class (30–35%)		Inconsistent attitudes — Unrealistic self-perception	Modest standard of living — Consumption of mass "material" and "symbolic" culture	Low participation in group life
Working class (40–45%)	Low occupational prestige	Greater prevalence of mental illness	Austere consumption	
Lower class (20–25%)	Stigma of worthlessness on the labor market		Physical suffering — Acute economic anxiety	Social isolation

TABLE 17-1. Continued

CLASS (AND PERCENTAGE OF TOTAL POPULATION)	POWER			
	PARTICIPATION IN POLITICAL PROCESSES	POLITICAL ATTITUDES	LEGISLATIVE AND GOVERNMENTAL BENEFITS	DISTRIBUTION OF JUSTICE
Upper class (1–3%)	High participation	Belief in efficacy of political action	Recieve the bulk of governmental benefits	Legal order biased in support of their interests and rights
Upper-middle class (10–15%)	in voting and other forms of political participation including monopoly on high governmental positions	Support for civil rights and liberal foreign policy		Much greater utilization of legal processes than classes below
Lower-middle class (30–35%)		Negative attitude toward governmental intervention in economy and toward welfare programs		
Working class (40–45%)	Tendency not to vote or participate	Tendency to discount value of political action Except for minorities, opposition to civil	Governmental neglect, some repression, some	Legal order biased against lower classes
Lower class (20–25%)	in politics	rights Support for more nationalist foreign policy and governmental programs that provide economic help and security	paternalism	Little utilization of legal processes

[a]This estimate is based on a variety of sources: the federal government; especially the Census Bureau; community, metropolitan, and national studies; and interpretive works. The proportion of the total population represented by each class is given as a percentage range to emphasize that this is an estimate. For expository purposes, racial and ethnic minorities are not included.

Slow economic growth, a stagnant standard of living, and a shrinking middle class may all point to a bipolar class system in the future.

However, it is too early to make dogmatic statements about the future of the American class system. What we do know is that the general relation between legitimate and illegitimate elements has not changed much and that there has been no significant increase in equality of opportunity, competition, or social justice (remembering, of course, that the civil rights and women's movements have simply moved blacks and females into the class system). Simply put, our social classes represent significant and enduring differences in the benefits Americans derive from society. By referring to these strata, therefore, one can predict outcomes in a wide range of areas, including family life; health; civic, political and cultural participation; voting; type and amount of crime; justice; and so on. Obviously, some overlap between the various strata, some differences within them, and some regional and local variations exist. Despite these qualifications, however, America's social classes are real because each is a network of social groups sharing unequally and often illegitimately in the totality of social benefits.

The Upper Class

It is safe to assume that the United States possesses a small collection of upper-class families that enjoy a thoroughgoing consistency of class, prestige, and power statuses.[1] More specifically, this class of families has great economic power derived from its ownership and control of economic enterprises; its wealth is secure over generations; and it enjoys high and dependable income. Furthermore, it enjoys high family stability, life expectancy, and mental health; high-quality socialization and education; high occupational prestige and satisfaction; high levels of comfort and diversion; high psychic satisfaction from material and symbolic consumption; high psychic satisfaction and high prestige from primary and secondary associations; and great access to, influence over, and protection from political and legal processes.

The basic causal process that maintains such families at the top is readily explicable; each of the foregoing categories of benefits reinforces the others, producing a web of causation that enables upper-class families to weather and prevail over adversity, whether in the form of economic depression, or an occasional mental illness or retarded child. No understanding of this group of families is possible if one restricts oneself to individualistic explanations. On the contrary, their social position derives from the historical accumulation and consolidation of advantage, including careful attention to the socialization structures and processes that ensure continuity from one generation to the next.

---

[1]Obviously, this definition excludes the new rich (instant business millionaires, entertainment celebrities) and the criminal rich.

It can be assumed that upper-class families are fairly self-conscious about their position in society, though they do not characteristically emphasize their superiority by demanding deference or recognition from society-at-large. The main evidence for imputing self-consciousness about social class to this group is the careful and comprehensive way in which they raise their children and manage their lives and the fact that membership in this stratum is restricted to those who qualify on both class and prestige criteria. This class also derives considerable unity and social power from common upbringing, education, intermarriage, socializing and associational membership, and overlapping economic statuses. Finally, surveys have shown that in general the upper classes are more conscious of social class than are the lower classes.

The upper class has not been subjected to exact empirical study, and we must infer most of its characteristics. It is tradition-conscious without being backward or reactionary; it is civic minded without being much interested in politics or public service. It is a leisure class, though its males work at occupations. It supports charitable, educational, and cultural activities and organizations, though its role may be declining as hard-pressed colleges, museums, service agencies, and research institutes become increasingly dependent on tax funds and business contributions to support themselves.

The power of the upper class derives from its wealth, which gives it control over the fundamental process of capital investment. The wealth of the upper class is intertwined and there is extensive overlap and cooperation among its various members. The upper class is also intertwined with the upper classes of other capitalist societies. The power of the upper class also derives from its ability to set the terms of membership for new wealth—here its control of both elite private schools and elite prestige groups is important. Its control over corporations and secondary organizations as well as government gives it the power to determine how the upper middle class should behave. Its power is also secured by good works (especially through foundations), by reform (corporate liberalism or support of moderate Republicans and Democrats), and by the liberal ethos of individualism, competition, and progress.

The Upper Middle Class

Families whose breadwinners are proprietors of substantial businesses or farms or upper-level managers or professionals, in either "private" or "public" life, enjoy a high level of sociocultural-personality benefits and a high level of consistency in their various benefits and statuses. In recent years women have increased their share of this group either alone or as the working partner of their spouse.

This class of families is distinguished from the upper class by its lack of certain prestige assets, but it appears not to suffer much on this account. As we have noted, one of the characteristics of a stable class system is the existence of many different ways by which individuals and families can obtain satisfaction. In any case, to join the ranks of the upper class, upper-middle-class families must learn to consume and to associate according to upper prestige standards and protocols. For real and lasting success in this regard, they must place their children in the socialization structures (especially private schools and prestige colleges) that old-rich families have established for their own offspring. In the meantime, upper-middle-class families participate in a full range of voluntary organizations, founding their own clubs and frequenting new resorts if need be. While they may occasionally experience discomfort when they consume or when they apply for membership in exclusive clubs, they tend to enjoy high consistency in all their statuses.

An upper-middle-class family is by definition characterized by high income, high education, high occupation (in terms of both prestige and other satisfactions), high participation in voluntary associations, and high awareness and participation in political life. Such families enjoy stable family life, privacy, pleasant surroundings, and stimulating associations. Their children of both sexes receive higher education as a matter of course, and their members enjoy the comfortable feeling that they are fully normal.[2]

Post-1945 America witnessed a significant growth in the absolute numbers of the upper middle class, though there appears to have been only slight growth in its relative size. Basically, the upper middle class is made up of individuals (and their families) who rode the wave of post–World War II corporate and professional expansion. Subject to the long-range process of rationalization, there has been a steady bureaucratization of the economy (the growth of corporate concentration), the professions (hospitals, law firms, universities, and so on), voluntary organizations (professionally run charitable organizations, foundations, trade and professional organizations, labor unions, churches, and so on), and, of course, government.

Thought of in terms of class (and not of the ideology of "nonegalitarian classlessness"), much of what has occurred in post-1945 America makes sense as class modernization, not as the reduction of ascription and the realization of merit and equality. As the upper and upper middle classes have grown in absolute numbers (not in relative size), elite institutions of higher education have been enlarged and others have been upgraded. As maturing industrial society has experienced long-term and short-term pressures and crises (technological displacement of labor and large-scale migration, boom and bust, labor unrest, war, racial conflict, student unrest, pollution, and the

---

[2]Remember that we are speaking about relative modal tendencies. The upper middle class obviously experiences trouble of various sorts, notably as a result of the pressure on children at this level to match or exceed the attainments of their successful fathers (and increasingly, mothers). And new difficulties have appeared at this level—for example, among dual-career couples as indicated by the fact that women with graduate-professional degrees have experienced high divorce rates.

like), it has increasingly turned to political solutions, which are defined by the upper middle class and its political allies—the rich, entrenched small-town business people and professionals, and small farmers. It is not surprising, therefore, that the upper middle class is a major beneficiary of most legislation, reform and otherwise. It goes without saying that this class is not a ruling class in any traditional sense. For one thing, it is too diverse in composition to have clear-cut common economic and political interests. Furthermore, it is too deeply committed to economic functions to be committedly political. On the whole, it is conservative on most domestic economic issues and liberal on foreign policy and civil rights.

The Lower Middle Class

The lower middle class is a very diverse group, unified loosely by the fact that it is not a manual (factory) laboring class, and, more importantly, by an overall level of social existence that places it above the working class and gives its children a much greater probability of rising to the upper middle class. The lower middle class includes small-business people and small farmers; various self-employed or marginal professionals[3] and semiprofessionals (teachers, clergy, local elected officials, social workers, nurses, police officers, firefighters); and sales, clerical, and middle-management personnel, both private and public. On the whole, members of this class enjoy stable family lives and a certain measure of occupational prestige; they are civic minded; and while they participate in political life less than the upper classes, they are more political than the classes below (each of the segments of this class can exhibit different shades of political behavior depending on issue and context). The various segments of this class have diverse histories, and each is potentially subject to various forms of inconsistency.[4] Small-business people, small farmers, and independent professionals are still committed to the laissez-faire ethic of rugged individualism, even though each of these groups has suffered a decline in relative class, prestige, and power status over the past century. Quasi-professionals, as well as sales, clerical, and middle-management personnel, enjoy a measure of prestige because of their education, because they are associated with valued social functions, and because their work is clean and allegedly cerebral, but their class position is not always congruent with their prestige. One of the persistent trends in this area is the growing unionization of teachers, firefighters, police officers, and lower-level white-collar servants on a "professional" basis—that is, without associating

---

[3]These same professionals could well be members of the upper middle class or even upper clan in their local class hierarchies but become lower middle class when ranked nationally. The reader will recall that professionals are themselves stratified internally on various grounds; see "Stratification Within Classes and Occupations" in Chapter 10.

[4]For a discussion of class inconsistency *within* class, see "America's Unique Class Politics" in Chapter 13.

themselves with factory and other service workers with whom they share many basic economic problems. Among these groups, small-business people and small farmers experience peculiar inconsistencies in their economic (class) positions. Small-business people are subject to many economic markets (credit, labor, commodity) as both buyers and sellers, and thus are unlikely to develop a coherent class ideology. The inconsistency of their position probably goes a long way toward explaining the appeal of that magical mechanism, the free market, for small-business owners. Farmers also have an inconsistent market relation: They are often buyers of credit in a seller's market and sellers of commodities in a buyer's market.

Both small farmers and owners of small businesses have made a considerable effort to shore up their difficult economic positions by stressing prestige factors. Both stress the moral value of their respective ways of life (self-sufficiency, competition) and both link their activities to the health of society. Neither group, however, is above using government to lower its costs—such as of transportation and credit—to stabilize the price of what it sells ("fair trade" laws, farm price supports), or to prevent collective bargaining by labor unions. The basic defensive posture of the semiprofessions, on the other hand, is collective action (increasingly collective bargaining) and the upgrading of their professional images, especially through increased and unnecessary educational requirements promoted by professional associations.

The Working Class

When we turn our attention from the lower middle class to the working class, we cross a rather deep cleavage in the American class system. The evidence points overwhelmingly to a significant gap between the level of social and cultural benefits received by blue-collar workers and those received by the classes above them. (A gap of similar magnitude separates the working class and the lower class.) The term *working class* obviously refers to a broad, diverse group of families encompassing highly skilled as well as semiskilled and unskilled workers—a group, in other words, that subsumes quite varied levels of income, work satisfaction, and prestige. If by *working class* one means workers who are steadily employed in manual or blue-collar occupations, regardless of other attributes, then inconsistency of class, prestige, and power statuses seems to be the normal condition of the working class. There is, first of all, the confining routine of work and the lack of prestige or public regard for manual work. Working-class marriages are significantly more unstable than are marriages in the classes above. At best, marriages at this level are deeply segregated into masculine and feminine roles; there is considerable isolation and even estrangement between working-class husbands and wives. In comparison with the classes above, working-class families manifest a significantly lower level of participation in community affairs and in the aesthetic and intellectual life of the nation. All in all, working-class life is seriously inconsistent with the American emphasis on freedom and individual choice; happiness; moral, political, and legal equality; and personal fulfillment and identity through work and success.

Some elite elements in the working class receive incomes in the middle-class range of income levels, and are thus somewhat difficult to classify. It is of great importance that this group accounts for the bulk of the working class with college-bound children. However, extreme caution must be exercised in interpreting high working-class incomes. The hourly wages of plumbers, steamfitters, bricklayers, and the like are quite misleading, since seasonal and other forms of underemployment make it difficult to translate hourly wages into true annual incomes. Secondly, a comparison of total work-related economic benefits (pensions, insurance, sick leave, material comforts and safety on the job, and paid holidays and vacations) and power-related economic benefits (taxation, housing policies, recreational facilities, public services in general) would undoubtedly differentiate many lower-middle-class and working-class individuals who earn similar incomes. And, of course, it is of the utmost importance not to confuse individuals with family income data: The bulk of high working-class incomes belong to families with two or more wage earners.

By and large, members of the working class earn incomes that permit only a modest level of comfort. Many working-class families live austere and even impoverished lives. Few can save—accumulation is very slow—and many live on credit. Economically, they are best characterized as living close to their incomes, which has obvious psychological implications. While members of the working class are less self-conscious about residential prestige differentials than the classes above, and do not worry much about being excluded from membership in middle-class clubs, they do face serious psychological insecurity and pain. Workers are typically not protected against serious medical illness, and historically their pensions were not vested—that is, workers lost all rights when they changed jobs or were laid off.[5] Many working-class males experience drudgery or heavy exertion (or both) in their work, compounded by the knowledge that they have little chance of improving their economic status. The working-class female typically faces a life of drudgery, revolving around too many children,[6] and isolation; she often remains closer to her relatives than to her husband.

Trade unions protect only 17 percent of the working class, and misconceptions about the power of unions to the contrary, many unskilled workers are not well paid—that is, they do not enjoy even a modest level of living—even when they are represented by unions. Trade unionism has not resulted

[5]Starting in 1974, Congress has strengthened pension rights for workers but much remains to be done.

[6]Family planning and legalized abortion may have modified this aspect of working-class life for some.

in a monolithic struggle between labor and management, as the popular image has it. Employers still find it possible to appeal to workers against trade unions, and employers and trade union officials often reach agreements against the wishes of workers (sometimes legally and sometimes not). The Reagan administration of the 1980s openly undermined labor strength through its appointees to the National Labor Relations Board, by its open promotion of overseas investment, its curb on social services, and its lack of interest in full employment.

Politically, the working class tends to be more apathetic than the classes above it; when it votes or otherwise participates in politics, it tends to be liberal on economic-welfare issues and conservative on foreign policy and civil rights (with the obvious exception of blacks and some other minorities). The working class gets into a great deal of trouble as a result either of criminal activities or of credit and marital-family problems, but its access to justice and public aid is deeply biased by class factors. Despite the pronounced particularities of the working-class life experience, however, it cannot be said that there exists anything resembling a working-class subculture. Nothing so poignantly expresses the plight of the American working class as the fact that it is subject to the full force of the middle-class ethos.

The Lower Class

The lower class in America is made up of a diverse collection of families and individuals: the permanently unemployed; the erratically employed; the underemployed; the badly underpaid; the old who are poor; abandoned mothers; and the physically, mentally, and psychologically sick, disabled, or different. This group is not united by any common consciousness, nor do its members have much to do with each other. What these individuals have in common, basically, is their worthlessness on the labor market, a class position that renders them fairly worthless in terms of prestige and power as well.

The lower class, therefore, is a composite of different types of individuals and families. Some are multigenerational members of the lower stratum who have inherited their class position as the children of migratory workers, seasonal laborers, hospital help, and the like. Others, unlucky enough to have physical characteristics that do not conform to the country's definition of normality, are destined from birth for the lower class. Still others gravitate downward as a result either of defeat in economic combat or of having or developing undesired or dysfunctional personalities. In the past two decades female-headed one-parent homes have burgeoned, many of which are poor (the feminization of poverty). And there are now significant numbers of young white males, often with families, who are among the poor. In 1987 the majority of the homeless were families with children.

The worthlessness of the lower class comes from the normal operation of capitalist institutions. The problems of the lower class result from the solutions that the upper classes have found for their own problems. The upper classes fight inflation with unemployment and bankruptcy. They favor technology over labor, oppose trade unions, and support immigration. Secure in their own identities and families, they stress individualism, thus making marriages and family life for those below them difficult. They oppose taxes for public services, helping to drive people into the labor market, creating yet another way to maintain labor surpluses. And they jealously guard their absolute right to control investment, including the right to use cheap labor overseas.

As Herbert J. Gans has argued, poverty is deeply connected to the structure of society.[7] The poor (by which Gans means mostly the historic poor of able-bodied workers, not the demoralized, apathetic underclass that has emerged recently) perform a number of functions for society. Their low wages, high relative taxation, and their work as servants directly subsidizes the well-to-do. The poor provide clients and customers for various businesses and professionals. They provide mobility for said businesses and professionals and allow the upper classes to gain prestige from sponsoring various charities. The poor built our cities and are dispossessed by urban renewal. The poor bore the costs of rural change as well. The poor are politically apathetic and their presence helps make possible a bland, noncompetitive political process.

Poverty, therefore, is a structural problem directly linked to the central institutions and power groups of American society. It is not a technical question to be solved by research and secondary reforms (such as welfare checks and food stamps). Gans argues that substitutes (functional equivalents) can be found for some of the functions served by the poor but most of the changes require a *change of power* and are a distinct and perceivable threat to the affluent. Though Gans may be overly optimistic about some aspects of his analysis, his overall conclusion appears sound: *Alternatives to poverty are dysfunctional to the nonpoor and thus cannot be changed without a reduction in the power of those who benefit from poverty.* Put differently, no inroads into poverty (or into many other social problems) appear to be possible unless American power groups accept economic and social planning, and put full (and meaningful) employment at the top of the political agenda.

THE CLASS SYSTEM AND MINORITY GROUPS

The foregoing characterization of the American class system contained almost no references to racial and religious-ethnic minorities. The following depiction of the positions of such minorities in the American class system is

---

[7]Herbert J. Gans, "The Positive Functions of Poverty," *American Journal of Sociology* 78 (September 1972): 175–189; widely reprinted.

again pitched at a high level of generalization. While broadly representative of empirical phenomena, it is not intended as an empirically based theory. Its purpose, rather, is to complete our summary of social stratification in the United States.

High Class, Prestige, and Power:
The Abnormal Norm

The norms and values governing majority-minority relations have been fully embodied historically only by a relatively small group of white, largely Protestant upper- and upper-middle-class families. At this level, remember, there is great consistency among the three hierarchies of social worth. The group that first achieved preeminence in America happened to be white, Anglo-Saxon, and Protestant, and its members simply assumed or asserted the superiority of all they did and believed in. Today, the upper class appears to contain significant numbers of Roman Catholics and Jews; however, because no exact studies exist, we cannot specify exact numbers or determine whether such newcomers are full or only partial members.

Normal Class, Prestige, and Power:
White Protestants

By *normal class* we mean families that do not exhibit unusually high or low achievement in the spheres of occupation, education, or income. White Protestants—both Anglo-Saxons of long duration in the United States and immigrant groups from Germany and Scandinavia—exhibit normal class achievement; in other words, they are well represented above the manual labor rank. As white Protestants, they also have normal prestige despite the fact that the occupations white Protestants hold and the churches they attend vary widely in class composition and prestige worth.[8]

Normal Class, Changing Prestige and Power:
European Roman Catholics

This category includes Roman Catholics of European origin (French, Irish, German, Polish, Italian) and European Roman Catholics who entered the United States via Canada (French Canadians). Thanks to their location in urban centers, Roman Catholics have been assimilated culturally, which is to say that socioeconomic status predicts more about a Roman Catholic than does religion. Even on basic issues such as birth control and parochial education, it cannot be said that there is a Roman Catholic position (among the laity) that varies much from the class views of non-Catholics. And in the field

---

[8]There is also a depressed white Protestant Anglo-Saxon group, largely rural but also concentrated in urban "hillbilly" enclaves.

of politics it appears that the historic proclivity of (underdog, working class) Roman Catholics to support the Democratic party has come to an end. As they diversify by class, Roman Catholics vote along the same class lines that divide other Americans. While basic religious attitudes have no doubt changed, there is still a prestige ranking that affects European Roman Catholics adversely. Because of both national origin (long associated with working-class status) and religion, European Roman Catholics do not mingle easily with other Americans outside the dimensions of class. Associational life in the United States is pervasively segregated along religious-ethnic lines, though such segregation is not necessarily enforced or characterized by feelings of resentment. Indeed, a relatively full way of life is available to the Irish of Boston, the French Canadians of Burlington, Vermont, and their counterparts elsewhere. While complaints may be expressed about this or that grievance or injustice, resentment of the system of society is minimal. Indeed, as we saw earlier, prestige segregation plays an important role in making the American system of stratification work.

Normal-to-High Class, Subnormal Prestige and Power: Jewish and Asian Americans

A number of minorities in the United States enjoy normal-to-high class achievement but suffer from subnormal prestige and power. This category of minorities includes Jews, Japanese Americans, Chinese Americans, and Americans from India. By and large, these groups have matched or exceeded the class achievements of majority Americans, but they suffer from adverse prestige evaluations on religious, ethnic, and racial grounds. While these groups have taken on the American cultural identity, they live and associate separately from other Americans. The position of Japanese and Chinese Americans in Hawaii is somewhat different from that of their counterparts in the continental United States: The latter has a deeper racist tradition than Hawaii, though no exact comparative studies exist.

Low Class, Negative Prestige and Power: The Oppressed and Depressed

It is no exaggeration to say that the United States possesses a substantial group of families and unrelated individuals who exhibit all the earmarks of a "permanent" proletariat. This category of minorities includes significant numbers of black Americans, Native Americans, Eskimos, Mexican Americans, Puerto Ricans, and to some extent Filipinos. It also includes a diverse group of white Protestants, who are not readily identifiable and thus not easily denied prestige; "hillbilly" is the most descriptive, though hardly the most flattering, term for this group.

Though each of these minorities is itself stratified, containing middle- and upper-class members, in the aggregate these minority groups have not made any significant relative gains vis-à-vis the class standing of mainstream white Protestants and white European Roman Catholics. They also suffer from a low prestige evaluation (largely associated with their historic economic subordination), which is largely expressed in racist terms. By force of class, prestige and power, these groups are barred from full or even adequate participation in American society. The vicious process in which low class (income, wealth, occupation, education) leads to low prestige (through racist values and beliefs, ethnic prejudice, residential segregation, interactional segregation), which in turn reinforces low class is an institutionalized pattern that will not be easy to break.

In addition, the power position of this group of minorities has been compromised throughout American history. Despite the rhetoric and the promises of American society, the most that can be claimed for the strenuous reform movements of recent decades is that they have lifted these groups out of "caste" subordination into class subordination. Though these minority groups achieved significant power mobility in the 1960s through the acquisition of a more effective franchise, they remain weak politically because they are weak economically; do not have access to politically relevant voluntary pressure groups; and are gerrymandered by the economics of transportation and housing, by discrimination, by various forms of public policy, and by explicitly drawn political boundaries.

HOW AND WHY THE SYSTEM WORKS

The United States falls short of its ideals by a considerable margin, and public opinion surveys indicate that the American people know this. Why then has the United States' failure in this regard not led to more popular disaffection? Why, for example, does the deep populist streak in American life not collide more violently with the inegalitarian (achievement-oriented and ascriptive) demands of our economic, familial, social, and political institutions? Why is the legitimacy of American institutions not subject to more widespread questioning, considering the deep and persistent ascriptive inequality that has characterized our history? Why does the irregular performance of the American economy not elicit deeper questioning of the economic system? The failure of the market economy to control pollution is only the latest chapter in a long record of failures to overcome poverty, produce full employment, achieve economic stability and harmony, integrate minority groups, and in general promote achievement and competition. Blatant disparities of wealth and power seem not to stir popular unrest, even though it is widely believed that the American reward system falls far short of matching traditional American norms of achievement. And why is there no concerted attack on the liberal *system* of society when Americans express widespread disbelief in the reality of its central legitimating ideal, equal opportunity?

What is it, therefore, that makes the United States work and what are the things that must be changed if its illegitimate elements are to be elinimated? Of first importance in understanding the United States' stability (as well as its tensions, dysfunctions, and inequities) is its economic system.

The Reality of Economic Growth

However difficult it is to interpret the social implications of economic growth, there is no denying that much of the loyalty of the American population to the American way of life is due to promises kept: Commitment and adherence to the American way of life has paid off in both psychic and material benefits for broad segments of the American people. Whether there is a better way to run an economy is not likely to become an issue as long as the economy by and large produces the satisfactions it promises.

Real economic growth produces an expectation of growth and a belief and faith in progress, and thus makes it easier for people to endure the hardships and disappointments of the moment. A future-oriented psychology is deeply rooted in the needs of capital formation (savings, thrift), socialization processes that stress deferred gratification, and in the middle-class sense of order, predictability, and control. All in all, the futurism inherent in an expansive economy is a potent solvent for pessimism and frustration.

The impact of American economic values and norms on the American personality has been deep and lasting in other ways as well. The American economy has always provided some measure of choice, which goes hand in hand with the ethic of individualism and personal responsibility for success and failure. American values have emphasized personal fulfillment from economic endeavor, and the nation provided the means of fulfillment for many: cheap, fertile land; a growing and diversifying business and occupational system; many and diverse forms of educational opportunity; and a congenial moral and political climate.

Stability Through Economic Expansion and Complexity

The specific economic processes that promote stability and forestall class struggle can be enumerated without lengthy explanation, since they recapitulate analyses made earlier:

1. Economic growth means a high and growing level of material satisfaction, a phenomenon that has played and continues to play an important role in sustaining the morale of the American population and in lubricating class relations. Readers will recall the highly developed system of differential and common consumption in which Americans participate. This payoff in goods and services is undoubtedly influential in disciplining workers to accept hateful work routines and in persuading others to undergo the arduous training for upper-level

occupations. While sizable segments of the lower classes do not believe that real equality of opportunity exists or that achievement lies at the heart of differential rewards, there is nonetheless widespread *personal* acceptance of the possibility of getting ahead, especially if one has what it takes.

This faith in the possibility of success is based on the realities as well as the illusions of American experience. It is due partly to rising living standards (without relative social mobility), partly to families' views of themselves as achieving mobility over more than one generation ("I want my kids to have what I didn't have"), and partly to actual vertical mobility, some of it quite spectacular and well publicized. Of considerable importance is the fact that a large proportion of economic growth is distributed within classes—that is, it is not necessary for a family or individual to change class in order to enjoy a rise in standard of living.

2. The American economy has not only continued to generate high levels of opportunity but it has done so largely by diversifying its occupational structure. Diversification and upgrading help to stabilize the American class system in a number of ways. For one thing, these processes make possible a variety of ways in which Americans can find work satisfaction, which is of special importance at the middle and upper levels of the occupational structure. The vast increase in the number and types of upper- and middle-level occupations has made it possible for large numbers of Americans to rise in economic status without having to challenge incumbents at higher class levels. The growth of the professions and semiprofessions is a fundamental aspect of the stabilizing process. Seen in another way, occupational upgrading and diversification are aspects of the deep functional specificity that serves to insulate and cushion relations between superiors and inferiors, professionals and clients, exploiters and exploited.

3. The growth of the American economy has also diversified class interests and affiliations. This aspect of the American class system has already been developed fully and needs no further elaboration. In a manner unprecedented in any previous system of social stratification, the United States has developed a rich variety of class relations through its labor, credit, and commodity markets. These class relations overlap and make it difficult for generic class interests to emerge and congeal. It is noteworthy that while new complexities are being added to American class relationships, old forms are not necessarily discarded or eliminated. The most important consequence of class relations of this complexity is to prevent metaphysical confrontations between self-conscious antagonistic strata while promoting a pragmatic, strange-bedfellow mentality.

4. The stability of the American class system also depends on both economic security and insecurity. Though the American labor force and the various economic interests are far from feeling secure, a certain measure of security has emerged in the form of pensions, Social Security, medical and life insurance benefits, seniority and tenure systems, and, of course, trade unionism. We have stressed the importance of collective bargaining as a co-opting process that contributes to the stability of the American class system. The advent and establishment of collective bargaining means that a large and potentially powerful segment of society has endorsed the validity of capitalism and of its relative position in the capitalist system. The rise in the level of tolerated unemployment, the movement of capital overseas (which, in effect, means that American workers are pitted against Third-World labor), the decline in real wages, and the virtual ineffectiveness of the labor strike may trigger changes.

It is highly likely that most members of the American lower middle and working classes lead marginal economic existences. They do not and cannot save, their pensions do not provide security, and for many there is the constant threat of unemployment. And insecurity is a way of life for many owners of small businesses and farmers as well. Given the tradition of Protestant-bourgeois responsibility, economic insecurity undoubtedly induces ritualistic conformity and self-blame for economic misfortune.

Heterogeneity Within Strata

The general thrust of the American economy has drawn large numbers of Americans of various economic, religious, ethnic, and racial backgrounds upward (and downward) into strata other than those in which they were born and raised. As a result, the various class levels of American society—the upper class, the upper middle class, the lower middle class, the working class, and the lower class—are heterogeneous in composition, though not all to the same extent or with the same consequences. Thus, in addition to the heterogeneous class (economic) interests that characterize the members of each of these levels, there exists a heterogeneity of religion, ethnicity, race, and previous class condition.

For example, the upper class is diversified by class since it includes holders of wealth in competitive industries and a variety of competitive elite occupations. And the upper class is further diversified by the entrance of Roman Catholic and Jewish families. However, diversification has probably not proceeded very far among the upper class. The smallness of that class and the fact that membership in it requires extensive socialization (elite education, manners, forms of consumption, and so on) ensures a general homogeneity of behavior and outlook, including consciousness of class. At this level, then, it is homogeneity that produces stability as the WASP upper stratum absorbs new elements into its way of life. Actually, the chief function of the small number of Roman Catholics and Jews at this level is probably not to provide religious-ethnic diversity but to serve as token proof that the United States is an open society.

The heterogeneity of American strata increases as one descends the class ladder, leading to a general conclusion that, while relative homogeneity produces stability at the top, it is relative heterogeneity that helps to stabilize the classes below it. It is difficult for a distinct consciousness of kind to develop or for concerted class action to take place when each economic class includes a variety of occupations and economic interests. How much more difficult it is when economic classes also contain Protestants, Roman Catholics of various nationalities, and Jews; whites, blacks, yellows, browns, and reds; and old-family achievers as well as new arrivals still bound by ties of blood, friendship, and locality to people and places belonging to higher or lower strata. It is impossible to account for the absence of a revolutionary working class in the United States or of the weakness of the American trade union movement, for example, unless this process of stratum differentiation is taken into account.

Insulating Processes

One of the outstanding features of the American system of social stratification is that the various strata do not interact as strata, as is more common in estate and caste systems. Actually, contact between strata is quite limited outside of carefully defined and functionally specific economic relations. By and large, each of the strata is insulated from the others by residential, associational, and political "segregation." In a real sense, the various strata lead full social lives without coming into contact with each other except in class-structured ways. Primary relations, which are heavily structured by class, absorb large amounts of time, and members of all class levels undoubtedly fall back on their primary groups to cushion themselves against the pressures and hurts of secondary, especially economic, relations. Outside their primary relations class members tend to associate with class equals and when they do not, they invariably interact in formally organized or functionally specific situations: work, shopping, education, voluntary groups, professional help. Relations between members of different classes are also smoothed and stabilized by the fact that work, education, professional needs, and voluntary activities are often under the control of members of one's own religion, ethnic group, or "race." The bitter conflicts over school integration through busing and mixed-class housing projects illustrate what happens when different classes come into contact outside class-structured channels.

This process of *institutional closure* varies from class to class and from one region of the country to another. But the existence of class-based subsocieties is quite real, and goes a long way toward explaining why social classes in the United States are not more conscious of or antagonistic toward one another. Marx thought that class consciousness would arise if members of the same class interacted (such as in a factory). Weber had the surer insight—class consciousness is more likely to arise when interaction *between* classes produces a sense of exploitation and oppression.

Stratum insulation occurs at all levels, but is most obviously manifested at the top and at the bottom. Upper-class families live in carefully isolated residential areas, and they are educated, worship, and engage in leisure activities with class peers. Breadwinners in the upper class and upper middle class often have no direct experience of how the other classes live. Even when they leave their residential areas, they often see little of the outside world. For example, commuters from upper- or upper-middle-class suburbs or towns see little of how other classes live on their way to or from, or even during, work.

An interesting variation on the process of insulation is created by class segregation combined with religious, ethnic, and/or racial segregation. Ghettoization is only one variant on this pattern, and the well-known separation of black and Mexican Americans from the rest of society need not be gone into again. But a word should be said about segregation at other class levels and of other minority groups. In a real sense, Jewish Americans and European-origin Roman Catholics are also segregated, though not as thoroughly as Mexican and, especially, black Americans. Our perception of this pattern is blurred, as is that of the affected minorities, because we associate a rise in the class (economic) system with freedom and independence.

The Expansion of Political-Legal Rights

The right of the general population to participate in political decisions is of paramount importance to the functioning and stability of the American class system. If we remember the vital role played by government in mediating and adjusting class-prestige interests, the role of the equal vote is apparent—it legitimates the far-reaching powers of legislators and political officials and their staffs. The extension of the suffrage during the pre–Civil War period, for example, went a long way toward stabilizing class (commodity, credit, labor) relations. It is of no little importance that American workers did not have to fight for the right to vote. By ending the formal identification of class with power (for example, by dropping the property qualification for voting), the extension of suffrage placed economic relations and conflicts in a wider moral, legal, and political context. As a result, class relations were disguised, and their potential for explosive confrontation was defused. Indeed, there is no better way of demonstrating the essential absence of change in the United States than to note how exactly our political and social history corresponds to Madison's argument in *The Federalist Papers*, number 10. Madison, remember, argued that property differences are due to the "diversity of human faculties," that conflicts are due mostly to property, that government cannot and should not eliminate property differences (which are natural) but only cushion or regulate conflicts, and that this is best done by removing the conflict from its immediate context (representative government).

The extension of suffrage to blacks (ineffective, however, until the 1960s), to women in 1919, and to eighteen- to twenty-year-olds in 1971 has also helped to defuse and diffuse class relations. The extension to blacks of political-legal rights and equality softens and disguises a heavily lopsided class relation. Similarly, the extension of the vote and the granting of a relatively full complement of legal rights to women serve to individualize American society and to disguise both the problem of the family (ascription and class advantage) and the subordinate social and economic position of women.

The lowering of the voting age to eighteen in 1971 was a response to a number of factors, the most obvious of which was the fact than an unpopular war was being fought by nonvoting conscripts. But the rise of educational standards and the variation in age requirements for performing various adult functions (voting, leaving school, working, driving a car, drinking, getting married, legal responsibility) also helped to persuade Americans to lower the voting age. A less consciously acknowledged factor is American society's failure to provide the young a coherent pattern of transition from high school to work. Giving eighteen-year-olds the vote has no doubt helped to defuse the potential for conflict inherent in high rates of unemployment among young males.

The political-legal rights of Americans are embedded in a normative system enjoying wide support,[9] and this too has a bearing on class stability. Public holidays (celebrating the birthdays of great national figures and commemorating great national achievements), public buildings and monuments, historical sites, state occasions, the mass media, religion, and, of course, education, all serve to promote this overriding normative tradition and to make it difficult for antisocial movements or ideologies to arise. Of considerable interest is Robert N. Bellah's depiction of these legitimating traditions as a civil religion.[10]

Power and the Economy

Though the state—at all levels—is a prime factor in the operation of the American economy, our awareness of its functioning is less full and sophisticated than it ought to be. One of the most interesting, and largely unnoticed, ways in which government interpenetrates with the class dimension is our money and credit system. Since the origin of the Republic, the issuance of currency has been a public responsibility, and the nature of the credit-banking system figured prominently in the early political struggles of the American nation. The outcome of these struggles was that the credit system of the nation was gradually placed under *fiduciary* structures, the trusteeship of government supplementing and supporting private banking. While this process was not completed until the 1930s, it now appears so normal that we fail to recognize that public money and credit, and public regulations and safeguards, have structured a specific kind of private class-based credit system.[11] By disguising a class relation in fiduciary terms, our political-legal system has helped to make this aspect of a capitalist economy seem normal. And by so doing, it has stabilized a class relationship (creditor-debtor) that has caused a great deal of trouble in our own history and in the histories of other societies.

---

[9]The broad American consensus on the Lockean liberal political tradition is amply documented by Donald J. Devine, *The Political Culture of the United States: The Influence of Member Values on Regime Maintenance* (Boston: Little, Brown, 1972).

[10]"Civil Religion in America," *Daedalus* 96 (Winter 1967): 1–21.

[11]Basically, those who have collateral pay less to borrow money than those who do not have collateral (when and if the latter can get credit).

Another notable political-legal adaptation relevant to the stability of the American class system has been the loosening of the definition of property rights. The gradual acceptance of the right of the power dimension to interfere with property rights through taxation, regulation, licensing, and sanctioning of collective bargaining represents a significant development in the history of the American class system. Its full import is only partially understood, however, if one thinks of public economic intervention as a struggle between the principle of class and the principle of equality. Basically, the growth of public authority over the economy and the legalization of collective bargaining were adaptive responses that supported the principle of class stratification. The vast growth of public fiduciary structures and functions is also largely understandable as a way of making the overall class system work. In sum, the growing array of regulatory commissions, licensing and certifying procedures, collective bargaining and mediation services, banking insurance, and presidential and congressional commissions as well as governmental purchasing and subsidization policies, tax and credit policy, moral exhortation, and wage-price controls, represent efforts to take the heat off class relations in one market after another.

The government also promotes economic well-being directly. The general (and always proportional) tax cuts in the post–World War II period were implemented by a public authority deeply responsive to the class system. The government also acts as an employer, often deliberately providing jobs for specifically depressed segments of society. (For example, the federal government employs a disproportionate number of black Americans.) And, of course, the government in its roles as the military, as a research and development agency, and as a dispenser of funds for research provides for the economic stability and advancement of different portions of our economy and labor force.

CLASS AND INTERNATIONAL RELATIONS

The American class system is also stabilized and redirected by developments on the intersocietal level. The United States has always benefitted from its foreign relations. It brought in 40 million immigrants of high quality (young, healthy individuals of working age and with considerable capital)[12] and has enjoyed a brain drain (foreign students do not return to their country of origin; professionals educated abroad immigrate to the United States). It exported staples and imported machinery in the nineteenth century and reversed the process in the first three-quarters of the twentieth century. It has also provided a way for American capital to prosper during the post–World

[12]Immigrants in recent decades may not have as much capital as in the past.

War II period through overseas investment. The government has various devices to promote overseas investment and maintains hundreds of military bases abroad to protect American investments and other interests. In the 1980s the government began to cooperate with other developed capitalist societies to regulate the international economy through the management of exchange rates, and domestic fiscal-tax-credit policies.

Intersocietal relations have also provided a way for American power groups to evoke and develop tribal loyalties against enemies real and imaginary, legitimate and illegitimate. Since 1945, for example, there has been a continuous exaggeration of the Soviet threat. And like other countries, the United States promotes solidarity by purging itself of both real and imaginary subversives.[13]

THE STRUCTURE OF SOCIAL POWER

Expressed in the vocabulary of stratification analysis, *social power* refers to a social class or classes possessing class, prestige, and power assets of such an order, intensity, and magnitude that it controls the structure and direction of society. The more sophisticated formulations of this idea specify the type of social system that produces such (social) power.

Three different images of social power can be distinguished: the power elite, the pluralist, and the semi-pluralist.

Is There a Power Elite?

C. Wright Mills argued that the main trend in the development of American capitalism is economic and political concentration. He argued further that there was already in evidence a small power elite drawn from and coordinating the upper reaches of the corporate world, the federal executive branch of government, and the military, which had come into being because of processes inherent in advanced industrial society. Perched atop the stratification dimensions of class and power, this group possesses, according to Mills, significantly more power than Congress, trade unions, farmers, small business, or the general public.[14]

G. William Domhoff, who has set himself the task of trying to substantiate Mills' thesis more fully, has investigated the upper levels of the various hierarchies in American society and offers what he considers conclusive evidence that a small homogeneous, stable, and interchangeable collection of

---

[13]Albert James Bergesen, "Political Witch Hunts: The Sacred and Subversive in Cross-National Perspective," *American Sociological Review* 42 (April 1977): 220–233.

[14]C. Wright Mills, *The Power Elite* (New York: Oxford University Press, 1956).

very rich individuals (and families) occupies the command positions of American society.[15]

Our study of social stratification found considerable concentration of power but not in the sense of a tiny power elite calling the tune by which the nation dances. The absence of a power elite does not mean, however, that the United States has approximated either a nonegalitarian classless society or a pluralistic self-equilibrating system of power, or that it is even making progress toward pluralism or a democratic meritocracy.

Is the United States Pluralistic?

Pluralists argue that social differentiation has led to a society whose various parts check and balance each other. They argue that American society is open and fluid, allowing individuals and groups to rise and fall according to ability. Pluralists see society as a natural, objective system, and oppose views suggesting that society has to be explicitly managed. When "artificial" human actions are taken, argue pluralists, they should be directed toward helping the natural society struggling to emerge from history.

American pluralists allege that no single group or combination of groups can dominate the others. The plurality of groups makes for overlapping group membership, which in turn inhibits groups from acting unilaterally. Our pluralist group structure, they argue, avoids cleavage between large contending blocs—there is stability if religious disputes occur among 200 denominations as opposed to two. A pluralist society produces a "strange bedfellow" set of relations. Those who want to ban abortion do not agree on the need for nuclear energy. Those who want gun control do not necessarily agree that school prayer is a good thing. The insurance company that argues against government interference in its investment policies wants the government to control hospital costs or require safer automobiles. Segments of Protestantism and Roman Catholicism oppose gay rights but other segments join secular groups to support them.

This criss-crossing of interests and values makes it impossible, argue pluralists, for arbitrary and unilateral power to emerge. A pluralistic power structure forces groups to make alliances with one another and promotes the arts of negotiation and compromise. Given this pluralistic power structure the public is always provided with alternatives to choose from and is constantly supplied with a wide variety of information to help it make up its

---

[15]G. William Domhoff, *Who Rules America?* (Englewood Cliffs, N.J.: Prentice-Hall, 1967), *The Higher Circles: The Governing Class in America* (New York: Random House, 1971), and *Who Rules America Now? A View for the '80s* (Englewood Cliffs, N.J.: Prentice-Hall, 1983). For a straightforward, sophisticated Marxist interpretation along the same lines, see Charles H. Anderson, *The Political Economy of Social Class* (Englewood Cliffs, N.J.: Prentice-Hall, 1974).

Other theorists—for example, Kees van der Pijl and Michael Useem, have found evidence that the American upper class has succeeded in linking its interests with the upper class of Great Britain and Europe. The evidence suggesting the existence of an international capitalist class (now including Japan) deserves further research. For an earlier discussion of links among the upper classes of capitalist societies, see Chapter 15.

collective mind about public issues. Under pluralism the public interest is guaranteed, or is at least being pursued and approximated.

Pluralist theorists defend both elites and ordinary people. American pluralism, they argue, allows the talented to rise to the top. Each area of human endeavor gradually develops standards to ensure competence, and society is led by its true aristocracy—the achievers in science, business, medicine, law, art, and so on. Ordinary people have their rights, including the right to compete for high position, and an indirect right as consumers, voters, or volunteer workers to influence how society works.

Pluralists argue that the United States is ruled by a shifting coalition of elite groups that comprise a moving equilibrium, not a unified upper class. Elites can get their way only in certain areas and have to yield to other elites on other issues. Ordinary Americans have at least some power to influence events in their everyday lives. But their real power derives from elite competition to gain their support, especially in economic and political markets. American society, pluralists argue, is flexible enough to achieve reforms when needed and no group will remain powerless or be victimized over the long run.

Semi-Pluralism: The Reality of Oligarchy

Our study of the American class system does not substantiate the pluralist argument. Indeed, it is probably true to say (judging from introductory sociology textbooks) that this position is now on the wane in sociology—few sociologists would argue that the United States is characterized by a relative equality of power, by responsible (professionalized) elites, or by a relative equality of opportunity and competition.

If American society does not conform either to the power elite or the pluralist model, to what model does it correspond? The best answer is that we are probably governed by an upper-middle-class to upper-class power structure with strong overtones of oligarchy.[16] The model of a "middle-class" establishment resembles the pluralist model up to a point. There is some truth, for example, in the argument that the liberal democracies are unique because the people rule. Power *is* shared by more people than was the case in the past. But this is not the same thing as saying that the people-at-large participate actively in the business of running society, which they do not, or that they have equal shares of power, which they do not. It is also true that the many groups in contemporary society tend somewhat to check and balance each other as they jostle for advantage. But closer scrutiny reveals that the articulated groups in American society are overwhelmingly middle and upper class in leadership, composition, and social philosophy. This fact is evidence of social power rather than of a natural distribution of ability,

---

[16]An *oligarchy* is a propertied or occupational power group, or collection of such groups, that consciously or unconsciously does not honor the ideals of its society.

since the processes and agencies of achievement in the United States are heavily ascriptive and arbitrary. Far from being a society based on equality of opportunity (with acknowledged gaps), the United States has no equality of opportunity—except among members of the same class—and cannot as long as children are raised in families steeply differentiated by class, and thus by prestige and power.

Stated differently, it is social power that explains individualism rather than the reverse: A minority of white males and their families from middle- and upper-class backgrounds (along with an increasing handful of their wives and daughters, the women's movement) has managed to monopolize important social positions in the name of nonegalitarian classlessness, or the philosophy of individualism. This has led to a hierarchy of ascriptive and arbitrary power in the United States because the dominant groups believe in achievement, excellence, and progress, and continously raise the norms required for admittance to upper-level occupations. Because these norms are largely unrelated to functional performance, their latent function is to maintain an artificial scarcity of qualified personnel. This practice is imitated at all levels as semiprofessionals and skilled workers use the state or their unions to establish unnecessary occupational qualifications. The net result is not pluralistic competition or power but a scramble for a socially created shortage of desirable positions in which the winners are largely preordained by the rules of the game.

The dominant power groups in American society have succeeded, by and large, in inculcating their explanation of how society works in the remainder of the population. Americans not only accept large concentrations of private power, especially corporations and the professions, but also regard this situation as normal and therefore legitimate. And the same thing is true of other basic features of American society: the primacy of economic status and occupation over other institutions; the stress on work and gain; the assumed validity of highly unequal rewards; faith in the automatic beneficence of science, technology, and education; the use of religion as a secular faith; reliance on an individualized and psychologized human nature as the ultimate explanation of behavior; and the assumed fiduciary benevolence of private power blocs.

Of course, there is evidence that Americans are highly critical of the specific ways in which their society works and, as public opinion polls have consistently revealed, have considerably less than full confidence in their leaders and institutions.[17] The important point, however, is that the lower classes find it difficult to articulate a philosophy that would challenge the existing system of power since their Americanism predisposes them away from the concept of power and the institutional explanation of behavior. And underlying the maintenance of the status quo is the fact the upper and lower

[17]See the section "Declining Legitimacy?" in Chapter 14.

classes are all implicated in the existing division of labor. Daily experience, interpreted in terms of the ideology of classless inequality and progress through reliance on existing processes (or variations on them), locates the various classes in orbits that seem normal and natural.

Within the upper and upper middle classes there is an intricate intermeshing of interests that the pluralist model invariably overlooks or slights. Interests are coordinated across competing groups in the same class by intermarriage; interlocking directorships; informal agreements; common experiences, such as schooling, socializing, religion, and business; and "fiduciary" organizations, such as law firms, banks, professional associations, voluntary organizations of various kinds, and governments. The intermeshing of interests can take the form of reciprocal backscratching and support, such as when the insurance industry supports the American Medical Association (AMA) in its fight against a public system of medical care and in turn receives support from the AMA in its own opposition to public insurance programs. Or it can take the form of reciprocal inaction, an important feature of our professional life. Indeed, the existence of noncompeting clusters of power within specific sectors of society, the economy, the professions, education, prestige groups, and politics is a salient feature of American society. These features, together with (1) economic insecurity and competition for scarce jobs and resources at lower levels, and (2) ethnic, religious, and racial hostilities, go a long way toward explaining the nature of social power in America.

It may be that the concept of a semi-pluralist structure of power, composed primarily of the upper class and the upper-middle class, is too broad and hides a more fundamental structure of power. Nonetheless, as will be apparent in the next section, basic changes in the upper class and upper middle class would go farthest in improving American society and wringing out its illegitimate elements.

DOES THE UNITED STATES HAVE A PERMANENT UNDERCLASS?

The Civil Rights Commission's report on minorities (discussed earlier), along with other evidence, raised disturbing issues that go considerably beyond left and right liberal understandings of the nature of minority inequality and what to do about it. Of the greatest importance is the fact that America's racial, ethnic, and female minorities have made no relative advance toward equality despite considerable legal and political help during the greatest and longest period of economic expansion in American history.[18]

---

[18]L. Paul Metzger argues that the traditional assimilationist perspective of sociology (and of left and right liberals) was shattered by the events of the 1960s—see his "American Sociology and Black Assimilation: Conflicting Perspectives," *American Journal of Sociology* 76 (January 1971): 627–647. The events of the 1970s and 1980s have done little to restore faith in it.

During this period the number of poor Americans (disproportionately made up of minorities) has remained fairly stable (roughly 15 percent of the total population). In addition, there has not been much improvement in the status of the handicapped. The stagnant position of America's various disadvantaged groups raises this question: Does the United States have a permanent underclass?

The evidence suggests that it has. The disadvantaged are not a temporary phenomenon but appear to result from the *normal operation of American institutions.* The workings of the economy and the polity have disconnected large numbers from the American mainstream. This insight leads to more questions. Do civil rights laws and other minority-oriented legislation have any effect on economic inequality? The answer appears to be no. Should minorities make a greater effort in education? The answer appears to be no. Are the civil rights laws and programs mostly a way for corporate capitalism to modernize its labor force? Over the past 600 years capitalism has developed a labor force composed of legally free individuals. In the United States it also developed first a slave and then a segregated labor force. Are the civil rights laws merely a way to turn minorities into legally free individuals who can then be held responsible for failure?

All evidence points to systematic and stable injustice for large portions of the American population. The evidence again points not only to the failure of American society to live up to its norms and values but to what appears to be an inherent inability to do so. The evidence suggests that American society cannot hope to achieve its values as long as Americans, especially power groups, continue to take the basic structure of the economy for granted. Ineffective poverty programs, giving minorities their civil rights, and underfunded, unenforced laws to help the handicapped may actually be more a process of legitimating exploitation than a real effort to help the American underclass. Little change can be expected until the working class and broad middle class realize that they too are forced to live in insecure and shrinking sectors of the American economy.

SOME SUGGESTIONS FOR IMPROVING THE AMERICAN CLASS SYSTEM

The Upper Class

The American public cannot expect to have a functional, adaptive society unless more public direction is given to capital investment. There are any number of ways to do this, from direct government investment in strategic industries and services to outright nationalization. There is also the option of socialism. Regardless of how policy in this area proceeds, the concentrated wealth of the upper class must be reduced through taxation. And political reforms, especially eliminating the role of wealth in the financing of political campaigns and abolishing the gerrymander, must be made to reduce the political power of the upper (and upper middle) class.

The Upper Middle Class

The question to ask here is: Must professionalism be wedded to a laissez-faire capitalist society, or can it serve a planned capitalist society or a socialist society? Certainly the crucial thing here is to stop the excessively abstract nature of professional education and focus it instead on policy. This requires a breakdown of artificial disciplines and an emphasis on relating professional problem solving to social causation, especially the economy.

One beneficial result of demanding performance from professional elites is that the excessive qualifications now required for elite occupations can be reduced and this can be followed by a reduction down the line. There is also a need to reduce the incomes of the presently overpaid members of the upper middle class: Executives in large corporations and elite doctors and lawyers come immediately to mind.

The Lower Middle Class

The value of small business to American society and to maintaining healthy local communities needs to be better understood. In addition, semi-professionals, such as teachers, police officers, and nurses, need better work environments.

The Working Class

America needs to follow practices developed in other capitalist societies and make it easier for workers to shift from one line of work to another. And there should be a greater stress on the value of manual work, something that will follow if the upper and upper middle classes are harnessed to social functions.

The Lower Class

The lower class is the creation of an unsatisfactory society. The reforms outlined above, especially if better public services for all are developed, will help cut down on the size of the lower class.

CHAPTER 18

Soviet Society:
Institutions
and the Structure of Power

THE HERITAGE OF ABSOLUTISM[1]

The great land expanse on which Czarist Russia and the Soviet Union emerged has few natural barriers against invasion (except for sheer space and the severity of its winters). Subject to constant invasion, Russia centralized under a czar who was theoretically omnipotent vis à vis nobles and clergy as well as peasants. Russian feudalism lacked the decentralized institutions that made rivalry between monarchy and nobles such a vital feature in the rise of Western constitutionalism. All land belonged to the czar, who assigned it to those who performed state functions. Christianity (Greek Orthodox Church)

---

[1]Soviet society is changing rapidly and general sources become dated quickly. *The U.S.S.R.: A Country Study* (Washington, D.C.: U.S. Government Printing Office, 1971), part of the comprehensive series on contemporary countries prepared by Foreign Area Studies of the American University, is badly dated but nonetheless provides valuable general information in the usual bland, nonpolitical manner of this series. For a fine, comprehensive source, kept reasonably up to date with new editions, see Vadim Medish, *The Soviet Union*, 3rd ed. (Englewood Cliffs, N.J.: Prentice-Hall, 1987). For a valuable series of articles designed to puncture the largely false picture that Americans have of the Soviet Union, written for the *Nation* magazine by an American Soviet specialist, and especially suitable for students, see Stephen F. Cohen, *Sovieticus: American Perceptions and Soviet Realities* (New York: W. W. Norton, 1986).

in Russia also developed as an agency of the state. Missing from Russian history are the conflicts between Caesar and God, State and Church, and society and individual conscience, which played such fruitful roles in the development of Western ideas of pluralism, toleration, and individualism. In short, Russia never developed a distinction between state and society, or society and individual. It was an Oriental despotism, or perhaps better, a despotism derived from and legitimated by need. In this sense the highly centralized Marxist system after 1917 continues the main thrust of Russia's historical development.

Russians are only one of many ethnic groups in the USSR. The expansion of Czarist Russia incorporated many radically different ethnic groups into Russian society. Czarist Russia's pressure against its neighbors has continued under Communist rule as well. Here again there is no break with the past—the pursuit and enhancement of national interests would find czar and commissar (and even a liberal government) in agreement on many things.

While ethnic diversity has led to distinct ethnic political entities in the Soviet Union (including the legal right to their own languages), there is also an insistence on the sovereignty of the national state. The Soviet Union is an *integrated* nation-state, which also means that Russians who make up a bare majority of the population are the dominant ethnic group.

LAND AND PEOPLE

Geography

The Soviet Union has 8 million square miles of relatively landlocked territory, most of it worthless. Much of its agricultural land is poor and its good soil suffers from frequent droughts. Soviet rivers often run the wrong way, and its resources are not located in close proximity to each other. The country's economic problems are further aggravated by the need to disperse its industry as a defensive measure. Nonetheless, the USSR is fabulously rich in natural resources and is largely self-sufficient save for tin, rubber, and coffee. Recently, it has also become aware that some resources are being depleted and that it must protect its natural environment. There is some evidence that planning includes environmental concerns and long-range energy conservation.

Population

The Central Intelligence Agency (CIA) places the Soviet population in 1988 at 286 million.[2] Population size and composition are important to a nation's economy and military strength. The population of Soviet Russia was

[2]U.S. Central Intelligence Agency, *The World Factbook, 1988* (Washington, D.C.: U.S. Government Printing Office, 1988), p. 216.

not known—indeed, kept secret—for a number of years following World War II. Soviet losses in the war were so immense (estimates place the war dead at 20 million compared to 300,000 for the United States) that the country understandably did not advertise its weakness.

The Soviet Union has pursued both antinatalist and pronatalist policies. Currently, it is concerned about prospective labor shortages and would like to increase its low birthrate, especially among its Slavic peoples. But, here as elsewhere, there are no easy answers. A growth of population would yield a dependent population group for the next twenty years. The extra cost of housing, child care, education, and loss of female labor would not bear fruit for two decades. For this and other reasons, one expert doubts that the Soviet Union will take further steps to increase the birthrate.[3]

Nationality Groups

A distinctive feature of the Soviet population is its racial, ethnic, and linguistic diversity. There are approximately 100 distinct "nationalities" and a wide range of linguistic groups, most of them very small. Russians make up only 53 percent of the population although they are clearly the dominant ethnic group. The major difference in the Soviet population is between the Westernized achievement-oriented European peoples, making up approximately 85 percent of the population, and the traditionalist rural people, largely Muslims, found in the Soviet Union's Asian republics (see Table 18–1). Given their higher birth rate, Asians have increased their relative size, and Russians will drop to a bare 50 percent of the total and Europeans to 71 percent by the year 2000.[4]

The Soviet Union has pursued a policy of Russianizing its population, which means not only an attempt to make Russian the primary language but also to bring non-Russians into the achievement-oriented world of industry and science. A number of the smaller "nationalities" have disappeared, but the Soviet Union is not a melting pot. Russification has led to a smaller number of ethnic groups, but these are now larger and more self-conscious and continued integration will no doubt become more difficult; indeed, it has already become more difficult with the liberalization of political expression under Mikhail Gorbachev. The number of Russians in non-Russian areas has increased, but the competition for jobs, housing, and other benefits, especially with the economic slowdown from the 1970s on, will accentuate ethnic differences rather than resolve them.[5] An idea of the language problem faced

---

[3]David M. Herr, "Population Policy," in Jerry G. Pankhurst and Michael P. Sacks, eds., *Contemporary Soviet Society* (New York: Praeger, 1980), chap. 3.

[4]Jeremy R. Azreal, "Emergent Nationality Problems in the U.S.S.R.," in Jeremy R. Azreal, ed., *Soviet Nationality Policies and Practices* (New York: Praeger, 1978), p. 381.

[5]Richard Pipes, "Introduction: The Nationality Problem," in Zev Katz and others, eds., *Handbook of Major Soviet Nationalities* (New York: Free Press, 1975), pp. 1–5.

TABLE 18-1. The Ethnic Diversity of the Soviet Union, 1979

ETHNIC GROUP	PERCENT OF TOTAL
Russians	52.42
Ukranians	16.16
Uzbeks	4.75
Byelorussians	3.61
Kazahks	2.50
Tatars	2.41
Azeri	2.08
Armenians	1.58
Georgians	1.36
Moldavians	1.13
Tadzhiks	1.11
Lithuanians	1.09
Turkmens	0.77
Ethnic Germans	0.74
Khirgiz	0.73
Jews	0.69
Chuvash	0.67
Latvians	0.55
Bashkirs	0.52
32 Other Groups Less than .5%	5.13

Source: Derived from Ralph S. Clem, "The Ethnic Factor in Contemporary Soviet Society," in Jerry G. Pankhurst and Michael Paul Sacks, eds., *Understanding Soviet Society* (Boston: Unwin Hyman, 1988), Table 1-1. Used with permission.

by the Soviet Union can be seen in the fact that only 59 percent of the population have Russian for their mother tongue, although an additional 17 percent know it fluently enough to call it a second tongue.[6]

Population, including rate of increase, is an important element in a nation's economic strength. One of the USSR's economic achievements (and one of the reasons for its economic success) is that it has fully engaged its European population, both male and female, in its economy. Given a declining birthrate among its European population, the Soviet Union faces labor shortages in the 1990s and beyond. Unlike the industrial nations of the West, the Soviet Union is not likely to benefit from an inflow of professionals, immigrants, guest labor, or illegal aliens.

Ethnic and racial diversity is a common feature of societies. Each society faces both unique and similar problems in managing ethnic diversity. All

[6]Jonathan Pool, "Soviet Language Planning: Goals, Results, Options," in Azreal, *Soviet Nationality Policies and Practices*, p. 224.

have found that ethnicity is reviving, not declining. Most experts agree that the Soviet Union faces a considerable drag on its future because of its multiethnic population.[7] The open restiveness of ethnic groups in Lithuania, Georgia, and elswhere since the liberalization of life under Gorbachev confirms their forecasts.

THE SOVIET ECONOMY

The Command Economy

The most notable features of the Soviet economy are that it is totally planned from above and the basic resources and productive capital of Soviet society are publicly owned. In short, economic growth follows the priorities laid down by government planners, which ultimately means the Communist party. Other economies are based on public ownership (for example, Yugoslavia) and others receive considerable direction by government (most developed nations). The Soviet model is distinctive in that public ownership is accompanied by central planning in the form of directives from above and compliance from below—a command, nonmarket economy. The USSR State Planning Committee (Gosplan) develops plans for the entire economy for a given period (usually five years), which when formally adopted have the force of law. Whatever its defects, centralized planning (as a type of centralized power) transformed the USSR into a superpower in less than half a century. Soviet centralized planning clearly gives priority to industrial growth (and military preparedness) and has clearly sacrificed living standards in favor of capital formation.

The Soviet command economy is a success in a number of respects. Under socialist auspices, the Soviet Union industrialized in a relatively short time. Accordingly, it has served as a model for some Third-World countries, providing a significant counter to liberal images of development. State socialism has also been a success if the Soviet economy is compared to other economies. Measured in terms of output growth the Soviet economy is in select company.[8] In any case, the Communist party's single-minded emphasis on heavy industry has made the Soviet Union the world's leading pro-

[7]Ralph S. Clem, "The Ethnic Factor in Contemporary Soviet Society," in Jerry G. Pankhurst, and Michael Paul Sacks, eds., *Understanding Soviet Society* (Boston: Unwin Hyman, 1988), chap. 1. For a collection of essays that sees multiethnicity as a major Soviet weakness, see S. Enders Wimbush, ed., *Soviet Nationalities in Strategic Perspective* (New York: St. Martin's Press, 1985).

[8]Paul R. Gregory and Robert C. Stuart, *Soviet Economic Structure and Performance*, 3rd ed. (New York: Harper & Row, 1986), chap. 11; Joint Economic Committee, Congress of the United States, *U.S.S.R.: Measures of Economic Growth and Development, 1950–1980* (Washington, D.C.: U.S. Government Printing Office, 1982), pt. I.

ducer of a wide range of basic industrial products—for example, coal, oil, steel, and a number of basic chemicals.

The Soviet Union commits far more of its annual production to capital investment than does the United States and even surpasses Japan's rate. Soviet gross national product (GNP) rose from 40 percent of the U.S. level in 1955 to 60 percent in 1977 and then fell to 55 percent in 1985 (GNP in 1986 was $2,357 billion and per capital income was $8,375).[9] The investment rate had to be cut in the late 1970s because of mass discontent with consumption levels, and for this and other reasons the Soviet growth rate has slowed considerably.[10]

The Economic Slowdown

The Stalinist model of economic growth (deliberate sacrifice of consumption goods in favor of investment) succeeded in establishing the Soviet Union as an industrial superpower. Central planning and direction must clearly receive some credit for the Soviet Union's spectacular economic growth. Clearly, too, an economy without private property and market mechanisms can succeed—indeed, the Soviet Union took less time to industrialize than did the capitalist countries.

However, the command or Stalinist model may be suitable only for the initial stage of industrialization. During the 1970s the Soviet growth rate slowed considerably (and is now on a par with that of the Unites States). From a broad perspective the slowdown represents the other side of the coin of economic growth. Initial economic growth, regardless of type of system, appears to be largely the result of employing unused, readily available resources: labor, land, raw materials, waterways, easily obtainable coal, oil, and other energy sources. Between the 1920s and the 1970s Soviet Russia succeeded in transforming its people and natural resources into economic forces. Now it faces the problem of maintaining productivity without being able to bring low-cost resources on line. Soviet oil production, for example, is the highest in the world, but its new oil fields cost considerably more to develop than its older ones. The Soviet labor force is already fully utilized and there are no prospects for fresh additions from immigrants, illegal aliens, women, or births. In all areas the Soviet economy faces the problems of mature industrialization: How to maintain growth in the face of markedly more expensive costs for all economic factors in the context of rising consumer expectations and rising social overhead (crime, alcoholism, broken families,

[9]Central Intelligence Agency, *The World Factbook, 1988*, p. 217.

[10]For a good comparison of the U.S. and Soviet economies, see Andrew Zimbalist, Howard J. Sherman, and Stuart Brown, *Comparing Economic Systems: A Political-Economic Approach*, 2nd ed. (San Diego: Harcourt Brace Jovanovich, 1989), pp. 151–174. For a full picture of the Soviet economy, see Gregory and Stuart, *Soviet Economic Structure and Performance*. An overall assessment of the Soviet economy and comparison with other countries may be found in Chapter 11.

absenteeism, and military expenditures). How much of the country's economic difficulties are due to the maturing of its economy and how much to its commitment to centralized planning is not easy to determine. A leading expert on comparative economies argues that centralized planning has inherent operational problems in the areas of "the transmission of user demand, quality, innovation, initiative, long-term responsibility, misleading prices, lack of objective criteria for choice."[11] Feedback from operational situations, especially from lower-level experience, is poor in a centralized system because of fear, careerism, and the dogma that the center knows best. Centralized planning makes it difficult to identify and replace incompetent personnel. Socialist full employment policies lead to an inefficient use of labor. And inefficiencies have a way of multiplying—for example, the shortage of consumer good means that a significant amount of time is lost by people standing in line waiting to shop.

Central planning, says Alec Nove, also has good features: a steady rate of investment, environmental planning, a more effective control of wages and prices, which provides stability and channels resources and labor into social objectives, and full employment. These virtues are to some extent due to the superior long-range time perspective that is inherent in centralized control and planning.[12]

Most experts on comparative economic systems agree that different economic systems, especially market capitalist and planned socialist economies, cannot be fully and precisely compared (the variables are too complex) and cannot be judged scientifically (at some point value judgments must be used). Both systems have impressive advantages and defects. While market economies are more adaptive, more technology oriented, provide high levels of quality consumption, and utilize labor more efficiently, they also suffer from inflation, wide income differentials, unemployment, economic ups and downs, economic insecurity, large amounts of frivolous consumption, and a significant neglect of basic needs (avoiding these defects is the good feature of the socialist system). Some similarities between capitalist-market and socialist-command economies, however, can be noted. Both are highly concentrated and both stress achievement as a qualification for occupation. And both use political means to achieve economic ends; both have developed welfare states to tie their populations into their respective ways of life.

The ascension to power of Mikhail Gorbachev in 1985 may be a new beginning for the Soviet economy. The three leaders prior to Gorbachev had been elderly and ailing. Gorbachev, relatively young and vigorous, also appears to be astute and capable. Domestically, he has launched a campaign

[11]Alec Nove, *The Soviet Economic System* (London: George Allen and Unwin, 1977), 377.

[12]Nove may be idealizing here somewhat. The Soviet Union is handicapped by a pervasive focus on short-term goals (the Five-Year Plan), and its superior environmental record appears to be largely a function of low consumption.

to reinvigorate the economy, including some distinct moves toward market mechanisms and decentralization. Clearly aware that the Soviet Union has failed to match the West's ability to grow through increased efficiency, Gorbachev has exhorted workers to work harder, has made it easier to voice grievances about incompetence, and has undertaken a campaign against the economic scourge of alcoholism. But there is no evidence that he is willing (or able) to decentralize the economy fully to permit greater on-the-spot decision making, give managers greater power to utilize labor more efficiently, or provide enough consumption incentives to spur work and performance.

Gorbachev's major thrust to invigorate the economy has been to liberalize political expression so that popular demands can put pressure on the Communist party hierarchy and the managers of state industries and services. Another major initiative by Gorbachev to reduce pressure on the Soviet economy has been to purchase consumer goods abroad and to borrow money abroad to purchase factories that produce consumer goods.

Still another initiative to spur the economy has been in the area of foreign affairs. Heavy military expenditures are a drag on the Soviet economy, and Gorbachev has worked hard to achieve arms control/reduction with the United States and to lessen tension with Western Europe and China (Western experts do not see much gain resulting from even a significant reduction of military expenditures).

Gorbachev has also intensified the USSR's entry into the world market that began on a large scale during the 1970s. In 1986 the Soviet Union applied to GATT (General Agreement on Tariffs and Trade) for observer status, and two years later applied for membership. Since GATT is mainly an organization of capitalist countries, the Soviet Union's request for membership signifies that it wants to become more involved in trade outside the Soviet bloc. It has also raised the possibility of joint ventures with capitalist companies and free trade zones. The one remaining stumbling block is the failure to make Soviet currency freely convertible—that is, to allow foreign companies to remove their profits.

Whether any of the above will revive the Soviet economy is problematic. The USSR will certainly benefit from exposing its economy to popular demands and to world competition. But all these initiatives are probably no substitute for opening its domestic economy to more competition, innovation, and on-the-spot decision making.

Clearly, centralized planning is not a pure economic act but is inextricably intertwined with political institutions and goals. The Soviet Union can be seen as a huge corporation in which the same president and board of directors simultaneously govern a total economy and use it to provide for defense, art, schools, sports, and justice, as well as food, housing, and clothing. Ultimately, the effective center of the Soviet economy is found in Soviet political institutions, especially the dominant Communist party.

THE SOVIET POLITY

From Totalitarianism to Rational-Legal Authoritarianism

The Soviet Union is a centralized, autocratic, one-party state. As such, it is clearly distinct from the presidential and parliamentary systems of representative government in the West. But comparisons among countries are difficult to make without slipping into moral judgments and empty abstraction. In analyzing a society one must clearly distinguish between an analysis that treats a society on its own terms and analysis that treats it in terms of differences and similarities with other countries.

Czarist Russia was only beginning to develop liberal political institutions when it suffered a crushing defeat in World War I. A small Marxist party, brilliantly led by Vladimir Lenin, seized power and managed to consolidate its grip on Russian society against considerable odds. The monopolistic one-party system that Lenin established was consistent with his aristocratic conception of socialist tactics and strategy (the party is the vanguard of the proletariat). It was also consistent with the mountain of problems that Soviet Russia faced and with Russian absolutism.

Soviet society is essentially an attempt to industrialize rapidly in order to build the economic abundance necessary for socialism. The only way to achieve rapid industrialization is through state action. The success of Germany and Japan in the nineteenth century (and say France in the twentieth century) in transforming themselves into industrial societies is largely because of state action. State action was also important for that matter in the industrialization of England and the United States, although obscured by liberal ideology.

Lenin's aristocratic style was transformed into one-person rule after his death. Soviet political development has two distinct periods: an initial phase of totalitarianism (largely under Joseph Stalin), which lasted until the 1960s, and its current phase of rational-legal authoritarianism.

Totalitarianism means systematic, explicit, total control from above by a willful leader. Totalitarian rule is unique to industrial society because only it has the technology that makes total political control possible. Totalitarian rule appears in twentieth-century societies when power groups are determined to destroy one order of society and replace it with another.

Totalitarianism was used by the Communist party to establish and consolidate power. Its essential ingredients are physical and psychic coercion. All enemies and even potential enemies of the socialist order were neutralized by executions, labor camps, or exile. Just as important was psychic control, not merely in the sense of propaganda and education, but through the cultivation of suspicion and distrust. Ultimately, totalitarianism must use terror to prevent the formation of solidarities that could oppose the central power. Terror is a social form that undercuts predictability and trust:

Its most obvious mechanism is the secret police, which can arbitrarily invade the home or office, imprison, and punish. Its ultimate form is the civilian spy or informer—people become afraid to speak or act for fear of being betrayed by co-workers, friends, or relatives.

Totalitarian rule, however, cannot be used to manage and direct a complex industrial system. Undermining the predictability of social relations to forestall opposition also undermines the essence of society. To cow people into submission means that personality features essential to industrialization will not be forthcoming: initiative, personal responsibility, methodical reasoning, ambition, and a concern for the future. Soviet totalitarianism must be sharply distinguished from Nazi totalitarianism. The Nazi party was not oriented toward building a new social order—at best it was nonrational; at worst, an irrational movement whose only future lay in war and conquest. Marxism is a rational social philosophy that seeks to build on and perfect the world-mastery orientation begun by liberalism. Its social goals and time perspective are abstract but also concrete. To reach its goals the Communist party must create a viable industrial society, and that means it must establish predictability, initiative, and voluntary commitment to the social order.

It was not surprising, therefore, that the various groups that make up the effective power hierarchy of the Soviet Union took the death of Stalin as an opportunity to curb the secret police and to curtail the power of the party leader to act arbitrarily. Both because Soviet Russia's internal enemies had been silenced and because of the need to develop a more positive institutional system, the 1960s saw a shift from totalitarianism to rational-legal authoritarianism.

Russian authoritarianism is somewhat different from authoritarianism in Bismarckian Germany, Franco Spain, fascist Italy, the Muslim monarchy in Saudi Arabia, the Muslim one-party rule in Libya, Syria, or Iraq, or the civilian or military authoritarianism present in Chile, Peru, Brazil, and Mexico. Soviet Russia is an industrial society and authoritarianism at this level of social development requires the systematic cultivation of dynamic, advanced skills on the part of ordinary citizens, including the ability to look at social problems critically. As we examine the political institutions of the Soviet Union, readers should anticipate a major theme that will emerge—the fundamental similarity to systems of representative government, especially in the United States. Similarities are not always apparent, and analysts must learn to think in terms of functional equivalents—for example, one-party rule in the USSR and two-party rule in the United States each functions to preserve a given social order and to prevent alternatives from arising.

Perhaps the simplest way to distinguish between totalitarianism and authoritarianism in Soviet Russia is to see it from the standpoint of the ruling party. To achieve a dynamic, expansionist economy the Communist party must allow structured groups to develop: government, factories, schools, labor unions, occupational communities, especially in the professions, and so on. The existence of such groups curtails its power; to coordinate them means politics rather than control through hierarchy, edict, and coercion. The most the party can hope for is authoritarian oversight. In turn, authoritarian oversight leads to explicit organization, in short, to bureaucracy or rational-legal administration, and that curtails arbitrary, willful, total power by a charismatic leader.

The Soviet Union has also been called *corporate pluralism*[13] and *welfare-state authoritarianism.*[14] The central insight behind any characterization, however, is that the dominant Communist party has so far been able to combine monopoly power with enlarged opportunities for policy input by outsiders while at the same time delivering on its overall promise that its rule is ultimately in the interests of the masses.[15] It has also succeeded by providing tangible benefits (housing and consumer goods) to its "middle class" of industrial managers, scientists, engineers, and civil-military administrators, a process going back to the 1930s but accelerated in the post–World War II period.[16] The story of recent years is that the Communist party has been forced to enlarge the opportunities for policy input by, and to deliver material benefits to, those below the "middle class."

Soviet Political Institutions

The Soviet Union is governed by a constitution and by a legal order. As in all complex societies, both feudal and industrial, the "people" are alleged to be the source of power, the legitimating force behind institutions. The various legislative levels, or "soviets," are made up of individuals "elected by the people." Until the Gorbachev reforms there was only one slate of candidates, and their fitness for office was debated during the nomination process. Elections were a formality and the soviets did not spend a great deal of time discussing policy. Legislative power was delegated to executive committees, and ultimately to government departments. In early 1989, however, voters were given a choice of candidates representing different policy stances, and a number of high-ranking party officials suffered defeat. The election's main result was to support Gorbachev's reform program by officially registering

[13]Samuel Huntington, "Social and Institutional Dynamics of One-Party Systems," in Samuel Huntington and Clement H. Moore, eds., *Authoritarian Politics in Modern Society* (New York: Basic Books, 1970), p. 35.

[14]George W. Breshauer, *Five Images of the Soviet Future: A Critical Review and Synthesis* (Berkeley: Institute of International Studies, University of California, 1978), chap. 2.

[15]For perhaps the best analysis of pluralism-at-the-top in the Soviet Union (which he refers to as *institutional pluralism*), see Jerry Hough, *The Soviet Union and Social Science Theory* (Cambridge, Mass.: Harvard University Press, 1977), Introduction and chaps. 1–7.

[16]For this implicit covenant, called the *Big Deal* by Vera Dunham, see Terry L. Thompson and Richard Sheldon, eds., *Soviet Society and Culture: Essays in Honor of Vera S. Dunham* (Boulder, Colo.: Westview Press, 1988).

significant popular discontent. A few months later, in yet another demonstration of his power, Gorbachev peacefully retired seventy-four old-line members of the 301-member Central Committee of the Communist party.

The Soviet political system is a federation of member republics but, in reality, is a highly centralized system. The Soviet state runs everything: the economy, education, arts, the press, television, publishing, and so on. Ultimately, all activities are in accord with the plan developed by the USSR State Planning Committee (Gosplan), which has the power to oversee ministries.

The Communist party is the reality or energizing force behind Soviet politics. It oversees nominations to legislatures and it makes appointments to the various government departments. It is a hierarchical organization much on the order of any bureaucratic group: the Roman Catholic Church, General Motors, the Chase Manhattan Bank, and so on. Western scholars have misdefined the Communist party's relation to Soviet society by thinking of it as a small, homogeneous entity separated from the Soviet people and imposing its will on them from the top. In one sense this is true—the party has a Central Committee of 301 members from which a smaller group, the Politburo, is derived. The Politburo is nominally controlled by the Central Committee, but the reverse is true. In turn, the Politburo is headed by a single leader, who also controls the party bureaucracy.

There is no doubt that the leader, presently Gorbachev, wields great power (as do presidents and prime ministers in the Western liberal democracies). But there is far more to this picture (as there is in the West). The Communist party is actually very large, enrolling a considerable percentage of the adult (male, over thirty) population. It is also far more representative of the broad mass of the Soviet people than the Democratic and Republican parties in the United States combined are representative of the American people. The Communist party is quite heterogeneous internally. It contains cleavages along generational, ethnic, educational, and above all, along lines created by functional specialization. The internal politics of the party reflect these differences as the various levels of the party with their various economic, political, and social specialists push and pull to establish their claims on resources and their sense of priorities. In a real sense, the party is the primary medium through which the different economic and professional interests of the Soviet society, along with the various interests of women, consumers, environmentalists, and others, exert and coordinate themselves. Thought of this way the one-party Soviet state is not different from political processes in the West.[17]

Participation in policy-debating and policy-making institutions by the Soviet population has increased significantly since the 1950s. One major

[17]For an analysis along these lines, see Hough, *The Soviet Union and Social Science Theory*, chaps. 3, 5.

reason for the increase is the Communist party itself. For many reasons the party needs public participation; it can keep power only if its links to the population are strong and positive. It needs to know how its policies are working and what the various factors are in any policy area. In this sense, the single party in the Soviet Union performs the same vital role played by multiple political parties in the West—keeping the political elite in touch with other elites and with the masses, allowing the differentiated population of industrial society a channel to voice grievances and become a part of national life.[18] The Communist party also needs links to the masses as a counterweight to the power of bureaucrats and professional groups. As such, it is continuously urging vigilance by ordinary citizens against red tape, corruption, nepotism, and incompetence. And in a more abstract sense the Communist party's very legitimacy depends on its ability to show that it is derived from the people and is in tangible ways serving their interests. Again, this need also exists in the West and underlines many of the practices of Western political parties.[19] The need is present in all polities for that matter—the Saudi absolute monarchy, for example, has a network of open-house hearings in which individuals voice claims and complaints, in effect, providing the monarchy with feedback and legitimacy.

The Soviet population is expected to engage in free and full debate on public issues and problems (but without criticizing the principle of Communist party leadership or maligning the top leaders). By and large, the populace is free to discuss and even criticize policies of any and all kinds, including ideas or policies of the party or leaders.

Most observers agree that there is considerable popular support for the Communist party, a testimony to its success in forging a superpower in its first half century of power. To appreciate the achievements of the Soviet Communist party is not to condone its excesses—but by any reckoning, its achievements rank with those of any of the great ages of social reconstruction.

The great similarity between Soviet and American political institutions should also be noted. Both are rational-legal systems of authority at least formally and to some extent in practice. The power of leaders allegedly derives from their ability to perform social functions and their recruitment to

---

[18]For a case study of the party's success at establishing a dense network of local political-voluntary channels for citizen mobilization, see Theodore H. Friedgut, "Community Structure, Political Participation, and Soviet Local Government: The Case of Kutaisi," in Henry W. Morton and Rudolf L. Tokes, eds., *Soviet Politics and Society in the 1970s* (New York: Free Press, 1974), pp. 261–296.

[19]For an analysis, see Hough, *The Soviet Union and Social Science Theory*, pt. I, especially chap. 4. For an interesting analysis claiming that there is wide popular participation in all aspects of power in the Soviet Union because under socialism there is no need for power groups to exploit nonpower groups, see Albert Szymanski, "The Class Basis of Political Processes in the Soviet Union," *Science and Society* XLII (Winter 1978/1979): 426–457.

office is allegedly based on merit. In both countries the effective flow of power is from the top down. Making allowances for differences in socioeconomic development, the effective holders of power are those at the apex of the economy (including the professions) and the state.

Considerable public discussion and citizen action takes place in both countries, but the formation of policy positions is conducted by those at the top, and these policy positions do not challenge the constituent principles of each country's social order. The power groups of each nation also dominate the political process. Only a handful of people are effective participants in the nomination of political candidates, in the day-to-day political process, and elections do not provide the broad public with clear policy choices. And in both societies a welfare state has been developed to provide ad hoc solutions within the system of society and to undercut and immobilize opposition. Despite their differences, therefore, political institutions in the Soviet Union and the United States are in many ways similar (even many of the differences are functional equivalents), yielding an identical result: an oligarchic polity in which the interests and ideology of the upper levels of power prevail over those of the lower levels. In recent years the similarities have increased. Gorbachev's reforms have produced what appears to be a significant step toward representative government. Elections in 1989 had rival candidates, and some high-ranking Communist party officials were defeated. However, representative government is not necessarily the same as or even the road to democracy (a society based on and for the benefit of ordinary people and the poor, that is, those without much economic power under all known forms of complex society)—it can also be thought of as a substitute for or a barrier to democracy.

The Legal System

Law varies with type of society. Above all, law reflects a society's level of industrialization and the route it took toward industrialization. Western societies, for example, developed over a long period of time and experienced a protracted struggle between feudal-religious groups and the middle class, followed by a long period of struggle among property groups and among property groups, workers, and minorities. Out of these conflicts emerged a rich body of law, intricate legal practices, professions and professional associations concerned with law, and public agencies assigned the task of adjudicating and enforcing the law.

The West's conception of law, therefore, reflects its unique history and should not be used in an unqualified way to think about law elsewhere. In contrast, for example, Japan's economic and social development was imposed from above and its people and culture remained homogeneous—in consequence, there was little need to develop elaborate legal solutions to problems of social integration and adjustment.

Having noted the importance of historical and sociocultural contexts, one can still distinguish three major legal systems among the various developed countries:

1. *Romano-Germanic law*—following Roman law, continental European countries have tried to develop an integrated, comprehensive code of law based on legal principles.
2. *Common law*—emerging in England and spreading to the United States and other former English colonies, the law in these countries is thought to be the result of individual court decisions.
3. *Socialist law*—developed in the USSR to promote a socialist society.[20]

Early Soviet thinkers saw the state and law as the instruments of coercion and exploitation characteristic of feudal and capitalist societies. Many of them thought that state and law would be unnecessary to socialism and would wither away. Today, Soviet thinkers have fully accepted the idea that the state and law are necessary to the formation, guidance, and day-to-day operation of even an (alleged) nonexploitative, nonantagonistic socialist society.

The developed capitalist and socialist (USSR and Eastern Europe) nation-states have many similarities in their legal systems. Czarist Russia was deeply influenced by Roman law, and today the Soviet legal system still shares many features with Romano-Germanic law. But the Soviet legal system is also different. Socialist law does not accept "bourgeois" concepts of ownership (property) and it does not accept the sharp distinctions made in Western law between private and public spheres or between individual and society. There is also a separate "legal" system for handling political cases— actually, a system in which arbitrary power is exerted against those who are seen to threaten socialism and Communist party dominance. But in all other matters, the Soviet Union, by virtue of being a complex (developed industrial) society has all the earmarks of legal systems in other developed societies.[21]

[20]For a good classification and description of these and other legal systems, see Rene Dair and John E.C. Brierly, *Major Legal Systems in the World Today: An Introduction to the Comparative Study of Law*, 2nd ed. (New York: Free Press, 1978).

[21]For a classic study, see Harold J. Berman, *Justice in Russia* (Cambridge, Mass.: Harvard University Press, 1950). For a general introduction, see E.L. Johnson, *An Introduction to the Soviet Legal System* (London: Methuen, 1969). For a collection of essays on contemporary legal developments, see F.J.M. Feldbrugge and William B. Simons, eds., *Perspectives on Soviet Law for the 1980s* (The Hague: Martinus Nijhoff, 1982). For a comprehensive reference work, see Donald D. Barry and others, eds., *Soviet Law After Stalin*, Vols. 1 and 3 (The Hague: Martinus Nijhoff, 1977, 1979), Vol. 2 (Alphen aan den Rijn, The Netherlands: Nijhoff and Noordhoff, 1978). For an informative analysis of one aspect of the Soviet legal profession, see Louise I. Shelley, *Lawyers in Soviet Work Life* (New Brunswick, N.J.: Rutgers University Press, 1984).

Mass and Elite Media, Sport, and Civil Ceremonies

The Soviet Constitution promises freedom of the press, but actual practice produces a press that is far different from what Westerners understand by a free press. Newspapers, magazines, radio, television, and books are all published by the government, which tightly controls all information. Journalists are government employees, more public relations experts than dispensers of independently collected information. Radio, television, theater, and film are also government run, and like the print media they are openly designed to glorify the nation and celebrate the achievements of the Communist party.[22] Under Gorbachev's reforms, the press, book publishing, and mass and elite media have blossomed to express a much wider range of opinion than has hitherto been allowed.

Sport is also state-sponsored—the Soviet Union has made the availability of free sport to the masses an integral part of a socialist society. Sport is promoted through the workplace and labor unions as a way of acquiring good health and socially valuable skills, of integrating the various nationalities, and even of emancipating Muslim women. Because it is free, it is also free of the class and commercial character of Western sports (although the stress on professionalism and mass spectator sport is somewhat contradictory of stated intentions).[23] The above advantages of sport to a power structure can also be framed somewhat differently. Fascist, capitalist, and communist countries all promote sport in a big way. The reason is simple: The discipline and morality of sports blend easily with any type of power structure. Especially valuable is the ability of sport to create the false impression that all of society is governed by rules and that all of society is a competitive race to uncover human nature's aristocracy.

Since the 1960s the Soviet Union has made a strong effort to develop a comprehensive set of social rituals to replace religion and to help socialize its citizens into socialism. These include family life-cycle rituals, initiation into political and social groups, and celebrations of the seasons, military-patriotic traditions, and political traditions. The Soviet Union's commitment to rituals as a way to socialize its members appears to be the largest in history. However, all countries make extensive use of rituals, and it is not at all clear, for example, that the United States does not have a comparable commitment to "political" rituals (for example, public holidays).[24]

---

[22]For a good description, see Medish, *The Soviet Union*, chaps. 9, 10.

[23]For a sophisticated analysis, see James Riordan, "Sport in Soviet Society: Fetish or Free Play?," in Jenny Brine and others, eds., *Home, School, and Leisure in the Soviet Union* (London: George Allen and Unwin, 1980), chap. 10.

[24]For an analysis of and a comparison of Soviet rituals with the United States and other countries, see Christel Lane, *The Rites of Rulers: Ritual in Industrial Society—The Soviet Case* (New York: Cambridge University Press, 1981).

THE SOVIET FAMILY

The Soviet Union's typical family structure is similar to that of other countries in a similar stage of social development. Marxism has a specific stance toward the family, and in the early years of communist rule the Soviet government attempted to create a new socialist marriage and family. By and large, Marxism sees the family as an inhibitor of the free personality, and early Soviet legislation sought to loosen marital and family ties. But the family performs vital social functions, and the Soviet government soon began to support the family: Divorce was made more difficult, abortion was banned (now legal), and in general the importance of family life was emphasized. Since the 1930s the Communist party and the Soviet state have emphasized the socialization responsibility of the family, especially mothers, and linked it to responsibility to the wider national community. Tangible support for the family has taken the form of child-support payments and child care for working mothers.[25]

The Soviet family is nuclear-neolocal. As in other industrial countries, the family consists of parents and children; when children become adults they tend to leave home and establish their own families. This ideal varies, of course, by class level, nationality, and is profoundly affected by the availability of housing. The extreme shortage of housing until the 1970s no doubt contributed to the low birthrate among the European portion of the Soviet population. But the fall in the birthrate is not abnormal—all industrial countries have experienced similar declines (it should be noted that Muslims in the Soviet Union have a high birthrate).

As in liberal society, the family is the transmission belt for class status over the generations.[26] Unlike the United States, the upper classes of the Soviet Union do not own the economy and, therefore, cannot pass it on to their children in the form of private property, (stocks, corporate bonds, real-estate holdings). But the upper classes control the economy of the nation, and control is passed on largely through education, the gateway to occupations with power and to valued group memberships. The upper classes also pass on significant amounts of money and personal property to their children.

---

[25]H. Kent Gieger, *The Family in Society Russia* (Cambridge, Mass.: Harvard University Press, 1968), and Vladimir Shlapentakh, *Love, Marriage, and Friendship in the Soviet Union: Ideals and Practices* (New York: Praeger, 1984), provide basic introductions to the Soviet family. Shlapentakh emphasizes the separation of personal, microlevel behavior from official Marxist morality and sociopolitical goals because of the anomie induced by the decline of communist ideology and repression. Most observers would probably refer to Soviet developments as normal to industrialization. For a richly detailed historical picture of Soviet women, and thus the Soviet family, in the context of Soviet economic, political, and ideological development, see Gail Warshofsky Lapidus, *Women in Soviet Society: Equality, Development, and Social Change* (Berkeley: University of California Press, 1978).

[26]For an analysis of social stratification in the Soviet Union, see Chapter 19.

Marxist ideology is somewhat ambiguous about sexual inequality and places far more emphasis on matters of class inequality. In a vague way, the ideal family is conceived as a cooperative venture by free individuals. In practice, however, the sexes are rather sharply differentiated. While Soviet women participate fully in the economy, unlike men they must also work at household and child-raising tasks. In imposing this burden the Soviet Union is similar to other industrial societies. The burden borne by women (and the Soviet family) is inherent in the primary economic goals established by Stalin. By stressing heavy industry and neglecting consumer goods and services, the family was forced to perform many economic functions that other industrial countries perform outside the home and to engage in many wasteful practices (such as standing in long lines to shop).

Despite the power of its highly centralized state it cannot be said that the Soviet Union's family policies have been more successful than other countries or that it even exercises that much control over the family. As in other countries, the Soviet family is a refuge from the world's troubles, and the Soviet people insist on using it to pursue interests as they see them. The Soviet family is where resistance to government policies develops, not in the sense of politics or subversion, but in the demand for better food and housing, grumbling about long lines at the stores, and the need for more day-care centers. The Soviet Union appears not to have had any unusual success in curbing domestic problems, juvenile delinquency, or in controlling the decline in the birthrate. Its very success in mobilizing both men and women for work outside the home has no doubt contributed to its limited successes in family policy.

RELIGION IN THE SOVIET UNION

Marxism is thoroughly naturalistic and thus opposes supernaturalism in any form. On the whole, the Soviet government's policy toward religion is one of discouragement rather than persecution. Churches still function openly but attendance seems to be low and mostly by older people, especially women. Christianity is the major religion, with the Greek Orthodox Church, Roman Catholicism, and Baptists as major denominations. There is also a significant number of Muslims in the Asian republics. After more than seventy years of Communist party rule and hectic industrialization, approximately 45 percent of the population remain believers.

During the early decades of communist rule, religion was openly attacked and discredited as "the opiate of the masses" and many churches were destroyed or allowed to fall into disuse. Official policies also led to a shortage of clergy, and in many new cities there are no churches at all. Religion has come into greater favor in recent decades, especially since it appears too weak to offer any serious resistance to the communist social order. Both because it feels more secure, and as part of its effort to enhance national strength and sentiment, the regime has not harassed religious worship and has even restored many old churches now considered part of its architectural heritage and as tourist attractions.

The decline of religion has also occurred because the Soviet state has actively promoted atheism and sought to substitute its own practices for those of religion. It has developed a comprehensive set of rituals for the major "crises" of life: birth, coming of age, marriage, and death. The heroic figures of Marxism have been canonized, especially Marx, Engels, and Lenin. Soviet education glorifies Soviet history and its successes. World War II and the monumental effort and victory over fascist Germany are an ever-present reality for Soviet citizens because of the commemoration of these events in word and marble.

The decline of religion in the Soviet Union has no doubt been accelerated by official policies. But the decline of religion is found in all industrial countries, and the major reason for its decline in the Soviet Union is undoubtedly the multiple attractions of secular life. Large portions of the Soviet population have experienced a spectacular growth in their life fortunes, and the heady excitement of occupational mobility along with a steady growth in the standard of living (at least up to the 1970s) have diverted Soviet citizens from religious to secular values.[27]

SOVIET EDUCATION

Marxism stresses the social nature of personality, and this has been reflected in Soviet educational policy. Marxism also stresses technical, scientific knowledge as the basis of economic growth and social self-direction, and this too has been reflected in Soviet education. After an initial period in which educational policy stressed the free, spontaneous unfolding of the personality, Soviet education restored the authority of the teacher and school, established classroom and academic discipline, and stressed personal responsibility.

Western countries have autonomous educational institutions, which are assumed to be performing positive social functions (as we saw, this is far from being the case). The Soviet Union has no such tradition—education is clearly a department of government and is organized to serve social purposes. It openly espouses values and seeks to create good character, and it openly glorifies the nation, socialism, and the Communist party.

The Soviet educational system is highly centralized and carefully monitored to ensure conformity with established programs. The Soviet Union has

[27]For background on religion in the USSR, including details on the emergence of religious interest groups, see Jerry G. Pankhurst, "The Sacred and the Secular in the U.S.S.R.," in Pankhurst and Sacks, *Understanding Soviet Society*, chap. 8.

invested considerable sums of money in education. One out of three individuals is enrolled in some form of education. Like all power groups, the Communist party is aware that control over the development of youth is the key to its power and to its ability to shape the development of Soviet society.

The Soviet educational system also has other purposes besides training compliant citizens and trained workers. Nursery schools and child-care centers help to free mothers for work. Educational opportunities help to integrate Asian minorities into the achievement ethic. But above all, the Soviet mass educational system (as in other countries) helps to legitimate power. The schools emphasize the central role of the Communist party and instill patriotic values. Power is legitimized in yet another, perhaps more fundamental, way. Like the United States, the Soviet Union claims to be classless. Because of its mass educational system, the Soviet Union, like the United States, can claim that those at the top are a natural elite recruited from the people in open, fair competition.

Finally, education is openly used for more sophisticated political purposes than mere patriotism. The Communist party promotes educational opportunities for the lower classes as a way of keeping families in the upper classes (high managerial, governmental, and professional groups) on their toes, and it has openly worked to ensure a large flow of individuals from working and peasant backgrounds into the upper reaches of the party and other elite groups. In the early years of communist rule this was done to counterbalance the need to rely on trained personnel in government, the economy, and the military whose origins lay in Czarist Russia. In recent decades, however, the policy of promoting upward mobility has also had as one of its purposes to offset the traditionalism inherent in elite positions that are not subject to competitive recruitment.

CHAPTER 19

Soviet Domestic Inequalities, Foreign Policy, and Their Interrelations

SOCIAL, RACIAL, ETHNIC, AND SEXUAL INEQUALITIES

Is the Soviet Union a Class Society?

Class inequality is an outcome of industrialization and appears in a variety of forms in all kinds of industrial society, capitalist and communist alike. Whether or not communist countries—also called *socialist, state socialist, state capitalist, classless,* and *elite versus mass societies*—are class societies is not settled, but our best analysts say yes.[1] The essentials of class society appear when science and human effort make mastery over nature feasible and turn it into a supreme value. The depiction of human destiny as inextricably bound up with the mastery of nature is common to liberal and Marxian thought, and both liberals and Marxists claim that the ideal society is classless—that is, unequal only because of functional differentiation.

[1] For a judicious examination of the various positions on this issue, which concludes that the key question about socialist society is whether it can maintain its openness in the long run, see Frank Parkin, *Class Inequality and Political Order* (London: MacGibbon and Kee, 1971), chap. 5. For an analysis that finds the similarities between systems of stratification in different industrial societies far outweigh the differences, see David Lane, *The End of Inequality? Class, Status, and Power Under State Socialism* (London: George Allen and Unwin, 1982).

Stanislaw Ossowski was perhaps the first to note the similarity among apologists for different social systems (for example, John of Salisbury, Adam Smith, James Madison, fascist corporate theorists, Joseph Stalin, and some contemporary functionalist sociologists).[2] Murray Yanowitch has traced the development of the functionalist position in Soviet theory since the original Stalinist conception. In the Soviet Union, says Yanowitch,

> *The vision of society as a set of functional, nonantagonistic social groups remains intact as an underlying conception. The distinct social groups, however, now include not only two classes and a stratum employed in mental labor but a multiplicity of "socio-occupational strata" within and overlapping the larger social groups. It has become a common practice for studies of social and cultural differentiation in the 1970s to encompass a variety of distinct strata (seven to nine seems to be a typical number), ranging from unskilled laborers to managerial personnel and technical specialists. Inequalities are seen as a function of location in social structure rather than as reflections of individual merit. The differential contributions of the various strata to the system's economic and cultural growth are the basis for (declining but still significant) inequalities in rewards, opportunities, and public esteem. Economic and technological change make for an increasingly "complex" social structure, and thus the precise boundaries of social groups are less clear-cut than formerly. The political dimension of stratification and inequalities in the distribution of power—unlike economic and cultural inequalities—remain largely ignored.[3]*

David Lane has also noted that

> *The "official" description of Soviet society is similar to the description that many structural functionalist sociologists make of Western liberal-democratic societies. Marxism-Leninism is a central value system rather than a "dominant" ideology as conceived of by Marxists. There is no fundamental conflict which could tear apart the society, though there are "deviations" from the central value system. The need for "politics," in the sense of making social arrangements or mobilizing people and resources, continues. The social system depicted in Soviet theory is very similar to Parsons' "ideal type" of industrial society. One might draw attention to the fact that the Soviet Marxist view of the U.S.S.R. and the Parsonian approach to the structure of American society are similar and might be conceived of as providing a kind of ideological "convergence."[4]*

Despite the ideology of classlessness, the central aspect of class—significant economic inequality and its transmission through the family—is present in all industrial societies. Despite historical variations in the emergence of industrialization, the overall impact of sustained economic growth is relatively uniform. State socialist societies may be under more direct political control (although the difference between them and liberal democracies in

---

[2]Stanislaw Ossowski, *Class Structure in the Social Consciousness*, trans. Sheila Patterson (New York: Free Press, 1963), pp. 172–180.

[3]Murray Yanowitch, *Social and Economic Inequality in the Soviet Union* (White Plains, N.Y.: M.E. Sharpe, 1977), 19f.

[4]David Lane, *The Socialist Industrial State: Toward a Political Ideology of State Socialism* (Boulder, Colo.: Westview Press, 1976), p. 28.

that respect should not be exaggerated), and may reveal more social mobility and less extreme cleavages between the various strata, but these characteristics are probably due to the rapidity of industrialization and the urgency of eliminating vestiges of the past. High technical and occupational competence is rewarded handsomely in all communist countries (as it is in capitalist countries), and managerial and professional groups have established themselves and developed considerable autonomy vis à vis the party machinery. Also noteworthy is the fact that both capitalist and communist countries have a high concentration of economic *control* despite their contrasting forms of property ownership and control.

We must assume, therefore, that regardless of previous cultural tradition or present ideology, any country that successfully industrializes has by definition changed its principle of stratification from caste or estate to class. Industrial countries also reveal marked similarities, again despite ideology and previous cultural tradition, in the relationship between class status (occupation, income, education) and responses to questions of belief and value.[5]

Despite obvious differences, the Soviet Union is similar to the United States in a number of fundamental ways. Both have a family system that is characteristic of other industrial countries at similar stages of development. Both rely heavily on laws and lawyers, although the Soviet Union has adopted European rather than Anglo-American legal practices. Similarities also exist in their medical establishments.[6] Both recognize and encourage achievement by *all* citizens in the struggle against nature and in the management of society. There are striking inequalities in economic, prestige, and power statuses in both countries, related (at least ideologically, and to some extent in practice) to functional achievement. In contrast to preindustrial society, and insofar as it can be measured, the two countries have considerable social mobility and similar problems of motivation, rigidity, and privilege. Both have pronounced tendencies toward the transmission of occupational (and, in general, stratum) position by means of the family and education. Both have extensive job dissatisfaction and many workers who are educated beyond what their occupations require.[7] In addition, both have inequalities by sex and among ethnic-racial groups.[8] And finally, both are

---

[5]For a classic compilation of cross-national data, see Alex Inkeles, "Industrial Man: The Relations of Status to Experience, Perception and Value," *American Journal of Sociology* 66, no. 1 (July 1960): 1–31.

[6]Vicente Navarro, *Social Security and Medicine in the U.S.S.R.: A Marxist Critique* (Lexington, Mass.: Lexington Books, 1977).

[7]Murray Yanowitch, *Work in the Soviet Union* (Armonk, N.Y.: M.E. Sharpe, 1985).

[8]Seymour M. Lipset, "Commentary: Social Stratification Research and Soviet Scholarship," in Murray Yanowitch and Wesley A. Fisher, ed. and trans., *Social Stratification and Mobility in the U.S.S.R.* (White Plains, N.Y.: International Arts and Sciences Press, 1973), pp. 355–391; Yanowitch, *Social and Economic Inequality in the Soviet Union;* Alastair McAuley, *Economic Welfare in the Soviet Union* (Madison: University of Wisconsin Press, 1979); and Lane, *The End of Inequality? Class, Status, and Power Under State Socialism.*

living beyond their means, experiencing sluggish economic growth, and finding it difficult to maintain living standards, let alone raise them.

Once these fundamental similarities are noted, their differences should also be highlighted. The Soviet Union does not have a capitalist class that derives large amounts of income from its property—thus, income distribution in the Soviet Union (and all Eastern European communist countries) is significantly more equal than in most capitalist societies (Sweden, Australia, New Zealand, all with strong socialist movements, also have more equality than the typical capitalist society).

Gerhard Lenski cites the greater income equality of the Soviet Union as one of its successes (another one is successful economic growth without private productive property or free enterprise ideology). Lenski also suggests that when both privileges and free public services are taken into account, living standards are also more equal in the Soviet Union than in capitalist societies. The Soviet elite (along with elites in other countries) receives more income than do ordinary citizens. But while the elite lives well, the ratio of its income to ordinary workers is far smaller than in capitalist countries. Lenski estimates that the ratio of highest to lowest wages (that is, excluding income from property in the United States) in the early 1970s was 50 to 1 in the Soviet Union and 300 to 1 in the United States (other ratios in communist countries were 40 to 1 in Poland and China, and 7.3 to 1 in Cuba). Using Lenski's findings, together with those of other analysts, one can say that manual workers receive more income in relation to nonmanual than in capitalist countries, and living standards between elite and nonelite and among the nonelite tend to be more equal.[9]

The Soviet Union (and other Soviet-bloc countries) also differs from the United States and most other developed capitalist countries in according manual workers more occupational prestige.[10] Social mobility is also high in the USSR, perhaps overall, even higher than in the United States. Especially noteworthy is the fact that mobility from the lower classes to managerial and professional ranks and into the elite is higher in the Soviet Union than in the United States.

The major reasons for these similarities and differences are essentially structural, that is, rapid industrialization. Manual workers make more and have more prestige because they are central to industrialization (and there are some labor shortages). Whether manual workers can maintain their position if and when the Soviet economy shifts to services remains to be seen. But

[9]Gerhard Lenski, "Marxist Experiments in Destratification: An Appraisal," *Social Forces* 57 (December 1978): 364–383. Lenski's position was anticipated (in an extended way) by Parkin, *Class Inequality and Political Order,* and Yanowitch, *Social and Economic Inequality in the Soviet Union,* chap. 2.

[10]Yanowitch, *Social and Economic Inequality in the Soviet Union,* p. 105. For similar differences in Czechoslovakia and Poland, see Roger Penn, "Occupational Prestige Hierarchies: A Great Empirical Invariant?," *Social Forces* 54 (December 1975): 352–364.

a good part of the greater income, prestige, and mobility of the lower classes, and thus the greater overall equality in the Soviet Union, is due to socialist ideology and practice.

Ethnic Inequality

Inequalities of income, education, prestige, and political power exist among Soviet ethnic groups. But these inequalities do not appear to be severe or immune to social policy. Russians are clearly the dominant group in all Soviet republics, but ethnic groups outside European Russia have benefitted from the industrialization of Asian Russia and income levels are not markedly different from one republic to another. The major reason for this is the deliberate dispersal of industrial development (and Russian migration). Another is that the government sets aside educational quotas for non-Russian minorities. And non-Russians, though not too well represented in central political positions, have done well at local levels.[11]

The Position of Women

Sexual inequality in the Soviet Union requires a separate word. Readers will remember that sexual inequality is different from social stratification. In the latter, some men and women and their male and female children are better off than both males and females in other families. In addition, parents tend to transmit their benefits and social rank to offspring of both sexes. Women may be unequal in important respects to men but some wives and daughters are better off than other females and many males.

The Soviet Union has made impressive gains in freeing women from their complete segregation from social life in Czarist Russia. Significantly more women work, especially at full-time jobs, in the Soviet Union than in the United States. In addition, they make up large portions of many important professions (though occupations in general are segregated by sex). Their representation in the professions (and their heavy representation at the lower levels of the Communist party hierarchy) may give them more political power than their absence at the upper reaches of political power may suggest.[12] All of these developments are the result of industrialization, not Marxist ideology. Indeed, others argue that the position of women in the Soviet Union is strikingly similar to that of women in the capitalist countries: They are increasingly absent as one goes up the ladder of power and they bear the

[11]Ralph S. Clem, "The Ethnic Dimension," in Jerry G. Pankhurst and Michael P. Sachs, eds., *Contemporary Soviet Society* (New York: Praeger, 1980), chap. 2; Lane, *The End of Inequality? Class, Status, Power Under State Socialism*, pp. 82–95; and Nancy Lubin, *Labor and Nationality in Soviet Central Asia: An Uneasy Compromise* (New York: Macmillan, 1984).

[12]Michael Paul Sachs, "Women, Work, and Family in the Soviet Union," in Michael Paul Sachs and Jerry G. Pankhurst, eds., *Understanding Soviet Society* (Boston: Unwin Hyman, 1988), chap. 4.

heavy burden of working and running a home.[13] As in all developed countries, women have simply been mobilized for work outside the home. By and large, women's civil rights serve to legitimate their pursuits outside the home. Because their rights are neither enforced nor operational, the vast majority of women in all industrial countries provide a huge pool of cheap labor.

DEVELOPMENTS IN THE SOVIET CLASS SYSTEM

Communist thought and policy in the first decade after the Russian Revolution tended toward substantive egalitarianism.[14] But by the early 1930s a systematic policy of encouraging social differentiation (by means of such practices as the increasingly precise definition of occupations, the establishment of piecework, large differentials in income between salaried and wage workers, and bonuses) led to a definite hierarchy of social classes. Alex Inkeles distinguishes ten such classes, ranked in the following order:

1	Ruling elite
2	Superior intelligentsia
3	General intelligentsia
4	Working-class aristocracy
5.5	White collar
5.5	Well-to-do peasants
7	Average workers
8.5	Average peasants
8.5	Disadvantaged workers
10	Forced labor

During and immediately after World War II, the process of formalizing the class system continued. Especially significant was the widespread adoption of civilian uniforms, the practice of awarding prizes and honors for outstanding achievement, and a tax system that allowed high-income groups to keep most of their money and even to pass it on to their children.

No exact picture of the contemporary class structure of the Soviet Union can be drawn. The general dichotomy of nonmanual vs. manual work has some reality across a number of dimensions including income, occupational prestige, and access to and success in school.[15] Recognizing that many non-

[13]Dorothy Atkinston, Alexander Dallin, and Gail W. Lapidus, eds., *Women in Russia* (Stanford, Calif.: Stanford University Press, 1977), and Gail W. Lapidus, *Women in Soviet Society* (Berkeley: University of California Press, 1978).

[14]For Soviet developments up to 1950, see Alex Inkeles, "Social Stratification and Mobility in the Soviet Union: 1940–1950," *American Sociological Review* 15 (August 1950): 465–479.

[15]Lane, *The End of Inequality? Class, Status, and Power Under State Socialism.*

manual positions are unskilled and poorly paid, Murray Yanowitch has proposed a three-tiered grouping of income groups:

> managerial personnel (plant directors and department heads) and senior scientific workers;
>
> skilled workers, technical workers (engineering-technical personnel below top management and higher-ranking office staff (economists, accountants);
>
> low-skilled manual workers and those in routine clerical and office jobs not requiring extended training.[16]

Both Lane and Yanowitch stress that differentials are accentuated by numerous hidden class perquisites: shopping privileges, use of cars, and, above all, housing subsidies. Most of these go to the top managerial and professional occupations. As in other industrial countries there is also considerable class ascription—children tend more or less to follow in the class steps of their parents. As in the United States and the other capitalist democracies, the crucial link in the chain of class ascription is the superior access to education of the upper classes. Class factors are also at work in consumption and in the choice of friends and marriage partners.

To the broad three tiers proposed by Yanowitch—a small "upper middle class," a heterogeneous middle tier of skilled manual and nonmanual workers, and a low unskilled group of manual and nonmanual workers—should be added a sizable poverty group, a distinct "lower class." Though not numerous there is also a small number of highly paid and privileged entertainers, sports figures, artists, and intellectual-scientists.[17]

Another aspect of the development of the Soviet class system has been apparent since the 1950s. Leadership and brain work cannot be emphasized in a universalistic achievement-oriented society without risking demoralization and deviance at the bottom levels. The position of the upper range of occupations cannot be shored up without risking the development of castelike obstructions to competition and achievement. And it is dangerous to monopolistic political power to allow a rigid hierarchal system to develop or to permit social groups to become too structured and thus somewhat autonomous. Recognizing all this, the Communist party has deliberately sought to prevent such developments by asserting the fundamental class principle of individual achievement.[18] It has appealed for "popular participation" to curb administrative incompetence and nepotism; it has abolished

---

[16]Yanowitch, *Social and Economic Inequality in the Soviet Union*, p. 47.

[17]For additional details, see Merwyn Matthews, *Privilege in the Soviet Union* (London: George Allen and Unwin, 1978). Caution should be exercised in reading Matthews; his concept of *privilege* creates the impression that all inequality in the Soviet Union is illegitimate and that Marxism in practice is a thorough fraud.

[18]And, of course, by the sytematic undermining of such groupings, in the earlier years of communist rule, through the use of terror, forced labor camps, and the like, and, since the 1950s, through censorship and harassment as well as positive economic and social programs.

many civilian uniforms; upheld the dignity of manual work; modified income structure in favor of lower-income groups (though differences in the distribution of economic values are still considerable and equalitarianism is still denounced); and increased opportunities for the lower classes, especially though educational reform.[19] Indeed, many of the internal political events in the Soviet Union since the 1950s bear striking resemblances to political struggles and reforms in the United States, such as the War on Poverty, federal aid to education, and the like.

Similarities between the USSR and the United States are also striking in another respect. Like their counterparts in the United States, Soviet policymakers do not understand how their society works. Based on false images, their policies have resulted in serious failures although they have continued to experiment and improvise. As in the United States, the attempt to define social problems in technical and administrative terms has run aground on political reefs. For example, to increase the opportunities of the poor in the United States or to alleviate their suffering means helping black Americans; but helping black Americans often entails depriving racists of their values or reducing opportunities for whites; understandably, the powerful white majority has made reform slow and difficult. In the Soviet Union, helping the poor often means helping the non-Russian ethnic groups, which runs counter to the interests of the dominant Russian majority.

The reformist ferment within the Soviet Union (and in the United States) is best understood as an attempt to maintain the momentum of industrial expansion by means of a differential reward system while preventing the least privileged from dropping behind or other levels from losing pace. As is true of the United States, internal reform in the Soviet Union appears not to have lessened the overall structure of social inequality or to have threatened the ability of the privileged strata to transmit their positions to their children.

COMPARING THE UNITED STATES AND THE SOVIET UNION

In discussing developments in the Soviet class system, similarities between the United States and the Soviet Union were emphasized. These similarities indicate that many conditions and problems are common to all urban-industrial social systems. They do not imply that the United States and the Soviet Union are identical, or that either one has created a classless system of individual merit and functional differentiation. Seeing the similarities is important to Americans because it enables them to view their own society better (that is, to see it in structural terms rather than in terms of the ideology of classlessness). It is also important to note differences, although here great

[19]For general background on the Soviet Union's struggle to deal with poverty and welfare, see McAuley, *Economic Welfare in the Soviet Union.*

caution must be exercised. The United States has an independent judiciary and equality before the law, but do the majority of the American people enjoy benefits from these differences? The United States has a strong civil rights tradition, but has the possession of these rights helped American minorities much and are they substitutes for good government and social justice?

In turn, the Soviet Union has free medical care, but does this really do much for the mass of the Soviet people? (What the Soviet people need for better health is better food, safer work, and less stressful lives.) Does it prevent the upper levels of Soviet society from getting superior medical care?

Another similarity between capitalist and socialist societies must now be raised—the way in which domestic pressures resulting from institutions and social classes (both their legitimate and illegitimate aspects) spill out into foreign relations.

SOVIET FOREIGN POLICY

The Continuity of Russian National Interests

All countries pursue national objectives as determined by the exigencies of geography, power, history, and internal pressures. Considerable continuity exists between Czarist Russia and the USSR insofar as certain national interests are concerned.[20] Regardless of the explanation offered, both Czarist and Soviet Russia have had much to fear from aggressive neighbors. Early Russian history saw continuous problems with the nomadic herding peoples of the Asian steppes. In more modern times, Russia suffered major invasions from Sweden, France, and Germany (twice).

After a period of almost complete withdrawal from world affairs between 1917 and the death of Stalin in 1953, the USSR has become active in all parts of the globe. In many ways Soviet foreign policy during the period between the world wars reflected Soviet isolation and weakness. World War II changed the USSR's relative world status. With the defeat of Nazi Germany, the Soviet army occupied Eastern Europe, and the USSR installed communist governments in Poland, Rumania, Bulgaria, Hungary, Czechoslovakia, and East Germany. This enlarged Soviet influence considerably, and it gave the USSR a buffer against the developed industrial capitalist nation-states of Western Europe, which Leninist theory and Russian experience had defined as inherently expansionist.

The Soviet Union, like all nation-states, pursues policies that serve its interests. A nation-state has many interests but none can be furthered without strength. Unlike the United States, which has no powerful neighbors to

---

[20]For valuable background, see Alvin Z. Rubinstein, *Soviet Foreign Policy Since World War II: Imperial and Global*, 3rd ed., rev. and expanded (Glenview, Ill.: Scott, Foresman, 1989).

threaten it and is surrounded by stable societies, the Soviet Union has always had unstable neighbors.

The Soviet government has achieved a number of Czarist Russia's historic objectives besides establishing a deep buffer zone between it and Western Europe. Long a landlocked giant, Czarist Russia searched for warm-water ports to enhance its naval power and to provide maritime transport to link its vast internal spaces. The Trans-Siberian Railroad was a spectacular achievement by Czarist Russia, although it could not prevent Russia's defeat by Japan in 1905. Still without warm-water ports, Soviet Russia has used modern technology and its economic strength to build large merchant, fishing, and naval fleets, and is now a global maritime and naval power.

Domestic Pressures and Constraints

Like all complex societies, the Soviet Union has conflicting domestic interests and problems that spill over into its foreign policy.[21] One observer says that the Soviet Union is "totalitarian" and that its freedom from internal pressure gives it an advantage in foreign policy.[22] Most other observers say that it is not as open to public pressure as the United States and the other liberal democracies (this may be based on an exaggerated sense of how open the American foreign policy-making process is). Nonetheless, Soviet foreign policy is (like all countries) subject to a wide variety of domestic pressures and is used (as in other countries) to further domestic interests. For example, during the initial stages of Soviet development, Joseph Stalin rallied the Soviet people by denouncing "capitalist encirclement." Stalin also conducted well-publicized political show trials to purge Soviet society of "subversives," an activity common to many types of society, including the United States.[23]

Russia's Changing Position in World Affairs

Soviet foreign policy is still determined by some of the constraints faced by Czarist Russia. Most of the Soviet Union's attention and foreign aid are focused on its immediate neighbors: Turkey, Iran, Afghanistan, Pakistan, India, and China (and, of course, Eastern Europe and NATO). But as the world's second largest economic power and a co-equal in military power

[21]For an interesting collection of essays on how domestic groups and needs (for example, the military, nationalities, the economy, Eastern Europe) influence Soviet foreign policy, see Seweryn Bialer, ed., *The Domestic Context of Soviet Foreign Policy* (Boulder, Colo.: Westview Press, 1981).

[22]Leonard Schapiro, "Totalitarianism in Foreign Policy," in Kurt London, ed., *The Soviet Union in World Politics* (Boulder, Colo.: Westview Press, 1980), chap. 1. Most observers would reject Schapiro's use of the term "totalitarian" (and would note that he fails to appreciate the pronounced pragmatism and flexibility of Soviet foreign policy in recent decades). The concluding essay by Kurt London is useful mostly as a good example of how right-wing (right-liberal) Americans view the Soviet Union.

[23]Albert James Bergesen, "Political Witch Hunts: The Sacred and the Subversive in Cross-National Perspective," *American Sociological Review* 43 (April 1977): 220–233.

with the United States, the Soviet Union is also different from Czarist or Stalinist Russia. Its only military threat is from the United States and it has exerted itself considerably (at the expense of both its productive capacity and living standards) to match American military efforts. The dramatic increase in the Soviet Union's relative world position has brought about significant changes in both its foreign and domestic policies.

Since the death of Stalin the Soviet Union has developed a far more pragmatic outlook on foreign relations. It now trades and has dealings with all types of regimes. Its need to trade abroad is deeply rooted in the imperatives of its economy—to maintain any pace of industrial expansion it must buy food and advanced technology from abroad. Until the death of Stalin the Soviet Union emphasized self-sufficiency and the need for internal discipline and vigilance because of "capitalist encirclement." Growing Soviet economic and military power has led to growing confidence in its relations with the rest of the world. From its inception, the USSR also proclaimed itself as the leader of the working classes and socialist movements everywhere in the world. Ironically, its new industrial economy has made it less able to identify with the developing countries. And the steady pursuit of national self-interest has alienated even other socialist countries and movements. In 1953 Yugoslavia defected from the Soviet camp; in the late 1950s a serious split developed with the People's Republic of China; and in the 1970s the large Communist parties of France and Italy asserted their independence from Moscow and their commitment to the political traditions of their respective countries.

The Soviet Union does not have relations with other countries through private firms, professional groups or through voluntary groups. Internally, the Soviet class system is more like the capitalist countries than it is different, but externally the Soviet Union's policies and relations are all official and coordinated. Nevertheless, a major thrust of Soviet foreign policy has been to mesh its economic needs (and those of the East European bloc) with the economies of developing nations. It has stressed mutual benefit, but its policies toward Third-World countries are very similar to those of the West— what it wants from them is increased raw material production; on-the-site processing of raw materials; light, labor-intensive industry, especially types related to staple production; and long-term credit and supply agreements. The Soviet Union's overall relations with developing countries, therefore, are largely the same as the capitalist countries. Marxist ideology denounces First-World (capitalist nations) policies as imperialist and dependency-creating, but the same policies are described as an international division of labor based on mutual benefit and respect when engaged in by the Second World (the Soviet bloc). The Soviet Union has also rejected the notion that it has an obligation to aid Third-World countries, arguing that such countries have problems created by the colonialism of capitalist nation-states. Socialist ideology aside, the Soviet Union has adopted a stance toward the rest of the world that is in its national self-interest, and, as in the United States and other First-World societies, it has studiously rejected attempts by Third-World countries to reorganize power relations in the world's economy. Soviet economic self-interest also coincides with its political-military interests—the bulk of its foreign and technical aid has gone to a narrow band of countries on its borders (though considerable aid has also gone to Cuba and Vietnam).

In recent years the Communist party and the Soviet government have downplayed ideology in their foreign relations. They are now the pragmatic managers of a vast corporation. Their focus is on their own economic problems and development and their foreign policy is designed with this in mind. A considerable trade has grown between the USSR and developed nations. The Soviet Union buys food and imports the latest technology and engineering-managerial skills that it can purchase (or steal). Interestingly, its partners in Eastern Europe have piled up considerable debts to First-World banks in their effort to keep up with the Western economies. All in all, there is little doubt that the Soviet Union and Eastern Europe are deeply implicated in the world-market economy.

It is also clear that Soviet theorists, researchers, and planners look upon the world in the above terms. Soviet paranoia, revolutionary rhetoric, and universalist propaganda still persist, but these are no longer characteristic of Soviet leadership.[24] Soviet economic thinkers now classify countries much on the order of Western economists, paying much less attention to a country's political forms or to its ideology. Soviet theorists recognize a global or one-world economy (with specialized subsystems).[25] The USSR has sidestepped the demand by the Third World for a new international order. Its basic philosophy is similar to that of the United States: All countries should promote international trade through cooperative efforts, each doing what it does best—in effect asking Third-World nations to remain suppliers of raw materials. The Soviet Union no longer espouses self-sufficiency and no longer holds up its own path to development as a guide for other countries. By and large, both in theory and practice, the Soviet Union has shifted from promoting revolution abroad to a world-market form of imperialism. Even its revolutionary efforts appear not to be aimed at promoting socialism abroad but as efforts to destabilize capitalist dependencies and cut off sources of raw materials to the West, thus enhancing its own relative power position.

---

[24]For a digest of how the Soviet Union views world developments on a daily basis, see *World Affairs Report* published quarterly by The California Institute of International Studies, Stanford University.

[25]For a comprehensive analysis of the shift from the Khrushchev era when the Soviet Union thought of itself as the defender of the Third World (who could also provide guidance and aid for a quick transition to socialism) to the present one-world outlook, see Elizabeth Kridl Valkenier, *The Soviet Union and the Third World: The Economic Bind* (New York: Praeger, 1983).

Soviet Foreign Policy Strategy and Priorities

Soviet foreign policy is debated continuously, and there are distinct and conflicting orientations in the upper levels of the Soviet power structure just as there are in all countries.[26] One basic division is between those who take a hard line against capitalism and imperialism and those who argue that détente and the liberalization of trade and cultural exchange are necessary now and in the best interests of the Soviet Union. Much of this debate revolves around interpretations of the "scientific-technological revolution." The Soviet elite believes that the world at large is being revolutionized by the advance of science and technology. It very much wants to be part of this revolution and to bend it to serve traditional Marxist-Leninist goals. But there are disputes about how to go about all this, with some emphasizing self-sufficiency and military strength and others pushing for détente and participation in the world economy.[27] As Jerry Hough points out, the Soviet leadership has even been told that the Brezhnev policy of relying on imported technology is a failure. Soviet experts have stated that the Soviet Union can learn from the export-oriented countries of the Third World. Only if Soviet industry tries to compete in the world market can it upgrade quality and lower costs, and thus gear Soviet industry to meet domestic needs. Adoption of such a policy, argues Hough, will further the already distinct movement of the Soviet Union toward being a "normal" member of the international community.[28]

Soviet military and foreign policy toward the West is heavily influenced by its relations with China. In recent years the Soviet Union has made a serious effort at reconciliation with China, and because it also suited China's interests, some warming of relations has occurred. Soviet leader Gorbachev's visit to China in May 1989 cemented the improvement in relations (the bloody repression of the student-led movement in June of 1989 made China an outcast with the developed capitalist world and may cause it to seek even closer relations with the Soviet Union). In addition to China, the Soviet Union must also deal with many complex issues of a more concrete nature—how to cope with separatist tendencies among some of its nationalities, how to maintain stability among its Eastern Europe satellites (many of which not only have higher living standards than the USSR has, but are more politically sophisticated and open to Western influence than it is), and how to relate to many diverse communist/Marxist radical nationalist movements around the world.

---

[26]For a comprehensive analysis, see Jerry F. Hough, *The Struggle for the Third World: Soviet Debates and American Options* (Washington, D.C.: The Brookings Institution, 1986).

[27]For a full discussion, see Erik P. Hoffmann and Robbin F. Laird, 'The Scientific-Technological Revolution' and Soviet Foreign Policy (New York: Pergamon Press, 1982).

[28]Hough, *The Struggle for the Third World*, 284–286.

The Soviet Union relies heavily on military strength for its foreign policy, as does the United States, but there is a clear and often creative practical strategy in its dealings with other countries. While the United States supports the status quo among Third World nations (many of whom are run by unstable, undemocratic, and often oppressive regimes), the Soviet Union's policy is to destabilize such regimes. American foreign policy is often badly handicapped by America's ahistorical, metaphysical outlook, by its economic power groups, and by its ethnic blocs. In some ways the Soviet Union's sociocultural, historical outlook is an advantage.

Soviet presence in the Middle East, Africa, and Asia has not been translated into influence or control.[29] Despite its heavy presence in Iraq, Egypt, and Afghanistan, for example, it has had no success in turning these nations into compliant allies. Iraq is continuously purged of communists and pursues policies often favorable to the West. Egypt renounced its Friendship Treaty with the Soviet Union and ousted Soviet advisors. Afghanistan remained stubbornly non-Marxist and unstable despite huge aid and even a Marxist government (both to protect its investment and to protect itself from Muslim revivalism, the Soviet Union invaded Afghanistan in 1979 but had to withdraw in defeat in 1989). The USSR has been successful in its policies toward India largely because both share a deep interest in restraining China and Pakistan.

The Soviet Union, however, has learned to get maximum use out of limited commitments and assets, something no doubt prompted by its various failures. The use of Cuba as a surrogate in Africa has been extremely successful. It is a major seller of arms, thus reducing the cost of its defense establishment while making allies abroad. Its worldwide fishing fleet no doubt brings home needed protein but also serves as an intelligence network and gives it vitally needed contacts with foreign ports and governments. Its presence in various countries or on the open seas gives it potent political and psychological power in the abstract. It also enhances its image abroad through sports, space exploration, and artistic-educational exchanges.

In any case, the Soviet Union clearly supports a policy designed to take as many countries out of the First-World orbit as possible, assuming, and probably correctly, that autonomous self-sufficient countries (such as Iraq, Syria, Libya), though not necessarily Marxist or Soviet satellites, are nonetheless more of a danger to the West than to the USSR. And there is little doubt that it has pursued (even as an alleged socialist society) an expansionist foreign policy of both empire and world-market forms.

Marxist theory holds that socialist society has no need to dominate or exploit either at home or abroad. In 1988 the Politburo's head of ideology, Vandim Medvedev, in a published speech, called for more experimentation

---

[29]This is the conclusion reached by the various essays in Robert H. Donaldson, ed., *The Soviet Union in the Third World: Successes and Failures* (Boulder, Colo.: Westview Press, 1981).

with markets at home and rejected the idea of a world struggle between communism and capitalism. "Universal values such as avoiding war and avoiding ecological disaster must outweigh the idea of a struggle between classes," he argued.[30] But theory aside, the same question we asked of the United States arises: Does the internal structure of power in the Soviet Union impel it toward foreign expansion and adventures? The two superpowers have each other as an excuse not to democratize their societies. The ultimate question that must be asked of any society is: Are its power groups willing to improve the lot of the masses, both materially and in terms of participation in policy-making, and thus lose power? Neither the power groups of the United States nor the Soviet Union show any signs that they are willing to do this (though each has some who understand that their rivalry postpones the day of peace through plenty).

THE USSR AS AN OLIGARCHY

The Communist party—along with the military, high government officials, the managers of industry, the scientific establishment, and the aesthetic and sports establishment—enjoy wide popular support and have considerable operational control over the institutions of Soviet society.

Soviet elites also enjoy high material and psychic benefits. To think of their unequal rewards as forming a system of privilege is a mistake. The Soviet Union has an explicit and open justification for inequality, one that is identical to the United States—those who do more for society deserve to get more. The question is, To what extent are the unequal rewards undeserved? The Soviet elites are secretive about their rewards, and observers must conclude that they are higher than can be easily justified. Beyond that it is not possible to go since there is very little hard data about how ordinary Soviet citizens feel about the hierarchy of rewards or how much they know about it. Our most important source of how ordinary citizens feel is the large number or emigrés (mostly Jewish) who report that there is considerable resentment and cynicism among the Soviet people.[31]

The hierarchy of reward is also based on illegal activities, everything from a flourishing black market and an underground economy to outright theft, bribery, and other criminal acts. There is also evidence of considerable sluggishness in the Soviet lines of communications, something not unrelated to the hierarchical command structure and the partially illegitimate hierarchy of rewards.

[30]*The New York Times*, October 6, 1988, p. 1.
[31]In this regard, see Matthews, *Privilege in the Soviet Union*.

In short, the USSR does not work the way in which its power group(s) says it works—in this sense it is oligarchic in the classic meaning of the word: The rule by the few is not totally in the interests of the many.

The Soviet Union may develop in a number of directions: toward liberal or market authoritarianism, social democracy, or toward reactionary authoritarianism. At present it appears committed to "technocratic socialism," the development of better, scientifically based techniques for running society from above. From 1986 on, under the leadership of Mikhail Gorbachev, a new openness in the arts and the mass media appeared—citizens are freer to express their views and to voice grievances. Government and party officials are openly criticized, and even the Red Army has not escaped censure. A more liberal policy in regard to civil rights and dissidents appeared. And far-reaching practices have appeared that have taken the USSR a good way toward representative government. Where all this will lead is not clear. It does indicate, however, that the Soviet leadership is aware of how stagnant the Soviet economy and polity have become.

Nonetheless, its initiatives for reform are careful not to question the essentials of Soviet-style socialism. In this sense, it shares much with the value-neutral social science, public and business administration, and public policy programs in the United States. However, the various forces that make up Soviet society are so numerous and so complex that it is not possible to form definitive judgments as to the country's future. Like all complex societies, the Soviet Union is a prisoner of its history (both before and after the Russian Revolution), and subject to outside forces over which it has even less control. As in all other complex societies, it is unlikely that Soviet power groups will enact policies that will undermine their power. Like all complex societies, the Soviet Union will more than likely remain an oligarchy, a permanent half-way house, a menace both to its own people and to others.

CHAPTER 20

Must Stratified Societies Always Fail?

WHY STRATIFIED SOCIETIES FAIL

History shows that complex societies are always stratified and, so far, have always succumbed to the problems generated by their system of stratification. Whether this fate will also befall the United States and the Soviet Union is the subject of this chapter. The problem-solving prospects of developing countries are discussed in our concluding chapter on stratification and world problems.

Stratified societies have failed in the past because their power groups developed practices that separated them from the performance of social functions. They failed because their upper levels had no direct experience with the problems of the lower levels. They failed because the upper class(es) thought their societies were rooted in human nature, nature, and supernature.

Three things about stratified societies can be cited to alert us to the deep structural problems facing American and Soviet societies:

1. Stratified societies from advanced horticulture to developed capitalist and socialist systems all exhibit a wide disparity between their legitimating norms and actual behavior. Deviance is widespread and occurs in its most important forms mostly among the upper classes.

2. The unworkable and illegitimate inner organization of stratified societies leads to imperialism and war.
3. The same unworkable and illegitimate elements force stratified societies to consume more than they produce, yielding a "fiscal crisis of the state." The power groups of stratified societies develop unproductive practices to protect their power structure, which at some point begin to drag down the society.

As we saw, the elites of capitalist and socialist societies, both developed and developing, are all struggling to improve the performance of their respective societies. Here it is important to distinguish between better policies with which to address problems, and policies designed to improve adaptive capabilities (our main focus will be on the latter). Societies do not unfold naturally nor do they improve (or decay) naturally. If we want a society to work, it must be designed to work. Ultimately, the sociologist must have an image of a workable society, one composed of groups and institutions that foster creative, competent, adaptive personalities.

THE IDEAL OF AN ADAPTIVE SOCIETY

An adaptive or functional society (not to be confused with functionalist social theory) is a problem-solving entity not a problem-free utopia. The members of a functional society can feed themselves, reproduce, settle disputes, and adjust to new conditions. Adaptive power groups are able to develop the motives, ideas, and skills needed for replenishing, sustaining, and adapting a given way of life to both old and new circumstances. A functional society has *legitimacy*, which means that people take it on faith that power groups deserve their power. Hierarchy, laws, taxes, unequal wealth and income, discipline, high standards, and competition are not suspect because ordinary citizens see direct and beneficial consequences flowing from them. Setbacks and failures are not resented because they appear to occur in a *just* society. A functional society has statuses and norms that, by and large, produce intended and desired results. The adaptive society is an ideal, but it is not beyond reach—to repeat, it is a problem-solving entity rather than a utopian one.

CLASS, POWER, AND AMERICA'S ADAPTIVE CAPACITY

Americans have always taken it on faith that they lived in a functional society. Americans have used various terms to express this faith (democracy, laissez-faire, achievement ethic), but the main concept used to justify faith in the adaptive capacities of the status quo has been *pluralism*. What does this term mean and how well does it stand up when measured against America's record?

Pluralism: The False Image of a Moving Equilibrium

Pluralist theorists believe that American society is adaptive because it is characterized by creative competition among relatively equal social actors. Pluralists argue that competition among individuals and groups (within the framework of free markets, law, toleration, and professionalism) transforms group diversity and conflict into social integration, stability, harmony, justice, and progressive adaptation.

Most sociologists would characterize the American power structure as *semi-pluralistic* (shying away from its synonym, *oligarchy*) and reject the power-elite image.[1] The evidence against pluralism (and a power elite) is large. In every sector of American society, there is competition but also hierarchical power. Business firms compete, but the economy is also deeply concentrated and excludes many from effective power and renders many powerless. The professions are based on significant competition and have developed achievement standards, but they are also deeply marked by artificial scarcity and incompetence, and by significant amounts of unethical and criminal behavior. The American polity is a hurly-burly of competition, but the economically powerful prevail while many are powerless. Government officials and legislators are drawn from the upper classes. Legislation and the law in general favor the powerful. Three-quarters of the seats in the U.S. House of Representatives are noncompetitive. Almost half of the eligible voters stay away from elections, many undoubtedly because they believe that they are powerless to influence events. The free press is useful in clarifying issues and protecting the rights of some, but it is also a powerful force in favor of the upper classes and the status quo. Education is not a fair contest to determine the natural elite, but deeply biased in favor of the upper classes and the status quo. Voluntary groups perform many functions and help to disperse power, but their policy-making boards and committees are dominated by the upper classes. All these institutions and groups work to depoliticize social problems, thus leaving their solution in the hands of those who cause them, the upper classes.

No matter what process, issue, or outcome is analyzed, the pattern is clear. The benefits of American life (income, wealth, occupation, education) are distributed unequally and with no close, positive relation to merit or functional outcomes. The lower classes bear the brunt of unemployment, insecurity, and occupational disease and disability, and it is their sons that bear the burden of war. And the government supports this overall process through its tax, spending, and other policies.

No assessment of power in the United States, therefore, can ignore three basic aspects of American life:

---

[1]For a previous discussion of the insufficiency of pluralist theory, see the section "Is the United States Pluralistic?" in Chapter 17.

1. the existence of significant amounts of powerlessness, exploitation, waste, and privilege;
2. the fact that these phenomena are deeply institutionalized and thus not easily eradicated; and
3. that oligarchic relations are *systemic*, that is, they characterize all aspects and apexes of American society.

Has the United States Become a Stalemated Society?

Something new may have emerged to reduce the adaptive capacity of the United States. Semi-pluralism has its drawbacks but it is not incompatible with a certain measure of adaptive behavior. The most significant change in American society may be the decline of whatever pluralism the United States has had and the emergence of a stalemated society. At present, many if not most sociologists would agree that much of the following is true about the United States:

1. No power group or combination of power groups has enough power to run society unilaterally. But coalitions of power groups that can solve problems are also scarce.
2. America's diversified oligarchy appears stalemated, adrift in a world it appears not to understand. Within a system of very unequal power, no one appears to be in charge; no one appears able to take charge.
3. The basic dynamic in the American power structure is rivalry among the very rich, and among the rich and their powerful auxiliaries, the near-rich and the well-to-do upper middle class.
4. Many American policies are made through an elaborate process of nondecision.[2]
5. That so far American institutions and symbolic culture have effectively depoliticized social problems and hidden illegitimacies.

There is more than a little evidence that the United States is not making progress against its problems. For over a decade the United States has no longer enjoyed the world's highest standard of living and many countries now have better health care, far less crime, and much more livable cities. Under the joint pressures of economic and political rationalization and reform, the general nature of group life has become even more hierarchical as more of life is run by professions embedded in bureaucratic structures. Almost no sphere of life has remained immune from this process, though the results are not unilaterally bad or easy to evaluate. Workers and professionals alike find themselves earning their livelihoods in vast impersonal structures. Political parties find it hard to build political followings as government welfare agencies and direct-action groups steal their former supporters. Volunteers find themselves drawn

---

[2]In this latter respect, see Peter Bachrach and Morton S. Baratz, *Power and Practice* (New York: Oxford University Press, 1970).

into bureaucratic structures run by career professionals. Voluntary organizations find themselves drawn into orbits controlled by governments. A large network of interest groups, many of them single-issue groups that practice a paranoid style of politics, clog up public life. And everyone finds a bureaucratic rationality substituted for individual rationality.

With the rise of a complex and interdependent economy and social system ever on the threshold of stalemate and conflict, economic power groups have resorted to political means (especially central governments) to achieve economic and social objectives even as they continue to denounce politics and government, uphold the virtues of self-reliance, and affirm the vitality of grassroots politics. Faced with the need to plan, American society has undertaken a considerable amount of "public" planning, often using personnel whose experience and outlook have been derived from a lifetime of affirming antiplanning, entrepreneurial values and ideas. When policymakers attempt serious planning or reforms, they find themselves deadlocked by an interlocked structure of veto groups that makes it difficult to enunciate any policy unless it is so abstract or compromised as to be virtually meaningless. Given the experience of much of its personnel and given the "veto" power structure contained in a mature industrial economy, the remorseless trend of turning politics into administration grows apace.

The irrelevance of American political institutions to social problems is now widely acknowledged. The ideology of relying on private actions to solve public ills is so deeply planted that no effective urban, state, or national politics or planning appears possible. The United States has no coherent and effective economic, energy, transportation, health, educational, housing, urban, family, or youth policy. Its system of taxation is inequitable and badly related to public purposes. The problems of retirement and the elderly are far from met. It has no meaningful, reality-oriented foreign policy, relying largely on anticommunism, military force, and the abstraction of a laissez-faire, world-market economy. From the late 1970s on, huge, chronic domestic and foreign trade deficits began to appear, indicating not only that the United States was living beyond its means but that it lacked the capacity to stop doing so.

Failure can be measured on many dimensions: The United States has been unable to provide full employment or equal competition and opportunity. There appear to be sizable amounts of poverty with no advances in reducing it since 1960. Minority groups have made no relative economic advances since they acquired their civil rights over two decades ago. The economy and the environment are still on a collision course, despite a quarter-century of warnings and efforts. The United States has a poor health-care system, perhaps the worst in the capitalist world. Its private and public educational system is largely irrelevant to the needs of contemporary citizenship and fails to provide skilled workers or competent professionals.

Few can argue that the natural and social sciences have produced the knowledge needed to run an advanced industrial system. Certainly the news media have not provided the knowledge or awareness needed by modern publics. And despite their profession of rationality and commitment to knowledge, American elites deviate considerably from the known world (see Box 20–1, "How Widespread Is Resistance to Knowledge Among American Elites?").

The image of a stalemated society may not be accurate, perhaps too static to capture the hustle and bustle of American society. But the images of incremental adaptation through pluralism and professionalism seem to be even further from the bull's-eye.

BOX 20–1 *HOW WIDESPREAD IS RESISTANCE TO KNOWLEDGE AMONG ELITES?*

The list of resistance to knowledge by elites is long. Here is a partial list:

Government has not acted on the knowledge that smoking is a menace to health.

Knowledge that education can be improved significantly only by improving the class conditions that students come from has been ignored.

Elites have not changed their belief that tax cuts improve savings and capital investment despite overwhelming evidence to the contrary.

Corporations do not reduce prices when demand slumps but raise them, giving the lie to ideas of market rationality and the alleged law of supply and demand.

The United States Air Force still believes in strategic bombing even though four of its own studies have found no strategic value in bombing.

Groups resist knowledge because they have interests that knowledge threatens. Resistance to knowledge in medicine provides details of this process. David Mechanic reports that research findings in biomedical research and technology tend to get accepted since they do not interfere with the interests of professionals and actually complement and extend them (and of course generate profits for business firms). Research in the area of health care and services tends to be neglected, and when done, ignored. Mechanic cites an example from a study at Yale-New Haven (a Yale University teaching hospital). Children scheduled for tonsillectomies were randomly divided into an experimental and control group. The control group received the normal care. Mothers of the children in the experimental group were admitted to the hospital and given a realistic picture of what to expect. The mothers in this group experienced less stress and their children had much better medical readings, made better adaptations to the hospital, and experienced a more rapid and better recovery after leaving the hospital. These findings are of added significance because tonsillectomies are widely performed and psychological problems are known to have important adverse effects on health. Neither Yale/New Haven nor other hospitals acted on the findings.*

*David Mechanic, "Sociological Critics Versus Institutional Elites In The Politics of Research Application: Examples from Medical Care" in N.J. Demerath *et al.*, eds., *Social Policy and Sociology* (New York: Academic Press, 1975), 99–108.

Were the 1960s a Watershed?

Our major concepts for understanding social change in the United States have been entrepreneurial and corporate capitalism. Within an unchanged capitalist society, the United States has moved from a small-scale entrepreneurial to a large-scale corporate economy and society. Has a further change occurred implicit in the concept of a stalemated society? The 1890s are usually cited as the watershed of change from entrepreneurial to corporate capitalism. Did the 1960s constitute a new watershed and did they herald a stalemated society? The post-1945 era produced a unique social tempo and a unique set of social expectations. America was suddenly saddled with world leadership, and after notable victories (for example, the Marshall Plan and the creation of a capitalist Japan), it was severely shaken by its defeat in Vietnam. Domestically, it found itself beset by novel problems. The costly Vietnam War had not been paid for—indeed, was actually accompanied by a surge of domestic spending in an effort to build support for the war. The result was serious inflation—indeed, a novel stagflation. The United States also found itself having to make good on meaningful social membership for its entire population. For the first time in their history American propertied and professional groups faced having to run a society in which all participate on an equal and equitable basis and it may well be that such a society is not compatible with a private economy.

The slowdown in the American economy and the relative stagnation in living standards from the 1970s on are unique occurrences in American history. Are they temporary or do they herald a more permanent condition? The easy optimism that has marked America's past, an optimism derived from unprecedented economic growth, may be a false guide. The United States may be facing a future that its past does not prepare it for. Not only are energy sources dwindling but all planetary resources are going to become increasingly scarce. America may no longer have the flexibility it once had as a white, Protestant, middle-class male monopoly. Today, a vast new array of groups are clamoring for their share of America's benefits and the American polity appears overloaded with demands. For the first time in its history, the United States cannot buoy its fortunes on a dependable supply of victims: the poor, racial and ethnic minorities, women, the young and the old, the handicapped, and those different in other ways.

Has the United States lost its enchanted world of Manifest Destiny and inevitable progress, its sense of being in tune with the cosmos? Forty years of prosperity seem to have created rather than solved problems. Not only have the consequences of prosperity contradicted basic American beliefs, but little has been done to prepare Americans for coping with what may be a no-growth future. Instead of a creative set of elites able to deal with problems one by one, the United States has an interlocked set of power groups that seem unable to tackle the deep tangle of intertwined social problems.

The elaborate welfare state erected during the past century is no doubt a source of stability for American society and has helped to correct some injustices and prevent some hardship and suffering. But the welfare state has also locked all power levels of American society into a structure of dependency and immobilization. The attempt by the Reagan administration to unclog American society by reducing the role of government and returning it to its past condition (an alleged era of individualism and free market competition) failed largely because of resistance by the wealthy and well-to-do who are the main beneficiaries of the welfare state and the main supporters of the Reagan administration.

The basic group dynamic in American society is competition among the various levels and types of propertied groups to maintain or increase relative advantage. The higher morality guiding rivalry among the "haves" is economic growth, not as measured by meaningful work, healthy consumption, or husbandry of resources (use economy) but in the abstract (exchange economy). Ominously, economic growth is no longer easily equated with rising levels of social welfare. Ever-larger portions of our gross national product are going into unproductive, unsatisfying social overhead: military preparations, fighting crime, repairing the physical and human costs of pollution, unsafe workplaces, and unhealthy life-styles, and welfare subsidies for unproductive people at all class levels, and debt service.

The 1960s may be a watershed by another criterion—it may mark new heights of formalism and reliance on myth. Our assorted indices and theories do not provide meaningful categories for judging economic and social outcomes. Expectations soar beyond what society can deliver, and widespread deviance is the order of the day. Absolutist, single-interest groups multiply as demands are unmet. Meanwhile, elites orient themselves to vague, often empty abstractions: freedom, excellence, research, economic growth, and so on. Far from being tied to social functions, elites have given themselves the right to look after their own interests and provide solutions to their own problems, under the master myth that both self- and public interest are the same. In the meantime, the public becomes alienated and the legitimacy of elites declines.[3]

Is Directed Change Possible?

Human beings have long dreamed of a society subject to human control and direction. Auguste Comte, a founder of sociology, thought of knowledge as a scientifically determined prediction about, and thus control over, collective existence. Despite disagreements on other matters, most sociologists agreed with Comte in this respect. Whether functional, conflict, or inter-

---

[3]For an earlier discussion of declining legitimacy, see the section "Declining Legitimacy?" in Chapter 14.

actionist, whether pure or applied in orientation, most sociologists have always thought of sociology as a way to help individuals and groups take conscious charge of their collective affairs. In adapting this outlook, sociology has been at odds with the main current of American society. By and large, American elites have argued that society needs no explicit direction. Our knowledge, they argue, should help us understand and conform to society's basic principles.

Today we know that the alleged principles of society are merely misplaced analogies between nature and society. All groups have used government to overcome problems despite their theories. Nonetheless, government intervention and social planning remain dirty words in the United States. Today, the United States is the only developed country in the world that has no open, officially acknowledged planning process. But the United States has always been planned—by Congress, corporations, professional associations, local governments, commissions, and institutes. All policy-making is an attempt to predict the future. *The choice is not between planning or not planning but between good and bad planning.* Perhaps things are changing—certainly policy occupations, policy research, and policy programs are booming.

Social planning gained some respectability in American history thanks largely to wars and depressions. During the Great Depression of the 1930s the United States actually committed itself to a limited form of planning. Ever since the 1930s the federal government has openly tried to direct the economy by using its monetary, tax, and spending policies to balance supply and demand (Keynesianism). Democratic administrations have favored stimulating consumer demand while Republicans favor producers. But Keynesianism appears to have failed. The reason is not difficult to undercover. Like so much else in American society the Keynesian state is abstract to a fault. Its purpose is economic balance and growth in the abstract leaving all the major decisions about how and where to invest resources up to private, self-interested groups. Reliance on broad abstractions is formalism not policy.

Lifetime habits are not shed easily. Freedom from government interference (free enterprise economics) and survival of the fittest (social Darwinism) have been the dominant philosophy of American elites for almost a century and a half. But the relative economic decline of American society, its apparent inability to make headway against its problems, and its frustrations abroad may be leading to changes. In the late 1970s some American leaders called for the United States to give its economy some explicit direction. The term used was *industrial policy*. The United States has always had an industrial—that is, economic—policy, but it has always been secretive, implicit, and on a backdoor basis. Now American leaders, especially in the Democratic party but also in the business world, are beginning to call for an explicit public policy to revitalize the American economy.

So far, however, American leaders have shown little interest in social planning in the full meaning of the term. Meaningful social planning would require control over the basic investment process by the organized public. It requires fresh approaches to basic questions. Can we achieve full employment *and* price stability? Can public investment make the economy more efficient and equitable? How should human resources be developed? What proportion of the economy should go into health services, education, recreation, food, clothing, housing, the military, research?

Improving Policy-Making Institutions[4]

Planning requires knowledge about how society works. But knowledge is acquired and used by social groups. People must do the planning but people see the world from their location in groups. Above all, directed change and better policy-making means structuring groups so that they can function better.

The major change needed is to put less faith in nonexistent market solutions. Basic decisions about the economy must be made by a public organized for that purpose. The second major change is to improve our political institutions, especially by freeing them from the power of private money (see Chapter 14). The third is to transform education to emphasize applied knowledge from kindergarten on with a view toward generating competent, adaptive citizens and improving our professions and occupations. And all reform must be guided by the overriding principle that policy groups are effective if they have heterogeneous memberships and are operating in a genuinely pluralistic system of power. Only when all social groups are adaptive will the Owl of Minerva fly by day instead of by night.

Electoral Reform

The stalemate of the American political process is evident to most people. There has been an ominous drop in political participation. People may have lost their sense that they have power to influence government. Many are aware and often cynical about the way government works to help the strong, the wealthy, and the educated more than their opposites.

Proposals to revitalize the American polity include the following:

1. Abolishing the gerrymander to force candidates and parties to compete in mixed electoral districts.

---

[4]No improvements in policy-making institutions are possible unless the economic power of the upper and upper middle classes are reduced (for an earlier discussion, see the last section of Chapter 17).

2. Financing all elections with tax money, thus curbing the special power that goes to those with money.
3. Making it easier to register and vote.

The overall thrust of electoral reform is to make politics more meaningful, and to make political actors accountable and their discourse clear and relevant.

Prospects for electoral reform do not look good. Those who benefit from existing arrangements are the same ones who must make the reforms, and that is asking a great deal. Existing arrangements fragment the electorate and allow entrenched power groups to veto electoral and other reforms. The gerrymander separates the population into relatively homogeneous enclaves that elect candidates tied to narrow interests. The financing and running of campaigns tends to emphasize candidates' personality, not issues or overall policy programs. Laws to control contributions to political parties and to limit campaign expenditures have not been effective—power groups ignore them for the most part or find it easy to go around them. In addition, the United States Supreme Court has declared that property interests (corporations) have the right to free speech (on ballot issues) thereby loosening the limits that reformers had hoped to place on the power of corporations to influence politics.[5]

The flow of money directly to candidates frees them from party discipline and makes them the agents of the suppliers of money. Public money to help finance presidential campaigns has been a step toward reforming elections, but Congress has refused to finance congressional elections with public money (for the obvious reason that incumbents have a huge advantage over challengers). The present arrangements benefit business and professional interests, and it is doubtful if their power over elections and candidates can be curtailed without strenuous effort. An aspect of this problem that is also detrimental to creative, pluralist politics is that over 90 percent of the money contributed to candidates goes to incumbents, and it is not uncommon for private power groups to contribute to *both* Republican and Democratic candidates. No wonder then that three-quarters of the seats for the U.S. House of Representatives are noncompetitive!

Reformers argue that curtailing the power of private money will force interest groups to argue their positions on their merits. Forcing power groups to explain why what they want is good for all is the meaning of a democratic polity. Reformers argue that Great Britain puts very strict limits on how much can be spent on elections and no harm has come to their democratic processes. Great Britain also allots free time on television for political parties (after all, the airwaves are public property). This reduces the party's need to solicit funds from private groups and it curtails the use of political commercials focused on irrelevant slogans and images.

---

[5]This continues the nineteenth-century legal fiction that corporations are persons entitled to constitutional rights.

Curbing Secrecy, Corruption, and Deception in Public Life

Secrecy, corruption, and deception could each receive separate treatment in this text. However, each makes the other possible and the three should be seen as a single problem.

Secrecy has been curtailed somewhat in recent years by the Freedom of Information Act and by the opening up of public hearings and legislatures. But, argue experts, there is still a large amount of unnecessary secrecy, especially among intelligence and law enforcement agencies.

Corruption in public life consists largely of private groups controlling public officials. This is a pervasive feature of the American polity especially at the local and state levels.[6] Corruption at the federal level is not absent, but here it takes a different form. If one thinks of federal politics and government as primarily ways to prevent change and to protect the interests of established groups, then much of what appears strange and backward at the federal level makes good sense: Regulatory agencies regulate in favor of their respective interest groups and against the public; executive agencies are often administered by officials who have private interests in their areas of responsibility and administer the law accordingly; a gerrymandered Congress is filled with people who owe allegiance to special-interest groups and with people who often have direct interests in matters that they legislate on.

Deception in public life takes many forms starting with the selling of candidates all the way to committee, commission, and government reports. The United States Army Corps of Engineers has a long history of misleading the Congress and the American people about construction projects favored by itself and other special interests. Few people believe proposals from the Department of Defense because of a long history of misleading and undependable estimates of military costs. American foreign policy is conducted without benefit of openly debated and carefully researched policy studies.

Public and private groups consistently exaggerate Soviet military buildups and American vulnerability. Myths about government spending, debt, size, and taxes continue because power groups find them useful. The Nuclear Regulatory Commission has a long history of deceiving the American public about nuclear energy. Even government agencies that collect scientific data mislead—government data on population, crime, unemployment, and so on are misleading unless the assumptions under which facts are collected are kept clearly in mind.

Secrecy, corruption, and deception go together and feed on each other. This is nowhere more apparent than in the behavior of our many unelected,

---

[6]For an excellent selection of readings in this area, see Jack D. Douglas and John M. Johnson, eds., *Official Deviance: Readings in Malfeasance, Misfeasance, and Other Forms of Corruption* (Philadelphia: J. B. Lippincott, 1977).

nonresponsible agencies, authorities, boards, and commissions that run so much of American public life. Secrecy, corruption, and deception emerge from even seemingly innocent and useful traditions. For example, a breeding ground of secrecy, corruption, and deception is our tradition of bipartisan foreign policy and nonpartisan politics and government. In effect, what these do is to let existing power groups remain in the saddle while public policies go unexamined and unevaluated.

The Reagan administration of the 1980s was the lowest point of federal politics since the Harding Administration of the 1920s. With its contempt for government and politics, the Reagan administration relaxed public supervision of federal programs and made no effort to improve the conduct of politics. No pay raises for Congress, federal judges, or federal civil servants, for example, resulted in a large loss of talent and violation of law—congressional members, caught in a financial squeeze and in the awkward, inconsistent position of having to deal with lobbyists who earned more than twice what they did, circumvented the law to increase their income. The result was the ethics scandal of 1989, which forced the Speaker of the House of Representatives to resign. The federal executive branch also oozed corruption as one political appointee after the other was forced to resign. The Reagan administration's contempt for public service and its open invitation to Americans to enrich themselves (under the false assumption that self-interest leads to the public good) resulted in a huge orgy of mismanagement at most federal departments, resulting in enormous costs to the taxpayer (or, rather, additions to public debt) and damage to the environment.

Corruption and incompetence are routine at the federal level and the Reagan administration's unusual record in these regards is not the issue. All federal administrations and all elected officials come from the American electorate, actually from the class system. The key thing to keep in mind, therefore, is the sociology of power. The defects of public life reflect the defects of private life. The key question to ask is: What illegitimate things are going on in private life that require the debasement of public ideals?

Economic and Social Planning

The American polity, argue reformers, must play a bigger role in explicitly guiding the development of American society. Our present policy is not working. Calling all this free enterprise and democracy obscures the issue: The lack of policies to run the country is itself a policy and deserves to be evaluated as such. The American economy must be directed, if not actually planned, so that recessions, unemployment, and bankruptcy can be prevented. Explicit government direction can help modernize and adjust the economy to new conditions—at present, threatened businesses dig in and use government to protect obsolete ways. Explicit government direction can help the professions evaluate their performance according to their own achievement criteria—at present, threatened elites dig in and use government to protect the incompetent and preserve obsolete practices. Once this process is started, labor unions, farmers, and other groups can afford to follow. The main objective is to make it possible for groups to adjust to new conditions. An important condition for developing adaptive personalities and an adaptive society is to create public confidence in which all have faith that losses and gains will be shared equitably.

Strengthening Social-Policy Research

Social-policy research has emerged in recent years as an encouraging development both in sociology and American public life. Despite impressive beginnings much remains to be done. Relations between social researchers and government data-collection agencies must be improved. A wide range of data must be recast to make fact-gathering relevant to policy formation. Relations between fact collectors and policymakers must be improved. And evaluation must be carefully built into our public policies and programs to ensure that they have their desired effects.

The use of advisory committees and consulting firms to formulate reports and make policy recommendations to our legislatures and political leaders must be reexamined. Such bodies are widely used and enjoy quasi-public standing. But, charge critics, such bodies help to disguise the exercise of power, allow partisan powerholders to appear disinterested and objective, and block or mismanage needed reforms.[7]

Public-policy educational programs must address the issue of how to infuse the exercise of power with knowledge, imagination, flexibility, and responsibility. At both the undergraduate and graduate levels, education for the professions must deal with the real world faced by problem solvers. They must recognize that running public affairs is not a matter solely for technical knowledge, not a matter to be approached only in a value-neutral way. Ultimately, problems make sense only if they are put in a sociopolitical context and solved through a mixture of cognitive and value judgments.[8]

SOVIET ADAPTIVE CAPACITY

Our analysis of the Soviet Union's adaptive capacity will be shorter than that of the United States. For one thing, its problems and deficiencies are in

[7] For an indictment of the federal government's use of private advisory and consulting bodies, see Daniel Guttman and Barry Willner, *The Shadow Government: The Government's Multi-Billion-Dollar Giveaway of Its Decision-Making Powers to Private Management Consultants, 'Experts,' and Think Tanks* (New York: Pantheon Books, 1976).

[8] For an indictment of Harvard University's Kennedy School of Government (which can also stand for most public-policy programs in the United States) along these lines, see Jonathan Alter, "Harvard vs. Democracy," *Washington Monthly* 15 (March 1983): 32–39.

many ways similar to those in the United States. For another, we do not know Soviet society as well as we know American society. We have almost no knowledge about the opinions, attitudes, and expectations of the Soviet people, and we lack reliable data about the incidence of many important social problems: nationality unrest, family instability, crime, deficit spending, poverty, and so on. Nonetheless, our knowledge is considerable and some generalizations about the Soviet Union's problem-solving record are possible (Gorbachev's reforms have also led to many new insights into Soviet social problems).

A society's adaptive capacity reflects its power structure. The most relevant image, therefore, for capturing the problem-solving capacity of the Soviet Union is one that analyzes power relations. Policymakers must have a wide range of information to be successful. They must have a sense of the multiple values implicated in every problem. They must be aware of the different perspectives that attach to every problem. They must have a channel that brings problems to their attention and feedback mechanisms to tell them how well policies are working. In short, a pluralistic social structure creates problems, and a pluralistic power structure is the ideal way to solve them. A first question to ask, therefore, is: How pluralistic is the Soviet Union's power structure? As we saw earlier, the best assessment appears to be that the Soviet Union has a fairly pronounced pluralism-at-the-top, or corporate pluralism. The second and most important question is: Does the Soviet power structure have what it takes to solve problems and direct Soviet society? Here it is important to focus separately on changes in the policy-making process (the power structure) and substantive issues, policies, and implementation.

Is Corporate Pluralism Enough?

The Communist party has succeeded in building a superpower for many reasons. One of these was its success in developing feedback systems so that it could tell how well its policies were working. It has permitted, even encouraged, the development of many political mechanisms that are functional equivalents of Western political institutions. The ultimate political problem it faces is whether corporate pluralism provides the party with what it needs to solve social problems. Perhaps a better way to frame this question is: Can the Communist party keep diversifying and liberalizing the Soviet social system without losing control of it?

The adaptive capacity of the Soviet Union is no doubt enhanced by the fact that its various elites find it much easier than their counterparts in the United States to think and act in terms of an interrelated whole. The Communist party's problem-solving record since 1917 must be characterized as outstanding, the equal of any power group in history, including those of Periclean Athens, Elizabethan England, Revolutionary America, or Bismarckian Germany. Its record is also unique because the problems it faced are not comparable to other times. And its past record is not a sure guide to how it will perform in the future because the problems it faces in the next ten to fifty years will be different from the problems of the past.

The Communist party has its dogmas and its metaphysics, which are sources of both strengths and weaknesses. Of special note, however, is the fact that in recent decades it has become more explicitly pragmatic and political rather than ideological and dogmatic. Also of interest is the fact that Communist party members are carefully recruited and apprenticed, yielding a political elite with no parallel in the Western liberal democracies. Internally, the Communist party is a congeries of "interest groups" rather than a monolithic, rigid hierarchy of similar-minded individuals—some segments of the Communist party favor heavy industry, others the military, others détente, others the consumer, and so on. It is also representative of the major powers outside the party. Above all, it appears to enjoy solid popular support.

Corporate pluralism encompasses "interest groups" outside the party and above the masses: the military, the scientific establishment, high civil servants, managers, conservationists, ethnic groups, historical preservation associations, and so on. These groups all make claims on Soviet resources, and the Communist party must coordinate, integrate, and ultimately make the compromises necessary to prevent conflict, stalemate, or drift. The general stance taken by the Communist party along with its actual interaction with Soviet society has led to impressive achievements. That same relation may not work too well in the future since Soviet problems have changed. The most important problem area is economic performance, and here the traditional posture of the Communist party, while successful for over a half century, seems to be failing.

The Stagnant Early Industrial Command Economy

All problem areas are interrelated, but perhaps the most difficult and the one most likely to cause problems (or have good effects) in other areas is the problem of the Soviet economy. Under Stalin the Soviet Union gave top priority to heavy industry and defense, and neglected industries that produce light and heavy consumer goods, service industries, transportation, and agriculture. In recent decades more emphasis has been placed on improving the levels and the quality of consumer goods and on increasing the productivity of agriculture. The Soviet Union has achieved a notable success in housing (which is still in very short supply) and there has been a slow but steady increase in the standard of living.

Policy changes have no doubt been prompted to forestall mass unrest. However, we do not know what ordinary Soviet citizens expect from their society—expectations are relative to experience, and living standards that Americans or Czechs might find burdensome could well be seen as improvements by the average Soviet consumer.

Today's stagnant command economy is a result of past success. Like the United States, the Soviet Union succeeded in building a mass-production economy. Like the United States, it assembled cheap resources via large bureaucratic structures and out poured huge amounts of steel, chemicals, energy, and so on. But it has been unable, again like the United States, to reorient its mass-production economy to changing domestic and world conditions.

Policy changes, therefore, have been prompted by the need for a more efficient program of economic development. Modern economies interrelate in many ways and neglected areas have a way of curbing development in emphasized areas. The Soviet failure to develop rail and truck transportation is now causing serious delays in industrial production. The failure to develop retail trade causes a huge loss of time spent waiting on long lines to shop. The failure to insist on quality housing construction will plague the Soviet economy with costly maintenance problems for decades.

A notable change since the death of Stalin has been a relatively full acceptance of the need to trade abroad. In effect, the Soviet Union has abandoned the concept of national self-sufficiency in favor of an international division of labor. It is more efficient for the Soviet Union to import food and advanced technology than to provide them for itself. It is also aware that it cannot hope to keep pace with the capitalist societies unless it participates fully in the world economy. Its application for member status with GATT in 1988 is evidence that it wants to participate more fully in the world economy.

The key to a more productive economy, however, is decentralization. In 1987 Mikhail Gorbachev proposed a set of wide-ranging reforms in the direction of a more market-oriented economy. Today, the Soviet Union allows cooperatives in many service businesses and will scrap collective farming to spur food production. It has admitted that its economy has experienced inflation and that its political economy has budget deficits (and has put state businesses and factories on notice that those not making the grade will be closed). It has invited foreign investment, allowing majority ownership, and is on the verge of allowing foreign companies to take profits out of the country. In 1988 the Soviet Union took out large loans from capitalist countries, in effect asking them to build consumer-oriented factories and services in the USSR. In 1989 it gave (government-controlled) labor unions the legal right to strike (largely to force management to improve its record of solving labor disputes). Whether vested interests will allow these reforms to take place remains to be seen. In any case, lagging economic growth will make it difficult to solve or mitigate problems in other areas. Here is another similarity with the United States.[9]

[9]For an analysis of Gorbachev's economic reforms, by a leading Soviet economist who helped formulate them, see Able Aganbegyan, *The Challenge of Perestroika*, ed., Michael Barratt Brown; intro., Alec Nove; trans., Pauline M. Taffen (Bloomington: Indiana University Press, 1988).

Problems of Political Succession

Transferring power peacefully is important to social systems. The liberal democracies use elections to transfer power and have provisions for succession in case leaders die or are incapacitated. So far the Soviet Union has been successful in transferring power after the death of its leaders and in one case from one holder of power to another (Khrushchev to Brezhnev).

Reviving Political Vitality and Legitimacy

That the Communist party enjoys wide support is undoubted. Nonetheless, the party is aware that its power is threatened by the long economic slowdown. To counter threats to its legitimacy, the party, under Gorbachev, has made some far-reaching reform proposals in regard to political institutions. Along with efforts to spur economic growth through more economic freedom, Gorbachev has proposed that the Soviet people have more say in choosing their leaders. Terms of offices will be limited. There must be a scrupulous regard for law even as personal rights and freedoms are expanded. The law must be changed to foster social development and everything not prohibited by law is to be allowed. The functions of the party and government must be carefully outlined so that they can always be seen as instruments of government by the people. And everything must be done to strengthen the self-regulation and self-government of society, and the initiative of citizens and social groups.[10]

Gorbachev's economic and political reforms are attempts to modernize the USSR, or rather, to bring its institutions abreast of the far-reaching changes that have occurred since Stalin. It would be a mistake, though, to think of the reform ferment of the Gorbachev era as an impulse from below or by civil society against an oppressive polity. The Community party and society are intertwined, and the new Soviet "civil" society is largely the creation of a dynamic party (building on an advanced feudal-authoritarian system). Today, the Soviet people are urbanized, educated, and highly political. The party, as always, is promoting reforms to keep power—but it is also doing so because the reforms are in line with the basic values of socialism. As always, the party is urging the people to support its fight against inefficiency and privilege. Thus, two perspectives on the reform ferment in the Soviet Union should be kept in mind:

1. As a rational authoritarian society (that is, a society in which the state has clearly established functions for the direction and welfare of society), the Soviet Union is further politicizing itself in response to the qualitative increases in the complexity of its problems (what this means is that nonfunctional bureaucratic routines are no longer tolerated). The shift toward representative government

[10]*The New York Times,* June 29, 1988, p. 1.

here has parallels with how representative government evolved in England and the United States and is evolving today in, say, Brazil and South Korea.

2. The reforms may be leading to a greater degree of Western-style representative government and reliance on market mechanisms, but they are basically attempts to shift from a socialist command to a socialist market society. It should be clearly noted that economic markets and political markets do not rest on equal power nor do they equalize. Their main function in all countries is to provide intelligence to the assorted power groups that run society, economic and political feedback to enable policymakers to make needed adjustments. In short, economic and electoral markets are ways to prevent social system change. They should be viewed in this manner both in the Soviet Union and elsewhere.

The Problem of Nationalities

Integrating its ethnic, religious, and linguistic minorities into its urban-industrial system will no doubt be a continuing problem into the foreseeable future. The Eastern European countries will also require considerable attention—much of the political future here depends on whether their economies can be wedded to the Soviet Union's. These countries have experienced a nationalist resurgence in recent years (except for Bulgaria and East Germany) and clearly belong in our next category as a foreign-policy problem for the Soviet Union.

Foreign Policy

Foreign-policy problems will continue to loom large for the Soviet Union. On its immediate borders, it faces restive Eastern-bloc countries, a still unreconciled China (despite the recent warming of relations), Muslim fundamentalism in Iran, and Turkey, which is a member of NATO and a military ally of the United States.

The Soviet Union has some important allies beyond its own borders. Vietnam helps it to outflank China and gives it access to Southeast Asia and the South Pacific. Cuba gives it presence in the Western Hemisphere and has proven an effective agent in Africa. But on the whole, it cannot be said that the Soviet Union has had any great success in foreign policy, something that no doubt accounts for the extraordinary emphasis it has placed in recent years on military preparedness. Its presence in the Middle East, Asia, and Africa is more appearance than substance. It has no control over the countries it deals with and even the ones it favors such as Iraq, Syria, and Libya are far from being compliant allies or peripheries. Its attempt to occupy Afghanistan was a costly failure.[11]

---

[11]The Center for Defense Information, "Soviet Geopolitial Momentum: Myth or Menace?," *The Defense Monitor* 15, no. 5 (1986), argues that Soviet world power is quite small and has been in decline since its high point in 1958.

Gorbachev has taken a number of initiatives to ease foreign pressures on the Soviet Union. During 1986 he put the United States on the defensive by proposing a series of arms control and reduction measures across a wide variety of areas, including both missiles and conventional arms. He also called for a moratorium on nuclear testing and stopped Soviet testing for extended periods. His unilateral reduction of the conventional arms facing NATO (small in number but large psychologically) and his repeated request for negotiations to reduce short-range nuclear weapons in Europe has appealed to continental West Europeans and separated them significantly from Great Britain and the United States. He has made overtures to China on easing border tensions and on establishing better relations, and his visit to China in 1989 was of great symbolic importance. In 1988, a trusted aide, the Politburo's head of ideology, Vadim Medvedev, in a published speech called for more experimentation with markets at home and rejected the idea of a world struggle between communism and capitalism. "Universal values such as avoiding war and avoiding ecological disaster must outweigh the idea of a struggle between classes," he argued.[12] Clearly, having an able and energetic leader will be an addition to the Soviet Union's adaptive capacity.

Social Problems

The Soviet Union is beset with the usual array of social problems found in all industrial societies. The exact nature and extent of these problems are difficult to determine because of the lack of research and reliable data. Leaving the future aside, analysts agree that Soviet problem solving up to the 1970s is impressive.[13] The story since the 1970s is different. An important perspective on Soviet social problems is gained if one compares living standards there with other countries. Soviet living standards are still far below American, European, and Eastern European standards. The Soviet standard of living is roughly one-third that of the United States and half that of France and the Federal Republic of Germany. And not only have there been no gains since the 1970s but, if anything, the Soviet Union is losing ground in one area after the other.[14]

Poverty

Poverty is an obvious place to start in discussing Soviet problems. With its heavy emphasis on capital formation and its burdensome military spend-

[12]*The New York Times*, October 6, 1988, p. 1.

[13]Vic George and Nick Manning, *Socialism, Social Welfare, and the Soviet Union* (Boston: Routledge and Kegan Paul, 1980) and Gordon B. Smith, ed., *Public Policy and Administration in the Soviet Union* (New York: Praeger, 1980).

[14]For a comprehensive analysis of Soviet living standards (goods and services, poverty, medical care, housing, education, and work), with extensive comparisons with other countries, see Horst Herlmann, ed., *Quality of Life in the Soviet Union* (Boulder, Colo.: Westview Press, 1987).

ing, it is not surprising that many Soviet citizens are poor. Ever since the death of Stalin a variety of antipoverty measures have been taken, in many ways resembling measures taken in the United States. On the whole, however, the Soviet Union cannot hope to make much headway against poverty unless it makes radical changes in its economic priorities.

The abstract problem of poverty (and near poverty) manifests itself in a number of concrete ways: housing hardships, family instability, alcoholism, delinquency among the young, and crime.

Cities and Housing

Soviet leaders have declared their intention to provide housing and to design cities so that egalitarian ideals can be achieved. Deliberately, they have spread industrialization into regions beyond European Russia in order to prevent regional imbalances or sharp differences between urban and rural areas (and for purposes of national defense).

Soviet urban planning has had some success in preventing the marked segregation of life-styles by class and income that marks Western cities. However, urban planning as such has not succeeded in establishing itself. State economic ministries still control a great deal of the investment in housing, transport, child care, schools, and medical facilities, and these often violate urban plans. In addition, Soviet citizens are not free to live where they want, and an elaborate system of domestic passports controls their movement in an effort to ration labor and housing, both of which are in short supply. This control has helped to protect older cities, which are relatively free of some of the pathologies that plague Western, especially American, cities (for example, crime—the newer cities with larger numbers of young males tend to have higher crime rates).[15]

Health

The Soviet Union has free health care for its citizens. Soviet leaders recognize that a healthy population is more productive and have stated their commitment to preventive medicine. The reality of Soviet medicine, however, reflects the scarcity of resources that is found everywhere outside heavy industry and the military. Here as elsewhere, the Soviet elite enjoy a higher level of benefits. This is similar to other countries, including the United States. Actually, the Soviet health care system has many similarities to the United States: reliance on doctors, technology, and large hospitals to take care of people *after* they become ill or disabled.

---

[15]For a fairly positive picture of Soviet urban achievements, see, James H. Bater, *The Soviet City* (Beverly Hills, Calif.: Sage, 1980). For a less positive picture, see Henry W. Morton and Robert C. Stuart, eds., *The Contemporary Soviet City* (Armonk, N.Y.: M.E. Sharpe, 1984).

The Soviet Union registered significant gains in health after the Revolution. In recent years, however, not only have there been no gains but, ominously, reversals have appeared. Infant mortality has increased and life expectancy for men has declined (and remained stationary for women).[16] The Soviet health care system, David and Feshbach argue, has not deteriorated, but they are unable to pinpoint the reasons why the earlier drop in infant mortality reversed itself in 1971. However, it now appears that no increase in infant mortality took place once attention is paid to differences in data collection and better reporting in the Asian republics.[17] The USSR has made mistakes in its medical investment strategy (more instead of better facilities, for example) and the proportion of GNP spent on health care has declined. Alcoholism is rampant in the USSR, and this no doubt has contributed to the drop in the male life expectancy (for example, drunkenness on the job and while driving has led to a large increase in deaths). The food supply seems adequate, but whether the population is eating the dull and bland diet is another matter. And there appears to be a widespread indifference to risks from industrial wastes, pesticides, and other hazardous materials. In any case, if the reversal in Soviet health statistics continues after the early 1970s it will be a unique case of a developed nation heading back toward the health levels characteristic of developing nations.

Crime

Although no exact data are available, a significant amount of crime takes a place in the Soviet Union. It is also clear that crime can no longer be explained as a vestige of Czarist Russia but clearly stems from contemporary Soviet society. It is also growing. There is much ordinary crime, especially by young males in the developing cities of the Far East and Far North. A good deal of it is associated with alcoholism. Of greater significance is crime by individuals in positions of power.[18]

Ordinary crime in the Soviet Union is largely a matter of society raising expectations and then not satisfying them. In this, it resembles crime in the capitalist world. And the most important types of crime, those committed by individuals in positions of power, also resemble those in capitalist societies. Because curbing crime means that power groups have to curb their own

---

[16]For an analysis of the latest data, which stop early in the 1970s, see Christopher Davis and Murray Feshbach, *Rising Infant Mortality in the U.S.S.R. in the 1970s* (Washington, D.C.: U. S. Bureau of the Census, 1980).

[17]Ellen Jones and Fred W. Grupp, "Infant Mortality Trends in the Soviet Union," *Population Development Review* 9 (June 1983): 213–246, and Barbara A. Anderson and Brian D. Silver, "Infant Mortality in the Soviet Union: Regional Differences and Measurement Issues," *Population Development Review* 12 (December 1986): 705–738.

[18]Louise I. Shelley, "Crime and Criminals in the U.S.S.R.," in Michael Paul Sacks, and Jerry G. Pankhurst, eds., *Understanding Soviet Society* (Boston: Unwin Hyman, 1988), chap. 9.

power, the chances of reducing crime in the Soviet Union are as small as they are in the United States.

Soviet Social Science and Adaptive Capacity

The social sciences in the Soviet Union are embedded in Marxism. Partly because Marxism is a rational philosophy committed to science and partly because all power groups in complex society, especially its industrial variant, need information about how society is working, the Soviet Union has developed an empirical sociological tradition similar to that in the United States.[19] In addition, there is considerable evidence that Soviet economists and foreign-policy analysts are now primarily pragmatists and empirical realists rather than dogmatists. The recent official abandonment of class struggle as the key relation in international relations and acceptance of state-centered political relations has antecedents in Soviet foreign-policy theory.[20] And considerable discussion has taken place about improving policy-making organs and administration.

Soviet thinkers have an overall image of Soviet society as being a sound functional system that requires time and research to iron out its problems. The similarity to how American theorists see the United States is startling. Also startling is the pronounced tendency to concentrate on deviance among the lower classes and to blame the victim for problem behavior. Because the system is fundamentally sound, pathological behavior must stem from the willful irresponsibility of the individuals involved.[21] The Soviet Union is no more likely than the United States to make inroads into its social problems as long as it fails or refuses to link them to the basic processes of industrialization and concentrated power.

Solving social problems requires considerable resources. Given the Soviet Union's present allocation of resources, it is unlikely that the resources needed to solve social problems will be forthcoming. Solving such problems also entails prevention and social reorganization. Given the present Soviet power structure these too are unlikely. It is already clear that Soviet ideologists, including Soviet social science, have developed the same orientation toward social problems that is found in the United States. Like mainstream American social science, Soviet social science is unlikely to connect social problems directly to Soviet institutions or to the power groups that create and benefit from them.

---

[19]For a depiction of Soviet sociology by two leading Soviet sociologists, see G.V. Osipov and M.N. Rutkevich, "Sociology in the U.S.S.R., 1965–1975," *Current Sociology* 26, no. 2 (Summer 1978): 1–60.

[20]Allen Lynch, *The Soviet Study of International Relations* (New York: Cambridge University Press, 1987).

[21]Walter D. Conner, *Deviance in Soviet Society: Crime, Delinquency, and Alcoholism* (New York: Columbia University Press, 1972), chap. 10.

Soviet leadership from Brezhnev on has emphasized the need to master the revolution in science and technology and bring it to bear on the overall management of society.[22] Soviet leaders and thinkers now talk of Soviet society as "developed" or "mature socialism." There is an urgent need to develop "scientific management" and to incorporate the latest findings in science and technology into the productive process. While affirming the continuing validity of political direction by the Communist party, the Politboro has widened elite participation in policy-making and encouraged mass participation in administration. But as Erik Hoffmann and Robbin Laird point out, the call for new ideas and innovative practices exceeds the actual development of policies, and far exceeds the development of new institutional arrangements. The Soviet leadership, these two researchers argue, is not committed to a democratization of Soviet society, which would bring goals and institutions into question, but to a more efficient, productive "technocratic socialism," which the Soviet leadership claims is a preparation for democracy (communism). The similarity with mainstream social science and mainstream professionalism in the United States (technocratic liberalism) is striking, with but one exception—American elites believe they are already in a democracy.

STRATIFICATION AND ADAPTATION: A SUMMARY

Stratified societies have a poor record of problem solving. Elites get separated from social reality, fail to solve problems, and often aggravate problems by acting inappropriately.

One must distinguish between policies to improve problem-solving institutions and personalities, and policies designed to address problems themselves.

Americans believe they live in a pluralistic society and that this ensures problem solving. However, sociologists no longer believe that the United States is characterized by *pluralism,* or competition among private individuals and groups directed by markets and refereed by government and law. Considerable evidence has appeared that the United States is *oligarchic* rather than pluralist. More evidence suggests that it is a *stalemated society* (one unable to solve its problems) and that it is losing its legitimacy (people no longer take it on faith that power groups deserve their power).

Directed social change is an old idea, but realizing it has eluded human beings. Whether the United States can control and direct social change depends largely on whether it can bring its economy under the direction of a public organized for adaptation.

[22]For a full discussion, see Erik P. Hoffmann and Robbin F. Laird, *Technocratic Socialism: The Soviet Union in the Advanced Industrial Era* (Durham, N.C.: Duke University Press, 1985).

The American polity appears unable to provide society with direction or to solve problems. Proposals to revitalize the American polity include: a more positive attitude toward government; electoral reform to neutralize the power of private money, curbing the gerrymander, and strengthening political parties; reducing secrecy, corruption, and deception; a more explicitly planned economy and society; and continued efforts to improve policy research and policy-making.

The Soviet Union has considerable pluralism at the top. The Communist party elite has an achievement record second to none. But it also presides over a deeply solidified class society and a top-heavy command economy. All in all, the Soviet power structure, while admirably suited to meet the problems of early industrialization, seems out of touch with the realities of a mature industrial economy dependent on the world market. Given its slowed economy and its top-heavy centralized society, the Soviet Union appears not to be keeping up with its problems.

CHAPTER 21

Stratification and World Problems

A WORLD OF STRATIFIED SOCIETIES

Imagine 165 stratified societies of all kinds. Imagine developed capitalist and socialist systems, each with their own mix of interests, each with interests running counter to the other. Multiply this world of conflict by the various developing capitalist and socialist societies, each of them with interests that differ from the others. Then imagine all 165 nation-states as having deep currents of illegitimacy in their systems of inequality. Imagine, too, that most have policy-making institutions that are inadequate for addressing today's problems.[1] And finally imagine all these societies implicated in an external world over which they have little control. Put together, these images results in the master image of an anomic world society.

THE ANOMIC WORLD SOCIETY

The planet is inhabited by 165 dissimilar societies, most of them problem societies. It is no longer easy for social analysts or elites to distinguish (or

[1]Three annual publications provide supplementary materials for world problems: Suzanne Ogden, ed., *Global Politics;* Robert M. Jackson, ed., *Global Issues;* and John Allen, ed., *Environment,* all from Dushkin Publishing, Guilford, Conn.

understand) internal from external relations. Societies, now more interdependent than ever, have few ways of interacting that can be relied on to solve disputes and satisfy mutual needs. Even the two superpowers cannot get their ways and have had great difficulty in coping with their external environment of other countries. In addition, the powerful thrust of technology has created many novel conditions for international relations. The destructiveness of contemporary military technology has produced an unprecedented situation—the possibility that war could end life on the planet. Even a limited nuclear war could usher in a nuclear winter. The basic processes of economic development spill out beyond national boundaries. Acid rain produced in Ohio contaminates Canada; acid rain generated in one European country affects ten other countries. The clearing of the Amazon rain forest could adversely affect the climate of North America. Industrial waste could gradually accumulate in the atmosphere, destroy the ozone that protects us from harmful rays from the sun, or block the escape of heat from the earth, in effect warming it, thus triggering a meltdown of the polar ice and creating catastrophic flooding.

With the emergence of the 165 new nation-states from the Middle Ages on (most of them since 1945), hundreds of territorial disputes have also emerged. Ethnic minorities and stateless people clamor for new arrangements. International struggles and regional disputes are more important to many countries than arguments between the United States and the USSR, though some regional disputes such as Vietnam and its neighbors and the Arab-Israel confrontation are also linked to superpower rivalry.

The bipolar confrontation between the superpowers is softened somewhat by the fact that the United States and the Soviet Union have a number of important common interests. Both see the developing nations as suppliers of raw and semi-processed materials. As naval powers, both nations have a stake in keeping the world's waterways open to international traffic. There is no better example of the strange bedfellow world of intersocietal politics than the fact that the United States, which banned the sale of wheat to the USSR and organized a boycott of the Moscow Olympics after the Soviet invasion of Afghanistan in 1979, continued to supply it with advanced oil-drilling and production equipment for fear that Soviet oil production would decline and thus create excessive demand pressures on world oil supplies.

Neither the United States nor the Soviet Union is acting to create international institutions that can solve problems. As the leader of the powerful bloc of capitalist societies, the United States bears a special responsibility in this regard. Like other societies, it pursues interests in terms of its internal power structure. Far from developing a framework for resolving world conflicts (which would require acknowledging its dependence on others and its fallibility), the United States has proclaimed itself the world's judge and declared its resolve not to share the land, the sea, or space with anyone that is not its ally or client.

In the unique multiple-system world, all actors are involved in a global system but in different ways. Some societies are interested mostly in local or regional interests. Some are involved in more than one region. Others are involved locally and in their own regions but are also interested in broadly defined world problems. Some are active at all levels and in all world problems. Nonetheless, the world's many dissimilar societies and blocs have few accepted ways of behaving toward each other. Worse still, all think of themselves as essentially sound and seek the causes of their problems in the malevolent actions of outsiders. This holds for the United States as much as any other society. The American foreign policy establishment has no idea that the world's major problem society is the United States. The American people and government have a long and settled faith that the United States is an exception to the corruptions that have always beset societies. The reality is otherwise.

In recent decades the American government (and national legislature) has reflected the growing complexities of American society. What coherence and unity there is in American foreign policy consists of simplistic slogans and well-intentioned blunders. In an important sense there is no American foreign policy. In another sense the reality of American foreign and domestic policy furthers the interests of American corporate and professional elites.

The incoherence in American foreign policy, reflecting the incoherence of American society, is also reflected in the organization of the federal executive and in the policy-making organs of the general polity. Large and diverse agencies formulate incoherent and ineffective policies under the assumption that order and stability are the natural condition of humankind. They accept no responsibility for being part of the cause of world disorders. Assuming order as a natural condition, American elites are constantly surprised by the frequency and seriousness of the outbursts against their country: Pearl Harbor, Korea, Cuba, Vietnam, Iran, Central America, Lebanon.

Private organizations have also failed to disabuse Americans of their conceit that their society is an exception to run-of-the-mill humanity. Private organizations are also powerful promoters of poor policies. The theory of intersocietal relations from about 1500 to 1945 focused narrowly on internation state relations. Even today it is not sufficiently recognized that the state-centric model of world affairs is much too narrow and that many other actors such as intergovernmental bodies, churches, ethnic lobbies, criminal groups, individuals, labor unions, militant liberation groups, professional associations, law firms, foundations, and a wide variety of powerful, geocentric corporations play a significant role in the fortunes of the world's peoples. Needless to say, such quasi-public and private groups add to the contradictions and confusions in the relations among societies.

American social science has not been much help in clarifying the anomic nature of intersocietal relations. Mainstream economics has simply extended the idea of laissez-faire to the world economy completely unaware that free trade is simply a cover to legitimate the selfish interests of powerful countries (like England in the nineteenth century and the United States in the twentieth) and multinational corporations. Mainstream political science and its sub-specialty—international relations—along with sociology have only limited conceptions of the real forces at work in the world. Introductory sociology texts continue to ignore foreign relations in their depiction of American society, and their concluding chapters on social change are an embarrassment to the profession. By and large, American social science takes the United States at face value and assumes that it is or can be a force for good.

A realistic assessment of intersocietal relations sees them as a dumping ground for internal frustrations and a way to divert attention from internal failure. Another cause of anomie in world affairs is that the elites of the world are sitting on different problems and cannot easily negotiate or cooperate. America's go-it-alone policy at the United Nations has isolated it in that forum. By and large, it has continued if not placed greater emphasis on the Cold War practice of linking all troubles to world communism. The United States has acted under the assumption that the Soviet economy, being social-ist, is fundamentally flawed and can thus be pressured and outspent into a fatal decline. The Soviets in turn have many false assumptions about the capitalist economy. Despite their many similarities and common problems, there is much pluralistic ignorance between the U.S. and USSR. Neither senses that all developed societies are problematic. Nor can modern society remain a taken-for-granted backdrop for sociology. Sociology's research, textbooks, teaching, social-type theorizing, and politics will all change once it begins to ask, Is an industrial society really possible, and if so, how?

PROSPECTS FOR A WORLD CULTURE

The industrial Western nations (along with Japan and even the developed socialist bloc) have sent elements of their cultures to the far corners of the earth. All countries now have cars, radios, television, powdered milk, soft drinks, and blue jeans. But many countries resist cultural elements that do not harmonize with their mores. Even Japan, an advanced industrial society, resists individualism and still does not yet have much of a feminist move-ment. But the greatest resistance is to industrialization itself. Of the non-Western countries, only those with a background in Chinese culture have really committed themselves to industry: Japan, South Korea, Taiwan, Hong Kong, Singapore, and now China. This is not to minimize the achievement of India, Brazil, and other countries, only to say that these latter nations have not yet made the transition to a viable industrialization.

We must not forget, therefore, that there has always been deep resis-tance to Western imperialism and to its cultural penetration and standardiza-tion. Today, religion is the foremost barrier to modernization (either toward capitalism or socialism). Certain forms of Islamic religion are especially hostile to the secular values of the West and industrial development. Religion is still a powerful force in all parts of the world and is far from having made its peace with modernity. Hinduism resists change in India. In Hispanic societies, Roman Catholicism is still a conservative force, although some elements of the Roman Catholic clergy have tried to promote reform. Even in the United States, powerful religious currents run counter to secularism, science, and humanism.

The various regions and blocs of the world are quite diverse. The Third World is filled with military and communist dictatorships. The Arab world is very diverse. Black African countries are having extreme difficulty in feeding themselves, let alone entering the modern world. And the rivalry between the superpowers shows no evidence that they understand that they have much in common and many mutual interests.

Thus, it is a mistake to think that a world culture is emerging that will integrate all the societies of the globe. True, the United Nations provides a common forum for discussion. Many dissimilar societies work in and derive mutual benefit from its many specialized agencies. The United Nations has had some success in its peacekeeping missions, especially in recent years. A body of international law has developed. All of the world's societies are dependent on the world-market economy and maintain a wide network of economic and other relations. But despite all this, the fact remains that the planet is now inhabited by 165 sovereign nation-states, most of which have very little in common and few accepted ways of interacting. The countries of the world have made little progress in establishing problem-solving mechanisms. And they have a long history of resorting to violence to redress differences. In short, the present intersocietal system has many of the earmarks of anomie.

But intersocietal anomie has its roots in the domestic power structures of the various societies. A world culture is in its infancy, but the prospects for cooperation and peace are not promising as long as the world's domestic power structures are not geared to democratically derived policies that ensure food, shelter, work, a protected environment, and meaningful social roles for all.

THE ALL-IMPORTANT DOMESTIC AND WORLD ECONOMY

The economy is the main determinant of how people behave. Today, the peoples of the world all share the same economic expectations—they desire and look forward to a better standard of living. The peoples of the world are also all implicated in the world economy—what happens to them domestically is affected by their economic relations to other nations. The countries of the world are all aware of this but find it difficult to manage their affairs. The

United States is no exception; indeed, it is uniquely handicapped by a metaphysical outlook that bears little correspondence to reality. American elites, including mainstream social scientists, continue to believe that America's economic and political institutions are something other than historical creations. From the mid- eighteenth century to the Great Depression of the 1930s, Western social scientists created a fictitious social world allegedly governed by natural laws. Economic theory was the stronghold of this fiction, though history, political science, and sociology were eager participants in it.

The Great Depression of the 1930s made clear what should have been apparent from the actual behavior of people—the social world is a created thing, and the economy, far from being natural, results from the selfish, often uninformed, often clashing actions of corporations, professions, consumers, workers, governments, citizens, churches, schools, research institutes, criminals, and cultural groups.

Today, the fiction of a natural economy continues under the names of free enterprise, market economics, free trade, and comparative advantage. Nonetheless, all societies openly accept the role of government in guiding the economy ("We are all Keynesians"). Even the United States under the Reagan administration of the 1980s was Keynesian (state management of the economy by favoring producers), a variant of Keynesianism that has been proven wrong (favoring producers through tax cuts led to reduced not increased capital investment during the 1980s and the resulting budget-trade deficits became a large drag on the American economy). Today, societies negotiate among themselves on a variety of economic matters and have set up a variety of international organizations to help coordinate their domestic economic systems. Even the Reagan administration, whose outlook on the world economy adhered to nineteenth-century laissez-faire economic and social theory, was eventually forced (from 1985 on) to act politically on the international scene in an effort to revive the sluggish American and world economy. However, the governments of the major capitalist industrial powers are under extreme pressure from their respective domestic interests and cannot easily do the things that are needed.

CHANGES IN THE ECONOMIES
OF THE DEVELOPED NATIONS

The developed capitalist and communist countries enjoyed a stage of economic development that appears to be historically unique, a perhaps one-time thing. Far from being a law of nature, the economic growth of the past few centuries and the rise in the standard of living in the West between the 1850s and the 1960s (and in the Soviet Union from 1917 to the 1960s) may be over.

Speaking broadly, economic growth occurred because inexpensive resources, technology, and cheap and eager labor could be united in easy and obvious ways.[2] People worked hard because they needed the essentials of life. Economic growth occurred because governments, religion, schools, and social scientists provided a congenial and supportive social context. Gradually, a general consensus developed that economic growth was not only good but a law of nature and that the same law would see to it that the fruits of growth would be distributed fairly. The emergence of trade unions (in the capitalist countries) and the welfare state in all countries was part of this consensus.

The 1970s ushered in a new era—slower economic growth, a decline in productivity, a stagnating standard of living. The economic boom of the 1950s and 1960s in the West had rested to some extent on the huge backlog of demand for housing, appliances, and automobiles created by World War II and the Great Depression of the 1930s. By the 1970s this demand, though still strong, had slackened. Resources had become scarcer and more expensive. Labor had also become expensive. Large-scale enterprise developed inefficiencies largely because management styles were inappropriate for emerging new problems.[3] And social overhead increased both in amount and in complexity. The general public wanted a large variety of services, including government initiatives to promote egalitarian values. The welfare state now included massive new interferences with market mechanisms: help to business, farmers, and professionals through a bewildering array of grants, subsidies, price supports, and tax preferences. And the state took on complex new services such as regulating medical services, safeguarding the environment, keeping advertisers honest, promoting research, and protecting the consumer.

The result was to narrow the options of government and to produce rigidity and stalemate. To make things worse, the domestic economies of the entire world were being increasingly affected by new developments in the international economy.

THE NEW INTERNATIONAL ECONOMY

The contemporary world of 165 nation-states began with Europe's outward expansion in the fifteenth century.[4] The great age of exploration also ushered in the great age of colonialism. That there was an international economy after

[2] For a deeper discussion of why economic growth started in the first place, see the section in Chapter 2 on the rise of capitalism.

[3] For a devastating indictment of complacency, greed, and incompetence in the oligarchic American automobile industry, see Richard Halberstam, *The Reckoning* (New York: William Morrow, 1986).

[4] Two books are especially useful as overviews of the present world economy: Lars Anell and Birgitta Nygren, *The Developing Countries and the World Economic Order* (New York: Methuen, 1980), and Lars Anell, *Recession, The Western Economies and the Changing World Order* (London: Frances Pinter, 1981).

1450 there is no doubt. The impact of the European colonial powers on most of the world was profound, as we saw abundantly in previous chapters. By and large, colonialism transformed the horticultural and agrarian systems of the non-European world into cash-crop dependencies. At the same time international trade had an impact on the internal development of the European nations, and later the United States and Canada. Profits from overseas provided additional investment funds for the emerging capitalist nations while their ability to import cheap food and other resources enabled them to shift their economy and labor force toward manufacturing and services.

Two things stand out about international trade from the nineteenth century to 1950:

1. The amount of economic activity among nations was small in relation to domestic activity and most of it was in terms of commodities.
2. The international economy was hegemonic, that is, England was the accepted pacesetter and standard-setter especially in the period up to World War I.

After World War II (climaxing trends that had occurred as early as World War I), the United States became the hegemonic power in the world economy. From the end of World War II to approximately 1970, the United States dominated the world economy, and this, combined with its military strength, also made it the dominant political actor on the world scene. However, its hegemony was short-lived. During the 1970s and 1980s, a new international order rose to the surface:

1. International economic activity had grown so as to dwarf the pre–World War II period.
2. The United States was no longer the dominant economic or political-military actor. The Soviet Union's rapid economic and military growth had transformed it into a world power. And Germany and Japan, thanks in measure to American support (much of it in the form of a free ride on defense), became significant industrial rivals to the United States. In addition, industrializing Third-World countries, such as South Korea, Taiwan, Hong Kong, Singapore, China, and Brazil, were providing significant inputs into the world economy. By the 1970s the world economy had no hegemonic leader, no center of gravity. By the 1980s, the United States' share of world production had slipped from 50 percent of the world's total to 20 percent.

The Capitalist World Economy

The basic world economy is essentially a capitalist system. The vast bulk of trade takes place among the developed capitalist countries and the same countries dominate trade with the Third World. The various groups that make up this economy are private corporations, governments, and international organizations (World Bank, International Monetary Fund, GATT, OPEC, commodity cartels). Lesser players are professional associations, labor unions, churches, and universities. It is clear that the Soviet Union, the

Eastern European countries, and the People's Republic of China are also in the world economy with both feet.

Not only is there a world economy (actually a world political economy) but economies have become increasingly intertwined. No longer does one have only a multinational company that is clearly a visible owner of a foreign plant. The new phenomenon is the multinational that uses the entire globe to perform its operations, manufacturing in different countries, assembling in still other countries, and selling everywhere. Also new is the practice of multinationals operating jointly and using each other's developed country as part of their own.

The world economy is massively affected by domestic policies, and states around the world openly intervene to pursue economic, political, and military goals. For example, the United States' basic policies give carte blanche to multinationals even as the United States practices selective protectionism. Taiwan and Korea manage their currencies and curb consumption so that their prices and imports remain low, thus helping them to build trade surpluses.

As countries experience difficulties all find it easy to blame foreigners rather than themselves or domestic groups, and this has led to increased protectionism and nationalism. Given the dense intertwining of many of the world's economies and our lack of knowledge about how the world economy works, most nations pursue policies in the blind.

The North-South Split

The nations of the world are deeply divided by economic status, especially the split between the industrial countries (capitalist and communist), which have diversified economies, and the Third-World countries (most of which are located in the Southern Hemisphere), which are still exporters of staples and only partially industrialized.[5]

The two most important new aspects of the stratification between the First World and the Third World is, one, the Third World is not only getting poorer in relation to the First World but that much of it is mired in absolute poverty; and, two, there is no longer an acceptance of low living conditions anywhere in the world.

Declining Productivity: The Global Economic Slowdown

In recent decades some countries have risen relatively and on an absolute economic scale (Japan, China, South Korea, Taiwan, Singapore, Hong

[5]Independent Commission on International Development Issues, *North-South: A Program For Survival* (Cambridge, Mass.: MIT Press, 1980)—the Brandt Report. For the history of negotiations between Europe and its former colonies in Africa and other places, see John Ravenhill, *Collective Clientelism: The Lome Conventions and North-South Relations* (New York: Columbia University Press, 1985).

Kong, Malaysia, and the oil-rich nations). Some have experienced continued growth but have suffered a relative decline (the U.S., USSR, Great Britain, France). Others have floundered or are in what appears to be chronic trouble unable to make either relative or absolute gains (examples are Argentina, Mexico, and Nigeria, the Philippines, but much the same is true of most of Latin America and Africa).

Beyond all these ups and downs by individual countries, however, lies the ominous slowdown in productivity of *all* the world's economies.[6] With no understanding of how the world economy works, with no established procedures for settling disputes or fostering cooperation, the world's societies are drifting.

Population Pressures

The inability of the world economy to provide for a large majority of the world's peoples or to hold out the promise of a better future is partly due to population pressures.[7] The population problems facing the countries of the world come in various forms:

1. Too many people.
2. Compositional problems. There are too many young, too many old, population segments with too many different cultural values.
3. Political problems posed by conflict over values (abortion in the United States, for example) or by conflict between ethnic-racial groups (for example, many African countries, Sri Lanka, Israel, South Africa).
4. High consumption practices and expectations. The developing countries now have populations that have tasted and expect a better life. The high consumption of the developed countries is a heavy burden on the planet (both on themselves and the developing countries) even as the peoples of developed countries expect more.

Population pressures and conflicts over population policy represent a drag on economic production and a threat to the environment. Significant steps have been taken by many developing countries to curb excessive population growth. The developed countries have provided a great deal of aid in helping countries adopt family planning programs. The United States government and private groups have been generous (though controversy over abortion has cut government funding). But the developed countries must do their part to ease population pressure on the environment. Their task is to curb excessive consumption.

---

[6]John Kendrick, ed., *International Comparisons of Productivity and Causes of the Slowdown* (Cambridge, Mass.: Ballinger, 1984).

[7]D. Gale Johnson and Ronald D. Lee, eds., *Population Growth and Economic Development: Issues and Evidence* (Madison: University of Wisconsin Press, 1987).

Environmental Pressures

Of special concern is the widespread and diverse impact of economic development on the natural environment. Here one need only list some of the problems to see the enormity of the pressure being exerted on the planet: deforestation as trees are cut for firewood and settlement; the spread of deserts (mostly because of inappropriate use of land); the pollution of air, water, and soil in all countries; the depletion of the ozone layer; the heating up of the planet; and the dumping of dangerous, long-lasting toxic wastes.

Strong support exists for environmental protection in many countries, and the United States has some tough, well-funded laws on the books that may yield significant gains if they are enforced. Some international cooperation has emerged in both population and environmental protection. By the 1980s the long decline toward an irreversible pollution of the Mediterranean Sea had been (perhaps) reversed thanks to international cooperation. In 1986 the Reagan administration announced it would seek international cooperation to cut back on the production of fluorocarbons, the chemical that depletes the ozone layer protecting the earth from harmful solar radiation, and by 1988 an important international agreement to phase out the use of flurocarbons was in place.

Nonetheless, it is clear that industrialization has put the planet's survival at risk. The United States is far from enforcing its environmental laws, and there has been on balance no halt to the degradation of the environment. The developing countries are not responsive to environmental concerns, seeing themselves as scapegoats for the excesses of the developed countries. With little scientific consensus on the extent of damage and no established procedures for the nations of the world to discuss environmental issues, the future does not look good.[8]

The basic outlook of environmentalists runs counter to the power structure and the nationalism that characterizes modern societies. Environmentalists think in terms of ecology and social ecology. *Ecology* is a branch of biology (and botany), which analyzes the interaction of microorganisms, plants, animals, and the general natural environment of water, soil, and air. Its concern ranges from the survival and adaptation of single organisms to that of the entire planet. *Social ecology* brings human beings into the equation: It focuses on various aspects of the natural environment (plants, animals, water, soil, terrain, energy, chemicals, microorganisms) and studies their impact on human life. Just as important, perhaps more so, it analyzes the impact of social life on the natural environment.

---

[8]For discussion of environmental problems, see William Ophuls, *Ecology and the Politics of Scarcity* (San Francisco: W. H. Freeman, 1977), Charles Pearson and Anthony Pryor, *Environment North and South* (New York: John Wiley & Sons, 1978), and Kenneth A. Dahlberg and others, *Environment and the Global Arena: Actors, Values, Policies, and Futures* (Durham, N.C.: Duke University Press, 1985).

Fundamental to the ecological perspective is the image of interdependence and exchange. Life forms exchange substances. We humans breathe air to get the oxygen that our blood needs and we exhale carbon dioxide as waste. Plants and trees do the opposite. The total "breathing" by plants, trees, and animals helps to keep the planet's atmosphere at livable levels. Invisible microorganisms help transform dead things into reusable ingredients. Worm tunnels help distribute needed air to the soil; bees pollinate both wild plants and farmers' crops. In short, nature and human nature are implicated in a far-reaching, complex, and largely invisible division of labor.

Social ecology focuses on how nature shapes social life and vice versa. Plentiful supplies of water are the basis of all the great agrarian civilizations. Cities develop in terms of geography: as ports, inland crossroads, or as military bases. In turn, social structures have an impact on nature, especially in the industrial era. Industry deposits wastes in air, water, and soil. Pesticides kill off birds and other organisms and contaminate the water supply. Paving over the earth to build homes, streets, shopping centers, and so forth causes flooding because the earth cannot absorb rain. The human impact on the environment can disrupt a part of the interdependent ecosystem: Cutting down trees and emitting waste into the air changes the composition of the atmosphere—when it rains, contaminated air falls as acid rain and destroys lakes, rivers, plants, and trees. Recreational vehicles can destroy the thin soil of semi-arid or mountainous areas, thus killing off plants and causing floods. Snowmobiles compact the snow on a lake and block the sun from reaching plant life in the water; plants cannot give off the oxygen fish need; eventually the plants die, thus consuming more oxygen; finally the fish die. Run-off of pesticides, acid rainfall, and ocean dumping of garbage have caused serious damage to the coastal waters of the eastern United States, threatening, for one thing, the supply of fish and thus endangering a vital source of human protein.

Today, environmentalism stresses the interdependence of each and every thing on the planet. It sees human well-being implicated in the rhythm of marshlands and the integrity of rain forests. It sees connections between industry and pollution, between pollution and disease, and between human sexual practices and pressure on resources. Environmentalism is especially concerned about technology. All technology poses a risk to humans and the natural environment. Animals are an important technology, but the pig was banned in the Middle East because it is ecologically destructive in that environment. The use of the hoe and plow to turn up the soil makes farmers much more productive; but clearing the land for farming can lead to soil erosion and depletion of nutrients in the soil.

Modern industry has expanded our ability to produce by a millionfold because it allows us to process nature, conquer its spaces, transform it, and create new materials, including new life forms. But the technology of the modern economy is also a warehouse of evils. In a brilliant sociological analysis, Charles Perrow has made an assessment of various forms of technology and ranked them in order of safety.[9] No amount of care, safety devices, training, or organizational restructuring, says Perrow, will make nuclear power safe. The reason is that the generation of nuclear power is "a system of high complexity and tight coupling", so high and so tight that a catastrophic accident is inherent in it (or normal). Because making nuclear power (and weapons) safe is hopeless, we should abandon it. Research into and production of DNA are also extremely dangerous, but here a large increase in safety procedures may do the job and allow us to reap the technology's considerable promise. Other technologies are dangerous, says Perrow, but do not pose the risk of catastrophe—for example, marine transport. Chemical plants, airline and automobile travel, dams, mining, power plants, and industry in general are also risky but lend themselves to improvement.

Perrow's assessment focuses on "systems" and not individuals, ideologies, or components. He also focuses on how we go about assessing risk. Power groups, he argues, impose technologies on us, and power groups have able defenders in the new science of risk assessment. The professionals who do risk assessment (risk-benefit analysis, cost-benefit analysis) tend to justify existing technology just as their predecessors (shamans, priests, court advisors, astrologers, lawyers) did for kings and landlords in the past. The pretense that precise quantitative figures about the relation of costs to benefits can be arrived at, says Perrow, should be abandoned because the attempt ignores a great deal that cannot be quantified. Risk assessment, with its stress on market principles and its focus on less government regulation (to provide elites but not ordinary people with more freedom), is essentially a defense of the existing structure of power. Instead of the formalism of expert risk assessment, says Perrow, we should focus on the concrete systems of technology and make political assessments of their role in the overall social system (how do they enhance or threaten personal and community values?).

The environmental movement is a broad coalition of specific-interest groups. Some environmental groups are concerned with the survival of particular kinds of plants or organisms: the whale, the tiger, marsh grass, rare birds. Others are concerned with the erosion of beaches or soil. Others worry about the shrinkage of farm acreage or the overuse of fertilizer and pesticides and the effect on the soil and water. Others are concerned about chemicals spewed into the air by smokestacks and automobiles. Others want wilderness areas protected against industrial, farm-ranch, extraction, and tourist businesses. Some focus on acid rain and the damage this is doing to forests, lakes, and rivers. Some worry about the chemicals that are being manufactured for consumption by humans, and also by the chemicals that go into the animals that feed us. Still others are concerned over the thousands of dumps holding chemical wastes or by the discharge of dangerous toxins into our

[9]Charles Perrow, *Normal Accidents: Living with High-Risk Technologies* (New York: Basic Books, 1984).

streams and drinking water. Some environmentalists are especially concerned about the dangers inherent in nuclear energy.

On a broader scale, many people worry about the so-called greenhouse effect—the warming of the earth by an atmospheric roof formed by industrial waste. (In 1988, climate experts testifying at congressional hearings stated that the greenhouse effect is inevitable and is already underway.) A different roof, the ozone layer that protects us against the sun's radiation has already been breached by human-made chemicals. Some environmentalists are concerned about what will happen to the planet's climate if forests are destroyed. Still others are worried by population pressures, both the smaller but high-consumption populations of the developed world, and the huge but low-consumption populations of the developing world. Finally, some environmentalists argue that we have already exceeded the planet's carrying capacity (see Box 21-1, "America Still Has Slaves: The Reality of Ghost Slaves").

Scholars do not agree on how much stress has been placed on the planet or how soon resources will be depleted. Most agree, however, that the planet is under threat. Perhaps our most reliable monitor is the Worldwatch Institute's annual report.[10] That we have exceeded sustainable levels is widely accepted. But how soon we will reach irreversible levels is not known. What to do is clear in general but breaks down when it comes to specific actions. Building a sustainable society means reevaluating the main thrust of American culture, and this will be difficult. But the United States also has a rich tradition of opposition to materialist modes of life that might prove helpful.[11]

The environmental movement has succeeded in arousing public concern about the environment. It has succeeded in making people aware that the despoilation and exhaustion of nature's resources pose a threat to human health and survival. It has succeeded in getting laws passed whose intent is to protect endangered species, clean the air and water, ensure workplace safety, and clean up toxic waste dumps. But enforcement lagged from the beginning. With the Reagan administration, the pretense that government would protect the environment was dropped. From 1981 on, enforcement of environmental laws at the federal level was relaxed and efforts were even made to weaken the laws.

Evaluating where we stand in the struggle to protect the environment is not easy. It is safe to say, however, that no overall progress can be reported in making the air or water cleaner, protecting nature in general, or in guarding human beings from various chemicals and harmful products. If anything, the situation has gotten worse, and we have come closer to the threshold of irreversible decline.

---

[10]Lester Russell Brown and others, *State of the World: A Worldwatch Institute Report on Progress Toward a Sustainable Society* (Washington, D.C.: Worldwatch Institute, Annual).

[11]David E. Shi, *The Simple Life: Plain Living and High Thinking in American Culture* (New York: Oxford University Press,1985).

BOX 21–1   *AMERICA STILL HAS SLAVES: THE REALITY OF GHOST SLAVES*

William Catton (along with other environmental theorists) has warned that industrial society is committed to a scale of living that exceeds the sustainable carrying capacity of our finite planet.[12] The industrial countries import food, raw materials, and energy, but no one worries about total supplies for the planet's population over time. These are "ghost" supplies, says Catton, based on ghost acreage. The industrial countries rely not only on "elsewhere" but on "elsewhen." The energy base of industrial civilization rest on fossil fuels that took hundreds of millions of years to develop. Converted to slave labor, this process equals the work of an incredibly large work force (tens of thousands of slaves stacking 2,300,000 blocks of stones each weighing 5000 pounds for twenty years would equal the energy spent in a few minutes by a three-stage Saturn V rocket!). The cost of using coal, oil, and gas has been cheap because no labor had to be paid to produce them. The cost of producing energy from our own sustainable resources (for example, from corn oil) would be thirteen times higher—high enough to prevent us from committing ourselves to a scale of living based on ghost slaves and exhaustible energy. Today, both the United States economy and society are based on eighty ghost slaves for each American (there are ten ghost slaves for each member of the world's population). The United States' standard of living is four parts phantom acreage and one part real carrying capacity. The world as a whole is based on 90 percent phantom carrying capacity. We are drawing ten times more from the earth, concludes Catton, than the earth is replacing (or we need ten Planet Earths to match present consumption).[13]

[12]William R. Catton, Jr., *Overshoot: The Ecological Basis of Revolutionary Change* (Urbana: University of Illinois Press, 1980).

[13]For a careful empirical survey that finds food production holding up for the foreseeable future but sees declines in fish and forestry products, and the disappearance of oil and the end of cheap energy, see F. Landis MacKellar and Daniel R. Vining, Jr., "Natural Resource Scarcity: A Global Survey," in D. Gale Johnson and Ronald D. Lee, eds., *Population Growth and Economic Development* (Madison: University of Wisconsin Press, 1987), chap. 8.

The reason why so little progress has been made is that environmentalism is fundamentally out of step with the logic of industrialism (whether capitalist or socialist). Powerful industries and agribusinesses, with the help of government, have blocked the environmental movement. Environmentalism is also out of step with the logic of development in the Third World. There, extensive damage to the environment has already occurred—soil erosion, the spread of deserts, deforestation, the decline of food production, and the pollution of air and water through uncontrolled industrialization and urbanization. The interdependence of the world economy is seen in the following irony: As Western nations raise pollution safeguards, capital flows to Third-World countries that lack pollution standards. The Third World is also a dumping ground for products that have been banned in the industrial world.

The environmental movement in the United States has stalled, or rather, has been depoliticized. Even most environmentalist groups have taken it for granted that they are dealing with solvable problems within the structure of capitalism. They have been only too ready to assume that laws will do the job and that technical solutions will be found. Few have seen the need for framing the problem of the environment in terms of an overall theory of society. But that, it appears, is what is needed.[14]

MANAGING THE WORLD ECONOMY: INTERRELATIONS BETWEEN THE INNER AND OUTER WORLDS OF THE NATION-STATE

The most important idea for understanding the contemporary world is that domestic power structures are under enormous internal pressures and constraints (that they may even be losing control of) even as constraints from the outside (that they have even less control of) have increased. This applies to giants like the United States and the Soviet Union as well as smaller countries.

The major capitalist societies have carefully stayed away from the United Nations as the forum for discussing the world's economy. Instead, they rely on the capitalist world banking system (private banks as well as the World Bank, International Monetary Fund, and so on), negotiations among themselves (annual economic summits), or negotiations among developed and developing countries in selected formats such as GATT (the General Agreement on Tariffs and Trade), which is a working consensus among approximately 125 countries on the rules of the economic game (which undergo periodic updating). Moreover, GATT is also an organization, and efforts are afoot to strengthen it so that parties to the agreement will have a mechanism to resolve their disputes.

In the past few decades GATT has worked fairly well. It has committed the majority of the world's nation-states to free trade, which is also an acknowledgment that their economies are interdependent (in 1986 the Soviet Union further acknowledged its dependence on the world market by asking to join GATT as an observer and in 1988 it applied for membership). Further, GATT has worked to prevent harmful protectionism through periodic meetings in which multilateral negotiations have succeeded in lowering trade barriers. A new round of negotiations began in 1986 in an effort to do something about the glut in farm products and to see if free trade in services could be

[14]For three overall views based on the assumption that overdevelopment is upon us, see Andre Gorz, *Ecology as Politics*, trans. Patsy Vigderman and Jonathan Cloud (Boston: South End Press, 1980); originally published 1975; Kirkpatrick Sale, *Human Scale* (New York: Coward, McCann & Geoghegan, 1980); and William R. Catton, Jr., *Overshoot: The Ecological Basis of Revolutionary Change* (Urbana: University of Illinois Press, 1980).

established. With its advanced service economy, the United States was pushing hard to open up world markets to its banking, insurance, engineering, construction, telecommunications, legal, mass media, and publishing companies.

The United States is still the most powerful country in the world with a GNP twice the size of its nearest competitor. It still has enormous power in world councils. But its experience and its beliefs and values are out of kilter with the world it faces. For one thing, it relies heavily on GATT, not realizing that GATT and the actual world economy are two very different things.[15] Its ritual enunciation of universalistic norms and values (formalism) also makes it difficult for the United States to understand the world's diversity. Its belief in natural economic laws and its equation of political-legal rights with democracy are not shared by most of the peoples of the world. Its belief in its exceptional status, while a source of strength, is also a blinding pride. The world faces a future in which its most powerful member wants stability when most of the world wants change.[16] For most of the post–World War II period the United States believed that the private economy of the nineteenth century, which consisted of an increased input of private resources and labor, referred by a neutral state, was the path to economic growth and prosperity. By the 1980s it learned that governments in Japan, Germany, France, Italy, and some of the industrializing Third-World countries such as South Korea and Brazil were developing policies and making capital available on a long-term basis so that their respective economies could be leaders in strategically important sectors of manufacturing. Now that the United States is aware of the uncompetitiveness of its economy (an awareness found in numerous reports), it seems unable to change from its commitment to nineteenth-century ideas and practices.

Whether the United States can learn to negotiate with other powerful countries (capitalist and socialist), to understand the varieties of society in its outer environment, to channel liberation movements into viable pluralistic systems (rather than relying on right-wing dictatorships), to share the planet's resources, and to accept its position as first among equals cannot be taken for granted.

STRATIFIED SOCIETIES AND WAR

War as a Sociohistorical Phenomenon

War is a social phenomenon and has little to do with human nature and little to do with the empty words spoken on its behalf by belligerents. Until

[15]Raymond Vernon, *Exploring the Global Economy* (Lanham, Md.: University Press of America, 1985).

[16]For a careful empirical study showing the deep isolation of the United States at the United Nations, see Miguel Marin-Bosch, "How Nations Vote in the General Assembly of the United Nations," *International Organization* 41, no. 4 (Autumn 1987): 705–724.

recently, it was widely believed that war would gradually disappear with economic growth and the spread of democracy. We now know that these are false assumptions. Essentially, war is a way in which power groups solve their problems.

War is found throughout history, varying in goals, form, and intensity depending on type of society. The fact that it varies in intensity and type (and is absent in some societies and periods) is very encouraging. This fact means that we are dealing with a sociohistorical rather than a fixed, natural phenomenon. For example, war is extremely uncommon among hunting-gathering peoples, and when it occurs its purpose is to alleviate some other problem by setting things right in the cosmos, to restore the problem-free status quo. War among simple societies is heavily ritualized (often it is enough to kill one enemy). It is not conducted to seize territory or large stores of booty.

Rather than stemming from our alleged innate aggressive nature, war comes from the way we humans have organized our various societies. The anthropologist Marvin Harris places the cause of war among primitive peoples in their economic system, or more specifically, in the lack of a natural equilibrium between human population growth and material provisions for sustaining life.[17] Population control occurs in various ways: abortion, abandoning the old, infanticide. Killing female babies is an effective way to control population, says Harris, and he adds, there is a basic connection between female infanticide and the male monopoly over hunting and war. Hunting and "war" are central to the life and survival of hunting-gathering societies, and by making them male monopolies, males become more important than females. This clears the way, says Harris, for female infanticide and for the general subordination of women.

Types of Stratification and War

How do stratified societies generate war? Max Weber's analysis of why Rome was imperialistic and warlike is instructive.[18] The Roman economy rested on male slavery. Rome could not generate its own slave labor force and was under chronic pressure to conquer other peoples to replenish its supply of male slaves. An economy based on slavery (and, in general, on a servile population) cannot motivate people for economic growth; hence, war is the way to increase wealth and pay for the overhead of war itself. As long as there is a plentiful supply of cheap labor, there is no incentive to improve technology and economic practices, and as long as economic and political institutions based on servile, cheap labor exist, war is inevitable.

---

[17]Marvin Harris, "The Origin of War," in his book *Cannibals and Kings: The Origins of Cultures* (New York: Vintage, 1978), chap. 4.

[18]Max Weber, *The Agrarian Sociology of Ancient Civilization*, R.I. Frank, trans. (London: New Left Books [now *Verso*], 1976), chap. 1.

Those who study war are now agreed that the great turning point in the development of war was the emergence of horticultural and herding societies. Horticulture produced enough surplus to enable a monarch and his retainers (eventually a noble class) to live without working. Warfare becomes much more frequent than in hunting-gathering societies, perhaps offering a substitute for the excitement of the hunt. Herding societies from the ancient Jews to the Mongols and Arabs were also warlike. Herding peoples have religions based on monotheism (God is a shepherd), which is also associated with a centralized political and military command structure (a Messiah among the Jews meant a military leader who would deliver them from their enemies). The herding economy easily leads to the encroachment on other people's territory and thus disputes that lead to war.

War appears to emerge when societies turn nature into "private" property. People who are used to taking what they want from nature cannot adjust easily to a world of boundaries. War is also not easy to distinguish from economic behavior in general—one lived by taking from nature or from others, one lived by violence either against animals or human animals (ethnocentric cultures prevented people from seeing themselves in terms of a common humanity).

Technological developments are important to war. Herding peoples learned to ride horses and camels and when this skill was turned to warfare it gave them an important edge. Bronze, an alloy, is far more durable than iron or copper, and bronze weapons gave those who had them an edge. Another innovation was the shift from militias to professional standing armies. The rise of capitalism meant new productive technology, but it also led to a continuous series of new and deadly weapons. It has also seen new organizational systems designed to make armies more efficient.

A qualitative and quantitative jump in militarization came with the far more productive agrarian society. Here, economic surplus is used to augment state power and to develop professional armies. The basic power structure yields a surplus that is then used to take what the masses produce away from them. Though force is ever-present, agrarian society develops symbolic justifications, especially religion, to legitimate the upward flow of economic surplus. But the overall thrust of the system retards productivity. There is little incentive on the part of the masses to work hard to innovate when the rewards go to others. Thus, while the first 2,000 years of the agrarian age (7,000 to 5,000 years ago) were extremely inventive and productive, there is a marked slowdown between 5,000 and 2,500 years ago as agrarian elites perfected the institutions that milked the masses. Once specialized to be parasitic and predatory, the feudal elite could not reverse itself or adapt to new conditions. A feudal nobility cannot engage in vulgar pursuits like working or even managing. The only way to increase its revenues was from war booty (and a further squeeze of its servile labor force).

War has persisted into the industrial age, and here too we must look to social institutions as the cause. Early liberals were wrong to think that economic growth, science, education, and political democracy would end war. War is a product of power relations inside society. Is there a relation between the capitalist economy and war? Is there something about the industrial economy common to both the capitalist and communist countries that causes inner tension, which is then projected outward? Have we so deeply institutionalized the military and weapon development that they now have a life of their own?

Today (the post–World War II period) war has become a many-sided phenomenon. Most wars are undeclared and nonlegal, often illegal. Though much of the thought about war centers on ways to avoid a nuclear confrontation, the world is filled with "dirty little" wars and has been for more than forty years. It is no longer easy to distinguish between war between nations and civil war. And wars do not end in peace treaties but more often in stalemate and exhaustion, peace being a mere interlude of rest before the next round of hostilities.[19]

Social Change, Insecurity, Anxiety

The past 600 years have seen unprecedented change as the capitalist West emerged and spread across the planet. First capitalist and now any and all of the world's societies routinely subject members to change, insecurity, and anxiety. The engines of development yank serfs, farmers, and peasants from their timeless routines. The village and town dweller meet the city dweller. Craft skills emerge only to become obsolete before the march of the machine. The machine owner finds his machinery obsolete. Prosperous farmers using the latest tools go bankrupt, undone by their success at producing more food than can be bought. Loyal workers are laid off as profit-oriented, faceless corporations move to another city or country.

The modern system of society must be seen as a breeder of anxiety. Or perhaps better, as a society with members who hunger for certainty and security and are thus a prey for power groups with simplistic answers. Here lie the reasons for the revival of religion, the spread of nationalism, and rival secular truths.

Hatreds from the Past

The confrontation between the superpowers stems partly from their histories; each has a long history of violence. But the many dirty little wars across the planet and many of the festering local conflicts also derive from the past. Here again we see the scars of imperialism; here again we have a developing planet living in the past: Arab-Israeli, Greek-Turk, Nicaragua-

[19]For valuable reviews of the causes and nature of war and for various views about war, see Martin Shaw, ed., *War, State, and Society* (New York: St. Martin's Press, 1984), and Seyom Brown, *The Causes and Prevention of War* (New York: St. Martin's Press, 1987).

United States, Vietnam-Cambodia-China-Thailand, Muslim vs. Hindu, Muslim vs. Christian, and a long list of stateless peoples, some very old, some new.

Arms Control and Reduction

Arms control and reduction are not new—the rival societies of Europe, the United States, and Japan held conferences and came to agreements, beginning with The Hague Conference of 1899 down to the naval agreements of the 1930s. The atomic bomb that exploded on Hiroshima in 1945 gave new urgency to arms control. Ever since the end of World War II, a large number of agreements have been negotiated, not only by small countries but also by the two superpowers (see Table 21–1).

Arms control and arms reduction are complex and difficult matters. Neither the United States nor the Soviet Union trusts the other. Each has its unique defense capabilities and problems. The USSR is a land power with large conventional forces and a heavy emphasis on long-range, land-based missiles. The United States places less reliance on conventional forces and has a three-part nuclear offensive force: nuclear missiles on submarines, nuclear bombs and missiles on airplanes, and land-based missiles. An obvious example of the difficulty of achieving arms reduction is the proposal for an across-the-board reduction in all nuclear weapons: That would give the Soviet Union's conventional forces a military edge. The United States relies heavily on maintaining a technological superiority to make up for its deficiency in conventional forces—thus, it has consistently refused to sign a treaty banning nuclear testing. Ironically, one way to reduce the chance of nuclear war is for the United States to increase its conventional forces.

The march of technology has already produced military capabilities that may be uncontrollable. Seen from each side, each advance is thought to provide superiority and invulnerability. By the 1990s, for example, the United States will have submarines that are undetectable and which for the first time will be equipped with accurate first-strike missiles. Beyond that the United States is pursuing a far-reaching defense system (SDI, or Strategic Defense Initiative, also known as "Star Wars"), which when put in conjunction with offensive weapons becomes an offensive system. Because few believe that SDI can ever provide an effective defense, SDI is a way for the United States to continue what it does best, rely on technological fetishism to avoid making political agreements with the Soviet Union.

Similarly, the argument that agreements are not worth pursuing because the Soviet Union violates them is a politically inspired falsehood. All thinking analysts including the Joint Chiefs of Staff and the CIA agree that the Soviet Union has abided by all the major provisions of all existing treaties and that alleged violations are minor and stem from ambiguities in the treaty.

TABLE 21–1. Arms Control Agreements and Partial Agreements Since 1959

1959: Antarctic Treaty demilitarizes the Antarctic. 23 nations.

1963: Limited Test Ban Treaty bans nuclear weapons tests in the atmosphere, in outer space and under water. 109 nations.

1963: U.S. Soviet Hot Line Agreement establishes a direct emergency communications link between the superpowers.

1967: Outer Space Treaty bans placing of nuclear or any other weapons of mass destruction in outer space and the establishment of military bases, installations or fortifications on the moon or other celestial bodies. 80 nations.

1967: Latin American Nuclear-Free Zone Treaty prohibits the testing, use, manufacture, production or acquisition of nuclear weapons in Latin America. Under Protocol II the nuclear-weapons states agree to respect the military denuclearization of Latin America. 22 nations, including all Latin American states except Argentina, Brazil, Chile and Cuba.

1968: Non-Proliferation Treaty (NPT) prohibits the transfer of nuclear weapons by states that have them and the acquisition of such weapons by those that do not and requires nuclear-weapons states to seek nuclear disarmament. 117 nations.

1971: Seabed Treaty bans placement of weapons of mass destruction on the seabed beyond a 12-mile zone outside a nation's territory. 68 nations.

1971: U.S.-Soviet "Accidents Measures" Agreement pledges each party to guard against accidental or unauthorized use of nuclear weapons and provides, *inter alia,* for immediate notification of any accidental, unauthorized incident involving a possible detonation of a nuclear weapon.

1972: Biological Weapons Convention prohibits the development, production, stockpiling or acquisition of biological agents and any weapons designed to use such agents. 90 nations.

1972: ABM Treaty and 1974 protocol limit U.S. and Soviet deployment of antiballistic missile defenses to a single site.

1972: Interim Offensive Weapons Agreement (technically expired October 3, 1977 but is still observed) froze the number of U.S. and Soviet strategic ballistic missile launchers for five years. (This agreement and the ABM Treaty are known as SALT I.)

1973: Agreement on the Prevention of Nuclear War provides that the United States and USSR will make the removal of the danger of war and the use of nuclear weapons an objective of their policies, practice restraint in their relations toward each other and all countries, and pursue policies dedicated to peace and stability.

1974: Threshold Test Ban Treaty limits U.S. and Soviet underground tests of nuclear weapons to 150 kilotons. Signed by both U.S. and USSR but not ratified by U.S.

1976: Peaceful Nuclear Explosions Treaty (PNE) limits U.S. and Soviet underground nuclear explosions for *peaceful* purposes to 150 kilotons. Signed by both U.S. and USSR but not ratified by U.S.

1977: Environmental Modification Convention prohibits the hostile use of techniques that could produce substantial environmental modifications. 32 nations.

1979: SALT II sets equal aggregate ceilings on a number of strategic nuclear systems, including the maximum number of strategic nuclear delivery vehicles (ICBMs, SLBMs and intercontinental bombers), the maximum number of launchers of ballistic missiles with multiple warheads (MIRVs) and the maximum number of launchers of MIRVed ICBMs. The treaty also bans construction of additional, fixed ICBM launchers and a number of other improvements to existing weapons. Signed by both U.S. and USSR but not ratified by the U.S.

Source: Alice Hughey, *"The Quest for Arms Control: Why and How,"* (Washington, D.C.: League of Women Voters, 1983), p. 2. In 1987 the United States and the Soviet Union signed the INF Treaty eliminating all intermediate nuclear missiles from their arsenals.

Incidentally, the treaties include a mechanism for resolving such differences, but the United States has refused to evoke them or participate in them.

Arms Control-Reduction as a Secondary Issue

The prevention of war through arms control (or through an arms buildup) is to turn war into a social problem on the order of crime, divorce, or poverty. Tackling a social problem directly assumes that it is solvable within the existing social order (much as Sherlock Holmes can solve a mystery because he lives in a predictable, supportive society). But social problems are now so interconnected and result so directly from a society's power structure that they cannot be solved on a piecemeal basis. The social-problem approach is probably obsolete, and social problems are now quite secondary to the problem of society itself. If there is any lesson to be learned from the comparative study of societies, it is that society itself is always the problem.

Another way to look on arms agreements is that they simply allow societies to modernize their arms, not reduce them. In addition, arms control lends legitimacy to the idea that national interests can be defended and promoted by force. It is the rival claims that societies make against each that must be examined and evaluated. Thinking of peace as the result of equitable arms agreements between the United States and the Soviet Union, therefore, may be a dead end. One must be prepared to assume that neither country can make the concessions needed for peace through arms negotiations. What then is needed? Or put another way: What initiatives should the United States take that will promote peace (and other social goods)?

CHANGING THE UNITED STATES TO ACHIEVE PEACE AND OTHER SOCIAL GOODS

Rethinking Mindless Economic Growth

The economic expansion of the West has had a large component of mindlessness. Economic growth has been given unqualified approval even though it means producing a large range of harmful products and services, harmful both to humans and the environment. The pursuit of economic growth under capitalism means that property owners and professionals must ceaselessly develop new products and services often with no regard for other social goods. It means that capital flows to the best sources of profit even if it means upsetting meaningful social routines both at home and abroad. And the spread of capital around the globe in the form of multinational corporations makes it difficult to hold these corporations accountable even as they ask for military protection and other political supports. Certainly the alliance of property groups across national boundaries far exceeds any counterpressure from labor, consumers, or governments.

Living Within Our Means

The United States has been running a large internal budget deficit and a large trade deficit since 1977.[20] These deficits appear to be structural—that is, they emerge from the fundamental American power structure. They appeared because public-policy decisions allocated American resources toward rearmament and away from enhancing productivity. They appeared because public policy allowed American capital to go overseas. To govern, American governments have cut taxes and kept interest rates high to attract the loans needed (from its citizens and from foreigners) to finance its deficits. High interest rates made the dollar strong, which made imports cheap. Americans enjoyed low-priced imports, which helped to keep inflation low. But while this made for political peace in some respects it also created unrest—low-priced imports, for example, hurt many American industries and communities.

Allowing easy access to the American market also promoted American foreign-policy objectives—by opening its markets the United States produced strong, friendly capitalist societies in the Pacific Basin and elsewhere. But its need to borrow to finance its deficits produced high interest rates, which also produced a debt crisis in Latin America and Africa.

The United States must make painful decisions in the coming years if it is to arrest the absolute decline in its standard of living that has already occurred and which will grow more noticeable with each passing year. Consumption must be curbed; problem-preventing public services expanded; corporations better managed; research and development (including environmental research) enhanced; and every effort must be made to cut the social overhead represented by idle people, crime, superfluous armaments, unnecessary illness and disability stemming from unsafe factories, and so on. None of this is likely, however, unless the United States is further democratized.

Promoting Democracy at Home

A major unfinished business for the United States is the establishment of full popular government. American elites talk largely to each other and hold periodic elections mostly devoid of meaning to give themselves legitimacy. The uncontrolled use of private money in conjunction with gerrymandered electoral districts and the new technology of television and computers have made it possible to hold elections in which few issues are discussed and no mandate for governance received. All this has led to a politics of stalemate and drift (for a fuller discussion and for suggestions about reforms, see Chapters 13 and 14). In its broadest context, democracy means politicizing issues, including the core values, beliefs, and institutions of society. This means that

[20]For a fine overview of where the United States stands (but which lacks concrete policy proposals for positive changes), see Sven W. Arndt and Lawrence Bouton, *Competitiveness: The United States in World Trade* (Washington, D.C.: American Enterprise Institute for Public Policy Research, 1987).

the American electorate must be given carefully reasoned alternatives to how the economy is now run. The United States must also reverse the general process found in schools, religion, civil ceremonies, popular culture, and social science (thinking of society in natural terms), which depoliticizes social problems, in effect, turning their solution over to the upper classes.

Loosening the Grip of the Iron Triangle

The United States has developed a potent military-industrial-political complex that has a stake in the conditions that usually lead to war. Keeping one's eye on the possibility that the United States may itself be a military-industrial-political complex, all that can be done to bring the iron triangle (Congress, the Pentagon, giant defense contractors) to heel should be done (for an earlier discussion, see Chapter 14).

Rethinking Foreign Policy

The United States relies far too heavily on anticommunism and military strength in its foreign policy. Its formalistic foreign policy has developed under the thought-numbing ideal of bipartisanship (the foreign-policy counterpart to nonpartisan domestic politics). All thinking analysts from the CIA to private scholars would probably agree with a recent study that the Soviet Union does not have much world power, that it has little ability to control events beyond its borders, and the high point of what little power it has was reached in 1958.

Domestic power structures that do not provide for the equitable distribution of the fruits of social life are the major cause of the world's troubles. World problems, including the threat of war, result from the imperialist actions of feudal, capitalist, and communist societies over the past centuries as power groups struggled to make their inequitable societies work.

The United States can protect itself and promote world peace by abandoning the fiction of a natural economy linking domestic and international economic transactions. America can promote world stability by focusing on viable economic development and popular government throughout the world, including at home. It was apparent during both the Carter and Reagan administrations that each was badly divided by contradictory forces. These came from the contradictory voices of a divided American power structure. To operate more effectively the United States must drastically improve its ability to understand other countries. The first barrier to be overcome is American ethnocentrism, seeing the world through American assumptions. The federal executive (State Department, Department of Defense, other civilian departments that deal with the outside world, and all intelligence agencies) is woefully deficient in its ability to read the outside world. Congress, not so directly involved in day-to-day operations, tends to see the world more clearly through its expert staffs and committees, but its voting record (subject to our oligarchic system of politics) is not consistent with its knowledge.

The United States has a dismal record in the Third World. One administration after the other has suffered defeats there (Vietnam, Lebanon, Central America, Iran, the Middle East) and there is little evidence that the United States has learned much from its experiences.[21] Americans must learn to understand the Third World, and the first step is to understand itself, especially the fact that it is not necessarily a relevant model for the rest of the world. It must also rethink its goals in the world arena, its "global commitment" outlook that says that interests are to be defended and our global credibility strengthened by making firm commitments to Third-World allies. Far from failing to live up to our commitments, says Bruce Jentleson, our problems stem from the fact that we have lived up to them only too well, with the result that our decision making became inflexible, the tail wagged the dog, and we have been forced into a misuse of military means (all these factors further undermining policy because it led to domestic opposition).[22]

Foreign policy is largely a matter of economic interests, and here the United States must reexamine its commitment to unmanaged economic growth, its furtherance of the conditions that allow free rein to multinational corporations, and its failure to address the domestic problems that keep the general public agitated and off balance. American trade policy (the political management of its economic policies toward other countries) must take into account the many "invisible" costs of so-called free trade. Far from leading only to efficiency and comparative-advantage benefits, free trade means that the Third World will have large and growing numbers of poor, large amounts of unemployment and labor repression, unmanageable cities, and no protection of the environment. To compete with such societies means that much the same takes place in the United States. On top of all these costs is the added expense of military expenditures to keep political peace.

The United States need not wait for prior agreements before undertaking tension-reducing acts. This does not mean that the concrete steps to be taken are easy—but certainly the philosophy that links all of the world's tension to communism must be abandoned. It also requires abandoning the assumption that the Soviets are absolutely untrustworthy (which simply breeds distrust) and building on the already effective inspection procedures that both sides agreed to in the INF Treaty of 1988. The logic behind breeding trust and progressive levels of tension reduction is TIT for TAT[23] (or responding in kind).

[21]For a classic case study of America's faulty policy-making structures and its failure to learn from experience, see Lloyd S. Etheredge, *Can Governments Learn? American Foreign Policy and Central American Revolutions* (New York: Pergamon Press, 1985).

[22]Bruce W. Jentleson, "American Commitments in the Third World: Theory vs. Practice," *International Organization* 41, no. 4 (Autumn 1987): 667–704.

[23]William F. Allman, "Nice Guys Finish First," *Science 84*, 5 (October 1984): 25–32.

Finally, perhaps the most difficult assumptions to rid ourselves of is the ideology of rational self-interest and the psychology of interest maximizing, both of which have failed in our domestic life yet are still thought to be somehow useful in international affairs. The rational pursuit of self-interest has been associated strongly with war from the nineteenth century on. The usual support for rational action is the parallel fallacy that wars come out of stress, mistaken views of opponents, and political-bureaucratic constraints on rational decision making.[24] The involvement of churches in foreign policy matters in recent years is encouraging (some fundamentalist Christian sects, ignorant of the social causes of war, are essentially covers for right-wing political extremists, and a better-managed economy and society will make it difficult for these sects and groups to find followers). And certainly the great cry for internationalizing the school curriculum at all levels is encouraging.

[24]For a creative look beyond this two-sided assumption, see Bruce Bueno de Mesquita, *The War Trap* (New Haven, Conn.: Yale University Press, 1981).

Name Index

Subject
Index